Justice Stanley Mosk

Justice Stanley Mosk

*A Life at the Center of
California Politics and Justice*

Jacqueline R. Braitman *and*
Gerald F. Uelmen

McFarland & Company, Inc., Publishers
Jefferson, North Carolina, and London

LIBRARY OF CONGRESS CATALOGUING-IN-PUBLICATION DATA

Braitman, Jacqueline R., 1953–
Justice Stanley Mosk : a life at the center of California politics and justice / Jacqueline R. Braitman and Gerald F. Uelmen.
  p.   cm.

Includes bibliographical references and indexes.

ISBN 978-0-7864-6841-6
softcover : acid free paper ∞

1. Mosk, Stanley, 1912–2001. 2. Judges—California—Biography. I. Uelmen, Gerald F. II. Title.
KF373.M63B73 2013   347.794'02092—dc23   [B]   2012040109

BRITISH LIBRARY CATALOGUING DATA ARE AVAILABLE

© 2013 Jacqueline R. Braitman and Gerald F. Uelmen. All rights reserved

No part of this book may be reproduced or transmitted in any form or by any means, electronic or mechanical, including photocopying or recording, or by any information storage and retrieval system, without permission in writing from the publisher.

On the cover: Stanley Mosk (courtesy Richard Mosk; photo credit: Albert C. Smith)

Manufactured in the United States of America

*McFarland & Company, Inc., Publishers
Box 611, Jefferson, North Carolina 28640
www.mcfarlandpub.com*

To my daughter Sara, who grew up with research-filled boxes
and conversations about Stanley Mosk; and to my family and friends
who provided their unconditional love and patient, enthusiastic support;
and to Stanley's devoted son, Richard.
—J.R.B.

To the memory of my mother, Trudy Uelmen (1916–2011),
and my friend and colleague Mary Emery (1937–2011).
You both live on in our hearts.
—G.F.U.

Contents

Preface and Acknowledgments	1
Introduction	3
1. "Walk Upstairs and Save"	9
2. "What This Fraternity Needs Is More Moreys!"	20
3. Lawyers "Who Should Be Thrown Out of Ten Story Windows"	28
4. "When the Plums Are Passed Out ... You Will Be Left Behind Again"	40
5. "I Crowded the War Off Page One"	53
6. "The Jewish Community Found a Leader"	72
7. "Use Their Heads Instead of Their Hob-Nailed Boots"	79
8. "Little Old Ladies in Tennis Shoes"	89
9. "A Great Democratic Rain"	109
10. "To Embarrass Them or Pressure Them Sometime in the Future"	120
11. "He Never Forgot What His Positions Were"	135
12. "The Mosk Doctrine"	149
13. "The Melancholy Truth"	159
14. "You Don't Have to Remove Your Shoes Before Stepping All Over Stanley Mosk"	164
15. "But I Blame Jerry Brown for Putting You Here"	177
16. "You Have Remarkable Sources!"	192
17. "I Am Now an Orphan"	204
18. "I Have Never Known Defeat at the Polls"	214
19. "They Have Exalted Principal Over Principle"	224
20. "Where Has All the Grandeur Gone?"	240
Epilogue	247
Chapter Notes	251
Bibliography	269
Index of Cases	273
General Index	275

Preface and Acknowledgments

During our years of collaboration to produce this biography, we frequently asked each other, "Is this really a history book or is it actually a law book?" Hopefully, it is both. We finally realized that when it comes to the life of Stanley Mosk, there is no contradiction between the two. As a law professor whose scholarship has focused on the work of the California Supreme Court, Professor Uelmen was well acquainted with Justice Mosk, an avid fan of his judicial opinions, and a frequent recipient of his advice. As an historian, Dr. Braitman found that decades of scholarly attention given to Los Angeles and California history had failed to notice how Stanley Mosk stood at the center, or very close to it, of epochal shifts in policy and politics, and how his voice had heralded defining moments of the last century. This biography thus offers the first comprehensive examination of Mosk's historical presence, and grounds him within diverse, and often conflicting, historical representations of twentieth-century Los Angeles, California, and America. The collaboration of a disciplined historian and an idealistic law professor enriched our mutual understanding of Stanley Mosk, as a man who not only reflected his times, but also profoundly shaped them. Because many of the headline-making issues he grappled with continue to shape today's policy debates, Stanley Mosk's story remains timely and will be relevant well into the new millennium.

While the historical documents we located and scoured support our interpretations, the input of those who shared his life and work was essential. Without the help of Stanley Mosk's son, Justice Richard Mosk, the full significance of many of the documents would be lost. Also significant were the unique perspectives provided by Richard's wife, Sandy Mosk, and their children Julie and Matthew. Stanley Mosk's sister-in-law, Fern Mosk (Mrs. Edward Mosk), provided valuable insight, and her son Tom generously shared his father's scrapbooks and photo albums. Viewing the early years of the Mosk clan through the eyes of cousin Harriet Perl was priceless, as were the affectionate recollections of Stanley Mosk's second wife, Susan Hines Mosk, and his widow, Mrs. Kaygey Kash Mosk.

Research for this project was generously funded by the Koret Foundation through the Department of History, UCLA, and supported by the John Randolph and Dora Haynes Foundation, awarded by both the Huntington Library and the Historical Society of Southern California. The support provided for faculty research by Dean Donald Polden and the Santa Clara University School of Law made a huge difference. The work depended on the help of dedicated archivists and library staffs throughout the country. We are greatly indebted to Fran M. Jones, Director of Library Services, for her immeasurable assistance facilitating our research in the Stanley Mosk Collection at the California Supreme Court Library in San Francisco. Her assistant Martha R. Noble, and colleague, archivist Andrea Hinding, also graciously aided initial research during processing of the Mosk Collection. Similarly, we owe thanks to the able associates who gathered, monitored, photocopied, and guided research in the following manuscript collections: Special Collections, the Bancroft Library, University of California, Berkeley (particularly David Kessler); the Department of Special Collections, Young Research Library, University of California, Los Angeles; The Stanley Mosk Library and Courts Building and the Library and Courts II, Sacramento; the Huntington Library, Pasadena; the John F. Kennedy Presidential Library and Museum; the Southern California Library for Social Studies and Research, aka Southern California Library; the People's Library; and the Urban Archives Center, California State University, Northridge. We also thank Luci Buda, a 2012 graduate of Santa Clara University School of Law, and Earl Horner, a 2014 graduate, for their editorial assistance.

We benefited from many suggestions and insights from Chief Justice Ronald M. George (ret.), Associate Justice Joyce Kennard, and Associate Justice Joseph Grodin (ret.) of the California Supreme Court, as well as Presiding Justices J. Anthony Kline and Norman L. Epstein of the California Courts of Appeal. Conversations with Greg Mitchell of *The Recorder*, author Ed Cray, and Tom McDonald, who as speechwriter for Attorney General Mosk helped to create his public and private narrative, all offered new insights. Journalist Josh Getlin offered early enthusiastic encouragement. Without others who shared their stories, this work would have been sorely lacking. Among them were Frank Burns (Robert Kennedy campaign and associate of Speaker Jesse Unruh); Richard Greene (attorney and Mosk family friend); Edna Mosk's confidant Mariam Perel; Steven Koblik (president, Huntington Library, and family friend); Melanie Lomax, daughter of civil rights activist and journalist Almena Lomax; Mosk's friend Dr. Edward F. Lewison; and Mosk's fellow partisans, Judge Stephen Reinhardt, Ninth Circuit Court of Appeals, and Stephen Zetterberg, Democratic Party officer.

We especially appreciated the suggestions from those who read drafts of the manuscript, including Tom Sitton, whose rich scholarship is well represented here; Malca Chall, whose own contribution to the voluminous oral histories of people important to California's past is extraordinary; California historian Andrew Rolle, writer Max Holland; Michael Millman of the California Appellate Project; Jake Dear of the Supreme Court staff; Professor Ken Manaster and Professor Stephanie Wildman of Santa Clara University School of Law; and San Francisco Attorney Jerome Falk, Jr. We are also grateful to the many lawyers and judges who shared treasured memories of working with or arguing in front of Stanley Mosk, including Dennis Fischer, Robert Gerstein, Jon Steiner, Ellis Horvitz, and Judge John McInerney (ret.). This project relied upon the sustained support of Martha Uelmen; and Dr. Braitman's mother, Mili Lang, her father, Hal "Tata," and stepmother, Selma Bates; along with Cristina Taccone, Stephen Braitman, and Tim Schwarz.

Introduction

> Mosk is California history with a heartbeat.
> — Marlene Adler Marks, *Jewish Journal*, October 30, 1997

Hundreds of mourners came to Los Angeles' majestic Wilshire Boulevard Temple in June of 2001. The massive, Byzantine-style structure and its hundred-foot-wide dome tower over the bustling mid-city corridor leading to the downtown hub of financial and corporate skyscrapers. Built in 1929, the historic synagogue symbolizes the bourgeoning pre–Depression prominence and wealth of the region's Jewish Reform congregants, including Hollywood moguls and business leaders. Filing into the rows of seats in the cavernous sanctuary were two generations of movers and shakers of post–World War II California politics, who helped to shape the course of history. Sitting among less recognizable faces were current and former governors and elected and appointed officials in the local, state, and national arena. Framed by the grandeur of the dais, family members, friends, and colleagues sat in ornate, stately chairs, and then each took to the podium to share their version of the essence of the life of California Supreme Court Justice Stanley Mosk. Together, their testimony established that there were few people who could rival the seventy years of influence Stanley Mosk had on the evolution of California law, the administration of justice, politics, and social policy. The City of Los Angeles, the State of California, indeed the United States of America had all been changed by his life, in ways both subtle and dramatic.

Jewish tradition requires that the headstones marking the graves of the dead be unveiled and placed no sooner than the first anniversary of death. This allows time for the soul to leave the body. Tweaking the tradition, to mark the first anniversary of Stanley Mosk's death, a smaller group gathered in the lush mezzanine of the grand Dorothy Chandler Pavilion of the Los Angeles Music Center. There, they witnessed the unveiling of the oversized, symbolic headstone which, rather than marking the gravesite, announced the naming of the Stanley Mosk County Courthouse, itself an iconic symbol of Los Angeles's pursuit of justice. This was soon followed with the renaming of the Stanley Mosk Library & Courts Building on Sacramento's Capitol Mall. A life-size statue of Mosk, attired in judicial robes, facing the State Capitol, was dedicated in front of the Stanley Mosk Library & Courts Building. An elementary school in Winnetka, in the heart of Los Angeles County's San Fernando Valley, was named Stanley Mosk Elementary School. Fellowships and honors were established in his name, and law school journals dissected his judicial legacy. The real monuments to Stanley Mosk, however, lie in the pages of the official *California Reports*, where the opinions of the California Supreme Court are available for public inspection. The crisp logic, passion, and eloquence of Justice Mosk's majority and dissenting opinions continue to influence the law of California and the nation.

The life of Stanley Mosk has much to teach us about politics and justice in America. It also offers a window into historic struggles that still reverberate in our times. Decades of scholarly attention given to Los Angeles and California history have barely acknowledged the evidence demonstrating that Stanley Mosk stood at the center, or very close to it, of the epochal, defining moments during seven decades of the 20th century. The longest-serving Justice in the history of the California Supreme Court (1964–2001), Mosk possessed a unique combination of political savvy, personal charm, sharp intelligence, and talent as a judge. Even before he became a Justice of California's high court, Stanley Mosk was a force to be reckoned with. From his arrival in California in 1933, he was fully engaged in the civic, social, and political life of his community, state, and nation.

As a neophyte lawyer during the Depression years, he allied with radical and progressive civic leaders, investigating and publicizing police brutality and anti-labor violence. He helped to catalyze a grassroots movement for municipal reform in Los Angeles during the 1930s, playing an instrumental role in the nation's first successful recall drive to oust a corrupt big city mayor, Frank Shaw. His efforts on behalf of farm-workers and labor unions, and the alliances he forged led to Mosk being labeled a "communist sympathizer," and for two decades, he successfully defended himself against the label that sidelined many aspiring political leaders.

His first political appointment began what came to be a sixty-two year career in public service. Democratic Governor Culbert Olson appointed Mosk as Executive Secretary, where he often took center stage as the voice of the governor's office and, among other duties, briefed Olson about clemency appeals from death row inmates. On the eve of his departure from office, Olson appointed Mosk to the Los Angeles Superior Court. He was the youngest person ever named to that bench. His sixteen-year tenure on the Superior Court captured a broad swath of public attention. As a family court judge, he made headlines presiding over scores of cases involving Hollywood celebrities like Judy Garland, Lana Turner, and Charlie Chaplin. The press followed his every move, and when he briefly left the bench to enlist in the U.S. Army as a buck private, they dubbed him "G. I. Judge." Returning to his seat, Mosk spoke widely about problems facing veterans and new African American residents to the region, such as access to housing and jobs. In 1947, he issued a precedent-shattering ruling declaring racially restrictive covenants unenforceable under the U.S. Constitution. His indefatigable community activism, a weekly newspaper column, "Judging the News," and his leadership posts in local affiliates of secular and Jewish national organizations made him a popular figure and a Jewish icon, which allowed him to help forge a political alliance among white liberals and African Americans that transformed Los Angeles and California politics.

Skillfully building upon this base, Mosk was elected as Attorney General of California in 1958. He won with the largest margin of victory of any contested candidate in the nation that year, which was a remarkable achievement for a Superior Court judge. As the first Jew elected to statewide office since the gold rush era, Mosk demonstrated that being Jewish could be a political asset in California, rather than a liability. Despite the climate of lingering McCarthyism, he warned citizens against the threat to freedom and civil liberties from extremist right wing groups, the threat to the constitutionally protected separation of church and state from religious zealots, and the threat to the rights of labor and consumers from powerful corporate conglomerates.

At each stage of his political and judicial career, Mosk dealt with recurring issues facing Californians and Americans in general, in a volatile climate of anti-communist hysteria, racial conflict, government corruption, and rampant abuse by law enforcement officials. While earning the wrath of F.B.I. Director J. Edgar Hoover, Los Angeles Police Chief William Parker, and like-minded minions of law and order, Mosk remained sensitive to the need to balance the crime-fighting goals and methods of law enforcement against the liberty of individual citizens. He worked closely with U.S. Attorney General Robert Kennedy to help formulate national policy regarding illicit drugs, and promoted a new framework for the nation's attorneys general to reign in the abuse of power by law enforcement agencies.

In the midst of the unprecedented, dynamic growth of California, Mosk seized every opportunity available to advance the causes of justice and tolerance. As a citizen activist, judge, political office holder, and Supreme Court Justice, he dedicated his life to protecting civil liberties and civil rights through advocacy, public policy, and the promotion and interpretation of state and federal law. Nearly every political campaign of note, from the rise of Earl Warren and Richard Nixon, through the administrations of governors Goodwin Knight, Pat Brown, Ronald Reagan, Jerry Brown, George Deukmejian, Pete Wilson and Gray Davis directly involved Stanley Mosk in one way or another. California Chief Justice Phil Gibson was a mentor to Mosk throughout his career, from his days as a law student through his tenure on the Supreme Court. Governor Pat Brown and Assembly Speaker Jesse Unruh were political enemies, but both were friends of Stanley Mosk. President John F. Kennedy and Attorney General Robert F. Kennedy were close allies, but Mosk's emulation of their playboy lifestyle cost him dearly. His intimate friendship with William Clark, President Reagan's Secretary of the Interior, was an odd coupling of a staunch conservative and an unrepentant liberal. Presidents, governors and senators valued his counsel, and local and state officials called upon his intellect and experience. He touched the lives of thousands, some famous, some obscure, some infamous, as he journeyed throughout the tumultuous years of the 20th century.

His life was not without controversy. Mosk's political popularity nearly propelled him to a seat in the U.S. Senate, an ambition that was quashed by an embarrassing lapse in his private life. In 1964, at the height of his political career, with polls suggesting a slam-dunk victory, and the late President Kennedy's endorsement, Mosk readied his followers to help him win the Democratic nomination for the United States Senate. Some even speculated he would soon have a shot at a vice presidential slot. Many still believe Mosk's withdrawal from the senate campaign changed the course of California history, and paved the way for the political ascendency of Ronald Reagan.

Stanley Mosk's political ambition, however, was vulnerable to a half-decade of spying and intelligence gathering by the FBI and the LAPD. Motivated by J. Edgar Hoover's obsession with the "communist menace" and Los Angeles Police Chief William Parker's zeal to identify threats to his visions of law and order, both agencies engaged in extensive surveillance of many public officials, especially those who were most outspoken in promoting respect for our constitutional values. Throughout this biography, we draw upon the extensive FBI file on Stanley Mosk. While many of the day-to-day observations or accounts of Mosk's activities reflect events that parallel newspaper and other published accounts, the accuracy of descriptions by others and the interpretations drawn by undercover agents should be read skeptically, within the context of the unbridled abuse of government resources, power, and reach administered by Director Hoover. Similarly, details derived from a 1960's report on detainees in custody of the Los Angeles Police Department do not purport to reflect truth, but they do reflect the LAPD's perceptions of events that helped to change the course of history. Justice Mosk's devotion to the right of privacy and the need for courts to enforce constitutional limits upon investigative activities by police may well have found inspiration in his own victimization.

Speculation abounded about the timing of Governor Pat Brown's appointment of Stanley Mosk to the California Supreme Court. It now appears clear that a seat on the Supreme Court was Mosk's consolation prize for agreeing to withdraw from the senate race. Regardless of how he got there, Mosk's intellect, personal charm and keen political sensibilities enabled him to survive several retention elections. With encouragement from long-standing supporters, he occasionally toyed with returning to partisan electoral office, even as he carved out an historic legacy on the Court. As a Justice of the most respected state supreme court in the nation, Stanley Mosk achieved national prominence through his reasoned arguments and brilliant prose, and his formulation of the "Mosk Doctrine" became a leading force in the revival of a modern interpretation of "states' rights." This doctrine of state constitutionalism advocates state constitutions rather than the federal constitution as the primary ground for state supreme court decisions, insulating state court decisions from review by an increasingly conservative Federal supreme court.

A stalwart opponent of racial quotas, Mosk challenged the policy of affirmative action, suffering through an abusive backlash from his liberal "friends." As a reviewing judge, he bowed to the overwhelming public will to uphold the death penalty, while carefully evaluating its fairness and accuracy. Many of his judicial opinions are still regarded as landmarks, forging changes in the law that have stood the test of time. Throughout his tenure, he was often a dissenting voice, criticizing the course taken by the court majority.

As the longest-serving justice in the history of the California Supreme Court, Stanley Mosk possessed a rare combination of political acumen and judicial talent. The court faced formidable opposition from powerful special interests that could finance expensive initiative campaigns. In 1986, under the auspices of opposition to the court's rulings in death penalty cases, their efforts led to the bitterest judicial election contest in the nation, which culminated in a purge that swept Chief Justice Rose Bird and Associate Justices Cruz Reynoso and Joseph Grodin off the bench. Justice Stanley Mosk survived that election, and managed to stay in office through many more years of political turmoil. Although his career path was singular, it can teach us a great deal about the politician as a judge in our legal system, as well as the need for every judge to be a "politician" of sorts.

Justice Mosk was not aloof from controversies; winning some, and losing some, but always emerging with his reputation for thoughtfulness and fairness intact. There were times, of

Rolla Hertzmark (Perl), pictured here sometime in the 1890s, was the irascible maternal grandmother of Stanley and Edward Mosk (courtesy Tom Mosk).

course, when he felt discouraged. "The Goddess of Justice is wearing a black armband today, as she weeps for the Constitution of California,"¹ he wrote in one memorable dissent. Despite disappointments, he continued to exhort his fellow judges and fellow citizens to "recognize what can be changed and what cannot."² Mosk's passion was tempered by political pragmatism, and his acceptance of practical limits distinguishes his judicial philosophy from other "liberal" judges.

Personally, Stanley Mosk has been described as shy, smart, charming, ambitious, witty, optimistic, and resourceful. He has also been described as cunning, duplicitous, opportunistic, elitist, and sexist. This work is filled with incidents that might fit any one of these descriptions. Some aspects of his life remain enigmatic. Viewing his life in its entirety, however, he emerges as a principled idealist, who truly valued liberty, equality, and justice, and who at every stage of his expanding influence, used the power of his position to ensure these values for the larger good.

Ultimately, Justice Stanley Mosk emerges from these pages as "one of that breed, few in number" that were not only

In marrying Morris Perl, pictured here sometime in the 1890s, Rolla believed the union was beneath her station. After migrating to America, she abandoned him and their three children but Morris eventually followed Rolla to Denver where he later died of tuberculosis (courtesy Tom Mosk).

skilled craftsmen, but also "architects" of the law. "Judges who are capable of perceiving how the particular case and the particular issue fits into the overall structure of the law; or, more broadly, ... how it fits within the framework of institutions and values that define our political community."³

Stanley Mosk's life is a window into the larger demographic, social, and political changes in California that helped to shape the cases coming before the court. Mosk arrived on the high court in the midst of a social revolution, when America's traditions, leaders, and authorities were often under attack. His tenure lasted until the new millennium, which found Californians still dealing with many of the same issues as the state struggled with new challenges posed by advancing technology, political polarization and the declining quality of the environment.

The California Supreme Court has long been recognized as the nation's leading state supreme court, due in large measure to strong leadership by its judicial giants. Justice Mosk knew them all, and now stands tall among them. To many, his death in 2001 signaled the loss of the last of the great liberals in a conservative era. In an era when nearly every court in the nation struggles to balance sharply different judicial philosophies, the life and career of Justice Stanley Mosk offers us a unique perspective into the dynamic interplay of law, politics and justice in America.

Chapter 1

"Walk Upstairs and Save"

After six botched attempts to assassinate Russia's Tsar Alexander II, the increasingly frustrated terrorist faction of the revolutionary organization Narodnaya Volya (People's Will) finally succeeded in taking his life. The deafening series of explosions on March 1, 1881, changed forever the lives of millions of Russian Jews, as well as the lives of their children and generations to come. This included the families of Rolla and Morris Perl, who were the maternal grandparents of Morey Stanley Mosk.

Rolla was born in a small town near Riga, Livonia in 1858. Livonia, on the shores of the Baltic, remained within the Russian empire until 1918, when its territory was divided between the newly independent states of Latvia and Estonia. Rolla's father, Elias Hartzmark, was a liberal reform Jew who educated his children in Hebrew and Yiddish.[1] The official language of Livonia was German. The Hartzmark family enjoyed special privileges awarded to university graduates and Jews who were engaged in "useful" professions. Rolla was twelve when her mother died. When her father later remarried and brought his 18-year-old bride home, teenaged Rolla left home to work as a seamstress in Riga, Livonia's most prosperous city. Industrious and determined, she eventually opened her own small shirtwaist factory.[2]

Morris Perl was born in Memel, Germany. He wore wire-rimmed spectacles set upon a prominent forehead with a dark bushy, handlebar mustache spread wide beneath his large nose. Morris moved to Hamburg to become a traveling salesman for a lamp company and during sales trips to Riga he met and wooed Rolla. After they married, Morris became a salesman for and then manager of Rolla's shirtwaist factory.[3] Despite his diligent efforts, Rolla began to look down on him, believing that she had married beneath her station. It was not a happy marriage. Nevertheless, the booming manufacturing base and prosperous market conditions brought the growing Latvian Jewish population a level of comfort, and the young couple prospered right up until the Tsar's assassination.

Following the murder of Alexander II, the Russian regime resorted to a time-honored tradition: blame the Jews. Police brutality and suppression of civil liberties resumed, even more ferociously than during the previous years of incremental social reforms. Draconian regulations began to reverse the freedoms and prestige enjoyed by the Jewish population of Riga. Livonia was "beyond the pale," the limited portion of the Russian empire where Jews were permitted to settle.[4] Now, restrictions were placed on Jewish worship, and Jews were excluded from holding public office and the practice of many professions. Those who were not employed in officially registered professions were ordered to leave the city, except for those like the Hartzmark family who could prove they lived in the city even before the province came under Russian rule.

Rolla's fortunes were now tied to those of her husband, and eventually Morris's German origins targeted him for expulsion. Pondering their options, Rolla insisted that returning to Germany was out of the question. The role of women in Germany would have confined Rolla to "kinder, kuchen and kirche" (children, kitchen and church). Even worse, the notion that she would be forced into civil and social subservience to her husband was a prospect for which she was much "too liberated."[5] As elsewhere in Europe, Jews reacted to growing hostility by forming Zionist groups, which urged Jews to prepare themselves for emigration to Palestine and to the United States, increasingly characterized as the "land of opportunity" for Europe's displaced and despairing populations. The wave of repressive edicts produced a flood of Jewish emigration to America that totaled more than two million souls in the ensuing quarter century. Rolla and Morris Perl were swept up in this flood of humanity.[6]

As with many immigrants at the time, the path to America had been prepared by previously settled relatives. Rolla's brother William Hartzmark and his wife Yetta were already living in Hartford, Connecticut, so Morris and Rolla settled near them. Morris went to work for a large grocery store, carting inventory back and forth between freezing storage units and the warmer store-front, where wooden shelves displayed the goods. They worked hard, and eventually saved enough money to buy their own small grocery store. When the children were old enough to count, they helped to operate the family enterprise. Three children arrived in rapid succession: Bessie (birthdate unknown), Minna (who became the mother of Stanley Mosk) in 1889, and David two years later.[7] Posing for a rare family portrait, the three siblings shared equally somber expressions. Minna's determination was suggested by the set of her jaw and her direct gaze. David's traditional black formal dress and dangling locks gave little indication of his idiosyncrasies and individualism. Rolla was hardly enchanted with her new American life, thinking she deserved better.

When Rolla's sister-in-law Yetta came down with tuberculosis, her husband William packed up and left for Denver, Colorado. At that time, TB accounted for ten percent of all deaths in America. Known as the "white plague," physicians recognized only one treatment for TB: clean air and sunshine. Denver, the Queen City on the Plains, with its mountain air and crisp climate, became the preferred destination for Jews infected with the disease. The city, however, was ill prepared for the arrival of these poor Jews and their families. In 1889, Frances Wisebart Jacobs, founder of the Denver Hebrew Ladies' Relief Society, pro-

Paul Mosk soon became mutually infatuated with Minna Perl, and unlike that of her parents, their marriage was a long and happy one (courtesy Tom Mosk).

posed building a Jewish-sponsored tuberculosis hospital. Although construction was completed in 1893, a precipitous drop in silver prices that year caused a depression in the western mining states, and the Frances Jacobs Hospital stood empty for lack of operating funds. In 1895, Louis Anfenger, the district president of national B'nai B'rith, asked that organization to adopt the tuberculosis hospital as a national project. On December 10, 1899, the Denver hospital finally opened its doors. Renamed the National Jewish Hospital, it was operated on a nondenominational basis. To reflect its openness to the impoverished of every back-

Minna Mosk's business acuity included renting out the top story of the Mosks' "Scotch Plaid Tailors" shop on 16th Street in Denver, seen here, c. 1907 (courtesy Tom Mosk).

ground, the hospital adopted the motto, "None may enter who can pay, and none can pay who enter." Yetta Hartzmark was one of the first patients of the new hospital.

Rolla believed that she too had contracted TB, but her fears were probably inspired by the opportunity it presented to escape her unhappy marriage. She followed her brother to Denver, leaving Morris struggling to run the grocery store with the help of their three children.[8] Rolla absolutely refused to return to Hartford. The small nest egg the couple had accumulated was soon depleted, and the family fell into an impoverished existence. Finally, Morris sold the store, packed up the children, and followed his estranged wife to Denver. There, he and oldest daughter Bessie worked in his brother-in-law William's china and glass shop until they could afford to rent their own establishment with living quarters in the rear. After years of exposure to extreme cold and heavy lifting, Morris was unable to withstand the challenges to his frail body, and so it was Morris and not Rolla who contracted tuberculosis. His health deteriorated rapidly. In 1904, while his son David studied for his bar mitzvah, Morris died in the Jewish National hospital.[9] Minna was fifteen when her father died.

Despite the loss of their devoted father, the three children thrived under Rolla's supervision. They were popular, attending parties and gatherings among the well-to-do. Morris had hoped his daughters would become teachers, but it was more fashionable for young women to drop out of high school to attend business school. Modern business management called on women to take over the expanding secretarial and clerical pools, while their fathers and brothers moved out and at times up in the burgeoning corporate culture. Mom-and-pop retail stores still dominated the economic landscape, though. After Minna enrolled in a bookkeeping course to learn typing and stenography, she was quickly hired by a small men's clothing outlet run by brothers Paul and Sam Mosk.

The Mosk brothers were adventurous and entrepreneurial spirits, and both were single. Paul, the youngest, was attracted to Minna and they soon began dating. They quickly became "a steady matter" and were married in 1910. Unlike her parents' marriage, Minna and Paul became a mutually supportive and devoted couple. Minna adored her husband.[10] Little is known about Paul Mosk's background except that his family name was originally

The youthful Mosk brothers sat still just long enough for this formal portrait. Stanley (left) wears matching stripes as he poses with toddler Edward, likely around 1918 (courtesy Tom Mosk).

The Mosk brothers opened their well-stocked Crown All Hat store in San Antonio, Texas, seen here c. 1914 (courtesy Tom Mosk).

Moskovics, and they came from a small Jewish "shtetl" named Lastovitz, in the present day Czech Republic near the German border. The "shtetl" was among the hundreds later destroyed during the Nazi era, and no trace remains. Sometime in the 1880s, the family began migrating to the United States, settling in Denver. Paul was born in 1880, and arrived in America in 1896. In addition to his brother Sam, he had three older brothers, Abraham, Earnest and Phillip.

Minna and Paul moved into a two-story house in Denver, and she capably managed the family finances by renting out the top floor.[11] The Mosk brothers were never content to stay in one place very long, however, and soon they sold their clothing store. Paul headed for Los Angeles, California, while Sam traveled to Houston, Texas. Paul and Minna briefly operated a men's clothing store in Los Angeles, but soon they also packed up for Houston, where Sam had opened another shop. Unhappy there, they then settled in San Antonio where they stayed long enough to open The Crown All Hat Company, and to give birth to the first of their two sons. Morey Stanley Mosk was born on September 4, 1912.[12] Minna couldn't have been more proud of her baby boy, whom she entered into "The Better Baby" contest in December, 1914.[13] He would be known as "Morey" to his friends and family for the first thirty years of his life, reversing the order of his name to Stanley M. Mosk when he first appeared on a ballot.

Then the largest city in Texas, with a population of 100,000, San Antonio was not unfriendly to the Mosks. In Texas, Jewish immigrants found relative freedom to practice their religion, follow their way of life, and seek opportunity for economic advancement. Just as they had in the Ottoman Empire prior to the First World War, they established a mercantile pattern in which individuals would arrive at a port or urban center and journey along well-established roads selling what they could. Finding a satisfactory business location, they would settle and, preserving their links to sources of supply, begin a chain that would grow, link by link. The Nieman-Marcus department stores, Zale's jewelry stores, and the Weingarten grocery stores (later Grand Union) are only a few of the well-known names that defined this pattern of entrepreneurial spirit in Texas.

By 1912, when Morey Stanley Mosk was born, San Antonio's Jewish population had grown to nearly 3,000. Amid rural hinterlands spotted with old-fashioned boarding houses and hotels and country general stores, Paul Mosk set up his hat shop. In those days, men never left the house without donning a hat, so he did a brisk business. Paul then entered a partnership with Harry Steele in a Galveston men's store. Harry tried to convince Paul there was a fortune to be made in Mexico, but Paul did not find the risk tempting. Steele rode off on horseback and made a fortune, controlling the importation of Swiss watches and clocks in Mexico. Paul then invited Minna's brother Dave, who was in California, to mind the hat store while he traveled to New York on yet another business venture. Shortly after his return, Paul sold the San Antonio store. The entire family, Minna, Paul, Stanley and Uncle Dave headed east. Grandmother Rolla, who had since moved in with them, stayed behind in San Antonio, and eventually remarried.

During a brief stay in Boston, the Mosk-Perl clan opened another small grocery store. Uncle Dave lived with the family, and became a soapbox orator, promoting the virtues of socialism. Boston audiences had little tolerance for socialists, and brawls were a daily occurrence. Frequently, Dave cut a deal: if the audience would let him finish his speech, he would agree to join them for a scrap in the seats when he was done. The fights and the grocery store soon took their toll on Dave and Paul, so the whole clan moved back to San Antonio. There, Uncle Dave began the study of law, and met and married Esther Radoff.[14] Esther and Dave lived in furnished rooms close to Minna and Paul, forming an extended nuclear family whose lives were intimately intertwined during the decades of Stanley's youth. Single again, Rolla moved in with Dave and Esther. The presence of the irascible Rolla in the newlyweds' home created a good deal of tension for Esther. Minna reached out to her, and the two formed a strong bond that lasted the rest of their lives. Stanley's younger brother Ed arrived on September 26, 1916, allowing both brothers to claim San Antonio as their birthplace, with birthdays two weeks apart.

In 1917, the extended family moved yet again, this time to Rockford, Illinois, in Northern Winnebago County. The original Swedish and Italian pioneers saw great potential for the fertile land located midway along the Galena-Chicago stagecoach run. Rockford's name reflects the shallow water meandering over rocks at a natural ford, an abundant source of natural power. The Pecatonica and Kishwaukee rivers run into the Sinnissippi; names reminiscent of the Native American tribes that had populated the lush green landscapes of the Rock River Valley. The Valley was the scene of the Black Hawk Indian War in the summer of 1832, when Colonel Zachary Taylor, Captain Abraham Lincoln, and Lieutenant Jefferson Davis helped drive the Sauk Indians from the Valley. By the time the Mosks settled, the city of Rockford proclaimed its distinction as the "metal fastener capital of the world," with a machine tool center second only to Chicago.

Paul moved to Rockford ahead of the family, to set up a new clothing store. He selected an upstairs location; a rather novel approach to retail sales. "Walk Upstairs and Save" seemed like a good idea to attract customers. Uncle Dave, Esther, Minna and the children soon followed. They all shared a two-story house and everyone helped in the store. Uncle Dave resumed his law studies, and this time his wife joined him.

The family arrived too late for the 1916 presidential election, when Rockford women voted for the first time, contributing to the narrow victory of incumbent President Woodrow Wilson. Wilson defeated a progressive Republican challenger, former New York governor and Supreme Court Justice Charles Evans Hughes. Voters perceived Hughes as more hawkish of the two, and Wilson's success was attributed largely to his promise to "keep us out of the war."

The first drive-in gas station in Rockford opened in 1917, and that year Sunday movies won approval to entertain a popula-

Part of Stanley Mosk's extended nuclear family included his mother Minna's brother David Perl, who married Esther in spite of her father's disapproval. Esther (right) is posing here with mother-in-law Rolla Perl in July 1927 (courtesy Tom Mosk).

tion hovering around 50,000. The United States entered the "war to end all wars" on April 2, 1917, and began drafting young men who would be shipped to France to fight in the trenches. Soon Rockford won a large military contract to erect what became known as Camp Grant, designed to train and house 41,160 military personnel.

In September, the first 2,000 recruits arrived and likely passed by the first busload of local draft dodgers carted off to the Winnebago County jail. Despite such protests, the war brought social and economic gains for both men and women to Rockford, which stubbornly retained its quiet town atmosphere. Rockford's economy took off soon after the outbreak of World War I. A 50 percent increase in industrial production meant jobs were plentiful, requiring nighttime shifts at the local plants. The following year, salaries increased along with the population, as auto production soared and bridge and other infrastructure construction surged.

Motivated by patriotic duty and a desire to help relieve the monotony of boot camp, the Mosks opened their door to men in uniform, and some became regulars at the weekend dinner table.[15] Paul came up with a new venture to sell tailor-made suits to military personnel on behalf of a nearby Chicago manufacturer. The enterprise lasted for well over a decade. Military men often wore civilian clothes during off duty hours, but they couldn't stray too far from base camp nor did they particularly like to shop. With limited budgets and few options, "Walk Upstairs and Save" provided a convenient alternative. Paul and Uncle Dave fitted servicemen with tailored suits, paid for through deductions from their monthly paychecks arranged through the local commanding officer. Paul's customers affectionately called him "the Colonel."

As the father of two young children, Paul Mosk was exempt from the draft. Uncle Dave came close to being inducted into the Army, but the world-wide flu epidemic intervened, reaching Rockford in the fall of 1918. Morey Stanley Mosk had just celebrated his sixth birthday when the epidemic struck. As one Rockford resident recalled,

> Death was everywhere. Schools, churches, theaters, and many businesses were closed. People on the street wore facemasks. Emergency hospitals were established in the Rockford Boys Club, Lincoln School, and the Knights of Columbus club. A downtown garage was turned into a morgue. Flag-draped coffins stood in huge stacks at train stations. Grieving families of dead soldiers poured into town to claim their loved ones. The city faltered under the strain, taking little solace in the fact that most of the nation and the world were suffering, too. A new round of attacks on local German-Americans occurred as rumors spread that the Kaiser's secret agents had deliberately started the pandemic.[16]

The production of coffins could not keep up with the number of deaths occurring each day. On Friday, October 4, 1918, with more than 100 bodies in the Camp Grant mortuary, officials negotiated with local undertakers to take the bodies at $50 each, but when one showed up with a flatbed truck to remove the dead, the Army quickly provided more dignified closed trucks.[17] Hospital officials summoned all officers on leave, converted barracks to hospital wards, and by "extreme effort" expanded the hospital capacity from "10 occupied beds to a capacity of 4,102 beds in six days."[18] By October 3, the combined death toll for Camp Grant and the city of Rockford stood at 63. In the next two days, it climbed to 234. On October 10 alone, 218 soldiers and civilians died. When the epidemic ended a few weeks later, as suddenly as it had started, fatalities numbered 323 in Rockford, nearly 100 more in the rest of Winnebago County, and more than 1,400 at Camp Grant, largely because the army inductees were more vulnerable in their close quarters and meager living conditions.[19] Camp Grant was closed to new recruits, including Uncle Dave. When Dave was finally ordered to report for duty on November 11, 1918, he instead joined the "explosive celebration" of news that the Armistice finally ended the war. Camp Grant was dismantled and postwar life could begin.

Paul and Minna were easy-going parents, and family and friends commented that their well behaved-boys were a pleasure to have around. Both Stanley and Ed were very bright, quick learners who shared a passion for baseball. In 1919, Uncle Dave and Esther gave birth to Harriet, who was more like a sister than a cousin, and provided the Mosk brothers with a playmate. Dave gave up on his aspirations for law and became a salesman for Brooks Brothers suits. On their days off, Paul loaded everyone into his Ford automobile and drove through Rockford's countryside. Stanley's hay fever inspired summer escapes up north to Lake Koshkonong, across the Wisconsin border.[20]

Stanley and Ed Mosk were free to enjoy their boyhoods, playing softball in a neighboring field every chance they could. When Minna called them home to practice the piano, it bred a lasting disdain for the instrument on Stanley's part.[21] Sports bonded the father to his sons, and the brothers to each other, and after buying a new Dart automobile, Paul would often load them into the back and drive to Chicago to see the White Sox play at Comiskey Park. Stanley remained a Sox fan, while Ed eventually rooted for the Cubs.[22] The boys were incessant scorekeepers and obsessive collectors of team minutia. Stanley acquired reputable skills in both table and court tennis, and developed a keen addiction to football during his well-rounded adolescence. Although Stanley was four years older than Ed, sports, and then politics became lifelong passions the brothers enjoyed together, relishing each other's company. Cousin Harriet observed that the Mosk household was calmer and warmer than her own. The free-flowing unconditional love of Paul and Minna instilled self-confidence in their sons, manifested in a lifelong rapport between them.[23]

As in Texas, the Mosks encountered very little anti–Semitism in Rockford. In fact, neighbors even invited Paul to join the local Ku Klux Klan, which in Rockford was a rather benign social club without cross burnings. The invitation was politely declined. Like many smaller communities in Middle America, Rockford had a sizable Jewish community of close to 1,000. The vast majority were German immigrants, most of whom were Reform Jews. As a result, English became the main language of prayer and rituals were simplified, often led by a layman rather than a rabbi. When the Reform Jews of Rockford were unable to obtain the services of a student rabbi for Passover in 1923, they cancelled their arrangements for a communal Seder. Temple Beth El had been built in Rockford in 1913, and conducted religious training which both Mosk boys regularly attended, and both were part of Temple Beth El's Confirmation Exercises, in 1926 and 1930 respectively. At the age of fourteen, Stanley was a featured speaker at his confirmation ceremony, speaking on "What Judaism Means to Us." During Edward's June 1930 confirmation four years later, he read an essay entitled, "I am A Jew." Rabbi Weinstein of the Austin, Texas, B'nai B'rith Hillel Foundation wrote Edward a heartfelt letter of congratulations. The Rabbi wrote fondly of both Stanley and Edward, concluding, "I'm going to watch your careers with great interest."[24]

Politics, more than piety, provided the vehicle to shape the Mosks' identities and places in their community. It fostered a strong sense of confidence, or political efficacy, which later inspired their lifelong activism on behalf of deeply held values of social justice. Minna was a Democrat, while Paul was a lifelong Republican. Minna cast her first vote in the 1920 election, when Democrats James Cox and Franklin D. Roosevelt lost to conservative Republicans Warren Harding and Calvin Coolidge. Although "they really canceled each other out in most elections,"[25] Paul identified strongly with the Progressive Republicanism characterized by neighboring Wisconsin's Senator Robert LaFollette. Minna was a firebrand and more vocal in her views than Paul, whose quiet demeanor disguised a steely determination. Stanley and Ed inherited traits from each of their parents, while the presence of Uncle Dave, the true revolutionary in the household, exposed them to more extreme facets of the political spectrum.

Uncle Dave often extolled the value of exercise, whole wheat bread, and regular bowel movements; and then launched into the glories of Marxist socialism. He progressed from a more generic communism to a Trotsky-as-the-devil, Stalinist bravado that lasted his lifetime.[26] News of the revolution in Russia and the establishment of the Soviet Union was cause to rejoice for Dave, and for him it "was the most exciting event" in his lifetime. He followed the birth of the new nation as if it were indeed his own child. He read everything he could about events abroad, and he gloated over Soviet successes and grieved over their failures and errors. His enthusiasm was risky, for the post-war Red Scare spread its own type of hysteria. One year after the armistice, Rockford paid a heavy toll during America's unprecedented wave of strikes, race riots, terrorist bombings, and flagrant violations of civil liberties. The city had a long tradition of tolerance for Socialists and labor organizers. A labor-Socialist coalition led by Alderman Oscar Ogren regularly polled 25–40 percent in mayoral elections. In January 1920, Rockford was a principal target of the infamous "Palmer Raids," coordinated by U.S. Attorney General A. Mitchell Palmer to round up "communist agitators." Between 140 and 180 Rockford residents were summarily arrested and charged with conspiracy and sedition. Clarence Darrow came to town to defend Arthur Person, who was put on trial in the Winnebago County Courthouse for sedition. Person was acquitted, and in the next election, Rockford citizens elected the Labor League candidate as their mayor.

Uncle Dave never wavered in his belief in socialism, and he held dearly to its tenets throughout his life. Although the Perls eventually went their own way, moving all over the country, the families reunited several times. Over the years Dave contributed to the Abraham Lincoln Brigade, supporting the Republican defense against Franco's Fascist takeover of Spain. He continued for many years to help refugees of the civil war who had fled to France after the fall of the Spanish Republic's government. Esther was her husband's disciple and together they joined such groups as the League Against Fascism, which became the League for Peace and Democracy, a notorious Communist front organization that dissolved when Stalin signed a non-aggression pact with Hitler in 1939.

Paul and Minna managed to resist Dave's attempts to convert them to either whole wheat bread or to communism. Minna revered her brother, but she was too preoccupied with her own husband and family to be swept up in his proselytizing. Nevertheless, Uncle Dave's influence and Minna's obvious admiration for him was absorbed by her sons. Edward appears to have embraced more of Dave's philosophy though, while Stanley remained somewhat aloof, feeling both attracted to and yet skeptical of Uncle Dave's radical views. Many years later, Stanley's increasingly public career might have been tarnished by his relationship to a man who expressed effusive and outspoken joy at the launching of Sputnik. Long after those who had once found hope in the Russian revolution turned into its staunchest critics, Uncle Dave held tight to his optimism. After two visits to the Soviet Union in the 1970's, he still believed in its ability to uplift mankind. There is little that directly connects Stanley to Uncle Dave during the rise of Mosk's public career, but there is much that resonates in the causes he fought as a youthful, left-leaning liberal often allied with those of more radical persuasion.

Throughout the 1920's, Stanley and Ed Mosk matured handsomely and made their parents proud. Cousin Harriet described Stanley as "grown up from the beginning." Brother Ed seemed warmer and more enthusiastic, with a smiling, happy disposition. He was rambunctious and at times, he was "like an overgrown puppy," whereas "there was nothing puppyish ever about Stanley."[27] Although somewhat shy, Stanley was ambitious and fiercely competitive. When his well-organized memory for detail was not focused on baseball statistics, he excelled as a student.

Stanley and Ed started an autograph collection, a passion that Stanley later passed on to his own son, Richard. The Mosk brothers wrote to every elected official alive, senators and congressmen, surviving presidents and vice presidents, Supreme Court justices, and anyone else they could imagine to add to their collection of autographed envelopes of "first day covers" with newly issued postage stamps. The boys eagerly awaited the delivery of each day's mail to see what treasures would enhance their collection. This hobby contributed to the close rapport the brothers sustained throughout their lives, which were filled with intense conversations about politics and law, and an almost obsessive preoccupation with sports. More importantly, it appears to be the beginning of Stanley's sustained writing of letters and notes, and his love of correspondence, which kept him linked to friends and acquaintances and leaders all over the world. Eventually, Stanley's autograph collection grew well beyond his boyhood requests for autographs from the ranks of politicians and government officials. Now in possession of his son Richard, it includes the riches of Stanley Mosk's personal correspondence with celebrated persons in all walks of life. It provides a vivid portrait of his intellect, his quick-witted sense of humor, his sometimes whimsical observations, and most certainly, his often biting critique of the persons and events that filled his days.

Over the years, Mosk would perfect the writing skills that were first honed by his Rockford teachers, whom he described as a "singularly unattractive" bunch of people. Nevertheless, he appreciated their ability to instill the skills he mastered. Rockford Senior High was among the largest high schools in Illinois at the time, with more than 1600 students. It was the second high school in the country to establish a yearbook, and the first to organize a band that played at halftimes during widely attended football games.[28]

The most helpful tool Morey Stanley Mosk took from his stint in high school was what he learned as a member of the Junior Press Club, where he developed his life long affection for journalism. The Club's arrangement with the local newspaper, *The Morning Star*, allowed him to work in the newsroom and to write an ongoing column about the school's activities. He got to know reporters and learned the fundamentals of the trade, writing journalistic style articles and adhering to deadlines. Briefly contemplating a career in the reporter's trenches, he abandoned this ambition when he found out that his hero, sports editor Frank Hicks, earned only $35 a week. Unquestionably, this early training facilitated his ability to garner a prolific media presence later in life.

By the time he graduated from Rockford Senior High School with his 384 classmates, it was perfectly clear that Morey Stanley Mosk was destined for great things. He had a lot of energy, and was able to balance many tasks at the same time and to excel in all of them. At seventeen he had already been elected senior class president and president of the student council, was a captain of the ROTC, a member of the debate team, vice president of the local branch of the National Honor Society, and editor of the school newspaper, *The Owl*.

A front-page school newspaper photo of Morey Stanley Mosk depicts a youthful but studious face, partially hidden by round, dark-rimmed glasses. His fellow students predicted his future in a "Class Prophesy" that he would take up aviation to break the recent record set by Charles Lindbergh, who had flown over Rockford after his historic trans–Atlantic solo journey.[29] He would also advance the field of transportation by "inventing the well-known machine that flies underground without causing the dirt to fly."[30]

At the commencement ceremony for the Rockford Senior High School class of 1929, the procession brought tears of laughter to Paul and Minna. Morey Stanley Mosk led the march of students, resplendent in their caps and gowns, carrying the banner which would be handed to the incoming senior class. As Mosk and the column of classmates came forward, the Mosks watched their son, the only Jewish kid leading hundreds of Scandinavian and northern European Protestants, as the band blasted out a chorus of "Onward Christian Soldiers!" No matter. Many immigrant Jews believed the key to success in America was to simply blend in; not to make a fuss that would point out their differences. It was better to be identified among the "us" than to be labeled one of "them." In later years, Justice Mosk often joked that such imposition on the religious views of a minority would probably provoke a lawsuit. Stanley Mosk became an ardent champion of respect for the rights of minorities, but not because of any discrimination or oppression he experienced in Rockford, Illinois.

Chapter 2

"What This Fraternity Needs Is More Moreys!"

Stanley Mosk came of age at the close of an era when experimentation by progressive social reformers altered the course of twentieth century American cities. Chicago in particular, and Illinois in general, ranked at the front of innovative environments where social welfare advocates and proponents of humanitarian public policy could have some influence over old-time political machines and statewide legislators. Rebuilding after the Great Fire of 1871, the "Windy City" flourished, becoming the Midwest's hub of industry and commercial enterprise. The changing cityscape provided an ideal laboratory to study America's modern multicultural populations, and to promote public policy designed to improve the lives of toiling immigrant families, with their armies of workers eager for any employment within the expanding manufacturing economy.

For the first time, academics worked with grassroot reformers, performing real-world field studies of men, women, and children forced to make their way in an unfamiliar world of dilapidated tenements, garbage-filled streets and the relentless cacophony of sounds and movement of big-city life. Among the most prominent reformers was Jane Addams, whose Hull House pioneered programs to hasten the assimilation of immigrants, and engaged in local politics to foster fulfillment of "the American dream." In this way, Chicago encapsulated the American experience, with its prosperity and modernism resting upon the shoulders of those most vulnerable to exploitation and abuse by the captains of industry. Socialist author Upton Sinclair's classic *The Jungle* vividly described the atmosphere of turn-of-the-century Chicago, depicting the lives of those who hustled to hazardous jobs in dangerous manufactories, railroads, and stockyards.

A Jewish boy applying to be a college freshman in 1929 would have been well aware that his opportunities for an Ivy League education were limited. Writers of the period report that by 1930 most private colleges facing a growing Jewish enrollment instituted some kind of restrictive scheme.[1] A public opinion poll taken at the time found that 41 percent of Americans believed "Jews have too much power in the United States," and 20 percent wanted to "drive Jews out of the United States."[2] Harvard, Yale and Princeton used "character" and "geographical diversity" to disguise their efforts to avoid the fate of Columbia University, which saw its Jewish enrollment soar to 40 percent before adopting a Jewish quota.

Universities in the Midwest were less likely to rely upon quotas to restrict the enrollment of Jewish students. The University of Chicago was in the vanguard of turn-of-the-century progressive leadership. It led the way in many things, especially when it came to admission policies that welcomed Morey Stanley Mosk in 1929. The University used grades and test scores to select its first-year students, which offered excellent opportunities for those excluded by the Ivy League universities.[3] With his record of academic achievement and high test scores, Stanley Mosk was easily admitted to the University of Chicago. Its nearby location and reasonable cost also fit the family budget, although it was still a stretch for his parents.

This is not to say, however, that anti–Semitism had been eradicated at the University of Chicago. Among Mosk's fellow undergraduate students in 1929 was 20-year-old Martha Dodd, the attractive and vivacious daughter of Professor William E. Dodd, Chair of the University of Chicago history department. She described a "subtle and undercurrent propaganda among the undergraduates" that promulgated hostility toward Jews. She found "that even many of the college professors resented the brilliance of Jewish colleagues and students." As for herself, she said, "I was slightly anti–Semitic in this sense: I accepted the attitude that Jews were not as physically attractive as Gentiles and were less socially desireable."[4]

Martha Dodd's attitude toward Jews was fully shared by her father, who was appointed American Ambassador to Hitler's Germany by Franklin D. Roosevelt in 1933. Before leaving with his family for Germany, Dodd dined with Charles R. Crane, the scion of a family that had grown wealthy selling plumbing fixtures. Crane was a generous supporter of Dodd's history department, endowing a chair for the study of Russian history. Dodd confided that "Jews had held a great many more of the key positions in Germany than their numbers or their talents entitled them to." Crane expressed great admiration for Hitler, and advised Dodd to "let Hitler have his way" with the Jews. He advised Dodd to "resist every social invitation" from Jews, telling him "the Jews, after winning the war, galloping along at a swift pace, getting Russia, England and Palestine, being caught in the act of trying to seize Germany, too, and meeting their first real rebuff have gone plumb crazy and are deluging the world — particularly easy America — with anti–German propaganda." Dodd later complained that the Embassy staff had too many Jews, and Martha confessed, in a letter to her friend Thornton Wilder, "We sort of don't like the Jews anyway."[5]

Mosk arrived at the University of Chicago the same year that Robert Maynard Hutchens came to serve as the university's fifth president. Although Mosk matriculated too early to benefit from most of Hutchens' reforms, he was a student at the university when the "New Plan" consolidated departmental structure, introduced general survey courses, and inaugurated comprehensive examinations. Mosk had the advantage of studying social sciences under a truly outstanding faculty of accomplished scholars. His economics professor was Paul H. Douglas, a Quaker convert who incorporated the work of social reformers like Jane Addams into his courses. Douglas later served with distinction as a U.S. senator for Illinois from 1949 to 1967. His political science professor was Frederick L. Schumann, a renowned author who went on to a celebrated teaching career at Williams College. Schumann's brief foray as a lecturer for the State Department landed him a spot on Senator Joseph McCarthy's infamous list of "known Communists" employed by the U.S. Department of State. Mosk's history professor was William Hutchinson, an authority on American constitutional history and historiography, who formulated a pioneering course on historical methods.[6]

As a freshman, Mosk pledged with Phi Sigma Delta fraternity, later merged with Zeta Beta Tau, the nation's first Jewish fraternity. Mosk moved into the frat house close to campus on Woodlawn Avenue. His fraternity brothers immediately recognized Morey's administrative skills. He served as the Master Frater of the "Mu" chapter. The fraternity quarterly journal *The Deltan* awarded him the Deltan Reportorial Prize, describing him as "a lover of ink with a nose for news, and with a fine sense of co-operaton." Lauded, for example, for his initiative to handle mail deliveries, Mosk was held up as a model for others: "Without

Morey Mosks the central body would be helpless, for it would not know what is going in the chapters.... What this fraternity needs is more Moreys!"[7]

Although Stanley was an attentive student, he pursued a "well-rounded" education beyond the classroom. He played on the freshman baseball team, and rarely missed a football game on Chicago's home field. Throughout his life, Stanley Mosk loved a good baseball or football game. While he was a student, the Chicago football teams coached by Amos Alonzo Stagg competed in the Big Ten Conference and produced the first winner of the Heisman Trophy, Jay Berwanger. Mosk called him "the greatest football player I ever saw."[8] One of his fraternity brothers, Sam Horwitz, was captain of the football team. Stanley was unhappy when President Hutchens later eliminated intercollegiate football games. Hutchens, he felt, was a consistent foe of organized sports. Speaking of Hutchens, he would joke, "Whenever he had the impulse to engage in any exercise, he would lie down until it passed."[9]

The college student newspaper, *The Phoenix*, was named for the mythical bird that is born anew from its own ashes. Referring to the Great Chicago fire of 1871 and the subsequent rebuilding with new steel-frame construction, the Phoenix was also the official mascot of the University of Chicago's athletic teams. *The Phoenix* provided Mosk with an opportunity to continue his passion for creative writing. He published articles about the future possibility of "Robust Robots" performing the daily tasks of humans, and about "Inter-Fraternity Playtime."[10]

The city of Chicago provided an excellent laboratory for Mosk to immerse himself in traditional urban politics. Chicago attracted a multitude of German, Polish, and Italian immigrants. Mosk's dive into the electoral arena occurred in the midst of great political upheaval at both the local and the national level. The "Great Crash" on Wall Street occurred during his first semester as a college freshman, and throughout his college years, the economic downturn altered the political landscape. Mosk used his summer vacations to travel with his fraternity brothers throughout the United States, gaining first-hand impressions of the national upheaval. Chicago's reliance on manufacturing and a large unskilled working class was devastated by the Great Depression. Only 50 percent of the Chicagoans who had worked in the manufacturing sector in 1927 were still working there in 1933. Forty to fifty percent of black workers in Chicago were unemployed. At the same time that the Chicago World's Fair opened, celebrating "The Century of Progress," and the first ever All-Stars baseball game was held at Comiskey Park, in which Babe Ruth's home run gave the victory to the American League, public school teachers were owed ten months' back pay, and throngs of demoralized inhabitants fell into poverty.

The 1931 election of Mayor Anton Cermak signaled that Chicago politics had turned sharply from Republican to Democratic. Cermak cobbled together a powerful organization of ethnic minorities to topple incumbent Mayor "Big Bill" Thompson. Thompson was famous for ethnic slurs, but his slur of Cermak hit a new low that backfired: "I won't take a back seat to that *Bohunk* Chairmock, Chermack or whatever his name is. Tony, Tony, where's your pushcart at? Can you picture a World's Fair mayor with a name like that?"

Cermak's victory ended Republican Party power in Chicago. Since Thompson's defeat, no Republican has ever been elected mayor of the "Windy City." Cermak did not get to preside over the 1933 World's Fair, though. On February 15, 1933, while Cermak was shaking hands with Franklin D. Roosevelt, at Bayfront Park in Miami, Florida, assassin Giuseppe Zangara pointed a loaded pistol at the president-elect. His aim was spoiled when a woman bystander hit his arm with her purse. The shot missed Roosevelt, but fatally wounded the Mayor. Cermak's final words to Roosevelt are inscribed on a plaque at Bayfront Park: "I'm glad it was me instead of you."

Stanley Mosk immersed himself in the hurly-burly of Chicago ward politics, joining a group of students working on behalf of James Cusack, a reform candidate for Alderman for the Fifth Ward. Cusack was elected and served on the Chicago City Council from 1933 to 1939. Mosk's choice to jump into politics at the ward level reflected a lifelong belief that "all politics is local," and that politicians needed to work their way up from the bottom to build a local base of support. There was never any question his political affiliation would be anything other Democratic, like his mother, and yet influenced by his father's progressive Republicanism and Uncle Dave's radicalism. In 1932, both the Democratic convention that nominated Franklin D. Roosevelt and the Republican convention that renominated Herbert Hoover met in Chicago. Stanley managed to talk his way into the Chicago Stadium to observe the Democratic Convention, shooting photos of the Al Smith delegates marching around the floor. Thirty-six years later he would return to Chicago to attend the 1968 Democratic Convention, at which his wife Edna was a delegate, and his son Richard was an alternate delegate.

The matriarch Rolla Perl, whose staunch independence was often the bane of the Mosk and Perl families, is seen here in a formal portrait perhaps during the late 1920s (courtesy Tom Mosk).

The University of Chicago law school permitted its undergraduates to commence legal studies after only three years of undergraduate study. The first year of law school would be substituted for the senior year of college work required for a bachelor's degree. During his senior year, Morey Stanley Mosk took advantage of this program.

Then as now, the University of Chicago School of Law was a pioneer in promoting an interdisciplinary approach to the study of law. It was among the first to recognize administrative law, legislation and comparative law as legitimate fields of legal study. During Mosk's first year in 1933, the University of Chicago published the first volume of its law review, offered its first courses in economics and law, and conducted its first "orientation" for beginning law students.[11]

Along with his formal education and ward politics, Chicago also offered opportunities to meet local luminaries. Attorney Clarence Darrow was a familiar figure around town. He often lectured on a host of subjects including "current criminal conditions," along with "an extensive program of vaudeville entertainment and a buffet supper," at the Jackson Park Post of the American Legion.[12] One April day, Stanley Mosk and classmate Jim Zacharias paid a visit to Clarence Darrow, who lived near campus. They wished him a happy 76th birthday, and told him of their lawyerly ambitions. He graciously invited them in, showed them his library, and told them a story of his having just come from a meeting with a doctor friend. "If you had listened to me," said his friend, "you would have been a doctor too."

Darrow replied there was nothing wrong with being a lawyer. "I don't say that all lawyers are crooks," responded the doctor, "but even you will have to admit that your profession doesn't exactly make angels of men." Darrow replied, "No, you doctors have the better of us there."

Like many of Mosk's classmates, Jim Zacharias went on to a successful business career. Not only was he an attorney, he was an entrepreneur who popularized the Dove Bar ice cream, and made a fortune in industrial plastics and plating. Like Mosk, his liberal politics never waned. He became a longtime member of the board of directors of the Illinois ACLU and in 1999 was awarded the group's Roger Baldwin Award for lifetime commitment to civil liberties.[13] Zacharias was one of the several lifelong friends who joined Mosk and other friends for yearly reunions, visiting vacation spots all over the world.

While Stanley was engrossed in his studies, his family was struggling to keep their heads above the rising floodwaters of the Great Depression. Army commanders were no longer allowed to deduct payments from personnel paychecks, so the lucrative tailor-made suit installment business abruptly ended.[14] Rockford lost most of what it had gained in the previous cycle of war prosperity. Many left the area for good and among those who remained, thousands of families joined the ranks dependent on public relief.[15] For a while, Uncle Dave had enough money to support both families because unlike the Mosks, who lost their savings in a bank account, Dave and Esther had put their money in the Post Office Savings Department. In December 1930, the Mosks left Rockford for good, only four months after Edward started Rockford Senior High School. During Edward's short time there, however, he followed his brother's footsteps, earning a spot on the sports desk of The *Owl,* and like Stanley, training in the Junior Star Press Club. The Mosks' departure inspired Rockford's principal, James E. Blue, to pen, "We are indeed sorry to lose Edward as he was a very valuable member of the High School."[16] Stanley attended classes at the University of Texas, while Edward completed high school in San Antonio. Edward returned to Rockford to attend the 1932 commencement ceremonies at Rockford High School, where he spoke about Albert Einstein.[17] The family then relocated to California, where they were joined by Stanley upon completion of his bachelor's degree at the University of Chicago.

Grandmother Rolla came to California too, apparently with much resistance. She was treated to a Pullman sleeping car for the long journey to Los Angeles from Cincinnati, where she had been living with Esther, Dave, and cousin Harriet. Upon finding her berth in the crowded coach, Rolla yelled for all to hear,

This more somber portrait of Stanley Mosk, c. 1934, might reflect recognition of the weight of his new status as a California Bar certified attorney, and his readiness to take on any case that walked through the door of his small office in downtown Los Angeles (courtesy Richard Mosk).

"Imagine that! Sending your own mother away to live with complete strangers!" Humiliated, Harriet wanted to explain that her grandmother was in fact going to live with her own daughter. With no trace of affection, she labeled her grandmother "a pain in the ass."[18]

Stanley moved in with his family, living on Horner Street in the Westside Jewish community known as the Pico-Robertson district. He completed two more years of law school at Southwestern Law School in Los Angeles. Ed enrolled as an undergraduate at UCLA and quickly found a network to immerse himself in the school's and the community's Jewish organizations. Edward won the Western Jewish Institute's annual essay writing prize and attended dances at UCLA's Council of Jewish Students, an organization in which he served as Director of Publicity, edited its "Council Bulletin," and the following year was elected president of the organization.[19] He attended "a communist talk" on Labor Day, sponsored a UCLA forum on "The California Youth Act," and maintained a steady schedule of meetings with groups such as the Hollywood League Against Nazism, the United Political Action Committee, and another to address Palestinian problems. It's likely that Edward and Stanley attended many these affairs together, and it's even more likely that Edward's extracurricular associations facilitated his brother's burgeoning political career.[20]

The dominant Midwestern Protestant communities of Los Angeles County hardly welcomed Depression-era migrants with open arms, and Jews found little opportunity in established political or social circles. Leaving the University of Chicago law school was a crushing blow for Stanley Mosk. At the time, Southwestern Law School offered only evening classes for struggling working class students who had few alternatives. Most members of the faculty were practicing lawyers who taught in the evenings after a full day at the office. It was a big step down from the University of Chicago, and for decades to come, Stanley Mosk was embarrassed to claim Southwestern as his alma mater. He identified the elite University of Chicago as his law school and shunned Southwestern's efforts to identify him as a distinguished alumnus. Nonetheless, Southwestern boasted a faculty of notable practitioners who were widely respected in the Los Angeles legal community. Among the classes in which Stanley was enrolled was a course taught by Phil Gibson, who later served as chief justice of California from 1940 until 1964, and who played an important role in Justice Mosk's political and judicial career.

Once settled into his new life, just as he had in Chicago, Mosk again jumped into local politics, supporting the campaign of George Rochester, who finished third in a four-man race for Los Angeles County District Attorney. The Mosks arrived in the midst of California's 1934 gubernatorial campaign of Upton Sinclair, whose bold program to "End Poverty in California" (EPIC) gained new recruits as hardships dragged on. Sinclair had moved to California in 1916, settled in Pasadena, and was employed as a screenwriter in an on-and-off relationship with Metro-Goldwyn-Mayer Studios. He made two runs for governor of California as a Socialist candidate in 1926 and 1930, polling around 50,000 votes each time. He changed his registration to Democrat and won the 1934 primary in a landslide. Sinclair's running mate was Sheridan Downey, and during the campaign, they were affectionately dubbed "Uppie and Downey."

EPIC had broad appeal in the depths of the Great Depression, but created a ticklish problem for Franklin Roosevelt and his New Deal. FDR refused to endorse Sinclair because his New Deal policies were under vociferous attack as socialism in disguise, so the election of an avowed socialist as the Democratic governor of California was a prospect the president did not welcome. Then, in their efforts to defeat Sinclair, the state's moneyed interests mounted one of the dirtiest campaigns ever waged in California. The "campaign of the century" forged a new alliance between mass media technology and political campaigns.[21]

Hollywood (including Sinclair's employer MGM) was enlisted to produce newsreels portraying trainloads of indigents arriving in California to take advantage of the largesse that Sinclair's election promised. Movie moguls threatened to take their studios out of California if Sinclair was elected. Sinclair was vilified as a communist, an enemy of religion, and a destroyer of business. Earl Warren, district attorney of Alameda County and state chairman of the Republican Party, led the party's campaign against Sinclair. Culbert Olson, the chair of the state Democratic Party, vigorously supported the Sinclair ticket. Sinclair lost to Republican Frank Merriam, who won 1.1 million votes to Sinclair's 900,000. As described by historian Kevin Starr, Merriam was an "exacting, humorless, Red-baiting number cruncher from Iowa,"[22] who was ill equipped to handle the challenges that beset California during his second term. The California Merriam now governed was a highly charged political battleground on which the haves and have-nots waged a war for survival. Southern California was a hotbed of virulent labor wars, and the city of Los Angeles was home to institutionalized terror and corruption. Voting for the first time in the 1934 election, 22-year-old Stanley Mosk cast his ballot for Upton Sinclair, and called EPIC "the acorn from which evolved the tree of whatever liberalism we have in California." His law studies precluded a very active role in the Sinclair campaign, but he attended meetings of the Young Democrats, and supported brother Ed's more active role as an EPIC campaigner.

After two years at Southwestern, Stanley felt ready to tackle the California bar examination. While studying for the exam, annotating Bernard Witkin's bar review outlines, he was invited by his friend Ed Rau to complete a foursome for a bridge game at the home of a "lady friend." The "lady friend" turned out to be Helen Edna Mitchell, who lived in Beverly Hills, and was enrolled as a student at UCLA. She was completely charmed by Stanley, and the attraction was mutual. With Ed Rau's approval, Stanley asked Edna out and their romance quickly blossomed. A year later, on September 27, 1936, they were married in an afternoon wedding ceremony at the bride's home on Lucerne Avenue, just west of the exclusive Wilshire Country Club and the historic estates in Hancock Park. The ceremony was attended by one hundred guests, and Stanley's brother Ed served as best man. Edna's family was well off, even in the midst of the Depression. Her father brought the family to Los Angeles from Winnipeg, Canada, where Edna was born in 1915. He developed and marketed a successful line of cosmetic products, including shampoos and after-shave lotions. Edna's Jewish upbringing was more formal than Stanley's had been. She was confirmed at the prestigious Wilshire Boulevard Temple. Her mother Katharine was active in national Jewish organizations such as Haddasah and the National Council of Jewish Women, as well as local institutions such as the Jewish Home for the Aged and the Vista Del Mar Association. Katharine Mitchell's connections would facilitate Stanley Mosk's growing visibility in Los Angeles' emergent organized Jewish community.

Stanley and Edna spent their honeymoon in Carmel, a romantic northern California seaside setting that contrasted sharply with the squalor of Depression-era Los Angeles. Mosk certainly improved his prospects for an upwardly mobile career when he married Edna, their love notwithstanding. But he had yet to establish his professional credentials, and no amount of family money could do that for him.[23] Edna's family moorings were more elevated than his own, but she embraced Stanley's unorthodox career path and ideological commitments, and became his biggest booster for a political career. She left UCLA without graduating, and was gainfully employed throughout most of their marriage.

Mosk's diligent study was rewarded with admission to the California bar on October 29, 1935. In California, as in many states, the legal profession responded to the Great Depression by substantially lowering bar pass rates. Between 1927 and 1933, the bar pass rate in California dropped precipitously, from 72 percent to 36 percent. 1935 was the nadir, putting a tremendous squeeze on the declining number of students managing to get through law school.[24]

Setting up shop in a downtown office on Spring Street, Mosk shared expenses with four other young attorneys. Describing his early professional career, Justice Mosk often said he returned home to his new wife at the end of the day, and proudly proclaimed, "I had a good day today; a $10.00 case and two smaller ones."[25] In a brief foray into criminal defense work, he undertook the representation of Gus Mohr, accused of abducting and molesting a 4-year-old child. Mosk unsuccessfully argued Mohr's confession to the crime should be excluded from evidence because it was obtained by police brutality during three days of incommunicado detention. His client was convicted, but Mosk did succeed in getting him deported to Canada instead of being sent to prison. He also made frequent appearances in divorce court, which occasionally got his name in the newspapers. Although his general practice simply relied on whoever came through the door, with an occasional referral from his father-in-law's factory, Stanley Mosk was not sitting behind his desk waiting. From the very beginning, he was out-and-about, achieving visibility in a community torn by dissension and political upheaval.

Chapter 3

Lawyers "Who Should Be Thrown Out of Ten Story Windows"

As a young attorney with sympathy toward labor and a passion for the protection of civil liberties, Stanley Mosk was eager to join the struggle for social justice in California. The Mosk family arrived in Los Angeles at the tail end of the period when some 683,000 migrants arrived in California, between 1930 and 1934. Most came by automobile; many of them dust bowl refugees. By the end of 1936, some 2.2 million Americans had joined "Townsend Clubs." After Sinclair's defeat, a motley assortment of reformers sought to lead these discontented and displaced citizens to challenge mainstream political parties at all levels of government. The "Townsend Plan," promoted by a 67-year-old physician from Long Beach, proposed a national sales tax to finance a monthly pension of $200 for the fifteen to twenty million Americans over 60. They would be required to spend the money before each new check arrived, thereby creating consumer demand with their spending to lift America out of the Depression.

Eventually, the California Townsendites morphed into the "Ham and Eggs" movement, which proposed to have the state issue scrip to unemployed Californians over the age of 50. The enactment of the federal Social Security Act in 1936 took some wind out of the sails of Ham and Eggs, but the federal law excluded huge categories of the employed, including most of those engaged in agricultural labor, domestic services, and other jobs dominated by women and minorities.[1] The Ham and Eggs movement started with a group that met regularly at Clifton's Cafeteria on Seventh Street in downtown Los Angeles. The name derived from the breakfasts served by owner Clifford E. Clinton, a liberal activist with whom Stanley Mosk became closely allied. Ham and Eggs became a potent political force under the leadership of Robert Noble, a controversial radio personality who later achieved notoriety as a Nazi sympathizer, and Willis and Laurence Allen, two Hollywood publicists. The Ham and Eggs initiative, Proposition 25, went to voters in November 1938. Although the initiative was narrowly defeated, its principal supporter, former Sinclair running mate Sheridan Downey, was elected to the United States Senate to replace conservative Democrat William Gibbs McAdoo, the FDR endorsed candidate.

While EPIC and pension movements mobilized the unemployed and the elderly, organized labor was engaged in a political struggle that often turned violent. Efforts to unionize migrant farm workers were met with fierce resistance. The New Deal came late to California. The strongest lobby in the state legislature was the Associated Farmers of California, which successfully opposed any legislation to improve living conditions for agricultural workers. The Communist Party USA sent dedicated and talented organizers into the fields and canneries of California to organize agricultural workers. Fear of a "Communist takeover" motivated repressive and violent countermeasures from property owners who felt threatened by the invasion of indigents, and the power they could wield at the ballot box.

The Associated Farmers of California mobilized friendly police and sheriff's deputies to oppose the supposed Communist menace with tear gas and arrests. In 1934, longshoreman Harry Bridges led a coast-wide maritime strike that shut down Pacific coast ports of Seattle, Tacoma, Portland, San Francisco, San Pedro and San Diego for over two months. When the National Guard marched into the port of San Francisco on "Bloody Thursday," July 5, 1934, the strike was crushed.

"Open shop" opponents of organized labor were not the only source of violence. Much of the labor strife of the mid–30s arose from the vigorous challenge to the dominance of the American Federation of Labor (AFL), by the newly formed Congress of Industrial Organizations (CIO). The CIO, similar in goals to the earlier industrial wide International Workers of the World (IWW), was built up in part by the fervor of Popular Front members or sympathizers, and soon became a special target of the House Committee on Un-American Activities (HUAC). The term Popular Front (or People's Front) was coined in the 1930s and referred to an alliance of the workers' parties (Communist and Socialist) with so-called "progressive" bourgeois parties (Liberals, Radicals, etc.). Other classic examples of this were in France and Spain. In 1931 and again in 1936, the Spanish Socialist Party (PSOE) joined a coalition with bourgeois parties. The same happened in France in 1936. Both the Communist and Socialist party leaderships played a role in holding back the revolutionary movement of the working class. This prepared the ground for the victory of reaction. In Europe, it led to Franco, Hitler and Mussolini. In California, repeated attacks on strikers elicited only a modicum of police protection. Roving bands of thugs beat up striking workers, broke up their meetings, and destroyed property.

At least one sympathetic government official took note. Los Angeles County Supervisor John Anson Ford asserted that the complicity of the police department in anti-labor violence went below the surface. He charged the Chamber of Commerce with using city funds donated for booster purposes to finance agents to "dissuade" business owners from entering into union contracts.[2]

Stanley Mosk weighed in to defend vulnerable farm workers and urban laborers alike. Equipped with his freshly minted license to practice law, his volunteer work brought him in contact with a large coterie of passionate zealots. Most of them were progressive and some were Communists. Many of them were lawyers fully dedicated to the goals of the still-young American Civil Liberties Union. Founded by pacifist lawyer Roger Baldwin in 1917 to support conscientious objectors during World War I, the ACLU was presented with challenging cases fighting police violence and political repression. His fellow activists were impressed by Stanley Mosk's obvious intelligence and dedication, and his innate skill at working the media. Mosk, in turn, had his conscience seared by the injustices he encountered, and was inspired by the lawyers with whom he worked in the trenches. Some of the attorneys and activists who became heroes or mentors to young Mosk were A.L. Wirin, Sam Yorty, John Anson Ford, Reuben W. Borough, Clifford Clinton, and Carey McWilliams.

Carey McWilliams was a young lawyer who gave up his successful Pasadena law practice to take up the cause of migrant farm workers. He observed violations of civil rights and unsanitary camp conditions and documented them in his classic, *Factories in the Field: The Story of Migratory Farm Labor in California.*[3] McWilliams argued that government provided extensive benefits to farmers in water subsidies and price supports, and very little to farm workers. He urged government to do more for migrants. The Associated Farmers regarded

McWilliams as public enemy number one and tried to discredit him as a communist sympathizer. To growers, McWilliams was "California's number one agricultural pest, worse than the pear blight or boll weevil." Although somewhat shy at first, Stanley Mosk made friends easily. Carey McWilliams and Stanley Mosk led parallel lives as they developed a mutual respect and friendship that lasted throughout their lives.

The reformers who fought battles in Depression-era Los Angeles have sometimes been characterized as simplistically waging old-fashioned wars of righteousness versus corruption. During Mosk's early activist years, however, a transitional period occurred when reformers began to utilize more sophisticated and nuanced interpretations of complex problems to advance innovative social policies.[4] He found an appropriate platform for his activism in the Los Angeles Chapter of the National Municipal League. From its inception in 1894, the Municipal League successfully initiated reform measures promoting direct democracy and modern municipal government. Its progressive agenda included a merit-based civil service, city commission government (until 1915), city manager government (after 1915), home rule, secret ballot, at-large commission elections, nonpartisan elections, and municipal control over utilities and public transportation systems. Decades earlier, the League helped to establish innovative reforms such as the initiative, referendum, and recall, all tools of direct democracy capable of undermining corrupt and entrenched boss rule.[5] The Los Angeles Chapter of the Municipal League had a long history of political reform in Los Angeles. It was instrumental in forcing the resignation of Los Angeles Mayor Arthur C. Harper in 1909, for his role in the official protection of vice operations in Los Angeles.[6] The widespread achievement of its initial goals inevitably led to declining membership and influence, but in 1930s Los Angeles, the League still played a formidable role in city politics. The National Municipal League survives today as the National Civic League.

Stanley Mosk was a witty conversationalist, well informed and opinionated about the issues of the day and, of course, current baseball standings. While essentially an optimist, he was well grounded, comprehending the political realities that required compromise and incremental progress. He was gifted with quick intellect and an incredible memory. While he was ambitious, he was well aware of the need to work his way up by displaying a mastery of minutiae before taking on bigger, more responsible roles. Soon after he began attending Municipal League meetings and events, senior members recognized his talents. Thrusting him into leadership positions early on, he became a member of the Executive Board as secretary, a member of Precinct and Telephone Committees, the Political Action Committee, the Industrial and Law Enforcement Committee, and Vice Chair of the Municipal Utilities Committee. He also headed the Attorneys' Advisory Committee, and he often served as the Leagues' legal representative. He was soon recognized as a key leader and spokesman for the League, forging alliances with other reform elements.

Mosk's work with the League allied him closely with the American Civil Liberties Union (ACLU) in documenting the extent and severity of police abuse, and made him a key player in the nascent challenge to the authority of Los Angeles Mayor Frank Shaw. Frank Shaw had been elected in 1933 on a "reform" platform that had turned out his inept predecessor, John C. Porter, a former automobile junk dealer. Numerous community, civic, labor and reform-minded groups, including the local branch of the National Municipal League, had heartily backed Shaw, who had previously served both as a respectable city councilman and a county supervisor.[7]

It soon became clear to liberals that Shaw's "personal corruption was deepened by a measure of viciousness," and they grew disenchanted with Shaw as they saw him leaning increasingly to the right.[8] Shaw's fears about Communist infiltration of the labor movement led him to support a repressive police regime in Los Angeles. Among Shaw's early appointments was his brother Joe Shaw, who became a "private secretary" on the city payroll. Joe Shaw emerged as the "chief fixer" in City Hall and was allowed to exercise authority over the police and fire departments. Under Joe Shaw, vice and corruption were allowed to flourish as police directed their efforts against labor unions and Shaw opponents.

Police Chief James E. Davis had headed the LAPD from 1926 to 1931, and was reappointed as police chief by Mayor Shaw in 1933. Davis was known as "two-gun" Davis for his flamboyant posing with two guns drawn, gunslinger style. Chief Davis established the Metropolitan Squad in 1933, to break up picket lines under the guise of keeping the peace and quelling disturbances.[9] The Squad became the tool of the city's open shop forces with Captain "Red" Hynes operating in close consultation with powerful citizens. Hynes denounced the local ACLU as made up of lawyers "who should be thrown out ten story windows" for representing Communists.[10] Strikers and picketers were frequently jailed for unruly behavior or threatening conduct. Police utilized tear-gas bombs, shot volleys over workers' heads, and employed coercive "interrogations" that would meet anyone's definition of torture.[11]

In 1935, Mayor Shaw permitted the organization of a special "Red" or "Spy Squad" within the Metropolitan Squad, to break up leftist meetings and spy on liberals. With its dedicated force of eighteen officers, the Squad preyed on organized labor and other opponents of the Shaw administration, earning its description as "the most sinister organization in America." Police Captain Earle E. Kynette headed the Spy Squad. Described as "a dough-faced, weak-eyed egomaniac with an army and medical background and considerable intelligence," he specialized in placing hidden dictographs to conduct surveillance of meetings of suspected troublemakers.[12]

The reach of the Shaw brothers and Chief Davis extended far beyond the borders of Los Angeles. In 1936, Davis dispatched 126 LAPD officers to sixteen highway and railway points throughout the state with orders to turn back any "indigent transients" who could not prove their California residence. Although patently unconstitutional, the action of Chief Davis was applauded by paranoid Angelenos. The blockade was disbanded after two months, following protests by the ACLU, the governor of Nevada, the attorneys general of Arizona and Oregon, and even the Chief of the California Highway Patrol.

On behalf of the Municipal League, in 1936 Stanley Mosk undertook preparation of a formal report documenting the "blatant favoritism" by police toward AFL labor organizations that had "strong tentacles reaching into the Shaw machine," and their hostility toward the competing CIO. Investigating police collusion with the AFL to oust CIO recruiters, Mosk and his committee held hearings, inviting public officials and an AFL spokesman to testify. Most refused, but the conclusions in Mosk's report still rested upon nineteen witnesses, accompanied by thirteen affidavits.

Groups favorable to the Shaw administration, the report explained, experienced less harassment at the hands of police. On the other hand, those seeking to "unite with other civic groups to clean up the local political mess," were more susceptible to abuse by police officers.[13] Mosk published accounts of his "sensational" revelations of violence carried out by civil authorities.[14] He wrote about an incident in the San Fernando Valley at a milk farm in Van Nuys. The Dairy Workers Union, a CIO affiliate, won workers' recognition by a vote of 87 out of 100, and hired workmen under their union hiring hall system. When Captain Hynes of the LAPD informed the workers that their union was instead going to be an AFL affiliate, a strike was called. During the walkout carloads of up to twenty-five men with clubs, all believed to be AFL Teamsters, attacked protesting picketers only seconds after two policemen arrived in a squad car. Another police car escorted a line of teamster's automobiles through the crowd, after which the police "retired to the sidelines while the fighting took place." Sixteen picketers were severely beaten. Mosk documented similar instances of police condoned violence, including police attacks against publicly employed workers.

Mosk's accounts included details of the brutal beating of Harry Mahoney, a young man in police custody, in a report he authored for the ACLU's *Open Forum*. Twenty-nine-year-old Harry Mahoney suffered a severe skull fracture during his incarceration in the Lincoln Heights jail. The police blamed Mahoney's skull fracture on an alleged fall from a streetcar. Mahoney's father, George, denied the accusation and initiated a civil suit seeking $50,000 damages against the city of Los Angeles. The senior Mahoney was a construction superintendent of the city's Board of Public Works. The ability of Mahoney's father to finance the suit may have inspired the Municipal League to take it as a test case.

Mahoney produced a witness to back up his claim that the police severely beat him while he was in their custody. A.H. Sweetman, himself arrested after a drunken domestic dispute, described how an officer had kicked Mahoney when he failed to leave his cell for breakfast, and left him lying on the cell floor for hours with his face bruised and bloody. Sweetman told the city attorney that he had also been beaten when he tried to help the severely injured young man. Dr. Erroll Moss, a police surgeon and attending physician the night of the beating, testified that he had observed Mahoney in an epileptic fit. He also said because Mahoney was wearing a hat, he had not noticed any head injury. Mahoney's parents angrily countered these claims, noting that their son was not an epileptic, and what's more, he did not even own a hat, nor did he ever tell anyone he had fallen from a streetcar.[15]

In preparing Mahoney's lawsuit, Mosk worked with renowned ACLU attorney A.L. Wirin, who had personally experienced the terror of mob violence when he was kidnapped and savagely beaten by vigilantes in the Imperial Valley. The press quoted "Morey Mock" [*sic*] who explained that the Mahoney case fell under a seldom-used clause in the penal code, which provided that any lack of care of a prisoner was a misdemeanor if the health of the prisoner was injured or impaired. The bottom line for "Mock" [*sic*] was that the code applied whether Mahoney had suffered a fracture before or after the police had seized him, regardless of its source.[16]

Mosk's suspicion was confirmed by the fact that the streetcar company had never investigated a fall by a rider, nor did it issue a report regarding any such alleged incident. He concluded that the denial of treatment for Mahoney should, at the very least, "in the interests of democracy and justice, be aired in court." Finally, he argued, "if the guilty were removed from the force ... example would be impressed upon other police officers who are disposed to use their uniforms as a shield for sadistic tendencies."

An important ally in Mosk's investigative work on behalf of the Municipal League was Samuel Yorty, a popular Democratic Assemblyman and future three-term Mayor of Los Angeles.[17] Yorty's then radical sympathies found a worthy ally in Mosk and the two became life-long friends. Their friendship endured even after Yorty became a "maverick" Democrat, directing sensationalist investigations to ferret out communist influence in labor unions.

Mosk and his allies used his Municipal League platform to help form coalition groups, such as the California Committee for Political Unity (CCPU), with its "Committee of 100."[18] Among the "100" were Sam Yorty, Ellis Patterson (later lieutenant governor) and Robert Kenny (later California attorney general), all of whom went on to significant, if politically divergent, careers.[19] At the time, it was hoped that CCPU could hold together the progressive coalition formed during the Sinclair gubernatorial campaign, and keep Democrats allied during the Republican administration of Governor Frank Merriman. Predating the larger but similar Americans for Democratic Action, the CCPU served as a model for Mosk's future agendas.

Another well-publicized leadership position assumed by Mosk was the organized opposition to the L.A. Board of Education's denial of a permit for the CCPU to use its facilities for meetings, because of its alliance with the communist Labor's Non-Partisan League. Moving front and center at a press conference called to rally supporters, Mosk assured the public that "the California Committee for Political Unity believed in the democratic guarantees of freedom of speech, press, religion, and the ballot." Democratic state senator and future governor Culbert Olson also spoke, defending the right of all of the members of the group to attend a meeting on school property. Don Healey, an acknowledged communist and CIO organizer, representing Labor's Non-Partisan League, also addressed the group. On May 5, 1938, the school board reversed its ruling.[20] The CCPU later joined those rallying around efforts to recall Mayor Frank Shaw.

Stanley Mosk also served as secretary of the Citizen's Committee for Industrial Justice (CCIJ), and became its loudest voice. He told reporters that the "public's patience" with the official "winking at violence" had "been exhausted." He said it was now time to show the administration that "public apathy exists no more." Mosk explained that the group was not set up to become "embroiled in labor disputes per se, but to gather leaders of civic clubs, political and labor groups, bar associations, employers' groups, chambers of commerce, AFL and CIO members, clergy, teachers, and public officials." Together these representatives would "establish a free interchange of thoughts between leaders."[21] The Los Angeles *Evening News* described the initial meeting of the CCIJ at the Angeles Hotel, where the organization called for the prosecution of anyone instigating violence in labor disputes, whether between unions or between unions and employers. The *Herald Express* reported that the group demanded public officials to refrain from taking sides in labor disputes, and a few days later the paper announced plans for a public rally.

Tensions were high in L.A., and the messianic zeal of the colorful cafeteria owner Clifford Clinton galvanized a merger of the diverse groups seeking reform into an alliance. Clifton's Cafeteria offered free meals to anyone who could not afford to pay. This profitable enterprise provided a venue for all kinds of reformers, offering them a forum for planning and strategy meetings, discussion groups, and speakers of liberal persuasion. Technocrats, Utopians, and the Municipal League were among the groups that came, not just to eat but also to "rendezvous" with "all intransigents with plans for a new world."[22]

Fueling Clinton's fury was his frustration with an aborted Los Angeles County grand jury investigation looking into the collusion of crime and City Hall. L.A. County Supervisor John Anson Ford, who had been defeated in a nasty mayoral campaign that re-elected Shaw in 1937, initiated an investigation. Ford then nominated Clinton to a grand jury appointed by Superior Court Judge Fletcher Bowron to investigate Mayor Shaw. During his tenure on the grand jury, Clinton was assigned to inspect the food service in the cafeteria of L.A.'s County General Hospital. Criticism of its operations brought what Clinton believed, correctly or not, were retaliatory inspections and fines for alleged abuses in his own establishment, along with a suspiciously timed raise in his business taxes. Clinton also charged that Negroes were being encouraged by Shaw to frequent Clifton's cafeteria in order to keep white customers away. The final report of the grand jury, however, praised the Shaw administration, and denounced Clinton as a "malicious, unbridled, reputation-smearing gossip."[23]

Clinton set up his own investigative apparatus, and threatened to issue a grand jury minority report. Unfortunately, he hired some local underworld thugs to assist him, a move he rationalized by their helpful first-hand knowledge of the city's affairs. This made him an easy target of ridicule. Supervisor Ford defended Clinton's zealousness, although he conceded Clinton was "activated by a religious, sacrificial zeal." The rabble-rouser was an amateur in politics, Ford said, but he was "learning fast," and he was "exceedingly shrewd," and above all "without selfish motives."

In the summer of 1937, Clinton pulled the discontented factions in Los Angeles together by forming the Citizens Independent Vice Investigating Committee (CIVIC) to serve as an umbrella organization. CIVIC carried on Clinton's corruption investigations, which rallied broader public support. Stanley Mosk believed in Clifford Clinton's leadership, writing, "Were the saga of individuals who have the courage to single-handedly rise up against the injustices of American municipal political machines published, the name of Clifford Clinton would deserve prominent mention." Echoing Supervisor Ford, Mosk praised Clinton's "sense of civic responsibility," by taking "his Grand Jury oath seriously." He heralded the restaurateur's "persistence to seek the truth about the Shaw brothers and to expose it," as well as to have "faith in his fellow citizens to help them do something about it." That Clinton asked for nothing in return for his investment of thousands of dollars is "but further tribute" to his "sincerity." Mosk thought Clifford Clinton was "not only a racket buster, but a man who [b]elieves citizenship implies duty as well as privilege."[24]

On January 14, 1938, a bomb exploded in the car of private investigator and former police officer Harry Raymond. Raymond had been investigating the Shaw administration for local anti–Shaw forces and was scheduled to give testimony before the grand jury. Despite being struck by more than 150 pieces of shrapnel, Raymond survived the blast. The media initially suggested the bombing was the work of the mob. Critics of the Mayor, however, immediately accused the Shaw administration. Beginning the reign of terror, the home of Clifford Clinton himself had been bombed three months before the Raymond bombing. While newsworthy, it was considered an isolated incident until the *Los Angeles Times* responded by suggesting that Raymond and Clinton themselves had staged the bombing as a publicity stunt. The answer emerged later when it was revealed that Raymond had been under surveillance for months, by one of the LAPD's secret police units. LAPD Captain Earl Kynette was indicted and convicted for illegal wiretapping in the surveillance of Harry Raymond. Suspicions remained that Kynette took his direction from somewhere in City Hall.

Other victims of violence followed, including Carl C. Hoskin, a close associate of Judge Fletcher Bowron who later managed his campaign for Mayor. Hoskin received mysterious phone calls threatening his life and those of his family, and then discovered a fire started under his car.[25] An exploding bomb terrorized Lyndon R. (Red) Foster after he accused Mayor Shaw of pressuring advertisers to control the editorial pages of Los Angeles newspapers. Still another bomb was aimed at Robert Noble, the Ham and Eggs Plan leader, and an outspoken critic of Shaw.[26] The popular but controversial Rev. Robert Shuler was yet another victim.

Three weeks after the Raymond bombing, the forces opposing Shaw and his "Gestapo-like" regime coalesced.[27] The parallel between what was happening in Nazi Germany and the excesses of police authority in Los Angeles was not lost on Stanley Mosk. He linked the events abroad with the happenings at home when he spoke under the auspices of the Hollywood Anti-Nazi League, entitling his talk, "Fascism in Our City Government."[28]

The *Los Angeles Times* made conscious efforts to play down the bombings in hopes of avoiding a scandal in the police department, while at the same time exploiting labor conflict to support its own decades-long open shop view. This spurred the formation of yet another group, the Federation for Civic Betterment (FCB). The Federation and its executive Committee of Twenty-Five soon supplanted CIVIC as the umbrella organization to galvanize public outrage against the Shaw administration.[29] Secretary of the Federation was bombing victim Carl C. Hoskin. The coalition included Methodist, Baptist, and Presbyterian pastors, a rabbi, and representatives of the Christian Youth Council, League of Women Shoppers, Labor's Non Partisan League, the local newspaper guild, CIVIC, the ACLU, the Women's International League for Peace and Freedom, the motion picture industry, as well as members of the "the colored race."[30] As a founding member of the FCB, Mosk attended the formative meetings where new community representatives were recruited. These included J. Frank Burke, future campaign manager for Culbert Olson, described as "America's foremost commentator on current events— and editor of the air."

Stanley Mosk became a member of the vanguard Committee of Twenty-Five, representing the Municipal League. In February 1938, over 2,000 Federation members voted to demand the ouster of Police Chief Davis. Because of the broad support for the recall, on March 13, the FCB's leadership council, the Committee of Twenty-Five voted to move forward and pledged to unify the good government forces behind a common mayoral candidate.

One of the first demands of the FCB was for Republican Governor Frank Merriam to appoint a special prosecutor to study the affairs in Los Angeles, preferably one experienced in such affairs, Thomas E. Dewey of New York.[31] Watching the tempest stirring, Mayor Shaw charged that Federation meetings were a "hubbub of prejudice, malicious gossip, vilification, and judging without evidence." His field secretary (and unofficial campaign manager) Harold Story described FCB's executive committee as made up of "eight labor leaders, seven ministers, six communists, and four crackpot reformers, all cleverly manipulated by Clifford Clinton."[32] He did not specify whether Stanley Mosk was one of the "six communists" or "four crackpot reformers."

Activities with the Municipal League and the Federation for Civic Betterment overlapped, and Mosk's efforts on behalf of both gave him valuable experience and exposed his organizational talents to the movers and shakers who would lead Culbert Olson's statewide gubernatorial campaign. In March, CIVIC and the FCB held mass recruitment rallies and scheduled major events. Plans were made for publicity and potential speakers, and steps were outlined to organize a radio "Committee of Four" and an advisory "Committee of Seven" among Negro ministers.[33] Clinton, who had a radio program, offered half of his regular KEHE airtime. Slated for one of the Friday night broadcasts was "Morey S. Mosk."[34] This was one of hundreds of such broadcasts between January and the September election. Loud, crashing sound effects recreating the Raymond bombing introduced the colorful and dramatic scripts. Hugely effective, one poll estimated that Clinton's nightly audience ranged between 250 — 300,000 listeners.[35]

Local newspapers couldn't help but take sides. The *Los Angeles Times* was, of course, against the recall, while Democrat Manchester Boddy's *Daily News* and Harlan Palmer's *Citizen-News* opposed Shaw and promoted the recall election. The Hearst papers, the *Herald Express* and the *Examiner*, remained neutral. The FCB set up its own editorial committee to write pamphlets targeting sectors of the city outlining how the recall would benefit labor or business.[36] Other less credible "throw away" papers surfaced with stinging attacks on recall leaders. The Shaw administration relied upon such "scandal sheets," and pseudo-community newspapers, which were usually edited anonymously and deceptively titled with progressive buzzwords.[37]

One month after CIVIC began its petition drive, the FCB officially took over the Mayor Shaw recall campaign in April 1938. This set in motion steps to hire professional signature gatherers, rather than relying upon volunteers supervised by Clinton. Clifton Clinton's parents had been Salvation Army missionaries and Clinton's workers adapted the "brass band-on-street-corner" techniques he learned from them. Females out in the field collecting signatures dressed in "flamboyant and red costumes" to conduct "personal tours of red-light districts" which flourished under the Shaw administration.

Shaw's supporters employed every avenue, legal and otherwise, to thwart the petition drive. City officials who opposed the recall tried to scare off otherwise willing signatories by telling them that libel suits would be filed against them the moment the petitions were officially filed, and anyone who affixed their signature to the petitions would be required "to come into court and prove these [libelous] charges." Furthermore, if the signers could not substantiate the charges, "they should be made to pay for the slanderous statements contained in the recall petition."[38] Fabricated petitions were also distributed and quickly disqualified by the city clerk. By June, only 55,000 signatures had been turned into the city clerk, and volunteer signature collectors were getting harder to find. A debilitating mood of "apathy and defeatism" set in among members of the coalition. The Federation decided to raise the compensation of petition workers from two to four cents a signature, and another committee was set up, chaired by Mosk, who was directed to accelerate the work of signature collectors.[39]

Suddenly, Mosk's task was made easier and everyone's spirits were lifted. Los Angeles District Attorney Buron Fitts had originally only charged Captain Earl Kynette with wire-tapping in the Raymond bombing case, and was unable to tie Kynette directly to the mayor. The discovery of additional evidence brought a second arrest and an indictment of Kynette for the attempted murder of Harry Raymond. Kynette admitted to spying on Raymond, but denied the bombing. Chief Davis fired him anyway. After a ten-week trial came the dramatic and unexpected announcement that LAPD Captain Earl Kynette and Lieutenant Roy J. Allen were convicted of attempted murder, assault with intent to kill, and malicious use of explosives against the private detective Harry Raymond.[40] District Attorney Fitts said the verdict was a "far-reaching" one "against secret political police and against political tyrants."[41] As Kynette began a two-year term in San Quentin, Chief Davis disbanded the spy squad.[42]

With news of the convictions, the recall movement finally made sense to the citizens of Los Angeles. With two police officials actually convicted for such a "preposterous act," public outrage grew and the momentum for the recall accelerated. Both CIVIC and the FCB were reinvigorated and they immediately called a "war council to take advantage" of the public clamor.[43] The goal was to qualify for an upcoming special election in which two opposing labor initiatives were already scheduled. It was anticipated that those measures would bring even more voters to the polls. Dramatic calls for action fueled the collection of 82,000 more signatures in just over twelve days. Angry citizens quickly signed petitions, and seventeen days later, the total reached 98,000, of which 55,000 were certified.[44] Over 75 percent of the required signatures came after the convictions were announced. The city clerk agreed to organize a special shift to ensure the official acceptance of the petitions from 6 P.M. until 6 A.M. on July 14, the last day for filing.

On that day, Clifford Clinton and members of the FCB carefully removed the remaining stacks of signed petitions from their safe-deposit vaults and transferred them under guard to the office of the city clerk. The local press captured the climactic moment when mounds of petitions were clumsily piled high on the clerk's desk. The photograph depicts the young fresh face of a handsome Stanley Mosk, wearing a slight smile of satisfaction, standing front-and-center surrounded by Clinton and the weary warriors exhausted by the long ordeal.

Until now, scholars have overlooked Mosk's role in Depression Era city reform efforts and his central role in the Shaw recall and subsequent events. Part of this oversight might be explained by students of the era not connecting the name of *Morey S.* Mosk to California's future Attorney General, and state Supreme Court Justice, Stanley Mosk. Mosk himself downplayed his earlier activism, possibly to avoid explaining his close association with the communists and other radicals engaged in the movement.

Nevertheless, the glow of victory lasted just as long as the flicker of photographer's flash bulbs. Someone had gotten into the clerk's City Hall vault, and when the verification of signatures began, it appeared as if alterations of many of the names had been made. "Smith" became "Smithson," and "John Jones" became "John X. Jones." Each altered signature had to be thrown out. When Mosk inquired on behalf of the coalition, he was told that no written or formal opinion by the clerk's office would be issued regarding tampered names. As a result he was assigned to chair yet another "legal committee" to deal with the problem. He was given "the privilege of selecting his committee members," in order to secure "the legal evidence in connection with the tampering of the petitions."[45] Less than two weeks later, however, the clerk processed all of the petitions and the tally of certified signatures came in with 3,490 more than the required number.[46] The attempted sabotage proved futile, and on July 26, the City Council enacted an ordinance calling for a special election at the same time the two labor initiatives were to be decided by voters on September 16, 1938.

Within days of the certification, Shaw's brother, Joe, resigned his position as secretary to the mayor and eloped with his own secretary to Reno, Nevada. He returned in an unofficial capacity to assist with his brother's defensive campaign. He was eventually indicted long after Mosk had moved on, but Joe's matrimony proved strategic in silencing his secretary-wife as a potential witness against himself or the mayor. Under California law, a wife could not be compelled to testify against her husband.[47]

The September recall ballot would potentially oust Mayor Shaw, and elect a new mayor as well, thus avoiding another election down the line. The FCB now turned its attention to the selection of a mayoral candidate to replace Shaw. With eighty-nine potential names thrown into the ring, the FCB's Committee of Twenty-Five detailed the list of qualifications for potential candidates. Clinton proposed that the various groups represented by the Federation be polled and a convention be held to sort it all out. Three top candidates quickly emerged: Supervisor John Anson Ford; Mr. Lawrence Larabee, member of the Board of Education; and Los Angeles Superior Court Judge Fletcher Bowron. Supervisor Ford officially withdrew his name for nomination citing his commitment to his current position. Judge Fletcher Bowron was at first reticent and indecisive; perhaps seeking to force his draft.[48] The lack of commitment by potential candidates and the obvious division among reformers over alternates was good news for the Shaw forces, who believed the inability of the recall proponents to rally behind one person would allow him to win back his post in the recall election.[49] At some point, the name of Assemblyman Samuel Yorty surfaced as a contender for the mayoral seat. Although some felt he was too young and inexperienced, his reputation as a respected progressive leftist, particularly in the Hollywood film colony, made him a viable alternative.[50]

After days of jockeying among the various church, political, labor, and citizen groups who sifted through the potential candidates, a secret meeting of the Federation's Committee of Twenty-Five was held at Clifton's Cafeteria. Clinton threatened to withdraw his faction and his money from the coalition if his choice of Judge Fletcher Bowron did not prevail. In hopes of avoiding a total collapse of the alliance, Communist labor leader Don Healey spoke up. He acknowledged that he would probably get his "head chopped off" for what he was about to say, and as distasteful as it was to him to support Judge Bowron, he wanted the group "to know that I have made such a decision because I know that Sam Yorty could never be elected."[51] He then sought a unanimous vote for the judge. Yorty supporters were furious. The local press reported that, "Despite heated disagreements before the nomination," including opposition from his own group, Labor's Non-Partisan League, Healey made "a spirited plea" to maintain a "united front for labor, church groups and progressive political organizations to defeat Mayor Shaw at all costs."[52]

Just moments before the vote of the secret meeting was to become public, Stanley Mosk, and others who feared erroneous reporting of a unanimous tally for Bowron, halted the proceedings. Refusing to remain silent, Mosk stood before the crowd gathered to watch the subsequent public meeting. He challenged what he saw as a blatant misrepresentation to the citizens of Los Angeles of the supposed "unanimous" support for Fletcher Bowron by the Committee of Twenty-Five. He boldly asserted, "I want to tell you how the [executive] committee voted today [in private session]." He said that there were thirteen votes for Judge Bowron; seven for Sam Yorty, three who chose not to vote, and two members absent. "I say that Yorty merits support and that your delegates should have a chance to vote for him." Even though the Mayor's office was non-partisan, he said that it made more strategic sense to run a New Deal Roosevelt Democrat for mayor than Bowron, who was a Republican.[53] He cautioned that, "the heavy Democratic registration in Los Angeles outnumbers Republicans two to one," and thus, "this heavy bloc of votes could be switched behind Yorty after the primaries."[54]

Applause filled the air. That is, until Mrs. Beatrice Reeves, a Negro representative of the Better Government Club, pointedly asked where the Democrats were in 1936, "when Democrat John Anson Ford was defeated by Republican Mayor Frank L. Shaw."[55] The house rocked with laughter until a representative from the Motion Picture Painter's Union rose in support of Mosk's motion, complaining that labor unions were being asked to make all of the compromises throughout the entire process. Another rose in a show of labor's support, and still another from the CIO Political Committee went so far as to say that he would prefer to keep Frank Shaw over electing Fletcher Bowron any day. The final choice was left to a vote of all of the delegates, who overwhelmingly chose Bowron (127) over Yorty (64).[56]

On September 16, 1938, almost fifty percent of the city's voters went to the polls where they threw Shaw out and elected Fletcher Bowron mayor. The recall was approved by a vote of 236,525 to 129,245, and Bowron was elected by 230,000 to Shaw's 122,000.[57] Shaw became the first U.S. mayor in history to be thrown out of office by recall. Proposition 1, the anti-picketing, anti-labor initiative, passed by over 40,000 votes, and pro-union Proposition 2 was resoundingly defeated, triggering another episode of labor strife.

Departing Frank Shaw called Mayor-elect Bowron "the official apologist for an unholy alliance of bigotry, communism, and rule or ruin defeatists," but he shook his hand, anyway, and wished him well. Police Chief Davis resigned and Bowron immediately dismissed twenty-three high-ranking LAPD officers. Many believed that the crime syndicate had finally been broken.

Two months after the vitriolic mayoral recall in L.A., another historic revolution bore fruit. For the first time in the twentieth century, a Democrat, State Senator Culbert Olson, was elected as governor of the Golden State. Supervisor Ford believed "The move which swept the Democratic state ticket into office has a great deal in common with the move that elected Fletcher Bowron over Frank Shaw's powerful machine." Mosk, along with many of the other strategists in both camps, noted how the removal of a Republican mayor in Los Angeles, and the proximity of the city and state elections, helped secure the victory of the Olson campaign.[58]

Clifford Clinton remained active in Los Angeles politics. Disappointed with Bowron's performance, in 1945 Clinton decided to run for mayor himself. There were 16 candidates in the primary, and Clinton ran second to Bowron. In his remaining years, Clinton achieved international renown as a humanitarian. He founded "Meals for Millions," an international organization that distributed 6.5 million pounds of multi-purpose food (MPF) through relief agencies in 129 countries in the years following World War II. Meals for Millions later merged with the American Freedom From Hunger Foundation, which still provides disaster relief on a word-wide basis.

Fletcher Bowron went on to preside over an energetic and successful administration for over fifteen years of distinguished service, earning Los Angeles a reputation as one of the best-governed cities in the nation. Bowron met with only varying degrees of success, however, in dealing with the rampant vice and perennial prostitution that characterized the City of Angels.[59] In 1950, he himself faced a recall election instigated by many of the same reform elements involved in the Shaw recall, including Stanley Mosk's brother Ed. Then-Judge Stanley Mosk wrote a warm letter to Bowron, assuring him that he would vote against the recall, and hoped the rest of the city would as well.[60]

Chapter 4

"When the Plums Are Passed Out ... You Will Be Left Behind Again"

Culbert Olson was a native of Utah, a lawyer who earned his law degree from George Washington University while working as a secretary for his cousin, Utah congressman (and later senator) William H. King. An ardent Bryan Democrat, Olson built a successful law practice in Salt Lake City, and won election to the Utah State Senate. Olson was not a Mormon, however, and he realized his political opportunities would always be limited in Utah. He moved his family to Los Angeles, and soon achieved prominence as president of the Los Angeles Democratic Club. While managing the statewide gubernatorial campaign for Upton Sinclair in 1934, he won election as a Democrat for the Los Angeles County seat in the State Senate. As a legislator, he assumed leadership of the EPIC-liberal bloc, and led the fight against Standard Oil's efforts to promote slant drilling of the state's tidelands oil reserves.[1]

When Olson announced his candidacy for governor, the Mosk brothers immediately volunteered. Stanley Mosk said he "just liked him and plunged into his campaign."[2] Throughout his political career, Stanley Mosk relied heavily on whether he "liked" someone or not to define his loyalties, and expected others to do the same. Being "likable" was a key factor in his own success. He never directed personal criticism at those who disagreed with him, and was often able to form close friendships with political adversaries.

Mosk had become quite active with the Young Democrats, and devoted almost full time to the Olson campaign. He was still deeply engaged in the recall of Mayor Shaw for the Municipal League, so 1938 became a very busy year for the 26-year-old Mosk. The director of finance for Olson's Southern California campaign was Judge Robert W. Kenny, who was also running for Olson's Los Angeles senate seat. Kenny won both the Democratic and Republican nominations, and was easily elected to the senate. He introduced Olson to Los Angeles lawyer and Democratic activist Phil S. Gibson, who had been Stanley Mosk's professor at Southwestern Law School, and Gibson became active in the Olson campaign. Stanley Mosk worked out of the West Hollywood campaign office directed by Florence "Susie" Clifton and her husband Robert. Campaign organization was crucial, given that 40 percent of the state's entire vote would come from L.A. County.[3] Susie Clifton was an excellent organizer, who rose through party ranks to eventually direct the southern California gubernatorial race for Pat Brown in 1958. Although Mosk was originally designated as director of organization, this appeared odd to Robert Clifton because Mosk lacked experience. Instead, Mosk was put in charge of the Speaker's Bureau, a position he held for the duration of the campaign. He never spoke to the press though, working out in the field recruiting precinct workers and district chairmen. "It was a people-to-people campaign, doorbell ringing with the modest contributors from liberal groups and clubs," he recalled.[4] In the August

30 primary election, Mosk made his first appearance on a ballot, listed with seven others as a candidate for a seat on the County Democratic Central Committee, which was chaired by Culbert Olson. He appeared in a display ad and on the ballot as "Morey Stanley Mosk, Director of the Los Angeles Municipal League," identified as a leader of one of the Democratic clubs in the 59th Assembly District. A news article summarizing the qualifications of the seven concluded, "These candidates have pledged themselves to fairly represent the Democratic party [sic], but not any faction and to campaign actively for the Democratic nominees in order that there shall be a Democratic state in 1938."[5]

Although Olson was widely supported by labor unions, the raging competition between the AFL and CIO intruded into his campaign when William Green, the national president of the AFL, endorsed Governor Merriam. This was direct retaliation for Olson's endorsement by the political arm of the CIO, Labor's Non-Partisan League. The Republican campaign against Olson advertised, "Vote Against Olson and CIO Domination in our State Government." Labor turned out en masse for the general election, rallying to decisively defeat Proposition 1, an initiative measure that provided severe restrictions on picketing, forbade hot cargo and secondary boycotts, and made unions liable for damages caused by members.

Throughout the campaign, opponents portrayed Olson as a political radical. Red and black billboards proclaimed, "Californians— Watch Your Step! Keep California Out of the 'Red'!" Reacting to continuous violence in the fields, ten days before the election Congressman Martin Dies convened the House Committee on Un-American Activities to hear the testimony of Harper Knowles, an officer of the Associated Farmers of California. Knowles testified that Olson "fraternizes with ... the Communist Party," that Downey was "the running mate of Communist Upton Sinclair," and that Ellis Patterson, candidate for lieutenant governor, was a member of the Communist Party. The Democratic response to these irresponsible accusations was ingenious. Another Dies witness had submitted a list of Hollywood personalities who allowed their names to be used for Communist fronts. The list included child star Shirley Temple. A widely circulated campaign ditty proclaimed:

> We're branded Red by Harper Knowles,
> But we refuse to fuss;
> What's good for Shirley Temple,
> Is good enough for us![6]

In September 1938, in the midst of his statewide campaign, Culbert Olson took a few days to rest at the Modoc County ranch of Roderick MacArthur. Joining him were Ellis Patterson, Phil Gibson, Robert W. Kenny, attorney Jesse W. Carter from Redding, and supreme court justice Emmett Seawell, whom Kenny was boosting to succeed Chief Justice William H. Waste, then seventy years old and quite ill. Kenny anticipated playing a significant role in the Olson administration, but his real ambition was to win a place on the California supreme court. Right after the November election, Wesley Barr, political editor of the Los Angeles *Herald Express*, wrote a column speculating that Kenny would serve as the "Grand Pooh-Bah" of the Olson administration. Olson was furious, and passed over Kenny in naming the new state chairman for the Democratic Party. He regarded Kenny as "too soft" on the conservative wing of the party, and was still unhappy that Kenny actually endorsed Republican Earl Warren in his successful race for attorney general. From then on, the relationship between Olson and Kenny went downhill, to the point that Kenny led a recall effort in the final year of the Olson administration. Kenny preferred to label himself a "Progressive." He explained, "A progressive is a man who is afraid to be a Democrat, and ashamed to be a Republican."[7]

The 1938 election of Culbert Olson as California's first Democratic governor since 1899 should have been a source of great jubilation for California Democrats. Olson won a decisive victory over Merriam, capturing 52.5 percent of the vote, to Merriam's 44.2 percent. Democrats held a majority in the State Assembly, but the State Senate was still controlled by the Republican Party. The truth was, however, that the Democratic Party was badly split into three factions. To the governor's right was a conservative wing still unhappy that Sheridan Downey took out William Gibbs McAdoo as U.S. senator in the primary.[8] In the 1938 Democratic gubernatorial primary, FDR's support was claimed by J.F.T. O'Connor, a McAdoo law partner and former comptroller of the currency, who finished sixth in the race. FDR endorsed both Downey and Olson in the general election.

To the governor's left were the Ham and Eggers and remnants of the Upton Sinclair EPIC campaign, opposed by the president and fully embraced by Senator Downey and Lieutenant Governor Ellis Patterson. Olson never endorsed the Ham and Eggs Initiative, nor did he ever repudiate it. He straddled the issue during the campaign, and it quickly came back to haunt him when, despite the initiative's defeat, the Ham and Eggers sought another special election a year later, and presented the signed petitions required to put it on the ballot.

After a forty-year drought for Democrats, the line for appointments was a long one. Governor Olson's choices were impressive. His choice for director of finance was Phil S. Gibson. The dynamic Carey McWilliams became the commissioner of housing and immigration and continued to be a lightning rod for opposition to Olson's administration by the politically powerful California Farmers Association. Four years later, when Earl Warren opposed Olson's re-election he promised campaign audiences that his first official act would be to fire McWilliams. McWilliams, in turn, became a sharp critic of Governor Warren, whom he described as "the personification of Smart Reaction."

Soon after the election, the emboldened Democrats held a two-day conference of the Young Democrats in Bakersfield. The newly elected slate of office holders and other "Democratic luminaries" such as actor Melvyn Douglas and Los Angeles Supervisor John Anson Ford, and scores of energetic partisans converged from all over the state to the Hotel El Tehon. Roundtable discussions covering the issues facing the new administration were on the agenda. Mrs. Robert (Susie) Clifton was in charge of mobilizing delegates. Morey Stanley Mosk from Los Angeles and Matthew Tobriner from San Francisco were among those who would head sessions on a variety of subjects including, "youth, labor, civil liberties, social security, monopoly, peace and agriculture, respectively."[9]

Although Culbert Olson was sympathetic to the concerns of women and minorities, they were hardly included among the high level appointments in his administration. Stanley Mosk was astutely aware of the "general legislative indifference" to minority concerns in Sacramento. Of the 120 state legislators, only two were "minority" legislators: one African American, Augustus Hawkins, from Central Los Angeles, and one Jew, Benjamin Rosenthal from Boyle Heights, a neighborhood on the East side of Los Angeles. Jews and blacks relied upon their alliance with organized labor and other groups within the Democratic Party coalition. According to Kenneth C. Burt, "Olson stayed true to his campaign pledge to 'affirm that all citizens everywhere, of whatever group, are entitled to equal social, political, and economic opportunities.'"[10] While blacks gained little, Jews and Hispanics did benefit from Olson's progressivism. The new governor appointed several prominent Jews to head various state boards and endorsed their efforts to reform outmoded practices. Olson appointed Isaac Pacht, lawyer and former judge, to the State Board of Prison Directors, where he spearheaded reforms of the state's penal system by "modernizing and humanizing the state's prisons and reformatories." Olson's Director of Institutions was Dr. Aaron J. Rosanoff, who pioneered research and early treatment of the mentally ill. While virtually denied participation at the local level of electoral politics, "Jews could play roles," beyond "the constricted political horizons of their own city."[11]

The other group to benefit "from having the governor's ear, the support of progressive Democrats, and the moral blessing of the official party platform" was the short-lived but impressive El Congreso (National Congress of the Mexican and Spanish-American Peoples of the United States; later changed to the Spanish Speaking People's Congress). Eduardo Quevedo, a member of El Congreso, had campaigned for FDR in 1932 and served as a spokesperson for Upton Sinclair's 1934 gubernatorial campaign. He also worked for the federal Works Project Administration and frequently spoke out against forced repatriation and discrimination. Quevedo had taken "a leadership role" in the Olson campaign. In appreciation of Quevedo's efforts on his behalf, Governor Olson invited him to his inauguration.[12]

For his personal staff, the governor appointed his son and law partner, Richard, to serve as his principal executive secretary. As assistant secretary, he appointed Kenneth Fulton, the Treasurer of his Southern California campaign. A third executive secretary position remained unfilled until the following February, when Stanley Mosk received a telephone call from Fulton inviting him to join the governor's staff. With a touch of hyperbole he recounted, "It took me 15 seconds to accept the offer, and 15 minutes thereafter to wind up my law practice and to move north to the state capital."[13] He went on the governor's staff at an annual salary of $5,000. Newly appointed Phil Gibson tried to lure Mosk out of the governor's office with an offer to serve as Deputy Director of the Department of Finance. Mosk turned down a 50 percent salary increase to stay in the governor's office, which he thought would be "more interesting." Mosk would make enough for he and his now pregnant wife to live comfortably and purchase a tract home in Sacramento. Edna traveled back to Los Angeles for the birth of their only child, Richard, on May 18, 1939.

Mosk joined the Olson administration while the governor was still recuperating from two weeks of hospitalization for "nervous exhaustion." During his first week in office, Olson collapsed while giving a speech to a crowd of 130,000 at the state fairgrounds. He did not make another public appearance until February 17, 1939, when he opened the 1939 Golden Gate International Exposition on Treasure Island in San Francisco. The Fair celebrated the completion of the city's two new bridges, the Golden Gate Bridge and the Oakland Bay Bridge.

Although Mosk started out as number three in a three-man office, he moved up to principal executive secretary within a year. The governor's son Richard, who served as Olson's spokesman during his illness, promptly put his foot in his mouth. He was quoted telling the San Francisco Junior Chamber of Commerce, "We all know most of the Senators are bought and paid for, bound and delivered." Although he was in all likelihood expressing an opinion his father had expressed on numerous occasions, he responded to a howl of protest from the president pro tem of the Senate by first denying he made the statement, then suggesting the Administration "may sometime ask the people to retire some members to private life." Richard himself resigned in April 1940, to return to private life. Kenneth Fulton was appointed Director of Natural Resources, leaving Mosk in charge of managing the office, and handling extradition, clemency, and other legal matters. David Foutz was brought in to oversee press and public relations, and Frank Sullivan joined the staff to handle patronage problems and appointments.

By then, the Olson Administration was off to a shaky start. Just days after his inauguration, the governor's first official act was to announce the pardon of labor activist Tom Mooney. Mooney had spent more than twenty years in prison for his conviction of murder for planting a bomb that had exploded and killed ten persons in the crowd that gathered for a Preparedness Day Parade in San Francisco in 1916. Mooney's struggle for vindication gained international support, but was repeatedly stymied by the courts. At Mooney's trial, two witnesses testified that they saw another man, Warren K. Billings, deposit the suitcase containing the bomb on the corner of Market and Steuart Streets, and then confer with Thomas J. Mooney just before they left the scene. Mooney presented an impressive alibi, documented by a photograph depicting him on the roof of a building a mile from the scene, with the clock on a building across the street reading 2:01 P.M. The bomb went off at 2:05 P.M. The jury convicted him anyway, and sentenced him to death. While his appeal to the California Supreme Court was pending, new evidence revealed that one of the witnesses had tried to induce a friend to supply false corroboration of his testimony. Based on this evidence, California Attorney General U.S. Webb stipulated his consent to a reversal of Mooney's conviction, but the California Supreme Court refused to accept the stipulation and held that the high court's jurisdiction was limited to a review of the trial proceedings.[14] After such a review, the high court affirmed the conviction and death sentence.[15]

Only after the unprecedented intervention of President Woodrow Wilson was Mooney's sentence commuted to life imprisonment. Mooney's San Francisco attorney George Davis continued to amass evidence that perjured testimony was presented at his trial, but to no avail until the United States Supreme Court agreed to hear the case in 1935. Then, in the landmark decision of *Mooney v. Holohan*,[16] the Court held that the knowing use of perjured testimony by state prosecuting authorities is an unconstitutional denial of due process of law. Because this ruling was based upon an assumption that Mooney's allegations were true, however, the Court sent Mooney back to the California courts to "make a proper showing" that he was entitled to relief. The California Supreme Court then appointed a referee who spent more than a year collecting twenty volumes of testimony.

In *In Re Mooney*,[17] the California Supreme Court reviewed the evidence, and concluded that Mooney had not met his burden of proving either that perjured testimony was presented at his trial or that the prosecution had reason to believe any testimony was false. In reaching that conclusion, the court had to reject as perjured the testimony of 16 witnesses produced by Mooney. In doing so, the Court's 85-page opinion was less than convincing. During his gubernatorial campaign, Olson had promised to promptly review the Mooney case. The newly-elected governor convened a meeting of the State Assembly on January 7, 1939, where he announced:

> I have made an extended study of the voluminous records of this case and I am convinced that Thomas J. Mooney is wholly innocent of the crime of murder for which he was convicted and that his conviction was based wholly on perjured testimony presented by representatives of the State of California. In view of my convictions, I deem it my duty to issue a pardon to Thomas J. Mooney.[18]

Lavish praise was heaped on the governor, but most of it came from sources outside the State of California. Strong opposition to the pardon came from Republicans, including the newly elected State Attorney General, Earl Warren.

Mooney's co-defendant Warren K. Billings could not be pardoned, because the State Constitution required Supreme Court approval to pardon someone with a previous felony conviction. Among Stanley Mosk's secretarial responsibilities were matters of commutations and pardons, so he was deeply involved in shepherding the Billings matter through the State Advisory Prison Board, which voted 3–2 against recommending a pardon. When Attorney General Earl Warren cast the deciding vote against Billings, Tom Mooney attacked Warren as a "virtual personification of the rotten, reactionary, corporate-banker-controlled, Republican machine."

Mosk then prepared the governor's request to the Supreme Court, and the Court replied by recommending commutation to time served. Olson followed that recommendation, releasing Billings on October 16. In the course of this work, Stanley Mosk met and conferred with Tom Mooney, whom he found disagreeable. He was right. Shortly after his release, Mooney abandoned the wife who had supported him throughout his ordeal, and announced his plans to marry another woman. His overblown ego and outrageous political pronouncements proved to be a continuing embarrassment to Olson.

Mosk's responsibility for reviewing pardon and commutation applications included a request to commute the death sentence of Mrs. Ethel Leta Juanita Spinelli, known as "The Duchess," convicted of the murder of a member of her own criminal gang. In a final letter to the governor asking for mercy, she outlined her family history, which included raising a grandson and her niece's baby. She requested permission to tape pictures of the children to her body prior to the execution. When Stanley Mosk presented his Spinelli report to the governor, Susie Clifton was sitting in Olson's office. She recalled that Olson impatiently said to Mosk, "Let her go," but wasn't sure if the governor meant "let her go to the gas chamber" or release her from her death sentence. It still wasn't entirely clear when a call to the governor from Superior Court Judge Raymond T. Coughlin prompted a last minute stay of execution just hours before she was to be put to death. While Mrs. Spinelli rejoiced at the news of her thirty-day reprieve from the gas chamber, Stanley Mosk told the press, "we have heard nothing here that changes the status of the case in the slightest," and thus he "couldn't help feeling the Governor has been imposed on in this matter." The headline in the Los Angeles Times read, "OLSON AIDE AND JUDGE IRKED OVER REPREIVE OF 'DUCHESS.'"[19] On November 21, 1941, she became the first woman to die in the California gas chamber. Her final request was granted, and she died with the photos of the children she had raised taped to her body.

In 1942, a San Francisco lawyer named Edmund G. "Pat" Brown wrote to Governor Olson urging the commutation of the death sentences of three young men scheduled to die in San Quentin's gas chamber. Brown suggested his knowledge of the case led him to conclude that "fate has played a terrible part in putting these boys in the gas chamber." He urged Olson to review the case carefully, to find a reason to spare their lives. "This act of mercy would live with you for the rest of your days," he concluded. On behalf of Governor Olson, Stanley Mosk responded to Brown's letter the day of the scheduled execution, explaining because the condemned men had prior felony convictions, the governor could offer no clemency without the approval of the state supreme court, and the justices had refused.[20] Eighteen years later, as governor, "Pat" Brown would face the same constitutional obstacle in his unsuccessful efforts to spare the life of Caryl Chessman. His Attorney General, reluctantly pressing for Chessman's execution, would be Stanley Mosk.

In the summer of 1939, the Associated Farmers accused Olson officials of contributing to "a reign of terror," in the Marysville orchard labor strife. The Association was responding to claims by the governor's office that picketers had been kidnapped and beaten by Yuba County peace officers. The Association president announced: "Although this incident involves only a small area of a [sic] agricultural county, it is a history making precedent, and the people of this State must awake to the realization that the office of our chief executive is being used for purposes certainly not prescribed by our Constitution, and for purposes evidently intended to create violence and strife at the expense of California farmers." The Oakland Tribune reported that "M. Stanley Mosk ... went to Marysville today to make a first-hand investigation for the Governor's office of the controversy."[21]

Throughout Olson's term in office, Lieutenant Governor Ellis Patterson was a constant thorn in his side. Patterson was an enthusiastic supporter of Ham and Eggs, and when a new Ham and Eggs initiative qualified for the ballot in 1939, Patterson campaigned for it all over the state. Governor Olson expressed his opposition to the measure in a reluctantly called special election in November. He said, "I would be false to my own conscience and sense of duty if I failed to here express my belief that, if adopted, this measure would fail to achieve its objectives, would disappoint the hopes of its supporters, and would retard instead of aiding our progress to a better economic order."[22] The revised version of Ham and Eggs went down to a decisive defeat by a two-to-one margin. Its sponsors blamed the governor, and proceeded with plans to recall him. They never succeeded in collecting the necessary signatures (12 percent of those who voted in the 1938 general election), but recall efforts continued throughout 1940.

When Olson backed a pro–Roosevelt slate organized for the 1940 Democratic National Convention in Chicago, Ellis Patterson bolted and formed a separate delegation. During the convention itself, Olson's friends promoted him as a possible vice presidential running-mate for FDR, but told him the chief stumbling block was that Patterson would become governor. In a telephone call to Patterson, Olson urged him to resign, and Patterson told him to "go to hell." Patterson then told reporters, "From now on, I'm going to be governor when I'm on the job; ... If Olson doesn't like it, he can come back and be the governor himself," by "putting some of those toothpick chewers in the corner office back to work." He further quipped, if Olson "would stay out of the State a couple of months longer I'd really show him how to run a government." Then, Patterson announced he was reappointing James K. Moffitt for another sixteen year term to the Board of Regents of the University of California. Patterson said, "Maybe Olson likes him and maybe he doesn't, but I don't care." Stanley Mosk let it be known that the appointment was not being made at the request of the still-absent Governor Olson.

The local press reported "the flaring feud" between Olson and Patterson. Another headline read, "'Bombshell' in Patterson, Olson Dispute." Patterson chartered an airplane hoping to reach the secretary of state's office before it closed at noon the next day. The next morning, Mosk had already filed a commission of appointment with his name as a Regent of the University of California and had been sworn into office a few minutes before Patterson's arrival. He told the press the governor had signed his commission before he left for the convention, and that the appointment would be temporary. In the meantime, the governor was "speeding across the country" by train, forgoing his planned visit to Washington, D.C., and the World's Fair in New York. It seemed obvious he had simply signed a number of blank commissions for Mosk to use in a case such as this if Patterson decided to act as governor. Stanley Mosk remained as a Regent until May 1941, when he resigned and was replaced by the governor's appointment of Brodie E. Ahlport.[23]

One of the more pleasant duties for the governor's executive secretaries was to escort groups on tours of the California State Capitol building, where the governor's corner office was located. In the winter of 1940, Stanley Mosk escorted a group of twenty students from a rural two-room schoolhouse in Ventura County that had been arranged by Bernice Clark, the mother of nine-year-old Bill Clark, Jr. Bernice and her husband, Bill, Sr., were active in Ventura's Democratic Party. The engaging young man who served as their guide impressed Bernice and her son, and they never forgot him.[24] Forty years later, Bill Jr. would serve as executive secretary to another California governor, Ronald Reagan, who appointed him to serve beside Stanley Mosk on the California Supreme Court.

Governor Culbert Olson made four appointments to the California Supreme Court during his term in office, and their outstanding quality may well have been the greatest legacy of his administration. The first vacancy occurred July 7, 1939, when Justice Emmet Seawell died of a sudden heart attack during a court session in San Francisco. Senator Robert W. Kenny immediately advised Olson of his interest in being appointed to the Seawell vacancy. A week later, Jesse W. Carter, who had also been elected to the State Senate, met with Kenny to tell him of his own interest in the Seawell vacancy. Kenny agreed to withdraw if he could get appointed to fill a vacancy on the Court of Appeal in Los Angeles. The two men went together that afternoon to present the proposal to Governor Olson. The next day, July 15, Olson announced the appointment of Senator Jesse W. Carter of Redding to the Supreme Court, and the appointment of Senator Robert W. Kenny as Presiding Justice of the Second District Court of Appeal in Los Angeles. Carter had chaired the planning committee for Olson's Northern California campaign. Both appointments were immediately challenged by the Commission on Judicial Qualifications, because the State Constitution provided that a person holding an elective position could not be appointed to any office other than an elective one. Carter then took the question to the Supreme Court, which ruled in a unanimous opinion that the position of Supreme Court Justice is an elective one, because the electorate had to vote to confirm or reject an appointment and to re-elect a justice for a subsequent term.[25] Carter served on the Court for twenty years, and was well known for the vigor (and occasionally intemperate language) of his dissents.[26] Five days before the decision upholding Carter's appointment came down, however, the heart attack and sudden death of Justice William H. Langdon created a second vacancy on the court.

Less than a week later, on August 16, Olson announced the appointment of his Director of Finance Phil S. Gibson to fill the Langdon vacancy. Robert W. Kenny, with some justification, felt that he was in line for the appointment that went to Gibson. In a fit of pique, he asked the governor to withdraw his appointment to the Court of Appeal, and Governor Olson promptly did so. Stanley Mosk attributed Kenny's subsequent bitter opposition to Olson to his disappointment over not getting the Supreme Court appointment that went to Gibson.[27] Gibson was only on the Court ten months before he was promoted to Chief Justice upon the death of Chief Justice William Waste in June of 1940. When he retired 24 years later, the entire judicial branch of California's state government had been transformed into a model of administrative efficiency and compassionate justice. Gibson is still revered as the greatest of California's Chief Justices.

The seat vacated by the promotion of Gibson to Chief resulted in one of the defining moments of Governor Olson's administration: a face-off with Republican Attorney General Earl Warren. Governor Olson announced the nomination of Max Radin, a widely respected law professor at the University of California at Berkeley. Unfortunately, Radin had commented on many of the legal controversies swirling around him in California, including the prosecution of three members of the maritime union for dispatching thugs to beat up a ship's engineer who subsequently died. They were convicted of second-degree murder in a case prosecuted by Earl Warren while serving as District Attorney of Alameda County. The case, known as the *Point Lobos* prosecution after the name of the ship, became a cause célèbre for CIO activists, who contended the unionists were framed. Professor Max Radin studied the case, and opined to friends that one of the defendants was innocent. When the Radin appointment came before the Commission on Judicial Qualifications, it was rejected without explanation by a vote of 2–1, with the deciding vote cast by Attorney General Earl Warren. Warren later justified his vote by pointing to Radin's lack of judicial experience. He expressed great personal animus toward Radin in a conversation with U.C. Berkeley President Robert Gordon Sproul. He took personal affront at Radin's apparent belief that the *Point Lobos* defendants had been "framed," since Warren himself would have done the "framing." Olson was furious with Warren, and reacted by undertaking a personal investigation of the *Point Lobos* case, even visiting the defendants at San Quentin. He did not grant a pardon, but two months later, his Board of Prison Terms and Paroles granted paroles to all three men. When they were released, Warren issued a bitter and inflammatory denunciation of the governor:

> The murderers are free today, not because they are rehabilitated criminals but because they are politically powerful Communistic radicals. Their parole is the culmination of a sinister program of subversive politics, attempted bribery, terrorism and intimidation which has evidenced itself in so many ways during the past three years.[28]

At Radin's suggestion, Governor Olson filled the Supreme Court vacancy with Roger J. Traynor, a distinguished Tax Professor who was then Acting Dean of the U.C. Berkeley law school. Olson was eager to name another professor without judicial experience to show that lack of judicial experience was not the reason Warren had rejected Radin. Traynor served thirty years on the Court, the last six as Chief Justice, when he served with Justice Stanley Mosk. Traynor is widely regarded as among the greatest Justices who ever served on the Court.

Governor Olson's relationship with the legislature was the greatest failure of his administration. Continually frustrated by maverick Democrats and reactionary Republicans, he compiled a "purge" list of those he targeted for defeat in the 1940 mid-term elections. With rare exceptions, those he targeted were reelected, and became even fiercer enemies during the second half of his administration. In February 1940, Assembly Speaker Gordon Garland dramatically announced to the Assembly that he had discovered a concealed microphone in his bedroom at the Hotel Senator. He noticed a pinhole of light coming through the valence holding the window drapes. He investigated, and found the microphone. Police traced the microphone wires to a dictograph in another room occupied by Robert E. Voshell, a private detective associated with Howard R. Philbrick in an earlier legislative graft investigation. Philbrick was prominent in the Olson administration, serving as the governor's director of motor vehicles. He admitted hiring Voshell's employer to continue the graft investigation, but denied any knowledge of the dictograph. Nonetheless, he resigned. It was soon revealed that Voshell had been paid with checks drawn on a governor's secret fund for "extraneous investigations." As executive secretary to Governor Olson, Mosk regularly signed checks issued by the governor's office. Mosk was summoned before the legislative investigating committee to give an explanation. While initially Mosk and the other witnesses from Olson's office refused to testify, challenging the authority of the investigating committee, they finally relented and answered the committee's questions. The committee subsequently reported it believed Mosk had been "truthful" when he denied he had any knowledge of the dictograph, but charged him with "gross negligence" regarding the funds under his jurisdiction and with "indiscretion" in his public comments. The committee excoriated Mosk for issuing a statement to the press claiming the dictograph incident was a "frame-up" instigated by enemies of the administration.[29]

Not all of Governor Olson's admirers became admirers of Stanley Mosk. Fellow Democrat John P. McEnery even went so far as to blame Stanley Mosk for Olson's troubles. "Stanley Mosk was a young guy who became secretary to Culbert Olson ... and I don't think that there was any-body [sic] did more to destroy Olson than Stanley Mosk did when he was his secretary. He thought he was running the whole office."[30] Years later, Stanley Mosk vividly recalled the hostile questioning he faced in the legislative committee, and explained that his signatures on all of the checks emanating from the governor's office was a routine matter. He did concede however that, "it was a little overzealousness on the part of some people in the administration who really did want to get something on Gordon Garland. Of course, that just wasn't a very nice way to do it."[31] Robert W. Kenny quipped that Olson wouldn't have needed concealed microphones if he hadn't isolated himself from "the ordinary ebb and flow of gossip." "I only had to make myself available regularly at Kearney's saloon, and enough people came up to volunteer more information than could have ever been obtained by a Dictaphone," he added.[32]

Perhaps the most personally disturbing episode Stanley Mosk experienced during his tenure with the Olson administration came with the publication of an article in the *American Mercury Magazine* in 1941. Entitled "A New Boss Takes Los Angeles," it was authored by Rena M. Vale. By this time, *American Mercury* was no longer controlled by H.L. Mencken. In an effort to prop up its sagging circulation, it was publishing sensationalist "exposes." Rena Vale claimed to be a former communist, and was a frequent witness before legislative committees investigating "communist infiltration" of government agencies. Among her more sensational "revelations" were her claims that she attended classes for new communists at the home of Lucille Ball, and that the fluoridation of water was a communist plot to weaken American children. She also leveled accusations of communist party membership against Carey McWilliams. Her *American Mercury* article attacked Clifford Clinton as a communist, and described the Citizen's Independent Vice Investigating Committee (CIVIC), which speared the Shaw recall, as a communist front. She included a paragraph describing Stanley Mosk as a communist associate who had been a member of CIVIC, claimed that he supported a communist magazine, and asserted that he had been named in a Dies Committee Report.

Stanley Mosk was hardly in a position to simply dismiss the *American Mercury* as yellow journalism that no longer carried any influence. He himself had proudly published an article in *American Mercury* five years earlier. In an article entitled *The Road to Dictatorship,* Mosk argued that under our form of government dictatorships were not unfathomable. He noted the recent shift away from a concept of constitutional law that saw government as a policeman, in a role that was "minor and peripheral." Ironically, he concluded that the "very flexibility" that permitted the Constitution "to withstand strain and to endure," would also permit a "Marxian socialist state ... to exist under our present Constitution." So too, he argued, if duly elected, "a dictatorship of an individual or of a social class, for example — would not [be] a violation but a vindication of our Constitution."[33]

Seeing the civic reformers he admired and emulated branded as communists, and seeing himself labeled a communist sympathizer, must have been a very sobering experience. Mosk was understandably upset, and fired off a letter to *American Mercury* demanding a retraction and threatening a libel action. Miss Vale had previously filed an affidavit with Governor Olson claiming Mosk's identification as a communist came from his own sister, who was going by the fictitious name of Lois Penniman. Olson dismissed the accusation out of hand, knowing Mosk had no sister.

When the editor of the *Mercury* asked for further clarification, Mosk explained defiantly that he never had even been a member of CIVIC, but if he had, it would have been a badge of distinction. He noted that the editor's source of information on California "is obviously cockeyed," and "not one of the four sentences is accurate in the third paragraph." Finally, he pointed out that his very own article previously published in that same magazine in May 1935, should have been evidence enough that he adamantly opposed the dictatorships of Hitler, Mussolini, and Stalin. He added, "This was so more than a dozen years ago when it wasn't as popular to be anti-fascist and anti-communist as it is today."[34] He countered that he had never been identified with communist-led causes, unless one believed that the Democratic Party is so led. Furthermore, he pointed out that, although a member, he was never an officer in the Young Democrats, and had consistently opposed the radical controlled Democratic Youth Federation when its faction had split with the Olson-supported regular group. Addressing other accusations in the Vale piece, he said that he had never been named in the Dies committee report, nor did he ever contribute to a party-line magazine, nor was he ever a member of any communist group.[35] This experience was a searing one for Stanley Mosk. The later excesses of Senator Joseph McCarthy in anti-communist witch hunting inspired similarly motivated zealots to paste the "communist sympathizer" label on many liberal Democrats, including Stanley Mosk.

When Justice Frederick W. Houser became too ill to serve on the California Supreme Court during the summer of 1942, Chief Justice Gibson appointed B. Rey Schauer, a Justice of the Court of Appeal in Los Angeles, to sit as a *pro tem* Justice of the Supreme Court during Houser's illness. Houser died three weeks before Governor Olson lost his bid for a second term to Republican Earl Warren. In December, as he prepared to leave office, Olson appointed Schauer to the vacancy, an appointment with which Governor-elect Warren concurred. Schauer was the most conservative of the Justices appointed by Olson, and served on the Court until 1964. Ironically, during Warren's ten years as governor, he made only one appointment to the California Supreme Court.[36] The Justices whom Culbert Olson appointed remained a majority of the California Supreme Court for the next seventeen years.

On April 9, 1942, Attorney General Earl Warren announced his candidacy for the governorship. Warren had grown increasingly frustrated with the Olson administration as efforts to mobilize the war effort produced jurisdictional disputes between the authority of the governor and the attorney general. Olson rarely consulted Warren before announcing wartime measures, including the declaration of a "state of emergency" one week after Pearl Harbor. The crowning blow came when Olson vetoed an emergency legislative appropriation of $214,740 for the Attorney General's wartime operations. One wartime measure upon which Olson and Warren agreed, however, was the internment of Japanese Americans. Not until the publication of his memoirs after his death did Earl Warren express regret for his role in promoting and organizing the internment. Governor Olson argued that "Because of the extreme difficulty in distinguishing between loyal Japanese-Americans, and there are many who are loyal to this country, and those other Japanese whose loyalty is to the Mikado. I believe in the wholesale evacuation of the Japanese people from coastal California."[37]

Earl Warren organized an aggressive and well-financed campaign. Culbert Olson did no campaigning in the primary, since he had no organized Democratic opposition. After Warren announced his candidacy for governor, Robert W. Kenny withdrew from the Democratic primary for governor and announced his candidacy for Attorney General. In those days, cross filing was permitted, and Earl Warren was the first gubernatorial candidate to take advantage of it. He was listed as a candidate in both the Democratic and Republican primaries. The result was a disaster for Olson. Although Olson won the Democratic primary with 514,000 votes, Earl Warren not only won the Republican nomination, he came in second in the *Democratic* primary with 405,000 votes![38] This took the wind out of the sails of any Olson argument that Warren was a reactionary Republican. Warren emphasized his lack of partisanship, arguing that the entire state needed to pull together to fight the war effort. He told the Republican state convention that the campaign "was not a contest between the Republican and Democratic parties, for Governor Olson, by his arrogance, his blundering, and his selfish manipulation of State government during a period of gravest emergency has jeopardized the safety and welfare of the people of California."[39] At the general election in November, Earl Warren decisively defeated Governor Olson 57 percent to 42 percent.

Earl Warren was subsequently reelected twice, the only person to serve three terms as California governor until Governor Jerry Brown was elected to a third term in 2010. In 1946, he won both the Republican *and* the Democratic primaries, defeating Bob Kenny for the Democratic nomination. In 1950, he defeated FDR's son, James Roosevelt. He was the Republican nominee for vice president of the United States in 1948, and in 1953 was appointed Chief Justice of the United States Supreme Court by President Dwight D. Eisenhower, who later called the appointment his "biggest mistake."

Stanley Mosk apparently had little use for Robert Kenny, although he publicly expressed admiration. In 1944, when writing to his brother Ed to express disappointment that Henry Wallace had not been renominated to serve as FDR's vice president, Mosk said, "My long-expressed views on Bob Kenny have once more been vindicated.... Bob's antics throughout [the Democratic convention] were really reprehensible, and clearly show him to be a conniving opportunist. He plays the game of the Kellys, Hagues, Pendergasts, Flynns and others who now control the party.... Remember when I wrote you that some day the tigers would find out he is a lion, and the lions that he is a tiger? Well, they're catching on."[40]

The restoration of Republican rule in the governor's office meant that every available appointment had to be filled by Olson before midnight of January 1, 1943, his last day in office. As a lame duck governor, Culbert Olson still had a few appointments he could hand out to some of his loyal friends. Stanley Mosk certainly qualified in that category. Last minute "midnight" appointments to the bench are an American tradition dating back to the judicial appointments by John Adams that were challenged in *Marbury v. Madison*.[41] There were three vacancies to be filled on the Superior Court in Los Angeles and two on the Municipal Court. Traditionally, a spot on the bench was the plum awarded to a long succession of lawyers who served California governors as executive secretary. Stanley Mosk pointedly reminded Governor Olson of this in a letter dated December 3, 1942:

> Yesterday a capitol newspaper man said to me, "Stanley, the staff has taken a half-dozen trips to the East in the past four years and you always seem to be the one left behind to keep the office operating. I will bet $10 that when the plums are passed out, that you will be left behind again."
>
> If I am the first executive secretary in California history not to be appointed to the Bench, I will be looked upon with suspicion for many, many years by lawyers, the Bench, by members of our own and opposing political party.
>
> "I do not contend that I am qualified to sit on the Bench solely because I have been your executive secretary. I have the necessary temperament and other qualifications, including education, sufficient years of trial practice, experience at holding hearings and writing legal and other publications. If you need convincing on any of these points, merely ask any of the judges on the Bench, from municipal court to Chief Justice Phil Gibson."[42]

The suggestion that the governor might still need convincing about Stanley's qualifications after working closely with him for four years implies that Mosk never felt completely secure in his relationship with Olson. He had witnessed Olson turn on his friends before, and Olson was a very self-contained man, who rarely offered praise or gratitude to others.

His service with Governor Olson taught Stanley Mosk that demonizing political enemies was not smart politics; you never know when you might need them as future allies. He later described Culbert Olson as among the most honest and highly principled men he ever met. "That, unfortunately, was his downfall. He could not compromise, and in the political world, some give and take is often necessary to reach ultimate goals. To Olson, however, if a legislator were with him 90 percent of the time, he was deemed a renegade because of his defection the other 10 percent."[43] With rare exceptions, Mosk maintained cordial relations with political opponents throughout his lengthy career. Earl Warren later became a lifelong friend.

On one of his final days in office, Olson called Mosk into his office and told him to prepare commissions to appoint Harold Jeffries, Harold Landreth, and Dwight Stephenson to the Superior Court, and Eugene Fay and Mosk himself to the Municipal Court. Mosk thanked the governor profusely. The Commissions were prepared and the governor signed them, but by then it was too late to file them. The secretary of state's office was closed, so Mosk locked the Commissions in his desk and went home, intending to file them early the next morning. In the middle of the night, the governor called to inquire if the Commissions had been filed yet. When Mosk explained they had not, the governor said, "Good. I cannot leave Bob Clifton off. Put him in your place on the Municipal Court, and you take Dwight Stephenson's place on the Superior Court." Thus, at the age of 30, Mosk became the youngest Superior Court judge in the history of California. He later noted with pride, "There can never be one younger. A subsequent law requires ten years of law practice before such an appointment can be made. I had been a member of the bar only seven years at that time."[44]

Chapter 5

"I Crowded the War Off Page One"

In January of 1943, Justice Jesse W. Carter of the California Supreme Court administered the oath to swear in Stanley Mosk as a judge of the Superior Court for Los Angeles County. As the youngest judge in the county's court system, Stanley Mosk became the darling of the Southland's Jewish community, and a favorite of the Hollywood film colony. But first, he had to adjust to the seniority system that governed (and still governs) assignments within Los Angeles' huge court structure, and survive a formidable election challenge.

When a very youthful and inexperienced Judge Stanley Mosk reported for duty, the presiding judge of the Los Angeles Superior Court refused to assign him to a courtroom. He thought Mosk was "too young." Mosk remained available for temporary assignments however, and soon Judge Alfred Paonessa requested Mosk's service for six months in the city of Long Beach. Because of wartime personnel shortages, Judge Mosk helped the court catch up on its probate and divorce dockets. The Long Beach press covered the arrival of the precocious and charming new judge, and the local legal community warmly welcomed him.[1] A quick study, he learned on the bench, having little courtroom or litigation experience under his belt. He heard civil jury and non-jury cases, and an occasional criminal matter came before him. Mosk found Judge Paonessa to be a charming man and a willing mentor. He was a lot of fun, besides. The court sat in the Jurgen's Trust Building overlooking the beach. Mosk often found his mentor sitting at a window with binoculars, checking out the pretty girls on the sand.[2] The Building also overlooked the site of the Long Beach Spit and Argue Club, a public forum on the Long Beach pier that functioned like a Hyde Park Speakers' Corner, where Dr. Townsend first presented his pension plan.

In the first jury trial ever heard by Judge Mosk, the family of a young man killed in a motorcycle collision with a taxicab sought damages for wrongful death. The insurance company for his employer also sought recovery of the death benefits paid to the family. Joseph A. Ball of Long Beach represented the defendants. Ball enjoyed a long and distinguished career as a trial lawyer, and later became a law partner of Governor Pat Brown. The jury returned a verdict of $3,377.76 for the insurer, and $1,000 for the family. In one of the very few reversals in Mosk's judicial career, both verdicts were set-aside on appeal because Judge Mosk failed to properly instruct the jury that the reimbursement to the insurer was to be deducted from the damages awarded the family.[3]

Judge Mosk resolved conflicts over private property, tried teachers accused of thievery, and presided over probation violation hearings. He ruled the exemption of truck pick-ups and deliveries from city taxes on laundry services was irrational, discriminatory, and therefore unconstitutional. Three decades before *Roe v. Wade*, he sentenced two chiropractors to prison for performing an abortion in the home of a 23-year-old client.

With an eye to the re-election campaign he would inevitably face, Mosk accepted invitations to address forums large and small concerning the courts and criminal justice system. He told the Long Beach Women's Democratic Club, for example, that when a comparison is made of the costs of probation and imprisonment, probation at $36 per year was a better bargain than the $225 per year it cost to keep someone in prison. He invited many of his listeners to "come down and see how things work at the court." One person who took him up on that invitation was Mrs. Kaygey Kash. "After all," she explained, "he was Jewish, and he was so gorgeous!"[4] A half century later, she became the third Mrs. Stanley Mosk.

It wasn't just women who found the charismatic young judge engaging. Upon his departure from Long Beach in July 1943, court employees organized a farewell banquet, which "started out as a small get-together of attaches and judges." It culminated in a large and representative gathering of the legal community. He was honored for being "patient and courteous with both litigants and lawyers, conscientious and studious in the consideration of litigation before him and impartial in the disposition of his work."

His reassignment to the Superior Court in Santa Monica placed him in the center of a wealthy, liberal community that would provide an excellent political base. Stanley and Edna moved into a comfortable 3 bedroom, 2 bath home built in 1926, centrally located at 1112 South Peck Drive, in the Cheviot Hills district of Los Angeles, just south of Beverly Hills and the Hillcrest Country Club, which provided Jewish residents throughout the city with a golf club and auxiliary activities. It originated during the decades when gentile only clubs discriminated against Jews, among others.

Stanley became a doting father to their son, affectionately called "Ritchie." In a wartime letter to his brother Ed, serving with the U.S. Army in Italy, Stanley boasted: "Ritchie is learning a little geography these days. We've shown him where we think you are, and he recognized other countries on the map. But he does get a bit confused when England is colored green on one map and orange on another! All in all, the little guy is getting quite sharp."[5]

Uncle Ed wrote to his nephew Ritchie, who was deeply impressed by the description of the conditions of wartime Italy. Stanley wrote to Ed, "Now, when [Ritchie] can't finish his meal, he always asks his Mommy to save it for him; he never suggests that any food be thrown out. Of course, it's sometimes difficult to save some slightly used post-toasties, or a bit of second-hand scrambled egg. But his intentions are of the best. And he feels very sorry for the little boys in Italy, he really does."[6]

Edward Mosk had graduated from UCLA in 1937, and attended law school at its legendary cross-town rival, the University of Southern California. After he graduated in 1940, his wartime experience included service with the Office of Strategic Services in Cairo, Algiers, Italy, and Austria. He worked directly under Arthur Goldberg, later appointed to the U.S. Supreme Court by President John F. Kennedy and a life-long friend of both Stanley and Edward Mosk.

On the home front, Paul Mosk's battle with tuberculosis and deteriorating health turned their father into a semi-invalid. Uncle Dave and his wife Esther moved to Los Angeles from Cincinnati, and Uncle Dave helped Minna care for his beloved friend and brother-in-law. The senior Mosks and the Perls occupied two huge, separate units in a Kingsley Street apartment house near downtown. Cousin Harriet, who was teaching in Lynwood, stayed with her parents in hopes of eventually finding her own place. Stanley's mother Minna took on the job of managing the building, which enabled her to take care of both her ailing husband and her aging mother, Rolla. Esther observed that her sister-in-law bore her care-taking responsibilities without complaint. Eventually, the near-blind Rolla moved into a convalescent home in her final days, and died in May of 1943, at the age of eighty-five. Her death brought relief and momentarily bonded Harriet with both of her cousins, when she realized she was not alone in loathing her maternal grandmother. Stanley, Ed and Harriet were given the responsibility to handle Rolla's funeral arrangements. They met the mortician, who tried to persuade them to upgrade the wooden coffin. In unison they moaned, "No! This is good enough! This is what she would have wanted." It was a rare moment of unspoken but shared sentiment

Six months later, in January, 1944, Stanley and Ed lost their father, "the Colonel." Their mother Minna did not take the loss of her partner of thirty-four years very well. Stanley thought she suffered from unwarranted depression and anxiety. He rather cynically thought she was suffering in part for appearance's sake. Stanley's letters to his brother Ed gave regular reports of her slow progress. He described her as "bitter about most everything and everyone." "Time," he added, "is probably the only possible cure. Our greatest fear, however, is that instead of a cure in time, her disposition may become like grandmother's was; there is that tendency at times."[7] Minna lost interest in socializing and found it difficult to distract herself from the grief of her loss. Stanley and Ed pondered how they could find something to provide her with income and spark her interest. The idea of a bookshop sounded promising. It could be financed through a combination of their assistance as well as her own savings.

Cousin Harriet now moved in with her beloved Aunt Minna, sharing the one-room flat with twin beds. Uncle Dave took a job with the local Office of Price Administration, and he helped Minna do the same. Adjusting to the lives of bureaucrats was difficult given their age and experience, so the idea of opening a bookshop was a welcome alternative. Dave and Esther helped launch what became the "Irolo Book and Gift Shop," on Irolo and Eighth Streets in Los Angeles. Things seemed to be going better for Minna until one day, while a passenger in the front seat of Stanley's car, she fell out onto the pavement. Apparently, she had been holding on the door handle, and when the car turned left at Warner and Wilshire Boulevards in Westwood, the door swung wide open and she toppled out. Stanley wasn't driving very fast, but this was before seat belts were required in automobiles. She sustained bumps and bruises, but no broken bones. Because she also suffered from severe osteoporosis, from then on she had to walk with a cane. Carrying on the Mosk-Perl shop keeping tradition, Uncle Dave opened another store, this time a handkerchief business on Olympic Boulevard, called David Perl Co. Handkerchiefs were an ideal product for his later, less robust years, since they didn't require heavy lifting. Uncle Dave died in 1976 at the age of eighty-five.

As Mosk was settling into his judgeship, he had to face the prospect of possibly losing his place on the bench. Then as now, Superior Court judges were appointed to serve only until the next general election, when voters would decide if they would win a full six-year term in office. In Los Angeles, that meant a county-wide election, in which public visibility and name recognition were the keys to success. Although most appointees ran unopposed, Mosk's youth and the defeat of the governor who appointed him made him a likely target for an election challenge one year after his appointment.

Just as he had done while working in Governor Olson's office, he rarely missed an opportunity to appear in the public eye at events for all occasions, big and small. Now, of course, such appearances could only aid him at election time. During a meeting of the Los Angeles Breakfast Club, Judge Mosk served as one of the judges to select the best costumes during "Albie's Radio Star Orchestra." The event was sponsored by the International Workers Order and featured folksongs about the United Nations.[8] He spoke at an Emergency Conference to promote direct relief to Jews in Poland, and he appeared before the Democratic Luncheon Club to speak about "Criminals I Have Known."[9]

Along with this hectic schedule, Mosk began writing a widely circulated weekly column, covering everything from jaywalkers to allied conquered areas and prisoners of war. His byline dropped the initial "M." for Morey, and simply read, "by Judge Stanley Mosk." "Judging the News" appeared for two years in a host of Southland newspapers, including *The Eastside Journal, Valley News, Compton News-Tribune, El Sereno News, Pico Times-Post, Azusa Herald, San Fernando Sun, Southeast Herald, San Pedro Shipyard Worker, Pacific Coast Shipyard Worker, Culver City Citizen, Robert's News,* and *Lynwood Press.* His light prose, infused with humor and proverbs, entertained and informed readers about education, equal rights for women, gas rationing, the proposed United Nations, stamp collecting, and more.

The column provided Stanley Mosk with a unique platform to present his philosophy about the world as he saw it, addressing some of the most controversial issues of the day. The holiday season of 1943 inspired him to ask his readers to bear good will to men, adding that this "obviously means all men," including next door neighbors, "the people across the tracks, those with white skin and those with colored skins," and those with opinions that differ from our own. He concluded, "When all people bear good will, the world will rise, new-bathed in the light of paradise," quoting Ida Coolbrith's *The Poet.* In one column entitled "Skin Colors," he quoted the findings of two noted anthropologists that "all races of men have four blood types ... and the color of skin does not tell which type one has." He then discussed recent research about "why some people are Negroid ... yellow and some are white." "We talk loosely about 'Negro blood' and 'white blood,'" he told his readers, often ignoring the fact that "every person, however light or dark his skin may appear, has some of [the same] materials in his skin...."

Addressing women's rights, he described the Equal Rights Amendment pending before Congress. He explained how the proposed constitutional amendment would remedy what "few of us may realize, that in many states of the nation the female sex is at a marked disadvantage in the eyes of the law." He said this was "particularly true of the East," while the West, where "the suffrage movement gained first headway-has always leaned toward greater equality." Mosk heralded women's incremental progress toward equality, telling his readers about a "new achievement" by the female sex: the appointment of a woman to serve as a law clerk to Associate Justice Harlan F. Stone. Justice Stone had also broken new ground a quarter of a century earlier when he hired the first female secretary. Citing evidence of California's "less backward" system of justice, Mosk listed three women serving in the state's judicial system, including Superior Court Judge Georgia Bullock, who presides over "the juvenile court and its many problems." Intentionally or otherwise, the name of Judge Ida May Adams, his opponent in his retention election, was not included. A few months later, Mosk applauded the state Supreme Court's decision to mandate that all persons under 21 convicted of felonies come under the "complete jurisdiction" of the Youth Correction Authority. Previously, the "tremendous power " and "grave responsibilities" of the Youth Authority were thought to be "merely permissive," leaving too much discretion to judges to determine when youthful offenders would be handed over to the three-man agency.[10]

As the war reached its climax, Judge Mosk used his column to promote the formation of "permanent international agencies to preserve the peace," including an International Court of Justice at The Hague, and to describe the plans for the trial of war criminals upon conclusion of the war. Judge Mosk's interest in international justice would grow throughout his career, and as his reputation achieved national and international proportions, he was called upon to work with developing nations in their quest to establish systems of justice. When his former boss, ex–Governor Culbert Olson, sought appointment as a judge on the U.S. Court of Appeals for the Ninth Circuit, Stanley Mosk addressed a letter of recommendation to the Assistant Attorney General in the U.S. Department of Justice. The effort proved futile.[11]

Mosk's judicial assignment in Santa Monica provided a steady source of press coverage. Even his blood drive donations captured media attention. The Wardsville Intelligencer for June 4, 1943, under the headline NINE JUDGES GIVE BLOOD FOR WAR, CLOSE COURT, reported that "nine superior court judges of this city demonstrated that they are really in the superior class when they closed their courts for a few hours and reported, in a body to the Red Cross for blood donations. They were Superior Court judges Clarence Kincaid, Edward R. Brand, Benjamin Scheinman, Clement D. Nye, Stanley Mosk, Thurmond Clarke, John C. Clark and Harold Landreth. Just to keep the records of the donation straight, Superior Court Secretary William M. Byrne went along and donated also, while reporting the proceedings." (Both Clarke and Byrne later served as federal District Court judges in Los Angeles).

In the era before no-fault divorce, Hollywood divorces were a staple, attracting widespread coverage in local and sometimes nationally syndicated papers. In Stanley Mosk's courtroom, Veronica Lake won an uncontested divorce from John Stewart Detlie for cruel and inhuman treatment.[12] The press described how "a sad-faced, pathetic-looking Veronica Lake, minus her famous peek-a-boo bob, ... summarized her troubles" to Judge Mosk. After he granted a divorce to Joe DiMaggio's first wife, actress Dorothy Arnold, the newspaper headline read, "Wife fans Joe out!"[13] Judge Mosk granted Judy Garland her divorce from orchestra leader David Rose, the first of her five husbands.[14] He wrote to Ed, "I had Lana Turner in for her divorce. She was beautiful, but the newspaper reporters were angry with her discourtesies." Lucille Ball sought a divorce decree from Desi Arnaz, but in their on- and off-again relationship, one month later she called it off, both in proceedings before Judge Mosk. Hedy Lamarr married Ted Stauffer in Judge Mosk's court and Ava Gardner, Zsa Zsa Gabor, and Joan Fontaine all appeared before him, as did the siblings of famous people, like the brothers of Bob Hope and Gene Autry, both of whom obtained divorces in Judge Stanley Mosk's court.[15]

Certainly the most celebrated case to come before him was the paternity suit against Charlie Chaplin. In 1942 Chaplin had a brief affair with actress Joan Barry (whose legal name was Joan Berry), whom he was considering for a starring role in a proposed film. The relationship ended when she began harassing him and displaying signs of severe mental illness. After giving birth, she filed a paternity suit against Chaplin in 1943. Her attorney agreed that if blood tests established that Chaplin was not the father, the suit would be dropped. Three doctors agreed that the blood tests were conclusive: Chaplin was not the father. Instead of dropping her suit, Ms. Barry retained legendary Los Angeles attorney Joseph Scott, who argued that the agreement to drop the suit was not binding on the child. On the basis of the agreement and the blood tests, Chaplin's attorney sought dismissal of the paternity suit. Judge Mosk took the motion under submission, and on March 8, 1943, rejected it. He declared, "[T]here is no sound reason to deny, and every sound reason to accept blood tests as a scientific advance of importance." But he added that until the Legislature ordains to the contrary, "courts must decline to accept any specific paternity test as conclusive, to the exclusion of other evidence." He then concluded:

To the adult parties to the action, this or any court owes only the obligation of impartiality and objectivity. But to the infant, unable to maintain its own rights under the law, the court owes the additional duty of protection. "That duty clearly extends to a scrutiny of a stipulation between the adult defendant and the minor's guardian ad litem.... [I]n the case of a minor, the court, in the exercise of that duty, and the ordinary discretion of the court, may determine the stipulation not controlling upon the minor."

Convinced "that the ends of justice will best be served by a full and fair trial of the issues," Judge Mosk denied the Motion to Dismiss. The case proceeded to a jury trial at which the jury rejected the blood test results. After Ms. Barry and the child were displayed in court to ascertain physical resemblances to Chaplin, the jury found Chaplin was the father, and he was ordered to pay child support. Ms. Barry's charges subsequently resulted in another sensational federal trial in which Chaplin was accused of violating the Mann Act for transporting her across state lines for immoral purposes. Defended by renowned Hollywood Attorney Jerry Geisler, Chaplin was acquitted on that charge, but in 1946, the Second District Court of Appeal upheld Judge Mosk's ruling, and sustained the jury's verdict in the paternity suit.[16] The California Supreme Court denied a hearing. Ten years later, the California legislature finally did "ordain to the contrary," adopting the Uniform Act on Blood Tests to Determine Paternity, which provides:

> In a civil action, in which paternity is a relevant fact, the court ... may ... order the mother, child and alleged father to submit to blood tests. If the court finds that the conclusions of all the experts ... are that the alleged father is not the father of the child, the question of paternity shall be resolved accordingly.[17]

Stanley Mosk was delighted with the publicity the Chaplin case brought him. He excitedly wrote to his brother Ed: "I crowded the war off page one throughout the country by denying Charlie Chaplin's motion to dismiss the paternity action against him, and ordering the case to proceed to trial." After noting that a friend in New Guinea had read about the case, he wrote again: "Apparently my fame as a jurist is reaching the most remote parts of the world. (I only hope it has reached the innermost recesses of Los Angeles County on May 16th)." That was the date set for the primary election in which voters would decide to retain or replace Judge Mosk.

Not only did Mosk encounter the rich and famous in his courtroom, but he socialized with them as well. Perhaps a bit star struck, he wrote to Ed about being invited to dinner, a "very ultra dinner" a "formal dinner mind you, at the home of a lawyer ... a nice guy." His host was Isidore Prinzmetal, former chief counsel for MGM. He described the twenty or so guests including "Betty Hutton, Keenan Wynn (son of Ed Wynn, and a fine actor himself), Stephen Crane (ex-husband of Lana Turner), Dave Rose (... ex-husband of Judy Garland)." The "curiosity of the evening," he reported, "was the fact that I had granted divorces to three of the guests ... Turner from Crane, Garland from Rose," and another unnamed.[18]

His experience in divorce court inspired him to write an article on the subject of divorce, citing statistics that showed 1943 was "modern history's darkest in the field of domestic relations, with 33,190 marriages and 24,222 divorces."[19] Judge Mosk told his readers "The breakup of homes and families is reaching alarming proportions." While the number of marriages in Los Angeles County set a new record, the number of "divorces, separate maintenance and annulment suits" also set a new high in the same period. For every five marriages, he reported, there was one divorce, and "after the war the number will likely rise." He supplied divorce rates among Allied nations following World War I, and explained that part of the reason for so many divorces was likely due to the number of marriages that were carried out in haste, along with the long separations for doughboy families, "the exodus of women from homes to war plants," and increased urbanization.

In another piece provocatively entitled, "How Immoral is Hollywood?," Mosk addressed concerns prominent in the public's imagination. "Is the Film Capital really A Sex-Mad, Haven for Adultery and Divorce?" he asked, offering what he called an "entirely unsolicited" perspective on Hollywood morals. "Hollywood is variously described as a sex-mad village, a haven for adultery and divorce, crime-ridden, and communist infested," he acknowledged. "Its detractors include members of Congress, would-be censors, many who failed to achieve their mark in the picture industry, the garden variety of gossips, adherents of the political and social lunatic fringe, and many innocently misled 'average citizens.'" He spoke with authority: "Through the paneled portals of my courtroom have passed most of the world famous celluloid personalities who have had domestic, civil, and criminal problems in recent years." From this, he concluded, "Official statistics do not indicate Hollywood to be any more evil or corrupt than other metropolitan communities in the nation, and, as a matter of fact, it is considerably more moral and law-abiding than most."[20]

The bitter racial strife during the war years did not escape Judge Mosk's attention. He frequently addressed race relations in his speeches and columns. One of the most blatantly racist incidents followed the 1942 trial of twenty-two Mexican-American youth accused of murder during a gang fight in the Sleepy Lagoon neighborhood, near Slauson and Atlantic Boulevards. After twelve of the defendants were convicted, during the week of June 6, 1943, Mexican-Americans, and other minorities were brutally attacked by roaming vigilante-style, uniformed servicemen. The violence became known as the Zoot Suit riots, referencing the faddish, oversized suits, hats, shoes, and accessories worn by young male African Americans and Mexican-Americans. To angry whites, the Zoot Suit culture was an unpleasant reminder of the growing presence of a restive minority population in their midst. Unchecked by local police, rowdy servicemen stationed at nearby military bases wantonly attacked Zoot Suiters and other innocent bystanders, beating up whomever crossed their path. The rampage terrorized the city as Americans in uniform rushed into darkened movie houses and dragged their victims into the streets, violently ripping the clothing from their bruised and broken bodies.

Governor Earl Warren appointed Joseph T. McGucken, then Auxiliary Bishop of the Roman Catholic Diocese in Los Angeles, to chair a committee to investigate the cause of the riots. Concluding their study, the Committee met with newspaper publishers and told them it was "an aggravating practice to link the phrase 'Zoot Suit' with the report of a crime. Repeated reports of this character tend to inflame public opinion on false premises and excite further outbreaks." The committee also met with police administrators and urged them to cease the mass arrests and dragnet raids on Mexican-Americans. The committee's report concluded, "It is significant that most of the persons mistreated during the recent incidents in Los Angeles were either persons of Mexican descent or Negroes. In undertaking to deal with the cause of these outbreaks, the existence of race prejudice cannot be ignored."[21]

As noted by historian Edward J. Escobar, the riots threw a harsh light upon the deteriorating relationship between the Los Angeles Mexican American community and the Los Angeles Police Department in the 1940s. The role the police played in condoning the racial violence closely mirrored the role they previously played in condoning violence in labor disputes.[22]

Today, when we face the turmoil of changing from war to peace, we must guard our Superior Court by retaining judges of proven impartiality, tolerance and understanding!

That is why the following prominent citizens and organizations endorse SUPERIOR Judge Stanley Mosk.

RETAIN

JUDGE

STANLEY MOSK

(Incumbent)

Judge of the SUPERIOR Court

VOTE NOVEMBER 7th

Headquarters: Room 909, 742 South Hill St., VA. 1814

The victor in every political race he entered, Stanley Mosk's first campaign in November 1944 to retain his judgeship on the Superior Court was won with aid of the broad spectrum of ideological factions within the Democratic Party including educators and movie stars, along with bi-partisan support of Republicans. Among those listed on this campaign flyer are educator Susan Dorsey; defense attorney Jerry Giesler; Democratic leader Mrs. Mattison Boyd Jones; noted author Carey McWilliams; Mrs. Edward G. Robinson, wife of the celebrated actor; the L.A. County Republican Voters League, labor leader Harry Braverman; legendary law firm partner John O'Melveny; and L.A. School Board member Fay Allen (courtesy Richard Mosk).

Governor Warren also appointed a Peace Officers Committee on Civil Disturbances, which was chaired by Attorney General Robert W. Kenny. Kenny retained Carey McWilliams to study race relations and race riots, and to make recommendations to the peace officers of the state. His report received widespread attention when race riots again broke out in Detroit in June 1943, leaving 34 dead, and two months later when five people were killed in Harlem. Los Angeles undertook a process to grapple with increasingly tense race relations. Under the auspices of the Institute on Community Relations for County Officials and Employees, a Committee for Interracial Progress was formed to organize a large symposium to promote racial harmony in Los Angeles. Judge Mosk chaired a panel entitled "The Problem of Inter-Group Relations in the Community."[23] The symposium addressed the effect of discriminatory covenants on housing, opportunities for minority groups, the impact of racial patterns of the county, regional planning, urban development, and employment opportunities for minorities.[24] All of these were issues that would persist throughout Mosk's judicial and professional career. During an era when the American legal profession was not a beacon of opposition to racism, Stanley Mosk was an outspoken critic of barriers based upon race.

Although he seemed to be joining every organization that would have him, Mosk persistently refused to become a member of the American Bar Association. It wasn't until the ABA's refusal to admit Negroes to membership was abandoned in 1943 that Judge Mosk became a member. He accompanied his payment of dues with a letter, published in the *Los Angeles Tribune*. In it, he declared that he originally refused to join because of the ABA's "notorious attitude of discrimination toward Negro attorneys," but he welcomed the impending change in policy because, "I have an abiding conviction that membership barriers based on race or color are improper, undemocratic and un–American."[25]

Early in 1944, the expected challenge to Mosk's Superior Court seat finally arrived when two well-regarded Municipal Court judges filed as candidates. Judge Ida May Adams had thirteen years of experience on the Municipal Court. She was elected to the Municipal Court in 1931, the first woman judge in the United States to be directly elected to office. She claimed responsibility for securing the 1927 amendment of the California Community Property Law that permitted California couples to file separate federal income tax returns. She was widely known as "the Marrying Judge," because she presided over so many courthouse weddings. In seeking election to the Superior Court, she noted it was currently occupied by 49 men and one woman. The other candidate, Judge LeRoy Dawson, was a decorated veteran of World War I, and the popular host of a weekly radio program. During his campaign, he referred to Stanley Mosk as "the child judge." Without missing a beat, Mosk retorted "better a child than someone in their second childhood."

Mosk called upon all of the constituencies he had carefully nurtured over the last decade. By the summer of 1944, he won formal support from business, labor, and church groups. To Judge Adams' chagrin, the local branch of the Business and Professional Women's Association endorsed Stanley Mosk. The AFL endorsed Mosk as part of a Democratic slate with Jerry Voorhees, Helen Gahagan Douglas, Ellis Patterson, Clyde Doyle, and Chet Hollifield.[26] The local political action committee of the CIO also endorsed him.

A month later, Mosk reported to Ed, "generally speak-

Stanley Mosk's brother Edward is seen in this photograph, perhaps from the late 1940s, with his wife Fern, who added an artistic, creative element to the Mosk clan, while Edward seemed to carry on Uncle Dave's dietary and political leanings (courtesy Tom Mosk).

ing, I have had two or three good stories every week lately, thanks to Judge Baird, who has really been pitching, and to the friendliness of the press boys on the beat." He received "encouraging assistance" from his sponsoring committee, including Joseph Scott, the lawyer for Joan Barry's child, and Jerry Giesler, who had represented Chaplin.[27] Giesler had previously offered Judge Mosk a position on the Commission on Civil Law and Proceedings of the Lawyers' Club of Los Angeles, which Mosk was honored to accept.[28]

Mosk wrote his brother, "My campaign has never really stopped. I'm constantly speaking before some political groups, more service clubs and nonpolitical outfits. I have been fortunate to get many fine publicity cases." He added that he was off to a Newspaper Guild event, with "of all things, a *Times* reporter."[29] At that time, the *Los Angeles Times* was still a rabidly Republican organ.

Edna Mosk was of enormous assistance in organizing her husband's election campaign. As he put it to Ed, "She has taken to the work remarkably well, and has given it new impetus; I sometimes procrastinate, but not her — everything must be done immediately — and she gets it done, too."[30] This turned out to be Edna Mosk's apprenticeship in politics, becoming not just her husband's primary source of campaign funds, but one of the state Democratic Party's most talented fundraisers. Even 5-year-old Richard Mosk was put to work, licking stamps for election mailers.

Although Mosk finished first in the primary with 240,000 votes, he was forced into a run-off by second place finisher Judge LeRoy Dawson, with 197,000 votes. He felt quite vulnerable, as incumbent judges forced into run-offs frequently lost. But Judge Ida May Adams, who pulled 165,000 votes in the primary, withdrew and a week before the general election she endorsed Mosk.[31] In a glowing endorsement, *The Free Press* reported that both political parties, and all factions of Los Angeles County labor backed Mosk, and described him as patient, kindly, industrious, courteous, scholarly, clear-thinking and possessing "no prejudices, no hatreds, no bias."[32]

California Supreme Court Justice Rey Schauer, who twenty years later would administer the California Supreme Court oath of office to Stanley Mosk, wrote Mosk a letter congratulating him on his primary victory and offered his view of Mosk's opponent in the run off. "Your opponent has been on the municipal bench for many years. I am satisfied that he received at the primary approximately all of the vote that he will receive at the final. He will pick up a few more of the anti-incumbent votes at that time, but there will be a far greater percentage of the electorate who will go to the polls then, and with your consistently increasing popularity I have no fear but that you will win out."[33] Mosk's former colleague Carey McWilliams inquired if there was anything he could do to help with the upcoming election.[34]

By November, *The Daily News, Los Angeles Times,* and *Santa Monica Outlook* all endorsed Mosk. So did the *Long Beach Press-Telegram*, although *The Long Beach Independent* did not.[35] The general election turned out 85 percent of registered voters, larger than in any previous county election to date. Mosk won with 740,227 votes to Dawson's 525,765, the largest vote ever received by a judge in Los Angeles County.[36] Justice Schauer again wrote to Judge Mosk: "The splendid majority given to you in your contest for election, as well as the result in the contest for President, certainly gives me new faith in the fairness and wisdom of the American electorate."[37] In the general election of 1944, President Franklin D. Roosevelt defeated Republican Thomas E. Dewey to win a fourth term in office.

With the election out of the way, Mosk was anxious to volunteer for military service, and even though his judicial position gave him an exemption from the military draft, he made repeated efforts to arrange his induction. Despite the success of the D-Day invasion in June of 1944, the war was far from over. The Battle of the Bulge had just been fought, and Japanese soldiers were stubbornly resisting the American advance in the Pacific. The shelling of an oil field near Santa Barbara by a Japanese sub in 1942 had created a sustained alarm that a West Coast invasion was possible, and the Coast Guard was mobilized to keep close watch on the Pacific shoreline. Edna was already volunteering for the Red Cross, so Stanley Mosk volunteered for the Coast Guard Reserve, spending twelve hours a week scanning for signs of Japanese submarines. By arrangement with other members of the flotilla, he served his duty on Saturdays and Sundays. Patriotism alone may not have been the motivation for Stanley Mosk's eagerness to volunteer for military service. He realized if he planned a political career, military service could be an important asset. Despite his eagerness, there was one obstacle standing in the way of his enlistment: his 20/800 eyesight. He expressed his concern to Col. Kenneth Leitch, the California Selective Service Director.

Judge Mosk must have made a profound impact on Col. Leitch, because he personally picked up Mosk in his official army vehicle, and took him to the induction center at Fort MacArthur. With Mosk sitting in the medical office, Col. Leitch called the medical director into the adjacent hallway. Realizing that he was being given the opportunity to memorize the eye chart, Mosk quickly memorized as much as he could. When the doctor returned, he asked Mosk to remove his eyeglasses and read the chart. Once pointed in the right direction, he rattled off the letters with amazing speed. "Well," said the doctor, "we must have made a mistake in the previous examination." Mosk was finally a buck private in the U.S. Army.

Everything Judge Stanley Mosk did received press coverage, including his induction into the armed services. Unbeknownst to him, his love affair with publicity now inspired both the Army and the FBI to initiate investigations into the background of the new doughboy. The military records at Fort MacArthur refer to the subversive files of the Los Angeles Police Department, which at that time provided scant evidence of Mosk's activities. Most of what the LAPD file included was taken from published accounts of Mosk's appearance at public events, including a *Los Angeles Daily News* article indicating Morey Stanley Mosk was chairman of the Citizen's Committee for Industrial Justice. It reported that the following year Mosk acted as an attorney for the California Federation for Political Unity and Labor's Non-Partisan League. The report noted Mosk's service as Culbert Olson's executive secretary.[38]

Always on the lookout for subversives in military ranks, the FBI reports

When the increasingly popular Judge Stanley Mosk finally passed the eye test to enlist into the armed services, the local press satirized the new Private Mosk's subservience to a superior officer who growls, "I'm the Law Around Here Bub!" (courtesy Richard Mosk).

concluded that Mosk was not a communist but was purported to be a "Communist political association sympathizer." This was only the beginning of their scrutiny of Stanley Mosk, and the agency left a vivid account of the remainder of Mosk's life, viewed through the lens of the FBI's obsession with a supposed communist conspiracy tearing at the very fiber of our democratic institutions. At every turn, the FBI found justification for tracking his activities. When Judge Mosk submitted the names of prospective jurors for the Los Angeles County Grand Jury, for example, the Bureau pointed out that when Mosk was informed that some of the names on his list were "much to the left," he refused to withdraw their names. Furthermore, when their names were put in nomination, it "aroused violent objection on the part of others connected with the Superior Court in Los Angeles County."[39]

Over the next two decades, the FBI utilized the observations of their own agents, as well as the insights of individuals providing volunteered or paid-for information, accurate or otherwise. Whomever the source, detailed accounts of episodes in Mosk's public and personal life were transcribed in memos, letters to the Director, or titled simply as "observation," which sometimes included expressions of the reporting agent's own feelings about Mosk. The FBI followed Stanley Mosk throughout the remainder of his Superior Court years, his tenure as Attorney General, and his early years on the Supreme Court. When serving as Attorney General, Mosk tried in to engage FBI Director J. Edgar Hoover in a collegial relationship, but was repeatedly snubbed.

Mosk's military service was short and he never left the mainland, completing his basic training at Fort Leonard Wood, Missouri with the Army Corps of Engineers, and then serving at Camp Plauche, Louisiana with the transportation corps. Only his commanding officers were aware of his civilian profession, but Mosk made sure that his enlistment and subsequent discharge were well covered by the Los Angeles press. He was photographed taking off his judicial robe, and the newspapers affectionately called him "G.I. Judge." Pointing out that Judge Mosk would serve "incognito" as a plain buck private, one newspaper cartoon was captioned, "I'm the law around here, Bub!" as Mosk cowers under the orders of his sergeant. Throughout his enlistment, he sent letters to newspapers back home describing his experiences. With tongue in cheek, he described his surroundings as "luxurious quarters." He had a "southern exposure" in a room "generously shared with thirty other men," with "a north, east and west" exposure as well. The men can "sleep as late as we wish, provided we are up by 6 A.M." He had a "fine barber ... with many years of training — as a veterinarian." In the First Regiment Table Tennis Championship at Camp Plauche, PFC Stanley Mosk defeated PFC Charles Young in the semi-final matches.[40]

After only three months service, and one month before the atomic bomb ended the Pacific theatre war, Chief Justice Phil Gibson informed Judge Mosk of the "difficulty in obtaining sufficient help to keep the [Superior Court's] calendars up to date," hoping Mosk would thus "feel justified in making application for a discharge" from army.[41] Mosk had applied for an Officer's commission, and anticipated being sent to the Phillipines. Congressman Ellis Patterson was "happy to hear he was relieved of service," and wished Mosk "a long period of service on the Bench in California, or, in any capacity you desire. You will always have the support and respect of your many friends in anything you do."[42]

Governor Warren magnanimously held Judge Mosk's seat open, in spite of others who coveted the position, so his return to the Superior Court was a simple matter. Mosk quickly resumed the hectic schedule of speeches, public meetings, and newspaper columns he had maintained during his election campaign. The *Eastside Journal* welcomed Judge Mosk back with a photo of him sitting in his old chair, "just to see how it felt."[43] Hardly catching his breath, Mosk took up the cause of returning G.I.'s. Mosk's views were supportive of President Truman's efforts to re-assimilate the nation's veterans, always adding his own twist. Speaking to the Los Angeles Chamber of Commerce, he proposed federal programs to assist Vets to find jobs and decent working conditions, "at a living wage," with possibilities for advancement. The National Youth Administration, the Civilian Conservation Corps, the Public Works Administration, and the Works Progress Administration were on his list of "government jobs" that returning G.I.'s would find were "not bureaucratic, communistic, or subversive."[44] Mosk said that although no consensus existed among servicemen's opinions, there was a "reasonable unanimity in three fields." Calling for "an alert progressive party" to take cognizance, Mosk told the crowd that servicemen had no patience with demagogues "seeking to divide by racism or religious bitterness." As a result of learning to live together during their military service, veterans were eager to live together in peacetime as well. Just as "there are no atheists in foxholes," Mosk said that there were "no war mongers on a battlefield or in an army camp," and we must learn to live with our allies. Most importantly, returning G.I.'s expected to find "productive employment, decent working conditions, and a living wage."[45]

Returning to his customary engagements, he served as the toastmaster to raise funds for a Jewish Center in Santa Monica, and later he was described as one "prominent in civic and Jewish affairs," when he chaired the American Jewish Congress's salute to Free France at the Los Angeles Philharmonic, attended by more than 2,000 Angelenos.[46] This and scores of other events brought Mosk increased public exposure and good will. He did not disappoint audiences or constituents, as he continued to grow in prominence in civic and Jewish affairs throughout the Southland.

Radio broadcasts facilitated Stanley Mosk's widespread familiarity and public esteem (courtesy Richard Mosk/Gene Lester).

When he wasn't out giving a speech or attending a dinner, Stanley Mosk could usually be found at a baseball or football game. With his son Richard in tow, he was a regular at Gilmore Field, to watch the Hollywood Stars of the Pacific Coast League, or at Wrigley Field to see the Los Angeles Angels. Richard remembers attending many athletic and sporting events: "I remember seeing a Sugar Ray Robinson fight at Wrigley Field, and he even took me to a Mr. America contest and a weight lifting event. We saw soccer, tennis, track and field and polo — all kinds of sports activities."[47] At an early age, Richard acquired his father's life-long love of tennis, as well as his father's passion for collecting: football programs, stamps, coins and comic books.

Stanley Mosk was not alone in his concern about returning G.I.'s. As elsewhere, the number of returning California residents along with throngs of newcomers swelled the areas where jobs had been plentiful, creating a severe housing shortage. More than numbers, new demographics altered the landscape as well. During the war, pressure from A. Philip Randolph, president of the Brotherhood of Sleeping Car Porters, inspired President Roosevelt to issue Executive Order 8802, which outlawed racial discrimination in wartime factory plants. Wartime employment in the aircraft plants of Los Angeles and the shipyards of Northern California became magnets for African Americans previously employed in dead-end agricultural work. During wartime, California's population had swelled by two million, a 27 percent increase, out of which approximately 200,000 settled in Los Angeles. Although some migrants returned to their home states or elsewhere, this represented an enormous shift of Southern blacks permanently leaving the South, and a new era in California history. Moore's Dry Dock in Oakland had 600 employees in 1936; in 1944, it employed 35,000. Kaiser Shipyards did not exist in 1940. Three years later, it employed 100,000 in the production of liberty ships. In the East Bay, the population of African Americans grew 400 percent during the war, from 14,000 to 60,000 residents. In 1945, 70 percent of them worked in one industry: shipyards. The pattern was identical in the aircraft industry in Southern California. At war's end, there were millions of white and black war-plant workers to reabsorb into the workforce, along with millions of soldiers coming home. Where would they find housing for their families? The answer was simple: they were confined to neighborhoods defined and reinforced during the pre-war years. By 1965, the population of African Americans in Los Angeles rose to 650,000, and most lived in the South-central area of the city, or a newly incorporated area of Watts.

The widespread use of racial restrictive covenants limited their access, not only to existing white residential areas, but also to most of the new housing developments sprawling across the suburbs of Southern California. Racial restrictive covenants were agreements between buyers and sellers of property recorded in the deed of sale not to sell, lease or rent the property to minority groups, usually blacks, but depending upon the part of country, Jews, Chinese, Japanese, Mexicans or any non–Caucasians. Their use became widespread after the U.S. Supreme Court ruled in 1917 that local governments could not directly segregate housing by use of zoning ordinances defining who could live in which part of town.[48] Since they were private contracts, these covenants were legally enforceable in court. In a 1926 decision, the U.S. Supreme Court declared:

> The constitutional right of a Negro to acquire, own, and occupy property does not carry with it the constitutional power to compel sale and conveyance to him of any particular private property. The individual citizen, whether he be black or white, may refuse to sell or lease his property to any particular individual or class of individuals.[49]

As a matter of California state law, racial restrictive covenants had been upheld in decisions of the California Supreme Court going back to 1919. The Court ruled that although sale of property to Negroes could not be restricted because that would be a restraint on alienation, restrictions on *occupancy* of the premises could be enforced.[50] Thus, the most punitive form of racial restrictive covenants permitted in most states, requiring the forfeiture of the property, was prohibited in California. But by enforcing the prohibitions of occupancy, California courts actually enjoined Negroes from occupying premises that they legally owned.[51]

Judge Mosk's views about such practices were well known from his columns and public speaking. Anyone who knew Judge Mosk was aware that intolerance for racism and bigotry ran deep in the Mosk household. As a Westside real estate broker, Edna Mosk helped break the color barriers in the Westwood neighborhoods surrounding UCLA. On one occasion, when a client expressed reluctance to purchase a home next door to an African American physician, she went to great lengths to persuade him that the doctor was a fine, upstanding gentleman. The client responded, "Oh, it's not the nigger I'm worried about; it's the kike who lives on the other side!" On another occasion, after she mailed invitations for Richard's birthday party, a mother called to complain that the invitees included a "colored youngster." Edna asked, "I didn't notice; what color is he?" Edna then gave her a lecture on tolerance. At the birthday party, Stanley organized a game of "Pin the Mustache on Tom Dewey" for the children to play. Although racial bias was pervasive in the well-to-do neighborhoods where they resided, the Mosks were outspoken in exposing and condemning it.

Now, as a judge on the Superior Court, Stanley Mosk had an opportunity to put his words into action. Activist lawyers and reformers sought test cases to transform Los Angeles into an open, upwardly mobile society for all of its residents. The case of *Wright v. Drye* came before Judge Mosk in 1947, involving a fight by three families against the injustice of racial covenants and the demeaning methods used to enforce them. The defendants included three African American families who had purchased homes in the tony Hancock Park neighborhood of West Los Angeles. The lead defendant was Frank Lloyd Drye, a talented musician who moved his wife and five children from Alabama to their "dream house," a five-bedroom, three bath, Mediterranean with an orange tree in the back yard. Frank Drye played the cornet with blues legend W.C. Handy, and after attending a Chicago music conservatory, he was hired as bandleader at acclaimed Tuskegee Institute. Drye even played taps at the funeral of Tuskegee's founder, Booker T. Washington. In 1918, he joined the U.S. Army's all-black cavalry, and won a Silver Star and Purple Heart for his service in the trenches of France. During World War II, Drye was re-commissioned as bandmaster at the Tuskegee Army Airfield, where the famed "Tuskegee Airmen" were trained. His band toured the nation selling war bonds.[52]

The deed to the Drye home included a racial restrictive covenant making their occupancy of the home they purchased unlawful. Two months after they moved in, nine white neighbors, led by Pastor Clarence Wright of the Wilshire Presbyterian Church, filed a suit to enforce the covenant by evicting the Dryes, as well as two other black families, the Stricklands, and the Stewards, who had also purchased houses in the neighborhood. The three families hired Loren Miller to defend them. Miller was a crusading black lawyer who had been representing families against racial covenants in Pasadena, and won a narrow victory in the "Sugar Hill" case decided by Judge Thurmond Clarke. Hattie McDaniel, the black actress who won an Oscar for her supporting role in *Gone With the Wind*, purchased a seventeen room house in the "Sugar Hill" West Adams District in 1942. When a small faction of white residents tried to enforce racial covenants against some of the black Sugar Hill residents, McDaniel and others organized opposition to the covenants. Superior Judge Thurmond Clarke decided to visit the disputed ground. The next morning, Judge Clarke threw the case out of court. His reason: "It is time that members of the Negro race are accorded, without reservations or evasions, the full rights guaranteed them under the 14th Amendment to the Federal Constitution. Judges have been avoiding the real issue too long."[53]

Loren Miller allied with Charlotta Bass and helped turn her newspaper, *The California Eagle*, into an influential and loud voice against "Jim Crow" laws in the Southland. Governor Pat Brown appointed him to the Los Angeles County Superior Court in 1964, where he served until his death in 1967.

Following the precedent established by the California Supreme Court would have required Judge Mosk to enforce the covenants, and evict the Dryes, Stricklands, and Stewards from their homes. Justice Mosk simply refused to do so. He courageously ruled that restrictive covenants were unconstitutional. He unequivocally stated: "Our nation has just fought the Nazi race superiority doctrine. One of these defendants was in that war and is a Purple Heart veteran. This court would indeed be callous if it were to permit him to be ousted from his own home by using 'race' as the measure of his worth as a citizen and neighbor." Mosk added, "We read columns in the press each day about un-American activities. This court feels there is no more reprehensible un-American activity than to attempt to deprive persons of their own homes on a 'master race' theory." He ruled the cause of action to enforce the restrictive covenant was "inconsistent with the guarantees of the 14th Amendment."[54]

African American newspapers heralded Mosk's action. The *Los Angeles Sentinel* banner headline read, "JUDGE STANLEY MOSK RULES RACE COVENANTS ILLEGAL, 'UN-AMERICAN.'" The *Sentinel* reported that the previous decision by Judge Clarke in the Sugar Hill case and Judge Mosk's in the Drye case were "the only two decisions rendered in the United States since 1892 which have found covenants violations of the rights guaranteed under the 14th Amendment."[55] Two months later, the *Sentinel* again referenced Judge Mosk's ruling, along with Judge Clarke and California Attorney General Robert W. Kenny, when it announced "RESTRICTIVE COVENANTS CHALLENGED NATIONALLY; Recommend 'End Abuse,'" referring to the report issued by President Truman's Committee on Civil Rights and the building momentum around the country that would eventually lead to a hearing before the U.S. Supreme Court.[56]

One year later, the United States Supreme Court decided the case of *Shelley v. Kramer,* coming to the same conclusion as Judge Stanley Mosk.[57] The Court did not overrule its prior decisions, holding that the restrictive covenants were private contracts not affected by the federal constitution, but it concluded that in *enforcing* the covenants state courts were engaged in state action, which violated the Fourteenth Amendment of equal protection of the laws. Chief Justice Fred Vinson authored the unanimous opinion. The United States Department of Justice, under Attorney General Tom Clark, filed an amicus brief in support of the petitioners, black families that were being ejected from their homes. Four Jewish lawyers in the U.S. Department of Justice wrote the government's brief. The Solicitor General's office omitted their names from the brief, however. Principal Assistant to the Solicitor General Arnold Raum, himself Jewish, later explained, "It was bad enough that Perlman's name has to be there, to have one Jew's name on it, but you have to put four more Jewish names on it. That makes it look as it a bunch of Jewish lawyers in the Department of Justice put this out." The case was argued for the petitioners by Thurgood Marshall, chief counsel for the NAACP and later a Justice of the U.S. Supreme Court, and Loren Miller, the lawyer who represented the defendants before Judge Stanley Mosk in *Wright v. Drye.*

Judge Stanley Mosk joined in the chorus of praise for the Supreme Court's decision in *Shelley v. Kramer.* "Naturally, I'm grateful that the Supreme Court saw fit to declare that neither federal nor state courts may enforce housing restrictions on race or color," he said. He added, "Judge Thurmond Clarke and I have consistently ruled that the Fourteenth Amendment of the constitution prohibited state courts from barring persons from their own homes on the basis of race or color," along with "courageous lawyers like Loren Miller, who have devoted years to waging a judicial war against discrimination in housing."[58] Several years later, one of the Hancock Park homes at issue in *Wright v. Drye* became the residence of Tom Bradley, the first black mayor of Los Angeles. The Drye family lived in their "dream house" for 57 years, until Frank Drye's wife Artoria, a retired schoolteacher, died at the age of 106.

During his sixteen years on the Superior Court bench, Stanley Mosk engaged in the trial and disposition of thousands of cases, seeing very few of his rulings overturned by a higher court. Among the exceptions was his ruling in *Beck v. Bel Air Properties*.[59] A homeowner filed a suit for mudslide damage attributable to the grading of land above his canyon location. Judge Mosk instructed the jury that grading of land was an "ultra-hazardous activity," for which strict liability could be imposed, without proof of negligence. In a divided opinion, a panel of the California Court of Appeal disagreed, concluding that earth moving operations incident to subdividing and grading hills and slopes into building sites were not ultra-hazardous. Thus, it held that Mosk erred in instructing the jury on strict liability, and because it could not be determined whether the verdict in favor of the homeowner was based on negligence or strict liability, the instruction was reversible error. As fate would have it, the ruling offered an excellent example of an important legal concept, and made it into at least one Torts casebook widely used in law school classes.[60] Six years later, when Judge Mosk's son Richard was a first year law student at Harvard Law School, he was chagrined to find *Beck v. Bel Air* in the Torts casebook he was assigned to read. He called his father to tease him about the embarrassment of finding his father reversed in his law school casebook. Judge Mosk explained that reversal of his decisions was a "rare occurrence," and said that he had warned the trial lawyer that risking an instruction on the then-untested theory of strict liability could jeopardize a favorable outcome. Mosk agreed that strict liability should be the law, however, and granted the lawyer's request to so instruct the jury.[61]

Judge Stanley Mosk sentenced only one man to death throughout his nearly two decades on the Superior Court. Mosk described the trial as "one of the most dramatic cases I heard as a trial judge.... The case had all the overtones of intrigue, love, sex, hate, rejection, frustration and finally violence."[62]

Newspaper readers followed the details of the case of John Crooker, who was accused of first-degree murder of Mrs. Norma McCauley, an attractive, wealthy divorcee, and mother of three, who lived in the fashionable Bel-Air section of West Los Angeles. During his first appearance before Judge Mosk, "The law student and former house boy stood silently ... until prodded into action by a slip of the tongue on the part of his attorney," who waived reading of the complaint saying, "There were several facets of the case requiring study before a plea of 'guilty' is entered." The lawyer corrected herself after "Crooker leaned over and whispered hurriedly" saying that she meant, "not guilty." Another attorney represented Crooker for the remainder of the case.

Ten years before the United States Supreme Court decision of *Miranda v. Arizona*,[63] Crooker's new lawyer argued that during Crooker's interrogation, the police failed to warn him of his right to an attorney, and therefore his written confession should be excluded from evidence. Crooker also claimed he wrote out a confession to the murder in order to escape a police beating. Crooker said he had been hit three times and threatened with more violence and as a result, he said he "would say anything they wanted me to say if they then would leave me alone." Although Mosk was well aware of such police practices, he credited the denials by police witnesses and admitted the confession in evidence.

Crooker testified that he had secreted himself inside Mrs. Cauley's nursery closet, waiting for her company to leave. Her company was a gentleman whom she had just met at another party and asked him to accompany her home out of fear that Crooker would harass her after she had ended their stormy, clandestine romance. Crooker said he hid in the closet from 3:30 A.M. until 5:00 A.M. on the morning of July 4th. When Mrs. Cauley was finally alone, he confronted her. They talked and argued for about an hour, but he insisted he was not at her home on the following morning when she was murdered around 5:00 A.M. on July 5th. In spite of Crooker's claim that he confronted McCauley the previous night, the timeline of the prosecution's witness's cleared up any doubts the jury might have had about Crooker's "far-fetched" claim that he spent all that time in the closet. During the trial, letters written by the murdered paramour were presented to the jury and recounted in detail by the press, reflecting how passionate the relationship once was and establishing that its dissolution provided strong motive for the murder. Another state witness, who knew Mrs. McCauley socially for the two months prior to her death, said that on several occasions she had mentioned her annoyance with Crooker, telling the witness, "he had threatened her again-that he knew enough about law to kill her and get by with it, that if Chessman can do it he can."[64] The Chessman to whom he was referring was Caryl Chessman, whose death penalty appeal from a kidnapping conviction Stanley Mosk would soon face as Attorney General.

When Crooker was convicted, the jury recommended the death penalty. Upon Crooker's appeal, the California Supreme Court, with Justice Jesse W. Carter dissenting, affirmed Judge Mosk's ruling and Crooker's death sentence.[65] On January 24, 1957, Judge Mosk set the date of execution for April 12.[66] He later confessed to his discomfort in doing it. "If we truly believe that only God renders such irrevocable decisions as life and death, then the judge who makes the pronouncement of the ultimate penalty is in fact playing God. He is ordering the elimination of a human being."[67]

Judge Mosk's ruling and Crooker's death sentence were affirmed by a 5–4 ruling of the United States Supreme Court,[68] with Chief Justice Earl Warren joining the dissenters.[69] The Supreme Court majority concluded that Crooker needed no warning of his right to counsel, since he had already completed a year of law school. Although only three years elapsed between the murder and the affirmance by the U.S. Supreme Court (compared to the 25 year average to dispose of California death appeals today), as Crooker's execution approached, Pat Brown had become governor and Stanley Mosk had become Attorney General. Crooker's petition for commutation of his death sentence was the first one heard by the newly elected governor. In explaining his decision to grant the commutation, he wrote:

When the Mosk family left Rockford, they briefly resettled in San Antonio, Texas, where in 1932 loyal Chicago White Sox fan Stanley Mosk posed wearing a generic pinstriped baseball uniform; in spite of his brother Edward's cheering for the Cubs, their passionate exchanges over sports and the law continued throughout their lives (courtesy Tom Mosk).

I listened carefully to all they had to say, but what really made up my mind was a note from Stanley Mosk in the report, stating that as the trial judge he would not object to a commutation of Crooker's sentence from death to life imprisonment. "This defendant's crime arose out of relationship with the deceased under a set of circumstances that would not likely happen again," Mosk wrote. "He is an intelligent young man of some cultural attainment, and if personality defects could be cured or contained, he could in the distant future become rehabilitated and become a constructive member of society."[70]

Eight years later, after receiving numerous reports of Crooker's rehabilitation, Governor Brown again commuted his sentence from life without parole to life with parole, and Crooker was paroled and released from prison in 1972. Shortly thereafter, then Justice Stanley Mosk received an invitation to John Crooker's wedding. He did not attend, but sent him a note to wish him well. Thereafter, every year without fail, he received a Christmas card from Crooker and his wife, updating him on how they were doing. Justice Mosk found one note particularly poignant:

> I thought you would be pleased to know that Valerie and I have bought a house. It is the first home I have ever owned. I have been promoted by my employer in the bay area and am now earning a guarantee of $25,000 per year. Things are really going well for us. I wish you continued success in your career.

Justice Mosk reflected that the rehabilitation of John Crooker to become a law-abiding member of society "would not have been possible were it not for the compassion of a Governor. Pat Brown — the original Governor Brown — was that type of human being."[71]

Chapter 6

"The Jewish Community Found a Leader"

As the late Journalist Marlene Adler Marks pointedly commented, the rarity of Jews in elective and appointed public positions in California during the 1940's gave Stanley Mosk's career special significance. "It was a time when the fact of being a Jew in public office really mattered."[1] Stanley Mosk became the rising star on which to hang a variety of hopes for the Southland's Jewish community and Jews throughout the state. He became, in effect, an icon of Jewish liberalism. The diverse demographics of Los Angeles could not have found a more dynamic Jewish ambassador than Judge Stanley Mosk. Mosk was an early participant in the rise of a powerful Jewish-black political coalition. The unique tapestry of Stanley Mosk's life was woven with the multi-ethnic strands of mid-twentieth century California.

The Jewish community in Los Angeles was dramatically transformed in the 1940's. The base of Jewish population until the Second World War had been the eastside's Boyle Heights' area. It was a multiethnic working class neighborhood, in which Jews, Hispanics, and Japanese-Americans shared their lives. Many Jews were active in the labor movement, and organized some of the most successful unions in downtown's garment district. Jewish labor organizing was particularly noteworthy because of the avid opposition of the powers-that-be in Los Angeles, including the *Los Angeles Times* and the notorious Red Squad of the Los Angeles Police Department. The Boyle Heights Jewish community was often militantly progressive in its politics. Massive migration after World War II created enclaves around Los Angeles of Jewish communities on the Westside and in the San Fernando Valley. The demise of racial restrictive covenants against Jews opened previously inaccessible housing, and many Jewish families left Boyle Heights for Beverly Hills and West Hollywood.

In 1940, the Los Angeles population of one and a half million included 130,000 Jews, or less than 9 percent. By 1950, when the population of Los Angeles had swelled to two million, an estimated 315,000 Jews lived there, making Los Angeles the second largest Jewish community in the United States after New York City, and the third largest in the world behind New York and Tel Aviv. At its height, the Jewish population of Los Angeles included 15 percent of the City's residents.

Although prominent Jews who helped to build up the city's business and commercial stature were frequently elected to the city council during the early history of Los Angeles, Jews elected to public office completely disappeared by the turn of the last century. In 1900, the entire Jewish population of Los Angeles was 2,500 in a city of 102,479 residents. That year, Herman Silver, a Jew who served four years as the president of the City Council, was defeated as the Republican candidate for Mayor. Until Rosalind Weiner (later Wyman), was elected to the Los Angeles City Council in 1953, no other Jews were elected to local government positions. Jews were, however, appointed to judgeships throughout the region, which provided an alternative to the vacuum of lower level elective office. Although not a monolithic voting bloc, the city's Jewish vote offered consistently strong support for liberal causes, often much stronger than the state as a whole. In November 1946, California voters turned down a ballot measure to establish a Fair Employment Practices Commission. Only thirty percent of the California electorate voted for the measure, but there was overwhelming support from Jewish voters,

Stanley Mosk had not grown up as part of the Jewish community in Los Angeles. In fact, he had not grown up in a Jewish community at all, but he arrived in Los Angeles along with thousands of other Jews who were eager to create

From left, Stanley, Minna, Paul, and Edward Mosk in a formal family portrait taken circa 1928 in Rockford, Illinois (courtesy Tom Mosk).

a community of mutual support that respected the cultural roots of all its neighbors. As his talent and willingness to serve became apparent, Mosk was approached to lead numerous drives, functions, and organizations throughout the Southland. Three months after the war ended, Mosk directed the southern California region for Yugoslavia Relief. Movie star Rita Hayworth, along with Stanley's wife Edna, took a leadership role in planning a winter clothing drive.[2] Mosk never lost touch with colleagues in the Shaw recall campaign, though. He spoke at Municipal League Luncheon Forums at Clifton's Cafeteria, on the topic of the returning veteran's future. He moderated a forum held at the Hollywood Women's Club as part of a series by the American Society for Russian Relief, where he compared the re-integration process for G.I. Joe's counterpart in the Russian Red Army.[3] Three days later, the *Eastside Journal* reported that Mosk would speak at an emergency conference promoting direct relief to Jews in Poland on behalf of the American Federation for Polish Jews Committee.[4] His never-ending round of appearances and speeches led to leadership positions in such groups as the Anti-Defamation League and the Jewish Federation, and to his heading up drives on behalf of war-torn Yugoslavia, European Jewry, Israel, and a host of local and international causes. Mosk immersed himself in the affairs of the Jewish community. His

Jewishness was secular and public-oriented; not theologically or ceremonially inspired. Later in life, he still knew little about Judaism and audiences would groan when he couldn't pronounce the Hebrew words during high holiday services. Even Shalom was difficult. Nonetheless, he had "a Jewish heart" in his commitment to civil liberties, civil rights, and other progressive issues, and his commitment to Israel attracted admirers of his ability to express deeply held convictions. Ed's wife Fern observed that the Jewish community found a leader in Stanley Mosk, whether he wanted to be one or not.[5]

Mosk must have realized that the Jewish community in Los Angeles could provide a launching pad for a political career that could carry him far beyond the confines of Los Angeles. When Jewish organizations called upon him to speak, he rarely said no. Appointments and accolades came at a dizzying pace. By way of just a few examples, *The California Jewish Voice* reported Mosk was the chairman of a new Speakers Bureau organized to publicize the need for blood plasma for Israel.[6] A month later Mosk, "one of the outstanding Jewish leaders in our community," was the featured guest at the Father and Sons Program for the Omaha Friendship Club.[7] Soon after, he was the featured speaker for the five-year birthday of the Wilshire Lodge of the B'nai B'rith.[8] B'nai B'rith International was and is the most widely known Jewish humanitarian, human rights, and advocacy organization, working for Jewish unity, security, continuity, and tolerance in 50 countries around the world.

Impressed with Mosk's comments during a KFI radio interview, the California Jewish Voice published his article on the upcoming war crimes trials. Responding to President Roosevelt's insistence on an unconditional surrender, and his pronouncement that no criminal will escape punishment, Mosk suggested the trials would be the greatest drama in the history of mankind—the drama of the apprehension, trial, conviction, and punishment of the high public officials of enemy countries. He proceeded to outline the legal difficulties involved in such an enterprise, however, and advised that strict adherence to international law was assured by relying on the newly proposed United Nations. While there was no guarantee of peace, he cautioned, his faith was nevertheless reinforced by knowing that members of the legal profession were devoting their energy and skills "to the construction of the mechanism necessary for a permanent peace, in effect an international bill of rights which may be the cornerstone for a fine, free world of the future."[9]

Mosk became a member of the Los Angeles Committee on Palestine headed by co-chairs Manchester Boddy and Byron C. Hanna. Boddy was the publisher of the chief Democratic newspapers in the state, the *Los Angeles Daily News* and the *Evening News*. Hanna was a former president of the Los Angeles Chamber of Commerce, and headed the group Southern Californians, Inc. As part of the national American Palestine Committee, revived in 1940 with the sponsorship of U.S. Congressional leadership, the cause attracted wide bi-partisan support. Mayor Fletcher Bowron, future mayor Norris Poulson, Hollywood notables Edward G. Robinson, David O. Selznick, and Helen Gahagan, as well as a host of rabbis, government, and civic leaders were enthusiastic supporters. The Committee called upon the president to take "immediate steps ... to open Palestine to unrestricted Jewish immigration and to establish that country as a free and democratic commonwealth," with an urgent appeal for state leaders to endorse "the righteous cause of a Jewish Palestine."[10]

Mosk was not just a passive member. After Britain's Labour Party came to power in 1945, Judge Stanley Mosk wrote Party leader Harold J. Laski to protest Laski's prediction that the Tory policy would lead to "a transfer of the scene of Jewish massacre from Central Europe to the Middle East." While "rejoicing" at the Labour Party's recent electoral victory, Mosk wrote that he felt "bewilderment bordering on chagrin" at the present foreign policy of their government. He protested "the latest blow to our confidence in your government; the inhumanity of your Palestine policy." He continued, "No people on earth have endured the suffering of the Jews of Europe ... only a natural homeland in Palestine holds forth any hope for the displaced Jews. They have the right to expect entry there, if not historically, then by virtue of the Balfour Declaration." He concluded, "Rising indignation in this country at Britain's Palestine policy is a blow to American-British relations." Laski responded that "My problem is the very simple one that I am not Foreign Secretary." The exchange was published the *California Jewish Voice*, and Judge Mosk forwarded copies of the correspondence to President Harry S Truman, who acknowledged receipt and thanked Mosk for sending it.

February 1948 found Mosk the retiring president of the B'nai B'rith Shield, and the newly appointed chaplain. Among the eight hundred guests at the installation-ceremony was its vice president, MGM's Dore Shary. Mosk spoke before the Santa Monica branch of the B'nai B'rith for the annual observance of American Brotherhood Week, which included the singing of the "Negro Spirituals of Calvary Baptist Church."[11] Along with activist Carey McWilliams, Mosk participated in a USC Hillel panel discussion, "Can You Outlaw Hate?"[12] Both men also sat as judges for the Brandeis composition scholarships,[13] and soon after Mosk favorably reviewed McWilliams' book *A Mask for Privilege: Anti-Semitism in America* for *The National Jewish Monthly*.[14]

For Stanley Mosk, the message of Carey McWilliams' book was particularly poignant. McWilliams argued that discrimination against Jews was a "top-down" phenomenon, rather than "bottom-up." It was most intense at the middle and upper class levels. Often disguised as "competition," it was chiefly manifested through old school ties and quota systems.[15] Although the setting for McWilliams' analysis was ostensibly Minneapolis, his thesis had much to say about anti-Semitism in Southern California. As noted by McWilliams' son, Wilson Carey McWilliams, in his introduction to the current edition of *A Mask for Privilege*:

> Southern California's anti-Semitism may have been less effective than that in Minnesota, but it was hard to miss. In 1947, when my father was working on *A Mask for Privilege*, I was a teenager about to enter high school, more interested in the fortunes of the Los Angeles Angels than in bias against Jews. Even so, I remember how often conversation among otherwise respectable adults took an anti-Semitic turn, in worries that Jews were "taking over" the Pico district, for example, or in sly references to the "connections" of Helen Gahagan Douglas' husband, Melvyn. In Southern California, Jews were the exception to the ethnic rule. Decentralized and sprawling even before the freeways, metropolitan Los Angeles rendered its minorities largely invisible. Anglos saw Mexicans on Olvera Street and Chinese in Chinatown, while middle-class Angelenos often had minority-group domestics, but the dominant social world was not only almost entirely white, but remarkably Protestant. Psychologically, the city faced west, toward the ocean and the beaches, and away from Watts and the ethnic neighborhoods on the East side. Jews, by contrast, were a minority that refused to be invisible: they intruded on Los Angeles's strange, half-Midwestern idyll, disturbing its contrived serenity in a way that decisively informs *A Mask for Privilege*.[16]

In *A Mask for Privilege*, Carey McWilliams notes that in most American cities, the reins of social control can be traced to a particular "prestige" club or similar institution, whose membership make up the dominant forces in the community. "In Los Angeles, where I live," he says, "everyone knows that the Athletic Club is less exclusive than the University Club, and that the latter is less exclusive than the California Club."[17] Although the founding members of the California Club in 1887 included prominent Jewish businessmen like Isias

Hellman, Leon Loeb and Jacob Loew, by the 1920's, the Club had become less inclusive, and Jews were not welcomed. Stanley Mosk seemed to join every club in Los Angeles, but he never became a member of the exclusive California Club.

When Darryl F. Zanuck, the head of Twentieth Century–Fox studios, was honored as Man of the Year in December of 1948, Judge Stanley Mosk co-chaired the awards committee of an affair attended by many Hollywood notables, including Ronald Reagan, Dore Shary, the Schenk brothers, David O. Selznik, and Mayor Fletcher Bowron. The following month Stanley Mosk's former boss, former Governor Culbert Olson, lectured on the "red peril" at a reception held in his honor hosted by his former executive secretary, Judge Mosk.[18]

Soon after, Stanley Mosk was elected as vice chair of the local chapter of the Anti Defamation League. Founded in 1913 by B'nai B'rith in the United States, the League's mission was "to stop, by appeals to reason and conscience and, if necessary, by appeals to law, the defamation of the Jewish people." Its ultimate goal is to put an end forever to unjust and unfair discrimination against and ridicule of any sect or body of citizens. Mosk was also elected to the executive board of the Southern California Council of Liberal Jewish Organizations' Assembly of Delegates.[19] Two days after Mosk's election, the Anti Defamation League began publishing a series of articles detailing the efforts to circumvent the U.S. Supreme Court decisions on restrictive covenants in the Los Angeles area.[20] The Legal and Civic Action Committee of the Los Angeles chapter of the American Jewish Committee undertook an investigation of the racial patterns of county housing projects.[21] Its published report described widespread discrimination against Negroes and Mexican Americans, who were sharply segregated into facilities inferior to those given to Anglo residents.[22] The following year, the L.A. County Committee on Human Relations announced formal charges brought by the American Jewish Committee, calling for the removal of five housing authority commissioners, whose continuation in office jeopardized the County's chances for additional federal funds. The L.A. Urban League, the Community Relations Committee of the Jewish Community Council, and the CIO endorsed the protest against "Jim Crow" segregation in Los Angeles.[23]

In many ways, Stanley Mosk was the archetypical Jewish liberal — a child of Eastern Europeans often radicalized and secularized by the persecution and terror of pogroms, and appreciating the many improvements to their lives under communism. As a child, he was exposed to socialist and communist ideologies through his Uncle Dave. Later, he distanced himself from such radical persuasions while at the same time defending his right to ally with those whose ideas were more radical than his own. His progressive-liberalism reflected a shift by many in the secular Jewish immigrant community whose politics emerged from historical exigencies as well as religious tenets.[24] Historian Marc Dollinger explains that during the years following World War II, some Jewish leaders feared their community's historic links to leftist politics might inspire an anti-Semitic backlash. Thus, he suggests, embracing anti-communism "would prove to skeptical Americans that Jews had abandoned leftism and joined the American political mainstream."[25] Although many of that generation, and the next, moved further to the right, Mosk remained a hold out to liberalism. He was clearly a man on the move and he soon inspired a following throughout the state. He built his reputation by endless public appearances and well publicized court rulings. His growing reputation was grounded in a passionate commitment to civil rights, civil and political liberties, and his unyielding ambition to educate, to inform, and to lead whatever audience he commanded or in whichever office he held.

While Stanley Mosk became a vocal and visible force in Los Angeles Jewish circles, he began to be identified as a leader in the cause of civil rights on behalf of the burgeoning post-war African American community. He presided over the California Conference for Democratic Action, held in November, 1946. Reminiscent of Mosk's previous reform alliances, he told the audience, "I hope it will be my privilege in the future to attend many meetings sponsored, not only by communists, doctors, lawyers, but also by named Republicans." Other speakers at the meeting included James Roosevelt, who announced his aspirations for office, and others from the National Lawyers Guild, the C.I.O. United Electrical Workers, the Fair Employment Practices Commission, the American Youth for Democracy, and the Screen Office Employees Guild.[26]

Some of the organizations with which Judge Mosk was affiliated became targets for a State Senate Committee on Un-American Activities chaired by Senator Jack Tenney, a notorious anti–Semite later affiliated with Gerald L.K. Smith and the "Christian National Party." Tenney sponsored the legislation requiring state employees to sign loyalty oaths. The Board of Supervisors of Los Angeles County, at Tenney's instigation, also enacted an Ordinance requiring all County employees to sign a loyalty oath which required them to swear that they had never been a member of, or directly or indirectly supported or followed any of an enumerated list of 145 organizations, including the California Conference for Democratic Action. Other organizations listed included the Bay Area Council Against Discrimination, Hollywood Cultural Committee, Hollywood Independent Citizens Committee of Arts, Sciences and Professions, Hollywood League for Democratic Action, Hollywood Theatre Alliance, Los Angeles County Political Commission, Los Angeles County Trade Union Commission, Motion Picture Cooperative Buyers Guild, and the Motion Picture Democratic Committee. Stanley Mosk's brother Ed had established an active law practice representing labor unions and many Hollywood producers, directors and writers. In 1947 he was elected to the Executive Board of the Progressive Citizens of America (PCA), a left-liberal coalition with a pro-labor and pro-civil rights agenda.[27] Among the other issues the PCA addressed was the Loyalty Oath required of County Employees. In September of 1947, the group resolved to call upon the Los Angeles Board of Supervisors to withdraw the oath requirement and to hold public hearings on the matter.[28] County employees who refused to sign the oath brought an action in Superior Court seeking relief from enforcement of the loyalty oath, represented by A.L. Wirin of the ACLU. The case went all the way to the U.S. Supreme Court, where it was dismissed because the plaintiffs had not exhausted state remedies against enforcement of the loyalty oath requirement.[29]

In 1950, Judge Mosk, Edna and Richard packed their bags for an adventurous tour of Europe, Stanley's first of many visits abroad. They flew to New York, saw some Broadway plays, then boarded the *Queen Elizabeth* to cross the Atlantic. Their whirlwind tour of London exposed them to both the bombed out remnants of World War II, and the frantic pace of rebuilding the city. When they got to Rome, Stanley arranged for a papal audience at the summer residence of Pope Pius XII in Castel Gondolfo. Richard remembers standing with his father and mother while everyone else knelt in the Pope's presence. The Pope posed for a picture with the family and blessed Richard, asking where he went to school. On the return trip, the Mosks were passengers on the *Queen Mary*.[30]

Mosk served as president of the Vista Del Mar Child-Care Service from 1951 to 1957. Formerly the Jewish Orphans' Home of Southern California, the institution officially opened its doors in 1909 and moved to several locations until it settled in the West Los Angeles community of Vista Del Mar on Motor Avenue in 1925. A former colleague from Olson's administration, Judge Isaac Pacht, preceded Mosk's term from 1937 to 1947. Vista Del Mar served children living on the streets of Los Angeles whose parents could not care for them because of illness, poverty, or death. By placing orphaned children in an innovative cottage setting with house parents rather than the institutional environment typical of the time, Vista became known as one of the finest residential programs in the country. Under Mosk's leadership, Vista Del Mar branched out into areas of foster care, adoption, and the treatment of children with mental health problems, emotional problems, behavior problems, social problems, or developmental difficulties.

From 1956 to 1957 Mosk was also Chairman of the Board of the Los Angeles Jewish Federation Council, again following Judge Pacht by a few years, and Mendel B. Silberberg by four. The Jewish Federation of Greater Los Angeles was and still is the largest Jewish nonprofit in the Los Angeles area. It identifies and funds social service, educational and humanitarian needs locally, in Israel and around the world. Through a network of agencies and programs, the Federation helps alleviate Jewish poverty, provides emergency relief, and supports the greater Los Angeles community. A list of Los Angeles' most influential Jewish professionals includes many with whom Stanley Mosk was allied over his life time, many of whom recognized Stanley Mosk as the titular head of the diverse Jewish community in Los Angeles, although he rarely attended services in a synagogue.

Chapter 7

"Use Their Heads Instead of Their Hob-Nailed Boots"

The 1950's saw the beginnings of a resurgence for California's Democratic Party, still smarting from the popularity of Governor Earl Warren and the statewide dominance of the Republican Party during the 1940's. As the party searched for new leadership, Stanley Mosk became a force to be reckoned with in California politics. In spite of his growing stature in mainstream politics, however, Judge Mosk stayed in close contact with his earlier compatriots. By now the Southern California branch of the ACLU was the largest branch of the national organization. Judge Mosk served as the principal speaker of the evening for its November, 1948 celebration of "Twenty-five years on Freedom's Front." Former gubernatorial candidate Upton Sinclair was among the others honored that evening. Mosk's popularity among civil rights groups and the African American community was stronger than ever, as a press release reminded event-goers that Judge Mosk was someone "whose innate sense of Americanism led him to anticipate the Supreme Court of the United States in a series of six restrictive covenant decisions."[1]

In 1948, James Roosevelt, the son of the now late president, was the chairman of Democratic National Committee. When Judge Robert Clifton told Roosevelt that Stanley Mosk was willing to assume a monthly sustaining membership for the next six months, Mosk and Roosevelt began a correspondence about Mosk's aspirations to become a delegate at the upcoming national convention. Roosevelt informed him that "while every effort [will be] made to secure" him a spot as a delegate, "he will instead accompany the delegation as his presence would mean much to the success of the work...."[2] The two men continued to correspond, appearing to be of like minds on any number of issues. Roosevelt found one of Mosk's communications a "splendid letter," and replied, "I feel so strongly that the Democratic Party must from within continue to push our national leaders along the paths of integrity and liberalism."[3] A friendship grew, built on mutual respect and support, and Roosevelt invited the Mosks to one of his children's weddings.

The 1948 presidential election battle was hard fought in California, a key state that year. Governor Earl Warren was on the Republican national ticket, as running mate to Thomas E. Dewey. The defeat of incumbent President Harry S Truman was widely predicted, in no small part due to the threat to his position in California posed by the Independent Progressive Party (IPP) candidacy of Henry Wallace, F.D.R.'s secretary of agriculture, and third term vice president. Playing a key role in the southern California organization of the IPP was its chairman, Stanley Mosk's brother Ed. Many loyal Democrats supporting Truman were upset with the Wallace candidacy, and by extension Ed Mosk. Truman outpolled Dewey by only 18,000 votes while Wallace captured 190,381 votes in California, or 4.73 percent of the total. Truman came within a hair's breadth of losing all of the state's electoral votes, carrying 47.57 percent of the vote, compared to Dewey and Warren's 47.13. Earl Warren's inability to deliver California for the Republicans was a major setback for his own presidential ambitions. The 1948 presidential election was also a setback for Stanley and Ed Mosk's relationship, at least as far as one informant of the FBI was concerned. According to the informant, Ed and Stanley were not very close and Ed Mosk's participation in the Independent Progressive Party was an occasion when Stanley did not support his brother because he was "too liberal."[4]

In June of 1949, the *Independent Review* suggested that the state Democratic Party needed a balanced ticket for the upcoming mid-term elections. The *Review* suggested Stanley Mosk as a candidate for Attorney General, along with James Roosevelt for governor, Eleanor Heller for secretary of state, Sam Yorty for the Board of Equalization, and Congresswoman Helen Gahagan Douglas for the U.S. Senate seat being vacated by Sheridan Downey.[5] Mosk wisely decided 1950 was not the year for a liberal Jew to become a candidate for statewide office. Governor Earl Warren crushed James Roosevelt by a 2–1 margin, and Richard Nixon decisively defeated Helen Gahagan Douglas in a campaign which borrowed the slam from conservative newspaperman Manchester Boddy that as the "pink lady," Douglas was pink down to her underwear.[6] The only Democrat elected to statewide office was San Francisco District Attorney Edmund G. "Pat" Brown, elected as Attorney General.

Judge Stanley Mosk was reaching a wider audience addressing many of the divisive social and political issues preoccupying post-war America. One controversial issue, however, that reflected the rising tide of McCarthyism was an issue upon which Stanley Mosk was discretely reserved. On October 3, 1950, the California Legislature enacted emergency legislation to take effect immediately, known as the Levering Act.[7] The Act created a new loyalty oath, to be taken within 30 days of its enactment, in addition to one to support and defend the constitution already required for teachers and all public employees. Failure to take the oath would prohibit further compensation. The new oath declared:

> And I do further swear (or affirm) that I do not advocate, nor am I a member of any party or organization, political or otherwise, that now advocates the overthrow of the Government of the United States or of the State of California by force or violence or other unlawful means; that within the five years immediately preceding the taking of this oath (or affirmation) I have not been a member of any party or organization, political or otherwise, that advocated the overthrow of the Government of the United States or of the State of California by force or violence or other unlawful means except as follows: (If no affiliations, write in the words "No Exceptions") and that during such time as I hold the office of (name of office) I will not advocate nor become a member of any party or organization, political or otherwise, that advocates the overthrow of the Government of the United States or of the State of California by force or violence or other unlawful means.

The state Democratic Party loudly and vociferously opposed the new oath, which was subsequently incorporated into the California constitution as a constitutional requirement.[8]

Although loyalty oaths were anathema to liberals, Mosk remained aloof of the controversy. Mosk did serve as the moderator for a University Synagogue Modern Forum, entitled, "Are Loyalty Oaths in the American Way?" The distinguished panelists opposed to loyalty oaths included A.L. Wirin, with whom Mosk was allied in the fields and in the courtroom during the labor struggles and recall of Mayor Frank Shaw two decades before, and John Caughey, a renowned UCLA historian.[9] Defending loyalty oaths on the panel were Norman Jacoby, the editor of *Alert Magazine*, and A. Weinberg, American Legion Coordinator of Veterans' Housing and the County Housing Authority. *Alert Magazine* was a "strident anti–Communist newsletter," and Jacoby promoted the idea that civic authorities should create "committees" to "watch the policy of their libraries in the circulation and promotion of subversive publications."[10]

The loyalty oath requirement was challenged in a lawsuit brought by an Associate Professor at San Francisco State University, but upheld by the California Supreme Court by a 6–1 vote in *Pockman v. Leonard*.[11] Justice Jesse W. Carter wrote a bitter dissent, accusing the majority of "forsaking its sworn duty to support the Constitution of the State of California, and [abdicating] its power, for the sake of expediency, to uphold an act which invades the constitutional guarantees of civil liberties of those affected by its mandates." He later said that Thomas Jefferson, who championed the right of those who would wish to dissolve the union to "stand undisturbed," in the atmosphere of fear and hysteria that then prevailed "would probably be labeled a subversive and possibly put in prison as being dangerous to national security."

If the views expressed in his 1936 *American Mercury* article reflected his true feelings, [that a dictatorship of the proletariat would be a "vindication of our constitution"], Stanley Mosk would have been in full agreement with both Justice Carter and Thomas Jefferson. One might attribute his ambivalence to his position as a sitting judge, but that didn't seem to be an impediment to his public statements on other controversial issues. In all likelihood, Judge Mosk concluded that opposition to loyalty oaths would render him too vulnerable to charges that he was a communist sympathizer. Fifteen years later, however, Justice Stanley Mosk joined in the California Supreme Court decision that overruled *Pockman v. Leonard* and held the Levering oath violated the First Amendment of the United States Constitution.[12]

One legal controversy about which Stanley Mosk did not mince words had to do with the methods law enforcement often used to obtain evidence used by prosecutors in criminal trials. The Fourth Amendment protects individuals from unreasonable searches and seizures by federal authorities, and the U.S. Supreme Court extended that protection to searches by state authorities in 1949, relying upon the Due Process Clause of the 14th Amendment. But that ruling did *not* require the states to apply the exclusionary rule that requires suppression of illegally seized evidence, even though the rule had long been applied in the federal courts.[13] States, however, remained free to impose the exclusionary rule under their state constitutions, and a growing number of states were doing so. The California Supreme Court took up the issue in 1955 in *People v. Cahan*.[14]

Charles Cahan was a Beverly Hills bookmaker who ran a $20,000 per day bookmaking syndicate. Los Angeles Police detectives burglarized his home and office to plant bugging devices without a warrant, and intercepted all his conversations for over a month. The California Supreme Court ruled 4–3 that evidence obtained by the warrantless bugging could not be used in court, reflecting the Court's frustration with police tactics that violated the California Constitution. The opinion noted that previous remedies had failed to "secure compliance with constitutional provisions on the part of police officers," and "under the old rule [we] have been constantly required to participate in, and in effect condone, the lawless activities of law enforcement officers." "Most of the incriminatory evidence introduced at the trial was obtained by officers of the Los Angeles Police Department in flagrant violation of the United States Constitution (4th and 14th Amendments), the California Constitution (art. I, sec. 19), and state and federal statutes." The ruling accused LAPD of "police state" tactics and said it was no more acceptable than "the rack, the screw, and other brutal means." The Court said it's a short-step from lawless but efficient law enforcement "to the stamping out of human rights."

The *Cahan* decision elicited a hostile and vocal reception from the California law enforcement community. Critics complained that the Court failed to adequately define what police practices would be deemed to be "unreasonable searches and seizures." One district attorney complained, "We are groping in the dark. We have no workable rules to go by. It's the most confusing situation we've ever faced." The passionate grandstanding of public officials, politicians, and law enforcement reflected the on-going struggle to balance the privacy rights of individuals against law enforcement's battle against crime. It was clear to observers that "the decision has divided the state into sharply opposing camps. Police agencies hold enforcement is breaking down, others argue the decision was necessary to protect the public."[15] State Attorney General Edmund G. Brown charged the high court with "usurpation of legislative power" and urged the Court to reconsider its decision "until such time as the legislature may enact laws to implement it." Alameda County Deputy District Attorney J. F. Coakley told attendees at the annual Peace Officers Association of California that the ruling could cause the public to lose confidence in law enforcement.[16] Coakley continued his attack against *Cahan's* "fallacious and unsound" exclusionary ruling at the subsequent State Bar Convention and before the State Senate. He urged an amendment to the penal code to admit proper evidence "irrespective of the manner in which it was obtained." California Governor Goodwin J. Knight agreed, claiming that changes in the court system "must and will be accomplished."

One state official called the *Cahan* decision "the Magna Carta of the criminal," in it's implication that "the activities of the police are a greater social menace than are the activities of the criminal." Over the ensuing months, Los Angeles Police Chief William H. Parker jumped into the fray, suggesting that "criminals are rejoicing" at the decision, and that the protection afforded criminals by limits on searches has resulted in a rise in crime rates which would find law-abiding citizens "consumed by a criminal army."[17] Writing to Stanley Mosk, Chief Justice Phil Gibson communicated more than his literal words suggest about the reactions to the controversial decision. He wrote that he could not comment on the "misleading and unintelligent attacks made on the *Cahan* decision."[18] On the other hand, Justice Jesse W. Carter responded directly to Parker's blustering. Carter said, "I am convinced that Chief Parker voiced opposition to the *Cahan* decision without mature deliberation, and has since endeavored to support his opposition by comparative statistics which are not supported by the facts."[19]

Vocal supporters and critics within both political parties were at odds with each other. Democratic National Committeeman Paul Ziffren called for the ouster of Chief Parker because "a man who believes it is more important to catch criminals than to protect our constitutional rights doesn't belong in this job." Ziffren accused Parker of trying to overrule the Supreme Court, to amend the constitution, and to abolish the Fourth Amendment, " just to catch a few lousy bookmakers, streetwalkers, and dope addicts."[20] In speaking out in support of the *Cahan* decision, Judge Stanley Mosk took a courageous stance, well aware that law enforcement opposition could undermine his future political prospects. Mosk praised the decision, remarking that "it will stand as a landmark decision "long after its detractors are forgotten," and that "'unreasonable searches' had long been 'the blind spot' in enforcement of individual constitutional rights."[21] In a speech to Town Hall in Los Angeles that year, Judge Stanley Mosk said:

> Everyone heaps praise on the early bird (who could catch the worm), but no one sheds a tear for the early worm. Only in a totalitarian state are the police beyond the reach of the law. Per-

haps law enforcement may be more deadly in that climate, but our founding fathers sacrificed efficiency for liberty. It was a wise choice. Essential though law and order may be, ominous though the inroads of crime may be, respect for our American legacy compels us to shelter the individual from an overzealous law enforcement agency. Now, in all fairness it must be said that in certain kinds of crime, the obtaining of evidence will be somewhat more difficult if law enforcement officers themselves obey the law — more officers may find it necessary to use their heads instead of their hob-nailed boots.[22]

It was no surprise that LAPD Chief William Parker was infuriated by Mosk's zinger about hob-nailed boots, and never let Mosk forget it. Thereafter, he opposed Mosk at every opportunity, and eight years later found the means to land a devastating blow to Stanley Mosk's political fortunes by using the fruits of his surreptitious surveillance of Mosk. For an audience in 1958, the reference to "hob-nailed boots" would surely have conjured up visions of nazis.

Charles Cahan did not make a very attractive poster boy for the protection of citizen's privacy rights. In the fall of 1955, Cahan lay in a hospital bed, fighting for his life after being shot six times by a man who claimed Cahan was trying to kill him, yelling he was going to kick the man's head off if he didn't get him some money. Cahan recovered but refused to testify against his attacker who went free, and described Cahan as a "dangerous man who broke peoples arms and took their money." In June 1956, Cahan was arrested and accused of illegally entering and stealing a watch and money from the apartment of a man who owed him for a horseracing bet. He was convicted on evidence obtained from a recording device affixed to the apartment telephone, which enabled police to overhear a conversation about the bet. Cahan's argument rested on his own earlier landmark case, that the recording was inadmissible in court. This time, however, the appellate court rejected his argument because the recording device had been placed in the victim's apartment with his consent.[23]

After their disappointing defeats in the 1950 state elections and the 1952 presidential race, California Democrats convened a conference in Northern California at the historic Asilomar retreat center to discuss "What's wrong with the Democratic Party?" Their conclusion reflected the famous Will Rogers quote: "I'm not a member of any organized political party. I'm a Democrat."[24] The need for organization was addressed by the formation of an independent structure of Democratic clubs that could, among other things, counter the influence of cross-filing by making pre-primary endorsements of candidates. The first president of the California Democratic Council (CDC) was Alan Cranston, whose dynamic organizing skills and fundraising abilities brought immediate success to the Party and the CDC. In the 1954 state elections, Democrats won the Democratic primary for every race, defeating numerous Republican cross-filers who had previously won Democratic primaries. In the general election, the party picked up six Assembly and five Senate seats, including the election of CDC-endorsed Richard Richards as state senator for Los Angeles County. Although incumbent Republican Governor Goodwin Knight was easily elected, so was Democratic Attorney General Pat Brown.

Knight, as lieutenant governor, had succeeded Earl Warren upon Governor Warren's appointment as Chief Justice of the United States. The CDC promoted a liberal agenda, including support of the United Nations, opposition to loyalty oaths, civil rights legislation, and increased funding for education. By 1957, Cranston reported that CDC had organized almost five hundred Democratic clubs with 40,000 members.

By the fall of 1957, Stanley Mosk had been a judge for fourteen years, and was ready to move on to bigger challenges. His son Richard was off to college, at Stanford University. Stanley drove him up and dropped him off with his luggage outside the dorm. On the way up, he pulled over to the side of the road and said to Richard, "I've never really talked to you much about sex or things like that." Richard cut short his lecture on protection by saying, "Don't bother." Stanley considered a race for the U.S. Senate, but accepted Pat Brown's decision that Clair Engle should be the party's Senate candidate. After weighing his options, in September 1957 Stanley Mosk announced that after Attorney General Pat Brown cleared the way by entering the race for governor, he would seek the Democratic nomination for State Attorney General. He said his judicial qualifications would provide "a unique benefit to me in the management of the largest law office in California."[25] Mosk pledged, "to adhere to the same high standard of public service established by Earl Warren and maintained by Brown."[26]

The following March, it became clear that Pat Brown would in fact vacate the Attorney General's office to make a run for governor. Stanley Mosk optimistically cross-filed his name for the primaries of both parties. Accompanying Mosk to the registrar's office were attorneys Joseph A. Ball of Long Beach, chairman of Brown's Southern California committee; Patricia Hofstetter, president of Southern California Women Lawyers Association, and Dianne Bregerson, also a member of the SCWLA. Mosk listed the issues he felt were "chronically confronting the Attorney General's office," including the protection of the state's rights in interstate water disputes, continuous war on organized and unorganized crime, and co-operation with local officials in combating juvenile delinquency and the war on narcotics."[27]

The only other Democrat who appeared interested in seeking the Attorney General position was Senator Bob McCarthy of San Francisco. Stanley Mosk thought he had several advantages over McCarthy in entering the race: Southern California was where the votes are; he could run with "Superior Court Judge" under his name, and he was better known than McCarthy. On the other hand, McCarthy was Catholic, and was close to Pat Brown. After convincing Pat Brown to remain neutral, Stanley Mosk sought the endorsement of the CDC.

Although Mosk was well known in Los Angeles, he needed more help in San Francisco, and he got it from Assemblyman Phil Burton and George Reilly, whose eleven terms on the State Board of Equalization set the California record for longest service in a single elected position. Burton's younger brother John questioned why he was supporting someone from Los Angeles against their friend and their own state senator. Phil Burton explained that there were things more important than the guys with whom he played pinball machines at O'Neil's Drugstore and told him, "You have to meet Stanley Mosk." Ann Eliaser also knew McCarthy, and recognized the senatorial districts in the Bay Area "had a lot of clout" (before one man-one vote). "Except for a few people in B'nai B'rith and Jewish philanthropy," nobody knew who Stanley Mosk was. To Eliaser, it "was heavy" that Mosk ran up against McCarthy, but she offered her support to Mosk, saying "the decision was made solely on merit and not on endorsement [of the CDC]." Eliaser worked with Charles O'Brien and others connected with the Golden Gate Democratic Club that got Mosk's northern primary campaign moving. Like Eliaser, his other campaign leaders and chairs were well known in the CDC, and introduced Mosk to Democratic clubs all over the state, usually in intimate home meetings. Soon, Mosk was making fourteen to fifteen stops a day in the Bay Area. Eliaser's skills were recognized again when she served as Finance Coordinator for Mosk's re-election bid four years later, and while serving as Democratic Party National Committeewoman, she was instrumental in building up a Democratic Party base in Southern California, along with Stephen Reinhardt, who later also served as National Committeeman.[28]

When Stanley Mosk won the CDC endorsement, Senator McCarthy tried to spin this to his advantage by condemning preprimary endorsements. He said he declined to appear before the California Democratic Council (CDC) because candidates seeking its endorsement must pledge not to run for office if they fail to receive the CDC's blessing. He persuasively argued that the weight of the CDC endorsement was disproportionate to the number of members in the organization, and it should not influence 3,500,000 Democrats statewide. Alienating himself from the growing and influential CDC, McCarthy said if he won the primary, he intended to focus on his own campaign, "and not tie [myself] to anyone else's coattails." Unlike Mosk, he wasn't "going to be tied in with any package."[29]

When Mosk began his primary race for Attorney General, Edna gave up her lucrative real estate business and devoted full time to the campaign. She organized supporters, handled logistics, raised funds, and kept "the troops happy and dedicated." The primary brought visibility to the disarming "whimsical touch" of her charm. During her first interview with a bay area newspaper, which was leaning toward Mosk's opponent, the reporter asked: "Mrs. Mosk, Senator McCarthy and his wife Betty have a wonderful family. They have nine children. How many do you have?" Edna responded, "We have one. But if elected we promise to have eight more."[30]

In anticipation of the June primary, Mosk's old boss, former Governor Culbert Olson wrote him a letter of support. By then Olson was the editor of *Progressive World*, the official publication for the United Secularists of America. He wrote, "I am alarmed at the extent to which the Catholic Church is taking over the Democratic Party," and added, "if you are not nominated and elected, it will be due to Catholic influence and political power." He also attached a copy of "An Open Letter to Alan Cranston" regarding an initiative to end tax exemption of private school property.[31] Stanley Mosk and Olson did share a deeply held belief in the separation of church and state, an issue about which Mosk frequently spoke.

Proving Olson's fears absurd, Mosk won what he called "the cleanest campaign I have ever seen," defeating McCarthy in the primary. In the Republican primary, Patrick Hillings won a decisive victory over Caspar Weinberger, who later served as Governor Reagan's Director of Finance and President Reagan's secretary of defense. The twenty-four hours following the closing of the polls must have been an emotional roller coaster for Mosk, his family and friends. Memorialized in a June 5, 1958, headline, "McCarthy, [Casper] Weinberger to Vie For State Atty. General in Fall," a premature announcement dubbed Robert McCarthy the victor over Mosk and Weinberger victorious over Hillings. "President Thomas E. Dewey would have been proud of this paper," Mosk wrote many years later to his son Richard, referring to the famous Chicago Tribune headline, "Dewey Defeats Truman."[32] The next day, all the votes were counted and Stanley Mosk was officially declared the winner, eking out a narrow victory from late returns from Southern Californians.

Mosk faced a formidable opponent in the general election. Patrick Hillings was a protégé of Richard M. Nixon, and had actually succeeded Nixon in the House of Representatives when Nixon won election to the Senate. Hillings capitalized on Mosk's continued silence regarding the controversial loyalty oath. "Everywhere I have been in California," Hillings told a San Joaquin Valley audience, "people have shown tremendous concern about the plank in the opposition's State platform that would abolish loyalty oaths for all public employees." He went on to cite the errors of Mosk's ways, such as his role in what by then was nearly a two-decade-old story about the secret dictaphone incident during Governor

Olson's administration, and Mosk's refusal to step down from the bench while he ran for office. Thus, Hillings argued, while Mosk has just shrugged off such controversies, when it comes to taking a public stand on the question of abolishing loyalty oaths, "he apparently favors it." In other words, Hillings suggested that because his "opponent doesn't let out a peep about where he stands," on the abolition of the loyalty oath, which was "one of the most dangerous proposals ever made," Mosk must be unmoved by the notion that, "we are engaged in a life and death struggle against the Communist conspiracy at home and abroad."[33] In the meantime, The *Los Angeles Times* provided Mosk with a headline story when he called for a new state commission to investigate the rising crime rate.[34]

Mosk kicked off his general election campaign with a large testimonial dinner at the Statler Hotel in Los Angeles. California Supreme Court Justice Jesse W. Carter, a strong supporter of Stanley Mosk, delivered the principal address. Carter concluded his remarks about the administration of justice with a ringing endorsement of Stanley Mosk:

> I have no hesitancy in stating that so long as we have men of the stalwart character and outstanding ability of Judge Stanley Mosk administering our department of justice, we need have no fear that our precious liberties will be destroyed or even restricted. In my opinion he is the type of man the poet Holland had in mind when he wrote these words:
>
>> "God give us men. A time like this demands
>> Strong minds, great hearts, true faith, and ready hands;
>> Men whom the lust of office does not kill;
>> Men whom the spoils of office cannot buy;
>> Men who possess opinions and a will;
>> Men who have honor, who will not lie;
>> Men who can stand before a demagogue
>> And damn his treacherous flatteries without winking;
>> Tall men, sun-crowned, who live above the fog
>> In public duty and in public thinking."[35]

Mosk's campaign literature bore a handsome, smiling visage of great confidence, wearing a judicial robe.[36] Although FBI sources posited that, "Mosk shows promise of becoming probably the most controversial figure in the state elections," his campaign actually generated lots of favorable press and very little controversy.

In appearances at press conferences, Edna did more than "stand behind her man." Edna Mosk's personality, beauty, and political savvy charmed the press and potential voters. One reporter suggested that candidate Mosk might have had "ideas of kibitzing his wife's first official bow to the local press but he was out of luck." In spite of her tailored style, Edna Mosk was comfortable with banter and small talk. In an appearance at the Biltmore Hotel in Los Angeles, she confessed that the "greatest strain of campaigning 'is on my feet,'" and said she was wearing her "lucky suit," i.e., the same one she wore when Mosk won the party's nomination. She immediately clarified that it wasn't because her husband needed the luck, but rather because she "was petrified." She then comfortably segued into a detailed portrait of her husband's extensive legal experience. She confidently explained how the Attorney General job is "a law job, " and therefore the mere nine months that Patrick Hillings had practiced law made him unqualified for the post, which should require, by constitutional amendment, that candidates have ten years experience in the practice of law."[37] Meanwhile, Judge Mosk was conducting his own press conference, naming prominent local Republicans who had lent their names in support of his campaign.

Republicans were having problems of their own that year. In what became known as "the big switch," incumbent U.S. Senator William Knowland decided to leave the Senate and run for California governor, and strong-armed incumbent Governor Goodwin Knight into running for the Senate rather that seeking reelection as governor. A "right to work" initiative on the ballot assured a strong labor turnout to defeat the measure. Both Knight and Knowland lost in a Democratic sweep, which aided Mosk and all Democrats who ran for office.

In the race for Attorney General, Judge Stanley Mosk proved to be the biggest vote-getter, not only in the State of California but in the entire United States. Mosk beat Hillings by 1,135,000 votes, exceeding Governor-elect Brown's total by 100,000.[38] Mosk was eager to interpret his election as a rebuke to Vice President Richard Nixon. He said Hillings "adopted all of the 'old Nixon' campaign techniques" and distributed "scurrilous literature." He charged the vice president with "personally intervening with financial contributions" and contacting one unidentified newspaper publisher on behalf of his "close friend and protégé."[39]

Journalist Marlene Adler Marks later gave Mosk's election added significance. She wrote, "[b]ecause of Stanley Mosk, Jewish candidates knew that their religion is not a factor in elections in this great state."[40] Hillings made a crude effort to take advantage of any anti–Semitism by sending a mailer to every voter in California, offering a point by point comparison between himself and Mosk. Listing "Religion," he identified himself as Catholic and Mosk as Jewish. It made no difference. Stanley Mosk became the first Jew elected to statewide office in California since the days of the gold rush. He had turned being Jewish into an asset rather than a liability. Mosk carried every county in the state with the single but not surprising exception of Orange County. Mosk's victory also signaled a shift in voting patterns for Northern California Jews, many of whom were Republicans who voted for Democrat Mosk and continued to vote for Democrats for the next several decades. According to David D. Dalin, as "the first Jew to win statewide elective office," Mosk "helped provide the organizational base for continued grass roots Democratic politics in," San Francisco. From then on, Jews there participated more often as Democrats than Republicans.[41]

Edna, Richard, and Stanley Mosk appearing understandably gleeful after casting their votes in 1958. The election resulted in Stanley Mosk's unprecedented margin of victory as California attorney general (courtesy Richard Mosk).

During the two-month interim before he assumed office, Mosk outlined his ideas about the obligations and responsibilities that came with his new job description. He called upon all citizens to assist with law enforcement problems. In an appearance before the newly merged AFL-CIO California Labor Federation at San Francisco's Fairmont Hotel, he thanked organized labor for its support and pointed out that he won November's general election "with approximately the same margin of votes by which labor forces defeated the right-to-work measure, Proposition 18," unlike its narrow defeat in so many battles before.[42] He told the crowd that "organized labor will be called upon to participate in citizen's groups" to address the issues he would tackle.

Soon after his election, the FBI updated their surveillance file on now Attorney General Stanley Mosk. Mosk's campaign rhetoric included the notion of establishing a regional law enforcement plan to coordinate resources in California, Washington, and Oregon. The agent explained. "Despite his pronouncements, the record of Stanley Mosk does not support the conclusion that he will turn from a civil libertarian to an aggressive criminal prosecutor simply as a result of his election as Attorney General. In the event that he establishes a multi-state program to coordinate west coast law enforcement activity as he proposes, it is logical to assume that his views would predominate in such an organization."[43]

In December 1958, he announced the Attorney General would no longer reside in San Francisco, as Pat Brown had, but at the state capital in Sacramento. "I have concluded that the law clearly requires the office of the Attorney General to be in Sacramento, and the Attorney General to reside in Sacramento," he said. Ending press speculation, after appeals from officials in both cities, Mosk said, "Those who believe the law is in error should seek a change of the statute, through legislative action."[44] He rented an apartment in Sacramento, but maintained his family home in Beverly Hills.

Aware of the need to coordinate the anti-crime efforts of his office with federal law enforcement, Mosk sought an appointment to meet with FBI Director J. Edgar Hoover before taking office. Mosk was unaware, however, that the FBI had been observing his every move and thus his efforts to reach out to Hoover proved futile. He was told that Hoover would be out of town and away the entire week Mosk was going to be in Washington. Subsequently released FBI files show that Mosk was deliberately snubbed. Hoover dictated that the new AG was not to be invited "in view of Mosk's reputation with law enforcement and [the fact that] some officers may be opposed to Mosk." After years of tailing his public appearances and documenting Mosk's public utterances, advisors to Hoover believed that Mosk was seeking legitimacy in his new position by gaining an appointment with the nation's most powerful law enforcement officer. They advised the Director that a meeting with Mosk "would greatly increase [Mosk's] stature in this state and benefit him politically by helping remove these stigma," referring to what they regarded as left-wing, communist sympathizing. Aware of the Director's dislike of LAPD Chief William Parker, however, they predicted Mosk's reaction to the controversial 1955 Cahan decision would come back to haunt him. They approvingly cited Mosk's view, "that it was not the business of police officers to challenge the edict of a court, but it was their duty, on the other hand, to find a way to perform their functions within the law interpreted." Mosk was said, "to support [the] view [of the] FBI as [an] example of ability to obtain high rate of criminal convictions while using only legally obtained evidence."[45]

In December 1959, a memo to the Director of the FBI discussed some sort of committee set up by Attorney General Mosk: "In essence, Mr. Mosk has picked forty public citizens throughout the state for the two committees and will utilize them as a sounding board for his very liberal views on the subject." It was said to be obvious from some of the individuals on the committee who are known progressives in the state, that Mosk, "was up on cloud 29" and was "being led by the nose by the pinks of the state."[46]

Chapter 8

"Little Old Ladies in Tennis Shoes"

The 1958 election of Governor Pat Brown and Attorney General Stanley Mosk also brought a Democratic majority to the state legislature. For the first time in the twentieth century, the Democrats controlled both the Assembly and the Senate. Celebrations at "the largest and grandest inaugural ball" attended by 6,000 people could put off a little longer the "unpleasant prospect" of addressing, among other things, the state's deficit and "what amounts to a political civil war between north and south over a water program."[1] At the swearing-in of both the new governor and the new Attorney General, Richard Mosk met Pat Brown's son Jerry for the first time. Jerry Brown attended the ceremony wearing the black robe of a Jesuit seminarian. Before Pat Brown was sworn in as governor, he issued his last opinion as the state's Attorney General which ruled that state supported colleges may not subsidize fraternities that restrict membership on racial or religious grounds.[2] Now, as governor, there was a full agenda of reform legislation, most of which succeeded, and all of which was fully supported by new Attorney General Stanley Mosk and the Democratically controlled legislature.

Most of the country's fifty heads of State Departments of Justice are traditionally addressed as "General," as is the Attorney General of the United States. Having never risen above Private First Class during his brief stint in the U.S. Army, California's new Attorney General loved being called "General" Mosk. On one occasion, however, he found it somewhat embarrassing. While attending a dinner hosted by Alfred Hart, the Los Angeles banker who served as his campaign finance chair, Hart introduced Mosk to his guests, saying, "General Mosk, meet so-and-so." Then, Hart approached an imposing figure and said, "General Mosk, meet Omar Bradley." As General Bradley reached out his hand, he asked the startled Mosk, "What outfit were you in, General?" Chagrined, Stanley Mosk mumbled something about the transportation corps and beat a hasty retreat.

The California Attorney General, to some extent, exercises a supervisory role over the work of the state's county District Attorneys, handling all of the appeals from criminal convictions obtained by county prosecutors, and even occasionally stepping in to handle the trial proceedings when the local district attorney asks for help or has a conflict of interest. Pat Brown had been a local District Attorney himself, and as Attorney General enjoyed a good relationship with colleagues around the state. Stanley Mosk had never been a prosecutor, and came into the office with no relationship of trust with California law enforcement. To the contrary, LAPD Chief William Parker, and many line prosecutors distrusted Mosk's liberal and outspoken positions about police activity.

To complicate matters, Governor Brown had his own agenda for the state's law enforcement community. In response to a request from Chief Parker to set up a statewide commission to study the parole system and its oversight by the Adult Authority, Pat Brown brought on Tom Lynch, his close friend and successor as San Francisco's District Attorney. He announced that Lynch would act as special personal advisor to the governor, and his opinions "will be personal, not official, but it will carry great weight with me." In an obvious slight to the Attorney General Mosk, Brown added, "I don't know anybody who knows any more about law enforcement and its problems that Tom Lynch."[3] In any event, Mosk worked smoothly with Brown throughout his administration. In August of 1959, the FBI, watching the relationship between Governor Brown and Attorney General Mosk closely, noted that "there was a strong undercurrent of discord between Brown and Mosk," and apparently "according to [Tom] Lynch," Brown was "seriously contemplating the appointment of Mosk to the circuit court rather than the [state] Supreme Court." When the press asked Stanley Mosk about the possibility of a judicial appointment, he replied, "I honestly don't know what I'd do if the Governor asked me to take the appointment." Furthermore, "there was no indication he would ask."[4] The FBI account went on to explain that "Mosk would be happy to obtain a judgeship, but not certain he would accept anything less than the State Supreme Court." One agent offered his prediction that "it appears that Governor Brown is going to get rid of Mosk, however, it might cost an appointment to the State Supreme Court rather than a lesser judgeship." The agent speculated that if the prediction came true, "the Bureau's relationship with the state Attorney General's office should improve."[5]

One of the legacies of Earl Warren's reorganization of the Attorney General's office was a statute that allowed the Attorney General to create new divisions within the office without legislative authorization. Stanley Mosk's priorities as Attorney General were quickly established by the formation of new divisions. Mosk created a new consumer fraud division, a new constitutional rights division, and a new anti-trust division. All three of these new divisions were aggressive in pursuing complaints of violations of the law, and utilizing creative dispute resolution.

By the time Pat Brown ran for governor in 1958, women had become a vital part of the national economy as workers and consumers, and their decades-long push for equal pay and equal representation in the nation's political parties had gained a momentum political leaders could ignore only at their peril. One of the major successes for California women's groups was the establishment of a state Commission on the Status of Women. Governor Brown also established a Department of Consumer Affairs in the governor's office, to educate consumers and to receive and investigate consumer fraud complaints. Keeping a campaign promise to appoint a woman "who knows the housewife's problems and finances" to direct the Department, he appointed Helen Nelson, an economist and prominent consumer advocate, to run the office. The governor could not bring legal actions to indict or prosecute offenders, however, so Nelson relied upon Mosk's office to establish policies that led to California having the strongest consumer protection laws of any state in the country. In his campaign to replace Governor Brown in 1966, Ronald Reagan promised the first thing he would do when in office was fire Helen Nelson, a promise which pleased the California Grocers' Association and the California Manufacturers' Association. It was reminiscent of gubernatorial candidate Earl Warren's promise to fire Carey McWilliams.

The Consumer Fraud Division received consumer complaints directly, such as the complaint that distributors of cosmetic products used containers with concealed false bottoms, to create the illusion that a jar or bottle contained more than it actually did. A woman from Ventura dropped a jar on her bathroom floor, and when it broke, she discovered it had a false bottom. She sent it to the Attorney General's office, writing, "What are you going to do about this?" The office's investigation revealed an industry-wide practice to use false bottoms in cosmetic containers, despite a California statute that clearly prohibited the practice.[6] Another statute authorized the Attorney General to seize jars or containers that violated the law. Mosk called and wrote to every cosmetic company that marketed products in California, suggesting they come to a meeting and bring their lawyers. At the meeting, he informed them their jars were in violation of California law, and asked how long they would need to change their jars. They protested that the jars were correctly labeled with the size of the contents, and that they could not make separate jars just for use in California. Mosk did not back down. He warned them that he would raid every drug store in California and seize all their jars if they did not make the change. As a result, with great cries of anguish, cosmetic manufacturers throughout the United States redesigned the jars and bottles in which cosmetics were sold. To commemorate their victory, Mosk's staff presented him with a plaque on which a cross section of a cold cream jar with a false bottom was mounted.

Taking over the office of Attorney General Pat Brown, Mosk was generally pleased with the staff he had to work with. There were only six positions exempt from civil service, so he was limited in making over the entire office staff. He brought on Richard Rogan as his Chief Deputy. Rogan practiced law in Burbank in a partnership with his wife, Mary Rogan. Charles O'Brien, a San Francisco prosecutor, was placed in charge of the criminal division. O'Brien later succeeded Rogan as Chief Deputy, but his ambition to become Attorney General was frustrated when he lost a 1970 run to Republican Evelle Younger. O'Brien faithfully served both Mosk and his successor Tom Lynch. Nancy Strawbridge was also very active in Mosk's campaign and she became his administrative assistant. Howard Jewel, a former Assistant Public Defender in Alameda County who lost a close race for Congress in 1958, was placed in charge of the Justice Department's Fraud unit. A romance blossomed between Jewel and Nancy and they were married in 1962. As his public information officer and principal speech-writer, Mosk hired Tom McDonald straight out of Loyola University in Los Angeles. Finally, to take charge of a new Constitutional Rights division, Mosk hired Franklin H. Williams, then serving as regional director for the NAACP. Williams had worked with Thurgood Marshall handling death penalty cases throughout the South. After two years in Mosk's administration, he resigned to help Sergeant Shriver organize the Peace Corps, and was later appointed Ambassador to Ghana by President Lyndon Johnson.

In hiring young lawyers to serve as Deputies in the office, Attorney General Mosk instinctively recognized great promise. He hired Samuel L. Williams, whom he mentored to later become the first black president of the California State Bar. He also hired Ronald M. George. George subsequently rose through the ranks of the California Judiciary to become the Chief Justice of California. Forty years later, he served with Justice Mosk until Mosk's death. Attorney General Mosk hired John L. Burton, the younger brother of then-Assemblyman Phil Burton, who succeeded his brother in the Assembly when Phil won the first of ten terms as a U.S. congressman. John Burton later served a president pro tempore of the California Senate. Burton later described his interview to serve as a Deputy Attorney General under Stanley Mosk:

> So I went down for an interview with a gentleman named Ted Westphal who was the head of the Civil Division. And for me, I was very well dressed. I had an alpaca sweater, a pair of clean khakis, some saddle shoes, and a nice new T-shirt. I went in for the interview, and I thought I kind of did all right until my brother told me that after it was over, Ted Westphal called Stanley and said, "General, this young Burton you sent in, he came in without a suit,

without a tie, and with a pair of saddle shoes." And Stanley listened to him and he said, "Well, Ted, I am very close to his family, and I hear he is a bright young man." He heard that from Philip, of course, because he didn't know me. And he said, "Even if he came in a bathing suit, we are going to hire him."[7]

Mosk was supportive of his staff, and fully confident of the quality of their work product. Deputy Attorney General Norman L. Epstein was assigned to draft Attorney General's Opinions. One day he was summoned to the Attorney General's office. Mosk was meeting with a lobbyist representing an association of bowling alley owners about the legal challenge to the practice of high schools and junior colleges charging fees for bowling classes for their students. (Yes, bowling classes). The lobbyist was bemoaning the potential impact upon revenues if the Attorney General offered an opinion that would declare such fees were illegal. Mosk turned to Epstein and simply asked what conclusion he had reached on the issue? He responded, "High school districts are expressly prohibited from charging fees for classes," to which Mosk said, "Well, there you have it," escorting the lobbyist from his office.[8]

Governor Brown's administration emboldened an aggressive legislative agenda to combat racial discrimination and protect civil rights and civil liberties. Mosk's Constitutional Rights Division provided a vehicle to continue his life-long challenge to unlawful racial discrimination wherever he encountered it. After a fourteen-year battle, Assemblyman Augustus Hawkins' efforts were successful with enactment of the Fair Employment Practices Law, which prohibited employers from discriminating based on religion or race. A Commission was established to hear and adjudicate complaints of violations. With the later enactment of the Rumford Fair Housing Law in 1963, discrimination in the rental and sale of housing was also prohibited, and a similar fair housing commission was established. In 1980, the two commissions were combined into the current Fair Employment and Housing Commission.[9]

Following up on his previous judicial declaration that racial restrictive covenants were unconstitutional, as Attorney General, Stanley Mosk faced difficulty in enforcing even the subsequent federal ban on such contracts. The new problem arose with the home loans funded under the Veterans Farm and Home Loan Act. In California, the state Department of Veterans Affairs oversaw the program. But, because the state had no power to enforce racial covenants under state and federal court decisions, he called for a new state law that would void restrictive real estate covenants. Mosk said, "The state becomes party to contracts administering loan funds," from the federal government, and "such contract clauses usually prohibit transfer of title to members of minority races or religions in subsequent sales of property." Furthermore, "By taking title and passing it without having purged such onerous restrictions," the state "sponsors the creation and extension of racial patterns," which was a violation of public policy and arouses constitutional objections."[10] Attorney General Mosk sponsored legislation which the California legislature enacted in 1961 to add Section 53 to the Civil Code. That section provides that real property restrictions based on sex, race, color, religion, ancestry, national origin, or disability, are void. Also in 1961, the Legislature added Section 782 to the Civil Code to make void such restrictions imposed by way of the payment of a penalty, forfeiture, reverter, or otherwise.

In 1959, the California Legislature enacted the Unruh Civil Rights Act, which broadly prohibited racial discrimination by any business establishment. While the power of his constitutional office gave Mosk the means to initiate significant changes in long-established practices, Mosk was personally committed to act decisively when he perceived injustice even beyond the borders of California.

A rare, undated, formal family portrait, and all appearing in good spirits: from left to right, Stanley Mosk, Fern Mosk, Edna Mosk, Edward Mosk, Richard Mosk, Minna Mosk (courtesy Richard Mosk).

In September of 1959, Stanley Mosk was playing golf at the Hillcrest Country Club, a prestigious gathering place for golf, weddings, and gala affairs known for its predominantly Jewish membership, which had historically been banned from the city's elite gentile clubs. Hillcrest was the only country club in Los Angeles that welcomed players of diverse race and ethnicity. Edna Mosk chided columnist Joan Winchell for never mentioning what Edna thought was "the best restaurant in L.A.—the Hillcrest Country Club on a Sunday night." Winchell went to see for herself, and was "flabbergasted" to find Edna was right. The "incredible" display must have "been a block long, with more than 30 hors d'oeuvres, 10 hot dishes, and 15 desserts."[11] Singer Billy Eckstine introduced Stanley Mosk to Charlie Sifford, one of the earliest and most successful black professional golfers.[12] Mosk was incredulous when Sifford told him he was not allowed to play in tournaments sponsored by the Professional Golfers Association, because of a "Caucasian clause" in their constitution. "You mean to tell me they actually have that in their organizational bylaws?" he asked. The next time Sifford visited Hillcrest, he brought a copy of the PGA constitution and left it for Mosk. Mosk contacted the PGA and verified that they continued to discriminate against non-Caucasians in admitting golfers to membership. In response to a protest from Mosk, the PGA informed Sifford it would make him an "approved tournament player," which would allow him to join the tour, but it would not make Sifford a PGA member. He would still face discrimination at golf courses where PGA tournaments were held. The Caucasian clause remained on the books. When Stanley Mosk learned that the 1962 PGA Championship was scheduled to take place at the Brentwood Country Club, he notified the PGA that a lawsuit would be brought to compel them to allow Sifford to play. He issued a public statement, announcing, "We intend to take every step available to us, both in and out of the courts, to force the PGA either to eliminate this obnoxious restriction or to cease all activity of any kind within our state." The PGA responded by announcing it would move the tournament out of California, to a private golf course near Philadelphia. Mosk responded by contacting his fellow attorneys general in other states, and encouraging them to keep the pressure on the PGA to change their constitution. The NAACP also joined in condemning the PGA, labeling the PGA Championship an "ugly tournament." In November 1961, the PGA finally relented and the "Caucasian clause" was repealed. Charlie Sifford was admitted to full PGA membership in 1964. In his 2002 autobiography, he wrote a moving tribute to Stanley Mosk for the key role he played in challenging the "Caucasian clause":

> The Caucasian clause eventually tumbled, and I was allowed into the game, but not because the rule was so inherently racist and wrong. It happened because I happened to meet a bright, liberal, Jewish man on a golf course at, of all places, a country club. His name was Stanley Mosk, and when he became attorney general of the state of California in 1958, he had a very powerful tool to wield on behalf of people like me. Within two years, Stanley accomplished something that no hot putter or public image could ever do. He threatened the PGA, and as the fifties drew to a close, some mighty thick walls began to come tumbling down, with me at the epicenter of what would be golf's biggest earthquake.[13]

In a photograph most likely taken during one of Dr. Martin Luther King, Jr.'s visits to California, he is seen here (perhaps in 1960) appearing to place an honorary pin on the lapel of California attorney general and state Democratic national committeeman Stanley Mosk (courtesy Richard Mosk).

In other battles over racial discrimination, however, Mosk was sometimes willing to compromise. He recognized that the law alone could not bring about the social change that a fully integrated community would require. Ping Yuen was a public housing project in San Francisco's Chinatown. Ping Yuen ("Tranquil Garden") opened its doors in 1951, symbolizing equality and civil inclusion for the Chinese, who had long been excluded from decent housing. Chosen out of 600 families for 232 coveted units, the favored residents of the complex were picture perfect Chinese American families, usually boasting fathers who had served in the armed forces during World War II and mothers eager to decorate their apartments according to the dictates of *Sunset Magazine*. Indeed, the Ping Yuen was a testament to the "ambivalent process by which ghettos created through racial segregation became valorized as ethnic cultural enclaves. During the middle of the twentieth century, descriptions of Chinatown as a site of danger, deviance, and epidemic disease were eclipsed by visions of sanitized exoticism." The underside of the Ping Yuen's inclusiveness and San Francisco's positive postwar reassessment of Chinatown was the fact that the housing project was segregated — open only to Chinese — and thus actually reinforced the city's divisions, which were often upheld by restrictive racial covenants endorsed by neighborhood improvement associations.[14] As Attorney General, Stanley Mosk was presented with complaints that although he opposed racial housing restrictions, he was apparently doing nothing about a public housing project exclusively for Chinese. On this matter, Mosk relented. A compromise was worked out to accommodate a gradual opening of Ping Yuen to non-Chinese residents.

In creating a new Anti-Trust division, Mosk reinvigorated California's Cartwright Act, the state anti-trust law that had been on the books for fifty years, but was seldom enforced. In Mosk's first year, four major anti-trust cases were filed. In 1960, the Anti-trust section of the state's Justice Department launched an attack on corporate price fixing and bid rigging. Mosk represented 33 counties in a suit against six national manufacturers of folding gymnasium bleachers for conspiring to fix prices charged to 82 school districts.[15] The suit resulted in a substantial judgment. Mosk reflected, "It was kind of gratifying to be Santa Claus and to send out checks to a number of local districts which had been overcharged."[16]

Although Mosk rarely appeared in court, soon after his election he was persuaded to argue a case in the California Supreme Court during a special session convened in historic Colton Hall in Monterey, where California's first constitutional convention met in 1849. Mosk was eager to show that he was going to be a "hands-on" Attorney General. Preble Stolz, then a young Deputy Attorney General (later a distinguished law professor at the University of California's Boalt Hall Law School), had written the briefs for the case of *Cash v. Superior Court*,[17] and briefed the Attorney General on the issues presented by the case. The prosecution was defending a lower court order denying the defendant pretrial discovery of a recorded conversation between himself and an undercover police officer. When the Court filed in to hear argument in the case, Chief Justice Gibson winked at Mosk, and then in a whispered aside to Mosk, asked, "Who gave you this turkey to argue?" From the outset of the argument, Mosk was in heavy weather, and lost the case in an unanimous opinion authored by Chief Justice Gibson. Stolz later recalled that "in his characteristically kindly way, [Mosk] assured [him] that it was his weak oral argument, not Preble's brief, that lost the case."[18] Soon after, Chief Justice Gibson asked Stanley Mosk to assign only his more experienced lawyers to argue cases before the California Supreme Court. Mosk declined, explaining it would be bad for office morale to disturb the traditional practice of deputies handling their cases from beginning to end, by substituting a more experienced lawyer if the California Supreme Court granted a hearing.

Mosk also made a personal appearance in one of the most important cases in the office before the United States Supreme Court. *Arizona v. California* involved the rights to the flow of water from the Colorado River. It was an extremely complex, and important case that wound on for eleven years after its original 1952 filing. The case had been tried before Simon H. Rifkind, a Special Master appointed by the Court, pursuant to the original jurisdiction the court exercises in disputes between states. By 1963, the controversy involved more than 300 witnesses, nearly 50 attorneys, 4000 exhibits, 25,000 pages of transcript, at a cost to the Golden State anywhere from two to three million taxpayer dollars. Governor Pat Brown understood the growing need for water in Southern California, and proposed a massive water project, which would move water from Northern California to the southern part of the state. The bond issue to fund the project had weak support in Southern California, however, which pinned its hopes on prevailing in *Arizona v. California* and meeting its need for water with Colorado River water.[19]

During Stanley Mosk's first campaign for Attorney General in August 1958, the state of Arizona announced its intention to amend its claim before the United States Supreme Court regarding the disposition of about one million annual acre feet in Arizona's Gila water system. Arizona contended that a 1922 compact the Colorado River states had adopted for allocation of water applied only to mainstream waters. California argued that the compact governed the entire Colorado River system, so Arizona's diversion of water from tributary rivers should be deducted from its allotted share.

Whether Arizona's effort to amend its claim would be allowed was unclear and the decision would be made by presiding Special Master Rifkind, at the center of the "longest, most complicated, most costly litigation in the history of water development."[20]

Grabbing an accompanying headline, candidate Judge Mosk responded to Arizona's new demand. If it is accepted, he proclaimed, it would mean that "the very future of California is at stake," and "our drinking cup from this river will be very dry indeed," and it would "mean the end of economic growth to a vast section" of California.[21] When Rifkin's ultimate decision favored Arizona, a banner headline announced that the new state's Attorney General Mosk was picking up the gauntlet. "State Starts Fight to Reverse Decision in Colorado River Suit," which was "the opening round," of

California Attorney General Stanley Mosk poses in front of the United States Supreme Court during his January 1962 visit to the nation's capital, where he opened the first session of oral arguments on behalf of the state's interest in the distribution of Colorado water in *Arizona v. California*. Mosk asked the justices, "Are we going to give Colorado River water to people of California to drink or to Arizona for asparagus?" The Court didn't give him an answer for another year-and-a-half (courtesy Richard Mosk).

Mosk's commitment to "make every effort to persuade the court that there is no legal basis for the adverse decision." Assisting in the case was a future law professor, Charles Corker, who was dedicated to winning the case for the state, or if the state lost, minimizing its impact.[22] B. Abbott Goldberg served as deputy and later assistant attorney general of California, handling the major litigation concerning the state's interest in Arizona's Central Valley Project. From 1961 to 1966, Goldberg served as deputy director and chief deputy director of the California Department of Water Resources. Goldberg believes that Mosk based his point of view about the water litigation from what he learned from Corker; because, "there was nobody else in his confidence to tell him differently."[23]

Mosk's office was ordered to file the state's exceptions to Rifkind's recommendations to the U.S. Supreme Court on May 22, 1959. Although this was merely a "preface to California's opening brief," Mosk submitted over 1000 pages of argument and supporting documents seeking "a decree denying Arizona's federal law suit for river water to operate its proposed Central Arizona Project to serve the Phoenix area."[24]

The water wars between Arizona and California involved local, state, regional, and federal interpretations of laws and practices about who had access to use water depending on how and where the point of origin was and the eventual path where the water flowed. It could flow above or collect below ground; it could be captured from vast ribbons of winding rivers or from smaller branch-like tributaries. It also depended on whether the water resided on open public lands or was located on federally protected Indian reservations. Decades of scholarly and journalistic accounts detail the convoluted layers of issues and battles, figuratively and literally, between diverse groups and individuals.

Water was particularly controversial for Southern Californians, who "had been preparing for years for a showdown" over Colorado River water. When the case was finally set for argument before the U.S. Supreme Court, the Court initially allocated sixteen hours spread over four days for argument, then reset the case for six more hours of re-argument. Accompanying the Attorney General's team were his wife Edna and several members of Los Angeles' Metropolitan Water District (MPA), as well as Mosk's friend Judge Shirley Hufstedler and Women's State Chair of the Democratic Central Committee, Carmen Warschaw.[25] A January, 1962 wire story from the nation's capitol reported that California Attorney General Stanley Mosk today launched a last-ditch fight in the Supreme Court to prevent any reduction in California's share of Colorado River water. Invoking principles of equity, Mosk opened oral arguments in what was to be the final clash in the bitter 10-year legal battle between California and Arizona over division of the river waters.[26] He intended to introduce his deputies to carry the argument, but the Court immediately started peppering him with questions. He asserted that the case should be decided by equitable principles, balancing the needs of the present population of Southern California against the future plans of Arizona to allocate the water to the Central Valley Project. In a thundering peroration, Attorney General Mosk concluded, "Are we going to give Colorado River water to people of California to drink or to Arizona for asparagus?"[27] Northcutt Ely, a brilliant water lawyer, and the Special Assistant Attorney General to Mosk, followed up to represent the interests of the California.[28] The Supreme Court Justices set the case for reargument in the following term and did not announce their decision until a year and half later, on June 3, 1963. The ruling, in favor of Arizona and asparagus, was based on the Boulder Canyon Act, not the compact of 1922. By referencing the Boulder Canyon Act, the Court stated that Arizona was entitled to its tributaries, and therefore authorized to use the one million acre feet disputed by California. Arizona had, through the Court's ruling, acquired nearly all it had set out to gain in the 1920s.[29]

The Colorado River case produced a rare disagreement between Mosk and Governor Pat Brown. According to Mosk, "we were fighting Arizona every bit of the way, and Pat ... took a more moderate position, which we always felt was sort of undercutting our litigation." Governor Brown would make speeches that did not conform to the position Mosk was taking in the litigation, resulting in some public disagreements with his Attorney General. Mosk later admitted that Brown was more moderate and objective about the issue, while his own passion reflected his appreciation of how important the water was to Southern California. Ultimately, the increased flow of water to Arizona resulted in the Central Arizona Project, the environmental consequences of which are still being sorted out.

Years later Stanley Mosk reviewed a 1966 publication detailing the history of the water wars. To Mosk, "the fundamental position was unassailably equitable: that existing uses deserve priority over future projects." He explained, "to put it more colorfully: water is more essential for present babies than for future asparagus." He also offered a broad view assessment of how the U.S. Congress and judiciary perceived the contest, seeing "Arizona as a modern unsullied David being frustrated by the wicked Goliath of the Coast. In this entire controversy California has been disadvantaged by its size and wealth, a curious anomaly."[30] Ultimately, Governor Brown persuaded voters to authorize a $1.75 billion bond issue to fund what was called the State Water Project, a vast assemblage of dams, pumping stations, aqueducts, and reservoirs that would bring millions of gallons of northern water to the thirsty south. Historian Kevin Starr calls it the "most ambitious water storage and distribution system in the history of the human race." Today, it is seen as the greatest legacy of Pat Brown's governorship.

Another dispute that began over water immersed Mosk in a nasty fight with ugly racial and anti–Semitic overtones in the popular Southern California resort town of Lake Elsinore. Proponents of funneling in Colorado River sweet water met stiff resistance from locals who depended on the tourist trade attracted to the area's sulfur mineral springs. Lake Elsinore had a long history as a mecca for working-class Jews attracted by resorts offering hot mineral baths. To serve this tourist trade, a large Jewish community developed, and half the businesses in town were Jewish-owned. Jewish residents and merchants sided with opponents of the Colorado River water proposal. The Colorado River water was believed to be an antidote to the high fluoride levels found in the sulfur water. Fluoride was believed to be part of the communist conspiracy. Anti-Fluoride and anti–Semitism became "hopelessly entangled," just as the confluence of anti-communism with anti–Semitism had increased throughout the twentieth century. Supporters of the Colorado River proposal were labeled right wing fanatics, who used the water issue to conflate their anti-communism with anti–Semitism. Several incidents of vandalism, anonymous hate letters, paint bombing of residences and businesses, and an isolated cross burning incident led Los Angeles television station KTLA-TV to broadcast a documentary entitled "City of Hate," which alleged vandalism of Jewish institutions, threats against local Jewish residents and a plot to purge Jews from the city. Letters to the Jewish Community Council of Elsinore from 1958 and 1959 made similar allegations.

California Attorney General Stanley Mosk undertook an investigation and issued a report, suggesting that much of the television documentary was greatly distorted and exaggerated. The report concluded that, "it is natural that people in a community with Elsinore's problems can become somewhat emotional in interpreting unusual events. It is disturbing when outside commentators encourage distortion and exaggeration." To Lake Elsinore's residents "initials scrawled on a wall, a hate letter in the mail, a rock thrown at night, can

Stanley Mosk proudly shared this photo capturing four generations represented here. He appears with his mother Minna Perl, his son Richard, and his maternal grandmother Rolla Perl (courtesy Tom Mosk).

assume a significance born of experience in places far from Elsinore. What appears to the objective mind as the senseless handiwork of a few disturbed hate mongers afraid to reveal their identity, to these elderly people [is] a very real threat of physical violence."[31] The controversy had sad consequences for the Jewish community of Lake Elsinore. The Jewish tourists stopped coming, and with rare exceptions, most of the Jewish residents and business owners left. Today, there are barely any Jews left in Lake Elsinore and few signs that a thriving Jewish community ever existed.

Debates about religious freedom frequently morph into the perennial contests over the separation of church and state. Mosk spoke often about the issue, as exemplified by his address before the Los Angeles Jewish Community Council in 1959. The newly elected Attorney General welded together the themes of housing discrimination, racism, and anti–Semitism. He told his audience of one-thousand, "the temptation to teach 'one God' in public schools is easy, until we begin to quarrel about which book, or whose book, is to be used for that purpose. The urge to read the Bible to school children in the name of morality is understandable until we begin to ask which Bible, and how to answer the natural questions which children raise regarding doctrinaire religious beliefs. Bible reading in public schools was ruled unconstitutional by my predecessor Attorney General Pat Brown, yet to many Californians the responsibility of religious education is too easily passed to public schools, which are ill equipped to teach religious creed. We dare not fall into the error of asking the state to do the impossible and satisfy the diversity of creeds and faiths by a watered down version of religion acceptable to no one."[32]

Attorney General Mosk was also the principal sponsor of a statute creating the Commission on Peace Officer Standards and Training (POST), an ingenious approach to elevating the professionalism of police agencies in California. The Commission sets minimum standards for the training of police officers, standards already met in most big-city departments. The Commission then funds training available to smaller police agencies throughout the state so they can meet the minimum standards. The Commission is financed by a 10 percent assessment on fines imposed as punishment for crimes, and requires no tax support from the general fund.

One of the most hotly contested issues to repeatedly come before the legislature during Mosk's tenure at the California Department of Justice was the California death penalty law. Stanley Mosk was profoundly opposed to the death penalty, but as an officer of the state, either as a judge or Attorney General, he believed he had to follow the law, as he did in sentencing John Crooker to death, and moving forward with the execution of Mrs. Spinelli while serving as executive secretary to Governor Olson. In seeking the office of Attorney General, he freely voiced his opposition to the death penalty, saying that as Attorney General he would have to enforce it, but he would do everything he could to eliminate it. Governor Pat Brown also was opposed to the death penalty, and although he presided over thirty-six executions as governor, he commuted the death sentences of twenty-three others, and repeatedly urged the legislature to repeal the death penalty, at great political cost.[33] Attorney General Mosk supported his efforts, testifying before the legislature to urge repeal of the death penalty in California. At the same time, however, he was supporting legislation proposed by the National Association of Attorneys General which would end the "interminable appeals" in death penalty cases. Speaking before Los Angeles County Grand Juror's Association, Stanley Mosk used the example of Caryl Chessman's case to decry the ability to "delay proper enforcement of a state court judgment." His support for a law that "would prohibit the use of the lower federal courts for appeals from state court decisions," was based on the need to "end seemingly endless appeals." He said, "with recourse to the lower courts available we find that petitioners can take seven bites at the public apple," and because "only a relatively small number of these petitioners have been successful," the "unnecessary burden" on the federal courts "greatly interferes with procedures of the state courts."[34]

The Caryl Chessman case brought the issue of life or death dramatically to public attention. Chessman was accused of being a notorious "red light bandit" who posed as a police officer, mounting a red light on his car to approach parked cars with romancing couples overlooking the panoramic vistas of the city on lovers' lanes. He raped the girls and robbed the men they were with. He eventually stood trial in 1948 and was convicted of kidnapping, which was then a capital crime in California, punishable by death. Kidnapping was defined to include any movement of victims for the purpose of robbing them, a definition which was broadly applied in his case. For fifteen years, Chessman's case wound through the California courts before a final execution date was set. While awaiting a final outcome, he authored a book entitled *Cell 2455, Death Row*,[35] in which he asserted his innocence and challenged the injustice of California's death penalty law. The book gained him an international following, and his case became a *cause célèbre*. In December of 1959, during the last stages of Chessman's appeals, Attorney General Mosk urged the United States Supreme Court to "reject the eighth and latest appeal of kidnap-rapist Caryl Chessman from his death sentence." Mosk's brief to the high court countered all of the contentions made in Chessman's appeal. These included Chessman's claim that he was denied a fair hearing in his challenge to the transcript of his original trial. The necessity for a forty-day hearing in November 1957 arose from the death of the official court reporter, which left two-thirds of his trial notes to be transcribed by a substitute court reporter. Chessman also asserted that his eleven year detention on Death Row, and "the setting and postponement of his execution date seven times constituted 'cruel and unusual punishment.'" Mosk countered that the hearing left "'no substantial issue remaining' to be decided." What's more,

Mosk added, at the time of the hearing, "Chessman himself stated he had been granted a 'full, fair and complete hearing.'"[36]

Perhaps most unsettling to Mosk, personally and professionally, was Chessman's accusation that the Attorney General and his staff had held secret meetings with justices of California's Supreme Court. Mosk pointed out such accusations were not "dissimilar to allegations against the district attorney, the substitute court reporter, both Supreme Court judges who participated in this case, the U.S. court judge and members of the U.S. Court of Appeals," and concluded, "The petitioner's allegations ... are legally groundless and factually false."[37]

Governor Brown would have commuted Chessman's death sentence, since he did not believe a death sentence was appropriate for a person who had not killed anyone. Just as in the case of Warren K. Billings, the California Constitution required the approval of a majority of the Justices of the state Supreme Court for a commutation if the defendant had a prior felony conviction, as Chessman did. Brown inquired whether the Court would approve a commutation in Chessman's case, and Chief Justice Phil Gibson informed him "that not only will they vote four to three against me, but they'll write a majority opinion kicking me in the teeth." Governor Brown was persuaded by his son Jerry to give Chessman a sixty-day stay of execution, and to ask the California legislature to enact a moratorium on the death penalty in California. Although the legislature had previously turned down moratorium requests eight times, Brown agreed to try again. Despite a valiant effort, supported by his Attorney General, the moratorium was defeated by an 8–7 vote of the Senate Judiciary Committee.

The sixty-day delay created a problem for the Attorney General. He felt obligated to reassure citizens of California that Chessman's death sentence had not been "altered" but merely postponed. On Monday morning, February 22, 1960, the banner headline in the *Los Angeles Times* read, "CHESSMAN WILL DIE IN 60 DAYS, MOSK PREDICTS." Assistant Attorney General Arlo E. Smith, who on behalf of the state had been overseeing the Chessman case in Mosk's office, requested that the original sentencing judge, Superior Court Judge Herbert V. Walker, set an execution date immediately. The unusual circumstances forced Los Angeles District Attorney William R. McKesson and his staff to pour over law books in an effort to find a precedent for a plan of action.[38] Everyone agreed that Chessman would not go to the gas chamber automatically at the end of the two-month reprieve, so a new execution date had to be set. Arlo Smith read the Penal Code to mean that the District Attorney is required to ask the Superior Court to set a new date "at least 60 days but not more than 90 days from" the date when Brown granted the reprieve. District Attorney McKesson disagreed. Calling this view "somewhat dubious," he was concerned that it would be embarrassing "to set a date, say 61 days from Friday (which would have been April 19) and then, after further study, find out we didn't have the power to set a date." He suggested that "maybe we have to wait another 60 days after the reprieve ends," or June 19. Smith prevailed, and a new execution date was set for May 2, 1960. No matter what the date, Mosk defended the governor's actions as being in line with the state constitution, which only denied pardons or commutations, but not stays for twice-convicted felons. Thus, Mosk pointed out, Governor Brown "has not granted a commutation — he merely in effect changed the date of execution."[39]

Surprisingly, the extraordinary Chessman saga also had implications for American foreign policy makers, and foreign relations. The schedule of Chessman's execution apparently concerned officials of the State Department because of its potential to exacerbate anti–

American demonstrations during President Eisenhower's upcoming goodwill trip to South America. Press accounts claiming that the State Department was meddling in California affairs led to denials by federal officials. The White House and State Department adamantly denied making any recommendation on behalf of Chessman, although shortly after federal officials informed him about potential international student reaction, Governor Brown had mentioned Uruguay in discussing the delay of Chessman's execution. FBI agents picked up a story about a Phoenix woman, a public stenographer, who supposedly knew one of Chessman's former cellmates. Between the three of them, Chessman was supposed to have dictated letters that were mailed to South America and then mailed back to the Governor Brown, "thus making it appear that there was a great deal of sentiment in the South American countries for leniency to Chessman." An FBI agent writing to Director Hoover conjectured that this may be the background of a newspaper report that the state department intervened in the Chessman matter to avoid disturbances in Uruguay incidental to President Eisenhower's visit to that country. Five days later, Hoover wrote to Vice President Richard Nixon detailing "vital facts concerning this criminal and his debt to society." He told Nixon that, "nowhere in Chessman's record is there the slightest mitigating circumstance which might serve as an excuse for leniency." Because Chessman had successfully thwarted the carrying out of his death sentence for twelve years, Hoover thought it worthwhile to examine the background of the persons spearheading Chessman's "latest attempt to defeat the interests of justice." Hoover asserted that "one of these men was Abraham Lincoln Wirin, a practicing attorney in Los Angeles" who was born in Russia in 1900. According to Hoover, "Wirin still continues to act as counsel for and has supported numerous subversive persons and organizations." Hoover's examples included Wirin's serving as counsel for Smith Act defendants, and his membership on the Executive Board of the National Lawyers Guild (NLG). George T. Davis, another Chessman attorney, Hoover said, "also has a long record of association with questionable activities in California. He was vice president of the NLG of San Francisco, and in 1936 served as attorney for Thomas J. Mooney. Davis was also indicted for smuggling out of San Quentin Chessman's second book." Hoover concluded with his long held view that when there is no shadow of a doubt concerning the guilt of the defendant, the public interest demands that capital punishment be invoked where the law so provides. "Based upon all available fact, these conditions most definitely appear to apply to the case of Caryl Chessman. Sincerely, Edgar." Hoover's investigation into Wirin and his colleagues alleged that Wirin had worked with many of the organizations that Stanley Mosk was affiliated with during his early professional career. This included representing what Hoover believed to be Communist Front organizations such as the Citizen's Committee to Preserve American Freedom, and the Los Angeles Committee for the Protection of the Foreign Born. A Southland Jewish organization, Women for Legislative Action was lumped in with Wirin's allegedly nefarious connections.[40]

A handwritten notation at the bottom of an FBI communication indicated that "as I anticipated this now backfiring on State Department. I now being concerned re: our action in transmitting to Brown information from England for next move." Attorney General Stanley Mosk commented that State Department denials couldn't refute the record of telephone calls and telegraphs to Governor Brown that were cleared with the White House. He suggested the State Department carry out its job to be "our diplomatic eyes and ears in foreign lands," instead of "trying to crawl out from under unjust criticism." Mosk expressed the hope that after the Department's USIA (United States Information Agency) "made inquiries in California for information, presumably to disseminate," they would use the sixty-days of Chessman's reprieve to "convey the true facts of the case abroad."[41]

Chessman was finally executed on May 2, 1960, and the delay made Governor Brown very unpopular. For the first time in his career, Governor Brown was booed at his public appearances at sporting events. Ironically, California law changed nine years after Chessman's execution. In *People v. Daniels*,[42] the California Supreme Court reversed a death sentence based upon a conviction of kidnapping for the purpose of robbery very similar to Chessman's case, holding that a death sentence cannot be sustained where the movement of the victim is merely incidental to the commission of the robbery. In authoring the opinion, Justice Mosk conceded that *Chessman,* and the intervening opinion in *People v. Wein*,[43] would require affirmance of the death sentence imposed on *Daniels*:

> The case at bar is the first to reach us on facts essentially identical to *Wein*: defendants here, in the course of robbing and raping three women in their own homes, forced them to move about their rooms for distances of 18 feet, 5 or 6 feet, and 30 feet respectively. Under the rule of *Chessman* and *Wein*, such brief movements of the victims would constitute "kidnapping or carrying away" within the meaning of the statute and would therefore be sufficient to support defendants' convictions of violating section 209.

Mosk's majority opinion in *Daniels* reflected his instinctive sense of assessing where the law was going:

> We believe, however, the time has come to reconsider the construction placed upon the statute in *Chessman* and applied in *Wein*. More than a decade has elapsed since the latter decision, and almost two decades since the former. During this period the law of kidnapping has not remained stagnant. There have been, as we will demonstrate, fresh judicial approaches, far-reaching legislative innovations, and considerable analysis of the problem by legal commentators and scholars. Out of this ferment has arisen a current of common sense in the construction and application of statutes defining the crime of kidnapping. *Chessman* and *Wein*, it now appears, stand as obstructions to the flow of that current in California.

Two rulings of the United States Supreme Court subsequently agreed with Justice Mosk and Governor Pat Brown. The death sentence for kidnapping was rendered unlawful under the Eighth Amendment prohibition of cruel and unusual punishment in the U.S. Constitution.[44] Thus, if Chessman's case were to come before the Courts of any state today, his death sentence would be set aside.

In 1961, the United States Supreme Court ruled that the Fourth Amendment exclusionary rule, requiring illegally seized evidence to be suppressed in criminal cases, was required by due process of law, and imposed the rule on all of the states in its 5–4 decision in *Mapp v. Ohio*. California had already adopted the rule as part of state Constitutional requirements in the 1956 ruling in *People v. Cahan,* a decision Stanley Mosk had applauded at the time, to the displeasure of LAPD Chief Parker. ("More officers may find it necessary to use their heads instead of their hob-nailed boots.") After the *Mapp* decision came down, during a social occasion in California, Attorney General Mosk discussed the impact of the case in California with U.S. Supreme Court Justice William O. Douglas. Their conversation became the subject of a lively exchange among the Justices of the high court. Justice Douglas wrote to Justice Tom Clark, the author of the *Mapp* opinion, with a "CC" to the other justices on the court, describing his recent conversation with Mosk. "Out of the blue," Douglas reported, Mosk said, "Thank the good Lord for *Mapp v. Ohio*." When Douglas asked him what he meant, Mosk gave him "an interesting account." Mosk told Douglas that since the Court's 4–3 *Cahan* decision the California court had two vacancies and two new appointees. Mosk explained that, "Phil Gibson and the others who were for the Cahan opinion held their breath until the nominees took office and until they could find out where these nominees stood on *Cahan*." Mosk said that it turned out that one of the two nominees supported *Cahan* and one was against it. Therefore, "so far as the Supreme Court of California went, *Cahan* was barely holding its own." Furthermore, Mosk said the newspaper campaign against *Cahan* "continued unabated," identifying Chief Parker as a source of the opposition. With the system of elective judges in California, he added, "pressure on trial courts was very, very great not to apply the *Cahan* case or to find there were more exceptions to it, or in other words, try to get around it." Mosk told Douglas, "in practical effect, the *Cahan* decision, while on the books, was not really given much life or vitality in practice." To sum it up, Douglas told Justice Clark, "The result of *Mapp v. Ohio*, according to Mosk, is to take the pressure off the local judges to create exceptions and to follow the exclusionary rule and all its ramifications."[45]

Justice Felix Frankfurter, who had dissented in *Mapp,* took issue with Stanley Mosk's reasons for approving of the decision. He was displeased that Mosk did not rely upon "the history of the Fourteenth Amendment or on what he conceived to be the juristic requirements of the Due Process Clause of that Amendment." He faulted Mosk for welcoming "the opinion because it will check a tendency of California lower court judges and, perchance, even the danger of the California Supreme Court, to make inroads upon the California doctrine regarding search and seizure, as expounded in the *Cahan* case. Coming from one of the most self-reliant of States, this attitude to look to federal authority for dealing with a local problem — for such was concern over the *Cahan* doctrine until *Mapp* came along — runs counter to one of my oldest convictions which time has only reinforced." As such, he was moved to commend the "so-called 'states rights' doctrine." Although Frankfurter described "states rights" claims as "the happy hunting ground of demagogues as well as of sincere reactionary minds," and had "no use for such claims," he did "care about the maintenance of our federalism," which was "indispensable for the protection of civil liberties to avoid concentration of governmental powers in one central government." In closing, Justice Frankfurter added, "Let me repeat. I am not addressing myself to Attorney General Mosk's approval of *Mapp v. Ohio*. I am not remotely adverting to the merits of that case. I do feel saddened, much as I respect him, by the ground of his satisfaction over the decision."[46]

Continuing the exchange, Justice Douglas wrote in a Memorandum to the Conference, "I did not ask Attorney General Mosk. But if I had put the question I am certain he would have also said, 'Thank God, California is in the Union.'"[47] Justice Frankfurter answered with a note to "Bill," suggesting, "When next you see Attorney General Mosk please ask him if California was not 'in the Union' before June 19, 1961" (the date of the *Mapp* decision).[48] Douglas shot back, "When I next see Stanley Mosk, I will put your question to him. My guess is he will say that California was not wholly 'in the union' before *Mapp v. Ohio*, as he thinks, I believe, that the Bill of Rights should be protective of all our constituent members."[49]

It might not be all that surprising that Stanley Mosk occupied such attention of members of the U.S. Supreme Court in light of his friendship over the years with several Justices of the High Court. Long time friend Chief Justice Earl Warren facilitated the blossoming of another friendship when he suggested to Professor Delmar Karlen, Director of the Institute of Judicial Administration at New York University, that he invite Mosk to join a distinguished team of American lawyers and judges to spend two weeks in London and Oxford studying British appellate procedure. Other members of the group were Justice William Brennan of the U.S. Supreme Court, Chief Judge Edward Lumbard of the U.S. Court of

Appeals for the First Circuit, Chief Judge William Desmond of the New York Court of Appeals, Chief Justice Walter Schaefer of the Illinois Supreme Court, and U.S. Solicitor General Archibald Cox. For Stanley Mosk, the highlight of this experience was being with Justice Brennan morning, noon, and night for two solid weeks. They became fast friends, and were tremendously impressed by the British judges they met. When Justice Brennan, as Chairman of the delegation, expressed admiration for the British practice of immediately announcing a decision from the bench at the conclusion of the argument of a case, their host Lord Denning responded,

> Well, that creates problems at times. I've got to tell you about a colleague of mine. He heard a case that went on for several weeks, and argument by counsel went on for several days. After oral argument, he immediately announced his decision right from the bench. He went back into his chambers and as his clerk helped him take off his wig and robes, he stopped, shook his head and slapped his sides. He said, "There I go ... I did it again. I said 'plaintiff' when I meant 'defendant.'"[50]

Stanley Mosk recalled that the group then and there decided that our more contemplative method had something to commend it. Professor Karlen authored a thoughtful comparison of British and American appellate procedure based upon this study, as well as a similar visit of British lawyers and judges to observe American appeals.[51]

Attorney General Mosk continued to vigorously defend the rights of labor unions, and took every available opportunity to express solidarity with labor's goals. He knew his stand was in line with the new president, particularly because Jack Kennedy had written to Mosk about passage of the Kennedy-Ives Labor Management Reform Bill, which according to Kennedy, "ought to make final one fact: That the Republicans will never again be able to denounce our Party as the protector of labor bosses and racketeers."[52]

In a February 1961 speech, Mosk said that "management and labor unions which are concerned only with the bread and butter approach to existence are not only neglecting their responsibilities to their country but are endangering their own future free position in a world that could go communistic." He praised AFL founder Samuel Gompers for steps taken early on to put American trade unions into the world peace movement by joining the International Labor Organization. With the elimination of sweatshop conditions and the end of the ten-hour day and sixty-hour week, bread and butter issues were largely resolved. Now, Mosk said, was the time for labor to expand globally to newly emerging nations in underdeveloped frontiers. He cited the importance of adding labor representation to all consular and embassy offices around the world, so that such ambassadors speaking the same language of laborers everywhere, could help guide trade unionists abroad.[53] In April, 1961 Mosk told the Amalgamated Clothing Workers that the strength and dignity of the labor movement "is a true and honest joining together of men and women who seek a better life for themselves and for all people of our nation." He recalled the "remote almost-forgotten days when unions were outlawed and the leaders were all seen as 'radicals' to the nation's leaders but who are now considered pillars of the community, and in those days closer to us-when unions were legal but beleaguered." He described how out of the struggles had come a "far greater, farther reaching, more permanent peaceful evolution based on the true dignity and worth of the working men and women than any bloody revolution based on values as meaningless today as they were in 1917." America's challenge, he said, is that our great unions must prove that democratic representatives and free labor unions offer the way to a life forever denied by the very tenets of the communist ideology.[54]

During the early 1960's, the proselytizing of extremist organizations like the John Birch

Society and the Christian Anti-Communist Crusade, both of which were widespread in California, once again ratcheted up latent anti-communist hysteria. The John Birch Society was founded in 1958 by retired candy manufacturer Robert Welch. He regarded liberals as "communist dupes" and called President Dwight D. Eisenhower a "conscious, dedicated agent of the communist conspiracy." At its peak in 1961, Birch membership was estimated as high as 100,000, and the organization had a staff of 60. The group campaigned for the impeachment of Chief Justice Earl Warren, and lobbied against civil rights legislation. Dr. Fred Schwarz, an Australian physician, founded The Christian Anti-Communist Crusade and moved his base of operations to California in 1960. The author of *You Can Trust the Communists (to be Communists)*, Dr. Schwarz lectured widely and organized "schools" to teach anti-communism. His Southern California School of Anti-Communism filled the 16,000-capacity Los Angeles Sports Arena from August 28 – September 1, 1961. A columnist for the *Los Angeles Times* reported, "evening sessions, featuring nationally known speakers, were televised, and those who should know tell me that some three million people listened in nightly. At any rate, I can honestly say that in my 25 years in Los Angeles I have never known a local event that so completely captured the enthusiasm of the city."[55]

Attorney General Stanley Mosk issued a widely publicized report examining the activity of secret right-wing extremist groups in California in 1961.[56] In describing the John Birch Society, the report characterized the Society's membership as "wealthy businessmen, retired military officers, and little old ladies in tennis shoes." The line got a huge play in the press, after the *New York Times* picked up on it. One columnist warned, "The next time you see Attorney General Stanley Mosk, don't sound off with 'Anyone for tennis?' With all those tennis shoes he has been receiving in Sacramento re his remarks about the John Birch Society ... [it] caused him to remark that 'I hope the shoes will not be for the right foot only. We prefer well balanced people, both at home and abroad.'"[57] Although the actual author of the report was Howard Jewel, he had heard his boss use the expression on many occasions. The term has since achieved a life of its own. Google "little old ladies in tennis shoes," and you will get 1,300,000 hits. Along with police officers in hob-nailed boots, Stanley Mosk got a lot of mileage out of footwear.

Mosk's attack on the John Birch Society drew a spirited response from right-wing Congressman John H. Rousselot, who asked, "How much longer will the people of California stomach Mr. Mosk's bitter and bigoted attacks against the John Birch Society, an organization the California Senate Fact Finding Commission on American Activities has found to be thoroughly dedicated to fundamental American ideals?" Fueling Rousselot's ire was Mosk's naïveté in failing to "wake up to the fact that one of the prime movers behind race riots and violent Civil Rights demonstrations in the U.S. is the Communist Party." According to Rousselot, Mosk was a "scare monger" who would go to any length to smear the Society and its founder, Robert Welch. What's more, by casting aspersions on the Society, Mosk was really trying to cover up the truth about the extent of Communist activities in our country.[58] Attorney General Mosk appeared on television station KTVU in Oakland, California, on February 5, 1962 to deliver a hard-hitting attack on Dr. Schwarz's Christian Anti-communist Crusade. He challenged the "non-profit" label attached to the Crusade, reporting that for ninety days following June 30, 1961, "the so-called Crusade took gross receipts in Los Angeles alone in the sum of $311,253. It expended $96,496 in rent, pay to its speakers, advertising, printing and so forth, leaving a net profit of $214,757. This is indeed big business; nearly a quarter of a million dollars net in 90 days.... No wonder this whole movement has been called 'Patriotism for Profit.'" He also derided the use of the term "school" by the Crusade, saying, "the Crusade was not a school but a promotion ... none of the alleged instructors have teaching credentials issued by the State of California." He concluded with a passionate defense of Chief Justice Earl Warren and President Dwight D. Eisenhower:

> They tell us we are losing the Cold War ... The orators of the radical-right have tried to preempt the term "patriotism" ... Is it patriotic to demand that the Chief Justice of the United States be impeached? It is patriotic to sow dissension by insisting that some of the very highest leaders of the United States are disloyal? It is patriotic to debase free and open debate by heckling, and shouting and hooting? It is patriotic to deride Democracy by calling it a perennial fraud? Does this help America or hurt America? ... Let us turn aside from these shrill-voiced apostles of despair. The leading anti–Communist is not to be found among them. He is to be found in the White House. He is the President of the United States of America. Every President of the United States.[59]

Dr. Schwarz responded by accusing Attorney General Mosk of "giving comfort and aid to the forces of Communism" with slander and deceit. An attack in his newsletter concluded:

> I do not know the mind or motives of Stanley Mosk. I do not know why he opposes so vehemently a program to teach American Citizens the philosophy, morality, organizational structure, tactics, and strategy of Communism so that citizens may be more effective in preserving freedom. I do know he has spoken falsely and slanderously. Slander is a strange quality in the custodian of justice. The statements of Stanley Mosk have given the enemy ammunition which is much more effective than any Communism could provide.[60]

Mosk continued to speak loud and clear about the dangers of right-wing extremism and the witch-hunting of cold war demagogues. His campaign against extremism inspired vitriolic attacks that questioned his loyalty. One such attack came from Karl Prussion, a former FBI counterspy who left the organization "to carry his story to the public." The FBI countered his claim, stating that he was not employed as a special agent of the FBI, but admitted that Prussion was among a few individuals who furnished information concerning subversive activity "for which they were compensated."[61] Nevertheless, Prussion's 1962 pamphlet entitled *California Dynasty of Communism*, playing on the name California Democratic Council, called on Californians to get the November 6 vote out to "return our state government to the so-called super-patriots." For Prussion, "The Golden State has been chosen to be the model Soviet State," and "Communist subversives" are pushing a "strong left-wing centralized hierarchy that must and will control the individual from birth to death." The triumvirate of evil was Pat Brown, Alan Cranston, and Stanley Mosk, along with other "Red Frontier" figures such as Gus Hawkins. Prussion called Mosk "a political gymnast." He argued that "this astute, opportunistic, slithering, political charlatan, casts a fraudulent shadow of his actual position to the people of California, and "remains the greatest single threat to the courageous patriotic anti-communist movement sweeping the state.... His record, past and present, reveals him to be a collaborator, appeaser, and consistent supporter of communist objectives in the state."[62]

Attorney General Mosk was well versed on matters regarding anti-communist propaganda. Such excesses of extremist's vitriol failed to deter Mosk from his own bully pulpit. Speaking at a conference held by the County Federation of Labor at the illustrious Ambassador Hotel in mid-town Los Angeles, Mosk charged that the right wing "Errs on Reds," by "oversimplifying complex economic and political problems." The "Devil Theory" of communism is "evangelistic zealotry," as advocated by Dr. Fred Schwarz and others, which then "freezes their policy proposals toward Communist nations" since they believe that negotiating with the Reds is "negotiating with the Devil or evil." Proponents of the "Devil Theory," see communists at home promoting their "international, atheist, communist conspiracy," through their "support of mental health clinics, fluoridated water, pornography, federal aid to education, narcotics and the sale of liquor."[63]

Two years after Mosk's report on the John Birch Society came out, he issued a statement about its origin. He said it was "written in response to a request from Governor Brown who wanted information on this new organization." At that time, the report "experienced a larger readership than we had envisioned," having been reprinted in newspapers and a national publication. "Requests continue to come in for copies which are provided with the caveat that, at the time of its writing, information within it are now over two years old and thus subject to the infirmities which that age lends to any description of American political phenomena."[64]

By 1963, Attorney General Stanley Mosk had achieved a national reputation as a thoughtful legal analyst. Governor Brown acknowledged Mosk's talents when he wrote Mosk that a speech at the Community Welfare Council was "a subject that seldom brings forth the kind of clear, straightforward speech you delivered," and he added, with Mosk's permission he will have it sent to all the editorial writers on his mailing list.[65]

When outgoing California Governor Culbert Olson appointed Stanley Mosk to the Superior Court, Judge Mosk was the youngest jurist assigned to the bench (courtesy Richard Mosk; photo by Albert C. Smith).

Chapter 9

"A Great Democratic Rain"

California Attorney General Stanley Mosk became a "player" in national politics as preparations for the 1960 presidential race took off. Stanley and Edna Mosk, along with Assemblyman Jess Unruh, the "Big Daddy" of California politics, were early supporters of Senator John F. Kennedy. Although he was not an announced candidate, two-time loser Adlai Stevenson also had a strong following in California, pushing for a draft. Governor Pat Brown was anxious to maintain control over the California delegation as a "favorite son," so he could play the role of "kingmaker" at the 1960 Democratic National Convention in Los Angeles. Supporters of JFK were convinced he could beat Governor Brown in a primary race, and sought to persuade him to enter the California presidential primary.

As early as October 1959, observers of California politics were already speculating that the Golden State would be, for both Democrats and Republicans, "the nation's major political battlefield," anticipating a "punching match" between Governor Pat Brown and John Kennedy for the state's Democratic delegation. After a long honeymoon period in office, many Southern Californians were becoming disenchanted with Governor Brown, perceiving him as lacking in attention to the region's needs. Numerous statewide issues contributed to this impression, such as his failure to place a reapportionment plan on the November, 1960 ballot which would help pass the water bond for his statewide water program.. Some believed that his alienation of powerful legislative leaders like Jess Unruh contributed to the divisive intraparty squabbling. It didn't help that supporters of Jack Kennedy asked him to speak at the annual Jefferson-Jackson Day dinner in November, 1959. The governor's office quickly responded with a request to withdraw the invitation. Ultimately, Kennedy stayed out of the California primary, and a slate pledged to Brown was elected.[1]

As the City of Los Angeles prepared to welcome the delegates to the 1960 Democratic National Convention, California Democrats were in a unique position to wield great influence in national politics. Unlike today, when national conventions follow the dictates of state party primaries and are usually indulgent self-congratulatory affairs, the 1960 Democratic convention actually picked the candidate. Right up to the point at which balloting began, the outcome was still in doubt.

Throughout the country, each state party elected one woman and one man as representatives to the party's national committee. The Democratic National Committeeman for California was Paul Ziffren. Ziffren was a successful tax lawyer from Chicago, who became a member of the national committee in 1953, and reactivated the Western States Democratic Conference, building a bloc of liberals in 12 states to offset the influence of conservative Southerners in the party. When his successful lobbying resulted in the announcement that the 1960 convention would be in Los Angeles, the *New York Times* reported that this accomplishment "is bound to focus national attention on Democratic triumphs in which Mr. Ziffren has had an important hand."[2] The continued loyalty of Paul Ziffren, along with National Committee president Paul Butler, to Adlai Stevenson was "beyond question despite their public protestations of being committed to none of the presidential hopefuls."[3] According to one close observer, oilman Ed Pauley was pulling Ziffren's strings, and because Pauley supported former President Harry Truman's choice of Senator Symington, it was likely the others wouldn't get into the best seats. Pauley did more than any other local leader to bring the Democratic conclave to Los Angeles, by his financing the $350,000 to pay for the "Big Show" to be held at the Memorial Sports Arena. As predicted, haggling ensued over the distribution of 3500 seats between, among others, Chairman Butler, Ed Pauley, Los Angeles Mayor Poulson, Supervisor Kenneth Hahn, and Ziffren. Eventually, however, Ziffren put together a new host committee and both Mayor Poulson and Supervisor Frank G. Bonelli agreed to support it." Thus, hopefuls like John F. Kennedy and Hubert H. Humphrey sought Ziffren out, knowing that he would determine which delegations would be seated and who would be admitted to the galleries.

Perhaps prodded by Jesse Unruh, Governor Brown began to view Ziffren with distrust, and to regard him as a threat to his own control of the California convention delegation.[4] On the eve of the national convention, the rift between Brown and Ziffren threatened to tear the Democratic Party to pieces. Brown blamed Ziffren for failing to rouse the Democratic clubs to "pull out all the stops in the primary election," but Brown supporters assured him that "convention delegates who hold state jobs," countered Ziffren's influence. At some point Brown learned that Ziffren had tried to persuade Senator Kennedy to enter the California presidential primary in opposition to Brown's favorite-son candidacy. Therefore, just three weeks before the convention, Brown sent shock waves throughout the Party when he announced he was removing Ziffren as National Committeeman. In California, partisans from the northern and southern regions of the state alternated in filling the position, and factional loyalties often created hotly contested, intraparty battles. As titular head of the state party, the governor had overwhelming influence over the vote for National Committeemen and women among party members. As "cover" for his removal of Ziffren, Brown pointed to media reports linking Ziffren to Chicago mobsters. Ziffren was a close associate of Sidney Korshak, alleged to represent Chicago mafia interests in the Hollywood film industry. Both Korshak and Ziffren were protégés of Chicago Alderman Jacob Arvey, notorious for mob connections dating back to Al Capone.[5] Years later Brown said that he regretted his actions, even though his divisive manipulation brought Mosk in as a like-minded liberal and Kennedy man.[6] State chairman and Brown confident Eugene Wyman may have had something to do with it, as he was apparently worried about how Ziffren antagonized key supporters in Southern California.[7]

To replace Ziffren, Brown announced the selection of California Attorney General Stanley Mosk. Apparently, after considering several well-known Democrats, "the Governor induced Attorney General Stanley Mosk to submit to a draft." Party insiders knew that Mosk was "like Ziffren, a dedicated liberal with a strong popular following," who seemed "like the ideal candidate." And both were Jewish, so any inference religion played a role was moot. In fact, by this time, many felt that "Stanley was the undisputed Jewish political leader of California," and "many people considered him really one of the top Jewish figures in the nation."[8] One political publication observed that, "In only a few short years, Mosk has emerged as the best Attorney General in California history. He has put together a superb staff, has ventured into fields where few prosecutors have dared to enter. He has gone after the overworld of crime as well as the underworld. He has cracked down on price fixers, phony stock peddlers, the financier," who plays fast and loose with other people's money.[9] Mosk's unusual dual role, serving both as Attorney General and the Democratic Party's National Committeeman, boosted his growing public image as one who could work well with all of the party's warring factions, in spite of the controversial method by which he had won the committee post.[10]

Governor Brown was grateful for Mosk's help in unseating Ziffren, realizing that Ziffren had strong support within the California Democratic Council. At the Democratic convention in Los Angeles, Pat Brown told Mosk, "Stanley, I cannot thank you enough; if there is anything I can do for you, I will."[11]

Brown was more candid during an interview with an agent of the FBI who was gathering information on California political figures for FBI Director J. Edgar Hoover. The agent reported that Brown talked about the state party's national committeeman (blacked out, but obviously Ziffren) and how he "had been flushed down the river as being a power any longer in California Democratic politics." (Much later, Ziffren regained prominence as chair of the Los Angeles Olympic Organizing Committee, which sponsored the 1984 Summer Olympics.) Brown said that, "a number of people must have been tremendously surprised" that he came out in support of Mosk. Most of them didn't realize that, although "Mosk would not have been his personal choice," he was the only "acceptable" choice to the "Los Angeles bunch." Brown found himself "more or less ... forced into the situation in order to have a unified group." Brown felt guilty for speaking to the agent "like this, being a Roman Catholic," but "there were some powerful Jewish interests which were backing Mosk and which could not be ignored." He said he would like to get Mosk "back on the bench" and "out of the Attorney Generalship so that he could appoint his close friend and advisor Tom Lynch in his place. He said he felt that Mosk was not generally acceptable to the law enforcement crowd in California but didn't know what he could do about it except to try to push him upstairs."[12]

Mosk enjoyed his new role as National Committeeman, although he regretted losing the friendship of Paul Ziffren, who bitterly resented being dumped on the eve of the convention. But this was all part of the game, and Mosk himself had previously experienced the political duplicity of Ziffren. In 1949, Ziffren promised to assist Mosk in pursuing appointment as a federal judge. Mosk later learned that Ziffren was seeking the appointment for himself.

Pat Brown was not a serious candidate for president. He had no national following. He did have serious hopes he would be considered for the Vice Presidency, however. That would not be a likely prospect if the nomination went to Kennedy, since both were Catholic. If Brown could hold the powerful California delegation in a brokered convention, he might see his hopes realized. He couldn't and he didn't. The California delegation was badly split between supporters of Adlai Stevenson and supporters of John F. Kennedy. When Brown became convinced Kennedy would win the nomination, he ultimately supported Kennedy, but was then unable to deliver as many delegation votes for Kennedy as he hoped. Brown was embarrassed when the nomination demonstrations revealed a gallery packed for Stevenson. Paul Ziffren got the blame for that, although the Kennedys thereafter regarded Governor Pat Brown as a "shlemiel."[13] When the roll was called on the first ballot, after some confusion, Pat Brown announced 33½ votes for Kennedy, 30½ votes for Stevenson, and a handful of votes for Johnson and Symington. In the end, the only sizable bloc of convention votes that went for Stevenson came from California. Stanley Mosk was an enthusiastic Kennedy supporter, and worked within the delegation to round up more Kennedy support, but the split created a good deal of antagonism that needed smoothing over after Kennedy narrowly won a first ballot nomination at the convention.

In the 1960 presidential race between Nixon and Kennedy, California was a key battleground state, although it was Nixon's home turf. Not having a high opinion of Governor Brown, the Kennedy campaign staff looked to Mosk and Assembly Speaker Jess Unruh for guidance. Kennedy frequently visited California, and whenever he came, he was accompanied on the campaign trail by the state's National Committeeman Stanley Mosk. The Mosks held fundraisers for their candidate, and Stanley Mosk, always attractive to women, held his own in the presence of the handsome and charismatic Kennedy. One of Mosk's friends sent a note after one fundraiser, gushing, "It was a joy to see you and Mrs. Mosk at the Kennedy reception," then adding that his wife, "confided in me that she thought our Attorney General had a lot more personality than the honored guest!"[14] Stanley Mosk regarded his time with Kennedy as the most pleasant duty of his position as National Committeeman, and the two developed a warm friendship. Richard Mosk was an undergraduate at Stanford University during the 1960 campaign. When John F. Kennedy spoke at Stanford, Richard introduced himself, and Kennedy mentioned he would be seeing his dad later that week. When he was later introduced to Edna Mosk in Fresno, Kennedy mentioned seeing her son at Stanford earlier that week. Edna was duly impressed.

Stanley Mosk was enthralled watching John Kennedy work the political hustings. He accompanied Kennedy on a train trip from Oakland to Bakersfield, watching the candidate deliver whistle-stop speeches along the way. Rather than the same canned speech, Kennedy frequently extemporized, and had something new of substance in every speech. Between stops, local delegations would be welcomed on board, and Kennedy charmed and chatted with them until the next station. While they stopped in Fresno, it started to rain just as Kennedy began speaking. Assuming farmers liked rain, he said, "There you are, ladies and gentlemen. This is a great Democratic rain!" The crowd groaned, because the last thing they wanted at that point was rain. Their grapes were all spread out on the ground for drying into raisins.

Frequent visits by Kennedy staffers Larry O'Brien, Ken O'Donnell and Steve Smith led

As California's Democratic Party National Committeeman, Stanley Mosk escorted U.S. Senator Jack Kennedy on his presidential campaign speaking tours traveling either by car, as pictured together here, or by train for Kennedy's whistlestop tours throughout the Golden State (courtesy Richard Mosk).

Mosk to remark, "In fact, it seemed like a good part of the state of Massachusetts moved out here during that period." Edna Mosk also campaigned, touring the Central Valley with Ted Kennedy's wife Joan, John F. Kennedy's sister Pat Lawford, and actress Janet Leigh. They visited small towns and met with women's groups, and like their husbands, formed bonds of friendship.

Edna Mosk was heavily invested in her husband's political fortunes. She was a very successful Los Angeles Westside real estate broker, and earned twice as much, or more, than her husband through her real estate commissions. She began as a partner with Betty Reddin, wife of future LAPD Chief Tom Reddin, then joined the firm of Douglas Adamson and Jack Hupp, who turned over a million dollars a week in high end residential real estate for a clientele of Hollywood celebrities. Edna's real talents emerged as a major fundraiser for the Democratic Party. Her ability to extract donations left no arm

During U.S. Senator John F. Kennedy's presidential campaign, the Kennedy entourage came to rely upon the talent of California's Democratic National Committeeman Stanley Mosk, who is seen here in 1960 standing between Kennedy brothers Robert and Ted, and who remarked of their visits that it seemed like a good part of the state of Massachusetts moved to the Golden State (courtesy Richard Mosk).

unbroken in Beverly Hills,[15] and her indefatigable energy was legendary. Speechwriter Tom McDonald said Edna's was the first voice he heard in the morning, and the last one he heard at night.[16] She was engaged, proactive, and relentlessly devoted to the job of promoting her husband. As she nurtured the important contacts Stanley was exposed to as national committeeman, Edna was poised to launch her husband to new political heights.

Mosk had the opportunity to discuss local politics with Kennedy, and brief him on issues of concern to California. One issue of particular concern to Mosk at the time was the growing problem of narcotics. Then, as now, California law enforcement was greatly concerned with the growth of illicit drug trafficking, and the misuse of prescription drugs.

Mosk openly cited the need for increased control of Percodan, stressing that the drug was creating a new class of addicts composed of otherwise honest, not criminally inclined persons. The arrest records for Percodan violations for the first nine months of 1961 was 50 per cent higher than violations involving all other licit narcotics combined. At the specific request of Governor Brown and Attorney General Mosk, and with the approval of the California Medical Association, Senator Edwin J. Regan introduced a bill which would have put oxycodone-containing drugs such as Percodan back on the list of drugs requiring triplicate prescriptions. A marathon of discussion then began among legislators. It continued on and off over a period of five months. The argument boiled down to an issue of conservative management of a dangerous drug versus matters of convenience, politics and finance. The bill passed the Senate but was killed in the Assembly Criminal Procedure Committee.[17]

In a rather clumsy political move, Mosk attempted to parlay law enforcement concern with drug regulation into a political advantage for the Kennedy campaign. Using the letterhead of the Attorney General's office, Mosk mailed a letter to state legislators and candidates to call attention to Kennedy's commitment to hold a White House conference on narcotics. The letter challenged Republican presidential candidate Richard M. Nixon to also commit to such a meeting, despite the fact that "the Eisenhower-Nixon administration has ignored a congressional resolution adopted unanimously on April 4, 1960," calling for a high level conference on illegal drugs. Mosk also asserted that, "while Kennedy is for stricter narcotic control, Vice President Nixon is not." In response, the state Republican national committee charged the Attorney General with "flagrant misuse of his office and public funds," and speculated that the postage for the letters had also been financed by public funds. Complaining that the Attorney General was "trying to serve two masters—the State of California and the Democratic Party," Mosk was asked to repay any misused funds and "to apologize publicly for the disgrace he has brought upon his office." In his

When Stanley Mosk befriended Jack Kennedy, he also socialized with the world famous 1960s "Rat Pack" which included Frank Sinatra, at left, and Dean Martin, far right. Second from right is Dodger baseball star Sandy Koufax (courtesy Richard Mosk).

defense, Mosk explained that the subjects of law enforcement and narcotics are non-partisan and non-political. Regarding the Congressional resolution, he asserted, "the 50 attorneys general of the United States" also passed a similar resolution in July of 1960. He said he felt it was his duty "to advise our legislators and candidates ... that one of the candidates for President had agreed to call such a conference and that I hoped the other would do so, too. This is a proper law enforcement activity." Furthermore, he added, the complaint involved "a total of 240 letters mailed at a cost of $9.00."[18]

Kennedy thought a national conference on narcotics was a good idea, and in 1962 he convened the first White House Conference on Narcotics and Drug Abuse. Mosk was invited to address the conference. This, in turn, led to the establishment of the president's Advisory Commission on Narcotics and Dangerous Drugs, chaired by E. Barrett Prettyman, Jr. The final report of the Prettyman Commission was on President Kennedy's desk in November of 1963. It recommended a significant restructuring of the federal response to drug abuse, much of which was subsequently enacted.

Ultimately, the California outcome was a disappointment for Kennedy. In the closest election up to that time, the contest was settled by absentee ballots, and Nixon carried California by only 13,150 votes out of the six and half million votes cast. The outcome of a very close election was determined in favor of Kennedy by the Illinois votes, where Kennedy's lead was only 6,397 votes, many coming from the cemeteries of Cook County.

President John F. Kennedy's inauguration in January 1961 was an historic event. Stanley and Edna Mosk proudly watched the inaugural parade in 26-degree weather, and then hosted a gala celebration in the Congressional Room of D.C.'s Statler Hotel. Newspapers described how Attorney General and Mrs. Stanley Mosk "provided warmth and good cheer for more than 500 friends from the Golden State," including most of the president's California appointees and several newly appointed cabinet members. Governor and Mrs. Pat Brown joined the festivities after leading the California delegation in the parade. Frank Sinatra served as program director for the party. He invited Sir Laurence Olivier, who cancelled that night's Broadway performance of *Becket* for the occasion, to recite a nineteenth century House of Commons oration praising the American presidency. When President Kennedy's staff and Olivier simultaneously realized that the oration was actually an attack on the British monarchy, the knighted actor instead read an unoffending passage from *Spartacus*.[19]

Just after President Kennedy's inauguration, the FBI noted that because Stanley Mosk had been very active in the recent presidential campaign he was "evidently aiming" for an appointment to the Ninth Circuit Court of Appeals as an interim position until he could be appointed to the next opening on the United States Supreme Court. The possibility of an appointment was very real, but it was not to be. California Supreme Court Justice Jesse Carter and Senator Henry M. "Scoop" Jackson endorsed Mosk for the Ninth Circuit post. By February 1, however, Bobby Kennedy acknowledged that Mosk was staying in his present position and continuing to work with Justice Carter on the upcoming conference on narcotics. Governor Brown told Mosk that he was happy that he turned the position down.[20]

After President Kennedy's appointment of his brother Robert to serve as Attorney General, Stanley Mosk dealt primarily with "Bobby" Kennedy, and formed a close relationship with him as well. As Mosk recalled, "I found I could call Attorney General Bobby Kennedy, make an appointment, and be back there and discuss problems without any difficulty any time I wanted to. I did frequently on criminal problems and that sort of thing."[21] One inquiry by Mosk to the U.S. Attorney General perhaps reflected Mosk's efforts to protect himself from the repeated accusations about his "communist tendencies." A Spanish language Mexican publication *Siempre!,* which appealed to Mexico's educated urban middle class, students, and intellectuals, extolled the promise of the progressive traditions of Mexican revolutionary nationalism, especially in regard to Mexico's relationship with the United States. Articles denounced Cold War geopolitical rivalries, defended the goals of sovereignty for Cuban revolutionaries, and asserted Mexico's role of leadership in Latin America and the Third World. Largely because of its anti–U.S. posture, the magazine and vendors who sold it came under attack by conservative Mexicans and the Catholic Church. Apparently, in 1963, Attorney General Mosk petitioned U.S. Attorney General Robert Kennedy to study "the danger represented [by *Siempre!*] for the well-being of the United States," arguing that it was "a magazine that praises the Cuban Revolution, criticizes the government of the United States and mocks [the U.S.] President."[22] Robert Kennedy answered Mosk regarding the "unsolicited Communist political propaganda, *Politica* and *Siempra*," indicating that the Mexican government "seeks not to antagonize intellectual left groups."[23] Mosk also discussed neo–Nazi agitation with Bobby who explained that the U.S. Justice Department could not stop George Lincoln Rockwell's Nazi Party activities, but that local enforcement was the key to deal with it if it was designated as a subversive organization.[24]

Among the other topics Mosk discussed was Bobby Kennedy's war on organized crime, and the impact of organized crime in California. For years, Mosk proudly boasted that organized crime did not have any sort of foothold in California. J. Edgar Hoover had been a skeptic as well, but Bobby Kennedy was tenacious in directing federal law enforcement efforts against organized crime. When the FBI succeeded in turning Joe Velachi into an informant, Mosk asked Bobby to share with him the names of any Californians identified by Velachi as part of the mob. Mosk retrieved the list and passed it on to local law enforcement, learning that "most of the names took them by surprise." Law enforcement was able to "keep an eye on these people, to make sure they weren't letting the Mafia get any foothold in California." Ironically, what Stanley Mosk did not know at the time was that local law enforcement and the FBI were keeping an eye on him.

Another topic of discussion with the Kennedy's was Mosk's political future. Mosk had declined an opportunity to serve in JFK's administration, either as General Counsel for the Defense Department or the FCC. He thought his prospects for political advancement could best be cultivated by remaining in California. One journalist suggested that the "most important accomplishment" of President Kennedy's trips to California was "the chance to meet and appraise" Attorney General Mosk, who, in the event Bobby Kennedy moved out of the U.S. Attorney General spot, could succeed him.[25]

Even before JFK's assassination in Dallas, Bobby Kennedy had urged Stanley Mosk to make a run for the Senate. The Kennedys' confidence in Mosk's chances was astute in its timing. Republican Thomas Kuchel and Democrat Clair Engle represented California in the U.S. Senate. Kuchel was a progressive Republican, first appointed by Governor Earl Warren in 1952 to replace Richard Nixon in the Senate after Nixon's election as vice president. Kuchel continued the Warren tradition of bipartisanship, refusing to endorse Republican candidates he regarded as "too far to the right." In this vein, Kuchel and Mosk were of like mind. At one point, Senator Kuchel wrote to Mosk, "Extremists do pose a threat to our country and to both our political parties. They do their work in shadows and cannot stand the light of day."[26] The radical right held tight to its obsessive belief that Mosk was at the helm of an encroaching communist conspiracy. Mosk and his assistants maneuvered around the tired drone of the anti-communist crusade, which continued long after the more rabid brand of McCarthyism subsided, but they also monitored a growth in organized terrorist groups, and private armies like the "minutemen.." In a speech before the California Democratic Council (CDC), Mosk was outspoken about his unequivocal opposition to such vehicles of hate, inspiring news stories such as, "Private Army Groups Need State Control."[27] He demanded, "the outlawing of private armies on a special legislative session call,"[28] and he continued to aggressively attack radical right-wing groups by calling for legislation to control the mail-order sale of firearms and the outlawing of paramilitary groups. Not surprisingly, such pronouncements inspired the Glendale Young Republicans to pass a resolution demanding the resignation of the Attorney General. They called upon the California legislature to conduct a thorough investigation of what they believed constituted "a complete disregard for the basic concepts of a free society and an incompetence seldom displayed by a public official."[29]

Mosk had been urged to run against Senator Kuchel in 1962, but wisely declined. Kuchel was overwhelmingly reelected to his second term in 1962, defeating Los Angeles County's State Senator Richard Richards. Stanley Mosk instead mounted a vigorous re-election campaign in 1962.

Governor Pat Brown was facing a formidable opponent in his race for reelection. Former Vice President Richard Nixon returned to California to orchestrate a political "comeback" after losing the presidency to John F. Kennedy, and won the Republican nomination for California's governorship. Along with opposition from the far right, Nixon's campaign was clouded by public suspicion about his apparent ambivalence about being California's governor because he viewed it as a "stepping-stone" to a higher office. Despite a strong initial lead in the polls, Nixon lost to Brown by nearly 300,000 votes, 52 percent to 47 percent. In an impromptu concession speech the morning after the election, Nixon blamed the media for favoring his opponent, and uttered the now famous words, "You won't have Nixon to kick around anymore because, gentlemen, this is my last press conference."

Attorney General Mosk easily won reelection in 1962, over his opponent Judge Tom Coakley of Mariposa County. Judge Coakley had served as a Deputy Attorney General under Earl Warren, who later appointed him to the bench. Coakley worked his way through college and law school as the leader of the hotel band at the renowned Palace Hotel in San Francisco. Although he was an able judge and lawyer, he was no match for Stanley Mosk. In August of 1962, Stanley Mosk

Former President Harry Truman surprised Stanley Mosk at Mosk's September 1962 fiftieth birthday celebration held as a fundraiser in the ballroom of San Francisco's chic Fairmont Hotel. Mosk later recalled, "It was a delightful evening I must say. Truman was in rare form and we just packed the Fairmont at $100.00 a head" (courtesy Richard Mosk).

was feted for his twenty-five years of "Distinguished Public Service," with a tribute dinner at the Beverly Hilton Hotel. While President Kennedy's recent visit to Los Angeles included a stay at the same hotel, his schedule prevented him from attending. The program for the event, however, included his personal tribute to Mosk: "Stanley Mosk has fully earned the high regard which this dinner symbolizes through the energy and good judgment which he has shown both as a public official and as a leader of the Democratic Party."[30] The 1500 guests dancing to Jerry Rosen's music included entertainers Phil Silvers, Polly Bergen, Sammy Khan, George Jessel, and Buddy Hackett. The host committee included many of the main organizers for his 1958 run for Attorney General. The actual kick off to Mosk's reelection campaign coincided with his fiftieth birthday, celebrated at a huge dinner at the luxurious Fairmont Hotel in San Francisco. The guest of honor was former President Harry S Truman.[31] Richard Mosk was sent to the airport to pick him up in his Plymouth, and recalls Truman was "all by himself, with no security." Over one thousand guests paid $100 a plate, giving Mosk an insurmountable fund-raising advantage for the campaign. When the votes were finally counted, Mosk again outpolled Governor Brown, beating Coakley by a margin of 56 percent to 44 percent. Impressed by his election victory, the Kennedys continued to press Mosk to seek a Senate seat. Stanley Mosk certainly did not envision his political career ending with the job of Attorney General of California. After his reelection, he more confidently believed just as Earl Warren and Pat Brown had before him, he would go directly from the Attorney General's office to the governor's mansion; or, he could move directly onto the national stage as U.S. Senator Stanley Mosk (D. Calif.).

Throughout his years as Attorney General, Mosk regularly informed Governor Brown about his activities and provided him copies of speeches that always heralded the achievements of Brown's administration. The governor passed on constituent letters more appropriate to the Attorney General's office, most of which were legitimate state matters, but sometimes not. Both men were obligated politically to do a bit of public relations on the other's behalf, and they did so with good humor. The two men boosted each other's careers, such as when Pat Brown was elected as Vice Chair of the Democratic National Committee in 1963 after Stanley Mosk nominated him for the post.[32] Both Mosk and Governor Brown received scores of anti–Semitic diatribes attacking Mosk's religion as a sign of some horrible impending doom. Mosk's frequent, outspoken views about the constitutional separation of church and state was a particular subject for obsessive letter writers. Unlike the 1958 campaign, in which his Jewish roots were barely mentioned, Mosk's high profile attacks on

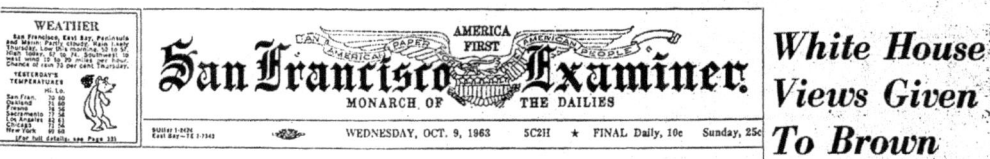

Just six weeks before President John F. Kennedy's tragic death, this October 6, 1963, *Los Angeles Times* banner headline announced "JFK for Mosk if Engle Out" which reflected Stanley Mosk's likely success over other potential candidates eager to replace the terminally ill incumbent, U.S. Senator Claire Engle (Huntington Library).

the extreme right provoked attacks heavily tinged with anti–Semitism in 1962. Mosk spoke to the national convention of the Council of Jewish Federations, urging the nation's Jews to take a stand against what he described as a "rapidly gaining drive on the part of significant numbers in our country who feel that they have the right to use the instrumentalities of the state to press home their religious points of view."[33] One hysterical letter writer beseeched Governor Brown to "stop this gang of debasers of our culture and morals," because our "Christian nation" is "being shoved to the ground by this ever grasping race," and "if the jews [sic] don't like it why don't they go over to Palestine which they grabbed from the Arabs and try to change the Moslems," but "this is what you get by appointing one of their race."[34] Noting the error of her assertion, Brown responded, "I might point out that Attorney General Mosk was elected to his position-not appointed by me. He is an independent constitutional officer responsible for writing his own opinions and free to make any comments, public or private, that he pleases." He added, "I have found him to be a splendid Attorney General."[35]

Another letter to Governor Brown from a Mr. Hill of the Veterans of Foreign Wars complained that Mosk had written a letter in defense of Carey McWilliams, labeling his detractors "well known in California as utterly irresponsible persons, who back in the 1930's labeled many patriotic California citizens as communists."[36] Mr. Hill found Mosk's explanation so contrary to a Senate report revealing "the [communist] affiliations of McWilliams," that it bothered him that the Attorney General "is not aware of the contents," or if he was, "he did not mention" it, along with his neglect to answer any questions put to him by "our District Commander." The obvious implication was that Mosk was covering something up, or more likely was a fellow traveler. Brown replied that Mosk's letter seems to "speak for itself," and as a constitutional officer, elected by the people, any further elaboration would have to come from Mosk himself.[37]

In 1963, it began to appear as though a Senate seat would soon be up for grabs. Senator Clair Engle was elected to succeed William F. Knowland in the 1958 Democratic sweep after the "big switch." Engle had previously served six terms in Congress, representing California's 2nd Congressional District. Tragically, in 1963 he was stricken with brain cancer. During the year it took him to die, his wife had stubbornly refused to consider letting him resign, insisting that he would be a candidate for another term in 1964.

The Kennedy administration was pressuring Governor Brown to appoint a replacement, and on October 9, 1963, six weeks before President Kennedy's assassination, a headline in the *San Francisco Examiner* announced, "JFK FOR MOSK IF ENGLE OUT."[38] The president had communicated his choice directly to Governor Brown. In November, Mosk received an invitation to attend a state dinner at the White House. He had to decline because of a long-planned trip to Japan with his wife Edna and Morton and Pauline Phillips. (Pauline Phillips wrote the syndicated "Dear Abby" advice column under the pen name Abigail Van Buren). They were in Japan when the news reached them that President Kennedy had been assassinated in Dallas on November 22, 1963.

Chapter 10

"To Embarrass Them or Pressure Them Sometime in the Future"

Chief Justice Earl Warren agreed to head up the Commission appointed to investigate the assassination of President Kennedy, which then became known as the Warren Commission. Richard Mosk was fresh out of Harvard Law School when Warren hired him as a staff attorney for the Commission. Over the years, Stanley Mosk and his family had grown close to the Warrens. Each New Year's, they attended the Pasadena Rose Bowl game together. As their friendship grew, Mosk regretted his vigorous opposition to Warren which had been inspired by his loyalty to Governor Olson. "As Warren developed into a great Chief Justice, we became good friends and our families became close, and I had an opportunity to apologize for every vote I cast against him."[1]

Throughout this period, the accolades kept coming, boosting Mosk's confidence. In January 1964, California Assemblyman Nicholas Petris wrote to Mosk, "Aristotle said, in POLITICS I, 'At his best man is the noblest of all animals; separated from law and justice, he is the worst.' Stanley Mosk, 'through his actions, has shown us man at his best.'"[2] The same month, Mosk was presented with an award from the Harry R. Sheppard Research Fellowship Fund. Carley V. Porter wrote to Mosk that he was being recognized for his work on behalf of consumer protection and water law, which Porter considered "a field in which you and I have for so long had a primary interest."[3]

It wasn't surprising that soon after, a Field poll among Democratic voters showed Mosk with a substantial lead as a potential candidate for the U.S. senate. Mosk had 54 percent, Cranston 17 percent, Unruh 11 percent, and undecided 18 percent. This put Governor Pat Brown in a very awkward position because he had already promised his support to Alan Cranston, and Cranston was absolutely determined to enter the race. The maneuvering among partisans was especially disquieting because the dying Clair Engle had not withdrawn from the race. Mosk continued to converse with the ailing senator, and after one conversation, he announced that he himself was not yet ready to declare one way or the other. He advised those encouraging him to run "to keep your powder dry." His underlying concern was that if Engle attended the upcoming CDC convention as the incumbent, he would likely reaffirm his own candidacy. Mosk sympathetically counseled that because this would be the senator's first foray into public since his surgery, to detract from this homecoming would be inappropriate.

Mosk's sensitivity was not self-interested strategizing. By June of 1964, Engle was unable to even speak, indicating his affirmative vote to close debate on the Civil Rights Act of 1964 by pointing to his eye. Nevertheless, Mrs. Engle felt that the "rats" were "leaving what they considered a sinking ship," but Mosk, Unruh, and Carmen Warschaw were among the few who stayed in close touch with the ailing senator. She resented how the others treated her husband, even though Engle went to the office everyday. "They could not wait ... it was indecent haste," she said. To her, the circling swarm was "so very greedy for the power in their own hands," especially at a time when Senator Engle was still physically able and believed he would "become more able" in the days ahead.

Outspoken opponents of the CDC's endorsement policy began to surface once again, and Governor Brown had to balance these competing factions within and outside of the CDC. He also had to handle an increasingly hostile relationship with Speaker Jesse Unruh and his supporters. Anticipating a brawl for the senate primary, Governor Brown told the press that he promised to remain neutral if both Cranston and Mosk sought the nomination. He said both were "fine men," that he liked "very, very much, and I think either one of them could make a great U.S. Senator."[4] Mosk's loyalties had so far bridged the Unruh and the Brown camps, but he soon found himself caught between the increasingly volatile warring factions.

In the skirmishing before the CDC convention in February 1964, Mosk and Cranston were already trading barbs. Mosk suggested that Cranston was exploiting the controller's office, by taxing his volunteer staff of estate appraisers to finance his campaign. Cranston accused Mosk of dredging up old news for political purposes. Although the same story had previously been reported, Cranston accused Mosk of "undignified conduct" and charged that his "ambitions are showing."[5] The Governor suggested that the Attorney General was "getting a little bit enthusiastic a little early in the campaign."[6] Cranston won the endorsement of the CDC, after an emotional convention full of tears for the departing Engle. Congressman James Roosevelt, still another contender for a Senate seat, then announced his withdrawal and endorsed Cranston. Mosk regarded this as traitorous, since he had always strongly supported Roosevelt in his races for governor and Congress.

Cranston's controversy didn't go away. In May, Mosk supporters were still calling for the Attorney General to investigate well-publicized charges made in the State Senate that Cranston forced his tax appraisers to contribute to his senate campaign. At least one other candidate for the U.S. Senate, George McLain agreed.[7] *The Long Beach Telegram*, a Mosk supporter, issued a challenge to the CDC, saying its members represented less than two per cent of the State's registered Democrats. The paper said it would donate $5000 to any charity of Mr. Cranston's choice if "he can prove to the satisfaction of the Attorney General's office that neither he nor his solicitors have accepted or requested substantial 'donations' from Inheritance Tax Appraisers appointed by him." The paper offered another $5000 if the CDC could prove it had a paid membership of 70,000 at the time it claimed these numbers.[8]

Governor Brown believed a divisive and expensive Senate primary fight in California would jeopardize the party's chances in the November general elections, and even affect Lyndon Johnson's hopes to carry California. Behind the scenes, Brown decided he had to convince Stanley Mosk not to announce his candidacy. Mosk was aware that Brown favored Cranston, and that his promise of neutrality could not be trusted. First, the governor sought to cut off Mosk's access to the campaign funds he would need to make the race. Mosk began receiving telephone calls from past supporters, indicating that the governor had twisted their arms and they would not be in a position to assist him to run against Cranston. Mosk remained confident he could raise the necessary campaign chest. He still had funds left over from his 1962 reelection campaign, and he already had pledges totaling $628,610. He was spending funds to reserve television and radio time and line up billboard space. He told reporters he planned to formally announce his decision in a pre-recorded taped press conference for release on Tuesday, March 4, 1964. Waiting until the last possible moment to publicly state his intentions, he directed his speechwriter Tom McDonald to prepare two speeches—one to enter, and the other to forego the race. A television crew was scheduled to tape on Monday, March 3, so Mosk's announcement could be released as a newsreel on the fourth.[9]

The *Los Angeles Times* reported that Mosk was counted as the "sure-fire candidate for the Senate seat" all the way up until Monday afternoon. Sunday night Jess Unruh met with Frank Burns, Vince Thorpe, and Tom McDonald to discuss details of the planned primary campaign. McDonald would continue as Mosk's principal speechwriter for the campaign. Burns, a Democratic activist, and Thorpe, an Assistant Attorney General in Mosk's Antitrust and Consumer Fraud division, were campaign volunteers. Recruitment of a "top-flight campaign staff" had begun, and Charlie O'Brien, Mosk's Chief Deputy in the Attorney General's office, was set to be his commander in chief.[10] The flurry of activity accelerated; the troops were readied to build upon the momentum generated by the upcoming press conference.

Suddenly, Governor Pat Brown pulled out the "smoking gun": a file of surveillance reports and photographs documenting that the Attorney General had been leading a "double life." The official report of the Los Angeles Police Department surveillance of Stanley Mosk began in December 1958, when, one month before taking office as Attorney General, his 1957 De Soto was observed parked at the West Hollywood home of a convicted bookmaker.[11] Mosk's was not the only car seen parked in front of the house. When the police tracked the license plates of the other cars, they came up with a rogue's list of individuals who had been convicted as major marijuana suppliers, heroin peddlers, burglars, pimps, prostitutes, forgers, and smugglers, along with "sex degenerates" and "advocates of the Communist Conspiracy." The police characterized the gathering as a "freak party." What was the newly elected Attorney General of California doing partying with the low-life of Los Angeles?

The answer to this question lies buried in a mix of humanity known as the "counterculture" of Los Angeles. In the late 1950's and early 1960's, the once glamorous Sunset Strip, the stretch of unincorporated land that passes through West Hollywood, became a favorite gathering spot for hippies, musicians and their groupies, and Hollywood hangers-on. The scene naturally attracted drug dealers, pimps, and prostitutes as well. It was eclectic and it was exciting, a magnet for tourists and locals looking for "action." A number of the era's major rock bands emerged from this milieu, and the bars and nightclubs were popular watering holes for celebrities on the prowl. Stanley Mosk was apparently attracted by the excitement of the Sunset Strip counterculture, but the main attraction soon became a beautiful young woman. Her name was Sabrina Jourdan. She was then twenty years old. The LAPD report tells us her husband, "by whom she has two children," was sentenced to state prison for 6 months to 10 years, "with an extensive record for narcotics and burglary from 1955 to 1966." Her sister was a "forger, narcotic smuggler and fraud expert," while her roommate was on parole and was a "prostitute, forger, and admitted user of cocaine," who according to the report, "states she has sniffed cocaine with Stanley Mosk." Apparently when it came to informants, the LAPD believed that being a prostitute, forger and cocaine user enhanced one's credibility.

Before Brown's surreptitious use of his knowledge about Mosk's affair, Stanley Mosk's connection to Sabrina Jourdan was documented by a letter on his official letterhead, addressed to the Los Angeles Police Commission on November 19, 1962. The Attorney General encouraged the Commissioners to issue an entertainment permit for Sabrina Jourdan to operate a Sunset Strip nightclub known as "Mr. Kon Ton's," assuring them it would be a "fine, clean establishment" and a "credit to the community." An FBI informant reported that Mosk's assistance to Sabrina's plans for a Sunset Strip Club went far beyond a letter. The informant told FBI Agents the application for a liquor license by "a very attractive dark-skinned woman" had been refused, perhaps because the application did not include fingerprints for her husband. The woman came in again, this time with "a negro," whose fingerprints were taken, and the application was denied again when he was found to have prior convictions. She appeared a third time, but now as a divorcee and applied for the license under her own name. The license was denied again until she could provide proof she had divorced her husband. Following the woman's fruitless efforts, according to the FBI source, Attorney General Stanley Mosk called, and for "thirty minutes berated" the unnamed person responsible for rejecting the license. Mosk also "charged" the individual "with discriminating against the colored race." The informant described how because of Mosk's subsequent pressure the license was finally granted. The FBI Report concluded by noting the initiation of an undercover investigation to "trace the ten-thousand dollars used by the woman in the purchase of the bar." Apparently whatever bank they contacted refused to furnish account information. At some point the Internal Affairs Unit of the LAPD became interested in the matter and conducted surveillance of the female on several occasions. Mr. Kon Ton's opened at 7180 Sunset Blvd., a site now occupied by the Seventh Veil Strip Club. Sabrina Jourdan and Irene Sampson became co-owners of "Mr. Kon Ton's," and Sabrina worked there nightly as a hostess. Sampson had dinner with Mosk on a number of occasions, and although Mosk was allegedly observed to drink heavily, "he never appeared to be drunk." One regular at the establishment had no idea that Mosk had any legal connection with the restaurant, but did notice how when bills were due and the waiters had not been paid, Stanley Mosk would visit "and suddenly there was enough money to pay the bills and the help."[12] One of the regulars later described the place as a "hang-out" for the "rounders"; "the hookers and the pimps and the thieves," who were according to some, "The scum of the earth, really." Tom McDonald described it as "a place where Mosk and all the boys could go to relax and mingle."[13] Mr. Kon Ton's became one of many nightspots promoting "Impact Music" in advertisements in the *Los Angeles Times*. While Johnny Mathis was appearing at the Ambassador Hotel's Cocoanut Grove, Liberace's Orchestra at the Hollywood Roosevelt Hotel's Cinegrill, and folk singers performing at the Ash Grove, Mr. Kon Ton's was showcasing jazz performers, such as musicians Mike Melvoin and Leroy Vinegar, who accompanied singers like Lorez Alexandria and David Allen.[14] In January 1963, Attorney General Mosk was observed entering the club in the company of Sam Yorty, then the mayor of Los Angeles.

Neither Mosk nor Sabrina made much of an effort to conceal their relationship. She would introduce him to her friends as "Stanley" or as "Stanley Mosk." On occasion, he served as co-host and bartender at her parties. "When people came in, she would say 'This is Stanley. What would you like to drink? Stanley will make it for you.'"[15] Some of her friends were known to boast of their acquaintance with the Attorney General.

LAPD intelligence officers, who were well known for their interest in the comings and goings of elected officials, took a keen interest in the relationship between Stanley Mosk and Sabrina Jourdan. On July 15, 1963, Stanley Mosk flew from Los Angeles to Mexico City, to participate in a drug law enforcement conference arranged by the Kennedy administration. The LAPD Intelligence File reports that Mosk met Sabrina at the airport, and once on the plane she was upgraded from tourist to first class to join him on the flight. The file also contained photos taken of the couple through a hotel window, although there was no explanation of who took the photos or why. The most plausible explanation is that one or more LAPD operatives boarded the plane and conducted photo surveillance of the couple during the trip, but Mosk later speculated it was someone closer to home. The photos have disappeared, but several who saw them describe them as depicting Sabrina disrobing in Stanley's presence.[16] The photos became the "smoking gun" used to derail the Attorney General's political ambitions.

The FBI had also kept a close eye on Stanley Mosk since his public career first gained momentum during the 1940s. Unlike the narrower concerns with criminal associations reflected in the LAPD intelligence gathering throughout Mosk's career, the FBI was concerned with his political ideas and connections to leftist groups and communist agitators. This reflected the obsession of J. Edgar Hoover with the "communist menace." The FBI regularly resorted to office burglaries, illegal wiretaps, and mail intercepts in its quest to "gather intelligence." During the 1960's, no one was immune, including the president of the United States, Dr. Martin Luther King, Jr., and other civil rights leaders.[17] Mosk's successful election as the state's Attorney General aroused even more concern among the Bureau's agents, because they came to view him as "a political and personal opportunist and therefore," they "could not trust him."[18] Sabrina Jourdan only confirmed their views of Mosk's character, but it still left them frustrated in their search for official misconduct with which to go after Mosk. They continued to follow his activities, and in December 1963, they noted both Stanley Mosk and Sabrina Jourdan inquired about purchasing a Pontiac and that he advised her about purchasing "her car." Later, when she made her choice for a 1964 Pontiac Le Mans convertible, the down payment was paid in three installments of traveler's checks of 250.00 each, signed by Stanley Mosk. At some point, he called the dealer and "appeared quite upset at the tactics used" to boost the price of the auto and hinted that he felt the dealership should be investigated because of their shady business dealings."[19] Almost two years later, and over a year after Mosk was seated as a Justice on the California Supreme Court, the FBI noted that after Sabrina had been delinquent in a few of her car payments, she was now current because Stanley Mosk had covered the delinquent amount.[20]

In November 1964, just two months after Stanley Mosk took his seat on the high court, a cocktail party hosted by Miss Sabrina Jourdan was held to celebrate the opening of the new Sabrina Gallery on La Cienaga Boulevard, where L.A.'s high end antique and designer shops and art galleries attracted Beverly Hills patrons and Hollywood personalities. Among those slated to attend the first local exhibition of the work of artist Don Weygandt, were Messrs. and Mmes. Freddie Fields, Barron Hilton, Steve Allen, Paul Caruso, Harry Karl, and Eddie Feldman.[21]

The FBI interviewed Sabrina Jourdan in October of 1965. She admitted knowing Mosk and being in Mexico City in 1962 during the time he was there, but denied traveling with him or staying at the same hotel. She said Mosk had been to her residence attending parties she hosted, and not with Mrs. Mosk. According to a decoded copy of a telegram noted in the FBI files, Stanley Mosk admitted the affair with Sabrina and believed a man named Lee Ettelson had photographed the couple at the Los Angeles airport as they boarded a Pan American flight."[22] Ettelson, a former editor of the *San Francisco Examiner*, had been appointed Deputy Director of the Department of Motor Vehicles by Governor Pat Brown.

By all accounts, the relationship between Stanley Mosk and Sabrina Jourdan was a warm and affectionate one, which lasted nearly a decade. Nevertheless, in reports filled with hyperbole, the FBI made note that Mosk "allegedly" was "playing around with a number of women," and according to one subject interviewed who supposedly had visited a location on a number of occasions, Mosk was found to be smoking pot. In fact, echoing the testimony of individuals associated with Sabrina Jourdan, the FBI subject said, "she would guarantee that he, Justice Mosk, would be found smoking pot." Another entry says that an informant "recently learned Mosk has a girl friend named "Phyllis" of Hollywood, California."[23] The public exposure of a prominent political figure carrying on a clandestine affair is now commonplace, but in the 1960's the media still respected the privacy of elected officials, and looked the other way when rumors of sexual dalliances circulated. This extended to most elected officials in Sacramento and other state houses, and even to presidents of United States. The clandestine dalliances of President John F. Kennedy with Marilyn Monroe and Judith Exner are just the most sensational examples. Stanley Mosk evidently felt confident that his relationship, although longer in duration than most, would remain a private matter, and the "newspaper boys" who were his friends and confidants would keep it that way. What made his affair different, however, were the alleged connections between his lover and the seedy underworld of Los Angeles. From the perspective of police intelligence officers, politicians who consorted with criminals were vulnerable to bribery and corruption. Stanley Mosk had made the connection himself in campaigning to recall Mayor Shaw during the 1930's.

Stanley Mosk as Attorney General and later as a Justice of the California Supreme Court, was a bold defender of the constitutional right of privacy, and a longstanding foe of intrusive and illegal police surveillance. Whether his legal and judicial views on these issues emanated from having himself been a victim of police surveillance makes for interesting speculation. It has even been suggested that Mosk should not have participated in Supreme Court decisions dealing with criminal due process, libel and privacy, drug use, obscenity, prostitution and related matters, at the same time he was continuing his clandestine affair.[24] But long before he met Sabrina, Mosk was an advocate for the protection of due process and the right of privacy . The double life he led for so many years is an important window into a full understanding of the man. By viewing what is known about the personal and sexual life of Stanley Mosk within the context of its historical, sociological, and cultural setting, a more nuanced and complex hypothesis emerges about the double life he lived.

Stanley Mosk certainly had a romantic side, which he made no effort to conceal. He was very attractive to women, who frequently described him as "charming." He kept himself physically fit with frequent games of tennis, and although somewhat shy at first, was a witty and thoughtful conversationalist. Despite his judicial and political experience, he may have been somewhat naïve in viewing romantic dalliance as unrelated to his official duties. He was also a partner in a marriage that locked two very ambitious people together into a powerful political alliance, but may not have offered much intimacy for either partner.

The affair continued even after Mosk's appointment to the California Supreme Court on September 1, 1964. Entries in the intelligence file that tracked surveillance of Sabrina Jourdan through 1964 reported observation of Justice Mosk's automobile parked in her driveway on October 18 and November 27, and that between those dates she made eight phone calls to the Court. On August 30, 1965, her car was pulled over by customs agents at the Mexican border and a companion was arrested. A search of Jourdan's purse revealed credit cards belonging to Justice Mosk and service-station credit card slips signed "Mrs. Stanley Mosk." She told customs agents she was not Mosk's wife, but admitted signing the credit card slips, insisting Mosk had loaned her the cards. The agents actually called Justice

Mosk at the state Supreme Court in San Francisco to confirm what she said, and he told them Jourdan had the cards with his consent, and asked them to mail them to him in San Francisco. This discovery led the LAPD to intensify its investigation, and during the following year, numerous phone calls and sightings of Mosk and Jourdan together were noted, as well as at total of $6,580 in checks to Jourdan written by Justice Mosk in 1966. In April of 1966, Jourdan's purse was found behind the Playboy Club on the Sunset Strip, and was turned over to LAPD. Once again, Justice Mosk's credit cards turned up, and again he requested they be returned to him by mail.[25]

Some who knew Edna Mosk simply assumed she must have known about the affair; others declared that she had lived with knowledge of it day in and day out. Not only did it affect their relationship, but that of their close friends as well.[26] Others have snidely suggested that knowing Edna made it readily understandable why Mosk would seek comfort in the arms of someone else. Her dominant personality was precariously balanced between being assertive and being just plain bossy. She was easily irritated and commanded attention, whether rushing into a restaurant for a family meal or dictating Stanley's daily activities. He usually responded with a "yes, dear," in his outwardly self-effacing manner, but Edna's criticism or dissatisfaction with her husband was often met with a passive acceptance of blame for whatever the offense, big or small. It has also been suggested that Stanley was merely acting out in reaction to something that Edna herself did, but no one could really say what.

The characterizations of the associates of Stanley Mosk and Sabrina Jourdan in police intelligence reports reflected the attitudes that dominated the police view of non-conformists. From 1950 until 1966, Mosk's old nemesis, Chief William H. Parker ran the Department and molded its modern image. He hired former Marines as drill instructors, and embraced a para-military police model that viewed the police as an army of occupation patrolling the ghettoized suburbs of Los Angeles to keep minorities "in their place." His supporters cite his "professionalization" of the police force, while his detractors contend that "To protect and serve" applied only to white people; blacks and latinos were routinely beaten into submission. Parker's detractors included FBI Director J. Edgar Hoover, who said he had "no use" for the man because Parker resisted federal intervention when his policies were called into question.

In 1965, one year before Parker died, the southwest Los Angeles neighborhood of Watts erupted in bloody rioting that left 34 persons dead. Parker's description of the riot was that "one person had thrown a rock, and then like monkeys in a zoo, others had started throwing rocks." With this mindset, the "counterculture" of the Sunset Strip was viewed by Parker as a threat to the morality and stability of the community.

The LAPD's idea of a "sexual degenerate" could simply have been a gay person or an artist who advocated sexual freedom. Drugs were rampant, and characterizing those who shared drugs among themselves as drug peddlers or dealers was common nomenclature. Characterizing someone with a single arrest for prostitution as a "known prostitute," or someone with a gambling arrest as a "known bookmaker" was the kind of hyperbole that recurred with alarming frequency in police reports. The characterization of harmless hippies as "advocates of the Communist conspiracy" is classic LAPD paranoia. Stretching back to the 1930's, the justification for police harassment of the counterculture has consistently been the need to root out Communists. Stanley Mosk would have been a target of particular interest for Chief Parker, and the officers conducting the surveillance would have been well aware of the Chief's interest. Mosk's criticism of LAPD tactics was particularly grating to

Parker, and the 1955 comment by Judge Mosk that the exclusionary rule meant that police "would have to use their brains instead of their hobnailed boots" was seen as a grievous personal affront to Parker and the LAPD.

One officer formerly employed as an LAPD Detective assigned to the Intelligence Division later claimed that under both Chief Parker and his successor Darryl Gates, LAPD targeted numerous prominent liberals, including Senator Alan Cranston, Governor Pat Brown, Governor Jerry Brown, Mayor Tom Bradley, Congressman Mervyn Dymally, Attorney General John Van de Kamp, and several members of the City Council. "The LAPD was conducting massive operations against non-criminals," he wrote, "for no other reason than to try to embarrass them or pressure them sometime in the future."[27]

When Tom Reddin became Chief of Police in 1967, he took a strong position against political intelligence, and closed down the surveillance of Justice Mosk. Reddin was a longtime supporter of Stanley Mosk, and a close friend of the Mosks; his wife Betty had been a partner in Edna Mosk's real estate business. He told reporters he never scrutinized the Mosk intelligence file. "About all I heard was that there was a relationship between a woman and the then attorney general," he said, " I never attached any importance to it." Chief Reddin did scrutinize his own intelligence file and commented that, "most of it was wrong."[28] Intelligence gathered from LAPD informants was frequently exaggerated, and sometimes false.

None of this is to excuse Mosk's behavior. His conduct deeply wounded his family and disappointed his friends and allies. It may even have rendered him vulnerable to corruption. No evidence has ever emerged that Mosk was politically or morally corrupt. Those who worked with Mosk have commented that he never discussed his personal life, and the line he drew between his work as Attorney General or as a Justice of the Supreme Court and what he did "after hours" was, at least to him, a very clear one which was strictly observed. Much later, Mosk did share some of the details about his relationship with Sabrina with his second wife, Susan. He confided to her that there was a side of him he always wanted to explore, and so when he met Sabrina through Jack Kennedy in Las Vegas, he seized the opportunity to expand the depths of his sexual experiences. Part of it was that every time he saw Kennedy in Los Angeles he saw some actress sitting in the corner wearing lingerie. It seemed to him as if everyone around him was having more fun than he was having.[29]

As with many successful political figures, his capacity for "compartmentalization" was capacious. There may have been occasional "seepage," where he was influenced to do semi-official "favors" for the denizens of his double life. The letter he wrote as Attorney General urging the Los Angeles Police Commission to license "Mr. Kon Ton's" is an example. Another is a letter he wrote as a Justice on the Supreme Court, addressed to a federal judge, urging leniency for a defendant awaiting sentencing for postal fraud, which can only be explained by the friendship between the defendant and Sabrina Jourdan.[30] These relatively minor transgressions are not evidence of corruption, but demonstrate that an occasional ethical lapse was more than a possibility.

Perhaps Stanley Mosk was aware of the ambiguity and hypocrisy in his attempt to straddle the establishment and the counterculture. Perhaps he was struggling with it. Perhaps Mosk simply thought, "everyone does it," knowing that other prominent political figures of his acquaintance, such as the "Kennedy crowd," engaged in a more promiscuous kind of sexual exploits. Perhaps Mosk was a closet hippie, who was born a little bit too early to roam the Sunset Strip. Perhaps he was truly in love. He was certainly attracted by this young, beautiful brunette with dark almond shaped eyes, with almost model-like features on a diamond shaped face with high-cheekbones, and a delicate nose accenting the sweep of her French-bun hair. He never offered an explanation. He denied the affair when he was confronted with public exposure of it almost three decades later.

There can now be little doubt about Governor Pat Brown's direct involvement in confronting Stanley Mosk and suggesting how embarrassing it could be for him if he stayed in the Senate race. Brown never admitted it directly. Decades later, during an oral history interview, he tried to explain why Mosk dropped out. He simply said, "I had been advised that he had some difficulties"—at which point the tape during the oral history interview was shut off and later resumed on another topic.[31] Contrary to later circumspection, just three days after Attorney General Stanley Mosk dropped out of the senate campaign, Pat Brown boasted to President Lyndon Johnson of his complicity in the scheme that derailed Mosk's senate run. Unknown to Brown, Johnson taped their telephone conversation. "One of these days I will tell you what I did to get Mosk out of it," Brown bragged to Johnson.[32] "Yep, yeh, but I know, I know, you told me," the only mildly attentive president responded. A perfunctory response was befitting, given Johnson's view of "that son of a bitch" Brown. In another tape, President Johnson told his top aide Lloyd Hand that he thought Governor Brown was "unreliable," "undependable," and a blabbermouth for "breaking the rules" by quoting the president — and a person who "leaked everything anyone ever told him."[33] As Brown's explanation to Johnson continued, he lamented that "it wasn't really a threat, per se," that got Mosk out of the race, but the governor didn't want California Democrats to spend a million dollars before the general election. Rather," Brown fawned he wanted to "concentrate on Lyndon, ... Lyndon Johnson."[34] Brown's suggestion that he got Mosk out to benefit the president was hardly convincing, even to Johnson. "That's right, that's right," the Texan drawled, as Brown described the quandary that justified stabbing Mosk in the back. Brown's reputation as a "blabbermouth" makes it likely that his explanation for Mosk's withdrawal was shared with many, and the affair became the subject of widespread rumors. Brown's biographer, asking whether Brown "personally spread word of Mosk's personal struggles," concludes:

> The evidence is mixed. But in numerous interviews, many sources told the author that the gossip was extremely widespread, regardless of Brown's involvement. One person close to Brown, speaking on condition of anonymity, remembered being approached by law enforcement officials who had copies of the pictures. It is not clear who took the pictures or to what extent they were distributed among the state's politicos, and the man involved never showed them to the governor. Brown believed the photos were in the possession of the Los Angeles Police Department; others thought that various political groups had them.[35]

Apparently, Governor Pat Brown was not the only person to confront Stanley Mosk with evidence of his "double life." In an interview of Frank J. Burns by Bill Boyarsky, Burns, a close political associate of Jesse Unruh, claimed that a picture of Mosk and Sabrina getting off a plane in Las Vegas fell into the hands of Hank Ridder, the publisher of the *Long Beach Press-Telegram*. Burns recalled, "The information I got was that Hank Ridder had called him [Mosk] in. Somebody had given the pictures to Ridder, and Ridder had a meeting with Stanley Mosk and showed it to him and said, 'What's this?'"[36]

At 6:00 A.M. Monday, March 3rd, 1964, Vince Thorpe called Frank Burns, who forty years later still remembered the startling words, "It's off! ... the campaign is off!"[37] At the same time, Stanley Mosk telephoned Tom McDonald directing him to bring the withdrawal speech to a new hastily arranged press conference to announce his decision to withdraw from the upcoming primary.[38] The call shattered the dreams of the team and the army of supporters who "were stunned" by what turned out to be an "abrupt reversal of plans."[39]

Sadly but defiantly, Stanley Mosk met with eagerly awaiting reporters at the Statler Hilton Hotel in Los Angeles where he simply stated that he would not enter the primary race "because it was just too costly.[40] Reporters already got wind of the "tremendous pressure exerted by Governor Brown" for Mosk to withdraw.[41] Although Mosk acknowledged this, he boasted that he could win the Democratic nomination just as the polls had shown, but he focused on the "astronomic" cost of running a general election campaign. Generously, he also countered rumors about Brown stabbing him in the back. He flatly refused "to accept the statement that Brown had tried to 'dry up campaign funds' in an effort to force him out of the race." Rather, Mosk said that Brown had twice spoken with him after the CDC had endorsed Cranston, but after apparently failing to convince him to withdraw, the governor had "managed to convey his feelings to a number of others high in Democratic ranks 'who in turn talked to me.'"[42]

Brown, in turn, explained to reporters that two Democrats at each other's throats would be bad for the party. He also saw Cranston's CDC endorsement and James Roosevelt's withdrawal and endorsement as a big boost to the Controller's bid in the general election.[43] The governor said that he changed his mind about remaining neutral because while "primary contests sometimes do good," he "could see this one had evil portents."[44] Later, the governor also told reporters that "if Mosk and Cranston had gotten into a campaign, it would have been a real donnybrook ... this would have been a rough one."[45]

Mosk's withdrawal from the Senate race was a huge disappointment for Edna Mosk, especially when she learned the real reason. After learning of the affair, she told Stanley she simply would not raise any money for a Senate campaign, and without her support there was nothing he could do. In Stanley's campaigns for Attorney General, his chief fundraiser had been his wife, who was much more aggressive than he in pursuing potential donors. Edna's former partner in real estate, Betty Reddin, said that her friend's crying indicated her grave disappointment.[46] Surely, her tears could have only hinted at the profound loss of so much, personally and professionally, for Edna. As her husband stood before the press announcing his withdrawal, she knew their lives would never be the same. Regardless, just two weeks later, Stanley and Edna Mosk, accompanied by Stanley's mother Minna, traveled to Worcester, Massachusetts for the wedding of their son Richard. Richard had met his bride, Sandra Lee Budnitz, while he was attending law school at Harvard and she was earning her Master's Degree in Education at Harvard. Richard and Sandy had no time for a honeymoon; he was back at work in the offices of the Warren Commission the following Monday morning. When Edna later saw Earl Warren, she chided him: "I'd just like you to know, Richard is really working hard. He didn't even take a honeymoon; he left on Friday and came back Monday." Warren responded, "Well, who let him off for Saturday?"

Despite Governor Brown's efforts, a political donnybrook was not avoided in California. Just two weeks after Stanley Mosk withdrew from the Senate race, and one day before the filing deadline, on March 19, 1964, Pierre Salinger, press secretary for both President Kennedy and President Lyndon Johnson, announced he was resigning in order to run for the Senate in California. The announcement took nearly everyone by surprise, including Ann Eliaser, who worked for Alan Cranston after Mosk withdrew. She found herself being blamed for Mosk's being "pulled off the ticket" in spite of her own belief that Mosk "would have been elected." As a result, her fundraising talents were largely overlooked in the general election.[47] Two California politicians who were not surprised by Salinger's announcement were Attorney General Stanley Mosk and Assembly Speaker Jess Unruh. Both had urged Salinger to get in the race, assuring him that his long absence and lack of residency in California would not disqualify him from running.

Pierre Salinger was 38 years old when he announced his candidacy. He was born in San Francisco, and graduated from the University of San Francisco in 1947. He served on a submarine chaser in the Pacific in World War II, and most of his journalistic career had been with the *San Francisco Chronicle*. He left California in 1957 to serve as an investigator for the Senate Select Committee looking into improper activities in labor-management relations, also known as the "Rackets Committee" chaired by Senator McClellan. Senator John F. Kennedy was a member of the Committee, and his brother Robert was its Chief Counsel. Salinger then joined the personal staff of Senator Kennedy in 1959, and after performing as press officer for his presidential campaign, was appointed White House press secretary in 1961. He continued in this position, serving President Johnson after Kennedy's assassination. By 1964, he was anxious to return to California. Sometime in February of 1964, Stanley Mosk was attending a dinner in Washington, D.C., and happened to be seated next to Pierre Salinger. Salinger confided that he was thinking about returning to California to run for Congress, but didn't think he would be eligible because he had registered to vote and voted in Virginia in the last election. Mosk assured him, "I don't think that would disqualify you, Pierre, if you really want to run for an office.... One, the qualifications in the state would not affect a federal office. Secondly, the important thing is your intent, and I assume it has always been your intent as a Californian to return to California."[48] Two weeks later, after Mosk's startling withdrawal as a contender in the Senate primary, Salinger called for reassurance that Mosk's advice was accurate, and after receiving it, told Mosk he was going to make a run for the Senate. Jess Unruh also had a hand in convincing Salinger to run. A longtime foe of Alan Cranston's efforts to control the Democratic Party through the CDC, Unruh was ready to support Mosk, and when Mosk withdrew, he jumped at the prospect of Salinger entering the race. He assured Salinger that a campaign staff and the necessary funding could be quickly pulled together. In making his announcement, Salinger noted he had discussed his candidacy with both Mosk and Unruh. President Lyndon Johnson was probably glad to see Salinger go. He gave Salinger his blessing, wished him well, and handed him part of the $450 California filing fee besides.[49] When Salinger flew to California to announce his candidacy, Tom McDonald met him at the airport and spirited him away.

Columnist Joseph Alsop wrote a "Matters of Fact" piece about Salinger's surprise announcement, and Stanley Mosk circulated it among his friends with the endorsement that it was "100 percent accurate." Alsop recounted that San Francisco Mayor John F. Shelley was the first to plant the seed in LBJ's head that Salinger should run for Congress from California. At that time, Salinger himself did not believe he was eligible, but found some people warm to the idea of his running. During a Bonds for Israel dinner, Mosk told Salinger that he could "stand for federal office," in California. According to Alsop, "Salinger made a joke about this," promising not to run against Mosk for the Senate, because "the attorney general was then the leading Democratic candidate." Alsop continued, "When hostile forces in" the party, "managed to push Mosk out of the race, on impulse, Salinger called Mosk to ask his opinion of his candidacy. Mosk told him it was wide open." He urged Salinger to enter the race, and he promised his support. Salinger spoke with Pat Brown's aide, Don Bradley, and then advised President Johnson of his plans just before he flew to California. Alsop saw the outcome of the race as "a decisive test of the political pulling power of the dead President's name." Democratic leaders, he added, including President Johnson, would likely understand that this will "surely affect many other matters conspicuously, including the Democrats' Vice Presidential choice."⁵⁰ The only thing left out of Alsop's account was the conversations and meeting with Jess Unruh, who said he could not publicly support Salinger's candidacy, but he would help raise money and get others to do so.

Shortly after Salinger filed as a candidate in California, Republican Secretary of State Frank Jordan refused to accept the filing, setting up a legal battle to be settled by the California Supreme Court. Although ostensibly represented by Quentin L. Kopp, later a San Francisco supervisor, state senator, and judge, the filings on behalf of Salinger were actually the work of Attorney General Stanley Mosk and his staff. As attorney general, however, Mosk was obligated to represent Secretary of State Jordan, and filed a rather bland brief on his behalf. An up and coming Democratic activist lawyer (now a judge of the United States Court of Appeals for the Ninth Circuit) Stephen Reinhardt was enlisted by Cranston and Governor Brown to present an "amicus" brief which would more forcefully support the secretary of state in rejecting Salinger's candidacy. The governor's son Jerry assisted Reinhardt in this endeavor. At issue was a state requirement that a candidate in a party's primary be a "member" of the party. Because Salinger was not registered to vote in California, he relied upon his Virginia registration to show he was a Democrat. Jordan argued that this did not make him a member of the California Democratic Party. There was also a constitutional argument in Salinger's favor, that the qualifications to serve as a United States senator were defined by the Constitution, and could not be altered by a state. In any event, even before Reinhardt's brief was filed, the California Supreme Court issued a terse two-line order announcing that Salinger had "substantially complied with the election laws," and requiring the secretary of state to place his name on the ballot. The race was on.

Salinger's candidacy was boosted by an endorsement from the wife of the dying Clair Engle, and a warm letter of support from Jacqueline Kennedy. Governor Pat Brown announced his support for Alan Cranston, despite an effort by Eugene Wyman, the Democratic powerful fundraiser and close friend of the governor, to persuade him to remain neutral. The race quickly took on all the trappings of a "showdown" between Jess Unruh and the remnants of the Kennedy cabal on one side, versus Governor Brown and the remnants of the CDC on the other side. The outcome was a real blow to Brown, when Pierre Salinger defeated Alan Cranston in the June primary with 53 percent of the vote, or 1,177,000 to Cranston's 1,037,000.⁵¹

On June 19, President Lyndon Johnson made his first California appearance as president at a gala dinner where Stanley Mosk introduced Pierre Salinger as the Democratic candidate for the U.S. Senate to the crowd of 2,500.⁵² When Clair Engle died on July 30, Governor Brown sought to boost Salinger's candidacy against Republican opponents in the general election by appointing him to the now vacant U.S. Senate seat, so Salinger could run as the incumbent. Ironically, he first sought the opinion of his Attorney General as to whether the appointment would be lawful under California law, which provided the governor could appoint an "elector" to fill an unexpired vacancy in Congress. Mosk obliged with an astute scholarly analysis upholding the legality of the appointment. The Republican candidate, George Murphy, a retired motion picture actor and dancer who defeated investment banker Leland M. Kaiser to capture the Republican nomination, challenged the legality of the appointment in a second trip to the California Supreme Court. Pierre Salinger, with the governor's appointment in hand, went off to Washington to be sworn in, only to find the validity of his appointment was being debated on the floor of the Senate. Minority Leader Sen. Everett Dirkson (R. Ill.) suggested sending the matter to the Rules Committee for a determination. Majority Leader Mike Mansfield countered with the suggestion that the Senate first swear Salinger in, then refer the matter to the Rules Committee for a report by August 13. The subsequent debate included two memorable and remarkable presentations. Senator Thomas Kuchel, the Republican senator from California, read into the record the opinion of California Attorney General Stanley Mosk, describing it as "a well reasoned legal document."

Senator Kuchel told his colleagues that they had a choice to make and that he was speaking to them not as a partisan but as a U.S. senator with responsibility to abide by the Constitution. He pointed out that the issue involved someone who was literally "waiting outside this chamber." He called upon his colleagues to honor the memory of Senator Clair Engle, to whom he recently paid his last respects. Recalling how Engle had been unable to perform his official functions, "except at those touching and poignant times when he came into the chamber in a wheel chair and sat over there, [likely pointing as he spoke] and voted." Even though Salinger was a Democrat, and he was a Republican, Kuchel thought it was more important that with only three weeks left to the current session, the state of California should be represented by two U.S. senators.

Next, North Carolina's Democratic senator Sam Ervin, later of Watergate fame, rose to commend the clarity of Kuchel's speech and the excellence of the legal opinion written by Attorney General Stanley Mosk, with whom he had periodically corresponded about bills. "I am of the opinion, as a result of such correspondence," he said, "that Mr. Mosk is one of the finest constitutional lawyers in the United States." In addressing the difference between qualifications for "membership" in the Senate, versus qualifications for a senate "candidate" to run in an election, Ervin declared that, in fact, the gap is not quite as wide as the distinction between "Tweedle-dum" and "Tweedle-dee."

Senator Ervin explained that by insisting the U.S. Constitution's qualifications of U.S. senators only apply to "senators who are elected" would result in the "absurd conclusion" that "appointed senators are not required to possess any qualifications under the U.S. constitution." He reasoned that appointees could therefore be required to possess traits that are either "wise" or "foolish" if prescribed by the state, even if they were inconsistent with the U.S. Constitution. In other words, if a state can add to the qualifications, it could then provide that only "baldheaded" or "redheaded" men be appointed; "Indeed, it could even pass a state law providing only idiots could be appointed to the U.S. Senate."

A roll call vote then tallied 59 yeas, including two Republicans, and 29 nays in favor of administering the oath of office to Salinger, with his credentials referred to the subcommittee for a report due by August 13. Pierre Salinger was sworn in as a member of the United States Senate on August 5. A subsequent hearing before the subcommittee featured a persuasive presentation by Attorney General Mosk, as well as statements by both Salinger and George Murphy and the attorneys representing them. Shortly thereafter, the subcommittee issued its report declaring the Senate's seating of Mr. Salinger legal and valid.

Although George Murphy's legal challenge to the Salinger appointment in the California courts became moot, Republican Secretary of State Frank Jordan subsequently refused Salinger's request to be designated the incumbent, listed first on the ballot. Yet, another trip to the California Supreme Court resulted in a ruling requiring that Salinger be listed first as the incumbent senator.[53] While Salinger was winning in the Courts and on the floor of the Senate, however, he was losing with California voters. All of the squabbling over his eligibility reinforced George Murphy's argument that Salinger was a carpet-bagging opportunist. Moreover, his presence in Washington for Senate sessions removed him from the campaign at home. Most important, he was on the wrong side of a very divisive initiative measure on the November ballot.

In 1963, the legislature enacted and Governor Brown signed the Rumford Fair Housing Law, a measure sponsored by Assemblyman William B. Rumford, the first African American elected to office in Northern California. The law broadly prohibited racial discrimination in the rental or sale of housing. The California Real Estate Agents' Association (CREA) responded with an aggressive campaign to qualify an initiative to repeal the Rumford Act by amending the California Constitution. It declared: "Neither the State nor any subdivision or agency thereof shall deny, limit or abridge, directly or indirectly, the right of any person, who is willing or desires to sell, lease or rent any part or all of his real property, to decline to sell, lease or rent such property to such person or persons as he, in his absolute discretion, chooses."[54]

CREA efforts gained the endorsement of conservative political groups such as the John Birch Society and the California Republican Assembly. Attorney General Stanley Mosk led the intense public condemnation of the repeal initiative and its promoters. He accused the CREA of prolonging race discrimination by "placing the constitution of this great state on the side of segregation."[55] In testimony before the State's Advisory Committee on Civil Rights, he said the measure would implicate the state as a party to the denial of constitutional rights. Firing back, the California Republican Assembly (CRA) and the Young Republicans used reverse logic to discredit liberals like Mosk, asserting: "The essence of freedom is the right to discriminate.... Discrimination is free choice."[56] After Mosk announced that he would seek a law to bar real estate dealers from racial blockbusting, the Glendale Young Republicans passed a resolution supporting the repeal of the Rumford Act. They deemed the Act to "deprive property owners of the freedom of choice."[57]

On a practical level, Mosk also argued that any repeal of the Rumford Act could threaten California's receipt of over 237 million dollars of federal urban renewal funds, and that the initiative "guarantees the tragic setback of moral ... and physical decay of our cities."[58] Republican Secretary of State Frank Jordan attacked both the Attorney General and the governor, arguing in a brief before the state Supreme Court that the two had violated their oaths of office when they urged California voters not to sign petitions for the repeal of the Rumford Act.[59]

The CREA's efforts were successful. Proposition 14 garnered over one million signatures, more than twice the 480,000 required, and was placed on the November ballot. It presented a real dilemma for candidate Pierre Salinger. Don Bradley, Joe Cerrell, and even Governor Brown, contrary to his own vocal opposition to the measure, all thought it a mistake for Salinger to take a clear stand on the issue while his opponent shied away from it. Salinger felt a moral obligation to attack the measure, having won the primary with 98 percent of the black vote, and identifying the fight for open housing with Kennedy legacy.[60] The initiative proved to be overwhelmingly popular, and was passed as Proposition 14 by a 65 percent majority vote in the November 1964 California election. Senator Pierre Salinger's opposition to the measure clearly contributed to his defeat at the polls. Murphy defeated Salinger 51.5 percent to 48.5 percent. Many observers agreed the outcome would have been different if Stanley Mosk had been the Democratic candidate, regardless of his obvious opposition to the proposition.

As Stanley Mosk had predicted, the enactment of Proposition 14 led the Kennedy administration Secretary of Housing and Urban Development, Robert C. Weaver, to cut off all federal housing funds to California. Soon after, Governor Brown wrote to Mosk about Proposition 14, "although we were not successful at the polls ... real advances were made towards acceptance of the principle of fair housing in California. We may have lost a battle, but the war against discrimination is not over and is still ours to win." The enactment of Proposition 14 was identified as one of the longer-term, underlying causes of the devastating Watts Riots that broke out in Los Angeles on August 11, 1965, just one week after President Johnson signed the Voting Rights Act into law. A constitutional challenge to the validity of Proposition 14 was quickly filed, and arrived in the California Supreme Court along with the arrival of Justice Stanley Mosk.

On August 10, 1964, Chief Justice Phil Gibson announced his retirement from the Supreme Court. Governor Pat Brown hailed him as one of the giants of American law, and then promptly appointed another giant to replace him, Associate Justice Roger Traynor. He also announced the appointment of Attorney General Stanley Mosk to take Traynor's place. Almost immediately, suspicion was voiced that Brown was delivering the inducement that got Mosk out of the Senate race. Both Brown and Mosk vehemently denied it, but neither of them were very credible in doing so. When the question of a "deal" was raised at the time Mosk announced his withdrawal from the Senate race, Mosk said he resented such a notion. He characterized it as "a disservice to a truly great court when we keep this rumor handy to bring out in a political sense." Furthermore, he added, at that time "there was "no vacancy on the court and there's no arrangement for a future vacancy."[61] Governor Brown later conceded the Supreme Court had been discussed prior to Mosk's withdrawal, explaining that he was careful not to make Mosk a firm offer, but instead pointed out that "since Cranston was not an attorney, it would not be possible to appoint" him to the Court."[62]

It is quite likely that both Brown and Mosk knew of Gibson's retirement plans by March of 1964, when Mosk was forced out of the Senate race. Gibson would not have sprung a surprise retirement on Governor Brown. Stanley Mosk apparently expected that he would be appointed Chief Justice, to replace Gibson, which lends strong credence to the rumors that a deal had been cut. If so, Mosk would have thought the deal was that he would get the next appointment to the Court, and the next appointment to the Court was the Chief Justice. Earl Warren had experienced a similar situation, when President Eisenhower tried to backtrack on the promise to give him a spot on the Supreme Court, after the "next spot" turned out to be the position of Chief Justice. Mosk was actually angry when Governor Brown announced the elevation of Traynor to be Chief Justice at the same time he appointed Mosk as an Associate Justice. He confronted Governor Brown about reneging on his promise, and stormed out of Brown's office after a loud argument.

Chapter 11

"He Never Forgot What His Positions Were"

On September 1, 1964, at the age of 52, Stanley Mosk was sworn in as the eighty-sixth Justice to serve on the Supreme Court of California. Justice B. Rey Schauer, who was preparing for his own retirement two weeks later, administered the oath. That same day, Governor Pat Brown sent the new Justice Mosk a letter with a handwritten note, "p.s. I will miss you as my lawyer very, very much. (Despite the Colorado!)"[1] Scores of congratulatory letters from near and far expressed similar sentiments. Typical was the letter from John W. Reynolds, governor of Wisconsin: "Congratulations on your ascension to the bench. We will miss you in the partisan political arena, but you have a great opportunity to make a contribution to the Californians and all of mankind in your new position."[2]

Mosk took over the seat previously occupied by Associate Justice Roger J. Traynor, the same seat that Justice Gibson had occupied years before, prior to his elevation to serve as Chief Justice. Traynor was that same day sworn in as the twenty-third Chief Justice of the California Supreme Court. Thus, two prior occupants of the seat Mosk assumed had gone on to serve as Chief Justice, a tradition Mosk often thought he was destined to maintain.

Traynor's elevation to Chief Justice was widely expected and well deserved. As the author of nearly 600 majority opinions and some 150 dissenting opinions, his liberal views were well known. His opinions were widely respected for their clarity, scholarship, and succinct reasoning.[3] He authored three of the most controversial landmark rulings of the Gibson Court, breaking new ground in the fields of tort liability of manufacturers for defective products, racial discrimination, and the use of exclusionary rules to deter unlawful police conduct. Regarding tort liability of manufacturers, in a concurring opinion authored in 1944, Traynor urged that manufacturers should be held strictly liable for defects in their products, without requiring proof of negligence.[4] Eighteen years later, he wrote the widely followed opinion in which the Court unanimously adopted this view.[5]

In 1948, the California Supreme Court became the first court in the country to invalidate miscegenation laws, which prohibited marriages between persons of different races. Speaking for a deeply divided court, Justice Traynor flatly rejected the claim that miscegenation laws applied "equally" to all races. "A member of any of these races," Traynor explained, "may find himself barred by law from marrying the person of his choice and that person to him may be irreplaceable.... Human beings are bereft of worth and dignity by a doctrine that would make them as interchangeable as trains." Thus, Traynor insisted, "the right to marry is the right of individuals, not of racial groups."[6] Nineteen years later, the United States Supreme Court agreed, this time in a unanimous decision written by

Chief Justice Earl Warren.[7] Traynor's decision served as the foundation upon which the California Supreme Court ruled six decades later that prohibiting marriage between persons of the same sex violated the California Constitution.[8]

Although Traynor was widely regarded as "the ablest judge of his generation,"[9] he fell short of the political and administrative talents of his predecessor. He lacked the warmth of Gibson's personality, and did not enjoy presiding over meetings or giving speeches, preferring to confine his eloquence to his published opinions. But this made little difference in the success of his tenure as Chief Justice. The smoothly running administrative machinery Gibson left behind continued to hum, largely thanks to the competent guiding hand of Ralph Kleps, appointed by Gibson in 1961 as the Director of the Administrative Office of the Courts (AOC).

Justice Mosk's tenure on the Court spanned the tenure of six governors—three Democrats and three Republicans. Each of them had the opportunity to modify the Court with the appointment of new Justices. At each stage, Stanley Mosk's relationship with his colleagues went through similarly remarkable transformations. He would serve on the Court for more than thirty-seven years, longer than any Justice before or since; he would serve under five Chief Justices, and thirty colleagues would come and go as fellow Justices.

For his first six years, Justice Mosk sat as a member of the "Traynor Court," an era of judicial hegemony still spoken of in reverential tones by California judges and lawyers. Stanley Mosk came to regard Roger Traynor with great admiration. Speaking at the memorial service following Traynor's death in 1983, Mosk said, "He brought luster to this Court. During and since the Traynor era we have been basking in the preeminence he earned for this institution."[10]

A judicial career of this magnitude and duration witnessed numerous transformations in the tenor of the court, and possibly his role as a judge. Throughout Mosk's tenure, however, he maintained a remarkable consistency. As Justice Joseph Grodin put it,

> He knew what he thought, what he believed, on a wide range of issues, and he would always remember what his views were. So you could be pretty sure that if Stanley had ever expressed a view on a particular question in some prior case, that would be his view today. Which is not to say he never changed his mind. Sometimes he did. But he had a long memory, and he never forgot what his positions were.[11]

On one occasion, when Justice Mosk *did* change his mind to reject an opinion he had authored as Attorney General, he borrowed a quotation from Lord Westbury: "I can only say that I am amazed that a man of my intelligence should have been guilty of giving such an opinion."[12] The evolution that Justice Stanley Mosk underwent can only be understood in the context of the transformations in the Court of which he was such a vital part—its history, traditions, and changing role in the government of a dynamic state.

The fellow Justice with whom Mosk should have felt greatest affinity was undoubtedly Justice Matthew Tobriner, appointed by Governor Brown in 1962. Tobriner and Pat Brown were close friends who practiced law together during the 1930's. Inspired by FDR's New Deal, they both changed their party registration from Republican to Democrat on the same day. Tobriner hailed from the German Jewish community of San Francisco and was active in the American Jewish Congress. Unlike Mosk who was an active member in the American Jewish Committee, which promoted Jewish assimilation in a pluralistic society, the Congress promoted Jewish interests at home and abroad, especially in Israel. Throughout its 114-year-history, few men of Jewish origin had sat on the court. Both Henry Lyons and Solomon Heydenfeldt served during the Gold Rush and Justice M. C. Sloss of San Francisco served from 1906 to 1919. The appointments of Tobriner and Mosk were harbingers of an increasingly diverse court in the years to come.

In addition to elevating Traynor to Chief Justice, Governor Brown had the unique opportunity to appoint five of the six Associate Justices of the Traynor Court.[13] In addition to Mosk and Tobriner, Brown appointed Raymond E. Peters, Louis H. Burke, and Raymond L. Sullivan. Peters was named to the Court in March of 1959 to replace Justice Jesse Carter. He had been the Presiding Justice of Division One of the First District Court of Appeal in San Francisco, where he had served for twenty years. He had a long history of association with the California Supreme Court, having served as chief law secretary to the justices from 1930 to 1939.[14] The most liberal of the Traynor Court justices, he sat as a justice of the Supreme Court until his death in January of 1973.

Justices Burke and Sullivan arrived after Justice Mosk took his seat on the Court. Governor Brown replaced retiring Justice Schauer with Justice Louis Burke, who had previously served as presiding judge of the Los Angeles County Superior Court, and a Justice of the California Court of Appeal. Burke, a gentlemanly conservative very much like Schauer, served on the Court ten years before his 1974 retirement. Brown had appointed Justice Paul Peek in 1962, but after only four years on the Court Justice Peek accelerated his retirement plans after Brown's reelection defeat in November 1966, in order to make room for Brown's final appointment to the Court. In December, Brown appointed a prominent San Francisco lawyer and a leader in the Catholic community, Raymond L. Sullivan, whom Brown had promoted to the First District Court of Appeal in San Francisco in 1961.

Justice Marshall McComb was thus the only Justice sitting on the Traynor Court not put there by Governor Pat Brown. McComb had been a Justice of the District Court of Appeal in Los Angeles, and after serving for thirty years, Governor Goodwin Knight elevated McComb, his only appointment to the high court, in December 1956. When Traynor took the reins in 1964, McComb was seventy years old and during Mosk's early years on the Court, McComb's increasing senility became an acute embarrassment for the Justices and the public's perception of the Court.

Stanley Mosk hit the ground running as a new Justice of the California Supreme Court. His first majority opinion appeared only nine weeks after he was sworn in,[15] and by the end of the year, he had published fourteen majority opinions and one dissent. During his sixteen years on the Superior Court, he had closely followed the work of the Supreme Court and on occasion, he had sat as a pro tem Justice of the California Court of Appeal.[16] His six years of service as Attorney General provided invaluable familiarity with the workings of the Court and the personalities of its members. His editing and issuance of 2,000 formal opinions as Attorney General gave him insight into supervising staff and polishing their work product. Most important, he recruited an outstanding line-up of judicial staff attorneys to assist him.

Associate Justice B. Rey Schauer left a parting gift for Stanley Mosk upon his retirement. He introduced Mosk to his chief staff attorney, Peter Belton, who joined Mosk's staff, and became the mainstay of the new Justice's chambers for the next 37 years. Peter Belton had four years of experience on the Court as staff attorney for Justice Schauer, and was already recognized as a superstar. Afflicted with polio while visiting Haiti as a college student, Belton was a paraplegic confined to a wheelchair. After graduating from Harvard Law School, he taught legal research and writing at Boalt Hall, and a year later joined the staff of Justice Schauer. Mosk hired Olga Murray as his second permanent staff attorney. After working her way through law school at George Washington University doing research for renowned columnist Drew Pearson,

Chief Justice Gibson hired Murray as a staff attorney, the first woman hired in such a position. With Gibson's retirement, she joined Mosk's staff, bringing her ten years of experience to Mosk's chambers. Murray was an avid hiker and traveler. While on an expedition to Nepal in 1985 she broke her leg and had a life-altering experience while recuperating in a Katmandu hospital. After she retired in 1989, she returned to Nepal to found and direct the Nepalese Youth Opportunity Foundation, devoted to helping the children of Nepal.

Mosk filled his third staff position with a one-year appointment of John Hansen, a classmate of his son Richard at both Stanford and Harvard Law School, and now partner with the Nossaman law firm in San Francisco. Justice Mosk relied upon Peter Belton and Olga Murray to draft his calendar memos and majority opinions. Belton developed an amazing capacity to assimilate and anticipate Justice Mosk's views. As fellow Justice Joseph Grodin observed, "They were intellectual, symbiotic twins. Peter knew what Stanley's view was about everything. I had the impression that all Stanley had to do was nod, and Peter would set out to write the opinion which he was sure that Stanley would want to have written."[17] More often than not, Mosk drafted his own dissenting and concurring opinions, sitting at his desk and pecking away at an old manual typewriter. He was efficient, finishing his work in less time than it took his fellow Justices.

In 1964, California Supreme Court Justices followed the nearly universal practice of hiring the best and brightest new law school graduates to serve as annual "law clerks," drafting memoranda and opinions under the direct supervision of each Justice. The list of those who served as annual law clerks to Justice Mosk includes many who went on to illustrious careers in law practice, public service, and academia.[18] Coincidentally, the two law clerks selected by Justice Tobriner for 1964–65 were Jerry Brown, Pat Brown's son and future California governor, and Richard, Justice Stanley Mosk's son. Richard had graduated from Stanford University with a Phi Beta Kappa key, and was a *cum laude* graduate of Harvard Law School. Thus, during his first year on the Court, Stanley worked in close proximity to his son, and Richard became a trusted adviser to his father, a role that assumed some prominence during the most controversial episodes the court faced during his father's tenure. Richard formed a warm and affectionate relationship with Justice Tobriner, and named his son "Matthew" in honor of Justice Tobriner.

Shortly after Justice Mosk's arrival, cases came before the Traynor Court in which the Court was called upon to determine the constitutionality of two popular initiatives. Proposition 15, known as the "Free Television Act," passed in November, 1964 by a 2–1 margin. Seeking to ban cable television, the rallying call was "If we have Pay TV, we'll lose the Dodgers and Ed Sullivan, and soon nothing will be free...." A constitutional challenge came before the California Supreme Court in *Weaver v. Jordan,* arguing that the measure violated the free speech and free press guarantees of both the federal and state constitutions.[19] In a thoughtful 6–1 majority opinion by newly appointed Justice Louis H. Burke, joined by Traynor, McComb, Peters, Tobriner, and Peek, the Court held the initiative was invalid. Justice Mosk authored a 17-page dissent upholding Proposition 15, which ranks among the lesser achievements of his otherwise distinguished judicial career. He argued that First Amendment guarantees were not impinged by the initiative because it regulated only the commercial market for television broadcasts. In other words, it did not prohibit anyone from distributing television programming by cable; it only prohibited them from charging for it. He wrote: "As I see it, however, my associates are vanquishing an illusory adversary. The target here is not speech; it is merely a matter of dollars and cents and the power of the people of the state to decide who gets them."[20]

With some misleading citations and out-of-context quotations of leading First Amendment scholars and Supreme Court decisions, Justice Mosk wove what many viewed as a questionable argument that economic activity fell outside of First Amendment protection. He ignored the authority cited by Justice Burke's majority opinion, which argued:

> The assertion ... that the Act does not invade freedom of expression because it does not prohibit subscription television, but merely forbids direct charges for programs transmitted to the home, is devoid of substance. The trial court correctly observed that "This is comparable to asserting that no prohibition of expression would exist in the case of newspapers or motion pictures if a statute were adopted requiring their distribution or showing without charge." When expression protected by the First Amendment is involved, "It is of course no matter that the dissemination takes place under commercial auspices."[21]

The United States Supreme Court promptly denied review[22] allowing the majority opinion in *Weaver v. Jordan* to stand, thus ushering in a new era of "Pay TV" which fostered new forms of home entertainment, consumer technologies, and cable based channels and independent program production to compete with the well-established national networks. While Justice Burke's opinion has since been widely cited and relied upon, Justice Mosk's dissent has been mercifully ignored and forgotten.

Justice Mosk redeemed himself just a year later, however, when he authored the opinion in *Wirta v. Alameda-Contra Costa Transit District*.[23] The case involved the alleged violation of the First Amendment right of freedom of speech by the prohibition of anti-war messages in paid advertising appearing on public buses. Ironically, the only dissenter from Mosk's majority opinion was Justice Louis H. Burke. Mosk struck down the restriction, beginning his opinion with the statement: "The fact that the message is proposed as a paid advertisement does not detract from the protection afforded."[24] He even cited the majority opinion in *Weaver v. Jordan*, noting, "the medium of subscription television ... is comparable to advertising on motor coaches owned by a transit district which has determined that advertising is an appropriate means of expression in its buses."[25] From this case on, Mosk's subsequent opinions earned him wide recognition as a champion for the protection of First Amendment rights even on privately owned commercial property.

The other popular initiative before the Court was the troublesome Proposition 14, purporting to create a "right to discriminate" in the rental and sale of residential property. An Orange County lawsuit brought by a black couple claiming a landlord refused to rent a vacant apartment to them in violation of the Unruh and Rumford Acts was dismissed when the court held that Proposition 14 rendered these Acts null and void. The California Supreme Court promptly granted a hearing. The plaintiffs argued that Proposition 14 violated the guarantee of equal protection of the laws under the United States Constitution.

Because of his prior involvement in enacting the Unruh and Rumford Acts, Justice Stanley Mosk recused himself from the case, and Justice Thomas White, who had resigned from the Supreme Court in 1962, was appointed to sit his place. In *Mulkey v. Reitman*,[26] a 5–2 ruling authored by Justice Paul Peek, the California Supreme Court ruled that Proposition 14 was unconstitutional. Justice White and Justice McComb dissented.

In the context of the times, the issue presented was not a simple one. The federal constitutional guaranty of equal protection of the laws applied to state action only, not individual discrimination. The ostensible purpose of Proposition 14 was to protect the "right" of *individuals* to discriminate. The Court reasoned that the elevation of private discrimination to a "right" offered state encouragement to private discrimination, thus supplying the requisite state action. This ruling, handed down on May 10, 1966, was roundly denounced by the political elements that promoted the initiative, placing the California Supreme Court in a very awkward position. Five of the Justices were scheduled to appear on the ballot for confirmation in the November, 1966 election six months later, and many supporters of Proposition 14 demanded that those who voted in the majority be ousted from the Court.

While his involvement in cases before the Court as Attorney General provided Mosk with experience, it also required frequent recusal after his appointment, and recently retired Justice Schauer was often appointed to replace him in these matters. As a result, during his first year on the Court, Mosk participated in few criminal cases, but when he did, his law enforcement experience as Attorney General inspired greater caution when it came to changing the rules police followed to gather evidence. In spite of his earlier lauding of the *Cahan* and *Mapp* decisions regarding the exclusion of illegally obtained evidence, he now was more inclined than some of his colleagues to conclude that errors in the admission of evidence in criminal cases were harmless, and did not require reversal of the judgment.

Two other cases required Justice Mosk's recusal because the lead counsel arguing the cases was his brother, Edward Mosk. Ed was representing citizens of the Soviet Union and Romania who inherited California land under the will of a California resident. Applying a California law that allowed non-resident aliens to inherit only if their country granted reciprocal inheritance rights to U.S. citizens, the trial courts in both cases had ordered forfeiture of the land to the state. Ed presented persuasive expert testimony that the law of the Soviet Union and Romania both permitted U.S. citizens to inherit land, and won unanimous reversals in both cases.[27] Ed had become an accomplished and successful appellate advocate on behalf of the left-wing clients and causes he espoused. He argued twice in the U.S. Supreme Court on behalf of a client who was refused admission to the State Bar of California for bad character because of previous membership in the Communist Party. In the first case, the Warren Court ruled 5–4 in his favor holding evidence of party membership seventeen years earlier or authorship of editorials denouncing U.S. participation in the Korean War did not support an inference of bad character.[28] After the case was returned to the State Bar, however, the client again refused to answer questions about his Communist Party membership, and this time he was refused admission on the ground that his refusals to answer had obstructed a full investigation into his qualifications. The case went back to the U.S. Supreme Court. This time Ed lost in a 5–4 ruling, holding that it was not unconstitutionally arbitrary for the state to deny admission because of refusals to answer.[29]

Throughout his service as Attorney General, the Mosks had maintained the family home in Beverly Hills, with Stanley renting an apartment in Sacramento. Stanley commuted among the three major Justice Department offices in San Francisco, Sacramento, and Los Angeles. With his appointment to the Supreme Court, he and Edna moved to San Francisco where they bought a spacious apartment on the ninth floor of a high-rise atop Nob Hill. The dramatic setting of the Mosks' unit was the unique wall of glass in the dining room where one was struck by the grandeur of the imposing Gothic, Grace Cathedral almost within reach just across the street. Completed around the time the Mosks moved in, it soon became an international pilgrimage center for churchgoers and visitors alike. Only after the awe wore off, one noticed the sweeping view of the San Francisco Bay stretching from the Golden Gate Bridge to the island hosting the infamous Alcatraz prison.

The Mosks employed Mary Benson, who migrated from rural Arkansas, as a full time housekeeper. Edna met Mary standing in line at the market. When she heard Mary lamenting over her predicament, Edna turned to her and said, "I need a maid and a cook," and that began Mary's long employment overseeing all things domestic in the Mosk household.

Edna took her under her wings to teach her culinary arts and social graces, and improve her vocabulary. Edna's style was a formal one. Mary wore a uniform and Edna asked her to wear a wig, more in line with the fashion of middle class standards. While the Mosks clearly saw Mary as an employee, maintaining a social distance, Edna did assist Mary's family in locating decent housing and getting them through some scrapes with the law. Mary often described Edna as "the best friend I've got."

The move to San Francisco and Stanley's new duties required both Stanley and Edna to make some lifestyle adjustments. Edna took up painting, and grew herbs on the balcony. It's likely that Edna found in such activities the necessary healing after the trauma of the aborted Senate campaign and Stanley's infidelity. She also became a prominent force behind the establishment of the Constitutional Rights Foundation. Apparently she heard about its success in Los Angeles, where it was started by lawyers from the American Civil Liberties Union who felt that material relating in the Constitution and the Bill of Rights was being neglected in the normal government studies that students received in high school. They organized young attorneys and law students to go into the social studies classrooms and work with the teachers in presenting issues and subjects related to constitutional protections. They would even organize a moot court, where the students would take a role. One would be an attorney for one side, one would be an attorney for the other, and one would be a judge. Students could see how the justice system works, in the context of contemporaneous issues that the students could understand and identify with.[30]

The change in Stanley's day-to-day lifestyle was more dramatic. The news column headline, "Finds Court Job Slower but Rewarding," captured the essence of his early impressions. He said that the pace of life as a Justice was much slower than he had been accustomed to, but to compensate, among other physical activities, he walked the two miles that separated the courthouse from his Nob Hill apartment. He said he was able to "readjust to his present duties after the vigorous speaking and traveling demands of his previous job." It wasn't just the pace that was different however: it was also his more circumscribed role in the public's eye, and the lack of public scrutiny of how his responsibilities were carried out. As Attorney General, his schedule included an average of five speeches a week "constantly advocating something," that could involve "prosecution on appeal or law enforcement legislation or testimony on water before a congressional committee." Now, as a Justice on the California Supreme Court, "one must rise above advocacy and be completely objective. You look at the issues and seldom note the names of the principals."[31]

Stanley and Edna Mosk both loved San Francisco, and soon became fixtures in the social life of the city's elite. They were frequent patrons of musical and theatrical presentation, and Stanley relished his proximity to his tennis club and major sporting events. Just one month before Mosk's appointment to the Supreme Court, Edna's mother Katharine passed away on August 4, 1964 at the age of 76. Stanley's mother Minna was still going strong, operating her bookstore at 8th and Irolo in Los Angeles.

The 1964 election kept Lyndon Johnson in the White House. Although Robert Kennedy soon left as Attorney General, many of the Kennedy appointees Stanley Mosk had gotten to know remained in office. By April of 1965, Justice Mosk felt secure enough in his new position to take off with Edna, for a seven-week mission to Africa. Mosk had volunteered to travel on behalf of the U.S. State Department, writing to his friend G. Mennen "Soapy" Williams, former governor of Michigan then serving as assistant secretary of state. The Mosks' first stop was The Hague, where he spent eleven days observing the proceedings in the Southwest Africa cases at the International Court of Justice in the Peace Palace. He found the entire experience fascinating, and explained the details to his friends in meticulously edited letters. The case pitted Ethiopia and Liberia against South Africa, challenging the introduction of apartheid policies as a violation of South Africa's trust mandate over the Southwest Africa Territory. The trip then proceeded to seven African nations to discuss the case, and to participate in seminars and meetings with judges and lawyers at each stop. In visits to Ethiopia, Tanzania, Zambia, Rhodesia, South Africa, Liberia, and Sierra Leone, he and Edna were wined and dined as distinguished American visitors. Throughout their itinerary, Mosk composed detailed letters, describing the politics and legal system of each country, as well as the highlights of their tourist adventures. They returned via Washington, D.C., where State Department officers debriefed Justice Mosk. After their return in June, *The Los Angeles Daily Journal* published his letters in a two-week long series.[32]

During his second year on the Court, Justice Mosk emerged as a reliable work-horse, producing a remarkable 32 majority opinions. Ten of those opinions were in criminal cases. He authored three majority opinions affirming death sentences,[33] and was a reliable vote for affirmance in nearly all of the death cases in which he participated. On twelve occasions during his first two years on the Traynor Court, Justice Mosk parted company with the Chief Justice, either dissenting to an opinion authored or concurred in by Traynor, or having Traynor dissent from an opinion authored or joined by him. In most of these cases, the position taken by Justice Mosk appears more conservative than the position assumed by Chief Justice Traynor, but occasionally the Chief Justice moved to the right of Mosk, siding with Justices Burke and McComb in dissenting.[34]

Stanley Mosk was again being considered for a high level promotion. In October, 1965, the FBI, at the request of the White House sent an urgent cablegram to the Director of Legal Affairs in their Mexico City office, "requesting expedited information regarding a presidential appointment: regarding a political function in Mexico; reportedly traveled with Sabrina Jourdan, born January 28, 1940, 6'1", 105 lbs., black hair, frequently died blond, olive complexion, very attractive. She was in contact with former presidential press secretary Pierre Salinger at this event. Possibility exists Mosk made this trip at expense of Mexican government."[35] At the same time, the background check developed "considerable derogatory information ... concerning Mosk's association with Communist Party front groups. Similar associations also developed concerning Mosk's brother, sister-in-law, and parents of his sister-in-law, and past association with admitted prostitute Laurelle Jane Stevenson (aka Sabrina Jourdan)."[36] Less than two weeks later, the FBI received information from an informant from the motion picture industry, who did not desire to disclose his name, reporting to the Bureau's agent that "Stanley Mosk had called on October 14, 1965, requesting the source to employ [unnamed] as an actress in motion pictures."[37]

Justices of the California Supreme Court were required to face the voters for an up-down confirmation vote at the first general election after their appointment. Thereafter, they face voters again at the completion of the remainder of the twelve-year term in which they were appointed, and then again in retention elections every twelve years. In September 1964, Justice Mosk replaced Traynor, who had been confirmed for another twelve year term in 1962. Thus, Mosk would be on the ballot in 1966, then again in 1974 when the term to which he had been elected expired. By coincidence, five of the Justices would appear on the 1966 ballot. Chief Justice Traynor, and Justice Burke would be up for confirmation. Although Justice Paul Peek had been confirmed in 1964, only two more years remained on the term of his predecessor, so he was on the ballot again for retention in 1966. Justice McComb's term was expiring, so he too was on the 1966 ballot for a new twelve year term.

In spite of Stanley Mosk's successful apprenticeship as a Supreme Court Justice, early in 1966, he approached Governor Brown with the suggestion that if Brown was ready to retire, he would be willing to retire from the Court and run for governor. Brown didn't encourage him. That November, former actor Ronald Reagan defeated Pat Brown in his efforts for reelection. Pat Brown later regretted his counsel to Justice Mosk. Years later, he wrote to Susan Mosk, Stanley's second wife, "This was the biggest mistake I have ever made in my life. I don't know if he could have beaten Ronald Reagan but he certainly could have given him one hell of a fight."[38]

The Supreme Court retention elections of 1966 marked the first time that California voters were urged to reject the confirmation or retention of Supreme Court Justices. The rulings throwing out both Propositions 14 and 15 after their overwhelming enactment in 1964 rendered the Justices quite vulnerable to attack. Although the legal standard for testing the constitutionality of an initiative is the same as for a statute enacted by the legislature, striking down an initiative is a politically perilous course. Often, the proponents of an initiative found to be unconstitutional train their sights on the offending Justices and target them for defeat in the next statewide election. Chief Justice Traynor and Justices Peek and Burke were roundly denounced for the Proposition 14 ruling, but they did not actively campaign for their retention. Hardly any Justice ever engaged in such self-promotion, because judicial confirmation was regarded as all but assured. Voters had never removed a sitting justice in all the years since contested elections were replaced with confirmation votes in 1934. This led to the phenomenon of Supreme Court Justices typically being confirmed by lop-sided margins. Traynor, for example, had been confirmed in 1962 with an affirmative vote of 89.7 percent. Paul Peek was confirmed in 1964 with a margin of 88.2 percent.

Although all of the Justices were retained, the results demonstrated the dramatic impact of the unpopular ruling on Proposition 14. Chief Justice Traynor received a disappointing 65.3 percent, with the lowest margin going to Justice Paul Peek, 62.1 percent.. Justice Stanley Mosk fared almost as poorly as Justice Peek, with a confirmation vote of only 63.2 percent, even though he had not participated in the Proposition 14 decision and dissented in the decision striking down Proposition 15.[39] Marshall McComb, was the top winner among the justices, with a 79.2 percent margin of victory.

During Mosk's early years on the high court, Edna Mosk continued her life filled with social and cultural activities. She was appointed to be a member of San Francisco's Economic Opportunity Council, and the city's Mayor John F. Shelley acknowledged her with reappointment to the Council in October of 1967.[40] In 1968, Edna was featured in *Good Housekeeping Magazine* with 17 other "smart women" commenting on what they thought of Ronald Reagan as California governor. She responded: "I believe California women are concerned over Governor Reagan's attacks on the state university, his cuts in mental-health funds and his failure to support the office of consumer council. But even more significantly, I sense a general spirit in Sacramento today that emphasizes money problems over human values. This, indeed, makes women apprehensive for the future."[41]

Justice Mosk was precluded by custom and ethical constraints from actively engaging in partisan politics, but Edna remained actively engaged. The year 1968 was an exceptionally turbulent one for Americans. Amidst growing disapproval and increasingly influential demonstrations against the Vietnam War, on March 31, President Lyndon B. Johnson announced he was bowing out of a reelection campaign. The following month, the assassination of Martin Luther King, Jr., fueled outraged citizens to engage in violent uprisings all over the country. At the same time, Justice Mosk briefly contemplated leaving the Court to run for the Senate seat of Republican Thomas Kuchel in 1968, but thought Kuchel was unbeatable. As it turned out, Kuchel was defeated in the Republican primary by State Superintendent of Education Max Rafferty. Alan Cranston finally achieved his senatorial ambitions, when he beat Rafferty. Meanwhile, Chief Justice Earl Warren of the United States Supreme Court announced his plans to retire. In discussing his own replacement with President Johnson, Warren suggested three men whom he thought Johnson should consider: Arthur Goldberg, Ramsey Clark, and Justice Stanley Mosk. It does not appear that any of these suggestions were seriously considered, but Stanley Mosk was the subject of another FBI background check at this time. Lyndon Johnson nominated his long-time friend and advisor Abe Fortas, but the nomination floundered in election year politics, leaving the position to be filled by newly elected President Richard Nixon. None of the California Supreme Court Justices were on the ballot in the 1968. A constitutional amendment provided that Justices would thereafter appear on the ballot only in the years in which gubernatorial elections were held.

While the turmoil swirled on the national stage, events unfolded in the life of Edna Mosk that would bring her to the center of the historical tragedy to come. With Johnson's retreat from the campaign, the Democratic Party struggled to place an equally formidable candidate in nomination. The New Hampshire primary held in March began the roller coaster ride of aspiring Democrats to win enough votes to sail into the August national nominating convention. In May, California Assembly Speaker Jesse Unruh, now chair of the Robert Kennedy Presidential Delegation, expressed his pleasure at Edna Mosk joining the delegation and provided her updates on the campaign in California.[42]

By the time of the June 4 primary in California, it was clear there was going to be a showdown between Bobby Kennedy and Eugene McCarthy. Kennedy narrowly defeated McCarthy in California, 46 to 42 percent. Stanley Mosk was not in attendance in the crowded ballroom of Los Angeles' famous Ambassador Hotel when Kennedy gave his victory speech. Thereafter, Kennedy and his entourage entered a kitchen pantry on their way to a banquet room to meet with reporters. Among scores of friends and colleagues in Mosk's circle, Jesse Unruh was there, as was the Mosks' close friend Frank Burns, who had been in the room ready to launch Stanley Mosk's senatorial campaign four years earlier. The night of Kennedy's victory celebration, Frank Burns was at the side of the jubilant Kennedy when just after midnight, he was mortally shot by Sirhan Sirhan. Burns helped to hold Sirhan down, while Unruh accompanied the dying candidate to the chaos of the emergency room of the Central Receiving Hospital.

The assassination, aside from its tragic and historic consequences, meant that the selection of a presidential nominee at the upcoming Democratic National Convention to be held in Chicago in from August 26 to 29, would be an even more volatile process. Edna Mosk turned her support to South Dakota's U.S. senator, George McGovern, who several years later wrote, "I'll always treasure that vote of yours in Chicago '68,"[43] but in July, prior to the convention, Vice President Hubert Humphrey also congratulated Edna on her delegate status.[44]

As the California delegation was preparing to attend the gathering in Chicago, one columnist observed, "the Democrats will kick up their heels for the next few days, stirring up enough sand to make a piker out of Mrs. O'Leary's cow." No one could anticipate the upheaval outside the International Amphitheater in the days ahead. Speaker Jesse Unruh was leading a state delegation of 172, including thirty women. The women included Carmen Warschaw, four-time delegate and former Southern California party chair, future Los Angeles Councilwoman and Supervisor Yvonee Braithwhite Burke, three-time delegate Trudy Owens, Assemblywoman March Fong (Eu), actress Shirley McLaine, and Hope Schecter (Mendoza). Also among the delegates was Edna Mosk, described as a member of the executive committee of the Economic Opportunity Council in San Francisco, and "a lively, petite and chic lady who managed her husband's campaigns for attorney general and the Supreme Court." Women delegates were advised to wear comfortable shoes in the Windy City, and the National Committee clarified that Democrats will welcome "bare-legged youth in sandals and mod ladies in fishnet hose and little girl slippers, as well as little old ladies in tennis shoes."[45] Stanley accompanied Edna to the Chicago convention, and their son Richard was an alternate delegate, so the entire family was together during this tumultuous time.

During her stay, Edna Mosk noted that "some of the delegates found it intimidating when they saw all the precautions the city took, but I am sure they did it to provide for our safety to make sure that nothing would happen." March Fong (Eu) "had no idea" anything untoward was occurring outside, until she and her 14-year-old son left the convention for their hotel and "saw the protesters squaring off with Chicago police in full battle gear."

The Chicago demonstrations doomed the Democratic ticket of Hubert Humphrey and Edmund Muskie, and in November of 1968, much to the disappointment of Stanley and Edna Mosk, Richard Nixon recaptured the White House for the Republicans.

During the subsequent trial of the iconic "Chicago Seven," Justice Mosk "condemned recent disruptive practices used in the courtroom," and suggested local bar associations "make it clear that defendants 'can not shove or brawl their way to vindication' in courts of law." He told members of the bar that, "they must show their feelings against these disruptive practices such as occurred during the Chicago Seven conspiracy trial," ensuring that "disruption in the courtroom" does not "become a trend."

Behind the scenes, Justice Mosk also expressed grave concern about the attacks upon the judiciary which characterized the 1968 presidential campaign. In July 1968, a memo from Mosk sounded a clarion call to Chief Justice Traynor. Mosk warned Traynor that, "to ignore the impending disaster to the courts is sheer masochism." The impending disaster Mosk feared "without being hysterical or an alarmist," was what could "well be the destruction of the independent judiciary process as we know it." Mosk envisioned "disquieted days ahead," because of the constant "harping on the theme that [the] courts are responsible for the permissiveness of contemporary society." The main culprits were the likes of Max Rafferty, George Wallace, Strom Thurmond, Richard Nixon, and Ronald Reagan. He told Traynor that it was impossible to rely upon [Senator Alan] Cranston to respond to attacks on the courts, suggesting it was problematical to answer political attack with political attack. Mosk suggested instead that several immediate and practical steps were needed to counter the negative campaign, which was, "of course, national in scope," because of Ronald Reagan and Wallace's most recent attacks. One possible source to rise to the aid of the courts was the American Bar Association, but Mosk noted "While I am not too sanguine about getting any effective action from the ABA," he reminded Traynor of Earl Warren's resignation from that organization because of its failure to defend the judiciary. Mosk then outlined steps and the reasons behind them to recruit the ABA and leading law firms, adding the caution that such steps should not be publicized."[46]

Meanwhile, Justice Mosk settled into the demanding routine of a very busy court. When Justice Mosk assumed the role of a Justice of the California Supreme Court, observers anticipated he would become a reliable fifth vote for the Traynor Court majority. He never did. The Court divided in a 4–3 split in 21 of its decisions, and in most such cases the majority consisted of the Chief Justice joined by Justices Peters, Tobriner and Sullivan, with the dissenters including Justices Mosk, Burke and McComb. Justice Mosk's rate of disagreement with the Chief Justice was 12.6 percent.[47] Mosk was positioned slightly to the right side of a left-leaning court. Although Chief Justice Traynor led from the middle, the tilt was to his left.

The most controversial decision of 1969 was one in which Justice Stanley Mosk did not participate. Mosk's recusal in *People v. Belous* was likely due to his brother Ed Mosk's participation in the setting up the case, and because Mosk was personally acquainted with Dr. Belous as a family physician. In *People v. Belous*,[48] the Court reviewed the criminal conviction of Dr. Leon Belous for assisting a patient to secure an abortion. The case attracted intense interest and numerous *amicus* briefs. The concern that Justice Mosk's absence would affect the outcome of the case was widespread.

Although California adopted the Therapeutic Abortion Act in 1967, legislation that Dr. Belous had vocally supported, prior to the enactment of the new law he had referred a 19-year-old, unmarried woman wanting an abortion to "an experienced Hollywood abortionist."[49] Belous apparently feared the woman would either try to abort the fetus herself, or seek an abortion in nearby Tijuana, Mexico—either of which would have involved a risk to her life. He was convicted of conspiring to perform an abortion, and sentenced to two years probation and a $5000 fine. His appeal, according *Time Magazine*, "attracted an awesome list of supporters."[50] At the time, Ed Mosk was vice president of the Southern California Branch of the American Civil Liberties Union. Although Ed was not listed along with 17 other prominent lawyers filing briefs in the final summary of the case, in January of 1969, he held a news conference to announce the ACLU was filing a "friend of the court" brief in the case of *People v. Belous,* asking the California Supreme Court to declare the state's abortion laws invalid. The ACLU brief argued among other things that abortion laws cater to "the dogma of the Roman Catholic Church and are an unconstitutional establishment of religion." Standing beside Ed Mosk was activist attorney Mrs. Norma G. Zarky, who was listed as one who submitted a brief on behalf of the defendant and appellant. She told the press, "The decision to bear children was a fundamental right of the mother."[51] Another friend of the court brief was signed by 178 deans and other professors of medical schools across the U.S."[52]

In place of Justice Mosk sat Justice Fred R. Pierce. Justice Mosk's former colleague A. L. Wirin appeared as counsel for the defendant and appellant.[53] With Justice Pierce signing with the majority, the Court reversed Belous's conviction on a 4-3 vote,, declaring invalid a law that for more than 100 years made it a crime to perform an abortion on a woman except when "necessary to preserve her life." The majority ruled that the law was both too vague and an improper encroachment on women's fundamental right to choose whether or not to bear children. Observers suggested that the ruling would make "it easier for a doctor to decide when he may legally perform an abortion," and provided "a weighty precedent for court action in other states," and affirmed "a legal trend" that at the time "would make all such intimate matters a private concern beyond the reach of the state."[54]

With one exception, California experienced a judicial moratorium on executions during the Traynor Court era of the 60's. In January of 1964, before Justice Mosk joined the Court, the California Supreme Court ruled in *People v. Morse*[55] that it was error to instruct jurors deciding the death penalty that, if they do not sentence the defendant to death, he might be paroled after seven years. Because this instruction was routinely given in death cases up to that time, the ruling required new penalty trials for all the occupants of death row. Thereafter, in 1968, the United States Supreme Court ruling in *Witherspoon v. Illinois*[56] also required routine reversals and retrials of the penalty proceedings of those awaiting execution, because of the exclusion of jurors with general objections to the death penalty. The only execution over which Governor Ronald Reagan presided was the April 12, 1967 gas chamber execution of Aaron Mitchell, a black man convicted of a Sacramento murder.

In September of 1969, Stanley and Edna Mosk enjoyed a month-long trip to Spain, Portugal, and Morocco, capping it with visits to Paris and London. Shortly after their return, Edna was diagnosed with breast cancer. She underwent a mastectomy in November. The cancer later recurred, and she was destined to fight a losing battle with bone pain and metastatic bone disease for the remaining years of her life. Throughout the 1970's, she sought to live as normal a life as possible, fully engaged in Stanley's active social life, and joining her husband on his international forays. Richard joined the Los Angeles law firm of Mitchell, Silberberg & Knupp.

Richard and his wife Sandy presented the Mosks with two grandchildren, Julie, born in 1966, and Matthew, born in 1969. The senior Mosks did not like being called "Grandpa" or "Grandma," so the children called them by their first names, Stanley and Edna. Court sessions in Los Angeles provided the Mosks with frequent opportunities to visit with their grandchildren. On occasion, Mosk would have to go into work, or play indoor tennis, and sometimes he took the grandchildren to show them off. During the December holidays, Richard and Sandy joined Stanley and Edna for the traditional festivities. Each year, Edna brought out the plastic Christmas tree with colored lights. Among the season's familiar guests were the Earl Warrens, followed by the New Year's Day Rose Bowl in Pasadena. Stanley Mosk loved to dine out, and one holiday the Mosks invited the owners of his favorite San Francisco Chinese restaurant, the Hu's, to join them for dinner on Christmas day, with their eight children. The Mosks liked to do things in groups, and every year the family attended the annual performance of *The Nutcracker*.[60]

Minna, Stanley's mother, had rebounded from her earlier accident, and continued to operate the Irolo Book and Gift Shop. She was always Stanley's biggest fan, a doting mother and grandmother, and an able campaign worker for his numerous electoral contests. She gladly babysat for both of Stanley's grandchildren, Julie and Matthew. Even though it was difficult for her to get around, Minna welcomed the little ones into her one room apartment, served them Hershey's kisses, and let Julie count her gray hairs as she sat in the mustard yellow rocking chair. Aromas of Minna's favorite foods, and the scent of flowers wafted through the books and conversations at Minna's home. Perhaps they covered up the smell of the cigarette she occasionally snuck out back with Ed's wife Fern.[15] As Julie became more psychologically astute, she concluded that her grandfather Stanley had really married his mother when he married Edna, because he liked to be taken care of, and both women were dedicated to that end.

In 1969, Justice Mosk was the most productive member of the Traynor Court, producing a total of 29 majority opinions and 16 dissenting opinions. Bernie Witkin, the widely acknowledged "guru" who carefully parsed every decision of the Court for his authoritative *Summary of California Law*, aptly summed up the personalities of the Traynor Court. With great wit, he introduced the Justices at the annual Supreme Court luncheon of the Lawyers' Club of San Francisco in 1968. He congratulated Chief Justice Traynor for "supplement[ing] his daytime product with truly magnificent moonlighting," a reference to Traynor's regular output of scholarly law review articles. He described Justice Tobriner as "Bold as Black, crafty as Cardozo, dogged as Douglas, flowery as Frankfurter, humble as Hughes, wild as

Warren." Justice Raymond Peters was likened to Paul Bunyan, "cleav[ing] through legislative dogma and judicial precedent" with a monstrous axe. He said Justice Louis Burke, anchoring the conservative minority, was "anchored to the proven past and working present." Newly appointed Justice Raymond Sullivan was characterized as "the bloc's solid fourth vote." He politely characterized Justice Marshall McComb as the Court's "only genuine lawman." When he came to Justice Stanley Mosk, Witkin paused and said:

> The next man is an enigma. Is he for or against the status quo and which? Is he a new or an old New Dealer? Why does he one day cuddle with the Chief and another day huddle with Burke? Is he a cautious liberal or a daring mugwump? The superior craftsmanship and persuasive style of this intransigent causes acute anguish in the bloc. And residents in the vicinity of 3494 Jackson [the Tobriner family home] have heard, in the still of the night, spectral tenor of Mathew, crooning in his Blooming boy:
>> *Can't you hear me yellin'*
>> *Your vote should be jellin'*
>> *Not just hanging on the vine;*
>> *Stanley, baby, won't you make up your mind and be mine?*[57]

Chapter 12

"The Mosk Doctrine"

In 1970, the Senate seat that eluded Stanley Mosk and ultimately went to George Murphy in 1964 was again up for grabs. Stanley Mosk was feeling restless, and toyed with the idea of leaving the Court and making a race for the Senate. The polls suggested Senator Murphy was vulnerable, and his lackluster Senate performance had left many Californians disenchanted. One columnist argued "this leaves one outstanding candidate for the Demos to take seriously," Stanley Mosk. "The Mosk candidacy would make sense, too," March Schwartz wrote. Mosk "has been an outstanding public servant," and "his recent court decisions have been masterpieces of good logic, and his stand is solid. He neither swings to the left nor to the right." What's more, the Party owed Mosk something after "party termites which allowed Alan Cranston to seek the party's nomination for the senate seat in 1964."[1]

When Mosk joined the Court in 1964, the campaign funds he had raised for a potential Senate race, along with funds left from his 1962 campaign, were placed in a trust fund. Mosk had used the funds to make contributions to other Democratic candidates, so he still had lots of political friends. Justice Mosk now used the funds to finance a public opinion poll to assess his potential strength in a race against Murphy. The poll suggested that the Mosk name and his record as Attorney General still carried clout. He was troubled, however, by the potential obstacle presented by Article VI, section 17 of the California Constitution, which provides:

> "A judge of a court of record may not practice law and during the term for which the judge was selected is ineligible for public employment or public office other than judicial employment or judicial office.... A judge of a trial court of record may, however, become eligible for election to other public office by taking a leave of absence without pay prior to filing a declaration of candidacy."

Although the term as a Supreme Court Justice to which he had been elected would not expire until 1974, Justice Mosk concluded that this problem could be avoided by simply resigning from the Court before declaring his candidacy.[2] But he was still haunted by the threat of public disclosure of his extramarital affair. He appeared on a radio show, and a caller (probably planted) asked whether public officials should have good morals. Mosk ultimately decided against a Senate race. On December 29, 1969, he issued a press release boasting that the poll results indicated "I could undoubtedly win the nomination and would be the most formidable candidate to win election to the Senate." He then explained his reasons for rejecting the urging of friends that he run:

> I have long been convinced that there is no greater distinction and no more gratifying opportunity to serve the cause of constitutional government than to be a member of what is univer-

sally recognized as the most prestigious court in the nation. Weighing the alternatives, I have concluded that I can best serve the people of our state by remaining on the Supreme Court of California and not becoming involved in partisan politics.

Justice Mosk was probably thankful he was far from what has been described as "one of the most bitter primary campaigns in California history," as John Tunney slugged out a victory by defeating fellow Democrat, Congressman George Brown, Jr. Tunney is the son of famous boxer Gene Tunney, and a close associate of the Kennedy family. During Tunney's campaign, he asked if Mosk would allow his name to be used on an endorsement letter. He summarized some of his views about his conviction that, "the retirement of George Murphy from the Senate is a crucial part of the effort to end the [Vietnam] war quickly, restore health to our economy, heal the divisions in our society and once again make Americans proud of their nation."[3]

While Brown and Tunney both questioned the expanding U.S. involvement in Vietnam, Brown opposed continuing the military draft while Tunney favored it. This conflict allowed incumbent Republican George Murphy to gain a lead in the early polls. However, Murphy was in his late 60s and his speaking voice was reduced to a gravelly whisper from throat cancer while Tunney was youthful and energetic, capitalizing upon his resemblance to the late Robert F. Kennedy, his friend and mentor. Murphy's staunch support for the Vietnam War also diminished his support. As the general election approached, Tunney overtook Murphy in the polls,[4] and defeated Senator Murphy in the 1970 Senate election.

The gubernatorial campaign that year has been described as "one of the most lackluster gubernatorial campaigns within memory," with Californians splitting their ticket by re-electing incumbent Governor Ronald Reagan who easily defeated Assembly Speaker Jesse Unruh, and giving Tunney a wide margin of victory over Murphy.[5] Humdrum or not, the mid-year election was good to the Democrats, who recaptured both houses of the state legislature and were now able to block Governor Reagan's reapportionment plans for the upcoming U.S. census. The state now had two Democratic senators, the first time since the Civil War, and Pat Brown's son, Jerry Brown, assumed his new post as State Controller.

Chief Justice Roger J. Traynor turned seventy on February 12, 1970, and announced his plans to retire. His frustration with the senility of Justice McComb made him acutely sensitive to the problem of judges not knowing when to retire, and he looked forward to enjoying more time for travel with his wife and visits with his six grandchildren. He felt confident that Governor Ronald Reagan was serious about making judicial appointments based on merit, and his confidence was justified by the appointment of Donald R. Wright to replace him. Mosk was named by Chief Justice Roger Traynor to serve as Acting Chief Justice during the three-month hiatus before Wright was sworn in on May 1, 1970.

The elevation of a sitting Justice to serve as Chief was not really an option for Governor Reagan, since all of the remaining Justices except Justice McComb were Democrats appointed by his predecessor, Governor Pat Brown. Eighty percent of Reagan's judicial appointments were Republicans, just as eighty percent of Pat Brown's were Democrats. Naming Donald Wright gave Governor Reagan a Republican who was a judge of long experience and widely acknowledged administrative skill. Appointed to the Municipal Court in Pasadena by Governor Earl Warren in 1953, he won election to an open seat on the Superior Court in 1961, and was later selected by his fellow judges to serve as presiding judge. Reagan employed William French Smith to carefully vet his judicial appointments, and Smith, in turn, had frequently sought the advice of Judge Donald Wright. Wright was elevated to the Second District Court of Appeal by Governor Reagan in 1968, and the governor was pleased by the praise which that appointment garnered. In announcing Wright's appointment as Chief Justice, Governor Reagan said he picked him "after an exhaustive search which encompassed the entire judiciary and legal profession of the state," and expressed his confidence that Chief Justice Wright would return the California high court "to a policy of judicial restraint."[6]

Wright was promptly confirmed by the Commission on Judicial Appointments, with Acting Chief Justice Stanley Mosk voting for confirmation. A few days before the official ceremony, Mosk told reporters, "Since a vacancy occurred on our bench, I've been sitting, at Governor Reagan's pleasure, as presiding justice. The governor's pleasure is limited. I'm being replaced Friday."[7] As his last official act as Acting Chief Justice, Stanley Mosk swore in Donald R. Wright as the new Chief Justice of the California Supreme Court on May 1, 1970.[8] In the November, 1970 statewide election, Chief Justice Wright was confirmed by a margin of 80.6 percent. Justice Sullivan was also confirmed, and Justice Peters and Burke were likewise retained with comfortable margins. The Justices were relieved that the lower margins of retention in 1966 were an aberration.[9]

Governor Reagan's call for "judicial restraint" reflected the national political agenda of the Republican Party. The 1968 presidential race had focused a good deal of attention on "activist" judges and their alleged contribution to dramatic increases in crime rates. President Nixon's first appointment to the U.S. Supreme Court was Chief Justice Warren Burger. By 1970, the Burger Court had begun dismantling many of the expansive Warren Court rulings established to deter police misconduct and expand First Amendment protections of dissent — a move resisted by some state supreme courts. By relying upon their state constitutions, these judges succeeded in preserving Warren Court protections, and insulated their rulings from United States Supreme Court review because they were based on "independent state grounds." More conservative judges closely followed the lead of the Burger Court, and construed their state constitutions in the same way the U.S. Supreme Court majority construed the corresponding protection of the U.S. Constitution.

Although Wright was not warmly welcomed by the sitting justices, he quickly won their friendship and loyalty. Justice Mosk expected the "typical country-club type," but soon realized Wright was "a man with a heart" as well as a brain. Wright's relaxed manner and easy accessibility fit well, and the Court continued on an even course. Wright was more conservative than Traynor, but not by much. During his first full year, there was no dramatic shift from the pattern of decisions under Chief Justice Traynor. Chief Justice Wright concurred in most of the landmark majority opinions authored by Justice Mosk during his reign.[10] Justice Mosk agreed with Wright more often than other Justices, and he and Justice Sullivan often served as bridges to form a centrist core. Chief Justice Wright skillfully avoided the formation of a divisive conservative minority through his astute leadership.

By 1971, Justice Mosk became a "swing vote," that determined the outcome in many of the cases that divided the Court.[11] Although Mosk deeply admired Justices Peters and Tobriner, he occasionally chafed at what he saw as their idealistic impracticality. In the 1971 case of *In Re Tucker*,[12] for example, the Court ruled 5–2 that there was no constitutional right to the presence of counsel for parolees at parole revocation hearings. Justice Tobriner and Justice Peters both authored dissenting opinions, which inspired an acerbic response from Justice Mosk. In a concurring opinion, he wrote:

Justice Tobriner implies that parole officers are malevolent functionaries dedicated to the deprivation of normal human existence by the parolees in their charge. Justice Peters asserts those of us in the majority adhere to a fiction "so divorced from reality that it cannot be tolerated by any fair-minded man." It is my two learned colleagues, with their gaze commendably fixed on the stars, who are tripping over reality.

Mosk presented a spirited defense of parole officers, and concluded that the regimen of parole revocation hearings contemplated by Tobriner and Peters "would impose an excessive burden on the machinery of the administration of justice."

In 1970, the California legislature enacted the California Environmental Quality Act, which required governmental agencies to file an environmental impact report before proceeding with construction projects that could affect environmental quality. In *Friends of Mammoth v. Board of Supervisors of Mono County*,[13] the California Supreme Court addressed the important question of whether CEQA applied to private projects, or was limited to government projects. At issue was the validity of building permits authorizing the construction of a huge condominium project (184 units) on a small five acre parcel of land in Mammoth Lakes, in Mono County, California. Mono County, then with a population of 4,016 persons, was historically oriented to the economy of cattle and sheep ranching, but was blessed with "nature's bountiful gifts of majestic mountains, lakes, streams, trees and wildlife [which] have produced in the area one of the nation's most spectacularly beautiful and comparatively unspoiled treasures." Writing for a 6–1 majority, Justice Mosk authored a landmark opinion calling for the broadest possible application of CEQA's requirements. As subsequently explained by Justice Cruz Reynoso, "of enduring importance to the statute has been the tour de force represented by Justice Mosk's opinion. In it, he recognizes the constant threats to the environment from a single-minded focus on the economy and the unique importance of protecting the environment. Consequently, *Friends of Mammoth* declares that CEQA must be interpreted "to afford the fullest possible protection to the environment...."[14] Justice Mosk noted the incongruous threat to the environment if small counties could avoid CEQA requirements by simply licensing private entities to undertake projects, rather than doing it themselves:

> More specifically, if private activities for which a permit is required were exempted from the operation of the act, projects with admittedly deleterious ecological consequences would be covered only if construction, acquisition or other development were undertaken by the governmental authority but not if the same authority allowed private enterprise to engage in the identical activity. The incongruity of such interpretation would be most vivid in the less populous counties, such as Mono, which because of limited economic capabilities might never engage in massive public works projects significantly affecting the environment, but could achieve the same result by permitting, licensing, or partially funding private activities.[15]

As Justice Reynoso aptly put it, "the principles articulated in [*Friends of Mammoth* and the cases following it] have compelled parties and courts to take the environment seriously and to take their obligations under CEQA seriously. The environment and the State of California have greatly benefited from the Court's early and insightful wisdom."[16]

During the early years of Chief Justice Wright's tenure, Justice Mosk began to counter the tendency of the Burger Court to more narrowly construe Warren Court protections by utilizing California's state constitution as the basis for the Court's ruling. While decisions could be based upon both the state and federal constitutions, by relying solely on the state constitution, the state court's decisions were insulated from review by the U.S. Supreme Court. As Mosk himself later explained in a 1993 law review article:

When the [U.S.] Supreme Court truck careens from one side of the road to the other, state courts have one of two alternatives. They can shift gears and change directions, thus achieving subservient consistency with Washington. Or they can retain existing individual rights by reliance on the independent nonfederal grounds found in the several state constitutions. A growing number of states have adopted the latter course. They have accepted Justice Brennan's cordial invitation in *Michigan v. Mosely*; he reminded us that each "[state] has power to impose higher standards governing police practices under state law than is required by the federal constitution."[17]

The Burger Court's retrenchment continued throughout the 1970s, sparking an interesting exchange between Justice Mosk and Senator Ted Kennedy. Mosk had sent him an article on the subject. Kennedy wrote back that, "in light of recent Supreme Court decisions cutting back on Warren court opinions," particularly cases "restricting access to the federal courts," he found confirmation of "the wisdom of Justice Brennan's advice to look to our state courts for relief."[18] Former Supreme Court Justice Arthur Goldberg wrote Mosk about three of the high court's cases that seemed to run contrary to Goldberg's theory about state versus federal constitutional protections. He said that he saw nothing that would prevent chief executives of states and state legislatures from adopting more liberal civil libertarian safeguards for citizens than the Supreme Court." He quoted what he described as a favorite expression: "What the Constitution does not mandate, it may nevertheless inspire." Offering his personal observation about the mood in Washington, D.C., he added, "I detect a considerable pique on the part of the Supreme Court of the United States against the state court's telling the Supreme Court what the Supreme Court has decided."[19]

In California, the practice of relying upon the state constitution to provide more expansive protection of individual rights than required by the Federal Constitution became known to many as "The Mosk Doctrine." Mosk gained renown for his consistent rulings that sought to guarantee individual liberties contained in the California Constitution independent from the Constitution of the United States. Mosk was influenced by a seminal law review article by Professor Hans Linde of the University of Oregon, arguing that state courts should look *first* to the protections of their state constitutions, rather than federal constitutional guarantees.[20] Professor Linde later served as a Justice of the Oregon Supreme Court, from 1977 to 1990. Justices Mosk and Linde became good friends, and both were at the forefront of a nascent movement to revive state constitutions as the primary protection for the rights of citizens.

The most important of these rulings came in a series of cases regarding the freedom of speech in privately owned shopping malls, which were open to the public. In a 1968 decision of the Warren Court, *Food Employees v. Logan Plaza*,[21] the U.S. Supreme Court ruled that the First Amendment right of assembly protected union members picketing their employer, and thus could not be curbed by a privately owned shopping center's wholesale or absolute prohibition of picketing on their premises. Two years later, the case of *Diamond v. Bland*[22] came before the California Supreme Court. The plaintiffs sought to keep the owners of the huge Inland-Empire, San Bernardino Shopping Center from interfering with their efforts to gather signatures for an initiative petition on the premises of the shopping center. Justice Mosk's majority opinion, joined by all of the Justices except Justice McComb, granted relief squarely based the Warren Court's *Logan Plaza* decision.

Justice Mosk noted that signature gathering in the *Diamond* case was not directly related to the operation of any of the seventy-five businesses located in the shopping center; and that the peaceful gathering of signatures did not disrupt any of those businesses. He concluded therefore, that reasonable regulations calculated to protect their business interests rather than absolute bans on all non-business-related activities would suffice in protecting the right of the petitioners and the concerns of the owners of the property. Although privately owned, "in many instances the contemporary shopping center serves as the analogue of the traditional town square," and thus his opinion emphasized that modern-day shopping centers serve as business districts for the surrounding residential communities, and have important public functions. The issue remained controversial and two years later, the Burger Court determined in the 1974 case *Lloyd Corp. v. Tanner*[23] that the owners of a shopping center in Oregon had a constitutional right to prohibit the distribution of political handbills unrelated to the operation of the shopping center.

As a result of the U.S. Supreme Court's *Lloyd* decision, the injunction the California Court upheld in 1970 against the Inland-Empire Shopping Center to permit the gathering of signatures on their property was immediately dissolved, and in 1974 *Diamond v. Bland*[24] was back before the California Supreme Court for a second round. This time, in a 4–3 split, the Court majority concluded that the Supreme Court *Lloyd* decision would have to be followed.[25] Justice Mosk wrote a spirited dissent, arguing that the Court should not "abjectly surrender" its prior position, but should instead base its ruling on independent non-federal grounds.

Justice Mosk's dissent was fully vindicated five years later, when the California Supreme Court overruled the *Diamond II* decision and ruled that the California Constitution protected the right to gather signatures for a petition in a privately owned shopping center in *Robins v. Pruneyard Shopping Center*.[26] In authoring the majority opinion, Justice Newman made note of the reasoning Mosk used in his dissent in *Diamond II*: "His observations on the role of [shopping] centers in our society are even more forceful now than when he wrote."[27]

It was gratifying to Justice Mosk to see his dissenting views gain majority support in so short a time, but the real test came when the Pruneyard decision was appealed to the U.S. Supreme Court. All of the Justices on the Burger Court concurred in an opinion by Justice Rehnquist affirming the Pruneyard ruling of the California Supreme Court, upholding the state's independent protection of a constitutional right to gather signatures on private property. Although this right was not protected by the federal Constitution, Justice Rehnquist concluded it did not unreasonably burden the property rights of the shopping center owners.[28] Justice Mosk became an admirer of Justice Rehnquist after the Pruneyard ruling, and when Rehnquist was nominated to become Chief Justice in 1986, Mosk wrote a favorable op-ed article for the *Los Angeles Times* urging his confirmation. Chief Justice Rehnquist responded with a personal note of thanks.[29]

The "Mosk Doctrine" was most frequently applied in criminal cases, however, resulting in the reversal of dozens of cases because the Court concluded a search or seizure was unreasonable under the State constitution, although it would have passed muster under the looser Fourth Amendment federal standards being applied by the Burger Court. Over the next few years, Stanley Mosk published dozens of articles laying out the principles behind what he viewed as a new Federalism, balancing the overlapping and distinctive jurisdictions of the Federal government and that of the various states. Mosk applauded the modern application of "states' rights" theory, and cautioned that previous exploiters of the Tenth Amendment to support constitutionally sanctioned policies of racism and prejudice had no place in today's revival of state constitutionalism. In fact, he was clear that unlike the era when an individual's civil rights and liberties were narrowly defined, thus needing the protection of the U.S. Constitution, present-day Federalism argues for an expansion of the protection of these rights. To Mosk, state constitutionalism had much to appeal to both liberals and conservatives who might be leery of turning such a historically explosive tenet as "state's rights" on its head. Writing in November 1985, Mosk said:

> For the liberal, there is the prospect of continued expansion of individual rights and liberties; the work of the Warren Court can be carried on at the state level. For the conservative, state constitutionalism represents the triumph of federalism; crucial decisions about the apportionment of rights and benefits are decided by state courts responsive to local needs, rather than by a distant United States Supreme Court, perceived as insensitive. The future of state constitutionalism depends on whether liberals and conservatives can put aside their traditional differences and join in supporting a concept that provides mutual benefits.[30]

He argued that liberals and conservatives "agree on the basic principle that state courts are appropriate guardians of individual rights. The difference is one of emphasis. Conservatives place paramount importance on the proper allocation of power between the state and federal governments. The protection of individual rights is subordinate to the overriding principle of federalism. Liberals, on the other hand, are primarily interested in protecting rights. They do not concern themselves with whether a federal court or a state court secures those rights. This difference in emphasis leads, of course, to a shaky alliance, easily shattered by changes in political or social conditions." If the alliance holds, then he said, "state constitutionalism prospers." However, an overreaction to an imagined threat to the use of state doctrine might inspire "further restrictive legislation or initiative action by political demagogues and Neanderthals, then the future of state constitutionalism is clouded."[31]

The California Supreme Court's embrace of the "Mosk Doctrine" was very frustrating for California police and prosecutors, who saw no reason to give greater privacy protections to criminals than the U.S. Supreme Court required under the federal constitution. In June of 1982, with the support of the California District Attorneys Association, an initiative measure was submitted to the voters entitled "The Victims' Bill of Rights." The measure included some provisions for victim participation in criminal proceedings, as well as a sweeping amendment to the California Constitution that declared, "relevant evidence shall not be excluded in any criminal proceeding."[32] Those ten words had the potential to abrogate nearly fifty decisions of the California Supreme Court that had relied upon the state Constitution to exclude evidence in criminal proceedings because of unlawful police conduct. In interpreting the protections of the Fourth Amendment of the U.S. Constitution, the United States Supreme Court had declared that only "reasonable expectations" of privacy were protected, and under Chief Justice Warren Burger the High Court took a restrictive view of what expectations of privacy were reasonable.

A good example was the case of *People v. Krivda*,[33] in which the California Supreme Court held that police needed a search warrant to rummage through a suspect's trash cans that had been placed at the curb for collection. Upon review, the United States Supreme Court concluded a warrant was not necessary for such searches, because any expectation of privacy was not reasonable. When the case was remanded to the California Supreme Court, the Court reaffirmed its prior decision, relying upon the state Constitution to give broader protection to privacy in California.

Justice Mosk was the author of many of the California Supreme Court's decisions relying upon the state constitution to give broader protection to privacy against police intrusion. In *Burrows v. Superior Court*,[34] he authored a ruling that police must obtain warrants before obtaining banking records from a suspect's bank. In *People v. Mozetti*,[35] he wrote police could not routinely search the contents of containers in automobiles that had been impounded. In *People v. Brisendine*,[36] his opinion declared that in taking a suspect into custody, the police could search for weapons or obvious contraband, but could not open containers. In *In Re Tony C.*,[37] he concluded a police stop-and-frisk could not be based only on suspicion of truancy. Other California Supreme Court decisions protected California citizens from police peering into toilet booths through peep holes, and extended protection against unreasonable searches to private security guards employed by department stores. By amending the state constitution to forbid the exclusion of relevant evidence in criminal cases, the Victims' Bill of Rights effectively overruled some fifty of these cases, eliminating the California constitution as a basis for excluding evidence and permitting California courts to apply constitutional exclusionary rules only when required to do so by the federal constitution. Ironically, the opinions in *Mozetti* and *Burrows* were among the most influential majority opinions authored by Justice Mosk. *Mozetti* was followed eight times by courts in other states, *Burrows* in five.[38] As a result of the enactment of the Victims' Bill of Rights, these rulings, along with fifteen other Mosk rulings, are no longer applied in California.

The Victims' Bill of Rights was approved by 56 percent of the voters in the June, 1982 election, and because of its breadth was immediately challenged by a lawsuit claiming it violated the constitutional rule requiring an initiative to address a "single subject." The case was heard by the Court in the midst of George Deukmejian's campaign for governor, and he was quoted as saying that any Justice who voted to strike down the initiative should be removed from office. Four Justices were slated to appear on the November, 1982 ballot for confirmation or retention. Justice Mosk was not among them. In a close and contentious 4–3 ruling, the California Supreme Court upheld the initiative, ruling that "victims' rights" was a single subject that united all of the various provisions of the measure.[39] In later reflecting on whether the pressure of political elections influences Supreme Court decisions, Justice Otto Kaus commented that as hard as judges try to ignore such pressures in deciding cases, "it's like trying to ignore a crocodile in your bathtub while shaving in the morning."[40]

Justice Mosk's dissent (joined by Justice Alan Broussard), lamented that vital protections of the California Constitution had been eliminated with the stroke of a pen. He concluded:

> Crime is indeed a serious problem of society. But it must be approached with determination and intelligence, not by destruction of the values that have made this the greatest nation on earth. It is not unduly dramatic to suggest that proponents of this initiative have yielded to "panic and myopia" in what they describe as a "war on crime." ... The Goddess of Justice is wearing a black arm-band today, as she weeps for the Constitution of California.[41]

The irony of the enactment of the initiative and the decision of the California Supreme Court upholding it was that the "Mosk Doctrine" could no longer be employed in criminal cases. Many other states continued down the path blazed by Justice Mosk, but in his own state of California, constitutional protections in criminal cases were now at the mercy of the United States Supreme Court, and its continued pattern of limiting the breadth of Warren Court protections.

Justice Mosk was in frequent demand as a luncheon or dinner speaker for bar association gatherings and conventions. His support for Israel was stronger than ever. As part of the November, 1974 nationwide protests of the U.N. recognition of the Palestine Liberation Organization (PLO), Mosk was the featured speaker at a rally sponsored by the Jewish Community Relations Council.[42] He enjoyed "taking off the gloves" on these occasions, and displayed greater candor than his formal legal opinions for the Court would permit. Commemorating "Law Day" before the Wilshire Bar Association at the Ambassador Hotel in

1972, Justice Mosk lamented the current state of the nation at large. He suggested that introspection "is dreadfully painful these days ... like asking the Boston Strangler to massage your neck." He said:

> Here we are, able to undertake exploration on the frontiers of the moon. We are the most affluent nation in the world. Yet we are unable to extricate ourselves from a war that nobody wants and few comprehend. Our cities are in disarray. Our prisons have become jungles. Our schools are political pawns. At a time when science is literally lifting us to the stars, the emotional issue of our day is the deceptively simple problem of law and order, and man's seemingly relentless inhumanity to his fellow man.[43]

Mosk remarked that using the term "law and order" was like "cheering for George Wallace at a NAACP meeting." He explained that when some employed that expression, however, they were really "making a subtle appeal for the preservation of the status quo, whatever its shortcomings, and others use the phrase as code for repression of minority and dissident groups, or as a means of resolving the conflict between the Old Guard and the avant-garde."

Mosk noted that his critique was inspired by "some Archie Bunker types on the extreme right and avowed revolutionaries on the extreme left who attempt to rationalize disorders on the basis of the validity of announced objectives." Mosk, however, believed that the "fanatical strong-arm brutes in the racist, reactionary and anti-intellectual cult are likely to be far more effective in the use of fear and force than those students, radicals and minorities whose avowed objectives of a better society may have some arguable merit." Furthermore, "For the Neanderthal extremists fear and force are not merely means, they are ends in themselves. The polarization toward which we seem to be moving helps not those with grievances, but those with guns."

Stanley Mosk's description of the state of the nation in 1972 was an eerie premonition of post–9/11 America. He complained about how "the current hue and cry over the deceptively simple slogan of 'law and order' has given rise to a series of federal laws that have been "euphemistically called safe streets and crime control measures," and "all of which would be unthinkable in more reflective times." He said, "we now have on the books federal laws that allow law enforcement officers, with court approval, to tap the telephones of and to bug anyone who has committed, seems to be in the act of committing, or is believed to be about to commit a crime punishable by a year or more in prison. The law also allows the President to order by-passing the court warrant requirement in cases involving threats to the 'national security,' an authority which has been very broadly interpreted by the Attorney General's office." What's more, "for the first-time in peace-time history, the criminal laws in the District of Columbia provide for a system of preventative detention." A defendant can be held for up to 60 days if prior to trial, and despite the presumption of innocence, the presiding judge during the arraignment feels the defendant "seems likely to have committed the crimes charged with and likely to commit other crimes if released on bail until he is tried." Washington, D.C., will also allow a "'no knock' provision permitting law enforcement officers to enter private premises, openly or stealthily, without identifying themselves."[44]

Throughout the 1970's, Stanley and Edna Mosk were off nearly every summer or fall for extended international travel, frequently combined with participation in educational programs and lots of tennis matches. In 1970, Justice Mosk enrolled in a two-week seminar at The Hague Academy of International Law, followed by a month of travel with Edna through France and Switzerland. In 1972, they attended a three-week session at the elite Wilton Park Conference in England, then toured England, Wales, Scotland and Ireland.

The trip also gave them the treasured opportunity to observe the semi-final and final championship tennis matches at Wimbledon for 1972. They saw Americans Stan Smith and Billie Jean King win the men's and women's singles titles. In 1975, they returned to Africa for a three-week camping sojourn in game preserves, where they observed and photographed a wide variety of African wildlife. They then went on to Egypt, Morocco, and Spain. Stanley had a mailing list of 41 recipients, who received lengthy "Dear All" letters with detailed descriptions of their travel adventures. He even authored an occasional feature for the travel sections of hometown newspapers. The *Los Angeles Times* rejected his article about tourist visits to Kinshasa, Zaire (the former Belgian Congo). The editors apparently concluded that a story that described what an awful place it was to visit did not fit their needs. In 1978, Edna accompanied her husband to Israel, where he participated in a conference of Jewish lawyers and jurists in Jerusalem. After that trip, Edna's illness and treatment demanded less rigorous travel. Their final trip together was an Alaska cruise in July of 1980.

Chapter 13

"The Melancholy Truth"

In 1972, there were 105 inmates on Califorrnia's death row, awaiting execution in California's gas chamber at San Quentin Prison. They included Charles Manson, leader of the cult that committed a horrifying series of grisly murders in Los Angeles; Sirhan Sirhan, who assassinated Robert F. Kennedy in 1968; and Gregory U. Powell, convicted of the execution murder of a Los Angeles police officer in an onion field near Bakersfield. As Attorney General, Stanley Mosk had consistently opposed the death penalty at the same time he was busily engaged in enforcing it as the State's chief law enforcement officer, representing the state in the automatic appeals to the California Supreme Court guaranteed to all death row inmates. *People v. Anderson*[1] presented the Wright Court with a broad challenge to the constitutionality of California's death penalty law. The case came before the Court for the second time, on the automatic review of a death judgment returned by a jury after Anderson's initial death sentence was reversed by the California Supreme Court because of errors in jury selection. This time, Anderson argued that the death penalty law was unconstitutional as both "cruel" and "unusual" under both the state and federal constitutions. The Court noted that the same issue was currently before the United States Supreme Court, but found it unnecessary to address the question of constitutionality under the federal Constitution, because it concluded that California's death penalty law violated the *state* constitutional prohibition of "cruel *or* unusual punishment." The ruling was not a complete surprise, because nearly every death judgment reviewed by the Court in the previous five years had been reversed. But the author of the opinion — Chief Justice Donald R. Wright — certainly surprised Governor Ronald Reagan. Anticipating the controversy the decision would engender, Justice Mosk and his fellow Justices sought to dissuade the Chief Justice from authoring the opinion. Mosk later reported, "We all said to him, 'Look Don, you were appointed by Governor Reagan. We know his attitude on the death penalty. We'll spare you the embarrassment of putting this out. One of us will be glad to do it, or we can put it out (unsigned) by the court and nobody will know who the author is.'" Mosk recalled Wright replying, "No, those are my views. I'm going to stand up and be counted."[2] Years later, Mosk described Wright's moving opinion as "a masterpiece of judicial writing," and he "considered it a privilege to sign it."[3] Chief Justice Wright's opinion in *People v. Anderson* spoke in broad, sweeping terms:

> We have concluded that capital punishment is impermissibly cruel. It degrades and dehumanizes all who participate in its processes. It is unnecessary to any legitimate goal of the state and is incompatible with the dignity of man and the judicial process. Our conclusion that the death penalty may no longer be exacted in California consistently with article I, section 6, of our Constitution is not grounded in sympathy for those who would commit crimes of violence, but in concern for the society that diminishes itself whenever it takes the life of one of its members.

Although the Chief Justice "gained great respect" for his courage from Justice Mosk and his other colleagues on the Court, he won bitter enmity from the governor who appointed him. Reagan publicly denounced the Chief Justice's opinion, labeling it "one more step toward totally disarming society in its fight against violence."[4] The public was outraged that the decision not only commuted the death sentence of Anderson, but spared the lives of everyone then on death row. An initiative measure was quickly proposed to amend the California constitution to abrogate the *Anderson* ruling by declaring the death penalty was neither cruel nor unusual. Proposition 17 was adopted by a 67 percent margin in the statewide election of November 7, 1972.

Meanwhile, in June of 1972, the United States Supreme Court handed down its nine separate opinions in the case of *Furman v. Georgia*,[5] prohibiting unguided discretion in the imposition of the death penalty by juries. This decision truly was a surprise, even to the Justices of the California Supreme Court. If they had simply waited four months, their controversial ruling in *Anderson* could have been entirely avoided. As Justice Mosk later explained, "We just sort of counted noses."[6] The California Justices assumed that the recent appointments by President Richard Nixon had shifted the United States Supreme Court so far to the right that the *Furman v. Georgia* challenge to death penalty laws would not succeed. But the California battles over the death penalty were far from over.

The Furman opinions were widely interpreted as prohibiting discretion in the imposition of the death penalty. In 1973, the California Legislature responded to Proposition 17 and the generally accepted interpretation of Furman by enacting a mandatory death penalty law, requiring that capital punishment be imposed in all cases of contract killings, murders of police officers or crime witnesses, multiple killings, and murders during the commission of rape, robbery, burglary, kidnapping or child molestation. During the next three years, another fifty persons were sentenced to death in California under this law.

In 1976, the United States Supreme Court upheld death penalty statutes that "guided" the discretion of juries, but ruled that the mandatory death penalty laws enacted in twenty states were unconstitutional.[7] Thereafter, in a ruling that surprised no one, the Wright Court declared the 1973 mandatory death penalty law unconstitutional in a unanimous opinion issued in December, 1976.[8] The California Legislature responded by enacting a new death penalty law modeled upon the laws upheld by the United States Supreme Court. The new death penalty law was authored by then–Senator George Deukmejian. The bill was vetoed by newly elected Governor Jerry Brown, but was re-enacted over his veto and became effective August 11, 1977. Fifteen months later, in November of 1978, the 1977 death penalty law was repealed and replaced by an initiative measure, known as the "Briggs Initiative," which broadly expanded the categories of cases in which the death penalty could be imposed. It was adopted by a popular margin of 72 percent.

The California Supreme Court finally addressed the constitutionality of the Deukmejian death penalty law in *People v. Frierson*.[9] Although Frierson's death sentence was set aside based on his claim he had been denied effective assistance of counsel, the majority opinion directly addressed the claims that the statute was unconstitutional, concluding that the issue was resolved when, in November of 1972, the people of California adopted a constitutional amendment (art. I, § 27) which clearly declared: "The death penalty provided for under those statutes shall not be deemed to be, or to constitute, the infliction of cruel or unusual punishments within the meaning of Article I, Section 6 nor shall such punishment for such offenses be deemed to contravene any other provision of this constitution." Only three Justices signed the majority opinion, however, which declared:

> It is proper that we promptly and clearly express our views either upholding the penalty or specifically defining any constitutional defects which we discern in the death penalty procedures. Since 1972 the sovereign people of this state twice directly, and through their elected representatives on other occasions, have mounted a continuous, strong, and joint effort to restore the death penalty as a permissible form of punishment. They are entitled to know whether they have adopted a valid sanction. Regardless of our personal moral or ethical convictions or preferences, and no matter how strongly held, fundamental principles of fairness demand that, as the final legal arbiters in this state to whom all death sentences are automatically appealed, we should speak on the issue of constitutionality. We should do so at the earliest practicable opportunity and when the procedural posture of the case is appropriate for the expression of our views. This has been our tradition.

Chief Justice Bird protested that the constitutional rulings were "dictum" and Justice Tobriner argued that:

> In my view our court should await a case in which a defendant actually faces execution under the 1977 law before addressing the basic constitutional questions raised by that enactment. The awesome question of whether a defendant will live or die should be framed in concrete, not abstract, terms; the decision must be reached with the realization that it will result in the designed death of an individual man or woman who stands before the court.

Thus, the majority ruling on the constitutional issues depended upon the concurrence of Justice Stanley Mosk and Justice Frank Newman. Newman joined the concurring opinion of Justice Mosk, in which he declared, "With the utmost reluctance, I have come full circle in my consideration of the death penalty in California." Justice Mosk wrote:

> The people of California responded quickly and emphatically, both directly and through their elected representatives, to callously declare that whatever the trends elsewhere in the nation and the world, society in our state does not deem the retributive extinction of a human life to be either cruel or unusual. "Cruelty" is not definable with precision. It is in the eye of the beholder: what may be perceived as cruelty by one person is seen as justice by another. Thus, this court, in ascertaining the permissible limits of punishment, must look in the first instance to those values to which the people of our state subscribe. That as one individual I prefer values more lofty than those implicit in the macabre process of deliberately exterminating a human being does not permit me to interpret in my image the common values of the people of our state.[10]

Thus, Justice Mosk bowed to the rule of law, recognizing that despite his personal moral reservations, the will of the people must prevail. With this memorable and quotable passage he concluded:

> The day will come when all mankind will deem killing to be immoral, whether committed by one individual or many individuals organized into a state. Unfortunately, morality appears to be a waning rule of conduct today, almost an endangered species, in this uneasy and tortured society of ours: a society in which sadism and violence are highly visible and often accepted commodities, a society in which guns are freely available and energy is scarce, a society in which reason is suspect and emotion is king. Thus with a feeling of futility I recognize the melancholy truth that the anticipated dawn of enlightenment does not seem destined to appear soon.

The interpretation and application of the California death penalty law would occupy the California Supreme Court throughout the remainder of Justice Mosk's tenure, and is still being litigated today. But the question of whether the death penalty is "cruel or unusual" under the California constitution was settled by the Frierson ruling.

Fourteen years later, on April 21, 1992, California conducted its first execution under the death penalty law enacted in 1978. Robert Alton Harris had been convicted of an execution style murder of two high school sophomores who were kidnapped while sitting in a parking lot at a San Diego drive-in eating hamburgers.. According to the testimony at trial, Harris boasted to a cellmate that he told one of the terrified boys to "quit crying and die like a man." When the boy started to pray, Harris said, "God can't help you now, boy; you're going to die." After shooting both boys through the head, he ate their half-finished hamburgers. The police officer who arrested Harris after a subsequent robbery was the father of one of the dead boys.

When Harris's direct appeal was rejected by the California Supreme Court in 1981, Justice Mosk had joined Chief Justice Rose Bird in dissenting, arguing that prejudicial pretrial publicity had tainted his right to a fair trial.[11] In a last-ditch challenge to the use of lethal gas as the means of execution, filed on the eve of the execution, Justice Mosk was the only one on the Court to dissent from the denial of a habeas corpus petition, arguing:

> Petitioner has made out a prima facie case. It is significant that all the exhibits, either directly or indirectly, support the proposition that today killing by lethal gas is extremely and unnecessarily painful. It is also significant that those same exhibits show that of the 38 states that provide for capital punishment, today only California effectively mandates use of gas.[12]

An appeal for clemency to California governor Pete Wilson was rejected in a live television news conference, where Wilson read a statement acknowledging Harris's abusive childhood but ended with a clear rejection of the clemency request, saying, "As great as is my compassion for Robert Harris the child, I cannot excuse or forgive the choice made by Robert Harris the man." Wilson then left without waiting for reporters' questions.

Harris' execution was originally scheduled for 12:01 A.M. on the morning of April 21, 1992. Pursuant to the Court's protocol, the Justices gathered in the chambers of Chief Justice Malcolm Lucas to respond to any last minute challenges to the execution, with an open line to the execution chamber. A series of four stays issued by individual federal judges delayed the execution until just after 6 A.M. In its order vacating the fourth stay of execution, the U.S. Supreme Court stated, "No further stays of Robert Alton Harris's execution shall be entered by the Federal courts except upon order of this Court." Thus, all of the California Supreme Court Justices spent over six hours of sleepless waiting. Halfway through this ordeal, Chief Justice Lucas noticed Stanley Mosk frequently checking his watch. He suggested Stanley go home and get some sleep, promising they would summon him if anything happened. Mosk replied, "I'm not worried about getting sleep. I have a 6:30 A.M. tennis match scheduled, and I'm concerned I may have to cancel it." After the execution was finally carried out and Robert Harris was declared dead at 6:21 A.M., Justice Mosk went directly to his tennis match, then returned to the Court to put in a full day's work.

Over the years, Stanley Mosk had frequently responded to requests from countries all over the world seeking his advice in setting up, refining, or reforming judicial institutions and procedures. Among others, Mosk earned the esteem of Israel's legal community, and in 1991, his views about the death penalty were published in *The Israeli Law Review*. He then wrote, "In a way, I suppose, everything has been said about the death penalty that can be said." Nonetheless, recognizing that the death penalty will continue to be a subject of discussion, he offered his perspective. "At the risk of appearing immodest, I claim to be particularly equipped to enter into this discussion because I have been on all sides of the issue — not, I hasten to explain, because of unconcern or ambivalence." Mosk proceded to briefly chronicle at which stages of his life he considered the issue of capital punishment:

> First, as an idealistic young man, I debated for abolition of the death penalty. Then, as executive secretary to the Governor of California, I had the duty of actually interviewing, in prison,

men — and one woman — under sentence of death and making a report to the Governor.... Next, I became a trial judge and had the tragic duty of sentencing a murderer to die.... My next public office was as Attorney General of California. In that capacity I was the chief law enforcement officer of the state and resisted the appeals of convicted defendants. Nevertheless, I testified on three occasions before our state legislature, urging repeal of capital punishment, to no avail. Finally, as a Justice of the Supreme Court of California, I took the oath of office to support the constitution and laws of the state as they are, and not as I might prefer them to be. Thus, on occasion I have concurred in opinions upholding convictions of murder and death sentences. As you can see, my perceptions have varied with my responsibilities. When called upon to enforce the laws as they are, I have done so. When permitted the indulgence of personal opinion, I have expressed a clear preference for elimination of capital punishment. Therefore, I claim a certain objectivity on the subject.

Mosk concluded with the "dismaying possibility," that "we can draw no conclusion," about the application of the death penalty in America. For him, it would remain "a serious moral query," that is, "whether a civilized society should proceed with executions when it has only imperfect procedures for determining which of its members it will deliberately put to death. The people, according to all available indicia, answer that question affirmatively. The courts merely seem to say, perhaps."[13]

Today, in 2012, California has 720 inmates on death row. There have been only twelve more executions since the 1992 execution of Robert Alton Harris. Two successive Chief Justices of the State of California have declared the death penalty law is "dysfunctional." The author of the Briggs Initiative now agrees it was a mistake. State Senator Ron Briggs, the son of the Senator John Briggs who sponsored the Briggs Initiative, wrote in the *Los Angeles Times* for February 12, 2012:

Back then, my future brother-in-law was Dad's district chief of staff and I proudly served as my father's personal aide. Today Dad is retired, my brother-in-law is a California Superior Court judge and I am in my second term as a county supervisor representing rural District IV in the county of El Dorado, east of Sacramento. Recently, the three of us sat together under a rose trellis in the quiet cool of morning to talk politics. Each of us remains a staunch Republican conservative, but our perspectives on the death penalty have changed. We'd thought we would bring California savings and safety in dealing with convicted murderers. Instead, we contributed to a nightmarish system that coddles murderers and enriches lawyers. Our initiative was intended to bring about greater justice for murder victims. Never did we envision a multibillion-dollar industry that packs murderers onto death row for decades of extremely expensive incarceration. We thought we would empty death row, not triple its population. Each of us, independently, has concluded that the death penalty isn't working for California.[14]

Perhaps, eleven years after the death of Stanley Mosk, the "dawn of enlightenment" is finally arriving in California. Senator Ron Briggs concluded:

There are few "do-overs" in life, especially in politics. With the death penalty, though, 34 years later I have an opportunity to set things right. The Briggs family has decided to endorse the SAFE California campaign, a fall 2012 ballot initiative that would replace the death penalty with a punishment of life without the possibility of parole. The state has another chance at real justice. We should embrace it.[15]

Chapter 14

"You Don't Have to Remove Your Shoes Before Stepping All Over Stanley Mosk"

Probably no single decision rendered by the California Supreme Court during the thirty-seven years of Justice Stanley Mosk's tenure engendered greater controversy than the case of *Allan Bakke v. Regents of the University of California*.[1] "Affirmative action" programs to address the long-term effects of previous racial discrimination first appeared at the federal level. President John F. Kennedy issued Executive Order 10925 on March 6, 1961, establishing the president's Commission on Equal Employment Opportunity (PCEEO) to oversee a new mandate that government contractors "take *affirmative action* to ensure that applicants are employed, and employees are treated during employment, without regard to their race, creed, color, or national origin." The Order, however, failed to clearly define the meaning of "affirmative action." It was largely interpreted to mean to "to take the initiative," or "to do something extra."[2] The term "Affirmative Action," was first coined during the Depression Era's New Deal policies designed to redress unfair labor practices.

While the federal government did not yet *mandate* affirmative action, state level Fair Employment Practices Commissions often ordered "affirmative action" by employers to comply with FEPC policies. Vice President Lyndon B. Johnson chaired the PCEEO and his vice chair was future Justice of the U.S. Supreme Court, and long-time friend of Stanley Mosk, Secretary of Labor Arthur Goldberg. Goldberg recognized the White House initiative as "a vigorous, positive program to ensure that all Americans ... will have equal access to employment opportunities." Goldberg announced "we are taking affirmative steps to acquaint members of minority groups with the opportunities for employment," and the Department followed suit, for the first time actively recruiting and hiring African Americans. Responding to concerns that Affirmative Action might "deprive qualified white students of job opportunities if improperly implemented," Goldberg stressed that the department would "follow the same staffing procedures, and qualify [the black students] in the same examinations or evaluations as others seeking employment or promotion." He said, "to do otherwise would in itself be a form of discrimination."[3]

Over the next two years, the Department of Labor developed guidelines and regulations supporting the Executive Order. One month after President Kennedy's assassination, the final report was published, to take effect mid–January, 1964. Nowhere did the document call for the initiation of "racial quotas." Instead it vaguely asserted that programs should provide "current opportunities for selection of qualified members' of minority groups."[4] Subsequently, President Johnson signed the historic 1964 Civil Rights Act, followed a year later by the Voting Rights Act and Executive Order 11246. Building on Kennedy's earlier executive order, the federal government broadened the groups protected and actually prohibited employment discrimination based on race, color, religion, and national origin (and two years later added "sex") by those organizations receiving federal contracts and subcontracts, and also required federal contractors to take *affirmative action* to promote the full realization of equal opportunity for women and minorities. The Office of Federal Contract Compliance Programs (OFCCP), under the Department of Labor, monitored this requirement for all federal contractors, including all University of California campuses, and developed regulations to which these contractors must adhere. For federal contractors employing more than 50 people and having federal contracts totaling more than $50,000, compliance with these regulations included disseminating and enforcing a nondiscrimination policy, establishing a written affirmative action plan and placement goals for women and minorities, and implementing action-oriented programs for accomplishing these goals. In addition, an official of the organization was to be assigned responsibility for implementation of equal employment opportunity and the affirmative action program.

In 1969, the faculty of the medical school of the University of California at Davis addressed the concern that its admission policies were perpetuating the underrepresentation of minorities in the student body, and ultimately in the medical profession itself. The faculty adopted a "special admissions program," under which 16 of the 100 places in each incoming class would be set aside for applicants from "disadvantaged backgrounds." Although white students were not barred from applying for the "special admissions program," all of the students admitted under the special program from its inception through 1974 were from identifiable racial minorities. The special admissions program operated with a separate committee, a majority of whom were members of minority groups. On the 1973 application form, candidates were asked to indicate whether they wished to be considered as "economically and/or educationally disadvantaged" applicants; on the 1974 form the question was whether they wished to be considered as members of a "minority group," which the medical school apparently viewed as "Blacks," "Chicanos," "Asians," and "American Indians." If these questions were answered affirmatively, the application was forwarded to the special admissions committee. No formal definition of "disadvantaged" was ever produced, but the chairman of the special committee screened each application to see whether it reflected economic or educational deprivation. From 1971 through 1974, the special program resulted in the admission of 21 black students, 30 Mexican-Americans, and 12 Asians, for 63 minority students. Over the same period, the regular admissions program produced 1 black, 6 Mexican-Americans, and 37 Asians, for a total of 44 minority students.[5]

Allan Bakke was a white student who applied under the school's normal admissions program, and was rejected in both 1973 and 1974. The normal admissions program assigned students a "combined numerical rating" based upon their undergraduate grades and their performance on the Medical College Admission Test (MCAT). Bakke had an undergraduate grade point average of 3.51, and scored above the 90th percentile in three of the four sections of the MCAT. In 1973, Bakke's combined numerical rating was 468 out of a possible 500, and in 1974 it was 549 out of a possible 600. He was able to demonstrate that the average scores on the MCAT test of the minority students admitted under the special admissions program in 1973 and 1974 were below the 50th percentile in all four areas tested. In addition, the combined numerical ratings of some students admitted under the special program were 20 to 30 points below Bakke's rating. He brought a lawsuit against the university seeking admission to the U.C. Davis Medical School, claiming he had been the victim of invidious discrimination because of his race, in violation of the equal protection clause of the Fourteenth Amendment to the United States Constitution. The University filed a counter-claim, seeking a declaratory judgment that its special admissions program was valid. The trial court ruled against the university, finding the special admissions program unconstitutional, but declined to order Bakke's admission because he could not demonstrate he would have been admitted even if the special admissions program did not exist. The California Supreme Court granted a hearing of the ensuing appeals without waiting for a ruling from the intermediate Court of Appeal.

The California Supreme Court was commonly thought to be the most liberal appellate court in the country. Supporters of the UC Davis program had every confidence the high court would overturn the Yolo County ruling."[6] The California Supreme Court had "an enviable reputation as one of the most active and progressive in the country." It had anticipated many of the most liberal rulings of the U.S. Supreme Court in protecting the poor and extending constitutional protections. In particular, one author noted, "On racial matters, it had rejected the high court's attempt to differentiate between de jure and de facto segregation, holding that all segregation violated the rights of black children." In other words, "This was a court that was viewed as a champion of the underdog and that gloried in its activist reputation."[7]

The case immediately attracted national media attention, and broad participation by civil rights organizations with the filing of "friend of the court" (*amicus curiae*) briefs. Six of the nine amicus briefs, including one from the NAACP, urged the Supreme Court to reverse the trial court and uphold the special admissions program. Three urged the Court to uphold the trial court and strike down the program: the Anti-Defamation League, the American Jewish Congress, and the American Federation of Teachers.

In the late 1960's and early 1970's over 100 medical schools throughout the country had set up similar special admission programs aimed at increasing the enrollment of minority medical students and producing a more integrated medical profession. Scores of law schools and other professional and graduate schools, as well as numerous undergraduate institutions, had implemented analogous "affirmative action" programs as part of a national effort to bring members of minority groups into the mainstream of American society. It was widely feared that a ruling striking down the University of California program would deliver a severe, if not fatal, blow to these voluntary efforts to integrate the professions and ameliorate the continuing effects of past discrimination.

The preparation of the conference memo for the *Bakke* case was randomly assigned to Justice Stanley Mosk, and after the Court granted a hearing, he was assigned to author the Court's decision to strike down the special admissions program and order the admission of Allan Bakke to the medical school of the University of California at Davis. His majority opinion focused on the rights of Allan Bakke as an individual. Directly addressing Bakke's claim that he was excluded because he was white, and that the special admission program was unconstitutional for that reason, Mosk wrote:

> It is plain that the special admission program denies admission to some white applicants solely because of their race. Of the 100 admission opportunities available in each year's class, 16 are set aside for disadvantaged minorities, and the committee admits applicants who fall into this category until these 16 places are filled. Since the pool of applicants available in any year is limited, it is obvious that this procedure may result in acceptance of minority students whose qualifications for medical study, under the standards adopted by the University itself, are inferior to those of some white applicants who are rejected.

From this perspective, Justice Mosk found the special admissions program impossible to distinguish from the hated "quota" systems that *limited* the admission of minorities in the past:

> While a program can be damned by semantics, it is difficult to avoid considering the University scheme as a form of an education quota system, benevolent in concept perhaps, but a revival of quotas nevertheless. No college admission policy in history has been so thoroughly discredited in contemporary times as the use of racial percentages.

With great satisfaction, he quoted his old friend Carey McWilliams in his *Bakke* opinion: "Originated as a means of exclusion of racial and religious minorities from higher education, a quota becomes no less offensive when it serves to exclude a racial majority. 'No form of discrimination should be opposed more vigorously than the quota system.' (McWilliams, *A Mask for Privilege* [1948] p. 238.)"[8]

In his classic study of anti-semitism in America, first published in 1948, Carey McWilliams had fully exposed the evil of racial and religious quotas aimed primarily at keeping Catholics and Jews out of Ivy League schools. Peter Belton, Mosk's principal staff attorney, attributed Mosk's views in the *Bakke* case to the Justice's "personal experience of being Jewish," and being himself a member of a group subjected to the hated quota system.[9] For Peter Belton, the "Bakke experience ... was quite an upheaval." Olga Murray worked on the opinion at great length, but Justice Mosk "took a strong hand in the case because [of his] deep feelings and opinions and thoughts about the issue." Belton explained that Mosk "had long believed that any quota system was of doubtful constitutionality. And this issue was presented to the court in Bakke in such a way that he thought he should express that view in forceful terms, so a lot of work was done on it." In fact, according to Belton, "everybody knew that it was going to be a landmark case, and indeed it went on to the United States Supreme Court."[10]

More than three decades later, Belton remarked, "Of course the issue is still alive in various ways. It's certainly far from a dead issue, and I suspect it will be a live issue for a long time to come. But that was the first salvo in the battle." Belton's view was that "Jewish people in America and other countries had long suffered from quotas," and therefore, "it was an article of faith of Jewish social philosophy that these kinds of quotas were unfair and unwise." Thus, for Justice Mosk, "it wasn't a big stretch for him to bring ... this predilection, if you will, to the table in this case." In other words, "It should have been, therefore, not as great a surprise as it was."[11]

Although it is true that many Jewish organizations had expressed hostility to affirmative action programs, it must be noted that the only Justice who dissented in *Bakke* was Justice Tobriner, who was also Jewish. Tobriner's dissent was a passionate defense of affirmative action programs, finding the need to fully integrate the medical profession a compelling necessity, and distinguishing "benign" preferences from the invidious racial discrimination that inspired the Fourteenth Amendment equal protection clause. When Chief Justice Donald Wright sided with Mosk in deciding the *Bakke* case, he explained that, "his heart was with Tobriner, but his head was with Justice Mosk," and sided with the majority opinion.[12] Mosk also had strong sympathy for the objectives of affirmative action, but felt that competition for college or professional school admission should be judged solely on merit. Most advocates seeking to fix the problem of underrepresentation in the upper echelons of academia agreed that the problem started in the lower grades, but that did nothing to overcome discrimination for the current generation of potential candidates to professional schools. Mosk was aware of the dilemma and he later explained his view that efforts to equalize educational opportunity should be focused on early education:

> I do have a gnawing sympathy for those who were disadvantaged because of race or color or economics, so that they cannot compete on a basis of equality with others. I've always seen the long-range solution to be roughly this: that those who have a disadvantage of any kind, whether it's race or economics or physical, ought to be given some special treatment during their early years of education in the public schools, so that when the competition begins later on for college admission, for professional school admission, or for employment, that they will be able to compete on a basis of equality. But I concede that it's going to take some special training for many of those people in the early days of public schools, and I don't think we're doing that today.[13]

The *Bakke* ruling did not foreclose the university from affirmative action programs that did not use race as a factor. As Justice Mosk put it in the majority opinion,

> The University is entitled to consider, as it does with respect to applicants in the special program, that low grades and test scores may not accurately reflect the abilities of some disadvantaged students; and it may reasonably conclude that although their academic scores are lower, their potential for success in the school and the profession is equal to or greater than that of an applicant with higher grades who has not been similarly handicapped. In addition, the University may properly, as it in fact does, consider other factors in evaluating an applicant, such as the personal interview, recommendations, character, and matters relating to the needs of the profession and society, such as an applicant's professional goals. In short, the standards for admission employed by the University are not constitutionally infirm except to the extent that they are utilized in a racially discriminatory manner. Disadvantaged applicants of all races must be eligible for sympathetic consideration, and no applicant may be rejected because of his race, in favor of another who is less qualified, as measured by standards applied *without regard to race*" [emphasis added].

The California Supreme Court also overruled the lower court's determination that Allan Bakke bore the burden of proving he would have been admitted if the special admissions program did not exist. The court concluded that because Bakke was the victim of unlawful discrimination, the burden shifted to the state to show he would not have been admitted. Because the state conceded it could not meet that burden, Allan Bakke was admitted to the incoming class of 1976.

Following the release of Mosk's Bakke opinion, the issue of whether UC Davis should appeal to the U.S. Supreme Court divided even those involved in the case on behalf of the university. For various reasons, groups like the NAACP Legal Defense Fund and the Mexican American Legal Defense Fund opposed moving forward to the U.S. Supreme Court. But Nathaniel Colley, as the general counsel of the West Coast NAACP, wanted to push forward. Colley suggested that had his organization been allowed to join the case, the NAACP could have produced evidence of past discrimination.[14] Colley also feared that the prestige of the California Supreme Court would induce other states to cite Mosk's opinion and follow it. Although his view was not widely shared, Colley found strong support in University of California Regent William Coblentz. After a closed-door meeting, the Board of Regents decided that if the California Supreme Court would not rehear their case, which it didn't, university attorneys had the go ahead to seek a hearing in the U.S. Supreme Court.

Some of Justice Mosk's good friends and colleagues politely disagreed with his Bakke opinion. U.S. Supreme Court Justice Arthur Goldberg tactfully wrote, "I enjoy your writings, even when I disagree with you, which is rarely. However, you have still not persuaded me about the Bakke case."[15] Others were not as civil. Justice Mosk's majority opinion subjected him to a barrage of liberal invective, which he took very personally. He liked to quote a remark by Los Angeles criminal defense attorney Marvin Part: "The difference between Stanley and the other type of mosque is that you don't have to remove your shoes before stepping all over Stanley Mosk." State Senator John Vasconcellos, a leading liberal, sent Mosk a draft memo in which he characterized Mosk's majority opinion as tortured, "like getting from Sacramento to Davis by going through Los Angeles." Mosk responded with "equally brutal frankness but not for publication":

> I gather your views were sent to me to aid you in assuming a stance of apparent objectivity. Actually, however, your observations are merely another version of what is obviously a shrill and well-orchestrated campaign to revive the long-discredited quota system in educational institutions.

He added that he was "disillusioned with professed liberals like you and Jerry Brown who sacrifice principle for expediency."[16]

Many academics addressed Mosk with uncharacteristic passion. The University of California, Los Angeles's noted historian John Caughey, an ACLU Board member, wished Mosk belated congratulations on the Bakke decision, adding "Surely, there can be no doubt that those 16 reserved spots were a quota from which the likes of Bakke were excluded." To Caughey, "the menace" that threatens the Fourteenth Amendment's equal protection clause comes from "generous-hearted persons with whom I like to associate," which then, "makes the threat to the constitutional principle all the more serious." He understood why the black caucus "was exercised," but criticized the ACLU for joining it. He then proffered a lengthy discussion about victimless alternatives to the quota method to accomplish the intent of affirmative action. Caughey offered a revealing observation that, "there is another strain of affirmative action that does victimize. Quota systems in staffing university faculties are a notorious instance. There the selection should be not at random but, as they say at Harvard, by finding the best candidate in the world. A merit system is especially important and quotas by definition are not that. Much of this argument carries over to graduate school entrance."[17] Mosk wrote back: "It is comforting to know that one with your civil rights' credentials sees the issue as I did."[18] Rodolfo Acuna, Professor of History at California State University, Northridge, also wrote to Mosk, copying to another UCLA history professor, Juan Gomez-Quinonez. Professor Acuna held nothing back. "Until recently I was one of your staunchest supporters. You were one of the few men whom I believed had integrity and understood the difficulties minority groups had surviving in this society. However, in view of the Bakke decision and your recent statements supporting the University of California, Davis, it is apparent that your own class and race interests have compromised your principles." Acuna challenged Mosk's statement in a recent interview explaining that he might have decided differently if it had been proven that the University of California, Davis had intentionlly discriminated against minorities, so the special admission program could be regarded as remedial. "Judge Mosk—you have lost touch with reality," Acuna asserted, and then went on to explain that after his twenty years of "continual contact with the Universities of this state," that he could "prove that discrimination has and does exist." Furthermore, "University authorities know it and so should you." He chastised Mosk to "leave your ivory tower for a minute," so he "might get another perspective and realize the harm that your ignorance is causing." In an offhand reference to the Jewish community, Acuna suggested it has shifted from its traditional liberal leadership to an "element" that "has grown very sectarian and has supported its own agenda at the expense of the minority community." Their leaders have evenly openly bragged that "Harvey Schechter of the Anti-Deformation [sic] League told a well known judge who told me that your court had taken his organization's brief almost verbatim in its rationale for Bakke." Acuna said he now "can clearly recognize the "arrogance of power," and that although he realized his letter was not going to change Mosk's mind, particularly because "you have too many chips to pay off," he wanted him "to know why so many of us are becoming disenchanted with the system and liberals in particular. Conservatives are at least honest.... But, liberals attempt to cloth opportunism behind the cloak of fairness, and justice while ignoring the truth." Acuna went on to describe how "disturbing" it was "that judges are influenced only by those who have money," and that "liberals think that by not eating grapes (referring to the grape boycott in support of Cesar Chavez's effort to win recognition of the United Farm Workers) that they have done their thing for Mexicanos. More important, he pointed out was the need for medical care. "I can introduce you to people in East Los Angeles and other colonias where specialist[s] and other medical doctors will not care for medicare or medical (Medi-Cal) patients. ... doctors from Mexico have [to be] imported to service Mexicans because your nice white liberal doctors only want to work in affluent areas (I wonder if Bakke will serve the poor)."[19]

Justice Mosk eagerly read the national media's treatment of his *Bakke* opinion, and thought much of it was ill informed. In an unusual move, he published an op-ed piece himself, offering a more detailed explanation of the Bakke decision. Entitled, "Why the California Court Ruled for Allan Bakke," it appeared in the *Baltimore Sun* for Sunday, May 22, 1977.

For the first time in his life, Mosk directly encountered protesters objecting to one of his decisions. Each year, the members of the graduating class at the School of Law at the University of California, Davis select their commencement speaker by a student vote. In the fall of 1977, the top vote-getters were Woody Allen, Coretta Scott King, Rose Bird, Barbara Jordan and Stanley Mosk. The Dean excluded Chief Justice Bird because she had been invited to judge the moot court finals for that year. Allen, King and Jordan all declined the invitation. Stanley Mosk accepted the invitation, and a group of minority students and others then urged the Dean to withdraw the invitation to protest Justice Mosk's *Bakke* opinion. The Dean replied that it was "unthinkable" to withdraw the invitation merely because some students disagreed with Mosk's decision in a single case. The students then sent a long letter to Justice Mosk, expressing their displeasure with his selection as commencement speaker. Justice Mosk responded with a letter reminding students of the First Amendment, and expressing the hope they would be present to hear what he had to say:

> I am sad that in 1978 there are third year law students with a lack of understanding of the First Amendment. I am sad that there are those with undergraduate degrees who failed to read Voltaire. ["I disapprove of what you say, but I will defend to the death your right to say it."] I am sad that there are young Americans who have forgotten the lessons of Thomas Jefferson. ["Error of opinion may be tolerated where reason is left free to combat it."] I am perhaps most sad that there are students hoping to enter the legal profession who apparently believe that picketing, pamphleteering and demonstrations are proper means to influence the judicial process.[20]

He compared the student threats of disruption of the commencement ceremonies with personal abuse he encountered from the White Citizens Council after striking down racially restrictive covenants in 1947. As campus tensions rose, the Dean reached an understanding with the students, that pickets would be allowed outside the commencement building, and those who felt strongly about *Bakke* could quietly leave the building during Justice Mosk's speech. On commencement day, there were as many as 75 pickets parading outside the building. As Mosk was introduced, 34 of the 139 graduates got up and left the room. As they did so, Mosk said, "I'm glad to be here at the siege of Fort Davis. Perhaps we can put our wagons in a circle and persevere. I understand that relief will be here from Washington in just a few days. [Referring to the anticipated U.S. Supreme Court ruling in *Bakke*]." In his speech, he said there were three things to be learned from the protest over his appearance: (1) Judges cannot be intimidated; (2) Lawsuits are won or lost in the courtrooms, not in the streets; and (3) In a democratic society all points of view deserve a thoughtful reception. As noted by Professor Edward L. Barrett, Jr., it was a "difficult day" for Stanley Mosk. But he "came with head high, delivered his speech, and maintained the dignity and strength of the judiciary. It was a sterling performance."[21]

Justice Mosk returned to this theme in a thoughtful address to a faculty retreat at Southwestern Law School in August of 1978. Noting the public demonstrations that occurred on the courthouse steps while the *Bakke* case was being argued before the California and U.S. Supreme Courts, he lamented:

> The disturbing aspect of these orchestrated outpourings of humanity in front of courthouses is not that they could have any actual effect upon independent justices of either Supreme Court, ours or the one in Washington, but that those who staged the demonstrations *believed* they would have an effect. Since many of the demonstrators were young people, it was disheartening to observe their apparent misguided notion that cases can be won or lost in the streets rather than in the courtroom.[22]

In March of 1980, Justice Mosk was invited to address the graduation ceremony at the University of San Francisco School of Law. The controversy over *Bakke* continued to haunt him and Mosk responded with a word of caution. He noted that Dean Paul L. McKaskle was "in a difficult situation being created by a small but aggressive group of militant students." Mosk "was disturbed," and was "fearful that if some ground rules are not laid down, the graduation exercises may become a shambles." Regardless, since he was being invited to an official U.S.F. ceremony, if he couldn't be "assured a courteous reception at the ceremony, I shall decline to attend." He said the "obstructionists ... need to be taught a lesson that such tactics cannot prevail, particularly by would-be lawyers, in a peaceful democratic society — but I do not see my role as being the teacher or the target." He went on to suggest the issuance of a directive about consequences for students who disrupt the graduation. While he considered it an honor to be asked, he saw no reason to "be subjected to the honor in a hostile atmosphere."[14] His commencement speech to the graduates of U.S.F. law school was greeted with pickets and protests. The experience still rankled a year later, when he wrote to Willis Hanawalt, expressing disappointment with the response of the organized bar to attacks on judges: "Not one word of comment came from the bar when I need actual police protection from aggressively obnoxious law student pickets at Davis commencement exercises one year and U.S.F. the next."[23] Justice Mosk found it ironic "that those with established liberal credentials become labeled racist and reactionary by the militant few."[24]

The United States Supreme Court promptly granted *certiorari* to review the *Bakke* decision during the 1977 term. The Court was anxious to address the issue, after its review of a prior ruling striking down the affirmative action program at the University of Washington in *DeFunis v. Odegaard* had been frustrated by the determination that the case had become moot.[25] The California Supreme Court deliberately avoided the use of state constitutional grounds in deciding *Bakke*, in order to assure U.S. Supreme Court review. In a note to Justice Hans Linde of the Oregon Supreme Court, a fellow champion of the use of state constitutional grounds, Justice Mosk wrote:

> I calculatingly relied on federal constitutional grounds for my *Bakke* opinion. Some of us are hopeful the United States Supreme Court will grapple with the issue so improvidently avoided in De Funis. Had I employed state constitutional provisions, our brethren in Washington would have had good reason to avoid certiorari. They now must consider the inevitable certiorari application on its merits. This is a rare exception to our normal desire to hasten finality of litigation.[26]

California Representative Henry A. Waxman wrote to Stanley Mosk and enclosed a copy of his amicus curie brief to be presented to the U.S. Supreme Court. He wrote:

> I have always been closely identified with the struggle of blacks and other victims of discrimination for equality. I share with the proponents of racial quotas deep concern over the slow rate at which certain minorities are obtaining college educations and entering such professions as law and medicine ... despite these concerns, I am thoroughly convinced that the answer does not lie with racial quotas ... in violation of the Equal Protection clause of the Fourteenth Amendment ... I plan to continue to fight against racial quotas.[27]

The Supreme Court received a flood of amicus briefs urging reversal of the California Supreme Court in *Bakke*, including one from the Bar Association of San Francisco. That led Justice Mosk to resign his honorary membership in the organization. He later explained that his resignation "was not merely for the filing of a brief in the *Bakke* case but for what I perceived to be the support for discrimination based on race."[28]

Anticipating the eagerly awaited U.S. Supreme Court ruling on the *Bakke* case, New York's *The Village Voice* ran a headline story: "THE MOST DIVISIVE CIVIL RIGHTS DECISION IN TWO DECADES: WHICH SIDE ARE YOU ON?"[29] The nine Justices of the U.S. Supreme Court were unable to agree which side they were on. There was no single majority opinion in the *Bakke* case; instead the Justices issued a bewildering array of six separate opinions.[30] But they did muster a majority of five to agree on two separate conclusions: (1) the California Supreme Court ruling that Bakke's rights had been violated and ordering his admission was upheld; (2) the ruling enjoining the University from considering race at all in its admission standards was reversed. The Court held that race could be considered among other factors in evaluating the qualifications of an applicant.

Justice Mosk was disappointed with the ambiguity of the United States Supreme Court ruling. By opening the door to the use of race as a factor in special admission programs, it invited universities and other public entities to continue doing exactly what the U.C. Davis Medical School had been doing, by simply avoiding any quantification of their goal. This would still permit the exclusion of white applicants who were objectively more qualified than specially admitted minority applicants, although it would be virtually impossible for them to show they were the victims of discrimination based upon race, who would have been admitted but for the special admissions program.

Justice Mosk was also quite annoyed that in quoting his *Bakke* majority opinion, Justice Powell inserted a "[sic]" into the quotation, suggesting the quote contained a grammatical error of which Powell was aware, but felt compelled to repeat in order to maintain the accuracy of the quotation. The alleged "error" was in treating the word "data" as singular, although the word, derived from Latin, is the plural form of "datum." Summing up the failure of the University to prove its affirmative action program would increase the availability of medical services in minority communities, Justice Mosk had written: "In short, there is no empirical data to demonstrate that any one race is more selflessly socially oriented or by contrast that another is more selfishly acquisitive."[31] In light of Justice Powell's "[sic]" Mosk assigned his staff to find support for the singular use of "data," and quoting several sources, wrote a polite letter to Justice Powell suggesting the "[sic]" was inappropriate. Justice Powell relented, and the "[sic]" was removed from the version of the United States Supreme Court Bakke opinion that appears in the official reports.[32]

Two years later, the issue of affirmative action was back before the California Supreme Court. In *Price v. Civil Service Commission*,[33] the District Attorney for Sacramento County challenged a remedial program the county instituted to increase the hiring of minority workers by imposing hiring ratios. Finding that the underrepresentation of minorities in county government resulted from "unintentional discriminatory employment practices," a county commission ordered that appointments to starting level deputy positions in the District Attorney's office must include at least one minority person for every two nonminority persons, until the total percentage of minorities in starting level positions reached 8 percent. The hiring plan established quotas that would clearly have been unconstitutional under the original *Bakke* ruling, but the U.S. Supreme Court version of *Bakke* left lots of room for "remedial" affirmative action plans designed to correct past discrimination. When the California Supreme Court votes were tallied, Justice Tobriner had picked up all three of the recent appointees of Governor Jerry Brown (Chief Justice Rose Bird, and Associate Justices Frank Newman and Wiley Manuel) to form a new majority, which upheld the Sacramento affirmative action plan. Justice Mosk, joined by Justices Clark and Richardson, authored a biting dissent expressing his continued opposition to racial quotas:

> The wry observation of Justice Rehnquist in his dissent in *Steelworkers v. Weber* [443 U.S. 193, 219(1979)] applies to this case: "In a very real sense, the Court's opinion is ahead of its time: it could more appropriately have been handed down five years from now, in 1984, a year coinciding with the title of a book from which the Court's opinion borrows, perhaps subconsciously, at least one idea." That one idea is "doublethink," the tortured abuse of words and phrases so that their meaning and effect become inverted. Thus here the majority purport to *eliminate* discrimination by means of *creating* discrimination; they construe *equality* of all persons regardless of race to mean *preference* for persons of some races over others; and a hiring program which *compels* compliance by a reluctant district attorney is described as *voluntary*. George Orwell is nodding complacently in his grave, as he wins vindication even before 1984 for his dire apprehensions about the misdirection of society.

Conscious of the personal attacks he endured after his *Bakke* opinion, Justice Mosk added:

> No member of this Court need apologize for his record in opposing racial and sexual discrimination. Over the years, we have forthrightly condemned unfair and discriminatory treatment of all persons, regardless of racial or sexual origin, whether that bias was manifest in racial restrictive housing covenants, prohibition of miscegenous marriages, judicial proceedings, employment opportunity or school segregation. We have consistently viewed sympathetically every effort to promote the American dream of equality of rights, duties and opportunity. That does not mean, however, that we must give carte blanche approval to every proposal, however undemocratic, made in the name of purportedly improving race relations.

U.S. Senator Orrin Hatch quoted from Mosk's *Bakke* opinion in proposing a Constitutional amendment designed to "restore the concept of equal protection" which he asserted, "has been substantially nullified" by the "federal bureaucracy's imposition of 'affirmative action'— racial and sexual quotas— right across American life."[34] Stanley Mosk graciously acknowledged Senator Hatch's efforts but firmly distanced himself from the senator's ultimate goals. First, because of the unlikelihood of a successful amendment to the U.S. Constitution on any grounds, he suggested perhaps an amendment to the Civil Rights Act itself that would "preempt any federal or state action to the contrary," would be more appropriate.

More importantly, however, Mosk pointed out that without exquisite clarity, supporters and opponents of civil rights equality might have more disagreement within each others' ranks and between each other. Mosk wrote: "I have read your statement expressing opposition to 'affirmative action.' The problem is that what constitutes 'affirmative action' is generally in the eye of the beholder. If the term means giving education, training, encouragement, or even financial aid to underprivileged persons of all races so that they may compete on a basis of equality, then 'affirmative action' is desirable and should not be condemned. That, I believe, is what President Johnson stated was his purpose in executive orders that were consistent with the Civil Rights Act of 1964. But if 'affirmative action' means bestowing racial preferences, instead of assuring racial equality, then it must be rejected as a gross distortion of equal protection values." He concluded that Hatch would know best how to ensure "the limitations or dimensions of 'affirmative action,' either by legislative statute, or resolution."[35]

Throughout his political life, Stanley Mosk was a "poll watcher." Writing to his former colleague, now Deputy Secretary of State William P. Clark, Mosk said that the Gallup poll regarding the Bakke, Price, and DeRonde opinions, "demonstrates you and I have been in step with the vast majority of Americans." He added, "It is particularly significant that even women and non-white minorities overwhelmingly oppose quotas and preferences."[36]

Justice Mosk's personal investment in the *Bakke* issue led him to respond favorably to a request from State Senator John Schmitz, asking for assistance in the drafting of a proposed state constitutional amendment to bar the use of preferential racial quotas by state agencies. This led to a call for his resignation from the Court by the National Association for the Advancement of Colored People, and a complaint to the Commission on Judicial Performance that his participation in the drafting of the proposal was unethical. The complaint was pressed by Maxine Waters, then a member of the State Assembly, now a member of the United States Congress. She laid out a detailed list of affronts for the Commission, suggesting that Mosk, as a sitting member of the California Supreme Court, acted in an unethical manner by participating in the drafting of the proposal. Waters claimed that "in agreeing to provide the draft, Judge [sic] Mosk violated several basic, interrelated principals of our governmental system: separation of powers, the independence of the judiciary, and the Code of Ethical Conduct." Furthermore, "Mosk could not have chosen a worse time to overstep his authority given the present public attacks on the courts. His conduct promotes the goals and activities of those who would weaken the courts for their own narrow political interests." Adding that because "he is one of he state's most senior jurists and as the issue is such a highly charged emotional, political and judicial controversy," his breach of judicial ethics is more serious," than any such potential affront involving, for recent example, the request for judges to comment on specific cases likely to come before the court.[37] Writing to Justice Mosk, Maxine Waters explained her actions in spite of how his "past record of support for minorities is well known by many," ... who "were as stunned as I was about the report of your assistance to Senator Schmitz in developing language to dismantle affirmative action." Furthermore, "the pain we all felt was because we felt a friend had indeed turned on us [and] the association with John Schmitz by you would help to give him undeserved credibility. I consider John Schmitz an extremely dangerous man with a right-wing, anti-Semetic [sic] and anti-minority philosophy who should not be assisted or supported in giving a platform to espouse his views. He does well enough on his own. My raged response to accounts of your actions is the kind of response we must all continue if we are to guard against erosion of our Constitutional rights and guarantees. From my point of view, silence is tantamount to acceptance. I cannot in good conscience ever be silent!"[38]

The Commission found there was no ethical lapse, but issued a press release that his action was "lacking in discretion" and ran "the risk of appearing insensitive." Justice Mosk chose a curious vehicle to respond, by dissenting from the Supreme Court's ruling upholding the Commission's censure of Judge Charles S. Stevens for employing racial epithets in judicial proceedings:

> [T]he Commission on Judicial Performance is seeking to impose on Judge Stevens its self-determined standard of appropriate taste and style in language. In so doing it reveals an imperious disregard for constitutional guarantees. Unfortunately this is not the first time this agency has demonstrated disdain for constitutional limitations.... As recently as February of this year, the Commission considered material sent by a judge to a legislative committee, and while it found the "facts do not constitute grounds for proceeding," it issued a didactic press release on February 23, 1982, declaring that communications "although not improper or unethical in a disciplinary sense, when indulged in by judges, run the risk of appearing insensitive and lacking in discretion." There can be no more clear indication that the Commission deems itself clothed with magisterial power to criticize any speech or writings of members of the judiciary that it unilaterally deems insensitive or indiscreet.[39]

In another ironic consequence of the Bakke case, Virna M. Canson, the regional director of the NAACP, called for Stanley Mosk's resignation from the Court. Supporting Representative Water's call for an investigation into Mosk's activities, Canson accused Mosk of "blatantly" and "unethically campaigning and lobbying to undermine the constitutional rights of racial minorities." She declared that "If Justice Mosk wishes to continue in his confrontation over preferential hiring, he should resign." What's more, "This recent maneuver reopens at a time that is so critical all the pain, controversy and confusion of Bakke."[40]

Mosk responded to the NAACP's call for his resignation from the Court by resigning from the NAACP. In an angry letter to Nathaniel Colley, Jr., he reminded Colley that "long before civil rights advocacy became politically attractive," he made a "substantial contribution to become a life member of the NAACP." He said he was proud to have been associated with Walter White, and "later became a personal friend of Martin Luther King [Jr.], all in furtherance of the principles of equality of opportunity and treatment." He pointed out that as California Attorney General he established the first Constitutional Rights Section in the office, to which he appointed as its head Franklin Williams, counsel for the NAACP. He concluded his letter with: "Unfortunately, the NAACP has changed, and now advocates not minority equality but minority preference. What is worse, it apparently cannot tolerate disagreement with its undemocratic program. Therefore, with regret, I resign my life membership in the NAACP."[41]

The ultimate vindication for Justice Mosk's views came in 1997, when California voters amended the state Constitution by approving Proposition 209. Article I, Section 31 of the California Constitution now states: "The state shall not discriminate against, or grant preferential treatment to, any individual or group on the basis of race ... in the operation of public employment, public education, or public contracting." In *Hi-Voltage Wire Works v. City of San Jose*,[42] the Court upheld the constitutionality of Proposition 209 and struck down a municipal program requiring contractors to use a specified percentage of minority and women subcontractors. The opinion was authored by fiery Justice Janice Rogers Brown, who managed to insult lots of liberal icons in her survey of cases dealing with racial discrimination. The 4–3 ruling was joined by Justice Stanley Mosk in a concurring opinion.

The United States' Supreme Court revisited the issue in 2003, with the nine Justices delivering nine opinions. In *Gruter v. Bollinger*,[43] the majority upheld a special admissions program at the University of Michigan Law School, while in *Gratz v. Bollinger*,[44] a different majority struck down the special admissions program used for University of Michigan undergraduates. The principal difference between the two programs was the use of a system of bonus points for racial minorities in the undergraduate admissions, which rendered the use of race "a decisive factor."

Justice Mosk always took great pride in Allan Bakke's success in medical school and subsequent career as a physician. He later recalled that "for four years, I was scared to death that Bakke would flunk out of medical school, and make our opinion look bad. But he graduated with honors."[45] Bakke invited Justice Mosk to his medical school graduation party with a personal note of thanks, but Mosk did not attend. When the Associated Press published a follow-up article reporting Bakke's employment as a doctor at the famed Mayo Clinic, Justice Mosk forwarded it to all of his fellow Justices on Christmas Eve of 1986, with obvious satisfaction.[46] In a sad sequel to the case, the press reported in 1997 that Dr. Patrick Chavis, the black student admitted in Bakke's place, lost his medical license after an administrative law judge found that he was grossly negligent and unprofessional in his care of three liposuction patients, one of whom bled to death hours after a lipectomy.[47] Dr. Chavis died in 2002, the victim of a botched robbery attempt.

The contentious issues posed by the *Bakke* case continue to haunt us nearly forty years later. On December 8, 2011, the *Los Angeles Times* reported that "A coalition of civil rights and student groups launched a statewide campaign ... to overturn California's Proposition 209, which prohibits public universities from considering race and gender in admissions decisions. The U.S. 9th Circuit Court of Appeals is scheduled to hear arguments ... from opponents that contend the measure is unconstitutional. Although the law has been upheld by the California Supreme Court, opponents cite a July opinion by the 6th Circuit of Appeals, which overturned a similar law in Michigan, as new ammunition for their case. 'We have an historic opportunity to repeal Prop. 209 if we can get the 9th Circuit to do the same as the 6th Circuit,' Leon Jenkins, president of the L.A. chapter of the National Assn. for the Advancement of Colored People, said at a news conference."[48] The NAACP's efforts were supported by Governor Jerry Brown, who filed an amicus brief in the Ninth Circuit urging the Court to strike down Proposition 209.

Chapter 15

"But I Blame Jerry Brown for Putting You Here"

Ronald Reagan labeled his appointment of Donald Wright to be California's Chief Justice as his "biggest mistake," echoing the regret President Dwight D. Eisenhower expressed over his appointment of Chief Justice Earl Warren to the U.S. Supreme Court. Reagan was determined not to make a similar mistake when the next court vacancy occurred with the sudden death of Justice Raymond E. Peters on January 2, 1973. Now the governor had an opportunity to replace the most liberal judge on the Court with a real conservative, but this time, he did not undertake an "exhaustive statewide search." He already knew who he wanted, and announced his appointment the day after Justice Peters' funeral.

William P. Clark was a small-town real estate lawyer who became an eager and early supporter of Ronald Reagan's political ambitions. After directing Reagan's highly successful 1966 gubernatorial campaign in Ventura County, Clark joined the Reagan administration as the governor's chief of staff. The next year, the governor appointed him to the Superior Court in Clark's hometown of San Luis Obispo. In 1971, he was elevated to the Court of Appeal in Los Angeles. Two years later, when Reagan announced his appointment to the California Supreme Court, it raised more than a few eyebrows. His judicial experience was brief and undistinguished, and the revelations that he had never finished college, flunked out of law school, and failed the bar exam the first time he took it led Chief Justice Wright to ask the State Bar to prepare a detailed report on Clark's background. As Chair of the Commission on Judicial Appointments, the Chief Justice would be one of three required to approve Clark's nomination before he could take office. The Report concluded that Clark had never misrepresented his educational background, and found nothing that would "disqualify" him from serving on the Supreme Court. Chief Justice Donald Wright was not impressed. At Clark's confirmation hearing, he voted against his appointment, expressing the opinion that "he is not qualified by education, training and experience to be confirmed as an associate justice of the Supreme Court."[1]

Governor Reagan was furious, but the affirmative votes of Attorney General Evelle Younger and Parker Wood, the Senior Presiding Justice of the Courts of Appeal, placed Clark on the Court. Governor Reagan attended the swearing-in ceremony, stating that his appointment of Clark "is one of my most satisfying acts since becoming governor." Although Clark was a congenial and likable man, his presence on the California Supreme Court was embarrassing for Chief Justice Wright, and he was viewed with awkward suspicion by most of the other Justices. Nevertheless, he and Stanley Mosk became close friends.

That friendship says a great deal about Mosk. While Mosk's failure to recognize Southwestern University School of Law as his alma mater revealed his own elitist tendencies, rather than looking down his nose at Clark's scholastic deficiencies, he admired his ambition and persistence in overcoming them. Clark's career path bore a striking resemblance to that of Stanley Mosk. Clark viewed Stanley Mosk as a role model of sorts, dating back to his schoolboy field trip to Sacramento in 1940, when Mosk served as his tour guide. Although Clark was a Republican, his parents were strong Democrats who gave Mosk important support in Ventura County in both runs for state attorney general. Just like Clark, Mosk's own loyal service on a governor's staff launched his judicial career. Although he and Clark were usually on opposing sides in the decisions that divided the Court, Justice Mosk rarely let rancor in the conference room affect his working or personal relationships with his fellow Justices. He welcomed Clark to the Court with warmth and genuine affection, and Justice Clark gratefully reciprocated. Their close friendship continued long after Clark's departure from the Court.

As Ronald Reagan reached the end of his second term in 1974, he tried to convince Chief Justice Wright to retire so he could appoint a younger successor. Wright said, "I might as well tell you that I'm not interested in retiring. I like the job." Wright later remembered, "I could tell he didn't like what I said. I don't remember whether he started eating any jelly beans, but it was clear he didn't like it."[2] Justice Louis Burke was more cooperative, timing his retirement so Governor Reagan could name his replacement. Reagan then promoted Justice Frank Richardson, whom he had appointed as Presiding Justice of the Third District Court of Appeal in Sacramento just three years earlier. Richardson's appointment did not disturb the liberal tilt of the Wright Court, but it did place on the Court an articulate judicial craftsman who expressed dissenting views in a forceful and persuasive manner.

Potential candidates for the 1974 statewide elections were now gearing up, and around this time Justice Mosk's campaign fund trust account provided fodder for critics of his ethical standards. Following the dictates of a new state law that required the filing of expenditure reports with the secretary of state's office, David P. Rousso, a certified public accountant and treasurer and trustee of Mosk's trust fund, filed an expenditure report on Mosk's behalf. The press had a field day with information about the previously undisclosed fund and Mosk's political contributions to others. Mosk had set up the account with the express purpose of advancing his political career, and by 1974, the fund's balance was around $23,000.00. Mosk explained the trust existed "only because there was always the possibility of a return to active political life." What concerned the press, and provided ammunition for his opponents, was that monies had been dispersed directly from the trust to other Democratic candidates.

Former Assembly Speaker Jesse Unruh received $1,000 for his gubernatorial race against Governor Reagan, as did the Democratic nominee for attorney general, Charles O'Brien. O'Brien had served Mosk as chief deputy attorney general, and he remained in that post under Mosk's successor Thomas Lynch. Justice Mosk's wife Edna and Mrs. Lynch had been named co-chairs of the Committee to Elect Charles O'Brien attorney general.[3] Mosk defended the use of the funds donated to 1970 candidates, saying, "Maybe they could have been helpful to me," if he followed through on a Senate race. In 1971, the trust fund contributions included a contribution to Dianne Feinstein's unsuccessful run for mayor of San Francisco.[4]

Mosk broke no law by holding the account, or having the trustee disperse funds to political candidates. But Governor Ronald Reagan suggested it was inappropriate for judges to contribute to candidates for partisan political offices. The state Judicial Performance Commission suggested that disciplinary action could possibly be brought against Mosk under a section of the California constitution that prohibited conduct by judges that is "prejudicial to the administration of justice that brings the judicial office into disrepute."

Stanley Mosk was pondering what to do with the trust fund when he spoke with Roger Kent, who followed up with a "personal and confidential" letter to Mosk on April 1. He wanted Mosk to be aware of the newly formed Northern California Political Action Foundation, of which he was an acting director. The purpose of the Foundation was to spend "some $18,000 left over from the McGovern campaign." Funds would be dispersed to county committees for registration drives based on need, budgets, and number of people involved. He said, "I am sure neither you nor your trustees would want any part of the funds raised for your campaign to be used for payment of the [Democratic Central] committee's debt." In other words, if Mosk donated his trust fund to the Democratic Central Committee, it could be specifically designated for the registration drive planned after the upcoming June primary.[5]

Reacting quickly to the press clamor, Justice Mosk asked his son Richard to do some research. Richard probed the reports of political donations filed on behalf of Ronald Reagan's campaign for governor, and found several contributions from sitting judges. Richard began calling newspaper editors around the state, and sharing his discovery with them. Mosk also responded directly to some of the newspapers which published articles critcal of his trust fund contributions. The tone of Mosk's communications can be gleaned from the response of one editor, who felt no need to apologize for publishing a story that he deemed newsworthy. He took exception to Mosk's characterization of the article in his newspaper as "chastising" Mosk for a breach of integrity. "As I told Richard in conversation last week," he said, "I think we were reporting about an unusual, if not unprecedented fund." He thought Mosk's references to how others have dealt with such money matters as "no more relevant (and please don't misinterpret this) than what Watergaters had to say about the sins of the other side." The midst of the Watergate scandal was not an opportune time to be accused of having a secret political "slush fund," or defending it by accusing the other side of doing the same thing.

In May, Republican candidate for Secretary of State Brian Van Camp called for the resignation of Justice Stanley Mosk for his "direct conflict of interest in his 1970 elections conduct." Van Camp hypothesized that a victory of Democratic candidate Charles O'Brien would have forced Mosk to recuse himself in untold numbers of cases the Attorney General handled before the high court, and would be "prejudicial to the administration of justice and bring the whole court system into disrepute."[6] Campaign hyperbole aside, the candidate was echoing an editorial in Long Beach's *Independent Press-Telegram* which pointed out that had O'Brien won for Attorney General or Jesse Unruh as governor, Justice Mosk would likely have heard state cases without bias, but "the suspicion of bias would have arisen, and it would have been difficult to dispel."[7]

On June 4, 1974, the ongoing Watergate scandals motivated voters to overwhelmingly approve Proposition 9, an initiative that created the California Fair Political Practices Commission. Governor Reagan's political reform measures, which included a ban on campaign contributions by judges, "so the public can be assured they are exercising their power 'impartially,'"[8] were rejected by the legislature, although an Assembly committee endorsed a Reagan-sponsored bill inspired by the controversy over Mosk's trust fund. Presented by the future long-serving Los Angeles County Supervisor, Assemblyman Mike Antonovich, the bill would have made it illegal for a judge to administer political funds for other candidates. The issue was finally laid to rest when the California Conference of Judges approved a new rule of ethics prohibiting judges from contributing more than $100 to campaigns other than their own.[9] In September, Justice Mosk's "controversial political fund" was turned over to the state of California for "unrestricted use" by the state. The $23,183.60 was transferred to the Controller's office and designated for use in funding of schools.

One might speculate as to how the constitutionality of restrictions on political contributions by judges would fare with the current U.S. Supreme Court, but a judge's contribution to the campaign of a party appearing in his or her court does risk the requirement of a recusal to avoid the appearance of bias. Fortunately, Justice Mosk never had to face this issue with regard the contributions made from his trust fund, since the candidates receiving his contributions lost. Today's judges are acutely sensitive to this problem, which also arises from their acceptance of campaign contributions to their own campaigns from potential litigants.[10] Apparently, in 1974 Justice Mosk was still thinking more like a politician than a judge.

In November, 1974, Chief Justice Donald R. Wright, Justice Stanley Mosk and Justice Matthew Tobriner were all retained for full twelve year terms, and Justice William P. Clark, Jr., was confirmed for the eight years remaining from Justice Peters' term. Chief Justice Wright served for two more years before retiring. But before leaving the Court, he took on the thorny problem of Justice Marshall McComb. As the most conservative Justice on a very liberal court, McComb did little to advance opposing views. He frequently dissented without opinion, or by adopting the views expressed in the Court of Appeals ruling that had been depublished after the grant of a Supreme Court hearing.[11] After Justice Burke joined the Court, McComb would often simply indicate that he voted the same way as Justice Burke, without expressing any understanding of the issues in the case. His assigned majority opinions were actually prepared by his staff, with competent but generally bland and tedious results. When the increasingly incapacitated and stubborn McComb refused to retire, Chief Justice Wright engineered a constitutional amendment to provide a specially convened panel of seven appellate justices to review recommendations by the Commission on Judicial Performance for the removal of a Justice of the California Supreme Court.[12] When the Commission recommended his forced retirement due to chronic brain syndrome (senile dementia), McComb appealed to the specially convened panel, which upheld the recommendation in May of 1977.[13]

If there is any blemish on the sterling reputation of the Traynor Court, it has to be the extent to which the Justices and staff cooperated in concealing McComb's incompetence from public view. As a frequent dissenter and the only holdover from the previous administration, forcing his removal would have appeared unseemly. Therefore, Traynor left this ticklish problem to his successor, Chief Justice Wright.

The issue of retirement was one frequently raised throughout the later years of Mosk's tenure on the Court, and his approach to his own retirement was strongly influenced by the Court's disagreeable experience with Justice McComb. For Mosk, the appropriate time to retire was when one could no longer competently handle the crushing workload. A Justice's failure to carry his or her load simply added to the burdens borne by colleagues. The now sixty-four-year-old Justice Stanley Mosk lived to work; he did not approach life like most Americans, who by their early-sixties are preoccupied with careful retirement planning. With gleeful anticipation or dreaded anxiety, they anticipate the grand vacation of a lifetime, or instead, worry about how to sustain a lifestyle that will provide for the basic, day-to-day necessities of an aging life. Grand vacations had been part of Mosk's life for decades, and he was in excellent health, regularly beating his law clerks on the tennis courts.

As a seasoned Justice, having already served ten years on the Court, he was at the peak of his productivity. He amply demonstrated his judicial independence and his elevated competence in mastering the job description of an Associate Justice. What's more, his convivial personality nurtured congenial relationships with his fellow Justices. Most of the friendships and political alliances he had established as Attorney General remained strong, and his administrative skills were exceptional.

While Mosk gracefully aged, however, the winds of political change arrived in the Golden State in January 1975, when the youthful Jerry Brown took his oath of office for what would become two highly charged terms as governor of California. Only thirty-six years old at the time, Brown had gained high visibility as California secretary of state, suing large corporations for violations of campaign finance laws. Only eight years after his own father Pat Brown was defeated for a third term by Ronald Reagan, the younger Brown won back the office his father had lost.

Reagan was already a harbinger of a rising conservatism, leading the increasing swell of an ideological tsunami, which continues to frame the discourse about America's national identity well into the early years of the twenty-first century. In the meantime, Brown Jr. grappled with California's environmental future, and Sacramento witnessed a sea change in a climate still dominated by the Watergate scandal that led, three months earlier, to the unprecedented resignation of President Richard Nixon. The new governor's bold leadership style and shake-em-up attitude, described with a measure of hindsight, was "stunningly youthful, heir to his father's name yet slightly at odds with his legacy, brash, serious and intellectually adventurous. Brown could seem flighty ... but he mirrored California as it was. He was a young governor in a young state, energetic, optimistic, a little off-kilter."[14] Jerry Brown's legacy remains controversial, in spite of his 2010 re-election victory for an unprecedented (non-consecutive) third-term as the elder statesman of the Democratic Party.

By the middle of his first term, Brown's administration had met with varying degress of success. He fulfilled his commitment to recognize talent from a broad pool among the state's diverse demographic profile. He set the record for selecting the highest proportion of women and minorities for office in state history.[15] This included the appointment of the state's first black Cabinet member, Leonard M. Grimes, as director of the Department of General Services. Out of 1,862 appointments, 575 appointments went to women. One of them was a close colleague of Brown's, Rose Elizabeth Bird, who as the new secretary of agriculture became the first woman to hold a cabinet level position in California history.[16]

When it came to making appointments to the massive state judiciary, however, Brown was at first slow to fill vacancies. During the first five months of 1977, Jerry Brown faced the challenge head-on, when he needed to fill, in rapid succession, three judicial vacancies on the state's Supreme Court. Initially, Justice Raymond L. Sullivan retired from the Court on January 19th. Then, less than two weeks later, on February 1, Chief Justice Donald R. Wright stepped down. Inherently, the most formidable challenge came with filling this second vacancy. No matter what choices Brown made, this moment in his administration could influence the course of judicial history for decades to come as well as the contours of his own legacy for historic statecraft. Finally, just three months later, on May 2, Justice Marshall McComb was forced to retire after losing his appeal.

To most followers of the Court, it seemed obvious that to fill the position of Chief Justice, Brown should turn to either Justices Mathew Tobriner or Stanley Mosk. Both were esteemed figures and both had been appointed by Brown's father, Pat Brown, but that could have just as easily worked against them, given Jerry's penchant to distance himself from the elder Brown's generational world-view and approach to governing. Justice Tobriner was considered the most liberal judge on the Court, and he was widely admired and respected for his strong commitment to compassionate justice. He authored many of the landmark rulings during the tenures of Chief Justices Traynor and Wright.[17] Although Tobriner was seventy-three years old, he was in good health and he continued his high level of productivity on the bench.

When Chief Justice Wright told the governor of his plans to retire, he recommended that Justice Mosk be appointed as his successor as Chief Justice. Brown refused to tip his hand to Wright, but appointing Mosk was an obvious option for Brown. Jerry Brown knew Stanley Mosk very well, both personally and professionally. During Mosk's and Pat Brown's simultaneous campaigns and years of service together, both families were brought together countless times. During Mosk's first year on the Supreme Court, his son Richard clerked alongside Jerry Brown for Mosk's colleague, Justice Mathew Tobriner. Jerry became a frequent visitor to Stanley and Edna Mosk's Nob Hill home, where they shared dinner and conversation.

Without any public revelation, Justice Tobriner took himself out of the running. He confided to a close friend that when Governor Brown offered him the Chief Justice seat, he declined to accept the honor.[18] A broad spectrum of Mosk supporters chimed in on his behalf. State Senator Nicholas C. Petris, from Oakland, urged Governor Brown to appoint Stanley Mosk as Chief Justice. Petris faithfully communicated to Mosk the details of a conversation he had with the governor. Brown responded to Petris that he needed "someone who's going to be innovative with new ideas." Senator Petris asked, "Have you talked to Mosk? I've talked to Mosk. He's got a lot of ideas on how to change things on the court and improve the process. Why don't you give it a try?"[19] In reporting this conversation to Mosk, Senator Petris apparently told him Brown said, "I could never appoint Justice Mosk because of the Bakke case."[20] Governor Brown never discussed the appointment with Mosk, nor is it likely he discussed the appointment with any Justice on the Court other than Tobriner.

Retired Chief Justice Phil Gibson indicated he would have recommended the appointment of Tobriner or Mosk if he had been asked: "Well, I don t think that our present governor consulted with anybody on the court except probably one member. He probably consulted with Justice Tobriner. The governor was Tobriner's research assistant. Tobriner is one of the ablest men ever to sit on a court. I thought he should appoint Tobriner and, when he retired, appoint Mosk. Mosk has the experience. After all, he had four years in Governor Olson's office, served with distinction as a superior court judge, sitting frequently by assignment on the court of appeal, and was elected attorney general by the largest majority any man had ever received for that office. Mosk is doing an outstanding job on the Supreme Court. He was a natural. Mosk is a top administrator as well as a good lawyer."[21]

It soon became apparent that Jerry Brown was eager to make history by appointing the first woman to the state Supreme Court. J. Anthony Kline, then serving as the governor's legal affairs secretary, urged the appointment of Shirley Hufstedler as chief justice. Unfortunately, after her stellar service on the U.S. Court of Appeals for the Ninth Circuit, however, she had recently accepted an appointment as President Carter's secretary of education. It was widely anticipated that Shirley Hufstedler would be President Jimmy Carter's first appointment to the U.S. Supreme Court, making her the first woman to sit on the High Court. As fate would have it, no Supreme Court vacancies occurred during Carter's single term, so President Ronald Reagan is credited for the historic appointment of the first woman, Justice Sandra Day O'Connor, to the U.S. Supreme Court in 1981.

Rose Bird's name quickly moved to the top of the short list. Brown thought placing Bird at the head of the Court would send a clear message he was "shaking up" California government from top to bottom, rejecting the "old boy" politics of his father. When word seeped out that Brown was seriously considering the appointment of Bird as Chief Justice, he was cautioned against taking such a risky step; in part because of the safer alternatives available to him, and in part because of the reputation that Rose Bird had earned among both her supporters and her opponents.

It wasn't that Rose Bird's skill and intellect had not already been amply demonstrated throughout her legal career. After graduation near the top of her law school class at the University of California at Berkeley, she spent a year clerking on the Nevada Supreme Court. She then joined the Santa Clara County Public Defender's Office, where she tried cases, argued appeals in both state and federal court, and taught part-time at Stanford Law School. When her college classmate Jerry Brown announced for governor, she volunteered to assist his campaign and frequently drove him to and from campaign events in the Bay Area. Brown was impressed by her outspoken independence. During the drive to an event held just three days before the 1974 election, the car in which Bird was chauffeuring Brown came side-by-side with car full of admirers. They were yelling to Brown their assurances that he was headed for a landslide victory over his opponent, State Controller Houston Flournoy, a progressive Republican. As they drove off, Brown asked Bird what she thought of their confidence, and she unhesitatingly countered, "I think you're going to lose, and I hope you do." She proceeded to berate him for backing off of some controversial positions he had taken earlier in the campaign.[22] After Brown's narrow victory, he immediately invited Bird to serve on his transition team, and subsequently appointed her to head the Department of Agriculture.

Her two years at the helm of the California Department of Agriculture were marked by both courage and controversy. The most notable success of Bird's leadership was her support for the goals of Cesar Chavez and the United Farm Workers when she marshaled through the state legislature the 1975 Agricultural Labor Relations Act (ALRA). The ALRA was designed to end a decade of strife and to "ensure peace in the agricultural fields by guaranteeing justice for all agricultural workers and stability in labor relations."[23] The three major mandates of the ALRA were to ensure the organizing and bargaining rights for farm workers; to address unfair labor practices when employers and unions interfered with these rights; and to establish the Agricul-

During one of Stanley Mosk's visits to Israel, he met Prime Minister Golda Meir, the two seen here most likely in 1978 (courtesy Richard Mosk).

tural Labor Relations Board (ALRB), to oversee elections for farm workers to decide for themselves if they want to be represented by unions.

Also under Bird's leadership, the state banned use of the short-handled hoe, which had inflicted disabling injuries upon generations of migrant farm-workers. The torturous tool kept thousands of field workers bent almost double for most of their working day. Most growers had abandoned the hoe for tools that allowed workers to stand upright, but California's lettuce growers insisted that it was needed for speed and efficiency. They had prevailed during previous administrations, despite physicians' reports of workers who suffered ruptured spinal disks, arthritis of the spine and other serious back injuries because they were forced to use what the United Farm Workers called "this despised tool." Growers and their Republican allies were outraged at Bird over the hoe ban. They were even angrier over her work in drafting the landmark Agricultural Labor Relations Act.[24]

Rose Bird was less successful serving as a team player in Brown's cabinet. Her regal demeanor alienated many in Sacramento who should have been allies, and occasionally the governor found himself employing intermediaries just to communicate with her. Marc Poche, the governor's legislative liaison, visited Bird in hopes of convincing her that whatever the reason she may be angry with the governor, she had to return his phone calls.

On February 12, 1977, Governor Brown announced his selection of Rose Elizabeth Bird to serve as Chief Justice of California, and Wiley Manuel to serve as an Associate Justice. Manuel, the first black appointed to the Court, was an Alameda County Superior Court judge and previously served as a division chief under Attorney General Stanley Mosk and as Chief Assistant to Attorney General Evelle Younger. Acting Chief Justice Justice Tobriner presided over the March 8 hearings of the Judicial Appointments Commission. The other two members were Attorney General Younger and Justice Parker Wood, the senior Justice of the intermediate Court of Appeal. Judge Manuel was quickly approved without opposition.

Justice Tobriner's support for Rose Bird was already assured. Justice Wood, however, was known to oppose candidates without judicial experience, and it was assumed he would vote against Bird's confirmation. Evelle Younger thus became the deciding vote, placing him in a precarious position. Younger had more than just Bird's qualifications to consider. His own political fortunes could be at stake. Younger already planned to challenge Jerry Brown in the next gubernatorial race. First, he had to win the GOP nomination over both the popular Mayor of San Diego, Pete Wilson, and the vocal, "law and order" Los Angeles Police Chief Ed Davis. Younger's reputation as a progressive Republican meant that he faced formidable challenges from more conservative rivals who were vocal opponents of Rose Bird. Younger was also aware that voting against Bird could potentially cost women's support in the Republican primary and in a general election. Many women's groups believed that the harsh criticism Bird elicited was solely because she was a woman. Influential Republicans made their views heard, urging Younger to vote against Bird's nomination. Organized opposition also came from Sacramento lawmakers in the form of letters signed by nineteen of the twenty-three Republicans in the State Assembly and seven of the fourteen Republican senators.[25]

Younger believed his responsibility as a member of the Judicial Qualifications Commission was a limited one. He thought it was important to respect the decision made by the governor about whom to nominate, and as a Commissioner to support or deny that choice based upon whether the minimal burden of qualification has been met or not. The

Commission received numerous letters of support and opposition from private citizens and organized groups, as well as from public figures. Roman Catholic Bishop Roger Mahony of Fresno, who later became the Cardinal Archbishop of Los Angeles, submitted the most troubling, confidential communication to the Commissioners. Governor Brown had appointed Mahony as the first to chair the newly formed Agricultural Labor Relations Board. As such, he worked closely with Rose Bird. Mahoney's letter opposed Bird's nomination based upon grave misgivings about Rose Bird's character. Drawn from his personal experience with Bird, he explained:

> My opposition to her appointment as Chief Justice centers on her questionable emotional stability and her vindictive approach to dealing with all persons under her authority. I experienced personally her vindictiveness on many occasions, when the ALRB, an independent state agency, chose to pursue a course other than that desired by Ms. Bird. She has a personal temperament which enables her to lash out at people who do not agree with her. Her normal approach is to become vindictive, then to transfer her feelings to a long phase of non-communication. She would refuse to take or return telephone calls or to acknowledge any attempts at communication. I am gravely concerned that the future Chief Justice of our state Supreme Court be a person of balanced emotional stability, of judicial temperament, and of co-responsible collaboration with the other Justices. In my experience and opinion Ms. Bird fits none of those requirements.[26]

When Commissioner Younger learned of the letter, he made its contents public because he could not "conceive of any letter being kept confidential." Along with providing the press with copies, he provided Bird with a copy in order for her to prepare a response. In the meantime, another influential group announced their support of Bird's nomination. The State Bar Board of governors concluded that Bird was qualified for the Chief Justice post by a vote of 12 to 3, with 5 abstentions. Six of the favorable votes were cast by new Brown appointees, sitting as public members of the Board.[27]

On the second day of the confirmation hearings, Attorney General Younger "reluctantly" voted to confirm Rose Bird, explaining that "the law does not require [the Governor] appoint a judge or the best-qualified or even a well-qualified person. My limited responsibility requires only that I determine if Rose Bird is qualified. Absent any significant evidence to the contrary, I am compelled to find that she is."[28]

Being rejected for the appointment as Chief Justice was perhaps Stanley Mosk's greatest disappointment, a wound that cut deep and seemed to never quite heal. He was fully justified in feeling that he was the most qualified person in California to assume leadership of the Court. Governor Brown's failure to offer even a semblance of personal and professional courtesy by broaching the subject with Mosk, left Mosk to speculate as to what had contributed to this outcome. Some have assumed, including Mosk, that Brown passed over his name because of the *Bakke* decision, which was profoundly anathema to Brown's sensibilities. Jerry Brown denies the Bakke claim, and he may have had very good reasons to pass over Justice Mosk, but his handling of the process left Mosk with a bitter taste in his mouth. Justice Mosk became an outspoken critic of Governor Jerry Brown's treatment of the judiciary. In candid remarks to a 1978 Faculty Retreat at Southwestern Law School, he complained:

> The current Governor of California throughout his term has assailed the judiciary for alleged profligacy — salaries, pensions, numbers and personnel ... the Governor's relentless barrage of criticism, his refusal to add personnel in accordance with caseload demands, his references to lawyers and judges as problems of society, all tend to undermine public confidence in the judicial process.[29]

After Jerry Brown announced the appointment of Rose Bird as Chief Justice, Stanley Mosk never spoke to Jerry Brown again. Thus, Jerry Brown stands out as a rare exception to Mosk's incredible ability to "kiss and make up" with political enemies. Despite Pat Brown's role in derailing Mosk's earlier senatorial ambitions, Mosk and the senior Brown were able to continue their collegial relationship. Richard Mosk found this puzzling, and asked his father, "how can you forgive Pat Brown for what he has done to you repeatedly — negative stuff to the FBI, the 1964 Senate election, appointing Traynor Chief Justice instead of him, etc.?" Stanley Mosk simply replied, "How can you hate Pat Brown?"

Former U.S. Supreme Court Justice Arthur Goldberg echoed the sentiments of many friends who offered their sympathy to Mosk. He expressed disappointment that Governor Brown "did not see fit" to appoint him as Chief Justice, writing, "It may be slight consolation for you, but I wish to recall that some of the greatest Justices in the history of the Supreme Court of the United States never occupied the center seat. The roll is a long and distinguished one: Story, Harlan the first, Brandeis, Cardozo, Holmes, Black, and others I could mention."[30]

The festive swearing in of Chief Justice Rose Bird was held on March 28, 1977, in the newly restored original courtroom of the California Supreme Court in Old Sacramento. In a departure from long-standing tradition that new Justices were sworn in by another member of the Court, Governor Jerry Brown insisted upon swearing her in himself. Stanley Mosk did not attend the ceremony. When Bird arrived at the Court's headquarters in San Francisco, Mosk informed the new Chief Justice, "I certainly cannot blame you for being here, but I blame Jerry Brown for putting you here." From that point on, it's not surprising that their relationship was a frosty, guarded one. "Rose Bird never let me forget that statement," Mosk recounted, explaining how their relationship devolved into one of distrust and suspicion.[31] The version of Mosk's greeting remembered by Rose Bird was even more chilling. She confided to a close friend that Justice Mosk concluded his "welcome" by saying, "You will rue the day you came."[32]

While Stanley Mosk started out with a preconceived prejudice against Rose Bird, her staffing changes soon sparked dissension among other members of the Court and its administrative employees. Bird's initial display of aggressive confidence in her administrative skills impressed no one. She exhibited little inclination to seek advice or consultation with her fellow Justices, and she antagonized career officers. Chief Justice Rose Bird had a very short honeymoon within the Court complex by generating a dramatically uncomfortable atmosphere. Six weeks after her arrival, Ralph Kleps submitted his resignation. Kleps had served as the Director of the Administration Office of the Courts for sixteen years, originally appointed by Chief Justice Phil Gibson. His abrupt departure troubled his friends and admirers in the judiciary. The careers of long serving Court secretaries were displaced, and some who served under Chief Justices Gibson, Traynor, and Wright, were "returned to the pool." The new Chief Justice brought in her own staff. State Bar president Ralph Gampell, who was a friend from her days as a Deputy Public Defender in Santa Clara County, replaced Kleps as AOC Director. She installed as her executive assistant Steven Buehl, her former student at Stanford Law School.

Bird's personal style also brought abrupt change to the Chambers. Unlike her predecessor Donald Wright, whose door was always open to fellow Justices and their staffs, Chief Justice Bird was available only by appointment prearranged with Buehl, who was always present, taking notes, in all of her meetings. Although she surrounded herself with a competent and intensely loyal staff, the brusqueness of Bird's aloofness and the manner in which her changes were implemented generated resentment among the other staff members and isolated her from the day-to-day collegial interactions and friendly banter in the hallways. One tradition in particular encouraged conviviality among the Justices. After their Wednesday conference, the Justices usually went out to lunch together. As Chief Justice, Rose Bird did not join her colleagues, missing an opportunity to ease some of the lingering tensions between her and the other Justices.

Unmarried, supporting her elderly mother, Chief Justice Bird worked long hours at the court, and was usually the last to leave. The Justices chambers are arrayed along one long corridor, so as she left she could see how late the other Justices were working by the light leaking through the glass transoms above their office dooors. When Rose made an off-hand comment about who was working late, Justice Mosk was furious that the Chief was "checking up" so see how late the Justices were working. He called in a carpenter to install a wooden panel over his transom, so the Chief couldn't see whether he was working late or not.

During her first two years in office, Bird exercised great influence over Governor Brown's subsequent judicial appointments. Professor Frank C. Newman filled the vacancy created by the removal of Justice Marshall McComb. Newman was a distinguished academic at the University of California at Berkeley Boalt Hall law school, where he also served a five year term as its Dean. Newman was Bird's favorite professor in law school, and he soon became her closest ally on the Court.[33] Newman's passion was international law and the international protection of human rights, and he found it difficult to adjust to the demanding regimen of producing Court opinions. He was the least productive member of the Bird Court, and after five years, he resigned his position and returned to Boalt Hall to teach.

Peter Belton reminds us that what distinguishes the Chief Justice from the other Justices is that the Chief Justice is responsible for the smooth running of the day-to-day administration of the Court. When it comes to deciding cases, however, the Chief Justice has only one vote, equal in weight to all the rest. "Their vote doesn't count any more or any less than the newest kid on the court," Belton explains. The Justices understand this, he continues, so "when you hear the phrase, 'the Warren Court' or even 'the Traynor Court,' ... it doesn't really imply much."[34]

Although any decisions made to grant review of a case and to decide the outcome of that review are made collectively by all of the Justices, there is remarkably little direct collaboration among them. They sit together for the weekly conference to decide what cases they will hear, and again for the oral arguments of those cases, but the real work of considering the petitions for

A formal portrait of California Supreme Court Justice Stanley Mosk; perhaps taken during the 1990s (courtesy Richard Mosk).

review and writing the opinions occurs in "chambers," the separate offices maintained by each of the Justices. They each have their own staff, and how each Justice uses his or her staff varies from one chamber to another. On the Bird Court, each Justice was assigned a staff of three lawyers, with a couple extra for the Chief Justice. Every Justice filled one or two staff positions with full time permanent staff, filling the remaining positions with "law clerks" hired on an annual basis for one-year periods. Today, each Associate Justice has five lawyers, the Chief Justice has eight, and a "central staff" of sixty more serves the entire Court. Only one of the Justices utilizes annual law clerks anymore.

At that time, civil cases were handled by Justices assigned by the Chief Justice to prepare "conference memos" summarizing each of the civil cases to be discussed at the weekly conference. In criminal cases, a small, central Court staff usually prepared the Conference memos. If a hearing was granted, the Chief Justice assigned one of the Justices who voted to grant the hearing the job of preparing a "calendar memo" for the oral argument of the case. If a majority of Justices agreed with the calendar memo, its author would prepare the majority opinion. The Court would sit for several days one week each month to hear oral arguments, alternating between San Francisco, Los Angeles, and Sacramento. Each Justice ordinarily authored between twenty and thirty majority opinions each year. Some Justices exercised the option to write separate concurring or dissenting opinions with greater frequency than others. If any Justice penned a separate concurring or dissenting opinion, it would set off another round of editing, so each Justice in turn could consider the effect of the new opinion upon his prior treatment of the case. When all of the Justices had signed an opinion, the decision would be ready for release. But this only happened after it had been circulated to all of the Justices for comments and suggestions, rolled from one Justice's chambers to the next on a cart carrying "the box"—containing the calendar memo and all of the briefs and filed documents—and the often voluminous "record"—the reporter's transcript of testimony and the clerk's transcript of documents filed in the lower court

According to Peter Belton, " theoretically" the Chief Justice "could make it uncomfortable" for Justices who may disagree with him or her. For example, "with respect to assignments ... [the Chief Justice] could assign them boring cases or such." But, Belton firmly believes "that has never happened. It doesn't work that way. These people are not so petty as that."[35] Belton's charitable view was not shared by all, however. Suspicions were rampant that the Chief Justice used her power to assign the authorship of opinions to reward her friends and punish her enemies, and Justice Mosk was never on her list of friends. The choicest plums were either kept by the Chief Justice for her own staff or assigned to Justice Tobriner. During this time, the Court's productivity declined. The Court produced only 98 published opinions in 1980, a dramatic drop from the 170–180 decisions per year produced by the Traynor and Wright Courts.[36]

As the most liberal judge on her Court, Chief Justice Rose Bird led from the left, but she frequently discovered no one was following.[37] Justice Mosk still served as a bridge between the liberals and the conservatives, but it was increasingly a bridge over troubled waters.[38] Justice Mosk authored 21 of the majority opinions, and 12 dissenting opinions during Bird's first year. An increasing number of the Court's opinions were divided, often by a 4–3 margin. Very few were unanimous. The Court rarely spoke with one voice.

In *City of Berkeley v. Superior Court*,[39] for example, Justices Clark, Manuel and Richardson all dissented from Justice Mosk's ruling that private owners of tidelands hold them subject to a public trust for public access and use. The ruling had broad impact in California, protecting public access for use of tidelands previously transferred to private owners.

One of Justice Mosk's most creative majority rulings was a lawsuit filed on behalf of women afflicted with cancerous vaginal and cervical growths because their mothers took the drug DES during their pregnancy. Since the harm occurred many years after the drug was taken, they were often unable to prove which of several manufacturers produced the drug taken by their mothers. In *Sindell v. Abbott Laboratories*,[40] Justice Mosk authored a ruling that persons unable to identify the particular manufacturer of the drug that injured them may jointly sue all of the manufacturers of that drug on the theory of enterprise liability, and damages may be apportioned among them on the basis of their market share at the time. The ruling was inspired by a student note in the *Fordham Law Review*, and was widely followed in other states to hold drug manufacturers responsible when devastating side effects of drugs showed up many years after the drugs are taken. Again, Justices Clark, Manuel and Richardson dissented from the 4–3 ruling.

One of Justice Mosk's landmark opinions did achieve unanimity, however. In the case of *In Re Marriage of Carney*,[41] the lower court ordered the custody of two young boys be changed from their father to their mother, concluding that despite a warm relationship between the father and his sons, "it would not be a normal relationship between father and boys." The father had been injured in a jeep accident while serving in the military reserve, leaving him a quadriplegic with paralyzed legs and impaired use of his arms and hands. The trial judge emphasized the physical demands of parenting, and a father's role in active play with his children. Custody decisions rest in the sound discretion of the trial judge, and reviewing courts rarely find the "abuse of discretion" required to reverse that ruling. But this case caught the attention of Peter Belton, Justice Mosk's head research attorney. Himself a paraplegic confined to a wheelchair, Belton, with his wife Nancy, was raising three children, and he was deeply offended by the stereotypes about handicapped parents that pervaded the lower court ruling. A hearing was granted, and Justice Mosk worked closely with Peter Belton in fashioning a truly remarkable legal landmark. In a memorable passage, they noted that mutual participation in sports was not essential to a healthy father-son relationship:

> For some, the court's emphasis on the importance of a father's "playing baseball" or "going fishing" with his sons may evoke nostalgic memories of a Norman Rockwell cover on the old Saturday Evening Post. But it has at last been understood that a boy need not prove his masculinity on the playing fields of Eton, nor must a man compete with his son in athletics to be a good father: their relationship is no less "normal" if it is built on shared experiences in such fields of interest as science, music, arts and crafts, history or travel, or in pursuing such classic hobbies as stamp or coin collecting. In short, an afternoon that a father and son spend together at a museum or the zoo is surely no less enriching than an equivalent amount of time spend catching either balls or fish.[42]

The passage is ironic in light of the importance that sports played in Stanley Mosk's relationship with his father, as well as his own relationship with his son. Turning to the realities of children's lives today, they added:

> The stereotype indulged in by the court is false for an additional reason: it mistakenly assumes that the parent's handicap inevitably handicaps the child. But children are more adaptable than the court gives them credit for; if one path to their enjoyment of physical activities is closed, they will soon find another. Indeed, having a handicapped parent often stimulates the growth of a child's imagination, independence, and self-reliance…. It is true that William may not be able to play tennis or swim, ride a bicycle or do gymnastics; but it does not follow that his children cannot learn and enjoy such skills.

Finally, and most important, they explained that the stereotype is false because it fails to reach the heart of the parent-child relationship. Citing contemporary psychology, they eloquently concluded the essence of the parent-child relationship "lies in the ethical, emotional, and intellectual guidance the parent gives to the child throughout his formative years, and often beyond. The source of this guidance is the adult's own experience of life; its motive power is parental love and concern for the child's well-being; and its teachings deal with such fundamental matters as the child's feelings about himself, his relationships with others, his system of values, his standards of conduct, and his goals and priorities in life."[43]

The unanimous court ruled that it is impermissible to rely upon a physical handicap as presumptive evidence of the parent's unfitness or of probable detriment to the child in child custody disputes.[44]

Twenty years later, in accepting an award as "Public Lawyer of the Year," Peter Belton described how his personal experience as a parent had pervaded Justice Mosk's ruling in *Marriage of Carney*:

> I contracted polio in 1954 and have been in a wheelchair ever since. Because I became disabled before my three children were born, they've never known me not to be in a wheelchair. Yet I feel that I fully participated, with their mother, in their upbringing. Like any parent, I read to them, played games with them, answered their questions about life and the world (usually in more detail than they wanted), drove them to school in my van equipped with a wheelchair lift and hand controls, helped them with their school work, and shared their adventures on weekends and family vacations. My being in a wheelchair was simply not an obstacle to normal family life, and certainly didn't prevent my children from participating in active sports—for example, they were competitive swimmers and won many ribbons and medals.[45]

Among the most influential majority opinions Justice Mosk authored during his four decades on the Court was the ruling in *People v. Wheeler*.[46] Justice Mosk broke new ground when the Court ruled that during jury selection for a trial, attorneys who exercised peremptory challenges in a discriminatory manner were required to explain their reasons for removing minority jurors. Although *Wheeler* was based upon Mosk's interpretation of California's state constitution, when the United States Supreme Court decided the same issue eight years later, it construed the U.S. Constitution to achieve the same result.[47] Justice Mosk took particular pride in his *Wheeler* opinion, noting that its breadth was quite deliberate. "The *Wheeler* opinion did not limit its scope to Blacks; it applied to women, Hispanics, Asians, any cognizable group in our society.... Our purpose, we made clear, was to obtain juries that were a representative cross-section of the community." He described the "inward satisfaction" he felt when the U.S. Supreme Court finally came around to his view: "To have refused to follow a High Court opinion we deemed improper, to have rendered a directly contrary opinion, and then to have the High Court recant some years later and adopt our view, is truly gratifying."[48]

In *People v. Shirley*,[49] Mosk was joined by Chief Justice Bird in a 5–2 ruling excluding the testimony of all witnesses who have undergone hypnosis to restore their memory. The witness in *Shirley* was a rape victim who was intoxicated at the time, and vaguely and inconsistently described many of the details surrounding the incident. On the eve of trial, the prosecutor asked a fellow Deputy District Attorney to place the victim under hypnosis, at which time she allegedly recalled the events in greater detail. Justice Mosk reviewed a great deal of scientific literature about hypnotism as well as the previously decided cases throughout the nation that had addressed the problem of enhancing a witness's recollection by hypnotic suggestion. He declined to address the problem by propounding "safeguards" surrounding how the hypnotic session was conducted, instead announcing a broad rule that flatly prohibited testimony by a witness who had been subjected to hypnosis regarding the subject of the testimony. The decision was widely criticized by police, who claimed hypnosis produced remarkable successes in their investigation of crime. A famous example is the 1976 kidnapping near Chowchilla, California, of 26 children in a school bus, which was then buried. Under hypnosis, the bus driver recalled most of the license plate number of a Dodge van he saw, which helped break the case. However, a committee of the American Medical Association concluded that recollections under hypnosis are too shaky for the witness stand. The committee reported that it found "no evidence to indicate that there is an increase of only accurate memory during hypnosis." Further, the committee's report said, "there is no way for either subject or hypnotist to distinguish between those recollections which may be accurate and those which may be pseudomemories." The problem is that hypnotism heightens the imagination. A mesmerized witness "sees" hypnotic suggestions in his mind. During and after the trance, nobody can distinguish such imagined scenes from actual memories. The witness, convinced his phony memories are true, in turn becomes convincing about them in court.[50] The Legislature subsequently incorporated Justice Mosk's concerns about hypnotized witnesses into the California Evidence Code.[51]

Chapter 16

"You Have Remarkable Sources!"

From the start, those who opposed Chief Justice Bird's appointment used every opportunity to generate negative public opinion towards her. Oversimplifying issues and at times misrepresenting or manipulating the court's opinions were common methods not just to engage the public's attention, but to arouse its ire. Within the first year of her tenure, roused by hostile, organized interests, the Court began to draw unusual media attention, especially about the opinions authored by Chief Justice Rose Bird. Much of this attention was focused on the upcoming 1978 general election, when she would appear on the ballot for confirmation.

Initially, media attention was focused upon a brief concurring opinion Bird authored in *People v. Caudillo*.[1] The controversy in that case became intertwined with another controversial case, *People v. Tanner*, which then ballooned into one of the most devastating episodes in the Court's history.

When the *Caudillo* case first came before the Court, dissatisfaction with the treatment of rape victims by the justice system was growing throughout the nation. Statistics indicated that while around 56,000 cases of rape were reported annually, the actual number of victims was closer to 250,000. The discrepancy was credited to the ordeal imposed upon a victim reporting a rape, as well as the lackluster record of convictions and negligible sentences of rapists. In California, as elsewhere in the nation, legislatures responded by increasing the maximum sentences for rape, often by adding "enhancements" where weapons were used or victims were physically harmed.

In the *Caudillo* case, the Court set aside a convicted rapist's sentence of 15 years to life for burglary and rape because the sentence was improperly enhanced by a jury finding that "great bodily injury" had been inflicted on the victim. The California Supreme Court concluded that the rape alone, without additional physical consequences, was not a sufficient showing of "great bodily injury" to permit the sentence enhancement. Chief Justice Bird concurred in the ruling to express her personal repugnance with the result, even though the law compelled her to join the majority in following the law as it was written. She concluded, "this court has no choice in this matter," and then she invited the Legislature to reconsider the issue.[2]

The *Caudillo* case attracted little notice until it was featured in an anti–Bird TV advertisement portraying a bloody, sobbing rape victim and announcing, "Next May, that rapist could be on the streets again because Rose Bird and the Supreme Court reversed an appellate court decision and said they did not think the victim had experienced 'great bodily harm.'"[3] In response to a protest from the Bird campaign, many TV stations refused to run the misleading ad. The campaign against confirmation of the Chief Justice (and Justice Newman) was directed by State Senator H. L. "Bill" Richardson, a doctrinaire conservative previously affiliated with the John Birch Society. He formed the "Law and Order Campaign Committee," with former LAPD Chief Ed Davis as honorary chairman, and announced a goal of raising $1 million to defeat Chief Justice Bird's confirmation. He told news reporters his goal was to have "a law enforcement oriented court for the first time in 30 years."[4]

The irony was that the *Caudillo* opinion reflected a "strict construction" of the law, and as such should have been embraced by conservatives who oppose activist jurists loosely interpreting legislative texts.[5] The exploitation of the *Caudillo* ruling became a powerful tool in the hands of supposed defenders of law and order, but several California legislators anticipated the Chief Justice's invitation to revisit the law. According to Judge Armand Arabian, a future colleague of Justice Mosk on the Supreme Court, several lawmakers had recently adopted a new "attitude of curative action in the area of rape," which evolved into "a package of laws that treat rape as the vicious crime that it is."[6] Unfortunately, most of their bills were defeated in committees in both houses of the legislature. After the Caudillo decision in June, 1978, however, "a mosaic of rape-law reform" quickly coalesced around the interpretation of the language of "great bodily injury" to include a rape victim's psychological and emotional trauma. Thus, Chief Justice Bird's opinion was a harbinger of reform, rather than the "soft on rape" spin her enemies put on it.

The use of sentencing enhancements to lengthen prison sentences was not limited to rape cases. "Use a gun, go to prison" became the mantra for advocates promoting a law to impose a mandatory prison sentence for any crime in which a gun was used. At the time, judges had full discretion in armed robbery cases to sentence defendants to state prison or to place them on probation, frequently on the condition they serve a short term in the county jail. The "use a gun, go to prison" law enacted by the legislature in 1975 was intended to eliminate that discretion and require a sentence to state prison for any offense where it was alleged and proved that a gun was used its commission. In *People v. Tanner*,[7] a defendant who was convicted of robbery with use of a gun argued the law requiring a prison sentence did not override another section of the Penal Code that gives judges discretion to *dismiss* a criminal charge.[8] The power to dismiss the charge, it was argued, included the power to dismiss a part of the charge, and the Legislature's failure to amend this dismissal statute contradicted its stated intention of precluding probation where a gun was used. Thus, the sentencing judge still had discretion to dismiss, or strike, the allegation that a gun was used in the commission of the offense, and sentence the defendant to probation.

When Tanner was sentenced in San Mateo Superior Court, the trial judge accepted this argument and followed a probation department recommendation that Tanner, a first offender, be placed on probation for five years on condition he serve one year in the county jail and submit to psychiatric treatment. On appeal to the First District Court of Appeal, this ruling was reversed and Tanner was remanded to the trial court to be resentenced to state prison.[9] Tanner then filed a petition for a hearing in the California Supreme Court, which the Court granted on July 21, 1977. The case was reserved pending resolution of another case raising the same issue, but that case was decided without addressing the issue. The Court did not decide to hear oral argument in *Tanner* until February 6, 1978.

The pre-argument "calendar memo" in the *Tanner* case, in reality a proposed decision in the case, was prepared by Justice Tobriner. It proposed reversing the Court of Appeal, and reinstating the probationary sentence. Tobriner relied upon a long line of precedents holding the Legislature is presumed to have knowledge of prior judicial rulings, and that no matter how "mandatory" the terms of a sentencing provision may appear, they do not curtail the trial court's statutory discretion to strike or dismiss a charge in the absence of unambiguous statutory language restricting that power. The calendar memo was circulated before oral argument, after which the Court met in conference for a tentative vote to decide the case. Justice Mosk and Chief Justice Bird agreed with Tobriner, while Justices Clark and Richardson were opposed. Justices Newman and Manuel were undecided. On March 3, Justice Tobriner circulated to his colleagues a proposed majority opinion.

The circulation of the proposed opinion in *Tanner* later became a crucial factor in determining whether the *Tanner* decision was deliberately delayed to prevent its release before the November 7, 1978, election. As the "box" containing a proposed opinion was circulated among the Justices, internal rules provided it would go first to any likely dissenter for preparation of a dissenting opinion. The proposed majority and dissenting opinions could then be circulated together among the remaining Justices. Pursuant to this rule, the box went to Justice Clark on March 3, 1978. Forty-five days later he sent the box to Justice Richardson who signed Clark's dissent. Just over two weeks later, Richardson returned the box to Tobriner. Tobriner made no change in his opinion to respond to the dissent and three days later sent the box back to Richardson.[10]

Stanley Mosk first received the Tanner box with its lead and dissenting opinions on May 10. He immediately signed on to Tobriner's opinion and after only one day, moved the box to Justice Manuel who signed with the two dissenters. Just under two weeks later, Manuel moved the box to Justice Newman, who signed Tobriner's opinion on May 30. By then, six of the Justices signed an opinion, with Clark, Richardson, and Manuel dissenting and Mosk, Tobriner, and Newman allied in the proposed majority opinion. Six days later, Newman sent it on to Chief Justice Rose Bird, who held the Tanner box for six weeks. On July 11, she issued a five-page concurring opinion relying upon a different ground than Justice Tobriner, arguing that a restriction of the judge's power to dismiss the enhancement violated the constitutional separation of powers. That started a whole new round of the box to circulate so that all of the Justices could respond to Bird's decision.

Complicating matters was Justice Clark's departure abroad on July 12. After his return to the office, he revised his dissent and circulated it on August 25th. The new dissent now included his reply to the Chief Justice's opinion, adding a footnote to point out that he thought her position was inconsistent with the position she had taken in the controversial *Caudillo* rape case. The Chief Justice's staff alerted the Justices that she felt the *Caudillo* research inserted by Clark was "politically motivated." Clark took great offense at the suggestion that he was using his opinion as a device to embarrass Bird shortly before the election, and was now motivated to explain why he thought *Caudillo was* apposite and why he thought the Chief Justice was being inconsistent. Mosk briefly viewed the box for less than a day near the end of July, and did not access it again until well after the November 7, 1978 general election. Clark's revised dissent first went to Tobriner who held it nearly a month without taking any action on it. On September 21 it was forwarded to Justice Manuel, who decided that rather than signing on to Clark's dissent, he would write his own, which took thirty-three days to complete. Then on October 24, two weeks before the election, the box was returned to Justice Tobriner. Presumably, each of the other Justices would have the opportunity to respond to Justice Manuel's new, separate dissent. Although Tobriner would author a revised lead opinion a month down the line, on the day of the election, the Tanner box was still sitting on its cart in Justice Tobriner's chambers.[11]

The morning of election day, an article appeared in the *Los Angeles Times* under the following headline:

Supreme Court Decision to Reverse Gun Law Reported
Sources Say Ruling, Completed by Justices Several Weeks Ago, Has Not Been Made Public.

The story, by *Times* Staff Writers William Endicott and Robert Fairbanks, cited "well-placed court sources" to claim that a 4–3 opinion with Chief Justice Bird in the majority overturning the "use a gun, go to prison" law had been decided by the Court but was being delayed by Justice Mathew Tobriner, identified as "one of Ms. Bird's strong supporters against a well-organized campaign to win voter disapproval of her appointment to the court." After quoting Justice Tobriner's comment that he could not comment, the article went on, "However, two other justices confirmed that individual decisions were signed some time ago by all members of the Court. The justices could not explain why the outcome had not been announced."

A newspaper article quoting two unnamed Justices allegedly revealing the internal proceedings of a still pending case was like a bomb going off inside the Court's hallowed chambers. When it was later revealed that the two sources were allegedly Stanley Mosk and Bill Clark, they had some explaining to do.

Later that day, as the polls were closing, Chief Justice Rose Bird issued "A Statement to the People of the State of California" denying the accusation, saying "There are *no completed cases* before this court where release has been delayed for political reasons or for any other reasons extraneous to the decision-making process." Her statement strongly defended Justice Tobriner, stating his refusal to comment was required by the Code of Judicial Conduct, and condemning the use of his silence to suggest he was delaying release of a case until after the election. Chief Justice Bird's reaction signaled some sense of urgency on her part to defend a charge of a serious ethical lapse "impugning the integrity" of Justice Tobriner. In reality, however, the Court routinely delayed opinions, evading a constitutional provision that forbids paying the salary of any judge "while any cause before the judge is pending and undetermined for 90 days after it has been submitted for decision."[12] The Court utilized the simple device of not "submitting" a case for decision until the final opinion was ready for filing. That practice has since been abandoned. Today, cases are submitted at the time of oral argument, and with rare exceptions in which an order vacating the submission is filed, the decision is announced within 90 days. The current practice, however, has the disadvantage of diminishing the importance of oral argument, since the case is not set for argument until the court has already reached agreement on a decision.

Election returns published the next day revealed Chief Justice Bird eked out a narrow victory, winning confirmation with only 51.7 percent of the vote. Justices Richardson, Newman and Manuel were all confirmed with more comfortable margins, ranging from 62.1 percent for Manuel to 72.6 percent for Richardson. Within the Court, however, there was little celebration. Justice Tobriner was livid that other Justices had allegedly breached the ethical requirement to abstain from public comment about pending cases by suggesting he was holding up an opinion for political purposes. He had one of his staff attorneys prepare a memorandum tracing the handling of the *Tanner* case, and personally circulated a statement to be signed by all of the Justices denying the charge. Justice Mosk signed the statement, but Justices Clark and Richardson declined. Although neither the memorandum nor the statement was released, someone leaked both and they became the subject of follow-up news stories.

On November 24, 1978, without discussing its advisability with the other Justices, or seeking their concurrence in her waiver of the secrecy of the Court's internal operations, Chief Justice Bird released a letter to the press that she sent to the Chairman of the Commission on Judicial Performance, requesting the Commission to undertake an investigation into whether the *Tanner* decision had been improperly delayed, and to issue a public report with detailed factual findings and conclusions. She assured the chairman, "As soon as the decision in the *Tanner* case is announced and has become final, you will be provided all necessary access to the internal records of the Supreme Court relevant to your inquiry." A rational debate over the propriety of manipulating the timing for the release of decisions might produce a strong defense for the practice. A judicial election is not supposed to be a referendum on the popularity of any particular decision, but an evaluation of an individual judge's qualifications for office. A particular controversial decision that might tip the balance arguably should not be injected into the decisional process shortly before voters go to the polls. Presenting that defense to the charges leveled by the *Los Angeles Times* on November 7 was not an option however. This was not a rational debate, but a bare-knuckle political brawl. As Senator H. L. "Bill" Richardson put it, "We're not playing patty-cake."[13]

On December 22, the *Tanner* decision was announced. It contained a number of changes in the Tobriner and Bird opinions, but the result was the same: the Court struck down the "use a gun, go to prison" law. A howl of outrage was heard from California's prosecutors and law enforcement agencies, who were still reeling from another decision handed down on November 9, two days after the election. In *Hawkins v. Superior Court*,[14] authored by Justice Mosk and joined by Justices Tobriner, Manuel and Newman, with Chief Justice Bird concurring, the Court ruled that a defendant indicted by grand jury is entitled to a post-indictment preliminary hearing. Previously, prosecutors could avoid a preliminary hearing by taking the case to the grand jury for indictment and then proceeding directly to trial. If they filed a felony complaint, a preliminary hearing was required to determine if the defendant should be held for trial. The Court ruled that the felony complaint option gave defendants a valuable advantage for discovery of the prosecution's case through the preliminary hearing, and depriving defendants indicted by the grand jury of this opportunity was a denial of the equal protection of the laws. The ruling resulted in the virtual abandonment of the use of grand juries in California, which prosecutors regarded as a valuable tool in organized crime investigations and child abuse cases. Because they had to go through a preliminary hearing anyway, there was little advantage in using the grand jury. The *Hawkins* decision was announced nine months after it was argued, leading to suspicions that it, too, had been held up until after the election. It turned out that the decision had been delayed by the same type of internal manuevering that held up the *Tanner* case. In his original majority opinion for the *Hawkins* case, Justice Mosk utilized a new "three tier" analysis of the equal protection clause, a revolutionary concept then being widely debated in academic and judicial circles. Although Justices Tobriner, Newman and Manuel signed on, the Chief Justice balked, and wrote a concurring opinion relying on the traditional "two tier" analysis. Justice Manuel then withdrew his signature from the original Mosk opinion, and signed the Bird concurring opinion. That deprived Justice Mosk of a majority, so he removed his "three-tier" analysis from the majority opinion and presented it in a separate opinion concurring in his own majority opinion. Justice Manuel then signed on to Mosk's majority opinion, and the decision was announced.

The antiquated use of "boxes" to circulate opinions among the Justices, since abandoned by the Court, could significantly delay a decision while a Justice was absent from the Court. Justice Allen Broussard expressed his chagrin upon returning from a two week vacation, and finding "the whole perimeter" of his desk was lined with "boxes":

And when I say with boxes, at that time on the court, when it was the justice's time to act on a case, either side on a majority opinion or side on a dissenting opinion, or write if you were going to write, when it came your time to participate, the box with the record of the opinions and everything came to you. The whole perimeter of that desk was lined with boxes. Sometime two or three boxes for one case.[15]

When the California Commission on Judicial Performance received the Chief Justice's request for an investigation, it asked the Judicial Council to adopt a change in its normal rules of practice to permit a public hearing of the charges. Although some misgivings were expressed, the Judicial Council responded by amending the rules to *require* a public hearing of the charges. From the moment he returned from travel abroad in early January, Stanley Mosk and/or his representatives fought to reverse the decision to hold public hearings. As early as the first depositions, held in private in February, Mosk challenged the Commission's authority to hold public hearings. He pointed out that the confidentiality of the Judicial Council's proceedings were guaranteed by the state constitution. To Mosk, "Simple language is tortured with Orwellian technique when it is claimed that confidentiality is provided by the device of eliminating confidentiality."[16]

The Commission engaged Los Angeles attorney Seth Hufstedler to direct the investigation. Hufstedler was an inspired choice. One of the most respected lawyers at the bar, and married to then–Secretary of Education Shirley Hufstedler, he could be counted on to conduct a fair and balanced investigation without turning the proceedings into the witch hunt they could easily have become. Hufstedler clearly but broadly defined the scope of the inquiry to include: "any possible improper conduct of any Justice of the Supreme Court of California arising out of (1) any irregularities or delays in handling the *Tanner* case; (2) any irregularities or delays in handling any other case prior to the election of November 7, 1978, caused or instituted for the purpose of delaying the filing of the Court's decision in any such case until after the date of the election; and/or (3) any unauthorized disclosure of confidential information regarding any of the above pending cases prior to the public release of the decision."[17] Thus, the unstated motives underlying any Justice's decision to delay a case by changing an opinion became "fair game" for the Commission's probe.

Hufstedler oversaw four attorneys who conducted sixty interviews, examined Court records, and took sixty-two depositions, including all of the Justices and most of the Court staff. Public hearings began on June 18, and all seven Justices were subpoenaed to testify. The hearings continued for sixteen days, until they were surprisingly halted by order of a specially convened session of the Supreme Court spawned by a lawsuit filed on behalf of Justice Stanley Mosk asserting that public hearings of the Commission were unlawful.

Richard Mosk and his law partner Ed Medvene represented Justice Mosk. They argued that under the California Constitution the Judicial Council had no authority to open proceedings of the Commission on Judicial Performance to public scrutiny. Mosk's suit, filed only on his own behalf, was undertaken to quash the subpoena issued to Justice Mosk, "so that he does not violate his oath of office by participating in what he believes to be an illegal proceeding." He had no objection to being deposed, and ultimately testified before the Commission in a secret, non-public hearing. Richard told Hufstedler that he intended to take the issue no further than the trial court, that no appeal would be taken if the trial court did not quash the subpoena. When the trial court ruled against Mosk, his father insisted an appeal be taken, saying he had not authorized Richard to make such a commitment. Justice Mosk's lawsuit succeeded before the Court of Appeal, and, on an appeal by the Commission, before the California Supreme Court. Six of the Justices recused themselves from hearing the appeal. The seventh was Frank Newman who refused to step down until he was ordered off the case, whereby an extraordinary panel of appointed Justices unanimously agreed that Mosk was right.[18] Richard Mosk raised a constitutional challenge to the authority of a court wholly composed of pro tem appointees to hear the case, but the challenge was rejected by Chief Justice Bird.

To many observers, the sixteen days of public testimony did little to enhance the reputation of the California Supreme Court or its Justices, who were portrayed as bumblers engaged in petty personality conflicts. Others saw the whole episode more constructively, placing the Court in the public's eye, permitting the same type of scrutiny to which the other two branches of state government were subjected.

The testimony of Justice Clark described the "cool but correct" stance adopted by Chief Justice Bird in her relationship to Justices Clark and Mosk:

> The relationship was such that when I went into her chambers for Wednesday conferences, there was no acknowledgment. And in other situations, when we came together, my attempts to even get into pleasantries failed. More concern to me, however, was the same treatment to my staff, which they were upset over.[19]

Clark went on to describe an incident in which the Chief Justice turned her back when his secretary greeted her in the morning on the elevator, as well as the "punishment" meted out to his secretary by denying her request to cover the linoleum in her office with carpet discarded when it was replaced in the Chief Justice's chambers. When Clark complained to Mosk, Mosk related similar incidents of a lack of acknowledgment from the Chief. All of these incidents provided titillating fodder for the press, which reported the proceedings like a peek behind the curtains.

By August, Stanley Mosk had threatened and then followed through with terminating his membership in the California Judges Association after its president, the Honorable Harry W. Low published an article advocating the Commission's publicized hearings. "While massaging the ego of the press may be a worthwhile project for the Association, or for you personally," Mosk wrote, "it is improper to do so in violation of the constitution which all judges have sworn to uphold."[20] That same month, in a speech to the American Bar Association while the proceedings were pending, Justice Mosk decried the indignity of the proceedings and he aggressively challenged the Commission's authority:

> The Commission decreed that it was not bound by the rules of evidence. Thus, it permitted reports of corridor gossip among law clerks, inquiries into intent, motivation, speculation, and the rankest type of hearsay.... The entire investigation became a media event that replaced daytime soap operas, and, not surprisingly, the press reveled with prurient interest in every juicy morsel relating to internal Court personality conflicts.... There is no more pathetic sight than learned judges cringing in fear of an aggressive investigative commission which is in turn pandering to an assaultive press.[21]

Coming to the defense of the Judicial Council was its special counsel, Pierce O'Donnell. Directly addressing Justice Stanley Mosk's speech in Dallas, O'Donnell said Mosk's criticisms were "unjudicious, insulting, and demeaning." To O'Donnell, "Justice Mosk would have us go back 20 years and begin the debate again of who shall judge the judges." What's more, "there is no imperial presidency, there can be no imperial judiciary."[22]

One positive outcome of the Commission hearings was exposing the irresponsibility of the *Los Angeles Times* and its reporters. Justice Clark testified that when Robert Fairbanks called him to get "confirmation" of the story the *Times* was running about Tobriner delaying the *Tanner* ruling, he declined to confirm or deny the story. Fairbanks told Clark that his fellow reporter William Endicott had already discussed the matter with Justice Mosk, who supposedly told him "they certainly have interesting sources or good sources." Then Fairbanks said, "Well, let me ask you another question. If in the morning you should read the story I have described to you, will you throw your coffee cup against the wall?" Clark indicated he might have responded with a chuckle.

The secret testimony given to the Commission by Justice Mosk has never been released. But when Betty Medsger published a passionate defense of Chief Justice Rose Bird entitled *Framed: The New Right Attack on Chief Justice Rose Bird and the Courts*, she quoted the testimony at length. Medsger was the wife of Justice John Racanelli, a member of the Commission on Judicial Performance, who recused himself from the Tanner investigation because of his close friendship with Chief Justice Bird. According to Medsger, Mosk testified that when Endicott called him for confirmation of the November 7 story, he said, "No comment." When Endicott said, "Well, we have got this from good sources that this is the situation," Mosk responded, "Well, you have remarkable sources."

The newspaper's interpretation of Mosk's response of "remarkable sources" and Clark's chuckle was a feat of journalistic jujitsu to claim that "two other Justices confirmed that individual decisions were signed some time ago by all members of the Court." Justice Clark's public testimony did confirm that he suspected the decision was being delayed to avoid embarrassing Chief Justice Bird by his *Tanner* dissent before the election, and his impression that Justice Mosk shared his suspicion. He testified that in January, 1979, Mosk said to him, "Bill, before election day, I told Matt that it was obvious that cases were being held for filing after [the] election and I told him it was obvious and if it were later revealed he would have to pay the consequences." This testimony was treated like the smoking gun, especially when Clark added that he reminded Mosk of this conversation just a week before he came to testify, and Mosk apparently responded, "Yes, Bill, that is correct. I had two such conversations with Matt."

But when Mosk testified behind closed doors, he shattered any confidence the Commissioners could place in Clark's recollections. Mosk's recall was also supported by a memo he sent to Justice Manuel. Mosk explained his January, 1979 conversations with Clark in these terms:

> The case that has troubled me has been the *Fox* case, and I have talked to Justice Tobriner twice and I brought it up in conference, as you will recall, about the long time it took in getting the *Fox* case out, and I even told Justice Tobriner I thought there would be some serious consequences for the court if the *Fox* case were delayed until the holiday season. There have been serious consequences. There was a bad reaction when the opinion was released on the 15th of December. I think the decision's right, but what atrocious timing for its release.

Mosk also confirmed the follow-up conversation with Justice Clark the week before Clark testified, but again stated that the conversation referred to the *Fox* case and not *Tanner*. He concluded that Justice Clark was confusing his concerns about the *Fox* case with comments he made about the delay of other court decisions in conference.

Mosk's testimony that he had concerns about the timing of the *Fox* decision was revealing. In *Fox v. City of Los Angeles*, the Court, in a 5–2 opinion by Justice Newman, upheld an injunction preventing Los Angeles from illuminating the windows of City Hall in the form of a cross during the Christmas season, as it had done for thirty years.[23] The Court concluded the display violated the establishment clause of the California Constitution, by preferring one religious symbol over others. The decision was released ten days before Christmas. After Mosk's testimony, Justice Tobriner was recalled to testify and confirmed that Justice Mosk had expressed concerns to him over the delay in the *Fox* opinion. Mosk did not want the opinion released close to Christmas. Thus, Justice Mosk apparently felt that potential public reaction to an opinion *was* an appropriate consideration in timing its release, and that his colleagues should consider forthrightly conceding that decisions were delayed for the very reason that the Court did not want them to affect public opinion shortly before the election. Mosk described to the Commission some thoughts he shared with his fellow Justices in conference:

> I said, "Let me offer a suggestion to any of you who may have held up cases because of the election." And the Chief Justice interrupted and said, "If anyone did." And I said, "Yes, if anyone did." And then I went on with this explanation, that I had been with Professor Paul Freund of Harvard in the Middle East. He had asked me what was going on here. I said justices were accused of having held up cases because of the election and his answer was, "What's wrong with that?" And I said, "Well some people seem to think it's wrong." He said, "I think that a court, if it has a politically sensitive case before it, has a right and perhaps a duty to hold the matter up until the election has passed.... I am convinced that if the United States Supreme Court had a case before it that would cause either the election or defeat of a sitting President of the United States it would not release the opinion in October; it would hold it up until after the November election." And I said, "Well, suppose however it's not the United States Supreme Court where they have life tenure, but it's a judge whose very election depends on this?" And he paused a moment and said, "Well, that changes the situation a little bit, but not particularly because," said he, "the issue in a judge's campaign for re-election is the judge's qualifications or temperament, and not the judge's opinion on a particular case the judge may have rendered. Therefore," said he, "if it doesn't involve someone sitting in jail who shouldn't be there or somebody's property being held up that shouldn't be, I think the court has a perfect right to hold up a case until after the election if it's going to affect the election." So I said to my colleagues, "I am passing that on to you for whatever it's worth. You may consider that, those of you who will have any problem in the forthcoming proceedings."

Mosk then told the Commissioners, "there was total silence after my presentation."[24]

During his "secret" testimony, Justice Mosk was pressed by Commisisioner Thomas H. Willoughby as to whether his "remarkable sources" comment was itself a breach of the confidentiality of Supreme Court deliberations. After clarifying that Stanley Mosk never felt he was one of the two Justices the *L.A. Times* authors claimed as their sources, Willoughby asked Mosk if his understanding of the judicial canons of ethical standards "permitted" him "to make the remark that you did, 'those are remarkable sources.'" Mosk repeatedly claimed he could not see the relevance of the question or how that comment related to the current case. Willoughby explained, "Well, I guess under certain circumstances it seems to me that phrase, that sentence might be taken as confirmation." If Willoughby's explicit confrontation appeared to identify a smoking gun and to undermine Justice Mosk's credibility, it was a short moment, indeed. "I don't see how you can," Mosk stated, "or anyone could draw that conclusion when *following* that expression Mr. Endicott said, 'But will you confirm or deny the story?' So he obviously did not deem it to be confirmation, any more than I deemed it to be confirmation."[25]

At the conclusion of Justice Mosk's testimony, Commissioner Willoughby took another shot. He noted the "obvious difference between your understanding of the conversation that you had with Justice Clark and Justice Clark's understanding of it." He then asked Mosk, prefaced by "This may be a little bit unfair," whether Mosk felt any ethical obligation to exonerate Justice Tobriner from the inferences that were being drawn from Clark's public testimony. He said Justice Tobriner "is at the least nearing the end of his career, has this cloud cast over him by first of all the Fairbanks and Endicott article, and then by the statement that Justice Clark made, I think in all good faith, in public, about the conversation that he, Justice Clark, felt had occurred between the two of you in January cast a further cloud, or darkened that cloud, if you will, I think over Justice Tobriner and Justice Tobriner's good name." The ultimate question he posed to Mosk was what did he feel was his obligation as a member of a collegial body to set the record straight? After a bit of wrangling by Mosk's counsel, Justice Mosk answered that all he could do is tell the truth to the best of his recollection, which was what he was doing.

Willoughby elaborated his point, saying, "What bothers me personally is that a very serious allegation emerged as a result of those public proceedings which does damage, I think not only to an individual justice, but perhaps to the Court as a whole, and from what we've heard you say, that allegation is based on an incorrect recollection of a conversation. How does that mistake that is now out in the public, how does that get corrected?"

Justice Stanley Mosk replied, "I would suggest to you that's the vice in having public hearings," to which Willoughby countered, "You mean — I don't mean this to be facetious, but are saying that Justice Tobriner now has no alternative but to twist slowly in the wind?" Mosk again replied, "I have to repeat my answer. That was one of the vices in having a public hearing in the first instance."[26]

After all of the testimony was gathered, it was clear there was insufficient evidence to support a finding of impropriety by any Justice of the Court. The Commission avoided saying as much in a cryptic report, which read more like a complaint that "under the compulsion of the decision in *Mosk v. Superior Court*, the Commission is not only prohibited from concluding the hearings in public," but it is also "prohibited from reviewing or commenting upon the testimony and other evidence." Furthermore, the Commission was prohibited "from public dissemination of the analysis and reasoning employed in arriving at a determination and disposition of the proceedings." The exoneration sought by Chief Justice Bird for Justice Tobriner eluded her, and the Court's public image was badly tarnished.

Commissioner Willoughby assured the public that "it's not an exoneration just because we didn't vote to bring charges." On the other hand, he also said there were still key questions left unanswered and the Court would have been protected from charges of a whitewash if the Commission could explain its actions. At the same time, it was reported that the Judicial Council decided to study proposals to substantially change its procedures in investigating charges of judicial misconduct.[27]

For Chief Justice Bird and her supporters, the villains of the piece were Justices Clark and Mosk. A forthright denial to the *Los Angeles Times*, they thought, would have prevented the entire imbroglio. Justice Mosk's assertion of constitutional objections to public testimony frustrated the goal of a public exoneration of Justice Tobriner. Chief Justice Bird remained suspicious of the motives of Justice Mosk throughout her tenure on the Court. She saw his hand in the opposition she faced for her confirmation election in 1978, and long after the Tanner hearings concluded, she frequently ascribed conspiratorial motives to him even regarding routine requests. When Mosk switched his vote to join a Grodin dissent, giving Grodin the four votes to make his dissent a majority, Justice Grodin asked Chief Justice Bird for permission to incorporate the statement of facts from what had been her majority opinion. She replied that he and Mosk were "conspiring" to deprive her of a majority opinion and refused permission.

For Justice Mosk, however, the entire Tanner debacle simply confirmed the ineptitude of Chief Justice Bird, who invited the Commission investigation without consulting any of her colleagues on the Court. For Anthony Lewis, astute legal analyst for the *New York Times*, the villain was the *Los Angeles Times*: "My guess is that [the reporters and editors of one of the country's best newspapers] were carried away by the lure of an exciting scoop — one whose significance would fade, moreover, if they did not rush the story into print the next morning. Just about every journalist knows that feeling of temptation. I have yielded to it myself, and later regretted what turned out to be a half-understood or inaccurate story. It is an explanation, not an excuse."[28]

Writing to a longtime supporter, Speaker of the Assembly Leo McCarthy, Mosk accused the Commission and the Judicial Council who of yielding "to the pressure from the media and from [the] lynch-the-judiciary mob." Citing the half million dollars the hearings cost the taxpayers and the unethical, unconstitutionality of the whole affair, Mosk asserted that "When members of the Commission donned their pancake makeup and opened their investigation to TV and the press, they were out of step with the entire nation and with California history." What's more, "it took protracted litigation and personal sacrifice by me to get the Commission back in step."[29] The irony of the outcome, cloaking the conclusion in secrecy, was aptly panned by Ed Lascher, a legal columnist whose trenchant wit was legendary:

> If one is contemptuous of one's colleagues and of their mental and ethical processes, but one still wants an aura of divine infallibility to cloak the group, then secrecy is the sine qua non. It won't do to let Dorothy see who is pumping the Wizard of Oz machine behind the screen.[30]

The ultimate victim could have been Tanner himself, who by then had completed his probationary sentence. On February 8, 1979, while preparations for the Commission hearing were underway, the Supreme Court granted the Attorney General's petition to rehear the *Tanner* case. A rehearing is rarely granted, but what made the difference in this case was that Justice Mosk, who voted with the majority, joined the dissenting Justices to provide the crucial fourth vote for rehearing. The case was reargued, and on June 14, 1979, four days before the public hearings of the Commission began, the California Supreme Court issued a new ruling in *People v. Tanner*.[31] The dissenting opinion of Justice Clark became the new majority opinion, upholding the "use a gun, go to prison" law. Clark was joined by Justices Manuel, Richardson, and Mosk. Mosk never explained his turnaround in the *Tanner* case, but it is quite likely he was influenced by the events subsequent to the opinion in the first *Tanner* case. Legislation had been immediately introduced to change the statutory language to reverse the effect of the first decision, and it passed the State Senate on a unanimous vote. Although the change languished in the Assembly, it was clear the first *Tanner* ruling would be reversed by the Legislature anyway. In the end, Mosk was probably mollified by one change Clark made in converting his dissent into a majority opinion. Clark added:

> However, given the unusual post-conviction manner in which the issue of judicial discretion has been presented and finally resolved, it follows Mr. Tanner should not necessarily be committed to prison. The uncertainty arising from the rule of law resulting in the trial court's erroneous disposition has created both an unusual burden on defendant and a dilemma for this court. Simply put, is it not unfair to require Mr. Tanner to now serve a second term for his criminal act? ... Mr. Tanner having complied with his conditions of probation — including one year's stay in county jail — we determine a second incarceration would be unjust.

Justice Newman, in a new dissenting opinion, gently chided Justice Mosk for not explaining his change of position:

> Indeed, the lead opinion's ultimate determination to relieve Tanner of a prison sentence is eloquent testimony to the strength of the traditional, underlying judicial policies in this area, recognizing that exceptional circumstances — unforeseen by the Legislature — may in rare cases warrant a departure from a generally appropriate sentence. I share those views, and that

four colleagues have not felt impelled to explain fully their reasons for disagreement is saddening.

Justice Newman then concluded, "The politicization of this proceeding after the summer of 1978 became phantasmagoric. A shrill, clamorous campaign — inspired and nurtured by experienced, well-financed, ambitious, and posse-like 'hard on crime' advocates— has had a still incalculable but dismal impact on the judicial process in California."

Chapter 17

"I Am Now an Orphan"

The years following the *Tanner* Commission hearings were difficult for Justice Stanley Mosk. Within a period of one year after the Tanner hearings, death claimed both Justice Mosk's wife, Edna, and his mother, Minna Perl Mosk. On May 22, 1981, Edna passed away at the age of 65 after a particularly painful final battle with her cancer. She had kept up a busy schedule despite chemotherapy treatments, blood transfusions, appointments with three or four different specialists, and the need to take more than a dozen pills a day. One month before her own death, she attended the funeral for her father in Los Angeles.

In many ways, Edna was very much like Mosk's mother, Minna — strong, independent, and devotedly caring for her husband as he moved up in his career. But Edna never really liked staying at home. Instead, she preferred to spend her days lunching and dining with friends, hosting dinner parties, and attending social and political affairs. She regularly attended the theatre, ballet, and symphony, and would have been out every evening if her health allowed. Always stylishly dressed, she had standing appointments for the hairdresser. Her calendar was filled with events and birthday reminders, all the way through the year 1981. The month before she died, she was meeting Mickey Ziffren, attending a B'nai B'rith dinner in Palm Springs, and traveling with Stanley to Los Angeles where he presided over the Loyola Law School Moot Court. She also participated in a weekly creative writing session with a cancer therapy group. In one session, she offered a poignant memoir of her suffering. The depth of her intimacy was reserved for Stanley alone:

> DEVOTION: Your love envelops me through all the tender motions — kissing, hugging, patting. Demanding nothing in return but my affection which is evident always. Your support and encouragement constantly keep me afloat. This disease is a nightmare — must keep fighting it with your help. Hold me tightly. — EDNA.

She utilized medicinal marijuana baked in brownies to alleviate her pain and the side effects of frequent chemotherapy during the final year of her illness. At the time, the use of medical marijuana was illegal in California, so the arrangements for her use of it had to be carefully concealed. Tucked inside a flap in Stanley Mosk's calendar for 1980 was a note in his distinctive handwriting. It read "1/4 oz. Columbian Pot." It was a shopping list.

Edna's courageous and compassionate oncologist, Dr. Ernest Rosenbaum, later became one of the leading advocates of California's Compassionate Use Act, an initiative measure which in 1996 legalized the medicinal use of cannabis for all California patients. In a sensitive letter to Stanley and his son Richard, Dr. Rosenbaum hinted at the difficulties the family faced during Edna's final illness:

> Cancer is not only a killer of the body but it somehow hurts the mind in a very subtle way to fear, anger and depression and it affects how a person acts and functions. I am sure that a lot of her dynamic personality was spent in just trying to keep herself afloat.[1]

A memorial service was held at Sinai Memorial Chapel in San Francisco, and Edna was interred at Hillside Memorial Park in Los Angeles. Harry Groman, the president of the city's leading Jewish Mortuary, directed the service himself.

Minna Perl Mosk died early in 1982. She had become a vital and connected mother, grandmother, and a source of pride to her family. Mosk's brother Ed and his wife Fern, their son Tom, Uncle Dave's wife Esther, and cousin Harriet remained a part of the circle around Minna, while Stanley and Edna led separate lives in San Francisco, trying to stay in touch by telephone calls and frequent visits. Stanley and Ed Mosk split the cost of her monthly rent. She managed to stay in her own apartment, spending only the last months of her life in a convalescent home, barely able to walk. Stanley Mosk tried to call his mother every day, and his work on the Supreme Court brought him to Los Angeles with some regularity. Minna's death was not a surprise. She was 93 years old.

Stanley Mosk had come to handle life's difficult moments with a sardonic humor, and that was how he responded to the news of his mother's passing. During dinner one evening while attending an annual reunion of his University of Chicago fraternity brothers in Jamaica, Mosk received an emergency phone call. He took it in another room and upon his return, the group waited to hear what was going on. He sat down and simply said, "I am now an orphan."[2]

After his mother's death, Justice Mosk fondly described her to friends as "a truly remarkable woman," a voracious reader who read nearly every book in the bookshop she operated for over thirty years, enabling her to advise customers. He was especially proud of her business acumen in managing the bookstore, calling her "Mrs. Irolo." He said she "handled the store remarkably well for a person who had no business training."[3] These remarks romanticized his mother in a way that devoted sons often do. He may not have remembered that Minna studied bookkeeping and was hired to keep accounts when she first met his father. She continued to perform as though she were a paid employee during her years of living, moving, and repeatedly setting up shop throughout the ventures of Paul Mosk and Dave Perl.

On January 5, 1981, Justice Wiley Manuel died unexpectedly, after serving only four years on the Court. At the Court's memorial service three weeks later, Justice Mosk bid farewell to "a kind, gentle, warm human being whom every one of us on this court loved like our own brother." When serving as Attorney General, Mosk had appointed Manuel as head of the administrative law section of the office. He joked that his Chief Assistant once suggested placing a plaque on Manuel's desk that would read, "Government Agencies Are Always Right." Wiley Manuel certainly didn't believe his former boss was always right, though. During his final year on the Court, he disagreed with Justice Mosk in one-third of the cases. Manuel was quickly replaced by Justice Otto Kaus, a well-regarded veteran of the Court of Appeal in Los Angeles. Kaus immigrated to the United States from Austria during the Nazi era. Although he spoke with a slight German accent, he was a true master of the English language, writing scholarly opinions with literary flair. Kaus was well known to Justice Mosk. In 1978, Justice Mosk's annual law clerk was Kaus' son, Mickey.

In March of 1981, newly elected President Ronald Reagan summoned Justice Clark to Washington, first to serve as deputy secretary of state, then as National Security Advisor, and finally secretary of the interior. Clark's appointment to Interior sparked fear in the minds of conservationists, hardly recovering from Secretary James Watt's hostility to environmentalism, and his controversial support for use of federal lands by foresting, ranching, and other commercial interests. Watt finally resigned after mocking affirmative action policies when he described a panel gathered to deal with coal leasing. He said, ""I have a black, a woman, two Jews and a cripple. And we have talent." Senator Alan Cranston expressed his feelings about Clark to Mosk. "I opposed this confirmation because the White House made it clear that the new Secretary of the Interior would carry on the policies of James Watt — policies with which I strongly disagree. Now that Bill has been confirmed, I hope to work with him and convince him of the need for change. Your confidence in Bill gives me encouragement."[4]

Justice Mosk strongly supported Clark's qualifications for the Interior post during Senate confirmation hearings, and received an appreciative note from President Ronald Reagan. Reagan took the occasion to "acknowledge your clear and courageous position relative to numerical quotas in hiring and college admission." The president added, "I agree with your observation that the equal protection clause of the United States Constitution does not suggest that some members of our nation shall be more equal than others."[5] Mosk and Clark continued to socialize, although they did so "covertly" because of Clark's new importance in Washington. One evening Justices Newman and Richardson joined them for a night out in San Francisco. Newman recalled, "we had the best evening together."[6]

After Clark's confirmation, Mosk was especially pleased when President Reagan accepted Bill Clark's recommendation to appoint his son, Richard, to be the American judge for the Iran–U.S. Claims Tribunal at The Hague. The position had first been offered to Justice Mosk, who indicated he did not want to leave the California Supreme Court, and recommended his son for the appointment. Richard took a leave from his law firm and with his family moved to The Hague to serve with distinction on the tribunal.

Justice Clark was replaced by Allen Broussard, then a Superior Court judge in Alameda County. Broussard restored an African American presence to the Court that had briefly disappeared with Wiley Manuel's death. Broussard and Manuel had been close friends, working together as leaders in bar association and Boy Scout activities. Although Broussard lacked appellate experience, he was a quick learner with a nimble mind.

In the wake of the Tanner Hearings, Stanley Mosk's relationship with some of his fellow Justices, especially Justice Mathew Tobriner, was severely strained. A siege mentality prevailed at the Court, as political efforts to unseat the Chief Justice continued. A petition to force her recall was circulated in 1981 by a group of disgruntled prosecutors. Six more recall petitions were circulated in 1982, including one filed by Senator H. L. "Bill" Richardson, who led the anti–Bird campaign in 1978. None of them qualified for the ballot, but the anti–Bird efforts made Rose Bird very wary of the media and suspicious of her "enemies" on the Court. The departure of four Justices from the Court created a dramatic realignment of the "Bird Court." Governor Jerry Brown's four second-term appointments reinforced the Court's diversity and brought some judicial "superstars" on board.

Nine months later, the greatly beloved Justice Mathew Tobriner retired, after twenty years on the Court. His health had rapidly declined after the ordeal of the Tanner hearings, and he died within four months of retirement. Although Justice Mosk was routinely invited to speak at the Court's memorial services for departed Justices with whom he had served, he was not asked to speak at the memorial for Justice Tobriner. The Tobriner family still harbored resentment toward Justice Clark and Justice Mosk over the injury to Tobriner's reputation caused by the Tanner hearings.

Tobriner was replaced by Cruz Reynoso, the first Hispanic to serve on the Court in modern times. In 1968, he came to national attention as the director of California Rural Legal Assistance (CRLA), a pioneering government-funded legal services agency that was to endure years of controversy and win wide acclaim for its efforts to serve the rural poor. Then-Governor Ronald Reagan sought to block CRLA funding, and Reynoso led a long fight to win support from the organized bar and in Congress, eventually gaining continued funding from the Nixon Administration. After briefly leaving California to teach constitutional and labor law at the University of New Mexico, he returned in 1976 to accept an appointment to the state Court of Appeal in Sacramento. In an unusual action, two Justices who served with Reynoso on the Court of Appeal publicly opposed his Supreme Court appointment. Justice Hugh A. Evans accused Reynoso of being too slow in producing opinions and of being a "true racist," showing bias in favor of Latinos, other minorities, and the poor. Retired Justice George E. Parras called Reynoso a "professional Mexican," whose lack of productivity had "bottlenecked" the court. After other appellate justices testified in favor of Reynoso, the Judicial Appointments Commission confirmed him on a 2–1 vote. Attorney General George Deukmejian opposed the appointment.

The fourth departure from the Court came in the fall of 1982, when Justice Frank Newman decided to return to his first love, law school teaching at U.C. Berkeley's Boalt Hall. His replacement on the Court was Joseph Grodin, a longtime professor at the University of California Hastings Law School, who was then serving on the Court of Appeal in San Francisco. Grodin was a protégé of Mathew Tobriner. After Grodin took his seat on the Supreme Court, Mosk called him into his chambers, and told him that despite his unhappiness with Justice Tobriner's support for Rose Bird, "you and I are starting out on a clean slate."[7] Grodin appreciated Justice Mosk's candor in describing the tensions on the Court, and admired Mosk's remarkable memory for detail.

During Governor Jerry Brown's second term, Republican George Deukmejian served as California's Attorney General, and thereby one of three members of the Judicial Appointments Commission. Deukmejian rose to prominence as author and chief proponent of legislation to restore the death penalty in California, and he was an outspoken critic of Chief Justice Bird and what he perceived as anti-death penalty bias on the Supreme Court. Attorney General Deukmejian voted against Brown's second-term nominations of Justices Broussard and Reynoso after they declined to respond to a "questionnaire" in which Deukmejian asked their opinions of fifteen Bird Court decisions with which he disagreed. Deukmejian did vote to approve the nominations of Justice Kaus and Justice Grodin.

On August 27, 1982, nearly a year and a half after Edna's death and two weeks before his seventieth birthday, Justice Mosk married Susan Jane Hines, an attractive woman 35 years his junior. The couple met at his tennis club in 1975, where they played mixed doubles. Mosk was still a vigorous tennis player, duly impressed with the professional level tennis skills which Susan demonstrated. Although Susan was at first unaware of who he was or what he did, she knew he was kind and gentlemanly, and he seemed a steady sort of man when she interacted with him, unlike her own more flashy and outgoing personality. She knew she liked him — not romantically, although she noticed there was always a twinkle in his eye. Eventually, she got to know Edna as well, since she lived across the street from their Nob Hill high rise, and the Mosks frequented the restaurant in her building. She knew Edna was ill, and for some reason Susan had a gut notion that she would marry Stanley Mosk when Edna's terminal illness played itself out.

Their relationship remained platonic but increasingly more intimate, filling a void in Mosk's emotional life. In spite of their age difference, they were suitably matched at this time in both of their lives. Stanley Mosk seemed to know instinctively what Susan later realized, the better she got to know him and learned about his relationship with Edna. It was that the relationship between Edna and Stanley was based upon their symmetry. Because they were so much alike, over time they could bring little to each other that was different. His relationship with Susan was based upon what they could give each other that was different.[8]

Susan's background was far removed from what Mosk had known. Susan was not Jewish. Both of her parents were Irish. Her father was an Irish orphan from Pittsburgh who became a Roman Catholic priest, then left the priesthood after meeting her mother, who was an Irish Protestant from Belfast. He served as a medic in World War II. As a young adult, Susan's talent as a pianist won her acclaim as a Julliard prodigy, who at one time stayed with Leonard Bernstein and his wife in their New York townhouse, and was a featured performer at a summer concerto festival. Then she pursued a business career with McGraw-Hill publishing house, where she earned a great salary, plus commission, and never touched a piano again — at least not until Stanley bought her a baby grand. Her skill on the tennis court continued to give her entre to interesting people and opportunities, and eventually she found herself as a speech writer for Senator Richard Stone, a one-term senator from Florida. When Stone was defeated for reelection in 1980, she joined the staff of California Senator John Tunney and moved to San Francisco.

As Edna's medical condition worsened, Susan's mother died. By then, Mosk had begun to hint that he was interested in a more permanent relationship. After Edna's death, Stanley Mosk remained stoic, reflecting his generational reticence to express feelings. Edna's debilitating illness had gone on for almost a decade and it had been wearing, but he coped; and he was sad. They had been married for a long time, and in spite of anything and everything, couples of their generation just stayed together. Edna and Stanley Mosk shared much, but their private lives were more formal and emotionally detached. Susan and Justice Mosk's friendship blossomed. Over time, he began to open up and his hilarious sense of humor returned.

After Edna's death, Mosk would have had his pick from a long line of women his age, but he was pleased that he was still attractive to a younger woman. With his remarriage, Mosk renewed his active social life and travel schedule. Two weeks after the wedding, he left his new bride behind and embarked on a month long trip to Asia on behalf of the Asia Foundation of San Francisco, a non-profit, non-governmental organization committed to the peaceful development of the Asia-Pacific region. He spent six days each in Thailand, Bangladesh, Korea, Sri Lanka and the Philippines, giving lectures and meeting with local lawyers and judges as a consultant on the American judicial system. He circled the globe to return home via Amsterdam, so he could visit Richard and his family at The Hague.

Mosk bought his new wife a beautiful fur coat, and boasted to friends at a football game tailgate party that she welcomed him home at the airport wearing nothing else. Susan enrolled as a law student at Hastings Law School, just two blocks from the high rise chambers of the California Supreme Court. Politically ambitious, she sought appointment to the San Francisco Board of Supervisors, but without success.[9]

The following year, Justice Mosk returned to Africa for a third time, again visiting the wild game preserves, this time with Susan. He and Susan rented a home in Napa for seven weeks in the summer of 1985, inviting some of his college chums to join them for a weeklong reunion. Jim Zacharias, the fraternity brother with whom he paid a call on Clarence Darrow in 1932, flew out from Illinois with his wife for the occasion.

In the November 1982 gubernatorial election, George Deukmejian defeated Los Angeles Mayor Tom Bradley. Deukmejian made crime the central issue of his campaign, criticizing the Supreme Court for its record on death penalty appeals. Tom Bradley's campaign emphasized his years as a member of the Los Angeles Police Department and his service on the city council to reassure voters he had solid credentials as a tough-on-crime candidate. Unfortunately, his support of Rose Bird, his opposition to the Victims' Bill of Rights, and quite likely, his being an African American took their toll. Deukmejian was able to exploit Bradley's weaknesses and tout his record for getting crime measures passed in the state Senate, his strong advocacy of capital punishment, and his outspoken opposition to Chief Justice Rose Bird.[10] All of the Justices on the ballot that year were retained. Justice Frank Richardson received an affirmative vote of 76.2 percent. The affirmative vote for the Brown appointees was much closer: Justice Kaus received 57 percent, Justice Broussard 56.2 percent, and Justice Reynoso 52.4 percent. When he was asked during the campaign why he wanted to be governor, Deukmejian replied, "The Attorney General doesn't get to appoint judges. The Governor does."

The enthusiastic use of California's broad death penalty law by the state's prosecutors meant that more and more of the Court's docket was being taken up by death penalty appeals. By June of 1983, the Court had decided only twenty of them, reversing all but two. There were 126 more in various stages of completion. Most had not yet been fully briefed, but concerns were frequently being voiced about the delays in processing these cases. Justice Mosk forthrightly addressed the issue in an Op-Ed article for the *Los Angeles Times*, published June 29, 1983.[11] He first described the crushing growth in the overall caseload of the Court, noting that total matters transacted by the Court rose from 4,673 in 1971 to 7,208 in 1981. He then argued against moving death appeals to the front of the line, and giving them priority on the Court's docket:

> There are some impatient legislators who insist that death penalty cases must receive absolute priority, that they must be heard and determined by the Supreme Court in preference to all other pending matters. This, I suggest, is an unrealistic tampering with the judicial process. Can it be said that a death-penalty case deserves to be heard before an appeal involving the care, custody and welfare of a minor child; or ahead of a matter concerning an imminent election; or a personal injury suit by one who became a paraplegic as a result of a drunken motorist's negligence; or an injunction sought by a business to prevent its destruction by unfair competition; or a judgment for millions of dollars against an industrial or commercial company that is accumulating thousands of dollars in interest while awaiting final decision; or ahead of a petition involving the license of a professional person whose conduct requires discipline to protect the public? Examples abound of other litigation that arguably may be more urgent than the ultimate fate of a murderer who has been convicted and is isolated on Death Row, thus presenting no imminent danger to society.

Finally, he proposed an expansion of the size of the Supreme Court to accommodate its growing backlog. Pointing to the establishment of separate Supreme Courts for civil and criminal cases in Oklahoma and Texas, he suggested a constitutional amendment to create two separate divisions of the state supreme court, one devoted exclusively to criminal matters, the other to hear only civil cases.

> In my plan there would be an increase from seven to eleven Justices. Five would sit as the Supreme Court/Criminal Division, and five would constitute the Supreme Court/Civil Division.... The Chief Justice would not be confined as a formal member of either panel, but would have administrative responsibility for supervising the total workload.

The proposal generated some academic debate,[12] but little support among the other Justices of the Court, the governor, or the Legislature. State Senator Quentin Kopp, a good friend of Mosk, introduced a proposed constitutional amendment to implement Mosk's plan, but it never emerged from committee. As a result, the death penalty backlog continued to grow, unchecked by any legislative or constitutional reform. At the time of Mosk's death eighteen years later, California's Death Row had grown to over 600 inmates, with only ten executions having taken place. The Court then had a backlog of hundreds of unresolved appeals and habeas corpus proceedings, with no relief in sight.

Governor Deukmejian had his first opportunity to make an appointment to the California Supreme Court in December of 1983, upon the retirement of Justice Frank Richardson. He appointed Malcolm M. Lucas, a federal district judge from Los Angeles. A courtly gentleman who looked like he had been sent by central casting for the role of Supreme Court Justice, Lucas had been the governor's law partner in Long Beach before his appointment to the federal bench. A graduate of USC Law School and the great-grandson of an Ohio governor, Lucas was widely known for the role he played in vetting judicial nominees for Republican politicians. He had chaired a committee that advised then–Governor Ronald Reagan in selecting trial court judges, served on then–Senator Pete Wilson's committee that recommended appointees to the federal bench, and frequently was consulted by Governor Deukmejian about judicial appointments. His own experience as a judge began when Reagan appointed him to the Los Angeles County Superior Court, where he presided over the criminal division. In 1971, President Nixon appointed him to the U.S. District Court in Los Angeles. Although both prosecutors and defense lawyers respected his ability as a trial judge, the severity of his sentencing earned him the nickname "Maximum Malcolm." Giving up a life-tenured position as a federal judge in Los Angeles for the state Supreme Court was a gamble, especially since he was then a strong contender for a presidential appointment to the U.S. Court of Appeals for the Ninth Circuit. But Lucas had every reason to believe that significant changes were in store for the California Supreme Court, and he could play a key role in its dramatic transformation.

With Justice Richardson's departure, Rose Bird and Stanley Mosk were the only remaining Justices who had served throughout the reign of the "Bird Court." Chief Justice Bird's closest supporters on the Court became Justice Cruz Reynoso and Justice Allen Broussard.[13] Justice Mosk, who was on the same side as Rose Bird in 78 percent of the 1980 decisions, by 1985 was agreeing with her in only 61 percent of the cases. Mosk's rate of agreement with the Chief Justice was lower than his rate of agreement with any other Justice on the Court, including Justice Malcolm Lucas.[14] Clearly, from 1980 to 1985, Justice Mosk was moving to the right, away from Chief Justice Bird. Justice Mosk was still a "bridge" of sorts, but now he was almost a bridge to nowhere. The only one further to his right was Justice Lucas. Despite their differences, Malcolm Lucas had a very high regard for Justice Mosk. When in 1984 the *Metropolitan News* observed Mosk's twentieth year on the Court by naming him "Person of the Year," Justice Lucas spoke with great admiration of Mosk's mental agility:

> He speaks with seeming total recall of past cases and the 'greats' of our court. His analysis of each case, each Wednesday, is direct, thorough and astonishingly perceptive. His intelligence is only exceeded by his intellectual curiosity and zeal for righting an injustice.[15]

Chief Justice Bird also submitted a tribute, but could not resist a subtle barb:

> Thanks to the effect of *Olson v. Cory*, Justice Mosk may well be the highest paid judicial officer in the world, and deservedly so as even this brief listing of his accomplishments illustrates.[16]

Olson v. Cory[17] presented a challenge by California judges to legislative repeal of automatic cost-of-living increases in judicial salaries. In a 6–1 decision authored by Justice Clark, the

Court held the Justices could not be disqualified from deciding the case by their obvious financial interest in the outcome, since the same disqualification would apply to all judges and thus a rule of necessity applied. The Court then declared the repeal unconstitutional as an impairment of existing contracts, but limited the effect of its ruling to judges who assumed office or began their current term prior to the effective date of the repeal, January 1, 1977. This meant that the only Justice then on the Supreme Court who received the automatic pay increases was Justice Mosk. Chief Justice Bird did not participate in the *Olson v. Cory* decision. Justice Mosk joined Justice Clark's majority opinion. Only Justice Newman dissented. Chief Justice Bird's statement that Mosk was the highest paid judicial officer in the world was probably true. Not only did his judicial salary exceed that of the other Justices, he also received an annual pension of nearly $100,000 for his service as Attorney General. He was certainly earning it. At the age of 72, Justice Mosk remained one of the most productive Justices on the Bird Court, filing 23 of the Court's 152 majority opinions in 1985. He cast dissenting votes in 26 percent of the cases, and authored 27 separate dissenting opinions.

One of Mosk's 1985 dissents addressed an issue that would haunt the Court for many years to come. In *Isbister v. Boys' Club of Santa Cruz*,[18] a 4–3 majority ruled that a nonprofit organization that operated a recreational facility for members, including a gymnasium and swimming pool, but restricted its membership to boys, was a "business organization" within the meaning of California's Unruh Act, which prohibited discrimination on the basis of race or sex "in all business establishments of every kind whatever."[19] Justice Mosk authored a vigorous dissent, foreseeing great mischief on the horizon:

> The majority's insouciance is disturbing. No girl's parents who are inclined to be litigious will fail to use this case as authority to demand their daughter's admission to other boys' clubs, the Boy Scouts, Cub Scouts, Young Men's Christian Association, and similar organizations that maintain camps or physical facilities. Conversely, boys could rely on this case to insist on their right to join girls' clubs, the Girl Scouts, Campfire Girls, Young Women's Christian Association, and like groups. There is no rational way to distinguish those situations.[20]

Chief Justice Bird responded directly to Justice Mosk's dissent in a concurring opinion quoting the Court of Appeal ruling of Justice Marc Poche, who protested that the interpretation of the Unruh Act that Mosk advocated would allow "the Ku Klux Klan or neo–Nazis to engage in the nonprofit, volunteer and fraternal offering of athletic facilities to some white children to combat the rise in juvenile delinquency."[21]

None of the opinions in *Isbister*, including Justice Grodin's majority opinion and Chief Justice Bird's concurring opinion, used the term "gender discrimination." While the case was pending, Justice Mosk addressed a memo to all of his fellow Justices objecting to usage of this term:

> It is true that many people use gender, possibly out of Victorian reluctance to talk about sex. While all of us are guilty of inadvertent grammatical error, I suggest this Court should not knowingly contribute to the corruption of the English language.[22]

Around the same time, in writing to a friend, Mosk displayed a touch of male chauvinism in his grammatical objections, and boasted of besting Chief Justice Bird on this score:

> My phobia remains against the creation of neuter words, such as "chairperson," merely to satisfy the overtly aggressive women of our modern world. I would still address a man as "Mr. Chairman" and a woman as "Madame Chairman." I refused to sign an opinion of our Chief Justice until she changed reference to "foreperson" to "foreman" of a jury. She needed my vote badly enough to capitulate.[23]

Ten years later, the Court revisited the applicability of the Unruh Act to sex discrimination in *Warfield v. Peninsula Golf & Country Club*,[24] holding that a country club could not exclude women from proprietary membership. Although Justice Mosk concurred in the result, he took strong exception to the majority's reliance upon *Isbister* to support its conclusion:

> Specifically, I part company with them when they reiterate with approval the misguided and illogical reasoning of *Isbister*. The concept that a small "swim and gym" club for boys is a "business establishment" was incomprehensible when proffered by a majority of this court and it has not gained stature or even plausibility with the passage of time.

Justice Mosk also objected to the use of the term "gender discrimination" in Justice Ronald George's majority opinion. A legendary stickler for correct usage of grammar, Mosk allied himself with Justice Antonin Scalia of the United States Supreme Court on this point:

> I also note that the majority euphemistically refer to "gender" discrimination, as if plaintiff were refused membership because of her femininity rather than her sex. (See *J.E.B. v. Alabama ex rel. T.B.* [1994] [dis. opn. of Scalia, J.].) In fact the Unruh Civil Rights Act says nothing about gender discrimination.[25]

In a footnote to his *J.E.B.* dissent, Justice Scalia had voiced a similar objection:

> Throughout this opinion, I shall refer to the issue as sex discrimination rather than (as the Court does) gender discrimination. The word "gender" has acquired the new and useful connotation of cultural or attitudinal characteristics (as opposed to physical characteristics) distinctive to the sexes. That is to say, gender is to sex as feminine is to female and masculine to male. The present case does not involve peremptory strikes exercised on the basis of femininity or masculinity (as far as it appears, effeminate men did not survive the prosecution's peremptories). The case involves, therefore, sex discrimination plain and simple.[26]

Associate Justice Joseph Grodin recalled an amusing incident with respect to Mosk's insistence on the use of "sex discrimination" rather than "gender discrimination." He received an issue of the *Chicago Law Review* containing a symposium on "gender discrimination." Knowing Mosk had attended the University of Chicago Law School, he took it into Mosk's chambers "with great glee," to tease him:

> There was Stanley sitting at his desk with this old typewriter that he used to bat out his letters and his opinions. He was writing a letter of complaint to the editor-in-chief of the Chicago Law Review for having abused the English language in that fashion.[27]

Years later, U.S. Supreme Court Justice Ruth Bader Ginsberg sent Mosk a copy of correspondence she had about the use of the terms "sex" and "gender." According to the correspondence, a secretary who assisted her at Columbia remarked, "'sex juts out in everything you write, and the first thing that word brings to mind for most people is not what you mean.' So, at her suggestion, Ginsberg started to use 'gender' and the Court sometimes followed along. She added, 'The word is wrong in one sense, but the choice of a grammar-book term, for its first association, was purposive.'"[28]

Justice Mosk defended his record on the matter of the " absolute equality of the sexes," as "not merely academic, nor of recent origin." He said he didn't choose the first female California Assistant Attorney General, or his law clerk of fourteen years (Olga Murray) and the current semester's three female externs "because they were women—i.e., the Jerry Brown statistical quota syndrome; they were chosen because they happened to be the best applicants at the time." He added, "the rights of women can be vindicated on merit without debasing the English language, which I consider a national treasure. To call a human being a 'chair' does little for equality of the sexes, but it does much to belittle both oral and written communication." He snidely extended the logic of neutered terminology, such as changing "manipulate to personipulate; man-of-war to person-of-war (even though ships are all female); mandate to persondate."[29]

Thirteen years after *Isbister*, Justice Mosk was the only one left from the Court that decided that case. In *Curran v. Mt. Diablo Council of Boy Scouts*,[30] a unanimous Court ruled that a social organization whose primary function was to inculcate values in its youth members, such as the Boy Scouts, was not a "business establishment" within the meaning of the Unruh Act.[31] Thus it permitted the Boy Scouts to reject the application of a former Eagle Scout to be a Scout Leader because he was gay. Chief Justice Ronald George distinguished the Boy Scouts from the situation presented in *Isbister*. Justice Mosk still had a bee in his bonnet, though. He authored a concurring opinion, arguing that *Isbister* should be overruled rather than distinguished. He added a cautionary note, however, that just because discrimination was legal did not make it right:

> But let us not ignore what lies behind. That the law does not prohibit the Mount Diablo Council from shutting Curran out cannot obscure the fact that he is the very kind of person whom it should receive most eagerly — a person whom it has itself honored as an Eagle Scout. Regrettably, the situation will remain such until the law changes. Or, perhaps, until the ideals of scouting transform its conduct.

Chapter 18

"I Have Never Known Defeat at the Polls"

For the California Supreme Court, 1986 was destined to be a political donnybrook. In an unusual combination of circumstances, the entire Court, with the sole exception of Justice Allen Broussard, would appear on the November ballot for confirmation or retention. Justices receive staggered twelve-year terms, but their initial term is only for the remainder of the term of their predecessor in office. Justice Mosk had won a full twelve-year term in 1974, which would expire in 1986. Although Chief Justice Bird had been on the Court only eight years, her 1978 confirmation gave her only the eight years remaining on the twelve-year term to which Donald Wright was elected in 1974. Although Justice Cruz Reynoso had narrowly survived a confirmation vote only four years before, four years was all that was left on the term of his predecessor, Justice Mathew Tobriner. Justices Joseph Grodin and Malcolm Lucas were appearing on the ballot for the first time, for their initial confirmation.

In 1966, the California Constitution was amended to provide that appellate justices would appear on the ballot only in gubernatorial election years.[1] This change had the unfortunate effect of tying the fate of the Court to gubernatorial politics. Because the appointments of Grodin and Lucas did not take effect until after the 1982 gubernatorial election, Grodin was on the court nearly four years, and Lucas nearly three, before they came up for their initial confirmation. The sixth Justice on the ballot was Justice Edward Panelli, who was appointed by Governor Deukmejian in 1985 after the departure of Justice Otto Kaus. Avoiding the ordeal of another statewide election motivated the premature retirement of Justice Kaus. In announcing his retirement, he said, "I concluded, frankly, that it is very, very difficult to reconcile the appellate process with the necessity of facing a retention election." Lamenting his loss as "the first justice to fall to the political atmosphere surrounding the court," the *Los Angeles Times* editorialized:

> [H]is opinions have been among the court's most scholarly and thoughtful. His has been a voice of reason and moderation. Everyone should heed the warning inherent in Kaus' statements on the danger of reconfirmation votes. The anti–Bird movement seeks to destroy the concept of an independent judiciary. Kaus' retirement shows that if Bird is removed next year, the real losers will be the court — and the people.[2]

Justice Panelli was the Presiding Justice of the Sixth District Court of Appeal in San Jose. His nomination to the Court of Appeal by Governor Jerry Brown had been blocked by Deukmejian as a member of the Commission on Judicial Appointments in 1982, because Deukmejian opposed the creation of a new division of the Court of Appeal at that time. When Deukmejian became governor, however, Panelli was his first Court of Appeal appointment. By nominating the moderate Panelli, an administration source explained, "Deukmejian can counter charges by the supporters of Bird that the campaign to turn her out of office next year is a right-wing effort to pack the court with conservatives."[3]

George Deukmejian was a candidate for a second term as governor in 1986, in a rematch with Los Angeles Mayor Tom Bradley, the Democratic candidate he defeated in 1982. The governor's opposition to Rose Bird became a centerpiece of his gubernatorial campaign. A *Los Angeles Times* poll released on February 7, 1986, suggested that Deukmejian's attacks on Rose Bird were increasing his popularity, and that supporting Bird could cost Tom Bradley the election. When voters were asked whether they were more likely or less likely to vote for the governor because of his criticism of the Chief Justice, the responses were 32 percent more likely and only 13 percent less likely. When the *Times* poll asked voters whether they would be more likely or less likely to vote for Bradley if he supported Bird, a third said they would be less likely, and only a tenth said they would be more likely. The governor launched his attack on the Court at a press conference a week later, on February 13, 1985, when he said, "People in the business community see a long line of cases that have now been coming down in recent years as creating that unfriendly, that negative impact on business in California." The governor's office then issued a list of 31 California Supreme Court rulings that had a "negative impact upon the private sector's job-producing capabilities."[4] The list was closely scrutinized by the press, to see whether Deukmejian would be targeting the entire Court, or only the Chief Justice.

The list was an eclectic one, hardly proving any pattern of anti-business bias on the Bird Court. Three of the cases involved workers' compensation issues, six involved tort liability, five involved taxation, one involved contract liability, two involved unemployment issues, three involved employer-employee relations, one involved environmental protection, and only two related directly to business practices. In eleven of the cases on the list, the lead opinion was authored by a Justice who was no longer on the Court. Chief Justice Bird wrote the majority opinion in only two of the cases. Justice Mosk was the lead author of eight of the opinions on the list, more than any other Justice on the Court. The list included Mosk's opinion in *Royal Globe Insurance Company v. Superior Court*,[5] a 4–3 ruling in which the Court held that an accident victim could bring suit directly against the insurance company that insured the person who caused the accident, for "bad faith" in not settling the lawsuit promptly and fairly.[6] If the list could be regarded as a "call to arms" to mobilize the business community to support removal of Supreme Court Justices, Mosk might have had reason to worry. He would emerge as one of the chief culprits, having joined the majority in 25 of the 31 cases.

Governor Deukmejian quickly realized that although business interests would be a reliable source of campaign contributions, the removal of Supreme Court Justices could not be sold to the voters on the basis that the Justices were too protective of employees and consumers and accident victims in disputes with California businesses. The issue that would define the campaign to remove Rose Bird would be her voting record on death penalty cases. Fifty-nine death penalty appeals had come before the California Supreme Court since the enactment of Deukmejian's bill to restore the California death penalty in 1977, and Chief Justice Rose Bird had voted to reverse every one of them. Although a death sentence had been upheld over her dissent in three cases, fifty-six cases had been reversed and sent back for retrial. In most cases, the reversal was required by retroactive application of the Court's ruling in *Carlos v. Superior Court*,[7] requiring a finding of intent to kill before a defendant could be subjected to a felony murder special circumstance that would make him eligible for the death penalty. Carlos was a 6–1 ruling authored by Justice Broussard, in which Justice Mosk joined the majority.

In August of 1986, Governor Deukmejian announced that in addition to opposing the retention of Chief Justice Rose Bird, he would also oppose the confirmation of Associate Justices Joseph Grodin and Cruz Reynoso: "A thorough review of the opinions and votes cast by Justices Bird, Grodin and Reynoso on death penalty cases indicates a lack of impartiality and objectivity. They have demonstrated a proclivity to substitute their judgment for the peoples,' as expressed through the legislative process, the initiative process and the Constitution." Many California judges and lawyers, including California Supreme Court Justices Malcolm Lucas and Edward Panelli, urged the governor to spare Justice Joseph Grodin and not target him for defeat. Although Grodin had generally voted with the majority to reverse death sentences, he was seen as a thoughtful and conscientious judge whose presence enhanced the scholarly prestige of the Court.

As a member of the Commission on Judicial Appointments, then–Attorney General Deukmejian had twice voted to confirm Grodin's appointments, first to the Court of Appeal, then to the Supreme Court. The governor's political advisors were apparently concerned, however, that an attack on the Court limited to Bird and Reynoso, the only woman and the only Hispanic on the court, would invite charges that sexism and racism were the real motivations for the governor's campaign, not his support for the death penalty. Justice Grodin could not be readily distinguished from Chief Justice Bird or Justice Reynoso when one counted up the votes in death penalty cases. Deukmejian's spokesman said research by the governor's aides showed that Reynoso had voted to overturn 44 of the 45 death penalty cases to come before him, and Grodin had voted against death in 38 of the 43 cases before him. Bird had voted to overturn all 59 of the death penalty cases she considered.[8]

Replying to a charge by Chief Justice Rose Bird that he was setting up a "quota" for death penalty affirmances as the determining factor in his endorsements, Governor Deukmejian explained that Justice Mosk had voted 17 times to impose the death penalty, while Grodin had voted to affirm the death penalty in only five cases. The governor noted that Mosk had long opposed capital punishment but in recent years had voted more than a third of the time to uphold death sentences. "I'm not looking for any quota," Deukmejian said. "What I am looking for are individuals who set aside their own personal view and in fact follow the law."[9] At the time of Deukmejian's announcement, the California Poll showed Bird trailing in voter sentiment by a margin of 24 points but Reynoso leading by 12 points and Grodin by 18. Mayor Bradley remained neutral on the Supreme Court retention elections, explaining that the Supreme Court had been "politicized enough." Senator Alan Cranston, seeking reelection, also announced he would take no position on the retention of Supreme Court Justices.

The governor's use of death penalty votes as a criterion in selecting his targets underlined an irony that is essential to an understanding of what happened to the Court in 1986. The targeted Justices were subjected to a well-funded campaign to remove them from office. The chief contributors to that campaign were corporations and insurance companies who believed Governor George Deukmejian would appoint replacements who were friendlier to their business interests. The entire campaign, however, was focused on the Justices' voting record in death penalty cases. Television ads suggested that votes against the retention or confirmation of Chief Justice Bird, Justice Reynoso and Justice Grodin would be "three votes for the death penalty."

In some quarters, the suggestion has been heard that Justice Mosk saved his neck in

1986 by strategically voting to dissent from the reversal of selected death penalty cases only when he was certain there were sufficient votes available to reverse the death sentence. As long as there were enough Justices available to achieve the result he really wanted, he would let them take the heat and join the dissenters. Although his vote would not make a difference in the outcome of the case, it would make a huge difference in persuading the governor, and ultimately the voters, not to target him for defeat. There is strong evidence to support this claim. Among the 59 death cases counted by the governor, Mosk cast a vote for death in only one case where his vote actually made a difference. In *People v. Stevie Lamar Fields*,[10] Justice Mosk joined in Justice Broussard's 4–2 majority opinion upholding a death sentence over the dissent of Chief Justice Bird and Justice Reynoso. Even then, he joined Bird and Reynoso in voting in favor of a petition for a rehearing. The governor's tally of 17 occasions when Mosk voted to "uphold" a death penalty actually included 16 cases in which he joined with one or two other Justices in dissenting from the reversal of a death judgment.

In December of 1985, the California Supreme Court issued decisions in thirteen death penalty cases, a remarkable year-end spate of death decisions. Every one resulted in a reversal of the death sentence. Justice Mosk dissented from the reversal in ten of those cases, along with Justice Lucas. Mosk's dissenting votes made the decision 5–2 in all ten cases, so his vote had no impact on the outcome; it simply shifted the margin from 6–1 to 5–2. Thus, on the eve of the 1986 election, Mosk clearly distinguished himself from Justices Reynoso and Grodin with a substantial string of dissents from death penalty reversals.

In a 1998 study of capital punishment and judicial decision-making in California, two political scientists who examined the death penalty decisions of Rose Bird and Stanley Mosk found that Mosk consistently voted to reverse death sentences during the period from January, 1981 through November, 1982. This was in stark contrast to his votes just prior to the 1986 retention election, when his votes to reverse death sentences declined by fully 34 percent.[11] In her University of Pittsburg Ph.D. dissertation entitled "State High Courts: Independent or Constrained Actors," Tara Wynn Stricko-Neubauer concludes: "These differences are consistent with a strategic explanation of judicial behavior. These statistics suggest that Mosk showed some awareness of the salience of capital punishment and the changes in political environment over time and adjusted his voting accordingly, particularly as the 1986 election neared. Bird's voting record on the other hand, shows no corresponding decline."

The pattern was remarkable enough to arouse the suspicion of Mosk's fellow Justices. At one point, Justice Grodin asked Peter Belton whether Mosk's votes to dissent from death reversals indicated a change in Mosk's longtime opposition to the death penalty. Belton replied that Mosk would not vote to affirm a death penalty judgment when his vote would make a difference in the outcome.

Careful analysis of the cases, however, suggests that shifting political winds alone may not have determined Justice Mosk's votes in pre-election death cases. The precedent of *Carlos v. Superior Court* required many of the Bird Court's death penalty reversals, as previously noted. Part of the underpinning for *Carlos* was a constitutional argument, based upon the 1982 U.S. Supreme Court ruling in *Enmund v. Florida*,[12] that permitting the imposition of a death penalty without a finding of intent to kill would violate the federal constitutional prohibition of cruel and unusual punishment, as well as equal protection of the laws. Support for that constitutional argument began to erode, however, when the United States Supreme Court granted *certiorari* and heard argument in the case of *Cabana v. Bullock*,[13] which directly raised the question whether a finding of intent to kill was constitutionally required for imposition of a penalty of death. The high court heard argument in *Cabana* on November 5, 1985, and speculation was rife that the death sentence in that case would be upheld. It is interesting to note that even though Justice Malcolm Lucas had been willing to join in reversals required by *Carlos*, believing he was bound to do so by the doctrine of *stare decisis*, he abandoned that position on November 18, 1985, two weeks after *Cabana* was argued:

> Although I have in the past concurred in reversals of some capital cases under the compulsion of *Carlos/Garcia* I can no longer characterize myself as "concurring" in these reversals. The *Carlos* and *Garcia* rulings are responsible for an increasing number of unnecessary reversals and retrials. I would join three of my colleagues in reexamining, and ultimately overruling, those decisions. Accordingly, I cannot join in the judgment of reversal.[14]

This voting shift by Justice Lucas might also be attributed to political motives. Up to that point, Justice Malcolm Lucas had participated in nine death penalty decisions. All nine had resulted in a reversal of the death penalty, and eight of them were unanimous. Thus, Justice Malcolm Lucas had voted to reverse 88 percent of the death verdicts he reviewed. If the governor was going after Bird, Renoso and Grodin for their death penalty votes, their counter-arguments that they were just "following the law" gained persuasive corroboration when one looked at the voting record of Justice Lucas, who had been placed on the Court by Governor Deukmejian. Thus the strategy of dissenting from death reversals in order to achieve a "voting record" that could be distinguished from Bird, Reynoso and Grodin would have been equally attractive to both Justice Lucas and Justice Mosk.

Most of the thirteen reversals in December, 1985 were based upon *Carlos* error. Justice Mosk may have been having second thoughts about Carlos as well, and joined Justice Lucas in dissenting for this reason. Although he did not explain his dissents as based upon a rejection of *Carlos*, he found a way to distinguish *Carlos* in most of them. After the United States Supreme Court ruling in *Cabana* and a similar ruling in *Tison v. Arizona*[15] made it clear that intent to kill was not constitutionally required, Justice Mosk ultimately authored the California Supreme Court decision overruling *Carlos*, a year after the election.[16] Thus, although the statistics suggest that Justice Mosk (and Justice Lucas) voted to affirm more death penalty cases as the 1986 election approached, an analysis of those cases and his post-election voting suggests that a significant shift of position by the United States Supreme Court had undermined support for the *Carlos* precedent, and Mosk's pre-election shift in death cases coincided with his own doubts about its continuing viability.

Between January 1, 1986 and the November, 1986 election, the Bird Court decided five more death cases, and reversed the death sentence in all five. Justice Mosk dissented in only one of these cases.[17] Two of the reversals were released only twelve days before the election. In one of these cases Justice Mosk authored the opinion for a unanimous court, finding racial discrimination in the prosecutor's peremptory challenges to black jurors.[18] In the other, which involved the execution murders of two California Highway Patrol Officers, Mosk wrote a concurring opinion urging outright reversal rather than a remand to rehear a modification motion.[19] Thus, his death penalty votes on the very eve of the election hardly suggest he was pulling his punches.

The 1986 campaign clearly demonstrated Stanley Mosk had lost none of the political savvy responsible for his previous overwhelming election victories. Mosk never lost an election in his life. The forces arrayed against Chief Justice Bird included Crime Victims for Court Reform, headed by Governor Deukmejian's former campaign manager Bill Roberts, and Californians to Defeat Rose Bird, which boasted an Executive Committee including tax reformers Howard Jarvis and Paul Gann, and State Senator (and former LAPD Chief) Ed Davis. Justice Mosk was well aware that some elements within these organizations wanted to target him along with Bird, Reynoso, and Grodin. Crime Victims for Court Reform issued statements referring to the "gang of four" offending Justices, and there was little ambiguity about who the fourth Justice would be. Robert Philibosian, then the District Attorney of Los Angeles County, recalls getting a telephone call from Justice Mosk's son, Richard, inviting him to lunch. Philibosian told Richard to "save the time," assuring him that he was doing everything he could to keep the senior Mosk out of the opposition's sights. A Bird campaign source suggested the possibility that Philibosian might be appointed Chief Justice if the governor succeeded in removing Bird. The Chief Justice replied that if that happened, he could replace the macramé plant hangers in her office with nooses.[20] Bill Roberts did accept an invitation to lunch from Richard, and was persuaded that Stanley Mosk should not be targeted. Ultimately, Californians to Defeat Rose Bird mounted a campaign to remove Mosk along with Bird, Grodin, and Reynoso. Crime Victims for Court Reform, however, limited their campaign to Bird, Grodin and Reynoso. Fred Karger, an aide to Bill Roberts, explained:

> A lot of district attorneys and people in law enforcement wanted to concentrate on the Jerry Brown appointees. (Mosk was appointed by Pat Brown). They feel that Mosk has proven himself as a former attorney general. He has lots of friends among conservatives and there's not the animosity toward him that there is toward the other three justices.[21]

In December, 1985, Kern County District Attorney Ed Jagels wrote to Richard Mosk:

> Crime Victims for Court Reform, of which I am steering committee chair, has elected not to oppose Justice Mosk's reelection. This position was confirmed at a recent steering committee meeting.... This does not mean that the law enforcement community is happy with your father's record in criminal justice matters.[22]

Justice Mosk realized at the outset that Chief Justice Rose Bird would not survive the election. Her campaign for retention suffered from the same defects as her leadership of the Court: obsessive control of every aspect of the campaign combined with paranoid secrecy and mistrust of the media. Although her supporters mounted a vigorous campaign to uphold judicial independence, they were outspent by more than $5 million dollars. In the end even a majority of California judges voted against Bird's retention. Justices Reynoso and Grodin found it impossible to separate their fate from that of the Chief Justice. Although they mounted separately funded campaigns, the anti–Bird forces succeeded in linking them with the unpopular Chief Justice.

Justice Mosk deliberately delayed announcing he would seek retention until the August deadline. Although he feigned uncertainty about whether he would run, it was clear he was planning strategy for a confirmation campaign two years before the election. In December of 1984, he inquired of California Secretary of State March Fong Eu in what order the names of the Justices would be listed on the November, 1986 ballot.[23] Apparently, he was concerned that if they were listed in order of seniority, his name would appear immediately below that of Chief Justice Rose Bird. When he learned that was the previous practice, he put his son Richard to work collecting information on the practice in other states. Richard submitted a memorandum to the secretary of state in June of 1985, demonstrating that a decision to rotate the order in which the Justices were listed would be consistent with the practice in other states as well as with good public policy.[24] That led to a decision to rotate the order in which the Justices were listed on the November, 1986 ballots. The historical pattern for judicial candidates suggested that voters frequently stop voting after the first few names, and that once they vote No on one candidate, they continue voting No. In any event, Mosk felt it would be to his advantage to appear further down the list, at least on some ballots. In February, 1985, Anthony Lewis wrote in his *New York Times* column that Justice Mosk might retire rather than go through a "nasty campaign" in 1986. Mosk quickly wrote to disabuse Lewis of the notion that the prospect of a nasty campaign could deter him:

> A campaign, nasty or constructive, has never deterred me before.... Fortunately, I have never known defeat at the polls.... I will be 74 years old in November, 1986, and will have served 22 years on this court. I have been eligible for retirement since 1977. My decision to run again will be determined by two factors: first, after 22 years in the same work, should I try something else, e.g., accept an invitation to teach at a law school, and second, is it morally defensible for a 74-year-old man to ask the voters for another 12-year term?[25]

Meanwhile, Mosk granted media interviews that emphasized the distinctions between himself and Rose Bird. Typical was the *Los Angeles Times* interview by Dan Morain, which appeared on Sunday, January 26, 1986. Headlined "Will Dean of High Court Hang It Up?," the article described Mosk as standing "apart from his brethren in part by his longevity, but also by his considerable political savvy and an independent streak that leads him to take frequent conservative stands."[26] The interview noted "he has voted to uphold about 20 death sentences since capital punishment was reinstated — more than any current justice. It is the law, he says, so he must carry it out."[27] Morain asserted, "Mosk has never been the Court's most liberal Justice. Mosk's more recent dissents suggest a more complicated temperament, such as his acid chastisement of his colleagues for giving school children rights against unreasonable searches by teachers; or ordering a Boys' Club to admit girls, and for letting cities with rent control restrict landlords from tearing down their buildings." Nevertheless, Morain concluded, "For the most part ... [Mosk] fits the mold of a liberal, activist judge." Explaining his decisions in such cases, Mosk said, "I have a resentment against government saying 'Thou Shalt Not.'" He told Morain that he rejected the notion that he was growing more conservative with age, except perhaps on questions of government encroachment into private property rights.[28] Mosk pondered whether his brand of New Deal liberalism "probably makes me a good deal more conservative today than the modern liberals." He said that "maybe time has passed me by, or maybe I have stubbornly adhered to a philosophy arrived at several years ago."[29] Morain also pointed out the irony that many of the opinions cited by critics of Chief Justice Bird, were actually opinions written by Mosk. "The irony is that while Bird is being pilloried in an unprecedented campaign to unseat her ... Mosk has been the beneficiary of glowing tributes in law journals."[30]

Speculation that he might retire worked to his advantage, and if he had announced early, there would have been enormous pressure for him to join forces with the challenged Justices. Thus, he waited until the last possible moment to announce his plans to seek another term. Then, he dramatically revealed he would not form a campaign committee or mount a campaign. "I expect neither to solicit nor to accept campaign contributions. My expenditures, to be assumed personally, will include the filing fee ($1,989.78) and 22 cents for a stamp to mail my declaration to the Secretary of State."[31] His announcement inspired numerous friends to send him a 22 cents postage stamp. But at the last moment, he feared his paperwork might not make it to Sacramento on time. Stanley's papers were delivered by overnight mail at a cost of $10.25.

In reality, Mosk mounted a very effective *sub rosa* campaign, with the help of his son, Richard. In November of 1985, Richard wrote to all radio station managers operating in

California to remind them that the FCC fairness doctrine required notification of parties being attacked on the airwaves, and an opportunity to respond.[32] During the fall of 1985, when the Court traveled to Sacramento and Los Angeles for hearings, Justice Mosk would call ahead to friends and political connections from his previous campaigns. Justice Mosk had always stayed "in touch" with the many friends and political associates he acquired in his statewide campaigns for Attorney General. Now, the many letters, friendly notes and telephone calls would pay dividends. He would call or write the editors or publishers of local newspapers, and say, "I'm going to be in town next week. I have a little time on my hands. Would you like me to drop by to chat with your editorial staff and answer any questions you may be interested in asking me, and give you a little interview that you could do with as you wish?"[33] These "chats" frequently resulted in favorable editorials even before endorsements were being announced. Typical was an editorial in the *San Jose Mercury News*, urging voters to evaluate each of the Justices on the ballot individually:

> Mosk, for example, may be measured by 21 years of opinions. One such analysis was recently published by the Hastings Constitutional Law Quarterly, in which such distinguished attorneys as former California Supreme Court Justice Otto Kaus and former U.S. Supreme Court Justice Arthur J. Goldberg pay tribute to a judge who cannot accurately be labeled either "liberal" or "conservative."[34]

Justice Mosk never openly criticized Chief Justice Rose Bird or other fellow Justices, but in private conversations or letters he was not so restrained. After the *Riverside Press Enterprise* ran an editorial concluding that Rose Bird "has been a poor administrator, a poor leader of the court," Justice Mosk wrote a personal letter to the editor praising the editorial for "being right on target." He added, "The diminished respect for the Supreme Court—indeed for the entire judiciary of California—is the legacy of Jerry Brown, a fact that should be remembered if he surfaces again."[35]

Mosk carefully followed the polls showing a decline in support for Rose Bird, and voiced strong objection to any suggestion that his fate was linked with hers. In May of 1986, in an interview with radio station KQED, Rose Bird casually mentioned that some groups were opposing the retention of Justice Mosk as well as herself. Mosk wrote her a terse memo, objecting to her "gratuitously injecting my name when the question did not call for it," and suggesting that "discomfort seeks companionship." He concluded, "From platforms and in media conferences, whenever asked I have made it clear that I am voting for all my colleagues. I hope I can continue to do so."[36] Chief Justice Bird responded with two separate notes of apology, explaining her comment was not part of any "strategy." She finally concluded, "I am saddened that you are not able to accept my sincere and truthful statement."[37]

In all of his media contacts, Mosk strongly emphasized the difference between his voting record in death penalty cases and the record of Bird, Grodin and Reynoso. He compiled and widely distributed, through his son Richard, an extensive list with citations to every case in which he had ever upheld a death penalty, affirmed a murder conviction, ruled in favor of the prosecution, and ruled against the defense. In a letter to the Editor of the *Claremont Review*, he protested:

> In the interest of accuracy, you might have noted that since I have been on the court I have written 26 opinions upholding death penalty judgments, more than any other appellate justice in the United States [anyone interested can write me for a list of citations].[38]

As the 1986 election approached, Justice Mosk also stepped up his speaking schedule, accepting more of the steady stream of invitations that came from bar associations and civic groups. His "stump speech" was a homespun mixture of self-deprecating humor, descriptions of the court's workings, and explanations of some of the landmark rulings in very understandable language. He loved to quote from the 1855 opinion of Justice Solomon Heydenfeldt, involving a claim for damages by a man who fell into a hole in front of a business establishment. The trial court instructed the jury that the plaintiff could not recover if he was intoxicated at the time of his injury. Justice Heydenfeldt (who incidentally was the first Jew to serve on the California Supreme Court) wrote: "a drunken man is as much entitled to a safe street, as a sober one, and much more in need of it."[39] He assured audiences that his championing of the independence of the state constitution did not mean he was a "state's rights" advocate like George Wallace of Alabama. "Beneath this forbidding exterior," he said, "remains the same, sweet, lovable liberal who has endeared himself to the Neanderthals of the state as a dart board."[40] When the question of the death penalty came up, as it inevitably did, Justice Mosk would reassure his audience that he would "follow the law," producing his list of citations to cases in which he upheld death judgments as evidence.

Mosk's campaign efforts paid off handsomely, with numerous favorable interviews, news stories, and editorial endorsements appearing in newspapers throughout the state. Public opinion polls confirmed that the level of support for Mosk was increasing, while the level of support for Bird, Grodin and Reynoso was declining. Still, voices were heard urging the voters to dump Justice Mosk along with Bird, Reynoso and Grodin. In September, 1986, the *Daily Journal* reported that the campaign had moved closer to adding a fourth target, Justice Mosk. University of California, Berkeley law professor Phillip E. Johnson told reporters that Mosk's record was "drifting and erratic," and that the Justice was "overdue for retirement." Although Mosk dismissed the criticism as the product of "just another disgruntled law clerk," Professor Johnson had, in fact, been a law clerk for men Stanley Mosk held in high regard, California Supreme Court Justice Roger Traynor and former United States Supreme Court Justice Earl Warren. As for the objectivity of Johnson's analysis, funding for his research came from the anti–Bird Supreme Court Project.[41] Nonetheless, Johnson argued that he was particularly singling Mosk out for removal because, "like the other three, Mosk believes the Court should reform society by redistributing wealth through steps the Legislature and the public have rejected." Without providing an example of this agenda, Johnson concluded that the deciding factor against Mosk was his age. At 73 years old, with twenty years on the Court, Johnson complained that Mosk's "standard of judgment" had "puzzled him for years." Mosk had written some "excellent opinions," Johnson admitted, but he also had authored "some incredibly capricious opinions."[42] Mosk dismissed the criticism by simply dismissing Professor Johnson. "Why [Johnson's] feelings about my 600 opinions should be worthy of any particular notice escapes me."[43]

In the November election, Governor Deukmejian roundly defeated Mayor Tom Bradley. Chief Justice Bird was rejected, winning approval of only 33.8 percent of the voters. Justices Cruz Reynoso and Joseph Grodin were also removed, respectively winning 39.8 percent and 43.4 percent of the vote. Justices Stanley Mosk, Malcolm Lucas and Edward Panelli were retained with comfortable margins. Mosk won the support of 73.6 percent of the voters, Panelli won 78.7 percent, and Malcolm Lucas topped the list with a "yes" vote of 79.5 percent. The fate of Chief Justice Rose Bird was aptly summed up by Bill Zimmerman, a campaign consultant who had been discharged by Bird early in the campaign. He saw her defeat as a self-inflicted wound:

In pursuit of a very personal wish, she closed her eyes to reality, marched ahead to the beat of a drummer only she could hear and squandered her seat as well as the seats of two other fine Supreme Court justices.[44]

For Justice Stanley Mosk, however, the election disaster could be justly laid at the feet of Jerry Brown. In a candid letter to his friend Stanley Sheinbaum, Mosk wrote:

> Throughout the administration of Culbert Olson, Earl Warren, Pat Brown and Ronald Reagan, the Supreme Court of California, and the entire judicial system, was the envy of every state in the nation. But as a result of Jerry Brown's whimsical appointments the prestige of the California judiciary is at its lowest ebb since the days of David S. Terry in the mid–19th century. The incompetence of many of his quota-inspired appointees is incredible to those who respect professionalism. And now, to bury the stiletto in deeper, the judiciary has been thrust into the political arena, with the likelihood of a monstrous effect not only on judges but on good candidates for many offices. In short, Jerry Brown may well have set liberalism in general, and political responsibility in particular, back a decade or more. The melancholy aspect is that he probably did not act out of malice, just whimsy pure and simple. That whimsy, however, disqualifies him from any serious consideration as a leader or prophet.

Sheinbaum, whom Jerry Brown had appointed to the University of California Board of Regents, responded expressing full agreement with Mosk's letter. He wrote, "You are nothing if not direct — and I appreciate it. Naturally, I am not surprised. It may surprise you, however, that my own thinking is very similar to yours." He added, "Indeed, Brown's behavior regarding the Regents' appointments was almost as bad in a less visible way than what he did to the courts."[45] Many agreed that the entire disaster would have been avoided if Brown had listened to those in 1977 who urged the appointment of Stanley Mosk as Chief Justice. As Lieutenant Governor Leo McCarthy wrote to Mosk in the midst of the campaign:

> I was proud to ask Jerry Brown in 1977 to pick you as Chief Justice. If you were Chief Justice today, the court would be projecting the balance and strength necessary to earn ample public respect.[46]

Chapter 19

"They Have Exalted Principal Over Principle"

The removal of Chief Justice Bird, along with Justices Grodin and Reynoso, gave Governor George Deukmejian an eagerly welcomed opportunity to reshape the California Supreme Court. He lost little time. On November 26, 1986 he announced the appointment of Associate Justice Malcolm Lucas to replace Rose Bird as Chief Justice of California. The appointment was a surprise to no one. Even before the election, speculation focused on Lucas as the most likely successor because of his long and close personal friendship with the governor. In commenting on his role as a frequent dissenter on the Bird Court, Lucas noted that a dissent often composes "the foundation stone for a future majority opinion once the issue is raised before a different panel of justices. Thus, even a dissenter may ultimately reap the fruit of his or her labor."[1] Under the leadership of Chief Justice Malcolm Lucas, the California Supreme Court reaped a lot of fruit from the dissents to Bird Court rulings.

On February 19, 1987, Governor Deukmejian announced three new appointments of Associate Justices to the high court, to fill the vacancies created by Lucas' elevation and the removal of Grodin and Reynoso. All three were experienced jurists who were well known to Malcolm Lucas, and he certainly was very influential in their selection. Both David Eagleson and John Arguelles had been appointed by Governor Deukmejian to the Court of Appeal, Eagleson in 1984 and Arguelles in 1985. Both had long experience on the Superior Court in Los Angeles County, and both had been put there by Governor Ronald Reagan: Eagleson in 1970, and Arguelles in 1969. Arguelles was Hispanic, thus filling a void created by the removal of Justice Cruz Reynoso, although much more conservative than Reynoso. Deukmejian's third appointment was the most impressive. Marcus Kaufman had served as a law clerk to Roger Traynor after graduating first in his class at USC Law School. Appointed to the Court of Appeal in San Bernardino by Governor Reagan in 1970, he was widely respected as an intelligent and thoughtful judge, although occasionally short-tempered and acerbic. Since all three Justices were quickly confirmed on the same day, they drew straws to determine their seniority—important for assigning their seats on the bench and assignment of chambers. They drew in the order of "AEK" (Arguelles, Eagleson and Kaufman). Thereafter, staff dubbed them the "All Electric Kitchen," after a common want-ad acronym.

Stanley Mosk enjoyed a cordial relationship with the new Justices, but was quickly disenchanted with their "judicial activism" in overruling or limiting Bird Court precedents. Most dramatic, and most welcomed by the insurance industry, was the 1988 opinion in *Moradi-Shalal v. Fireman's Fund Ins. Companies*.[2] Chief Justice Lucas, joined by Justices Panelli, Arguelles, Eagleson and Kaufman, overruled a decision authored by Mosk (and joined by Bird) less than eight years earlier, *Royal Globe Ins. Co. v. Superior Court.*³ Justice Mosk, joined by Justice Broussard, wrote a stinging dissent that began:

> "Royal Globe (1979–1988), may it Rest in Peace. During its life it served the people of California well, particularly the victims of unfair and deceptive practices. The majority have now replaced Royal Globe with a 'Royal Bonanza'" for insurance carriers, i.e., total immunity for unfair and deceptive practices committed on innocent claimants. They have exalted principal over principle. It will be interesting to observe whether this judicial largesse causes insurance premiums to decrease or insurance profits to increase.

Accusing the majority of "judicial activism," he characterized their willingness to limit the retroactivity of their opinion as "merely applying a thin sugar coat to their cyanide pill."⁴ The decision demonstrated that the insurance industry had made a wise investment with its contributions to the 1986 election. It now had a Supreme Court more to its liking. Justice Mosk concluded his Moradi-Shalal dissent by noting:

> The insurance industry, with a lavish public relations and media campaign, has failed to persuade the people of California that it should be immune from responsibility for unfair and deceptive acts. Up to now no court has so held. The industry, with the service of dozens of lobbyists, failed to persuade the Legislature that the statute was improperly imposing liability for unfair and deceptive acts. Now, regrettably, the insurance industry has succeeded in persuading justices of this court that it is entitled to immunity from the same type of responsibility required of every other business and individual that commit deceptive practices. The question, unanswered by the majority because it is unanswerable, is why this one industry is entitled to be above the law that applies to every other segment of society. I do not believe it should be, or is.⁵

Yet another landmark precedent in tort law bit the dust in the case of *Thing v. LaChusa*,⁶ disallowing bystander recovery for a mother at the scene of an auto accident in which her son was seriously injured, because she was not there when the accident happened. Bystander recovery had been steadily expanded since *Dillon v. Legg*,⁷ a landmark Traynor Court ruling authored by Justice Tobriner. The 5–2 ruling was authored by Justice Eagleson, joined by Chief Justice Lucas and Justices Panelli, Arguelles and Kaufman. Justice Mosk joined the dissent authored by Justice Broussard, but added in his own dissent:

> I disagree with the majority opinion not merely for its conclusion ... but with its wholesale criticism of past opinions of this court and of the Courts of Appeal, some prevailing for three decades. Such callous disregard for the doctrine of stare decisis does not constructively serve the judicial process, nor does it contribute to the guidance of the bench and bar. As Justice Cardozo wrote in The Nature of the Judicial Process (1921) page 34, "Adherence to precedent must ... be the rule rather than the exception if litigants are to have faith in the even-handed administration of justice in the courts."⁸

Justice Mosk's refuge in *stare decisis* was somewhat ironic, since he himself authored the Lucas Court opinion that did most to undo the death penalty jurisprudence of the Bird Court. As previously noted, Justice Mosk authored the California Supreme Court decision in *People v. Anderson*, overruling *Carlos*.⁹ Genuflecting to one of his own prior decisions extolling the virtues of stare decisis, he wrote:

> Defendant contends the court failed to instruct in accord with *Carlos v. Superior Court*, that intent to kill was an element of the felony-murder special circumstances. In response, the Attorney General urges us to reconsider Carlos. We would generally be reluctant to do so: "stare decisis and respect for the judicial process require adherence to decisions rendered so recently by a substantial majority of this court." *People v. Hamilton* (1985) 41 Cal.3d 408, 439 [conc. & dis. opn. of Mosk, J.].) But because, as we shall explain, one of the bases of Carlos

has proved to be unsound, we undertake a reexamination of that decision. As will appear, we conclude that the broad holding of Carlos that intent to kill is an element of the felony-murder special circumstance cannot stand, and that the following narrow holding must be put in its place: intent to kill is not an element of the felony-murder special circumstance; but when the defendant is an aider and abetter rather than the actual killer, intent must be proved before the trier of fact can find the special circumstance to be true.

Only Justice Broussard dissented, suggesting that "political winds" may have had more to do with the Court's ruling than intervening decisions of the United States Supreme Court. "Periodically," he said, "when the political winds gust in a new direction, it becomes necessary to remind all concerned of the virtues of a steady course. As lawyers and judges, we sometimes deliver our reminder in Latin: stare decisis."[10] The dramatic shift in the death penalty rulings was the most immediate and obvious consequence of the change in the Court's composition. From March of 1987 through March of 1989, the Supreme Court of California reviewed seventy-one judgments of death. Fifty-one of them, or 71.8 percent, were affirmed. In two short years, the California affirmance rate for state Supreme Court review of death penalty judgments moved from the third lowest in the United States to the eighth highest.[11] Most of the affirmances were unanimous, with Justice Stanley Mosk joining in.[12]

In September, 1989, Mosk was feted at bar association dinners in both San Francisco and Los Angeles to celebrate his twenty-fifth anniversary as a Justice of the California Supreme Court. Co-chairs of the San Francisco bash held at the Meridien Hotel were former Governor Pat Brown and television personality, Judge Joseph A. Wapner. Judge Wapner and his wife, Mickey, were long-time friends of Mosk, impressed early on with his charm and intellect. Members of the Dinner Committee were friends and colleagues from previous decades, as well as current public officials and other notables.[13] *California Lawyer* magazine marked the occasion with a cover story entitled, "The Elusive Stanley Mosk."[14] A probing interview by Philip Carrizosa, a lawyer-journalist who closely followed the work of the California Supreme Court, challenged Justice Mosk to explain his reversing field in his death penalty decisions. Mosk replied with a litany of his most important decisions. "The test is whether today I would write Bakke, Wheeler, Friends of Mammoth, Hawkins, the public trust doctrine cases, Marriage of Carney and some 600 other opinions in the same manner. The answer is emphatically yes. That's about the only answer I can think of. I think it's too simplistic to look at these things in terms of somebody's concept of philosophy. We're looking at individual cases involving individual parties who are involved in litigation." Admitting he did change his mind about the correctness of the *Carlos* decision, he explained:

> I can't tell you the precise time, of course, but it troubled me that a person who actually did the killing could nevertheless require at trial that the prosecution show an intent. It seems to me that the act itself evidenced the intent. That's what we ultimately held in Anderson.

The article quoted some harsh criticism of Mosk by unidentified criminal defense lawyers. Said one, "He's not just hypocritical, he's worse. There's no getting away from the fact that he's one of the most brilliant justices who's been on that court. Yet whenever it gets tight and there's any danger to his continuing as a justice, he chickens out." Said another, "His only consistency has been the chameleon-like quality of his opinions." Mosk replied to this criticism by defending the consistency of his work. "I look at each case as an individual matter before us. I did that before and I do it now, regardless of the other members of the court." Rejecting the suggestion that his shifting positions were inspired by the need for self preservation, he said, "If one is fearful of public reaction or some kind of retribution, then he doesn't deserve to be on the court."

Reiterating his lifelong opposition to capital punishment, he said, "If I were a legislator, I would vote against the death penalty." But he felt the overwhelming public support of the death penalty in California required him to affirm death sentences when the law was complied with. On a later occasion, he expressed the hope that public opinion on this issue would change. "Some day we may get a governor, a legislature, and an electorate that will take a truly dispassionate look at what the death penalty costs in treasure and in its effect on society and the judicial process and will objectively determine whether it is worth it."[15]

Justice Mosk suffered still another sad loss on October 1, 1989, with the death of his brother Ed. Despite their occasional political differences, the brothers enjoyed a warm, affectionate relationship. As Ed's son Tom described it, they had a "legal love affair." They shared a lifelong love for the law, and both held tight to a vision of compassionate justice. Despite a lifetime as a vegetarian, Ed succumbed to the ravages of colon cancer at the age of 73. Stanley Mosk was then 77, still in excellent health, and still an avid tennis enthusiast. With his wife Susan, he toured Eastern Europe in 1990 on behalf of the Central and Eastern Europe Law Initiative (CEELI) of the American Bar Association, visiting Warsaw, Budapest, and Dubrovnik.

In October 1989, former Governor Pat Brown wrote Mosk a note acknowledging his recent visit to Stanley and Susan Mosk's home. "I am thankful that I had the opportunity to appoint you to the California Supreme Court. You are one of the greatest justices in the history of this state," he wrote, adding, "furthermore, and more important, your wife sings beautifully and is beautiful!"[16] At one of the 25th anniversary parties, Susan sang a musical tribute to "my husband, the justice." The humorous lyrics revealed much about their relationship:

> Have you met my husband, the justice?
> Judicial to the 'Nth Degree.
> Even at our wedding, when asked "Do you take her?"
> Instead of "I do," he said "I concur."
>
> Stanley loves his high position,
> He reminds me even when he's away.
> He always faithfully writes to me,
> And he always signs "Love, Mosk, J."
>
> Stanley's a stickler on word use.
> Foul it up and he sees red,
> And if you don't want to become his victim,
> Never say "dicta" when referring to a dictum.
>
> Stanley brings his work home with him,
> Telling war stories galore.
> Sometimes for hours he waxes nostalgic,
> About an instruction he banished from CALJIC.
>
> He conducts while we are driving,
> Waving his arms with great feeling.
> His passion for music, the law ... and me,
> Makes life with him, well ... appealing.
> I affirm it!
> Life with him is so appealing.
> Love ya!

Seven days later, the "shake-up" of the Court's composition and its precedents was closely followed by a "shake-up" of the courthouse itself. At 5:04 P.M. on October 17, 1989,

Stanley Mosk served under five chief justices during his 37-year tenure on the supreme court of California (1964 — 2001), including Chief Justice Malcolm M. Lucas, seen here to the right of Justice Mosk on the far left, c. 1991; along with the other Justices David N. Eagleson, Armand Arabian, Edward Panelli, Joyce L. Kennard, Marvin R. Baxter, and Allen E. Broussard (courtesy Richard Mosk/Albert C. Smith).

Stanley Mosk was sitting in the stands at Candlestick Park, waiting for the third game of the 1989 World Series to begin. The series featured both of the Bay Area's Major League Baseball teams, the Oakland Athletics and the San Francisco Giants. The stadium began to shake, as the Loma Preita earthquake registered 7.1 on the Richter Scale. Forty-two people died in the City of Oakland where a double-deck portion of the Interstate 880 freeway collapsed, crushing the cars on the lower deck. One 50-foot section of the San Francisco—Oakland Bay Bridge also collapsed into the Bay, leading to a single fatality on the bridge.

The venerable Earl Warren Courthouse building at 350 McAllister Street, principal home to the California Supreme Court since 1923, suffered substantial damage in the earthquake. Stairwell walls buckled, bookcases pitched out the collected volumes of the Court's output, and a large bronze light fixture crashed to the floor next to the Chief Justice's desk. Although entry to the damaged structure was forbidden, Justice Mosk insisted on entering to retrieve his working files from his Chambers. The Court moved to "temporary" quarters in a high rise office building on Second Street, while the Earl Warren Building was renovated. It took ten years.[17]

The high priority the Court gave to the death penalty decisions put enormous pressure on the Justices, and Justices Eagleson, Arguelles and Kaufman soon decided that spending the remainder of their careers plowing through the death penalty backlog was not what they had in mind. Justice Arguelles retired in March, 1989, after only two years on the Court, and both Eagleson and Kaufman were gone a year later. None of the three ever faced the voters for confirmation, departing prior to the next gubernatorial election, when they would have been on the ballot. This, of course, allowed Governor Deukmejian to name all of their replacements, and he replaced them with younger appointees with more lasting power.

In March of 1989, Governor Deukmejian replaced Justice Arguelles with Joyce Kennard, whom he had appointed to the Municipal Court in 1986, the Superior Court in 1987, and the Court of Appeal in 1988. Her meteoric rise through the judicial ranks underlined the governor's commitment to appointing both women and minorities. Kennard was the first Asian-American to serve on the high court, and the second woman. She was born in Indonesia, to a Dutch-Indonesian father and a Chinese-Indonesian mother, and was imprisoned by the Japanese during World War II. A graduate of USC School of Law, she worked as a Deputy Attorney General for five years, then spent seven years as a research attorney for the Court of Appeal. She served with Justice Mosk until his death in 2001, and still sits as the most senior Justice on the Court today. Any lurking suspicions that Justice Mosk's rocky relationship with Chief Justice Bird related to her being the first woman on the Court was laid to rest in the warm welcome he extended to Justice Kennard. She was quickly invited to dine with the Mosks, and Susan baked a huge cake to fete her. Her relationship with Stanley Mosk was warm and affectionate, and for most of his remaining years on the Court, he was seated beside Joyce Kennard during oral argument sessions. During one session, an Orange County prosecutor responded to a question from the Court by saying, "That will be up to you guys." Chief Justice Malcolm Lucas asked icily, "When you say 'you guys,' to whom are you referring?" Justice Kennard sought clarification as well, "Does that include me?" The prosecutor quickly apologized, but Justice Mosk was incensed, and remarked to Kennard as they left the courtroom, "In all my years on the Court, that's the first time I heard us referred to as 'you guys!'"

Justice Kaufman was replaced in January, 1990 with Armand Arabian. A graduate of Boston University School of Law, Arabian was first appointed to the Los Angeles Municipal

Court by Governor Reagan in 1972, then after serving on the Superior Court for nine years, he was placed on the Court of Appeal by Governor Deukmejian in 1983. Justice Eagleson was replaced with Marvin Baxter in January, 1991. Baxter had served Governor Deukmejian during his first term as appointments secretary, advising the governor on the appointment of judges and executive officers. In 1988, Deukmejian appointed him to the Court of Appeal in his home town of Fresno. Baxter was Governor George Deukmejian's final appointment to the California Supreme Court. Deukmejian was succeeded by Governor Pete Wilson in January, 1991.

None of the five Justices on the 1990 ballot was challenged, and all were confirmed, although the margins were somewhat lower than the favorable margins achieved by Lucas, Panelli and Mosk in the 1986 election. Chief Justice Lucas was confirmed for another eight years, with a yes vote of 69 percent. Justice Joyce Kennard was confirmed with a 68 percent margin, Justices Baxter and Panelli with 66 percent, and Justice Armand Arabian with a 56 percent margin. Those with foreign-sounding names are often most in jeopardy in judicial elections, where the voters frequently know little more than the judge's name, so vote on the basis of ethnic stereotypes.

After four years at the helm, Chief Justice Malcolm Lucas was in firm control, with a solid majority of five. Associate Justices Arabian, Baxter, Kennard and Panelli agreed with him at rates ranging from 89 percent to 97 percent. Dissent rates were declining, even by Justices Broussard and Mosk, who each dissented in one fourth of the cases, although not necessarily the same one-fourth. Broussard and Mosk disagreed with each other in 12 percent of the cases. Justice Stanley Mosk was writing fewer of the Court's landmark decisions, although he did win unanimous support for his opinion in *Henning v. Industrial Welfare Com.*,[18] striking down a two-tier minimum wage system that authorized a lower minimum wage for employees who work for tips, and gained the support of the Court's conservatives for his 6–1 ruling in *Molko v. Holy Spirit Assoc.*,[19] holding that former "Moonies" had the right to bring an action against the Unification Church for fraud and intentional infliction of emotional distress.

In the June, 1990 primary election, the voters approved Proposition 115, an initiative which threatened to foreclose any California Supreme Court opinions interpreting any constitutional protections more broadly than they were interpreted by the U.S. Supreme Court. Article I, section 24 of the California constitution, added in 1974, provided that "Rights guaranteed by this Constitution are not dependent on those guaranteed by the United States Constitution." Proposition 115 would have added the proviso that:

> In criminal cases the rights of a defendant to equal protection of the laws, to due process of law, to the assistance of counsel, to be personally present with counsel, to a speedy and public trial, to compel the attendance of witnesses, to confront the witnesses against him or her, to be free from unreasonable searches and seizures, to privacy, to not be compelled to be a witness against himself or herself, to not be placed twice in jeopardy for the same offense, and not to suffer the imposition of cruel or unusual punishment, shall be construed by the courts of this state in a manner consistent with the Constitution of the United States. This Constitution shall not be construed by the courts to afford greater rights to criminal defendants than those afforded by the Constitution of the United States, nor shall it be construed to afford greater rights to minors in juvenile proceedings on criminal causes than those afforded by the Constitution of the United States.

What remained of the "Mosk Doctrine," interpreting the state constitution independently of corresponding protections in the federal constitution, would be abrogated if the initiative's language was given effect. Although the Court upheld most of the measure against a single subject challenge in *Raven v. Deukmejian*,[20] the unanimous ruling by Chief Justice Malcolm Lucas held that the limitation of the Court's authority to independently construe the state Constitution was so broad that it amounted to a "revision" of the Constitution. Although an initiative measure can amend the California constitution, the constitution itself requires a constitutional convention or a legislative submission to the voters in order to revise the constitution. Although concurring in this ruling, Justice Mosk dissented from the portion of Lucas' opinion that rejected the broader single subject challenge. He would have invalidated the entire measure, on the same grounds relied upon in his "black armband" dissent in *Brosnahan v. Brown*. Recalling the painful history of that case, Justice Mosk wrote:

> I part company with my colleagues on the single-subject issue. I do not agree that this case is controlled by *Brosnahan v. Brown* (1982). If it were, we should forthrightly overrule that discredited four-to-three decision and restore the constitutional single-subject rule to its appropriate role. Parenthetically, one cannot fail to observe widespread disenchantment with the modern initiative process. At the November 6, 1990, General Election, 10 of the 13 initiatives on the ballot were defeated by the voters, some perhaps on the merits, but some undoubtedly because of prolix texts that were perplexing to all but the measures' authors. *Brosnahan v. Brown* dealt with only one initiative on the June 8, 1982, Primary Election ballot, and magnanimously held the measure did not violate the single-subject rule. The opinion, however, did not give carte blanche to initiative promoters to join together numerous disparate topics into one 'grabbag' proposal, held together with a seductive title designed for voter appeal. Indeed, the four justices in the majority warned that they were not suggesting "that initiative proponents are given blank checks to draft measures containing unduly diverse or extensive provisions bearing no reasonable relationship to each other...." In short, they were considering one proposition only and not devising a rule requiring approval of subsequent measures.

One effect of Proposition 115 was to abrogate Justice Mosk's landmark ruling in *Hawkins v. Superior Court*, which had put criminal grand juries out of business in California by requiring post-indictment preliminary hearings. The initiative amended the state Constitution to abolish that requirement, and California grand juries were back in business, investigating and indicting in criminal cases.

In December of 1990, Justice Mosk sent a birthday card congratulating crooner Frank Sinatra on his 75th birthday. Sinatra responded a month later with an affectionate note, writing, "I often reflect on the 'good old days,' too and your name always brings a smile."[21]

The validity of yet another major initiative was presented to the Court in the 1991 case of *Legislature v. Eu*.[22] In the November, 1990 election voters approved "The Political Reform Act of 1990," which mandated three major changes in state government: term limits for all elected state office holders, except the Insurance Commissioner; a constitutional limit on legislative budgets; and a restriction on the retirement benefits for legislators. The measure was challenged as a violation of both the "single subject" requirement for initiative measures, and the prohibition of constitutional "revision" by initiatives. With Justice Stanley Mosk as the only dissenter, the initiative was upheld by a 6–1 vote. Only the restriction on retirement benefits was struck down. The majority opinion by Chief Justice Malcolm Lucas went out of its way to rub salt in the wounds of the legislature, creating a rather hostile climate for the Court in Sacramento. He labeled the Legislature an "entrenched dynasty." Citing an amicus brief of the conservative Pacific Legal Foundation, he concluded that a $70 million cut in the legislative budget, or 38 percent, "will contribute in a positive manner toward eliminating excessive legislative spending and terminating surplus or inefficient personnel." The State Assembly responded by voting a 38 percent cut in the Court's budget.

Justice Mosk blamed the Court's lax enforcement of the single subject rule for creating a climate in which initiatives were out of control. He noted that in 1988, proponents and opponents of initiative measures spent more than $130 million in attempting to persuade the voters of the merits of their respective positions. He argued that the three separate measures combined in the Political Reform Act initiative violated the single subject rule on its face. He conceded that the prior decisions in *Brosnahan v. Brown* and *Raven v. Deukmejian*, in both of which he had dissented, gave some support to the use of a "common theme" to meet the single subject requirement. But he rejected the reasoning of those decisions as "demonstrably faulty," and said, "It is never too late, or too early, to correct error." The "common theme" identified by the majority, "incumbency reform," he rejected as a sham:

> Such a theme is not "unifying"; such a purpose is not "common." The term "incumbency reform" is nothing more, and nothing less, than a seductive label of indefinite scope—a label that can be applied to any "grab bag" containing any provisions, no matter how numerous or heterogeneous, that relate to some office-holder in some way. It begs reality to hold that an initiative that "makes three major changes to the California Constitution" (Ballot Pamp., supra, analysis of Prop. 140 by Legis. Analyst, at p. 69) embraces only one subject. But the majority cavalierly do so.

Justice Mosk concluded that the Political Reform Act of 1990 also violated the prohibition of constitutional revisions by initiative. It would "fundamentally alter a fundamental component of the state constitutional system by effecting a substantial change in the nature and character of the Legislature," he said. Chief Justice Lucas had fully expected that his opinion in *Legislature v. Eu* would be unanimous, and was heard to remark that "Stanley's L.A. friends at the Hillcrest Country Club must have gotten to him."[23] The subsequent political history of California strongly confirms the prescience of Mosk's views, however. In 2009, Chief Justice Ronald George attributed the dysfunctional chaos of California state government to the constraints imposed by initiative measures. He complained that the initiative process burdened the justice system with years of litigation where a measure's intent is unclear, and subjected the Justices of the Supreme Court to the wrath of the voters if they invalidate an initiative in whole or in part. "Californians may need to consider some fundamental reform of the voter initiative process," he said. "Otherwise, I am concerned, we shall continue on a course of dysfunctional state government, characterized by a lack of accountability on the part of office holders as well as the voting public."[24]

In August of 1991, Mosk authored a biting dissent to a 4–3 ruling rejecting the claim of the *Los Angeles Times* that it was entitled, under the state Public Records Act, to Governor George Deukmejian's calendars and schedules. Citing the "lessons of history," Justice Mosk wrote, "secrecy in government, *except as provided by law*, causes lack of public confidence and various other ills. We would do well to heed the words of Justice Brandeis: 'sunlight is said to be the best of disinfectants.'"[25] Writing for the majority, Justice Armand Arabian responded to Mosk's dissent with a zinger:

> In his dissenting opinion, Justice Mosk asserts that "secrecy is inconsistent with the duty of officials to keep the public informed of their activities..." and suggests that our holding represents a departure from both democratic principles and judicial precedent. On the contrary, express statutory and constitutional provisions recognize the need for confidentiality in governmental deliberations. Thus, it has been held that the activities of judges *under investigation* by the Commission on Judicial Performance—activities which the public would presumably be most interested in learning—are nevertheless not subject to disclosure pursuant to the provisions of article VI, section 18 of the California Constitution and for reasons of "sound public policy" [*Mosk v. Superior Court* (1979) 25 Cal.3d 474, 491, 499 (159 Cal.Rptr. 494, 601 P.2d 1030)].

The reference to *Mosk v. Superior Court* was, of course, a citation to the case in which Justice Mosk himself had insisted on the secrecy of the testimony gathered during the Tanner Investigation. Mosk responded by adding two lines to his dissent:

> The majority, in their footnote 14, observe that the Commission on Judicial Performance conducts its investigations in confidence, pursuant to a constitutional provision. They make my point: if there is to be governmental secrecy it must be pursuant to law. There is no statutory or constitutional provision specifically granting the right of secrecy to the Governor.

The decision inspired an outraged editorial in the *San Francisco Examiner*, which quoted Mosk's dissent and argued, "The Supreme Court should be well ashamed of this decision, which is clearly against the public interest." The editorial strongly suggested that political loyalties affected the outcome:

> Adding to the stench was the insider nature of the decision: All four votes in the Duke's favor came from his appointees: Armand Arabian, who wrote the tortured thing, Chief Justice Malcolm Lucas, plus Justices Panelli and Marvin Baxter. To make matters worse, Baxter served as the Duke's appointments secretary (although that job deals with appointing judges among others, not scheduling), but he denied a conflict of interest and refused to disqualify himself.[26]

The 1991 retirement of Justice Allen Broussard gave newly elected Governor Pete Wilson his first chance to make a Supreme Court appointment. He appointed Court of Appeal Justice Ronald M. George, whom he later promoted to Chief Justice upon the retirement of Malcolm Lucas as Chief Justice in 1996. After graduating from Stanford Law School in 1964, George had been hired as a Deputy Attorney General by Stanley Mosk. He excelled as an appellate advocate, arguing six cases before the United States Supreme Court. At the age of 32, he was appointed to the Municipal Court in Los Angeles by Governor Ronald Reagan. He was elevated to the Superior Court by Governor Jerry Brown in 1977, and appointed to the Court of Appeal by Governor George Deukmejian in 1987. Justice Mosk welcomed Ron George to the Court with a warm note of congratulations. He added, "My only advice for what it is worth — based on 27 years on this Court — is to be your own self, totally independent. Although ours is a collegial group, do not walk in lock-step with others and you will earn the recognition you deserve." He enclosed with his note a copy of the *San Francisco Examiner* editorial critical of the opinion protecting Governor Deukmejian's calendars and schedules, pointedly noting, "Enclosed is an article that relates what happens when blind conformity exists." Obviously, Mosk was concerned that George would ally himself with the Deukmejian appointees. His concern was well founded. During his first year on the Court, Justice George voted in lock step with Chief Justice Lucas, agreeing with him in every case that was decided. He later moved to a more central position on the Court, and then succeeded Lucas as Chief Justice. Chief Justice George became a warm friend and great admirer of Justice Mosk, and the moderation of his views was likely influenced by Justice Mosk.

The departure of Justice Broussard left Justice Mosk as the only dissenter in many of the Lucas Court opinions, and his dissent rate rose sharply. He dissented from 40 percent of the Lucas Court opinions in 1992, and racked up the highest dissent rate of his career, 47 percent, for the cases decided in 1993 and 1994. Producing dissenting or concurring opinions for nearly half of the Court's output was a daunting task, and the five years of the Lucas Court from 1991 to 1996 were the most productive years of Justice Mosk's entire tenure. During those five years, he produced 60 majority opinions, 68 concurring opinions, and 140 dissenting opinions. Not unlike Justice Oliver Wendell Holmes, Jr., who produced many of his most memorable dissents after he was eighty years old, Justice Mosk greeted his eighth decade with renewed energy. His eightieth birthday was celebrated on September 12, 1992. His health was excellent, although he was slowing down somewhat on the tennis court.

Justice Mosk's dissents frequently "called the roll" of the previous Justices whose venerable precedents were being cast off by the Lucas Court majority. In *Kowis v. Howard*,[27] for example, he lamented:

> I cannot join the majority in unnecessarily reaching out to overrule a decision of this court that has been the prevailing law for almost 30 years. *Pigeon Point Ranch, Inc. v. Perot (1963) 59 Cal.2d 227* was authored by Chief Justice Gibson and concurred in by Justices Traynor, McComb, Peters, Tobriner, Peek, and White. I doubt that we are more competent to determine the rather simple rule of law involved than was one of the most distinguished courts in California history. Its opinion was sound when written, and three decades later it is not an obstacle to the result in the instant case.

Occasionally, Mosk's dissents grew shrill, accusing the majority of "flouting the authority of the United States Supreme Court" by its "insubordinate" refusal to apply a United States Supreme Court precedent.[28] But his persistence and forceful logic attracted his more conservative colleagues with growing frequency, and persuaded them to join him in dissenting. Justice Kennard's dissent rate grew, achieving a high of 25 percent in 1995. In many of her dissents, she was in agreement with Justice Mosk. Mosk's rate of agreement with his colleagues was highest for Justice Kennard.

Justices Kennard and George, for example, joined his dissent in *Alfredo A. v. Superior Court*,[29] arguing that no state interest justified holding juveniles longer than adults after a warrantless arrest. Although relying upon different arguments, Justices George and Kennard also joined Justice Mosk in dissenting from Chief Justice Lucas' majority opinion in *Hill v. NCAA*,[30] a landmark ruling defining the right of privacy under the California Constitution. Stanford University athletes, joined by the University, objected to the drug testing program for athletes imposed by the National Collegiate Athletic Association. Under the NCAA's drug testing program, randomly selected college student athletes competing in postseason championships and football bowl games were required to provide samples of their urine under closely monitored conditions. Urine samples were chemically analyzed for proscribed substances. Athletes testing "positive" were subject to disqualification. The majority concluded that although the constitutional protection of privacy rights extended to private enterprises in California, a student athlete's already diminished expectation of privacy was outweighed by the NCAA's legitimate regulatory objectives in conducting testing for proscribed drugs. Justice Mosk was not impressed by the "regulatory objectives" of the NCAA. He wrote:

> The NCAA is now free to use in California the weapons it had chosen for its "war on drugs." "What better way to show that" it "is serious about its 'war on drugs'" than to subject "student athletes" to this invasion of their privacy and affront to their dignity? To be sure, there is only a slight chance that it will prevent some serious ... harm resulting from "student athlete" drug use, but it will show to the world that "it" is "clean," and — most important of all — will demonstrate "its" determination ... to eliminate this scourge of our society! I think it obvious that this justification is unacceptable; that the impairment of individual liberties cannot be the means of making a point; that "symbolism, even symbolism for [a] worthy ... cause..., cannot" justify an abridgment of the right of privacy.

To please his son Richard, a Stanford University graduate, Justice Mosk inserted a curious footnote extolling the glories of Stanford's athletic program:

It may be noted in passing that "[f]or the inaugural issue of College Sports Magazine, 110 sports information directors (SID's) were asked what three college athletic programs they admired most. The magazine asked the SID's to take into account athletes' competitive and academic success, facilities, men's teams and women's teams, major and non-revenue sports, and all other aspects of a well-rounded program" [*Stanford Athletics #1* (Nov. 1993) College Sports Magazine, at p. 6]. Stanford finished first with 26 first-place votes and 164 total points. The institution that came in second was far behind, with only seven first-place votes and only seventy total points [*ibid.*].

Like Justice Oliver Wendell Holmes, Jr., Justice Stanley Mosk appreciated brevity in majority opinions, and frequently achieved it. His longest Lucas Court opinion, however, came in *20th Century Insurance Co. et al. v. John Garamendi*,[31] upholding regulations drafted by the California Insurance Commissioner to implement an initiative measure requiring roll-backs in automobile insurance rates. The careful 113-page majority opinion won unanimous support of all the Justices. Justice Mosk could not resist adding a three page concurring opinion, however, to express a view that none of his colleagues agreed with: that no insurer, through the operation of Proposition 103's rate rollback requirement provision, could suffer confiscation under the takings clause of the Fifth Amendment. Because they were "service providers" voluntarily participating in a price-regulated activity, he argued, the Fifth Amendment offered no protection at all.

Not all of Justice Mosk's dissents were written for posterity. Some were written for the State Legislature. An example was his pointed dissent to Justice Ronald M. George's majority opinion in *People v. Whitfield*,[32] holding that a defendant accused of second degree "implied malice" murder for recklessly causing the death of another motorist while driving drunk could offer evidence that his extreme intoxication prevented him from having the subjective awareness of the risk required for implied malice. Justice Mosk dissented, arguing that getting extremely intoxicated was itself the act that supplied the requisite implied malice:

> [A]wareness of the potential consequences of excessive drinking on the capacity of human beings to guage risks incident to their conduct is by now so dispersed in our culture that we believe it fair to postulate a general equivalence between the risks created by the conduct of the drunken actor and the risks created by his conduct in becoming drunk.[33]

One year after *Whitfield*, the California Legislature amended Section 22 of the California Penal Code to reflect Justice Mosk's view, limiting the admissibility of voluntary intoxication to rebut a showing of express malice, but not implied malice.[34]

In March of 1994, the free, award winning publication, the *L.A. Weekly*, then with a circulation of around 50,000, and a tradition of editorial board endorsement of Justice Stanley Mosk, published a front-page report entitled, "The Judge, the Photos and the Senate Race."[35] It dredged up the role of Mosk's affair in his withdrawal from the Senate Race thirty years before, in salacious detail. When called to comment on the article, Justice Mosk told the reporters he had "never heard of" Sabrina Jourdan, and said, "I don't know. Someone's making a story up. There's not a word of truth in that. That's 30 years ago, and entirely untrue." He then threatened a lawsuit that would put the paper out of business "if you publish anything of that sort, 30 years after it is alleged to have happened."[36] The story was published, and Richard Mosk mobilized to minimize the damage. No lawsuit was ever filed. The revelation ignited interest by the *Los Angeles Times* and the *San Francisco Chronicle*, however, and Richard went to extraordinary lengths to squelch it. He met with the editorial board at the *L.A. Times*, and he and Mosk's wife Susan met with the board at *The Chronicle*. They convinced the editors that the story was not newsworthy, and its publication would only serve to tarnish the reputation of a dedicated public servant in the twilight of a distinguished career.[16]

Times have changed. Up until the exposure of presidential candidate Gary Hart in 1984, the sexual dalliances of political figures were considered irrelevant, and news reporters simply didn't go there. Today, candidates and elected officials are knocked off their pedestals on almost a weekly basis, by the exposure of extracurricular sexual activity. In large part, this reflects changes in the media, and the public's expectation that such disclosures about the sexual lives of their political leaders and cultural icons contribute to their "need to know." News reporters are no longer a close-knit fraternity, but a highly competitive conglomeration feeding a bewildering array of delivery mechanisms, and daily feeding frenzies, often triggered by political opponents. Although it might appear that fewer political figures lead exemplary moral lives, it is more likely that political figures fail to recognize the need to take greater steps to conceal or disguise their dalliances.

In the summer of 1994, after twelve years of marriage, Stanley and Susan Mosk quietly divorced. Over the years, the difference in their ages began to put increasing strain on their marriage. Their long-term goals and day-to-day needs and interests were less and less compatible. Perhaps Susan began to recognize the reality that both of them had ignored in the early years of their genuinely passionate relationship — that is, her unavailability to care for her aging husband as her own burgeoning legal career demanded long hours at the office and the kind of dedication demanded of younger, recent law school graduates. For those who didn't already know, columnist Herb Caen tipped off *Chronicle* readers about a "not so much funny" situation. Writing in May 1994, Caen said that, "after a twelve year marriage State Supreme Court Justice Stanley Mosk and his wife Susan, a prominent lawyer, and who moved out of their Nob Hill apartment, are undergoing 'what we euphemistically call a trial separation.'"[37] Their trial separation ended when Susan filed for divorce. Susan embarked upon her law practice as Susan Hines Mosk. She kept the baby grand piano Stanley Mosk had given her as a gift. She frequently was asked if she was Justice Mosk's daughter.

Justice Mosk was represented in the divorce proceedings by Michael C. Tobriner, Justice Tobriner's son. Later that year, Mosk was anticipating his yearly reunion with his college mates and he felt the need to write to them to explain his new domestic situation. "The rumor is true that Susan left me." He explained, "Though damaging to my ego, I must note two things. First, our parting was without acrimony and we both still act civilly. And, second, I can comprehend Susan's underlying frame of mind, though never so declared: at age 47 she does not want the burden of being married to a husband in his 80s. Selfish perhaps, but understandable." He went on: "So, I have reluctantly accepted the fact that 12 happy years of marriage apparently are all I may presently deserve. (As an aside, in that period I served a Pygmalion role in overcoming Susan's health problem, putting her through law school and enjoying her progress in the profession — she is due to become state president of California Women Lawyers.)" "Fortunately," he added, "I have not been bereft of all romance in my life. By remarkable fortuity, a Los Angeles woman whom I have known and admired for some 40 years suffered the death of her husband shortly before my marriage collapsed." Kaygey Kash was a longtime friend whom he had first met while serving as a Superior Court judge in Long Beach forty years before. There was an immediate attraction back then, but their feelings were put on hold for almost a half century. They served together in several Jewish community organizations, and when he was Attorney General, he invited her to serve on a number of advisory committees.

Mosk told his friends, "at first, we tended to cry on each other's shoulder. Lately that mutual feeling has progressed to a serious and perhaps permanent relationship. By additional fortuity, we both become available for matrimony at the same time, if we ultimately choose that route: I at the end of the statutory divorce period, she at the end of a religious traditional year of mourning. Both occur about the first of the year." He described Kaygey, whom they would all meet when he brought her to their reunion in Santa Fe, as "a tiny, very quiet, unassuming person, but she has an impressive string of accomplishments in community service. Some years ago she spent two years in Washington as international president of the B'nai B'rith Women's organization." He closed his letter with noting that his "current story," boring as it may be, was just something he wanted them to know in case there was any embarrassment when he showed up with Kaygey "and [we] stay together."[26]

On January 15, 1995, the eighty-two-year-old Justice Stanley Mosk bounded down the aisle for the third time, marrying Kaygey Kash. Once again, Herb Caen whispered to his readers a "well-kept secret" about Mosk tying the knot with his "longtime friend Kaygey Kash of Los Angeles," and they were then honeymooning in Australia."[38] Susan had filed for divorce just six weeks before, after a two year separation. Unfortunately, it took eight weeks for the divorce papers to be processed, so when Susan learned that he had remarried, she advised him that he was a bigamist because the divorce had not yet been finalized. Susan was able to get the divorce certificate back-dated, and no one was the wiser.[39] He described his new marriage to friends as a "more appropriate" marriage than his second. Day-to-day life returned to the more traditional lifestyle that Mosk had shared with Edna, a mutually satisfying companionship with a formality more befitting an elder statesman and his well-established wife. Kaygey accommodated her husband's need for reassurance before he headed off to the Court. "Stanley was always careful about his appearance — not because of vanity, but because he respected his position in public life. When he was ready to go to work each day — always well groomed and wearing a nice suit — he would turn around for my inspection, and I would say: 'Okay; Okay; today you're even more beautiful than I am.' Then his face would break into a radiant smile and he would leave the house with his usual parting remark: 'Well, I'm off to make a living for us.'"[40] At the Court's memorial service for Stanley Mosk, Kaygey presented a delightful snapshot of a typical day in their life:

> In the early morning I would often hear Stanley jogging or two-stepping to his own tune. When he saw me watching him exercise, he would call out: "Kiddo, I'm hungry!" I took this as a signal to prepare breakfast. He loved food — any kind of food — and was very tolerant of my limited cooking skills: Even when I burned his toast and eggs, he would exclaim, "Delicious! What a meal!" In the evening Stanley would usually bring home a briefcase bulging with court materials. After changing into casual clothes, he would point to a chair next to his and say, "Why don't you sit there while I get this reading done." I was always surprised he could work with the television on; but it was usually a baseball or football game, and he seemed to follow it with one ear, occasionally responding to the play with a small groan or cheer. Eventually I would say, "Stanley, it's really quite late. Let me finish the reading for you, and make the decisions, too." He got the message: He would quickly turn off the television and snap his briefcase shut — only to open it again early the next morning to finish his work.

Throughout the Lucas Court years, Justice Mosk maintained his busy routine of off-the-bench speeches, bar convention panels and law school moot court judging. An article on the death penalty which he published in 1994 inspired a March 7 response from U.S. Supreme Court Justice Harry Blackmun, noting that "the tide, of course, is running strongly the other way." Ironically, Blackmun announced his retirement from the Court one month later, after issuing his dissent in *Callins v. Collins*.[41] In that case, Justice Blackmun famously declared that "[f]rom this day forward, I no longer shall tinker with the machinery of death." During his final six months on the Court, he adopted the practice begun by Justices Brennan and Marshall of issuing a dissent from denial of *certiorari* in every death penalty case, citing and reiterating his *Callins* dissent.

As the senior Justice on the Court, and an accomplished speaker, Mosk was in wide demand. He loved to pepper his conversation and speeches with humor and jokes. Throughout his professional life, he carried a small pocket diary. In the front, he pasted a typed script for marriage ceremonies. In the back, he scribbled the punch lines of jokes he wanted to remember. An example:

> PROSECUTOR: This man is married to three women at the same time. We are charging him with bigotry.
> JUDGE: You oaf, that's not bigotry. That's trigonometry.

By his own count, as Attorney General Stanley Mosk spoke to groups from 10 to 3,000 on an average of four times a week, and on many occasions he spoke three times in one day. During the 1960 presidential campaign, he gave fourteen talks in one day.[42] As a Justice of the Supreme Court, his speaking schedule was less rigorous but more philosophical and restrained in tone. Dennis Peter Maio, a Yale Law School graduate who served as an attorney on Justice Mosk's staff from 1984 until Justice Mosk's death in 2001, and assisted in writing hundreds of his opinions, noted that the staff never had anything to do with any of his speeches. "His speeches sounded one voice, and one voice alone, and it was his."[43] In his speeches, and often in short articles for law reviews as well, he addressed issues of the day from a deep reservoir of experience. Maio, in introducing a collection of Mosk's speeches, aptly summed up the spirit that energized them:

> He lived a long life.... In living that life he engaged himself fully in public affairs, from the Great Depression, through the Second World War, and into the Civil Rights Era and all that accompanied and succeeded those times. And how was it that he engaged himself in public affairs? With principles and pragmatism. He was principled, committed unabashedly to the American liberal tradition and its ideals of a society that is not only open but also caring. He was also pragmatic, choosing to do what he could to make things better now rather then stake all on a chance to make things perfect sometime in the future. His principled pragmatism filled him with a passionate generosity that left no room for small-mindedness or mean-spiritedness.[44]

Justice Mosk had begun the task of collecting and editing many of his speeches and other writings for publication as a book, which he intended to entitle *Myths and Realities in the Law*. Among the "myths" he addressed were that common sense prevails in courts, and that the rule of law is safe in the world. Just as he collected baseball cards and autographs throughout his life, he collected historical examples and quotations that illustrate "where we are, how we got here, and where we should be going." In 1995, he published them in the only book that bears his name as author. He titled it, *Democracy in America — Day by Day*. Offering a "teaspoonful of knowledge each day," the book collected "365 thoughts for 365 days, some mine, mostly of others," related to events that actually occurred on that day. His entry for August 25, however, did not relate to anything that happened on that date. Instead, it offered his reflections on the value of judicial dissents. He wrote:

> A dissenter is basically a nonconformist, one who views a universally accepted concept with skepticism. In 1491, the world was flat with only Columbus, J., dissenting. Later, in England, a "dissenter" was one who left the established church. In America, the term became associated with politics; dissent is endemic in a country founded in revolution by men committed to

freedom of conscience and freedom of expression. Thomas Paine and Patrick Henry were card-carrying dissenters. But today, dissent denotes a high court opinion critical of the prevailing majority and dedicated to posterity. Justice Cardozo once put it this way: "The voice of the majority may be that of force triumphant, content with the plaudits of the hour and recking little of the morrow. This dissenter speaks of the futures, and his voice is pitched to a key that will carry through the years." It is, as Justice Hughes said, "An appeal to the brooding spirit of the law, to the intelligence of a future day."[45]

Chapter 20

"Where Has All the Grandeur Gone?"

On April 19, 1995, a truck bomb driven by Timothy McVeigh destroyed the Alfred P. Murrah Federal Building in downtown Oklahoma City, claiming the lives of 168 victims and injuring more than 680. The blast destroyed or damaged 324 buildings within a sixteen-block radius, destroyed or burned 86 cars, and shattered glass in 258 nearby buildings. The bomb was estimated to have caused at least $652 million worth of damage. Among those whose offices in the Murrah Building were destroyed was Judge Robert H. Henry of the United States Court of Appeals for the Tenth Circuit, a friend and admirer of Justice Stanley Mosk. Mosk was deeply moved when he received a note from Judge Henry describing the damage to his office. The windows were blown out and the ceiling collapsed, but Judge Henry only sustained bruises. He wrote: "A letter from you which I have framed and hung on the wall about 20 feet from one of the windows remained proudly displayed, though with a few nicks in the frame." His wife, a dentist, was volunteering in the morgue to help with identification of bodies.[1]

Despite this sad reminder that "the anticipated dawn of enlightenment does not seem destined to appear soon," Justice Mosk remained upbeat and sanguine about America's future, although some wistfulness occasionally crept into his off the bench reminiscing. In 1997, he was especially pleased by an invitation to deliver the "Brennan Lecture" at New York University, an annual event honoring the memory of Justice William Brennan of the U.S. Supreme Court. Mosk began his lecture by recalling the delightful two weeks he had spent with Bill Brennan studying British appellate courts in London thirty years before. He was in a nostalgic mood, beginning with a description of "a few of my current phobias." They could more accurately be described as "pet peeves," including his longtime war against the use of the term "gender discrimination" rather than "sex discrimination." He said, "I may sound like an old Victorian, but another phobia is court opinions that employ unimaginative, or worse, unacceptable prose. I grimace when reading an opinion that fails to recognize dictum is singular, dicta the plural. It may be unrealistic to expect Benjamin Cardozo or Robert Jackson brilliance in a fairly pedestrian case, but the fact that opinions enter the bound volumes on library shelves should require at least an elementary devotion to literary quality." After expressing his displeasure with current legislation and U.S. Supreme Court rulings limiting the access of prisoners to habeas corpus and increasing the length of prison sentences, he ended on a note of uncharacteristic pessimism:

> When I look back on the origins of our nation, I feel a deep sense of pride — but also a feeling of apprehension for the present and the future. Bear in mind that the original 13 states consisted of a mere 2,205,000 people, not much more than the current population of many metropolitan areas. Out of that tiny pool of inhabitants, there was produced Washington, Jefferson, John and Samuel Adams, Hamilton, Franklin, Tom Paine, Madison, Monroe, John

Marshall, John Jay—all cultured, articulate, intellectually brilliant men. They had studied and understood the principle of democracy, and lived with respect for democracy. Now look around us, in this nation more than 100 times larger, more than 250 millions of people, and we search in vain for leadership of that intellectual quality. One is compelled to ask, as Archibald MacLeish did so plaintively: "Where has all the grandeur gone?" Sorry, I have no answer.[2]

A similar note was struck in a note to Almena Lomax, a leader in the Los Angeles African American community that he deeply admired, decrying the current lack of leadership in the ongoing struggle for civil rights:

Where are the Adlai Stevensons, John Kennedys, Martin Luther Kings, Roy Wilkins, Bill Douglases, Earl Warrens, Thurgood Marshalls, Bill Brennans, today? Dole, Gingrich, Clarence Thomas—what dim prospects we have for the immediate future.[3]

His longing for the past did not distract him from the prodigious pace of work he maintained at the California Supreme Court, however. Justices Ronald George and Edward Panelli were beginning to move to more centrist positions, but both still agreed with Chief Justice Lucas in 90 percent of the cases. The retirements of Justice Panelli in 1994 and Justice Armand Arabian in early 1996 barely caused a ripple in the line-up of the Court. Panelli was replaced with Justice Kathryn M. Werdegar, who had served as one of Panelli's staff attorneys before her appointment to the Court of Appeal. She graduated first in her class from Boalt Hall, and was the first woman to serve as Editor in Chief of the *California Law Review*. Arabian was replaced by Justice Ming Chin, who previously served on the Alameda County Superior Court and the First District Court of Appeal. A major shift came about later in 1996, when Chief Justice Malcolm Lucas retired after ten years at the helm. He was replaced by Justice Ronald M. George, and the vacancy created by George's elevation was filled with the appointment of Justice Janice Rogers Brown. The appointment of Chief Justice George was widely anticipated, but Brown's appointment created controversy. After serving as Governor Pete Wilson's Legal Affairs secretary, Brown was appointed by Wilson to the Third District Court of Appeal in Sacramento. When he nominated her to the California Supreme Court two years later, the State Bar Commission on evaluation of judicial nominees rated her "unqualified," criticizing her lack of judicial experience. Upon her confirmation, she restored an African American presence to the Court, missing since the departure of Justice Allen Broussard. But her strong libertarian views aligned her most closely with Justices Baxter and Chin.

The appointment of Ronald George as Chief Justice signaled a remarkable realignment of the Justices that dramatically transformed the role of Justice Stanley Mosk. Throughout the ten year reign of Chief Justice Malcolm Lucas, there was a solid conservative phalanx of five votes, with Mosk as the old "liberal" war-horse who frequently dissented. Least predictable was Justice Joyce Kennard, but the only difference her dissents would make was whether the decision would be 6–1 or 5–2. Very few cases were decided by a 4–3 margin. From 1993 to 1997, however, Justice George's rate of agreement with Justice Mosk crept steadily upwards, from 60 percent to 75 percent. Justice Kathryn Werdegar also moved steadily to the left, and the number of 4–3 decisions dramatically increased. The most common configuration in these decisions put Justices Mosk, Kennard and Werdegar on one side, Justices Baxter, Chin and Brown on the other side, and the Chief Justice in the center, casting the deciding vote. During the first eighteen months of the George Court, there were eighteen 4–3 decisions, and Chief Justice George was in the majority in all of them. While he tended to side with the conservatives, the liberals won his vote with increasing frequency.

For Justice Mosk, this meant he was back on the winning side in more and more of the Court's landmark decisions, and had the opportunity again to write important majority decisions. His dissent rate steadily declined, falling below 20 percent. In 1997, he led the Court in production of majority opinions, authoring 21 of them.

One 4–3 split that deviated from the normal voting pattern became the most controversial decision of the early George Court. In *American Academy of Pediatrics v. Lungren*,[4] the Court struck down as unconstitutional a law requiring parental consent for abortions for juveniles. The majority opinion was authored by Chief Justice George, joined by Justices Chin, Werdegar and Kennard. Surprisingly, Justice Stanley Mosk dissented in an opinion that reads as though it was written to be the majority opinion. In strongly disagreeing with the majority, Mosk wrote that he was "setting aside any personal beliefs concerning the morality — and politics— of abortion." He then argued that the constitutional right of privacy upon which the majority relied was a more limited right for juveniles than for adults:

> With respect to whether an unemancipated minor has a legally protected privacy interest concerning reproductive choice, our consistent precedents compel the conclusion that she has such an interest but it is neither coequal with that of an adult, nor, in the case of an immature unemancipated minor, absolute even in the early stages of pregnancy. It is not the case, as the plurality erroneously conclude, that the legally protected privacy interest in procreative choice does not vary based on the maturity or cognitive ability of the person whose choice is at issue.

Justice Mosk's dissent in *American Academy of Pediatrics* distinguished the strong defense of the constitutional right of privacy he presented in his dissent in *Hill v. NCAA*, arguing *Hill* involved the privacy rights of adults, not minors. He claimed that he was following *Hill* while Justices George and Kennard were not.

> The test crafted by the majority in Hill was obviously intended to confine privacy litigation in the area of personal autonomy rights to invasions that are truly serious, i.e., offensive to a reasonable person. The majority in Hill appears to have been particularly concerned that, unless we so confined the right to privacy, it would become a "back door" legal theory in employment cases. I was the only member of the court dissenting in Hill [7 Cal. 4th at pp. 73–110 (dis. opn. of Mosk, J.)]. Two members of the present plurality filed concurring and dissenting opinions.

He then concluded that the requirement of parental consent for abortions did not constitute an "egregious breach of the social norms underlying the privacy right" of unemancipated minors, as required by Hill.

In another 1997 opinion, Justice Mosk authored a 6–1 majority ruling on a procedural issue regarding the designation of juvenile convictions as felonies or misdemeanors.[5] In his dissent, Justice Marvin Baxter chided Mosk for disregarding a precedent that he himself had authored fourteen years before. Justice Mosk always prided himself on remembering what position he had taken in virtually every case that had come before the Court during his tenure. He replied to Justice Baxter in an amusing separate opinion concurring in his own majority opinion:

> I concur, of course, in the majority opinion that I authored for the court. I write briefly to respond to the dissenting opinion, which refers to my dissenting opinion in In re Kenneth H. (1983) 33 Cal. 3d 616. In Kenneth H., I expressed the view, as a matter of personal belief, that remand was unnecessary under the specific facts of that case, and that literal compliance with Welfare and Institutions Code section 702 represented "but one more step in a seemingly inexorable process ... of converting juvenile proceedings into formal criminal trials."
>
> I have not succeeded, however, in persuading my colleagues of the soundness of that view.

> After reflection, I have decided not to beat a rataplan, but to join with the majority here as a matter of stare decisis. Moreover, in light of the increasingly serious consequences of a determination that a so-called "wobbler" would, in the case of an adult, be a felony, I do not share the view of the dissenting opinion that remand under these circumstances is merely a redundant exercise. Even if one can perceive an inconsistency between a previous point of view and the court's conclusion in this case, I am reminded of the philosophy of Justice Frankfurter, subsequently quoted by Justice Rutledge and Justice Jackson: "Wisdom too often never comes, and so one ought not to reject it merely because it comes late."

Justice Mosk's highest rate of disagreement on the George Court was with Justice Janice Rogers Brown. They voted on opposite sides of 40 percent of the cases. In one such case, Justice Brown cited a pantheon of legal philosophers in upholding injunctions of gang activities even when the activities themselves were not criminal.[6] Justice Mosk opened his dissent with a memorable line:

> No doubt Montesquieu, Locke, and Madison will turn over in their graves when they learn they are cited in an opinion that does not enhance liberty but deprives a number of simple rights to a group of Latino youths who have not been convicted of a crime. Mindful of the admonition of another great 18th century political philosopher, Benjamin Franklin, that "[t]hey that can give up essential liberty to obtain a little temporary safety deserve neither liberty nor safety," I would, unlike the majority, in large part affirm the judgment of the Court of Appeal.

As he approached his 86th birthday, Stanley Mosk filed papers to seek retention in the general election slated for November 1998. He told reporters that he could always withdraw his name before the August 15 deadline, but he added, "I still haven't firmly made up my mind. I just thought I ought to stay on for a few more years." No vocal or organized opposition had surfaced yet. Another electoral victory would put him only two years away from the January, 2000 date that would break the record of Justice John Shenk, who served on the high court for thirty-five years, from 1924 to 1959. Once again, he was on his way to foil anyone who anticipated his retirement, including Governor Pete Wilson, who would have relished the opportunity to fill another seat on the Court.[7] Because of their participation in the majority ruling in *American Academy of Pediatrics*, both Chief Justice George and Justice Chin were targeted for defeat by right-to-life forces in the retention election of 1998. Justices Mosk and Janice Rogers Brown generated no opposition. Justice Mosk was concerned that his age might become an issue in the election, and made the rounds of newspaper editorial boards to demonstrate how alert he still was. He received the endorsements of all of California's leading newspapers. His friend former Los Angeles Police Chief Tom Reddin circulated a letter extolling the Mosk decisions that conservatives would like. He listed fourteen items as reasons conservatives should support the retention of Justice Mosk, not the least of which was his sentencing of "a West Los Angeles murderer to death," and how he "vigorously fought to affirm death penalty convictions," and how "he has probably voted to affirm more death penalty cases than any other judge in the country." Reddin also included "favorable articles" by conservative columnist Max Boot, heralding Mosk's reaffirmation that the Unruh Act was not applicable to the Boy Scouts and thus the organization "could maintain its rules regarding gays and atheists." The election results demonstrated that California voters strongly supported the incumbent Justices regardless of where they stood on the abortion issue. Justice Brown led the pack with a 76 percent approval rate, closely followed by Chief Justice George with 75 percent. Justice Mosk, at the age of 86, won another twelve-year term with 70.6 percent of the vote, while Justice Ming Chin was retained with a 69.3 percent margin.

On Sunday, December 26, 1999, Justice Mosk broke the record as the longest serving Justice in the history of the California Supreme Court. Anticipating Mosk's historic landmark just two days away, a *Los Angeles Times* editorial provided some perspective, citing one legal scholar who noted "with a modicum of hyperbole," that Mosk has been ... one of the most influential members in the history of one of the most influential tribunals in the Western world."[8] The *Los Angeles Times* also marked the occasion with the publication of a lengthy interview by Maura Dolan. She noted that, "the pictures on Mosk's office wall attest to his many years of prominence. There are photographs of him with JFK, Harry S Truman, Adlai Stevenson II, Indira Gandhi and Martin Luther King, Jr., who played the piano as a guest at a dinner party Mosk attended in Los Angeles." She described Mosk as a small man, with receding white hair. Although his gait has slowed and at times his breathing is more labored, and his physique more frail, she said, he continued to be regarded as a legal giant. Asking him directly about his health, Mosk quipped, "I sometimes can't stand at cocktail parties as long as I used to, and I had to give up tennis, which I enjoyed very much." His only complaint about aging was his grief over dying friends, explaining that he lost three in one recent month. "If I find at some point that I am not being productive for the court, I would then consider retiring," he said, "but thus far, and I don't say this boastfully, I have been the most productive member of the court every year." His son Richard reported that he had been unsuccessful in trying to convince his father to lift lightweights to stay fit. His father replied, "Listen, I got along without your advice for 87 years. I am not going to start taking it now." A *Times* editorial added, "Californians are fortunate that this strong defender of civil rights, civil liberties and press freedom has proved to have such staying power."

On January 7, 2000, Chief Justice Ronald George convened the California Supreme Court for a special celebration session honoring the record service of Justice Stanley Mosk.[9] Among those who spoke were his son, Richard, and Peter Belton, who had served as his staff attorney for all 35 years of Justice Mosk's service on the Court. Belton summed up the amazing productivity of Justice Mosk with these words:

> As of this morning, Justice Mosk has authored no less than 710 majority opinions and 776 minority opinions, for a grand total of 1,486 opinions of this court. A precise division of his minority opinions into concurrences and dissents is difficult, because some are both; but a fair reading indicates they are composed of 285 concurring opinions and 491 dissents ... Justice Mosk's grand total very likely gives him a second record as well: the most productive justice in the history of the court. Finally, and the most startling figure of all, Justice Mosk's current total of 1,486 opinions works out to an average of one opinion filed every eight days of the last three and half decades.

Thus, in terms of quantitative output, Stanley Mosk holds the record as not only the longest-serving Justice in the history of the California Supreme Court, he also holds the record for being the most productive. He enjoyed the satisfaction of seeing many of his opinions embraced by judges of the appellate courts of other states. A recent study established, that the California Supreme Court remains the "most followed" Supreme Court in the nation, in terms of its rulings being cited and followed by the courts of other states. The study identified 160 opinions authored by 33 different Justices as the "most influential," followed three or more times. Justice Mosk authored 27 of those decisions, more than any other Justice who ever sat on the California Supreme Court.[10]

Justice Mosk concluded the ceremony with a moving tribute to his wife, Kaygey. "My helpmate, my companion, my adviser, my lover, and the one person who is indispensable to my well-being," and to Chief Justice Ronald George, whom he thanked for his splendid leadership of the court: "No one," he said, "at least in modern times, has done more for judicial administration than our current Chief Justice."

Throughout this period, he never banked his fires, leading the Court in the production of majority opinions and dissents in his final year. His colleagues on the Court marveled at his continued productivity, and Chief Justice Ron George assured him that "having you performing at 95% capacity is worth more than 100% of the other Justices." He frequently found himself in agreement with the Chief Justice, agreeing with George in 86 percent of the cases. Justice Mosk's Nob Hill apartment was just a couple blocks from the apartment that was home to Chief Justice George and his wife, Barbara. When George remarked that he lived "a stone's throw" from Justice Mosk, Stanley joked that he occasionally would like to throw a stone at George. But the relationship between Chief Justice George and Justice Mosk was a warm and affectionate one. He also found himself in agreement with Justice Janice Rogers Brown in one of the most divisive cases, *Hi-Voltage Wireworks, Inc. v. City of San Jose*.[11] Striking down a municipal program requiring contractors to use a specified percentage of minority and women subcontractors as a violation of the Proposition 209 prohibition of affirmative action programs, Justice Brown managed to insult lots of liberal icons in her survey of cases dealing with racial discrimination. For example, she characterized the late United States Supreme Court Justice William J. Brennan's dissent in *McCleskey v. Kemp*[12] as a low point in the effort to articulate a coherent vision of civil rights, classifying it along with the Dred Scott decision. But her majority opinion was amply sprinkled with citations and quotations of the opinions of Justice Stanley Mosk regarding affirmative action. Chief Justice George, joined by Justice Kennard, wrote an outraged dissent, and Justice Werdegar also dissented, but Justice Mosk concurred fully in the majority opinion.

In his final majority opinion, Justice Mosk was joined by Chief Justice George and Justices Baxter and Chin in upholding the conviction of a three-strikes defendant who received a life sentence for possession of PCP, over the dissents of Justices Brown, Kennard and Werdegar protesting prosecutorial misconduct in the case.[13] As he was throughout his judicial career, Justice Mosk was somewhat unpredictable to the end, and capable of delivering surprises.

His final published work was not a Supreme Court opinion, however. His by-line appeared in the June 11, 2001, issue of *Sports Illustrated* magazine, under the title "My Shot: The Tour's fear of carts is the same form of bigotry that caused the Caucasian-only clause." The article recounted his role in pressing for full integration of the PGA on behalf of Charlie Sifford.

In March of 2000, the San Francisco Giants began the baseball season in a brand new stadium, overlooking San Francisco Bay at the foot of the Oakland-Bay Bridge. Later that year, Richard secured tickets to take his 88-year-old father to see the Giants play in the new stadium. No one ever kept count of how many baseball games Stanley Mosk watched during his lifetime, but it probably exceeded the number of majority opinions he authored. Surely, as he enjoyed the afternoon sunshine and the thrill of the game, he remembered playing first base at Rockford High School and the University of Chicago. In reflecting on his love affair with sports, Mosk wrote:

> From my early childhood days, as a collector of baseball cards, to this very day, I have been a hero worshipper of athletes and a fanatical fan of sports events. Knowing Gene Washington, Sandy Koufax, Hank Greenberg, Archie Moore, Willie Mays has been more important than knowing most public officials. I am not sure I can explain this phenomenon, for at least superficially, I consider myself more cerebral than macho.[14]

During the last few years of Justice Mosk's life, his daughter-in-law Sandy Mosk observed that he had a sense he was aging and that life was becoming more difficult. He didn't express any anger about it, he rarely expressed anger about anything, but he "got quieter," as if he felt things were more of a struggle for him.

At the age of 88, Stanley Mosk was still driving a car. He shouldn't have been. One crisp morning in January of 2001, he lost control of his state-issued Ford Taurus while parking in the underground garage of the Supreme Court headquarters in San Francisco. He plowed into the side of a brand new Infiniti owned by Ron Overholt, then Deputy Director of the Administrative Office of the Courts. Overholt recalls being called out of a Judicial Council meeting by a CHP officer who informed him there was a problem with his car. He replied, "But it's right downstairs in the garage." When informed that Justice Mosk had collided with his car, his first concern was for Justice Mosk. Assured that Mosk was not injured, he asked the extent of damage to his car. "It's not good," he was told. His car was not drivable. Justice Mosk was greatly embarrassed by the incident, but never apologized to Overholt. That was the last time he drove a car. Stanley's son Richard asked Chief Justice George to take the car away. Arrangements were quickly made to provide a driver to transport Justice Mosk between his apartment and the courthouse.

Mosk still met on an occasional basis for lunch with his former wife Susan. Sometime during the late part of May or early June of 2001, Susan and Stanley had lunch. He started to cry when he told her that in two weeks he was going to resign from the court. Susan said, "There is nothing you love more than the court — and you're going to give it up? What are you going to do with yourself?" He simply said, "I've done it, and that's what I'm going to do." He showed her the resignation letter he had in his pocket and she cried as she read it.

Justice Mosk's son Richard had applied for appointment to the California Court of Appeal, and Mosk was anxious to see Richard's appointment before he retired. He contacted Governor Gray Davis to speed the process along, but Richard Mosk's appointment as a Justice of the Court of Appeal was not completed until after his father's death.

On Monday, June 18, 2001 Justice Mosk put in a full day at his Supreme Court chambers. His driver delivered him to his Nob Hill condo. When he walked through the door, he kissed Kaygey on the cheek and said he was going to lie down for a few minutes before dinner. As she walked with him down the hallway, she asked him if was feeling all right. "Yes, yes, dear," he replied with the same words he had used to reassure her so many times before. She watched him walk down the hall with a feeling of dread streaming through her body. He usually came home with so much energy, more than for a man half his age. She prepared for their usual evening cocktail before stepping out to one of their favorite restaurants. Kaygey removed her apron and lit the candles on the counter. She walked down the hall toward the bedroom. She sat down on the bed next to her husband, and when he did not stir, she realized he was gone. She realized she had probably felt him fading away when he kissed her on the cheek. She held him tightly, as if trying to reverse the last moments in time, and she cried deep, mournful tears. She truly loved Stanley Mosk.

When she noticed something sticking out of his shirt pocket, she opened the folded paper and read the letter of resignation and his expression of gratitude to the people of California for giving him the opportunity to serve. He had intended to personally deliver it to the governor on the morning of the following day.

Epilogue

We began this book by suggesting that the life of Justice Stanley Mosk has much to teach us about politics and justice in America. It is appropriate to end it by reflecting upon the interplay of political experience and legal acumen in the career of a judge. In testimony before the United States Senate Judiciary Committee, before his confirmation as Chief Justice of the United States, John Roberts said, "Judges are not politicians who can promise to do certain things in exchange for votes." Rather, he said, "judges are like umpires. Umpires don't make the rules; they apply them."[1] Chief Justice Roberts not only greatly oversimplified the role of judges in our system; he oversimplified the role of politicians. The vision of a politician merely as someone "who can promise to do certain things in exchange for votes" can be contrasted with the Merriam Webster definition of politician as "a person experienced in the art or science of government; especially one actively engaged in conducting the business of a government." A broader view of the skills of politicians has produced a chorus of recent comment suggesting that a "politician" is precisely what the United States Supreme Court needs right now. As Professor Gordon Silverstein of the University of California, Berkeley, put it:

> While the instinct in choosing a justice for the highest court in the land is to find the most qualified judge or legal scholar, there is a powerful case to be made that the court very much needs an experienced elected official among its ranks. Someone with the appropriate legal experience who also has faced voters and listened to constituents, someone who has rounded up votes to pass legislation and has actually implemented policy, would bring to the bench an intimate knowledge and understanding of the American political system, its institutions, and how they actually work, on the ground, in the 21st century.[2]

In joining this chorus, *New York Times* columnist Linda Greenhouse, an astute observer of the United States Supreme Court, looked to the example of the late Judge Frank M. Coffin of the United States Court of Appeals for the First Circuit, whose career closely paralleled that of Justice Mosk:

> When President Lyndon B. Johnson, at the urging of Senator Edmund S. Muskie of Maine, named Frank Coffin to the First Circuit in 1965, he chose a World War II veteran, a Harvard Law School graduate — and a politician. The nominee was a former state Democratic Party chairman who had played a strong role in breaking a century of Republican domination of Maine's state government and who had served two terms in the House of Representatives before running unsuccessfully for governor.[3]

Greenhouse noted how Judge Coffin's political experience influenced his pragmatic approach to the task of judging. Skeptical of overarching theories of jurisprudence, Judge Coffin believed that even federal judges, with lifetime tenure, remain accountable to the public and are constantly obliged to demonstrate the legitimacy of the judicial enterprise. The same could certainly be said of Justice Stanley Mosk.

Another frequently cited example of the successful politician as successful judge is Earl Warren, three-time governor of California, who had never been a judge before his appointment as Chief Justice of the United States by President Dwight D. Eisenhower. Warren used his political skills to forge unanimous agreement to the Court's revolutionary ruling in *Brown v. Board of Education*, ending segregation in the nation's public schools.

We should not confine our search for examples of successful politician-judges to the federal courts, however. The 326 other men and women in the United States who bear the title of "Justice" of a Supreme Court will offer many examples. Each of our fifty state constitutions places a "Supreme Court" at the top of its judicial pyramid.[4] Those who serve as Justices on these courts deliver the final word for most questions of law. Their decisions can be reviewed by the U.S. Supreme Court only when questions arise under the federal constitution. The U.S. Supreme Court reviews only a handful of State Supreme Court decisions each term.

Justice Mosk was fully cognizant of the significant role Supreme Court Justices play in *making* law, but found that to be a normal consequence of the nature of the judicial function:

> It has been said that judges are rulers, albeit rulers in a different sense than legislators or officials of the executive branch, but rulers nevertheless. When called upon to resolve disputes between individual litigants, or between litigants and the government, judges render decisions that often affect the basic economic, social and political order of the nation or of a state. Thus, in the very nature of settling controversies, superficially an inocuous task, judges play a significant role in shaping broad public policy.[5]

Relatively few of the Justices of state supreme courts ever become known beyond the borders of their states. Some achieve fame by elevation to service on the U.S. Supreme Court, although recent presidents have rarely looked beyond the federal appellate courts in making appointments to the highest court. In the past half-century, only Justices William Brennan and David Souter had previously served on a state supreme court. In the earlier history of the Court, many of its greatest Justices were elevated after service on the highest courts of their state: Oliver Wendell Holmes, Jr., and Benjamin Cardozo come immediately to mind. Because the average tenure of a state supreme court Justice is less than ten years, and most states have a mandatory retirement age of 70, few state court Justices have the opportunity for national reputation that lengthy service affords. Still, these positions are eagerly sought and often bitterly contested. In twenty-eight states, including California, there are only seven Justices on the state supreme court. Only five states have as many as nine Justices, like the U.S. Supreme Court.[6] Another seventeen states limit their highest court to five Justices. These are positions of great prestige, at least within the ranks of the legal profession. Justices are feted and fawned over, and their judicial opinions are widely quoted. They are also positions of awesome power, not diluted by the double digits required for legislative majorities. On appellate courts, judges must often become advocates themselves, seeking to persuade each other. Judge Frank Coffin aptly described the collegiality of an appellate bench:

> In applying the term collegial to an appellate court, we are using it with maximum precision, for the judges on such a court are a small and intimate band of brothers and sisters.... Collegiality has several faces. One is intimacy. But it is intimacy beyond affection. It begins with a deep if selective knowledge of one another; no one knows our societal values, biases and thought ways better than a colleague, even though he may never master the names of our children. It is fed from the spring of our common enterprise. It manifests itself in an abiding

concern for each other and the court, with the ardent hope that there need never be a choice between the two. If there were, however, the latter would prevail, not despite intimacy but because of it.[7]

From this vantage point, we can find in the model of Justice Stanley Mosk some answers for three questions that every modern judge must face.

First, how does a judge reconcile his personal, moral views with his oath to "follow the law"? Stanley Mosk was a life-long opponent of capital punishment, and on several occasions, he urged the California legislature to abolish it. Yet as a trial judge he was called upon to impose a sentence of death, as Attorney General he was in charge of enforcing the death penalty law, and as a supreme court Justice he rendered life or death decisions in hundreds of cases, and frequently voted to uphold death sentences. The history of California's dysfunctional death penalty law is inextricably intertwined with the long career of judge, then Attorney General, and then Justice Stanley Mosk. When offering his personal opinions, he was quite critical of the U.S. Supreme Court opinions he had to follow. He thought one such opinion was "indefensible," and another was "incomprehensible." Ultimately, he concluded that punishment is a matter of legislative judgment, and any effort to limit or eliminate the death penalty must have the support of public opinion. "If abolition of the death penalty is to occur it must be by virtue of a current movement based on current ideals."[8]

Although he twice concurred in California Supreme Court rulings declaring California's death penalty law unconstitutional, and deeply admired the courage and scholarship of Chief Justice Donald Wright, who authored those opinions, Mosk also recognized that public opinion in reaction to those decisions was loud and spoke with "unmistakable clarity." Thus, he realized that his moral reservations about the death penalty must find expression in settings other than his judicial opinions. His willingness to express his views in those other settings was one mark of the courage of Justice Stanley Mosk. He found unpersuasive the arguments that we were in poor company among the other nations that utilized the death penalty. "The voting public sees the extreme penalty as a means of protecting society," he said. The task for opponents of the death penalty, as he saw it, was to persuade the public that the "protection" they perceived they were gaining was illusory. Ultimately, he thought, the public must become aware of how imperfect our system of justice is. For him the serious moral query was "whether a civilized society should proceed with executions when it has only *imperfect* procedures for determining which of its members it will deliberately put to death." He upheld numerous judgments of death when he concluded that the law had been followed, but whenever he was asked if California should have a death penalty law, Justice Mosk consistently said no.

Second, what does it mean to "follow the law"? For Stanley Mosk, the first question was always "where is the law going?" Following the law occasionally requires acute sensitivity to where change is occurring, and how quickly it is progressing. Some call this a "political sense," but whatever we may call it, Stanley Mosk had it. When he went out on a limb, and ruled in a way that could not be reconciled with precedent, he was very careful to assess the strength of that precedent in terms of the shifting groundswells of judicial thought and popular support. In this sense, Mosk was fundamentally a pragmatist. He instinctively knew how far the envelope could be pushed. Most often, he was vindicated. His refusal as a trial judge to enforce racially restrictive covenants in property deeds anticipated a similar decision by the U.S. Supreme Court one year later. His ruling that lawyers could not use peremptory challenges to eliminate minority jurors came several years before a similar ruling by the U.S. Supreme Court. His ruling that university "affirmative action" programs could not use numerical quotas to deny admission to otherwise qualified applicants was affirmed by the U.S. Supreme Court a year later, and adopted as an amendment to the California constitution twenty years later. Occasionally, he pushed the envelope too far, beyond what the voting public was willing to accept. His interpretations of the California constitution to give broader protection to expectations of privacy against governmental intrusions than required by the U.S. Constitution were rejected by the voters in a popular initiative.

If pushing the envelope makes one an "activist" judge, then Mosk clearly fit the label. Mosk was not an apostle of "judicial restraint," if that concept means judges should never disturb the status quo or challenge the conventional wisdom. In this regard, Mosk's role model was Earl Warren, whom he counted as a friend although, when he began his career, he was a political enemy. Mosk admired the "personal courage, progressive conviction, and human understanding" demonstrated by Warren's judicial career, and praised his "vision for American democracy."[9] He thought the "deliberate speed" with which *Brown v. Board of Education* was implemented was, however, "much too slow." His admiration for Warren was reciprocated. When Warren retired as Chief Justice of the U.S. Supreme Court, one of the three persons he recommended to President Lyndon Johnson as potential replacements was Justice Stanley Mosk.[10]

Third, what should a judge do when he or she sees the law heading in the wrong direction? For Justice Mosk, the moral imperative to dissent was just as strong as the moral imperative to follow the law. On this point, he quoted Justice Sutherland of the U.S. Supreme Court, who said the oath which a judge takes "is not a composite oath, but an individual one.... He cannot subordinate his convictions and keep faith with his oath and retain his judicial and moral independence."[11] Justice Mosk sharply distinguished majority opinions, a "watered down consensus," from the more personal dissents:

> The writer of a dissent has no one to please but his own conscience. He may wax eloquent, resort to hyperbole, predict dire results when the majority view prevails, and at the same time try to affect the future of the law. I must confess it is often much more personally rewarding to write a dissent than a consensus majority opinion.[12]

Justice Mosk personally wrote all of his dissenting opinions, rather than relying upon his staff. Thus, these opinions reveal more unadulterated Mosk than any other source available to us. Fortunately, there are a lot of them. Justice Mosk authored 507 dissenting opinions, as well as 741 majority opinions and 290 concurring opinions.

One might argue that political ambition is the bane of judicial impartiality. In the case of Justice Stanley Mosk, one is left with the impression that his political ambition occasionally intruded, and affected his conduct as a judge. He certainly became a more courageous and independent jurist when he finally put his political ambitions aside, manifested by his liquidation of his trust fund of campaign contributions. His ambition to become Chief Justice clearly affected his relationship with Chief Justice Bird, whom, as he saw it, took "his" place. But ambition is often the defining element that leads to a judge's appointment in the first place, and judges, like everyone else in life, often strive to be promoted to more exalted positions. The practice of electing judges in most states means that a judge's rulings will likely impact their prospects for confirmation or reelection, as much as they try to ignore that fact of life. Thus, ambition is a peril for every judge, whether he or she is a politician or not. Every judge must struggle with the demon of personal ambition, and for many, the ultimate test comes when their conscience calls for a decision that will not be popular. For Stanley Mosk, that point recurred several times in his career. On each occasion, he met the challenge that judicial independence poses, and put his personal ambitions aside.

Chapter Notes

Introduction

1. *Brosnahan v. Brown*, 32 Cal.3d 236, 299 (1982).
2. Dan Morain, "Interview of Justice Stanley Mosk," *Los Angeles Times*, January 26, 1986.
3. Grodin, Tribute to Mosk, 26 Cal.4th at 1250.

Chapter 1

1. Hertzmark traced to 1795; Genealogy sent to Stanley Mosk; Mosk Papers, California Judicial Library, San Francisco (hereafter CJLSF); Hertzmark may be related to Hartzmark, which according to family legend came from a Jewish scribe facing anti–Semitic persecution who affixed his signature with the image of a heart and thus became known as "heart" "mark." Harriet Perl interview by Braitman, October 16, 2003 (hereafter Perl int.).
2. "Remembering David Perl" (hereafter *Remembering*) unpublished family account written by Minna Mosk and sister-in-law Esther Perl. In Personal, Mosk Family History, Mosk Papers; CJLSF, p. 1.
3. Perl int.
4. Catherine the Great created a "Pale of Settlement" in Russia in 1791; a western border region of the country in which Jews were allowed to live. The motivation behind this was to restrict trade between Jews and native Russians. Some Jews were allowed to live, as a concession, beyond the pale.
5. *Remembering*, p. 2.
6. Livonia remained within the Russian Empire until the end of World War I, when it was split between the newly independent states of Latvia and Estonia. In 1918–1920, both Soviet troops and German Freikorps fought against Latvian and Estonian troops for control over Livonia, but their attempts were defeated. In independent Latvia between the World Wars, southern Livonia became an administrative region under the traditional Latvian name Vidzeme, encompassing the then much larger counties of Riga, Cēsis, Valmiera, and Valka. (Wikipedia).
7. David, the youngest, was born July 1, 1891.
8. *Remembering*, 2.
9. Ibid., 4–6.
10. Perl int.
11. Samuel Mosk managed Glasgow Woolen Mills, and Paul ran the 933 [sic] 15th Street "Scotch Plaid Tailors." 1907 Ballenger & Richards Denver City Directory; Western History/Genealogy Dept. Denver Public Library, Denver, CO.
12. *Remembering*, pp. 5–10; contrary to Mosk's recollections in the Levy-Bakken interview, n. 15, *infra*, p. 175, he did not leave San Antonio "as a precocious child" but moved to Rockford.
13. *The Galveston Daily News*, December, 1914 (Mosk Scrapbook, CJLSF).
14. *Remembering*, p. 10.
15. Margaret Levy and Gordon Bakken, interview with Justice Mosk, CSCHS Yearbook, 1996–97, vol. 3 (hereafter Levy-Bakken); p. 182.
16. "Looking Back at the Flu Pandemic of 1918," posted online April 28, 2009 by Pat Cunningham.
17. Carol R. Byerly, Ph.D., "The U.S. Military and the Influenza Pandemic of 1918–1919," *Public Health Rep.* 125 (Suppl 3) 2010: 82–91.
18. Ibid.
19. "Looking Back at the Flu Pandemic of 1918" by Pat Cunningham; Carol R. Byerly, Ph.D., "The U.S. Military and the Influenza Pandemic of 1918–1919," *Public Health Rep.* 125 (Suppl 3) 2010: 82–91.
20. Levy-Baken, p. 184.
21. Ibid.
22. Letter from Morey S. Mosk to Ed Mosk, 1944 (on file with Richard Mosk).
23. Perl int.
24. June 1, 1930, Temple Beth El Religious School Confirmation Exercises, Rockford, Illinois. Scrapbook to Edward Mosk from Mother and Father, 1932; Sixth Commencement, May 20, 1932. Courtesy of Edward's son, Tom Mosk.
25. Levy-Bakken, 184.
26. Perl int.
27. Perl int.
28. Mosk's classmates included at least one other youngster destined to become a giant of American law. J. Willard Hurst was a graduate in the class of 1928, one year ahead of Stanley Mosk. After Hurst graduated from Harvard Law School, where he was Professor Felix Frankfurter's research assistant, he clerked for Justice Louis Brandeis on the U.S. Supreme Court. During his years as a professor of law at the University of Wisconsin Law School, Hurst's scholarship laid the foundations for the study of modern American legal history. Quentin "Bud" Ogren, the Alderman's son, was a freshman during Stanley Mosk's senior year. He later became a Professor of Constitutional Law at Loyola Law School in Los Angeles.
29. August 20, 1927; Rockford Website.
30. June 1929 *The Owl*, Rockford High School newspaper. (Mosk Scrapbook, CJLSF).

Chapter 2

1. Steinberg, "How Jewish Quotas Began," *Commentary*, September, 1971.
2. Breitman and Kraut, *American Refugee Policy and*

European Jewry, 1933–1945 (Bloomington: Indiana University Press, 1987), p. 88.
  3. Jerome Karabel, *The Chosen: The Hidden History of Admission and Exclusion at Harvard, Yale and Princeton* (Boston: Houghton-Mifflin, 2005).
  4. Erik Larson, *In the Garden of the Beasts* (New York: Crown Publishers, 2011), p. 41.
  5. Ibid., at pp. 38–39.
  6. Margaret Levy and Gordon Bakken, interview with Justice Mosk, CSCHS Yearbook, 1996–97, vol. 3 (hereafter Levy-Bakken).
  7. *The Deltan, The Phi Sigma Delta Quarterly*, March 1932, Vol. XI, No. 1. CFJLSF.
  8. Ibid.
  9. Ibid.
  10. Morey Mosk, *Phoenix*, March 1933, p. 15, and April 1933, p. 8. CJLSF.
  11. The FBI tracking Mosk's life, listed Mosk's educational background on October 8, 1965 as follows: "University of Chicago, Ill.-Autumn 1929 to Autumn 1930; University of Texas-February 1931 to June 1931; Re-enters University of Chicago-August 1931 to June 1932, when he transfers to law school."
  12. Talk scheduled for May 23, 1929; *Southtown Economist* April 19, 1929. NewspaperArchives.com
  13. James L. Zacharias, Ph.D. '33, JD '35, a retired businessman and legal activist, died October 29, 1999, in Winnetka, Illinois, at age 87. After practicing law for three years, Zacharias entered the plastics industry, served in the Army, and then joined his brother as a partner in Precision Plating Company. He retired in 1989. Zacharias was a member of the board of directors, executive committee, and advisory council of the ACLU and in 1999 was awarded the group's Roger Baldwin Award for longtime commitment to civil liberties. Zacharias also helped to develop the Dove Bar ice-cream bar. Survivors included his wife, Bobette; two daughters; a son; and a grandchild.
  14. *Remembering*, p. 31.
  15. Apparently, the town never recovered; by 1981 it led the nation in unemployment at 11 percent. Congressional testimony, 2004.
  16. James E. Blue, "To Whom It May Concern," December 1, 1930; Scrapbook to Edward Mosk from Mother and Father, 1932. Courtesy of Edward's son, Tom Mosk.
  17. Scrapbook to Edward Mosk from Mother and Father, 1932; Sixth Commencement, May 20, 1932. Courtesy of Edward's son, Tom Mosk.
  18. Perl int.
  19. In 1935, among the members of the Board of Trustees of UCLA's Council of Jewish Students were Mendel Siberberg, Rabbi E. Magnin, and Marco Newmark.
  20. Two provocative entries in Edwards 1935–36 datebook list on one page: Manchester Boddy, Stephen O' Donnell, Rockey, G. Johnson, and Taft with ACLU next to Taft. The very next page has a list with the following names: Irwin Shaw, Samuel Orditz, Paul Muni, Edward G. Robinson, Rabbi Weinstein, New Provost, Lewis Brown, Rabbi Magnin, Walter Cohn, Dr. Lubonov, Irving Pichel, Jed John, Irving Stone, Pete Lorrie, Carey McWilliams, Louise Ranier, Mae Robson. Examples: Western Jewish Institute, June 14, 1936; Vodvil Nite and Dance, Jewish Council House, December 1, 1935. Scrapbook to Edward Mosk from Mother and Father, 1932. Courtesy of Edward's son, Tom Mosk.
  21. Greg Mitchell, *The Campaign of the Century* (1992).
  22. Kevin Starr, *Endangered Dreams: The Great Depression In California* (1996), p. 149.
  23. Perl. Int.
  24. Kidder, "The Bar Exam and the Dream Deferred," *Law & Social Inquiry* 29 (2004): 547, 556.
  25. Levy and Bakken interview, *supra* n.6; Remarks of Seth Hufstedler, 21 Cal. 45h at 1329; and recounted in many places.

Chapter 3

  1. Women made up 90 percent of the domestic labor force in 1940 and two-thirds of all employed black women were in domestic service. Social security exclusions exempted nearly half the working population; nearly two-thirds of all African Americans in the labor force, and just over half of all women employed were not covered by Social Security.
  2. Carey McWilliams, *Factories in the Field*, reissued by Peregrine Smith in 1971, p. 146.
  3. Ibid.
  4. Max Vorspan and Lloyd P. Gartner, *History of the Jews of Los Angeles* (Philadelphia: Jewish Publication Society of America, 1970), p. 200.
  5. The preamble of the ML constitution, October 10, 1901; *MLBulletin*, 1912; Article II, July 3, 1930; Esther Van Vleet Story, *The LAML*, undated, Fletcher Bowron Papers, Box 56, Huntington Library, pp. 1–5.
  6. Tom Sitton, *The Haynes Foundation and Urban Reform Philanthropy in Los Angeles* (Los Angeles: Historical Society of Southern California, 1999), p. 29.
  7. During its early days, the primary mover in the Municipal League was Dr. John Randolph Haynes, who, as a commissioner on the Department of Water and Power had worked closely with Shaw. Over time, however, it was common knowledge that the Shaw brothers made the Department of Water and Power a "spawning ground for their patronage." Haynes' support of Shaw, in fact, is alleged to have been instrumental in aiding Shaw's narrow victories in both 1933 and 1937 primaries. Tom Sitton, *John Randolph Haynes, California Progressive* (Stanford, CA: Stanford University Press, 1992) at 243. Sitton says that the change in attitude toward the Mayor by the Municipal League corresponded to a transformation in its leadership. The moderate-to-liberal composition of the executive board in the 1920's and early 1930's began to change in the mid-1930's, as more leftists joined the League and rose to leadership positions within it. The leftists were welcomed because of dwindling membership and finances, out of which arose conflicts in the 1940's brought on by the leftist direction which destroyed the organization. Ibid. at 144.
  8. Vorspan and Gartner, *History of the Jews of Los Angeles*, p. 200.
  9. Jerry Saul Caplan, "The CIVIC Committee in the Recall of Mayor Frank Shaw," master's thesis, UCLA, June 1947, p. 102.
  10. Walker, p. 95; Judy Kutulus "Pretty Darn Chic: The ACLU in the 1930's," *Mid-America* vol. 83, no. 3 (Fall 2001) on early ACLU and communist connections which give rise to later vulnerability of Mosk and ACLU members.
  11. McWilliams, *supra* n.2 at 272–3.
  12. Dwight F. McKinney and Fred Allhoff, "The Lid Off Los Angeles" Part I *Liberty Magazine* Sept. 1, 1939, Clifford Clinton Papers, YRL, UCLA.
  13. *Municipal League Bulletin*, June 1938, p. 3. (Mosk Scrapbook, CJLSF).

14. Morey Stanley Mosk, LSCIR Secretary, "League Sifts Alleged Discrimination by Local Government in Labor Disputes," Sept. 1937 *Municipal League Bulletin*, pp. 5–6. (Mosk Scrapbook, CJLSF). Reuben W. Borough Papers (Collection 927). Department of Special Collections, Charles E. Young Research Library, University of California, Los Angeles.
15. ACLU Open Forum, 1938 (Mosk Scrapbook, CJLSF).
16. Ibid.
17. Municipal League Stationery, Aug. 1937, Box 69IV Relations, 3. State Relations, K. Municipal League; in JAF; Huntington Library.
18. Olson, p. 5; October 1937.
19. October 17, 1937, *Fresno Bee* (Mosk Scrapbook, CJLSF).
20. John Anson Ford Papers, May and June, 1938, *Municipal League Bulletin*.
21. October 22, 1937, *The Industrial Unionist; The Los Angeles Evening News*, n.d.; *The Herald and Express*, n.d.; October 25, 1937, *The Evening Herald and Express*; Rally set for November 1, 1937; Ibid.(Mosk Scrapbook, CJLSF).
22. Sitton, *supra* n.6 at. 165.
23. George Creel, "Unholy City," *Collier's*, Sept. 1939, p.12.
24. June 1938, *Light* (Mosk Scrapbook 1928–1944; CJLSF).
25. Coates; McKinney and Allhoff, *supra* n.12 at 60.
26. Noble has been described as "one of the most interesting and unprincipled men in California public life," who used one reform movement or racket after another to enrich himself with the organizational dues of his followers." Shuler, on the other hand, was an opponent of Catholics, Jews, blacks, liberals, and alcohol, as well as the theory of evolution. He praised the KKK and private ownership of utilities. His growing influence from radio and monthly publications aided his promotion of John C. Porter against Mayor Cryer. In early 1934, Shuler started the Citizens Recall Committee initiating an aborted recall movement against Mayor Shaw. Sitton, *Urban Politics*, pp. 127–8, 275–8.
27. Ibid.
28. Wed. May 25, Fountain Ave. 15 cents; *Hollywood Now*, May 20, 1938. (Mosk Scrapbook, CJLSF).
29. "Anger at L.A. Times..." *Open Forum*, vol. XV No. 6 (1938). Huntington Library.
30. Office of Morey Stanley Mosk at 541 South Spring Street. In file: Committee of 25 of the Federation for Civic Betterment; Clifford E. Clinton Papers (Collection 2018). Department of Special Collections, Charles E. Young Research Library, University of California, Los Angeles; *Municipal League Bulletin*, Feb.-Dec. 1938, John Anson Ford Papers, Huntington Library.
31. *Open Forum*, Vol. XV, No. 7 (1938), p. 1; Huntington Library.
32. Caplan, *supra* n.9 at 81; *Open Forum*, Vol. XV, No. 7 (1938), p. 1; Huntington Library.
33. *Los Angeles Daily News*, March 28, 1938. Louise Ward Watkins Collection, Huntington Library.
34. Ibid., March 29, 1938, and April 6, 1938.
35. Caplan, *supra* n.9 at 113; Roper Poll, May 18, 1938; *L.A. Examiner* May 19, 1938, p. 4, pt. 1.
36. Federation for Civic Betterment minutes, June 13, 1938. Clifford E. Clinton Papers (Collection 2018). Department of Special Collections, Charles E. Young Research Library, University of California, Los Angeles.
37. Caplan, *supra* n.9 at 116.
38. *Hollywood Clipper*, April 28, 1938, p. 1; Clifford Clinton papers, Special Collections, YRL, UCLA.

39. Federation for Civic Betterment minutes, May 25, 1938. Clifford E. Clinton Papers (Collection 2018). Department of Special Collections, Charles E. Young Research Library, University of California, Los Angeles.
40. February 26, 1938 *Open Forum* vol. Xv. No. 9 states that Fred A. Brown and Roy J. Allen were indicted along with Kynette. It is assumed that it is Roy Allen who was convicted, but the subsequent fate of Fred A. Brown is not clear; see also McKinney and Allhoff, *supra* n.12 at 60.
41. June 25, 1938 *Open Forum* vol. Xv, no. 26.
42. July 2, 1938 *Open Forum* vol. 27.
43. Caplan, *supra* n.9 at 85.
44. June 29, 1938; Interviews with signatories indicated that 30 percent had signed up before the convictions and 75 percent after the announcement. Caplan, *supra* n.9 at 85 and from July 6, 1938, Federation for Civic Betterment minutes.
45. Mosk also seconded a motion to bring before the next mass meeting in July, "the matter of changing the city charter to pattern that of the county," July 21, 1938. FCB Minutes, Clifford Clinton Papers, YRL, and Caplan, *supra* n.9 at 86.
46. On July 21, the FCB count showed 65,119 certified out of 108,046, only a 607 difference with the city clerk's office. Federation for Civic Betterment minutes, June 27, 1938. Clifford Clinton Papers, YRL.
47. Sitton, *Urban Politics*, pp. 196–7 footnote.
48. Caplan, *supra* n.9 at 88–91
49. Ibid., 91–2.
50. The Workers' Alliance was the leading organization of the unemployed in this period. It fought vigorously in behalf of its membership, including issues involving relief payments and relief workers as strikebreakers. It is described as militantly left wing, but it had 120 locals by 1938, and 186 the following year. There were 12,000 paid-up members and 42,000 members in all. Robert Burke, *Olson's New Deal for California*, p. 83 (1953); Sitton, *Urban Politics*, 198.
51. John Constantinus Bollens and Grant B. Geyer, *Yorty, Politics of a Constant Candidate* (1973), p. 22.
52. Unnamed newspaper clipping "United Drive to Elect Judge Bowron; L.A. Reform Groups Bury the Hatchet to Defeat Shaw" Aug. 10, 1938; Culbert Olson Papers, Box 7, CB442, Bancroft Library.
53. *People's World*, August 9, 1938.
54. August 12, "United Drive to Elect Judge Bowron; L.A. Reform Groups Bury the Hatchet to Defeat Shaw" Aug. 10(?) 1938; Culbert Olson Papers, Box 7; Bancroft Library.
55. Ibid.; *People's World*, Aug. 10, 1938.
56. Yorty went on to a noteworthy, but even by California standards, controversial career. After losing two campaigns for the U.S. Senate running as a Democrat, in 1960 he endorsed Richard Nixon over John F. Kennedy for president, and in 1961 ran for mayor of Los Angeles as an independent populist. He defeated incumbent mayor Norris Poulson, and was reelected in 1965, defeating James Roosevelt. He challenged Governor Pat Brown in the Democratic primary in 1966, then joined in congratulating Ronald Reagan for defeating Brown in the general election. He was reelected to a third term as mayor in 1969, defeating city councilman Tom Bradley. In a rematch four years later, Bradley prevailed. John Constantinus Bollens and Grant B. Geyer, *Yorty, Politics of a Constant Candidate*, p. 22.
57. 52 percent of city's voters with 232,000 Bowron, 122,000 for Shaw, *Los Angeles Times*; Dorothy Healey reports 233,427 for Bowron and 122,692 for Shaw with

only 46.6 percent going to the polls; Dorothy Healey and Maurice Isserman, *Dorothy Healey Remembers, A Life in the American Communist Party* (Oxford: Oxford University Press, 1990), p. 67.

58. Letter from John Anson Ford to Walter R. Jones Nov. 19, 1938; Box 46, BIII 110 aa (5) JAF papers, Huntington Library; Sitton, *Urban Politics* at 217.

59. Sitton, *Urban Politics*, 201.

60. Letter from Stanley Mosk to Fletcher Bowron, Mosk Papers, CJLSF.

Chapter 4

1. Robert E. Burke, *Olson's New Deal For California* (Berkeley: University of California Press, 1953). Hereafter Burke.

2. Interview by Amelia Fry with Stanley Mosk, in "San Francisco, CA, California Constitutional Officers" (Mar. 1, 1979), available at http://ia700301.us.archive.org/22/items/caliconstitutoff00morrrich/caliconstitutoff00morrrich.pdf.

3. Interview by Carlos Vasquez with Augustus F. Hawkins, Member of the U.S. House of Representatives, in Los Angeles, CA, Online Archive California (Dec. 10, 1988).

4. Interview by Amelia Fry with Stanley Mosk, *supra* note 2.

5. August 26, 1938 *The Tribune-West Hollywood*, Mosk Scrapbook, CJLSF.

6. Burke, p. 30.

7. Interview by Doyce Blackman Nunis with Robert Walker Kenny, "My First Forty Years in California Politics, 1922–1962" (1963).

8. FDR supported McAdoo, a longtime friend. Their friendship went all the way back to the Woodrow Wilson administration, when McAdoo (married to one of Wilson's daughters) served as Secretary of the Treasury and FDR served as Assistant Secretary of the Navy.

9. *Los Angeles Times* December 11, 1938. ProQuest Historical Newspapers.

10. Kenneth C. Burt, "The Search for a Civic Voice: California Latino Politics—The Birth of California Latino Politics," *Goodreads* (June 15, 2008), www.goodreads.com/story/show/18912-the-search-for-a-civic-voice-california-latino-politics.

11. Max Vorspan and Lloyd P. Gartner, *History of the Jews In Los Angeles* (Philadelphia: Jewish Publication Society of America, 1970), 201

12. Burt, *supra* n.10.

13. Interview by Germaine LaBerge with Stanley Mosk, CA Supreme Court Justice, in San Francisco, CA, State Government Oral History Program (1998), available at http://www.sos.ca.gov/archives/oral-history/pdf/mosk.pdf.

14. *People v. Mooney* (1917) 176 Cal. 105.

15. *People v. Mooney* (1918) 177 Cal. 642.

16. *Mooney v. Holohan, Warden*, 294 U.S. 103 (1935).

17. *In the Matter of Application of Thomas Mooney for a Writ of Habeas Corpus,* 10 Cal.2d 1 (1937).

18. Burke, p. 55.

19. *Los Angeles Times*, p. 1, June 21, 1941.

20. Ethan Rarick, *The Life And Times Of Pat Brown: California Rising* (2005), p. 158.

21. "Olson Has Stirred 'Near Terror' in Orchard Area, Says Farm Leader," *Oakland Tribune*, July 26, 1939, at 4.

22. Burke, p. 109.

23. Burke, p. 145.

24. Paul Kengor and Patricia Clark Doerner, *The Judge: William P. Clark, Ronald Reagan's Top Hand* (San Francisco: Ignatius Press, 2007), 34–35.

25. *Carter v. Commission on Qualifications of Judicial Appointments et al.*, 14 Cal. 2d 179 (1939).

26. J. Edward Johnson, *History of the Supreme Court Justices of California*, Vol. 2 (1966), 161–169.

27. Interview by Amelia Fry with Stanley Mosk, *supra* note 2.

28. Jim Newton, *Justice for All: Earl Warren and the Nation He Made* (2006), 118.

29. Burke, pp. 123–126.

30. *Oral History Interview with John P. McEnery, Member of California State Democratic Central Committee, 1944–48; and Vice-Chairman, 1946–48 Monterey, California; March 11, 1970; James R. Fuchs* http://www.trumanlibrary.org/oralhist/mcenery1.htm.

31. Interview by Amelia Fry with Stanley Mosk, *supra* note 2.

32. Interview by Doyce Blackman Nunis with Robert Walker Kenny, *supra* note 7, pp. 134–35.

33. Morey Stanley Mosk, "The Road to Dictatorship," *American Mercury*, May, 1935, pp. 63–70.

34. Letter from Stanley Mosk, CA Supreme Court Justice, to Eugene Lyons, Editor, *American Mercury* (Apr. 2, 1941) (Olson Cabinet Correspondence) (on file with the California Judicial Center Library, Special Collections and Archives).

35. Ibid.

36. In 1945 Governor Earl Warren appointed Homer R. Spence to serve on the California Supreme Court. Spence had previously served for fifteen years on the Fifth District Court of Appeal. He retired from the California Supreme Court in 1960, and died in 1973.

37. *San Francisco News*, March 6, 1942.

38. Burke, p. 217.

39. Burke, p. 219

40. Stanley Mosk Collections, Mosk Letters (on file with the California Judicial Center Library, Special Collections and Archives).

41. *Marbury v. Madison*, 5 U.S 137 (1803).

42. Stanley Mosk Collections, Mosk Letters (on file with the California Judicial Center Library, Special Collections and Archives).

43. Interview by Germaine LaBerge with Stanley Mosk, CA Supreme Court Justice, in San Francisco, CA, State Government Oral History Program (1998), available at http://www.sos.ca.gov/archives/oral-history/pdf/mosk.pdf.

44. Ibid.

Chapter 5

1. *Long Beach Press Telegram*, Jan. 11, 1943.

2. Interview by Germaine LaBerge with Stanley Mosk, CA Supreme Court Justice, in San Francisco, CA, State Government Oral History Program (1998), available at http://www.sos.ca.gov/archives/oral-history/pdf/mosk.pdf.

3. *Eckman v. Arnold Taxi Company*, 64 Cal.App.2d 229 (1944).

4. Kaygey Kash Mosk interview with author Braitman.

5. Mosk Letter to Ed, July 4, 1944.

6. Mosk Letter to Ed, May 20, 1944.

7. Mosk Letter to Ed, June 30, 1944.

8. Flyer, International Workers Order (Nov. 11, 1944) (on file with UCLA Charles E. Young Research Library).

Notes — Chapter 5

9. John Anson Ford, John Anson Ford Papers Box 47 B.III e.bb (5) (March 1944) (on file with The Huntington Library).
10. The columns are collected in Mosk Scrapbook (on file with the California Judicial Center Library, Special Collections and Archives).
11. Letter from James P. McGranery, judge of the United States Dist. Court for the E. Dist. of Pa., to Stanley Mosk, CA Supreme Court Justice (Jan. 5, 1944) (on file with Richard Mosk).
12. "Veronica Gets Divorce," *The Pittsburgh Press*, Dec. 2, 1943.
13. L.A. *Daily News & Evening Herald*, May 12, 1944.
14. *Los Angeles Examiner*, June 8, 1944.
15. *L.A. Times*, June 3, 1944. Elaine Barrymore ruled to return panels; Benny Rubin, Comedian found in contempt for falling behind in child support payment (to ex-wife Mary O'Brian of silent screen).
16. *Berry v. Chaplin*, 74 Cal.App.2d 652 (1946).
17. Calif. Code Civ. Proc., § 1980.3, 1980.6.
18. Mosk Letter to Ed, Jan. 8, 1945.
19. Mosk Scrapbook, *supra*, n.10.
20. Ibid.
21. Eduardo Obregon Pagan, *Murder at the Sleepy Lagoon: Zoot Suits, Race, and Riot in Wartime L.A.* (2003).
22. Edward J. Escobar, *Race, Police, And The Making Of a Political Identity* (1999).
23. February 22, 1945 Box 72 IV 5 a dd (4) JAF papers, Huntington Library. See Shana Bernstein, *Bridges of Reform, Interracial Civil Rights Activism in Twentieth Century Los Angeles* (Oxford: Oxford University Press, 2011).
24. Stanley Mosk Collections, Mosk Scrapbook (on file with the California Judicial Center Library, Special Collections and Archives).
25. Ibid.
26. Among those who signed letters of support were Amerigo Bozzani, Susan Dorsey, Jerry Geisler, Lawrence Harvey, Jack L. Rau, William Mosley Jones, Mrs. Mattison Boyd Jones, Carey McWilliams, J. Edward Keating, Mrs. Ed. G. Robinson, Lawrence Larabee, Harry Braverman, John O'Melveny, Helen Melinkoff, Fay Allen; July 17, 1944, *L.A. Daily News* and *L.A. Times,* July 17, 1944. CJLSF.
27. Mosk Letters to Ed, July 20 and 24, 1944. Courtesy of Richard Mosk.
28. Letter from Jerry Giesler to Stanley Mosk, March 1, 1944. Courtesy of Richard Mosk.
29. Mosk Letter to Ed, July 30,1944. Richard Mosk collection.
30. Mosk Letter to Ed, July 31, 1944. Richard Mosk collection.
31. November 2, 1944, *L.A. Daily News*, CJLSF.
32. Nov. 3, 1944, *The Free Press*, Mosk Scrapbook.
33. May 22, 1944, Letter from Justice B. Rey Schauer to Stanley Mosk. Richard Mosk collection.
34. June 27, 1944, Letter from Carey McWilliams to Stanley Mosk. Richard Mosk collection.
35. Mosk Letter to Ed, Nov. 8, 1944. Courtesy of Richard Mosk.
36. February 20, 1948 *Evening Outlook*. 1948 Scrapbook Mosk Papers, CJLSF.
37. November 13, 1944, Letter from Justice B. Rey Schauer to Stanley Mosk. Richard Mosk collection.
38. Stanley Mosk, ASN39739440, George K. Hartwick, Agent, SIC, 9SC, from Department of Army, U.S. Army Intelligence, April 22, 1977 Privacy Act request; Richard Mosk.
39. Page 7, FBI Files. Richard Mosk Collection.
40. June 28, 1945 *The Nope News*, Mosk Scrapbook, CJLSF.
41. September 5, 1945, Letter from Phil Gibson to Stanley Mosk. Courtesy of Richard Mosk.
42. September 17, 1945, Letter from Ellis E. Patterson to Stanley Mosk. Courtesy of Richard Mosk.
43. September 19, 1945, *The Eastside Journal*, CSCLSF.
44. June 1945 "Of Home and Jobs," *Political Reporter*. CJLSF.
45. Ibid.
46. January 22, 1945, *Valley Jewish News*; February 26, 1945; *Santa Monica Outlook*, Mosk Papers, CJLSF.
47. Richard Mosk, Oral History, p. 7.
48. *Buchanan v. Warley*, 245 U.S. 60 (1917).
49. *Corrigan v. Buckley,* 271 U.S. 323 (1926).
50. *Los Angeles Investment Co. v. Gary*, 181 Cal. 680 (1919).
51. *W.B. Wayt v. Paytee*, 205 Cal. 46 (1928).
52. Rasmussen, "Dream Home Came With Racial Restrictions," *Los Angeles Times*, Nov. 11, 2007.
53. *Time*, Dec. 17, 1945.
54. December 4, 1947 *Los Angeles Sentinel*, Sec. 2, p. 1; JAF, Huntington Library. The same paper indicates Judge Thurmond Clarke had dismissed a suit in December, 1945 in the well-known Sugar Hill case and Attorney General Robert W. Kenny argued in a brief before the California Supreme Court the following year that state court enforcement of restrictive covenants would violate the 14th Amendment.
55. October 30, 1947, *Los Angeles Sentinel*. John Anson Ford Papers, Huntington Library.
56. *Los Angeles Sentinel*, December 4, 1947. John Anson Ford Papers, Huntington Library.
57. *Shelley v. Kramer,* 334 U.S. 1 (1948).
58. Unknown Labor or Progressive Paper, Mosk Scrapbook.
59. *Beck v. Bel Air Properties* 134 Cal.App.2d 834 (1955).
60. Warren Abner Seavey, Page Keeton, and Richard E. Keeton, *Cases and Materials on the Law of Torts* (St. Paul: West Pub. Co, 1964) p. 378.
61. Celebration Session Honoring the Record Service of Justice Stanley Mosk (1964-Present), 21 Cal. 4th 1316, 1320 (remarks of Richard Mosk) (Cal. 1999).
62. Mosk, unpublished book manuscript.
63. *Miranda v. Arizona,* 384 U.S. 436 (1966).
64. "Both Sides Rest in Crooker Trial: Surprise Witnesses, Including Victim's Mother, Rock Defense," *Los Angeles Times*, Dec. 7, 1955, at 4.
65. *People v. Crooker,* 48 Cal. 2d 348 (1956).
66. "Date Set for Crooker Execution," *Los Angeles Times*, Jan. 24, 1957, at 5.
67. Mosk unpublished book manuscript.
68. *People v. Crooker,* 48 Cal. 2d 348 (1956).
69. *Crooker v. California,* 357 U.S. 433 (1958).
70. Edmund (Pat) Brown with Dick Adler, *Public Justice, Private Mercy: A Governor's Education on Death Row* (1989), p. 13
71. Mosk unpublished book manuscript. Governor Pat Brown described a 1978 visit to his office by John Crooker: "Two more years passed, and then came that day in 1978 when John Crooker, the very first man who death sentence I'd commuted, came to my office in Beverly Hills for a visit. One of the things we talked about was Eddie Wein. 'I wish there was a way you could have asked me about him before you granted that second commutation,' Crooker told me. 'I would have warned you against it. The man was very sick, very dangerous,

Chapter 6

1. Marlene Adler Marks, *Jewish Journal*, October 30, 1997.
2. *Hollywood Press-Time*, Nov. 25, 1945, Mosk Scrapbook, CJLSF
3. *Hollywood Press-Time*, Nov. 28, 1945, Mosk Scrapbook, CJLSF.
4. *Eastside Journal*, Dec. 1, 1945, Mosk Scrapbook, CJLSF.
5. Interview with Fern Mosk by Braitman (2002).
6. June 25, 1948 *The California Jewish Voice*, Mosk Scrapbook, CJLSF.
7. Omaha Friendship Club, L.A. June 1948, Mosk Scrapbook, CJLSF.
8. Sept. 1948, *Wilshire Bulletin*, Mosk Scrapbook, CJLSF.
9. *The California Jewish Voice*, Mosk Scrapbook, CJLSF.
10. John Anson Ford, John Anson Ford Papers Box 72 B.IV 5 a dd (4) (August 1, 1944) (Letterhead of Los Angeles Committee on Palestine) (on file with The Huntington Library) (Hereafter JAF).
11. February 20, 1948, *Evening Outlook*. Mosk Scrapbook, CJLSF.
12. February 2, 1948, *The Record*; speaker at Hillel-Lites USC Hill; Mosk Scrapbook, CJLSF.
13. Feb. 1948, Mosk Scrapbook, CJLSF.
14. May 1948 *The National Jewish Monthly*, Mosk Scrapbook, CJLSF.
15. Letter from Stanley Mosk to Mr. Samuel R. Cohen, February 17, 1964 (on file, Carton 710, Brown Papers, Bancroft Library).
16. Wilson Carey McWilliams, introduction to Carey McWilliams, *A Mask For Privilege* (New Brunswick, NJ: Transaction Publishers, 1975), x–xi
17. Carey McWilliams, *A Mask For Privilege*, 117–118.
18. November 8, 1948 *Los Angeles Examiner*, Mosk Scrapbook, CJLSF.
19. Jan. 14, and Jan. 21, 1949, *The California Jewish Voice*, Mosk Scrapbook, CJLSF.
20. January 22, 1948 *Los Angeles Tribune*; January 15, 1949 *Mirror;* January 20, 1949 *California Eagle*; January 21, 1949 *B'nai B'rith Messenger*; JAF Papers, Huntington Library.
21. Memorandum to Board of Supervisors and County Counsel of L.A. County; JAF.
22. Published Chapter Newsletter Report, June 1948. JAF.
23. For Release September 7, 1949; JAF. (Material related to sequence of events found in letter from Armando Torres to JAF, Aug. 25, 1949; JAF.
24. Louis Sandy Maisel, Ira N. Forman & Donald Altschiller, *Jews in American Politics* (2001) 82
25. Dollinger has argued that Jewish political influence grew from that community's desire, "to secure the most elusive prize ... social, economic, and political inclusion in the larger Jewish community." He says that Jews used liberal politics to power their move from the margin to the mainstream of American life. Marc Dollinger, *Quest for Inclusion* (2000) 4–5.
26. November, 1946; Mosk Scrapbook, CJLSF.
27. Among its members were: Mary McLeod Bethune; Mrs. Marshall Field; Max Lerner; Frieda Kirchway; Dorothy Parker; Gifford Pinchot; Orson Wells; Charlotta Bass; Augustus Hawkins; Carey McWiliams; Lena Horne; Gene Kelly; Thomas Mann; Frederick March; Gregory Peck; Paul Robeson and E.G. Robinson. PCA Bound Volumes, 1947; Ed Mosk Box 2 of 3; Edward Mosk Papers, Southern California Library for Social Studies and Research. "MRS. EDNA MOSK" was listed on the ballot for Executive Board Members, but it was later denied she had any involvement. Possibly she was confused with Ed's wife, Fern, who is noted as attending a May 27, 1947 meeting. The ballot also listed the name of Paul Ziffren. Official Ballot # 1139, February 11, 1947.
28. October 3, 1947, Letter from Mildred B. Peck, Rec. Sec. PAC to John Anson Ford, Board of Supervisors; JAF Papers, Huntington Library
29. *Parker v. Los Angeles County*, 338 U.S. 327 (1949).
30. Richard Mosk, Oral History, pp. 7–8.

Chapter 7

1. ACLU Press Release, announced Oct. 2, to be held Nov. 8; Mosk Scrapbook, CJLSF.
2. February 4, 1948, Letter from James Roosevelt James to Stanley Mosk. Richard Mosk collection.
3. January 8, March 19, and July 27, 1948; Letters from James Roosevelt to Stanley Mosk. Richard Mosk collection.
4. FBI Files, page 10.
5. June 24, 1949, *Independent Review*, Mosk Scrapbook, CJLSF.
6. Greg Mitchell, *Tricky Dick and the Pink Lady* (1998).
7. California Government Code section 3100–3109 (2012).
8. Calif. Const. Art. XX, Sec. 3.
9. University Synagogue Modern Forum, Feb. 3, 1950, Mosk Scrapbook, CJLSF.
10. Media Villa, *The War On Books & Ideas*, 337.
11. *Pockman v. Leonard*, 39 Cal.2d 676 (1952).
12. *Vogel v. County of Los Angeles,* 68 Cal.2d 18 (1967). In that ruling, the Court upheld a decision invalidating the oath authored by Superior Court Judge Robert W. Kenny, the former attorney general who succeeded Earl Warren.
13. *Wolf. v. Colorado*, 338 U.S. 25 (1949).
14. *People v. Cahan*, 44 Cal.2d 434 (1955), superceded by Constitutional Amendment, Proposition 8 (Victims' Bill of Rights (1982).
15. "Coakley Attacks Evidence Ruling," *Oakland Tribune*, May 22, 1956.
16. Ibid.
17. *Long Beach Press-Telegram,* May 5, 1956; *The Independent*, Pasadena, CA July 13, 1956.
18. July 5, 1955, Letter from Phil E. Gibson to Stanley Mosk; Courtesy of Richard Mosk.
19. *The Independent*, Pasadena, CA July 13, 1956.
20. *Long Beach Press-Telegram,* June 2, 1955.
21. *Van Nuys News* March 4, 1956.
22. Stanley Mosk, Address to Town Hall, 1955, CJLSF
23. *The Independent*, Pasadena, CA June 28, 1956.
24. Joseph Carter, *The Quotable Will Rogers* (2005).
25. *Los Angeles Times*, p. 21, October 8, 1957, ProQuest Historical Newspapers.
26. *Los Angeles Times*, p. 26, October 31, 1957, ProQuest Historical Newspapers.
27. *Los Angeles Times*, p. B3, March 18, 1958, ProQuest Historical Newspapers.
28. *Ann Eliaser: From Grassroots Politics to the Top*

Dollar: Fundraising For Candidates and Non-Profit Agencies, pp. 67–8; 139. Interviewed by Malca Chall, 1983; Women in Politics Oral History Project, Regional Oral History Office (ROHO), Bancroft Library, UC Berkeley.

29. *Los Angeles Times*, p. B2, May 7, 1958, ProQuest Historical Newspapers.

30. Typed essay about Edna Mosk written by Stanley Mosk. CJLSF.

31. May 2, 1958, Letter from Culbert Olson to Stanley Mosk. Courtesy of Richard Mosk.

32. *Los Angeles Metropolitan News*, June 5, 1958. Courtesy of Richard Mosk.

33. "Mosk Accused of Ducking on Loyalty Oath," *Los Angeles Times*, October 26, 1958, p. 29.

34. "New Crime Board Expected as Sequel To Dope Inquiry," *Los Angeles Times*, June 18, 1958.

35. The poem by American poet Josiah Gilbert Holland (1819–1891) was written with Lincoln in mind. The same poem was recited by Senator Sam Ervin at the final news conference of the Senate Watergate Committee in 1974. It's interesting to note that Justice Carter, with uncharacteristic diplomacy, left out the final stanza of the poem: "For while the rabble, with their thumb-worn creeds, / Their large professions and their little deeds, / Mingle in selfish strife, Lo! Freedom weeps, / Wrong rules the land and Justice sleeps."

36. The Canons of Judicial Ethics have since been amended to forbid judges from appearing in robes in campaign literature.

37. *Los Angeles Times*, p. 2, November 10, 1958, ProQuest Historical Newspapers.

38. From G.A. Nease, November 2, 1958. FBI Files. CJLSF.

39. *Los Angeles Times*, p. 14, December 5, 1958, ProQuest Historical Newspapers.

40. Marlene Adler Marks, *Jewish Journal*, October 30, 1997.

41. David G. Dalin, "Jewish and Non-Partisan Republicanism in San Francisco, 1911–1963," *American Jewish History* 68 (1978): 492–495.

42. *Los Angeles Times*, p. 6, December 11, 1958, ProQuest Historical Newspapers.

43. November 25, 1958, FBI Files, page 4, 6. CJLSF.

44. *Los Angeles Times*, p. 17, December 23, 1958, ProQuest Historical Newspapers.

45. FBI Files. CJLSF.

46. Ibid.

Chapter 8

1. January 5, 1959; *Oxnard Press-Courier*, ProQuest Historical Newspapers.

2. Ibid.

3. Press Release March 26, 1959 from the Governor Edmund G. Brown (on file with Brown Papers, Bancroft Library).

4. FBI quoting *Los Angeles Mirror News*, August 12, 1959. Page 2, FBI Files, CJLSF.

5. August 17, 1959, Letter from W.C. Sullivan to A.H. Belmont, FBI files, CJLSF.

6. Cal. Bus & Prof. Code §12606 (2012).

7. John Burton, President Pro Tempore of the California Senate, Speaker at the Rededication of the Library and Courts Building as the Stanley Mosk Library and Courts Building (November 6, 2002).

8. Epstein to Uelmen, Sept. 29, 2009. See Attorney General Opinion 61-137, 39 Calif. Attorney General's Opinions 136 (1962).

9. In 1959, the Unruh Civil Rights Act was adopted, prohibiting racial or religious discrimination by any business enterprise operating in California.

10. "No Damages for Breaking Clauses; Att'y General Wants Restrictive Covenants Barred," *The Press Courier* February 3, 1961, Mosk Scrapbook, CJLSF.

11. August 13, 1961, *Los Angeles Times*.

12. *John H. Kennedy, a Course of Their Own: A History Of African American Golfers* (University of Nebraska Press, 2005). After turning professional at age 17 on the former United Golf Association Tour, Charlie Sifford won six Negro National Open titles, and served as golf instructor to singer Billy Eckstine. Sifford began his golf career as a caddie in Charlotte. For looping 18 holes Sifford got paid only 60 cents. "I'd give 50 cents to my mother, and then I'd go get me a cigar," Sifford told the *Charlotte Observer*. PGA Media Center, www.pga.com.

13. Charlie Sifford and Jim Gullo, *Just Let Me Play: The Story of Charlie Sifford, the First Black PGA Golfer* (1992), 91.

14. Nayan Shad, *Contagious Divides: Epidemics and Race in San Francisco's Chinatown* (2001).

15. John K. Van De Kamp, *California Dept. of Justice, A History of the California Attorney General's Office* (1988), 63.

16. Interview by Amelia Fry with Stanley Mosk, CA Supreme Court Justice, in "San Francisco, CA, California Constitutional Officers" (Mar. 1, 1979), available at http://ia700301.us.archive.org/22/items/caliconstitutoff00morrrich/caliconstitutoff00morrrich.pdf.

17. *Cash v. Superior Court of Santa Clara County*, 53 Cal.2d 72 (1959).

18. Ira Michael Heyman, "A Tribute to Professor Preble Stolz," *Calif. L. Rev.* 80 (1992), 801, 803.

19. Marc Reisner, *Cadillac Desert: The American West and Its Disappearing Water* (1986), 361–363

20. Arizona-California Lawsuit, *Colorado Water Congress Newsletter* (Official Publication of the Colorado Water Congress, Denver, C.O.), June 25, 1963, at 1 of Vol. 6, No. 6.

21. August 14, 1958, *Oxnard Press Courier*, Mosk Scrapbook, CJLSF.

22. Charles E. Corker taught at the University of Washington Law School from 1965 to 1987, notably in the areas of water resource law, contracts, and constitutional law. After graduating from Harvard Law School, he taught at Stanford Law School. He then served for eleven years in the California Attorney General's office, for many years as a deputy attorney general on the special legal staff for the Colorado River Board and then as Assistant Attorney General in charge of the Southern California Office.

23. B. Abbott Goldberg also acted as special counsel to the governor on the legal problems of water development. He was appointed a judge of the Municipal Court in Sacramento in 1966 by Gov. Edmund G. Brown. B. Abbott Goldberg, California Water Issues, 1950–1966: Oral history transcript and related material, 1979–1981, p. 13; Interviews Conducted by Malca Chall in 1979, 1980. Regional Oral History Office (Hereafter ROHO); The Bancroft Library, University of California, Berkeley, California; Governmental History Documentation Project; Goodwin Knight/Edmund Brown, Sr., Era.

24. April 2, 1959, *Oxnard Press Courier*. Mosk Scrapbook, CJLSF.

25. January 15, 1962, *Los Angeles Times*. ProQuest Historical Newspapers.

26. January 8, 1962, *Scottsdale Daily Progress*. Mosk Scrapbook, CJLSF.

27. *Arizona v. California*, 373 U.S. 546 (1963). U.S. Supreme Court; No. 8, Original Argued January 8–11, 1962; Restored to calendar for reargument June 4, 1962; Reargued November 13–14, 1962; Decided June 3, 1963. Chief Justice Earl Warren recused himself, and Justice Douglas dissented. Ibid. at 602, 627.
28. Arizona-California Lawsuit, *Colorado Water Congress Newsletter* (Official Publication of the Colorado Water Congress, Denver, C.O.), June 25, 1963, at 1 of Vol. 6, No. 6.
29. For additional information on the Arizona v. California cases, see Norris Hundley's *Water and the West: The Colorado River Compact and the Politics of Water in the American West* (University of California Press, 1975).
30. John Upton Terrell, *War for the Colorado River Vol. I: The California-Arizona Controversy,* and *Vol. II: Above Lee's Ferry—The Upper Basin* (1965), reviewed by Stanley Mosk, *The Historical Society of Southern California*, at 310–312.
31. Attorney General Report, Mosk Papers, CJLSF.
32. January 18, 1959 Filed in former speechwriter Tom McDonald's collection of "Speeches of the Attorney General Stanley Mosk, First Term 1959–1962," Vol. III, 1961, copy one.
33. Edmund (Pat) Brown, with Dick Adler, *Public Justice, Private Mercy: A Governor's Education on Death Row* (1989) xii.
34. *Los Angeles Times*, April 2, 1959 p. A39; ProQuest Historical Newspapers.
35. Caryl Chessman, *Cell 2455, Death Row: A Condemned Man's Own Story* (Carroll & Graff, 2006. First edition New York: Prentice-Hall, 1954).
36. *Los Angeles Times*, Dec. 4, 1959 p. A1; ProQuest Historical Newspapers.
37. Ibid.
38. *Los Angeles Times*, February 22, 1960, courtesy of Richard Mosk.
39. Ibid.
40. Memorandum from Mr. A.H. Belmont Re: Caryl Chessman to Mr. Parsons and Director of the FBI from SAC, Phoenix (Feb. 20, 1960).
41. *Los Angeles Times*, February 22, 1960, courtesy of Richard Mosk.
42. *People v. Gene Daniels and Archie Simmons*, 71 Cal. 2d 1119 (1969).
43. *People v. Wein*, 50 Cal. 2d 383 (1958). Wein's death sentence was commuted by Governor Pat Brown, just as he would have commuted Chessman's death sentence if he could. He simply did not believe death was an appropriate sentence for a crime not involving loss of life. Wein was subsequently released on parole, and then, using the same unique means of subduing his victims (when they answered the door, he would be groping around on the front porch claiming he had just lost his watch stem; the victim would instinctively assist him by joining the search for the watch stem, at which point he struck the victim from behind), he raped and murdered a Westchester woman. Governor Pat Brown later reflected, "I was racked with guilt and doubt. I had made mistakes before—anybody who makes decisions as part of his job finds our later that some of them were wrong—but this one had cost a woman her life." Edmund (Pat) Brown, with Dick Adler, *Public Justice, Private Mercy: A Governor's Education On Death Row* (1989), p. 102. Cf. supra, chapter 5, n.75.
44. *Coker v. Georgia*, 433 U.S. 584 (1977) and *Kennedy v. Louisiana*, 128 S.Ct. 2641 (2008).
45. January 25, 1962 Letter from William O. Douglas to Tom Clark, CJLSF.

46. January 30, 1962 Letter from Felix Frankfurter (F.F.) to "Dear Brethren," CJLSF.
47. January 30, 1962 Memorandum from William O. Douglas to the Conference in re: *Mapp v. Ohio*, CJLSF.
48. January 31, 1962 Letter from Felix Frankfurter (F.F.) to "Dear Bill" William O. Brennan, CJLSF.
49. January 31, 1962 Letter from William O. Douglas to "Dear Felix," CJLSF.
50. Mosk, Memorial Dedication to Justice William O. Douglas, *Loyola* (L.A.) *L. Rev.* 31 (1998), 769–70.
51. Delmar Karlen, *Appellate Courts in the United States and England* (1963).
52. May 4, 1959, Letter from John F. Kennedy to Stanley Mosk; Congressional Speech on bill enclosed. CJLSF.
53. February 5, 1961 Stanley Mosk speech before Histadrut Annual Dinner, St. Francis Hotel, San Francisco. He described Histadrut as a labor, management, social and political organization. Filed in speechwriter Tom McDonald's private collection, "Speeches of the Attorney General Stanley Mosk, First Term 1959–1962, Vol. III," 1961, copy 1. (Hereafter McDonald, Speeches, Vol. 3).
54. April 22, 1964 Stanley Mosk Speech before the Amalgamated Clothing Workers Honoring Jerry Posner. McDonald Speeches, Vol. 3.
55. Morrie Ryskind, *Los Angeles Times*, Sept. 1, 1961.
56. Attorney General Report, Mosk Papers, CJLSF.
57. August 18, 1963, Doug McMann column, *Pasadena Independent*.
58. "A Birchist vs. Mosk," *San Francisco Examiner*, August 18, 1963, p. 8.
59. Speeches of Attorney General Mosk, Feb. 5, 1962, CJLSF.
60. "Christian Anti-Communist Crusade Newsletter," Mosk Scrapbook, CJLSF.
61. FBI Files on Stanley Mosk (December 11, 1961) (on file with California Judicial Center Library, Special Collections and Archives).
62. Karl Prussion, *California Dynasty of Communism* (San Diego: Heads Up, 1962); Minna Mosk papers (CJLSF) and Walter Ely papers, Huntington Library.
63. April 21, 1963, *Los Angeles Times*, p. 10, Sec. B.
64. August 1, 1963; received by the University of California, March 9, 1964. CJLSF
65. May 8, 1963, Letter from Edmund G. Brown to Stanley Mosk. Courtesy of Richard Mosk.

Chapter 9

1. *Los Angeles Newsletter*, Joseph M. Quinn, Editorial Director: August 8, 1959, No. 258; June 6, 1960; June 11, 1960, No. 302.
2. *New York Times*, Jan. 19, 1959.
3. Ibid.
4. Joseph Cerrell, recorded interview by Dennis O'Brian, June 13, 1969, pp. 19, John F. Kennedy Library Oral History Program.
5. Dennis McDougal, *The Last Mogul: Lew Wasserman, MCA and the Hidden History of Hollywood* (1998).
6. Brown interview.
7. Levy/Bakken interview, p. 411; Fry interview, p. 543.
8. Joseph Cerrell, n.4, *supra*.
9. June 11, 1960, # 302, p. 1.
10. Frederick Tuttle, "The California Democrats: 1953–1966," UCLA Ph.D. Diss., 1975, p. 163.
11. Richard Mosk to Braitman.

12. Interview by Eleanor Glaser with Richard Kline, "Governor Brown's Faithful Advisor, in the Governor's Office Under Edmund G. Brown, Sr." (1977, on file with the Regional Oral History Office, The Bancroft Library), available at http://www.archive.org/stream/underedmundbrow00rowlrich/underedmundbrow00rowlrich_djvu.txt.

13. A schlemiel is a word of Yiddish origin defined as an awkward and unlucky person for whom things never turn out right. *Random House Webster's College Dictionary* (2nd ed. 2000).

14. November 4, 1959, Letter in Richard Mosk collection.

15. Tom McDonald to Braitman, 2002.

16. Ibid.

17. Edward R. Bloomquist, M.D., "The Addiction Potential of Oxycodone (Percodan)," *California Medicine* 99 no. 2 (August 1963): 127

18. "Mosk Accused of Using Office to Aid Kennedy," Mosk Scrapbook, CJLSF.

19. Joann Lynott, "Party Warms Up Cold Californians," *Los Angeles Times*, January 21, 1961.

20. Feb. 2, 1961, Letter from Attorney General Robert Kennedy to Stanley Mosk; Mar. 22,1961, Letter from Governor Edmund G. Brown to Stanley Mosk; Mar. 6, 1961, Letter from U.S. Sen. Henry M. Jackson to Stanley Mosk. Courtesy of Richard Mosk.

21. Interview by Amelia Fry with Stanley Mosk, CA Supreme Court Justice, in *San Francisco, CA, California Constitutional Officers* (Mar. 1, 1979), available at http://ia700301.us.archive.org/22/items/caliconstitutoff00morrrich/caliconstitutoff00morrrich.pdf

22. "Siempre! ¿Un peligro para Estados Unidos?" (Letter to Editor), *Siempre!*, 1 May 1963, 4.

23. June 28, 1963, Letter from Robert F. Kennedy to Stanley Mosk. Courtesy of Richard Mosk.

24. April 16, 1963, Letter from Robert F. Kennedy to Stanley Mosk. Courtesy of Richard Mosk.

25. "Bard's Stratford by Leonard Lyons," *The Sumpter Daily Item*, August 28, 1962,.

26. May 9, 1963, Letter from Thomas H. Kuchel to Stanley Mosk. Courtesy of Richard Mosk.

27. January 15, 1964, *Southern California Democratic Report*, Vol. 3, No. 1, pt. 2, 4; Political, 1963–4; Walter Ely Papers, Huntington Library.

28. January 19, 1964 *San Francisco Chronicle*, 17/4.

29. January 7, 1964, *San Francisco Chronicle*, 1/1; Glendale Young Republicans Resolution No. 64–5; Box 710/F., AG; Brown papers; Bancroft Library.

30. Program for Civic Tribute Honoring Attorney General Stanley Mosk for his 25 years of "Distinguished Public Service." August 15, 1962. Courtesy of Richard Mosk.

31. "Truman's closest associate was David Noyes, who was a long-time friend of mine. Through him the invitation was delivered. So Truman came out for my fiftieth birthday party in September, 1962." See Fry ROHO interview with Stanley Mosk, p. 12. Along with the other veritable "who's who?" of the Democratic Party were Assemblyman "Big Daddy" Jesse Unruh, Honorary Co-Chair, Chairman Edwin W. Pauley, Vice Chairs the enormously wealthy Howard F. Ahmanson, who had been a liberal Republican who supported candidates of both parties; Bart Lytton, a financier and an active partisan, Coordinator Joseph R. Cerrell. Heading the Lawyers' Committee was co-chair Warren Christopher, future secretary of state. His Southern California re-election committee drew on the formidable strength of the areas Jewish political clout. Under the Chair of the Executive Committee, Jesse Unruh, Louis Warschaw, a wealthy businessman, who was both Finance chair and Treasurer, and his wife Carmen, wealthy daughter of Leo Harvey of Harvey Aluminum, and was co-chair of women's activities, while L.A. City Councilwoman, and one half of "the darlings" of the party, Rosalind Wyman, who was the honorary chair of the latter. Mickey Wapner, wife of the famous "Judge Wapner," and Lester Ziffren, brother of Paul. Other prominent officials around the Southland included Augustus Hawkins, Mrvyn Dymally, Ed Roybal, Ed Elliot, Charles Warren, George E. Brown, as well as the lesser known party stalwarts Hope Schecter (Mendoza), Knox Mellon, and Madale Watson. Flyers from Huntington Collection and The Southern California Democratic Report, Knox Mellon Papers, UCLA

32. February 6, 1963, Letter from Edmund G. Brown to Stanley Mosk. Courtesy of Richard Mosk.

33. Speeches of Attorney General Stanley Mosk, CJLSF.

34. Letter from Mary McGuire to Governor Edmund G. Brown, Nov. 27, 1959; Brown papers, Bancroft Library.

35. Letter from Governor Edmund G. Brown to Mary McGuire (December 2, 1959); Brown Papers, Bancroft Library.

36. Letter from Stanley Mosk, CA Supreme Court Justice, to Samuel R. Cohen, Edmund Brown Papers, Box 710/F (February 17, 1964) (on file with the Bancroft Library).

37. Feb. 27, 1964 Joseph W. Hill to Hon. *Edwin* Brown, Governor (writing from New Jersey, he could be excused for not knowing the governor's first name); March 17, 1964; Jack Burby, Press Secretary for the Governor; Box 710/F. AG; Brown Papers; Bancroft Library.

Chapter 10

1. October 9, 1963 *San Francisco Chronicle*, p. 1 Huntington Library, *Los Angeles Times* Newspaper Archives.

2. *California Legal History* 163 (2009) p. 4.

3. January 9, 1964, Letter from Sen. Nicholas Petris to Stanley Mosk. Courtesy of Richard Mosk.

4. January 16, 1964 Letter from Carley V. Porter to Stanley Mosk. Courtesy of Richard Mosk.

5. January 29, 1964 *San Francisco Chronicle*, p. 11.

6. February 10, 1964, *San Francisco Chronicle*, p. 6.

7. February 12, 1964, *San Francisco Chronicle*, p. 6.

8. Letter from George McLain, to Stanley Mosk, CA Supreme Court Justice (May 20, 1964) (on file with the California Judicial Center Library, Special Collections and Archives). Attorney General File, Alan Cranston, 1964, Mosk Papers, CJLSF.

9. "$10,000 to Nothing," Currents of Opinion Editorial, *Long Beach Telegram*, May 25, 1964, p. 10; Attorney General File, Alan Cranston, 1964, Mosk Papers, CJLSF.

10. Charles Rappleye and David Robb, "The Judge, the Photos and the Senate Race," *Los Angeles Weekly*, March 4–10, 1994, at 20.

11. March 3, 1964, *Los Angeles Times*, p. 1, 21.

12. All of the information in this chapter is from the LAPD file on Stanley Mosk unless otherwise indicated.

13. FBI Files, page 12. Stanley Mosk Papers, CJLSF.

14. Tom McDonald to Braitman, 2002.

15. *Los Angeles Times*, May 19, 1963 and April 14, 1963; ProQuest Historical Newspapers.

16. Charles Rappleye and David Robb, "The Judge, the Photos and the Senate Race," *Los Angeles Weekly*, March 4–10, 1994.
17. Ibid.
18. Tim Weiner, *Enemies: A History of the FBI* (2012).
19. FBI files, Page 14, Stanley Mosk Papers, CJLSF.
20. Ibid., p. 22.
21. Ibid., p. 5.
22. *Los Angeles Times*, November 12, 1964.
23. October 25, 1965, telegram-decoded copy FBI Files, page 5.
24. Page 25, FBI file; Pg. 11 subject says "also knows the identity of another girlfriend other than Sabrina Jourdan with whom J? Mosk is alleged to be currently involved," which eliminated J.? Mosk as a senate candidate.
25. Rappleye and Robb, *supra* n.16.
26. Ibid. The authors prefaced their 1994 expose with this Editor's Note: "Legal precedent established by the California Supreme Court, in an opinion joined by Justice Stanley Mosk, puts news organizations at financial risk for printing factual information about private figures who have committed past crimes. For that reason alone, three names known to reporters have been replaced in this article with ... pseudonyms."
27. Miriam Perl to Braitman, 2003.
28. Mike Rothmiller and Ivan G. Goldman, *L.A. Secret Police: Inside the LAPD Elite Spy Network* (1992).
29. John, Buntin, *L.A. Noir: The Struggle for the Soul of America's Most Seductive City* (2009).
30. Susan Mosk to Braitman.
31. Letter from Stanley Mosk to Judge Jesse Curtis, 1967.
32. Interview of Edmund G. Brown by Malca Chall with B. Abbott Goldberg, "California Water Issues 1950–60" (1979, 1980, on file with the Regional Oral History Office, The Bancroft Library), available at http://www.archive.org/stream/califwatertapere00chalrich/califwatertapere00chalrich_djvu.txt.
33. LBJ tape: LBJ with Governor Edmund G. "Pat" Brown; March 6, 1964 LBJ Library and CSPAN website recording, available at http://www.c-span.org/search.aspx?For=lbj+tapes+listen.
34. LBJ tape: LBJ with attorney and presidential aide Lloyd Hand; 1964; LBJ Library and CSPAN website recording, available at http://www.c-span.org/search.aspx?For=lbj+tapes+listen.
35. LBJ and Pat Brown tape, n. 33, *supra*.
36. Ethan Rarick, *The Life And Times Of Pat Brown: California Rising* (2005), p. 437, n. 29
37. Bill Boyarsky, *Big Daddy: Jesse Unruh and the Art Of Power Politics* (2008), p. 137
38. Frank Burns telephone interview with Braitman, 2003.
39. Tom McDonald to Braitman, 2002.
40. March 3, 1964, *Los Angeles Times*, p. 1.
41. March 5, 1964, *San Francisco Chronicle*, 1/1.
42. March 3, 1964, *Los Angeles Times*, p. 1.
43. Ibid.
44. March 4, 1964, *San Francisco Chronicle*.
45. Ibid.; Rappalye and Robb, n. 17, *supra* at p. 23.
46. Text of Press Conference, June 4, 1964, Reported by Alex C. Kaempfer, CSR. Unruh, State Archives.
47. Betty Reddin to Braitman, 2003
48. Ann Eliaser: *From Grassroots Politics to the Top Dollar: Fundraising For Candidates and Non-Profit Agencies*, pp. 67–8. Interviewed by Malca Chall, 1983; Women in Politics Oral History Project, Regional Oral History Office (ROHO), Bancroft Library, UC Berkeley.

49. Interview by Amelia Fry with Stanley Mosk, CA Supreme Court Justice, in "San Francisco, Ca, California Constitutional Officers" (Mar. 1, 1979) (on file with the Regional Oral History Office, The Bancroft Library), available at http://ia700301.us.archive.org/22/items/caliconstitutoff00morrrich/caliconstitutoff00morrrich.pdf
50. Gladwin Hill, *Dancing Bear: An Inside Look at California Politics* (1968) 187; Frederick B. Tuttle, *The California Democrats, 1953–1966* (1975) 260: Pierre Salinger, *With Kennedy* (1966) 378.
51. Editorial by Joseph Alsop, *Salinger Chief Campaign Asset: Late President's Reflected Glow, San Francisco Examiner*, April 3, 1964; Mosk Papers, Pierre Salinger Campaign (1964), CJLSF.
52. Gladwin Hill, *Dancing Bear* 187.
53. June 19, 1964, Walter Ely Papers, V Box DD (4) (5), on file with Huntington Library.
54. *Salinger v. Jordan, as Secretary of State*, 61 Cal.2d 824 (1964). Salinger won the right to be designated "incumbent" on the ballot in the general election, but lost the right to list his occupation as "Presidential Secretary" in the primary. The case was decided September 15, 1964, after Stanley Mosk had already been appointed to the California Supreme Court. Justice Mosk, of course, recused himself and did not participate in the decision, which was unanimous.
55. Proposition 14 (Rumford Fair Housing Initiative) in California Ballot Pamphlet, General Election 13–14, 18–20 (Nov. 3 1964).
56. January 13, 1964, Remarks by Attorney General Stanley Mosk to California Advisory Commission; *San Francisco Chronicle*, 18/7 February 17, 1964; *Democratic Report*; Box DD (2), Walter Ely Papers, Huntington Library.
57. CRA president Nolan Frizelle as quoted in Schiesl, p. 61.
58. On two occasions, one during a speech before the County Conference on Human Relations in Los Angeles, and one before the consolidated Realty Board in Los Angeles. *San Francisco Chronicle*, February 2, 1963, at 22; *San Francisco Chronicle*, February 5, 1964, at 5,13.
59. Memorandum to the Press, February 7, 1964, Attorney General; Brown Papers, Box 710/ F AG Feb, Bancroft Library; February 19, 1964 *San Francisco Chronicle*, 6/6.
60. Feb. 2, 1964, *San Francisco Chronicle* 6/7.
61. *San Francisco Chronicle*, July 11, 1966, at 5 (on file with Richard Mosk); Pierre Salinger, *With Kennedy*, 361–62.
62. Frederick B. Tuttle, *The California Democrats, 1953–1966*, 269.
63. Ibid.

Chapter 11

1. September 1, 1964, Governor Edmund G. Brown to Stanley Mosk, CJLSF.
2. October 5, 1964, Wisconsin Governor John W. Reynolds to Stanley Mosk. Courtesy of Richard Mosk.
3. For an excellent account of Traynor's influence on the law, see Ben Field, *Activism in Pursuit of the Public Interest: The Jurisprudence of Chief Justice Roger Traynor* (Berkeley Public Policy Press, 2003). The voice of United States Chief Justice Earl Warren was heard among the chorus of prominent judges, lawyers and law professors that greeted the appointment of Roger Traynor as Chief Justice of California. He said, "Californians can ... rejoice because of the elevation of this greatly talented

man to their highest judicial position. Boalt Hall can be most proud of its former student and teacher, and all who follow the course of judicial decisions in the solution of the infinite number of legal problems that arise in our complex society can continue to benefit from his erudition and humanitarianism."

4. *Escola v. Coca Cola Bottling Co.*, 24 Cal. 2d 453, 461 (1944).
5. *Greenman v. Yuba Power Prod. Inc.*, 59 Cal.2d 57 (1963).
6. *Perez v. Sharp*, 32 Cal. 2d 711 (1948).
7. *Loving v. Virginia*, 388 U.S. 1 (1967).
8. *In Re Marriage Cases*, 43 Cal. 4th 757 (2008). The ruling was subsequently abrogated by adoption of a constitutional amendment, Proposition Eight, in the 2008 election. The constitutionality of Proposition Eight is still being litigated.
9. Remarks of Judge Henry Friendly, Traynor Memorial Proceedings, 39 Cal. 3d 953.
10. Remarks of Justice Stanley Mosk, Traynor Memorial Proceedings, 39 Cal. 3d 953.
11. Interview prepared by Committee on History of Law in CA with Justice Joseph R. Grodin, CA Supreme Court Justice, in San Francisco, CA, Retrospect Oral History: Justice Joseph R. Grodin (Sept. 28, 1987) (on file with Hastings College of Law, State Bar of CA: Committee on the History of Law in CA), available at http://hastingsconlawquarterly.org/archives/V16/I1/Zakheim.pdf.
12. Gerald Uelmen, CACJ Forum, Vol. 28, No. 3, p. 23 (2001).
13. Governor Pat Brown made eight appointments to the California Supreme Court. Two of his appointees, Thomas White and Maurice Dooling, Jr., were on the court for very brief periods prior to the appointment of Roger Traynor as Chief Justice.
14. The chief law secretary position was the predecessor of the current court administrator/clerk, appointed by the court to serve as the court's executive officer. The court administrator/clerk is responsible for overseeing the administration and management of the court's non-judicial functions, including supervising and directing the Clerk's Office and the Calendar Coordination Office, administering the court's personnel and budget systems, and overseeing activities relating to information systems, purchasing, and other business services.
15. *Nunes v. Nunes*, 62 Cal.2d 33 (1964).
16. See, e.g., *Traders etc. Ins. Co. v. Pac. Emp. Ins. Co.*, 130 Cal.App.2d 158 (1955).
17. Grodin, *supra* n.11.
18. Justice Stanley Mosk's annual law clerks included John Hansen (1964–65), David Friedland (1966–67), Joel Klevens (1969–71), Larry Rubin (1971–72), John Levin (1973–74), Brian Lysaght (1974–75), Dick Rothschild (1975–76), Mickey Kaus (1976–77), Marvin Pearlstein (1977–78), Wendy Shiba (1979–80), Craig Labadie (1981–82), Andrea Asaro (1982–83), Jake Dear (1983–84), Ellyn Lindsay (1984–85), and Dennis Maio (1984–85). [Partial List provided by Jake Dear].
19. 64 Cal.2d 235 (1966).
20. Ibid. at 249.
21. Ibid. at 246, citing *Smith v. California* (1959) 361 U.S. 147 and *New York Times Co. v. Sullivan* (1964) 376 U.S. 254.
22. *Jordan v. Weaver*, 385 U.S. 844 (1966).
23. *Frances Wirta v. Alameda-Contra Costa Transit District et al.*, 68 Cal.2d 51 (1967).
24. Ibid. at 54, citing *New York Times Co. v. Sullivan* (1963) 376 U.S. 254.
25. Ibid. at 60.
26. *Mulkey v. Reitman*, 64 Cal.2d 529 (1966).
27. *Estate of Larkin*, 65 Cal.2d 60 (1966); *Estate of Chichernea*, 66 Cal.2d 83 (1966).
28. *Konigsberg v. State Bar*, 353 U.S. 252 (1957).
29. *Konigsberg v. State Bar*, 366 U.S. 36 (1961).
30. "Justice Abroad," *Los Angeles Daily Journal*, July 9–21, 1965.
31. *People v. Jacobson*, 63 Cal.2d 319 (1965) (6–1, with Justice Peters dissenting); *People v. Mathis*, 63 Cal.2d 416 (1965) (5–2, with Justices Peters and Tobriner dissenting); *People v. Reeves*, 64 Cal.2d 767 (1966)(unanimous).
32. In *Otsuka v. Hite*, 64 Cal.2d 596 (1966), for example, bona fide conscientious objectors who resisted the draft during World War II were denied registration as voters because of their prior convictions of "infamous crimes." In an opinion joined by Justices Peters, Tobriner and Peek, Justice Mosk construed the term "infamous crimes" to require moral corruption or dishonesty, and ruled that the plaintiffs should be permitted to register and vote. Chief Justice Traynor and Justice McComb joined a dissent by Justice Burke.
33. October 8, 1965, FBI Files, CJLSF.
34. October 11, 1965, FBI Files, CJLSF.
35. October 26, 1965, page 2, FBI Files, CJLSF.
36. Former California Governor Edmund G. "Pat" Brown to Mrs. Stanley (Susan) Mosk (1982).
37. Gerald F. Uelmen, "Supreme Court Retention Elections in California," *Santa Clara Law Review* 28 (1988) 333.
38. October 24, 1967, John F. Shelley to Edna Mosk. Courtesy of Richard Mosk.
39. *Good Housekeeping Magazine*, January, 1968.
40. May 3, 168 Jesse Unruh to Edna Mosk. Courtesy of Richard Mosk.
41. April 10, 1970, Letter from George McGovern to Edna Mosk. Courtesy of Richard Mosk.
42. July 24, 1968, Letter from Hubert H. Humphrey to Edna Mosk. Courtesy of Richard Mosk.
43. August 25, 1968, *Los Angeles Times*; Maggie Savoy.
44. Memorandum to Chief Justice Roger Traynor from Stanley Mosk, July 23, 1968. Courtesy of Richard Mosk.
45. Mosk's highest rate of disagreement was with Justice McComb, who dissented in 35 percent of the 1969 Traynor Court opinions. Ironically, however, aside from Justice Burke, Justice Mosk had the highest rate of agreement with McComb of any Justice on the Court. Dissenting in 11 percent of the opinions, Mosk racked up a high rate of disagreement with Justice Sullivan (13.1 percent); Justice Tobriner (13.7 percent) and Justice Peters (13.7 percent).
46. *People v. Leon Phillip Belous*, 71 Cal.2d 954 (1969).
47. *Time Magazine*, September 19, 1969.
48. Ibid.
49. *Pasadena Independent Press-Telegram*, January 14, 1969.
50. *Time Magazine*, September 19, 1969.
51. Fred Okrand, Zad Leavy and Beilenson & Leavy for the defendant and appellant; McCutchen, Doyle, Brown & Enersen, Burnham Enersen, Robert A. Blum, Terry J. Houlihan, Norma G. Zarky, Howard H. Jewel, Paul N. Halvonik, William Kelly, Barbara N. Armstrong, Charles E. Beardsley, George A. Blackstone, A. Stevens Halsted, Jr., Roderick M. Hills, Leonard S. Janofsky, Herma Hill Kay, Frederick R. McBrien, Charles T. Munger, Stuart T. Peeler, Samuel O. Pruitt, Jr., Charles

E. Rickershauser, Jr., Graham L. Sterling, Charles E. Stimson, Jr., and Francis M. Wheat as Amici Curiae on behalf of Defendant and Appellant. Thomas C. Lynch, Attorney General, William E. James, Assistant Attorney General, and Phillip G. Samovar, Deputy Attorney General, for Plaintiff and Respondent. Charles H. Clifford, Walter R. Trinkaus, J. J. Brandlin, Thomas J. Arata, Richard D. Andrews, Cyril A. Coyle, Mazzera, Snyder & De Martini, John F. Duff, William R. Kennedy, Richard G. Logan and Curran, Golden, McDevitt & Martin as Amici Curiae on behalf of Plaintiff and Respondent.

52. *Time Magazine*, September 19, 1969.

53. *People v. Joseph Bernard Morse*, 60 Cal.2d 631(1964).

54. *Witherspoon v. Illinois*, 391 U.S. 510 (1968).

55. Bernard Witkin, "Through Bernie's Binoculars," *The California Supreme Court Historical Society Newsletter*, Spring–Summer, 2007, p. 2.

Chapter 12

1. March Schwartz, Editorial "Murphy or Mosk?" (Collection of Richard Mosk).

2. That conclusion is open to question under subsequent court rulings. See *Lungren v. Davis*, 234 Cal.App.3d 806 (1991).

3. John V. Tunney to Stanley Mosk, September 1, 1970. (On file with Richard Mosk).

4. Lou Cannon, *Governor Reagan: His Rise to Power*, pp. 222–223.

5. "Beach Combing," column by Malcolm Eply, April 29, 1970, *Independent Press Telegram*.

6. May 1, 1970, *Modesto Bee*.

7. Totton J. Anderson and Charles G. Bell, "The 1970 Election in California," *The Western Political Quarterly* Vol. 24, No. 2 (Jun., 1971), pp. 252–273.

8. Chief Justice Wright concurred in most of the notable majority opinions authored by Justice Mosk during his reign, including *Associated Home Builders, Inc. v. City of Walnut Creek* (1971) (holding constitutional a requirement that developers of private land dedicate open space to public use); *Vasquez v. Superior Court* (1971) (extending the availability of class actions to consumer fraud suits); *Cobbs v. Grant* (1972) (adopting the doctrine of informed consent, requiring doctors to inform patients of the treatments available and the risks inherent in each); *Friends of Mammoth v. Board of Supervisors* (1972) (holding that developers of private building projects needing a governmental license or public funds must comply with the California Environmental Quality Act); *In Re Lynch* (1972) (holding that the penalty for a crime can be so disproportionate to the offense that it violates the constitutional prohibition of cruel or unusual punishments); and *Rodriguez v. Bethlehem Steel Corp.* (1974) (holding that the spouse of an injured worker can bring an action for loss of consortium). Chief Justice Wright dissented, however, from Justice Mosk's majority opinions in *Schweiger v. Superior Court* (1970) (holding that tenants may defend against unlawful detainer actions on the ground they were evicted in retaliation for exercising their statutory right to ask for repairs) and *Parr v. Municipal Court* (1971) (holding that a "Keep Off the Grass" ordinance designed to discriminate against hippies violates the equal protection clause).

9. The Wright Court split 4–3 in nineteen cases in 1971. The Justice most often in the majority in these splits was Justice Stanley Mosk. Much like Justice Anthony Kennedy on the current United States Supreme Court, he became a "swing vote," often determining the outcome in the cases that divided the Court. In fifteen of these cases, Chief Justice Wright was on one side while Justices Tobriner and Peters were on the other. Justice Mosk voted with the Chief Justice in five of them, and with Justices Tobriner and Peters in ten.

10. *In Re Tucker*, 5 Cal.3d 171 (1971).

11. *Friends of Mammoth v. Board of Supervisors of Mono County*, 8 Cal.3d 247 (1972).

12. Cruz Reynoso, CEQA: A Judicial Perspective, in *Thirty-Five Years of the California Environmental Quality Act*, 164 (Planning and Conservation League Foundation, 2005).

13. 8 Cal.3d at 263–64.

14. Cruz Reynoso, n.14 *supra*.

15. Mosk, "Nothing Succeeds Like Excess," *Loyola (L.A.) L. Rev*. 26 (1993), 981, 988.

16. July 6, 1976, Edward M. Kennedy to Stanley Mosk. (On file with Richard Mosk).

17. Writing in March 1977, Goldberg clarified, "I suppose in the judicial area it really comes down to what your court did some time ago in the death cases, namely, decide cases enlarging federal rights on the basis of the interpretation of your own constitution and refrain from commenting on SC decisions interpreting the Fed Const. which are less civilized." March 23, 1977, Letter From Arthur J. Goldberg to Stanley Mosk. (On file with Richard Mosk).

18. Hans A. Linde, "Without 'Due Process'—Unconstitutional Law in Oregon," *Or. L. Rev*. 49 (1970), 125.

19. *Food Employees v. Logan Plaza*, 391 U.S. 308, 313, 315 [20 L.Ed.2d 603, 608, 610, 88 S.Ct. 161 (1968).

20. *Diamond v. Bland*, 3 Cal.3d 653 (1970).

21. *Lloyd Corp. v. Tanner*, 407 U.S. 551 [33 L.Ed.2d 131, 92 S.Ct. 2219] (1972).

22. *Diamond v. Bland*, 11 Cal.3d 331 (1974).

23. The majority opinion was authored by Justice Burke, joined by Chief Justice Wright and Justices McComb and Justice William Clark, Governor Reagan's second appointment to the Court.

24. *Robins v. Pruneyard Shopping Center*, 23 Cal.3d 899 (1979).

25. Ibid. at 910.

26. *Pruneyard Shopping Center v. Robins*, 447 U.S. 74 (1980).

27. Letter from William Rehinquist, Chief Justice of the U.S Supreme Court to Stanley Mosk, CA. Supreme Court Justice (June, 1986) (CJLSF).

28. Stanley Mosk, "State Constitutionalism: Both Liberal and Conservative," *Texas Law Review* Nos. 6 & 7 (March/April 1965), 63.

29. Ibid.

30. Calif. Const. Art. I, Section 28(d).

31. *People v. Krivda*, 5 Cal.3d 357, overruled by *People v. Kaanehe*, 19 Cal. 3d 1 (1977).

32. *Burrows v. Superior Court*, 13 Cal. 3d 238 (1974).

33. *Mozzetti v. Superior Court of Sacramento*, 4 Cal. 3d 699 (1971).

34. *People v. Brisendine*, 13 Cal. 3d 528 (1975).

35. *In re Tony C.*, 21 Cal. 3d 888 (1978).

36. Jake Dear and Edward W. Jessen, "'Followed' Rates and Leading State Cases, 1940–2005," *U.C Davis Law Review* 41 (2007), 683; Jake Dear, *The Influence of Justice Stanley Mosk's Opinions* (2008).

37. *Brosnahan v. Brown*, 32 Cal.3d 236 (1982).

38. Gerald F. Uelmen, "Crocodiles in the Bathtub: Maintaining the Independence of State Supreme Courts

in an Era of Judicial Politicization," *Notre Dame L. Rev.* 72 (1997) 1133.
39. 32 Cal.3d 236.
40. *San Francisco Jewish Bulletin,* November 4, 1974.
41. Stanley Mosk, CA. Supreme Court Justice, Law Day, 1972 to 1984, Address at the Wilshire Bar Association and Wilshire Chamber of Commerce, Ambassador Hotel, Los Angeles (May 11, 1972) (CJLSF).
42. Ibid.

Chapter 13

1. *People v. Anderson,* 6 Cal.3d 628 (1972).
2. Dan Morain, "Both Sides Point to Death Penalty Decision of 1972," *Los Angeles Times,* Feb. 18, 1986.
3. Stanley Mosk, "The Current Profile of Capital Punishment," *Israeli Law Review* Vol. 25, nos. 3–4, 1991, 498.
4. Betty Medsger, *Framed: The New Right Attack on Chief Justice Rose Bird and the Courts* (1983), p. 20.
5. *Furman v. Georgia,* 408 U.S. 238 (1972).
6. Morain, *supra* n.2.
7. *Gregg v. Georgia,* 428 U.S. 153 (1976).
8. *Rockwell v. Superior Court,* 18 Cal.3d 420 (1976).
9. *People v. Frierson,* 25 Cal. 3d 142, 189 (1978).
10. Ibid.
11. *People v. Harris,* 28 Cal.3d 935 (1981).
12. *In Re Harris,* 1992 Cal.Lexis 1788 (April 21, 1992).
13. Stanley Mosk, "The Current Profile of Capital Punishment," *Israeli Law Review* Vol. 25, nos. 3–4, 1991, pp. 488–504.
14. Senator Ron Briggs, "California's Death Penalty Law: It Simply Does Not Work," *Los Angeles Times,* February 12, 2012.
15. Ibid.

Chapter 14

1. *Bakke v. Regents of the University of California,* 18 Cal. 3d 34 (1976).
2. Judson MacLaury, "President Kennedy's E.O. 10925: Seedbed of Affirmative Action," *Society for History in the Federal Government* 45 (January, 2010), http://shfg.org/shfg/wp-content/uploads/2011/01/4-MacLaury-design4-new_Layout-1.pdf.
3. Ibid.
4. Ibid., at 56.
5. The chairman normally checked to see if, among other things, the applicant had been granted a waiver of the school's application fee, which required a means test; whether the applicant had worked during college or interrupted his education to support himself or his family; and whether the applicant was a member of a minority group. Ibid. at 65–66.
6. Howard Ball, *The Bakke Case: Race, Education, and Affirmative Action* (2000), p. 58.
7. Joel Dreyfuss & Charles Lawrence III, *The Bakke Case: The Politics of Inequality* (1979), p. 68.
8. In a letter to McWilliams dated October 15, 1976, Mosk wrote, "I quoted you in my opinion in Bakke—*A Mask for Privilege,* p. 238." Letter from Stanley Mosk, CA. Supreme Court Justice to Carey McWilliams (October 15, 1976) (CJLSF).
9. Interview by Germaine LaBerge, with Peter J. Belton, C.A Supreme Court Staff Attorney, "A Senior Staff Attorney Reflects on Four Decades With the California Supreme Court (1960–2001) And a Lifetime with Disability" (2003) (on file with the Regional Oral History Office, The Bancroft Library), available at http://www.archive.org/details/staffattorney4dec00beltrich.
10. Ibid. at 208.
11. Ibid.
12. Interview by Germaine LaBerge with Stanley Mosk, CA Supreme Court Justice, in San Francisco, CA, State Government Oral History Program (1998) (on file with the Regional Oral History Office), available at http://www.sos.ca.gov/archives/oral-history/pdf/mosk.pdf.
13. Ibid.
14. Gloster B. Current, "The 69th: The Post-*Bakke* Convention," *The Crisis,* October 1978, p. 270; October 27, 1976, *Merced Sun Star.*
15. Letter from Arthur Goldberg to Stanley Mosk (Private Collection of Richard Mosk).
16. Letter from Stanley Mosk, CA. supreme court justice, to John Vasconcellos, state senator (1978) (CJLSF).
17. Letter from John Caughey to Stanley Mosk, September 21, 1977; CJLSF.
18. Letter from Stanley Mosk to Professor John Caughey, September 26, 1977; CJLSF.
19. Letter from Dr. Rodolfo Acuna to Stanley Mosk, September 26, 1977; CJLSF.
20. Letters from Stanley Mosk to Carolyn Y. Williams, Third World Coalition, Feb. 8, 1978; CJLSF.
21. Edward L. Barrett, Jr., *Stanley Mosk, Bakke and the Davis Commencement,* 12 Hastings Const. L.Q. 379–81 (1985).
22. Stanley Mosk, "The Mask of Reform," *Southwestern Law Review* 10 (1978) 885, 888.
23. Letter from Stanley Mosk to Willis Hannawalt, Nov. 19, 1981; CJLSF.
24. Ibid.
25. *DeFunis v. Odegaard,* 416 U.S. 312 (1974), was dismissed as moot because DeFunis graduated before the ruling requiring his admission could be argued to the Supreme Court.
26. Letter from Stanley Mosk, CA. Supreme Court Justice, to Hans A. Linde, Oregon Supreme Court Justice (Oct. 15, 1976) (CJLSF).
27. Aug. 15, 1977, Letter from Henry A. Waxman to Stanley Mosk. (On file with Richard Mosk).
28. Letter from Stanley Mosk to Willis Hanawalt, July 12, 1978. CJLSF.
29. Nat Hentoff, October 17, 1977, *The Village Voice.*
30. *Regents of the University of California v. Bakke,* 438 U.S. 265 (1978).
31. *Bakke v. Regents of University of California,* 18 Cal.3d at 56.
32. See 438 U.S. 265 at 311. Thereafter, Justice Mosk abided by Justice Powell's initial ruling, and treated "data" as a plural word. In a note to Gerald F. Uelmen, after the publication of a summary of the annual output of the California Supreme Court which acknowledged, in a footnote, that data for the article "was" collected by his research assistant, Justice Mosk suggested that Uelmen inform his research assistant that data "were" collected. Letter, Stanley Mosk to Gerald Uelmen.
33. *Price v. Civil Service Commission,* 26 Cal. 3d 257 (1980).
34. Letter from Senator Orrin G. Hatch to Stanley Mosk, October 15, 1980. (Richard Mosk Papers).
35. Letter from Stanley Mosk to Senator Orrin G. Hatch, November 12, 1980. (Richard Mosk Papers).
36. Letter from Stanley Mosk to William P. Clark, May 21, 1981, including *San Francisco Chronicle,* Thursday, May 21, 1981 "Preferential Job Hiring Opposed" (Richard Mosk papers).

37. Letter from Maxine Waters, Assemblywoman, 48th District to John T. Racanelli, Chairman, Commission on Judicial Performance; October 29, 1981. CJLSF.
38. Letter from Maxine Waters, Assemblywoman, 48th District to Stanley Mosk, April 23, 1982; CJLSF.
39. *In re Charles S. Stevens, a Judge of the Superior Court, on Censure*, 31 Cal. 3d 403 (1982).
40. October 25, 1981, *The Press Courier*.
41. Letter from Stanley Mosk, CA. Supreme Court Justice, to Nathanial Colley, Jr., Esq, West Coast President NAACP (October 27, 1981) (file with California Judicial Center Library in San Francisco in Mosk Papers)
42. *Hi-Voltage Wire Works, Inc., v. City of San Jose*, 24 Cal.4th 537 (2000).
43. *Grutter v. Bollinger*, 539 U.S. 306 (2003).
44. *Gratz v. Bollinger*, 539 U.S. 244 (2003).
45. Interview by Germaine LaBerge with Stanley Mosk, CA Supreme Court Justice, in San Francisco, CA, State Government Oral History Program (1998) (on file with the Regional Oral History Office), available at http://www.sos.ca.gov/archives/oral-history/pdf/mosk.pdf. Mosk, Oral History.
46. Memorandum from Stanley Mosk, on Bakke's Employment as a Doctor at the Mayo Clinic to CA. Supreme Court Justices (Dec. 24, 1986) (CJLSF).
47. *Los Angeles Times*, June 20, 1997, "Doctor's License is Suspended," at B1.
48. *Los Angeles Times*, December 8, 2011, at AA3.

Chapter 15

1. Betty Medsger, Framed: The New Right Attack on Chief Justice Rose Bird and the Courts (1983), p. 25
2. Ibid. at 29.
3. September 17, 1970, *Oakland Tribune*.
4. March 22, 1974, *Daily Enterprise*.
5. Letter from Roger Kent, to Stanly Mosk, CA Supreme Court Justice (April 17, 1974) (on file with Richard Mosk).
6. May 9, 1974, *The Van Nuys News*.
7. March 31, 1974, *Long Beach Independent Press-Telegram*.
8. April 20, 1994, *The Fremont-Newark Argus*.
9. September 25, 1974. *Metropolitan News*.
10. *Caperton v. A.T. Massey Coal Co.*, 556 U.S. 868 (2009).
11. The California Supreme Court practice of depublishing the opinion of the Court of Appeal after a hearing is granted prevails to this day. While depublished opinions are now preserved in online research systems, they are not found in the official reports of the Courts of Appeal. Thus the views McComb was adopting have not been preserved. Occasionally, he would republish the Court of Appeal opinion in his Supreme Court dissent, so the opinion was preserved in the official reports of the California Supreme Court.
12. Proposition 7 (Judges. Censure, Removal, Judicial Performance Commission) in California Ballot Pamphlet, General Election 30–31, 60–61 (Nov. 2 1976), available at library.uchastings.edu/ballot_pdf/1976g.pdf.
13. *Marshall F. McComb v. Commission on Judicial Performance*, 564 P. 2d 1 (1977).
14. "Jerry Brown, Then and Now," *Los Angeles Times*, November 4, 2010.
15. The Brown Administration's unofficial attitude toward Affirmative Action was revealed by Greg Lipscomb, who, in two General Services memorandums stated that, "division chiefs are not to pick the best qualified per current rules but will select minorities or women, if possible, even though he or she may be further down the list," and, "so long as a minority/woman meets the minimum qualifications, pick them." *Sacramento Union*, March 7, 1976.
16. Governor Brown appointed or elevated sixty women, bringing the total number of women in the state judiciary to eighty-four. Still, women judges in California comprised only 7 percent of the 1192 authorized judgeships.
17. Among Justice Tobriner's landmark rulings were *People v. Woody* (1964), upholding the right of native Americans to use peyote in religious ceremonies; *Green v. Superior Court* (1974), requiring landlords to maintain leased dwellings in a habitable condition; *Dillon v. Legg* (1968), limiting bystander recovery for emotional distress, and *Tarasoff v. Regents of the University of California* (1976), imposing a duty of care upon psychotherapists to warn those who are threatened with bodily harm by their patients. *Dillon* and *Tarasoff* are the two precedents of the California Supreme Court most widely cited and followed by the courts of other states.
18. Joseph Grodin interview with Gerald Uelmen, Nov. 3, 2009.
19. Interview by Gabrielle Morris, with Nicholas C. Petris, C.A state senator, in "Sacramento and Oakland, CA, State Government Oral History Program: California" (1988–89) (on file with the Regional Oral History Office), available at http://www.archive.org/details/petrisnicholascali00petrrich
20. Interview by Germaine LaBerge with Stanley Mosk, CA Supreme Court Justice, in "San Francisco, CA, State Government Oral History Program" (1998) (on file with the Regional Oral History Office), available at http://www.sos.ca.gov/archives/oral-history/pdf/mosk.pdf.
21. Interview by Gabrielle Morris with Phil S. Gibson, CA Supreme Court Chief Justice, in "Carmel Valley, CA, California Constitutional Officers" (May 12, 1977) (on file with the Regional Oral History Office, The Bancroft Library), available at http://ia700301.us.archive.org/22/items/caliconstitutoff00morrrich/caliconstitutoff00morrrich.pdf
22. Marc Poche interview with Gerald Uelmen, Sept. 23, 2009.
23. California Agriculture Labor Relations Act (1977), codified in the Cal. Lab. Code §1140.
24. Dick Meister, "The Courage of Rose Bird," *Labor-And a Whole Lot More: Articles by Dick Meister*, http://www.dickmeister.com/id111.html.
25. Preble Stolz, *Judging Judges: The Investigation of Rose Bird and the California Supreme Court* (1981), p. 88.
26. Ibid. at 89.
27. Ibid. at 91.
28. Ibid. at 93.
29. Stanley Mosk, "The Mask of Reform."
30. Letter from Arthur J. Goldberg to Stanley Mosk, March 23, 1977 (on file with Richard Mosk).
31. Interview by Germaine LaBerge with Stanley Mosk, CA Supreme Court Justice, in "San Francisco, CA, State Government Oral History Program" (1998) (on file with the Regional Oral History Office), available at http://www.sos.ca.gov/archives/oral-history/pdf/mosk.pdf.
32. Jerome Falk, Jr., interview with Gerald Uelmen, Feb. 14, 2012.
33. He voted with the Chief Justice in 90 percent of the cases.

34. "These judges, by the time they get into the highest court of the biggest state in the union, or the highest court in the federal system, they are pretty independent people, if not prima donnas. Not to say they are all prima donnas some of them are that too, but at least they are very independent. They are not easily led. It's like herding cats; they don't herd too well. They have their own mind and their own opinions. The Chief can urge that they reach consensus, but he only has persuasive powers; he doesn't have any sanctions. If they don't want to do it, they don't do it. There's nothing he can do about it. After all, any other Judge can go up and down the hall and try and persuade other Judges to join him. The Chief is not the only one who can do that. There were some who did a lot of that, and maybe still today, who try to achieve a consensus to support their view. He doesn't have any more power or any more votes." Interview by Germaine LaBerge, with Peter J. Belton, CA Supreme Court Staff Attorney, "A Senior Staff Attorney Reflects on Four Decades With the California Supreme Court (1960–2001) And a Lifetime with Disability" (2003), p. 138 (on file with the Regional Oral History Office, The Bancroft Library), available at http://www.archive.org/details/staffattorney4dec00beltrich.
35. Ibid.
36. Not including state bar disciplinary cases.
37. In 1980, her dissent rate was 20 percent. Chief Justice Donald Wright, much more conservative than Bird, dissented in only 4 percent of the cases. Justices Clark, Richardson and Manuel were most often in the minority when the Court split 4–3, as it did 26 times in 1980. These close decisions, where one vote determined the outcome, occurred with much greater frequency on the Bird Court. Under Chief Justice Wright, only 11 percent of the decisions were divided 4–3. Under Chief Justice Rose Bird, more that one-fourth of the cases divided the Court 4–3.
38. He had a high rate of disagreement with Chief Justice Bird, parting company with her in 22 percent of the cases. Although 40 percent of the decisions were unanimous, concurring opinions appeared with greater frequency, often niggling over obscure procedural differences. Even the routine unsigned per curiam opinions began drawing dissents. In 1980, four of the state bar disciplinary cases were decided by 4–3 margins.
39. 26 Cal.3d 515 (1980).
40. *Sindell v. Abbott Laboratories,* 26 Cal.3d 588 (1980).
41. *In re Marriage of Carney,* 24 Cal.3d 725 (1979).
42. Ibid. at 737.
43. Ibid. at 739.
44. While the case was winding its was through the appeals process, production began on what became a two-hour television CBS docudrama- "The Ordeal of Bill Carney," written by Tom Lazarus. As one columnist noted, the ruling by the California Supreme Court supplied a happy ending for what at the time was not yet written. December 23, 1981 *Pittsburgh Post-Gazette.*
45. Interview by Germaine LaBerge, with Peter J. Belton, CA Supreme Court Staff Attorney, "A Senior Staff Attorney Reflects on Four Decades With the California Supreme Court (1960–2001) And a Lifetime with Disability" (2003) (on file with the Regional Oral History Office, The Bancroft Library), available at http://www.archive.org/details/staffattorney4dec00beltrich.
46. *People v. Wheeler,* 22 Cal.3d 258 (1978).
47. *Batson v. Kentucky,* 476 U.S. 79 (1986).
48. Stanley Mosk, "Stanley Mosk of the California Supreme Court (1964–2001): Fifteen Papers by Justice Stanley Mosk," *California Legal History* 4 (2009), 155.
49. *People v. Shirley,* 31 Cal.3d 18 (1982).
50. Malcolm Ritter, "Hypnotized Witnesses Spark Legal Dilemmas," *Los Angeles Times,* Feb. 10, 1985.
51. California Evidence Code, Section 795.

Chapter 16

1. *People v. Caudillo,* 21 Cal.3d 562 (1978).
2. The majority opinion was authored by Court of Appeal Justice Bernard Jefferson, assigned by Bird to replace the absent Justice McComb before the swearing in of Justice Newman. Justices Mosk, Tobriner and Manuel joined Justice Jefferson's majority opinion along with Chief Justice Bird.
3. Preble Stolz, *Judging Judges,* p. 49.
4. Ibid., p. 48.
5. Tom Wicker, *New York Times,* October 9, 1978.
6. Judge Armand Arabian, "Rapists Find the Judicial Odds Changing," *Los Angeles Times,* September 27, 1978, p. 11.
7. *People v. Tanner,* 151 Cal.Rptr.299 (1978).
8. California Penal Code Section 1385 (2012).
9. *People v. Tanner,* 139 Cal.Rptr. 167 (1977) (depublished).
10. "In the Matter of Commission Proceedings Concerning the Seven Justices of the Supreme Court of California"; Background Report of Special Counsel, June 11, 1979; CJLSF.
11. "In the Matter of Commission Proceedings Concerning the Seven Justices of the Supreme Court of California; Background Report of Special Counsel, June 11, 1979; CJLSF.
12. Calif. Const. Article VI Section 19.
13. "Rapists Find the Judicial Odds Changing," *Los Angeles Times,* September 27, 1978, p. 11; Betty Medsger, *Framed,* p. 76.
14. *Hawkins v. Superior Court,* 22 Cal.3d 584 (1978).
15. Interview by Gabrielle Morris with Allen E. Broussard, C.A Supreme Court Justice, "A California Supreme Court Justice Looks at Law and Society, 1964–1996" with an Introduction by Carl B. Metoyer (1991, 1992, 1995 and 1996) (Regional Oral History Office, The Bancroft Library, University of California, Berkeley), available at http://texts.cdlib.org/view?docId=kt0v19n4dr&doc.view=entire_text.
16. Letter from Stanley Mosk to Hon. Bertram D. Jones, Chairman, Commission on Judicial Performance, February 15, 1979. CJLSF.
17. Stolz, *supra* n.3 at 176–177.
18. *Mosk v. Superior Court,* 25 Cal.3d 474 (1979).
19. Stolz, *supra* note 3 at 327.
20. Stanley Mosk to Honorable Harry W. Low, August 7, 1979. CJLSF.
21. Stanley Mosk, "When the Supreme Court of California Became Exhibit A," *Judges J.* 18, no. 4 (1979): 40.
22. "Special Counsel Defends High Court Probe, Press," Los Angeles *Daily Journal,* September 24, 1979; CJLSF.
23. *Fox v. City of Los Angeles,* 22 Cal. 3d 794 (1978).
24. Hearing in the Matter of Commission Proceedings Concerning Justice Stanley Mosk of the Supreme Court of California, Volume II (July 25, 1979) (on file with California Judicial Center Library in San Francisco).
25. Ibid.
26. Ibid.

27. "Court Wasn't Exonerated, Judicial Panel Member Says," *Los Angeles Times*, November 7, 1979, p. 1, 23. CJLSF.
28. Anthony Lewis, foreword to Preble Stolz, *Judging Judges*, p. xv.
29. Letter from Stanley Mosk to Honorable Leo T. McCarthy, November 14, 1979. CJLSF.
30. Edward Lascher, "Lascher at Large" Column, Los Angeles *Daily Journal*, available at http://www.lascher.com/large.php.
31. *People v. Tanner*, 24 Cal.3d 514 (1979).

Chapter 17

1. Letter from Dr. Ernest Rosenbaum, to Stanley Mosk, CA Supreme Court Justice (June 2, 1981) (CJLSF).
2. Interview by Amelia Fry, with Stanley Mosk, CA Supreme Court Justice, in "San Francisco, CA, Constitutional Officers" (Mar. 1, 1979) (on file with the Regional Oral History Office, The Bancroft Library), available at http://ia700301.us.archive.org/22/items/calico nstitutoff00morrrich/caliconstitutoff00morrrich.pdf.
3. Ibid.
4. Letter from Alan Cranston, CA. democratic senator, to Stanley Mosk, CA. Supreme Court Justice (December 12, 1983) (on file with Richard Mosk).
5. Letter from Ronald Reagan, 40th president of the U.S, to Stanley Mosk, CA. Supreme Court Justice (Feb. 17, 1981) (CJLSF).
6. "Oral History Interview with Frank C. Newman," California State Archives State Government Oral History Program, January — July 1991, p. 186. Interviewed by Carole Hicke, ROHO.
7. Interview prepared by Committee on History of Law in California with Justice Joseph R. Grodin, CA Supreme Court Justice, in "San Francisco, CA, Retrospect Oral History: Justice Joseph R. Grodin" (Sept. 28, 1987), on file with Hastings College of Law, State Bar of CA: Committee on the History of Law in CA, available at http://hastingsconlawquarterly.org/archives/V16/I1/Zakheim.pdf.
8. Jacqueline Braitman interview with Susan Mosk.
9. Letter from Susan Mosk, to Dianne Feinstein, Mayor of San Francisco (Dec. 4, 1986) (CJLSF).
10. Joseph Malhluf, "Jerry's Judges and the Politics of the Death Penalty: 1977–1982" (2010) (Second Place Entry, California Supreme Court Historical Society 2010 Student Writing Competition) (CJLSF).
11. Stanley Mosk, *Los Angeles Times*, June 29, 1983.
12. Stanley Mosk, "Opinion: A Two-Part State Supreme Court," *Pepperdine L. Rev.* 1 (1983), 11; Gerald Uelmen, "Dissent: Supreme Court Reform: Diversion Instead of Division," *Pepperdine L. Rev.* 5 (1983), 11.
13. Reynoso voted with Bird in 81 percent of the cases decided in 1985, while Broussard agreed with her in 74 percent of those cases. Justices Grodin and Kaus voted with her in 67 percent of the cases.
14. Justice Lucas had a very high dissent rate, agreeing with only 43 percent of the Bird Court decisions. But he and Justice Mosk were in agreement in 69 percent of the cases.
15. Letter from Malcolm Lucas, CA. Supreme Court Chief Justice, to Roger Grace (Dec. 13, 1984) (CJLSF).
16. Letter from Rose Bird, CA. Supreme Court, Chief Justice, to Roger Grace (Dec. 1984) (CJLSF).
17. *Olson v. Cory*, 26 Cal. 3d 672 (1980).
18. *Isbister v. Boys' Club of Santa Cruz*, 40 Cal.3d 72 (1985).
19. Cal. Civ. Code § 51 (2012).
20. 40 Cal.3d at 93–94.
21. Ibid. at 92.
22. Memorandum from Stanley Mosk on Objecting to Usage of the Term "Gender Discrimination" to CA Supreme Court Justices (May 8, 1985) (CJLSF).
23. Letter from Stanley Mosk, CA. Supreme Court Justice, to "John" (Dec. 16, 1985) (CJLSF).
24. *Warfield v. Peninsula Golf & Country Club*, 10 Cal. 4th 594 (1995).
25. Ibid. at 632.
26. *J.E.B v. Alabama, ex rel. T.B.*, 511 U.S. 127, 157 n. 1 (1993) (Scalia, J., dissenting).
27. Interview prepared by Committee on History of Law in California with Justice Joseph R. Grodin, *supra* note 7.
28. Letter from Ruth Bader Ginsburg to Stanley Mosk, CJLSF.
29. Stanley Mosk, Unfinished book manuscript, CJLSF.
30. *Curran v. Mt. Diablo Council of Boy Scouts*, 17 Cal.4th 670 (1998).
31. In a companion case, the Court ruled that the Cub Scouts could exclude children who were atheists. *Randall v. Orange County Council*, 17 Cal.4th 736 (1998).

Chapter 18

1. CA Const. art. VI, § 16(a).
2. *Los Angeles Times*, July 3, 1985.
3. *Los Angeles Times*, Nov. 3, 1985.
4. Endicott, "Governor Cites Cases in Assailing State Court," *Los Angeles Times*, February 14, 1985, Pt. I., p. 3.
5. *Royal Globe Insurance Company v. Superior Court*, 23 Cal.3d 880 (1979).
6. *Royal Globe* was subsequently overruled in *Moradi-Shalal v. Firemens' Fund Insurance Cos.*, 46 Cal. 3d 287 (1988).
7. *Carlos v. Superior Court*, 35 Cal. 3d 131 (1983).
8. *Los Angeles Times*, Aug. 26, 1986.
9. *Los Angeles Times*, Oct. 18, 1986.
10. *People v. Stevie Lamar Fields*, 35 Cal.3d 329 (1983). Justice Mosk dissented in the only two other cases in which the Bird Court affirmed a death judgment. In *People v. Earl Lloyd Jackson*, 28 Cal. 3d 264 (1980), a majority composed of Justices Richardson, Manuel, Clark and Newman upheld the death sentence over the dissents of Chief Justice Bird, Justice Mosk and Justice Tobriner. Both Bird and Mosk, joined by Tobriner, expressed the opinion that the 1987 death penalty law violated federal constitutional requirements. In *People v. Robert Alton Harris*, 28 Cal. 3d 935 (1981), a majority composed of Justices Clark, Richardson, Newman and Tobriner upheld the death sentence over the dissents of Chief Justice Bird and Justice Mosk, who argued that a change of venue should have been granted. Justice Tobriner concurred, explaining that although he still felt the statute was unconstitutional, he was bound by the *Jackson* majority decision. Robert Alton Harris was executed on April 21, 1992. The finding of special circumstances and death sentence imposed on Earl Lloyd Jackson was set aside in a federal habeas corpus proceeding. See *Jackson v. Brown*, 513 F. 3d 1057 (9th Cir. 2008).
11. Carol Ann Traut and Craig F. Emmert, "Expanding the Integrated Model of Judicial Decision Making: The California Justices and Capital Punishment," *J. Pol.* 60 (Nov. 1998): 1166, 1166–1180.

12. *Enmund v. Florida,* 458 U.S. 782 (1982).
13. *Cabana v. Bullock,* 474 U.S. 376 (1986).
14. *People v. Guerra,* 40 Cal.3d 377 (1985).
15. *Tison v. Arizona,* 481 U.S. 137 (1986).
16. *People v. Anderson,* 43 Cal. 3d 1104 (1987).
17. *People v. Smallwood,* 42 Cal.3d 415 (1986).
18. *People v. Turner,* 42 Cal.3d 711 (1986).
19. *People v. Rodriguez,* 42 Cal.3d 730 (1986).
20. "Philibosian Profile," *Los Angeles Metropolitan News-Enterprise,* Jan. 14, 2008.
21. Bud Lembke, *Political Pulse,* March 8, 1985. (CJLSF).
22. Letter from Ed Jagels to Richard Mosk, Dec. 19, 1985.(CJLSF).
23. Letter from Stanley Mosk to March Fong Eu, Dec. 13, 1984.(CJLSF).
24. Letter from Richard Mosk to March Fong Eu, June 14, 1985.(CJLSF).
25. Letter from Stanley Mosk to Anthony Lewis, Feb. 11, 1985. (CJLSF).
26. Dan Morain, "Will Dean of High Court Hang It Up?," *Los Angeles Times,* Jan 26, 1986.
27. Ibid.
28. Ibid.
29. Ibid.
30. Ibid.
31. Announcement, Stanley Mosk, Announcing Plan to Seek Another Term (Aug. 11, 1986). (CJLSF).
32. Letter from Richard Mosk to Radio Station Managers, Nov. 1985.(CJLSF).
33. Interview by Germaine LaBerge, with Peter J. Belton, C.A Supreme Court Staff Attorney, "A Senior Staff Attorney Reflects on Four Decades With the California Supreme Court (1960–2001) And a Lifetime with Disability" (2003, on file with the Regional Oral History Office, The Bancroft Library), available at http://www.archive.org/details/staffattorney4dec00beltrich; Letter from Stanley Mosk, CA. Supreme Court Justice, to Copley (Sept. 17, 1985); Letter from Stanley Mosk to *San Francisco Chronicle* (Sept. 11, 1985); Letter from Stanley Mosk to *San Jose Mercury* (Dec. 19, 1985) (All at CJLSF).
34. *San Jose Mercury,* Dec. 19, 1985. (CJLSF).
35. Letter from Stanley Mosk to Howard Hayes, Feb. 14, 1986. (CJLSF).
36. Letter from Stanley Mosk to Rose Bird, May 21, 1986. (CJLSF).
37. Notes from Rose Bird to Stanley Mosk. (CJLSF).
38. Letter, Stanley Mosk to Editor, *Claremont Review,* May 6, 1986. (CJLSF).
39. *Robinson v. Pioche,* 5 Cal. 460 (1855).
40. Stanley Mosk, "Whither Thou Goest — The State Constitution and Election Returns," *Whittier L. Rev.* 7 (1985): 753, 754
41. September 18, 1986, *Daily Journal,* p. 21. (Collection of Richard Mosk).
42. Ibid.
43. Ibid.
44. *The San Francisco Recorder,* Nov. 24, 1986. (CJLSF).
45. Letter from Stanley K. Sheinbaum to Stanley Mosk, May 8, 1986. Collection of Richard Mosk.
46. Letter from Leo McCarthy to Stanley Mosk, Jan. 7, 1986 (CJLSF).

Chapter 19

1. Morain, *Los Angeles Times,* Oct. 1986.
2. *Moradi-Shalal v. Fireman's Fund Ins. Companies,* 46 Cal. 3d 287 (1988).
3. *Royal Globe Ins. Co. v. Superior Court,* 23 Cal. 3d 880 (1979).
4. 46 Cal. 3d at 313–314.
5. Ibid., 320.
6. *Thing v. LaChusa,* 48 Cal. 3d 644 (1989).
7. *Dillon v. Legg,* 68 Cal. 2d 728 (1968).
8. 48 Cal. 3d at 681–682.
9. *People v. Anderson,* 43 Cal.3d 1104 (1987).
10. 43 Cal. 3d at 1152.
11. Gerald Uelmen, "A Tale of Two Courts," *Loyola* (L.A.) *Law Rev.* 23 (1989): 237.
12. During the first two years of the Lucas Court, the Court lined up, left to right, Broussard, Mosk, Kaufman, Panelli, Arguelles, Eagleson and Lucas. Justices Panelli, Eagleson and Arguelles were reliable allies of Chief Justice Lucas, voting with him in 94.3 percent, 94.8 percent and 96.3 percent of the cases, respectively. The leading dissenter was Justice Broussard, disagreeing with 29 percent of the outcomes, closely followed by Justice Mosk, dissenting in 27 percent of the cases.
13. Program, "The Anniversary Tribute Honoring Justice Stanley Mosk," September 22, 1989. (Collection of Richard Mosk.)
14. Philip Carrizosa, "The Elusive Stanley Mosk," *California Lawyer Magazine,* March, 1989, p. 63.
15. Stanley Mosk, "Nothing Succeeds Like Excess," *Loyola* (L.A.*) Law Review* 26 (June 1993): 981, 991.
16. Letter from Edmund G. Brown to Stanley Mosk, October 10, 1989. (Collection of Richard Mosk.)
17. Jake Dear, "150th Anniversary Celebration of California Supreme Court," *4 Cal. Sup. Ct. Hist. Society Yearbook* 63 (1999–2000).
18. *Henning v. Industrial Welfare Com.,* 46 Cal.3d 1292 (1988).
19. *Molko v. Holy Spirit Assoc.,* 46 Cal.3d 1092 (1988).
20. *Raven v. Deukmejian,* 52 Cal.3d 336 (1991).
21. Letter from Frank Sinatra to Stanley Mosk, December, 1990. Collection of Richard Mosk.
22. *Legislature v. Eu,* 54 Cal.3d 492 (1991).
23. Interview of Ronald M. George by Gerald F. Uelmen, 2012.
24. Ronald M. George, Address to American Academy of Arts & Sciences, October, 2009.
25. *Times Co. v. Superior Court,* 53 Cal.3d 1325, 1348 (1991).
26. *San Francisco Examiner,* August 30, 1991, p. A-22.
27. *Kowis v. Howard,* 3 Cal.4th 888 (1992).
28. *People v. Bacigalupo,* 6 Cal. 4th 457 (1993).
29. *Alfredo A. v. Superior Court,* 6 Cal.4th 1212 (1994).
30. *Hill v. NCAA,* 7 Cal.4th 1 (1994).
31. *20th Century Insurance Co. et al. v. John Garamendi,* 8 Cal.4th 216 (1994).
32. *People v. Whitfield,* 7 Cal. 4th 437 (1994).
33. Ibid. at 475.
34. Cal. Penal Code 22 (1872) (amended 1995). 1995 Cal.Stat. ch. 793.
35. Charles Rappleye and David Robb, *L.A. Weekly,* March 4–10, 1994.
36. Ibid. at 28.
37. Herb Caen, "Back in the Real World," *San Francisco Chronicle,* May 2, 1994.
38. Herb Caen, *San Francisco Chronicle,* February 2, 1995.
39. Jacqueline Braitman interview with Susan Mosk.
40. Kaygey Kash Mosk, Memorial Service for Justice Stanley Mosk, before the California Supreme Court, 26 Cal.4th 1242 (2001).

41. *Bruce Callins v. Collins, Director, Texas Dept. of Criminal Justice*, 510 U.S. 1141, 1144 (1994) (Blackmun, J., dissenting).
42. Mosk Papers, 1964 U.S. State Dept. Biographical Form. (CJLSF)
43. Dennis Peter Maio, *Fifteen Papers by Stanley Mosk*, California Legal History 4 (2009): 47, 48.
44. Ibid., 49.
45. Stanley Mosk, *Democracy in America–Day by Day* (1995), 239.

Chapter 20

1. Letter from Robert H. Henry to Stanley Mosk (CJLSF).
2. Stanley Mosk, "States' Rights—And Wrongs," *N.Y.U. L. Rev.* 72 (1997): 552, 559–565.
3. Letter from Stanley Mosk to Ms. Almena Lomax, March 16, 1995. Courtesy of Richard Mosk.
4. *American Academy of Pediatrics v. Lungren*, 16 Cal.4th 307 (1997).
5. *In Re Manzy W.*, 14 Cal.4th 1199 (1977).
6. *People v. Gallo*, 14 Cal.4th 1090 (1997).
7. Harriet Chiang, *San Francisco Chronicle*, July 30, 1998.
8. *Los Angeles Times*, December 24, 1999.
9. 21 Cal.4th 1316 (1999.
10. Jake Dear and Edward W. Jessen, "'Followed' Rates and Leading State Cases, 1940–2005," *U.C Davis Law Review* 4 (2007) 1683; Jake Dear, *The Influence of Justice Stanley Mosk's Opinions* (2008).
11. *Hi-Voltage Wireworks, Inc. v. City of San Jose*, 24 Cal.4th 537 (2000).
12. *McCleskey v. Kemp*, 481 U.S. 279, 343–44 (1987).
13. *People v. Morales*, 25 Cal.4th 34 (2001).
14. "Stanley Mosk of the California Supreme Court (1964–2001);" "Fifteen Papers by Stanley Mosk," *California Legal History* 4 (2009): 50; 168.

Epilogue

1. "'Judges Are Not Politicans,' Roberts Says," *Washington Post*, September 13, 2005.
2. Silverstein, "Bench Politics," *The New Republic*, May 15, 2009.
3. Linda Greenhouse, "A Judge and a Politician," *New York Times*, Dec. 31, 2009.
4. In some cases, as in New York, it is called a "Court of Appeals," although in most states the Court of Appeals is an intermediate appellate court below the Supreme Court. In Oklahoma and Texas, there are separate high courts for civil and criminal appeals. The court for civil appeals is called the "Supreme Court," while the court for criminal appeals is called "Court of Criminal Appeals."
5. Stanley Mosk, "The Mask of Reform," *Southwestern Law Review* 10 (1978): 885, 892.
6. Alabama, Mississippi, Oklahoma, Texas and Washington.
7. Frank M. Coffin, *The Ways of a Judge: Reflections From the Federal Appellate Bench* (1980).
8. Mosk, "Myths and Realities in the Law," unpublished manuscript, p. 13. (CJLSF).
9. Mosk, *Democracy in America—Day by Day*, p. 175.
10. Ed Cray, *Chief Justice: A Biography of Earl Warren* (1997), 497. The other two were Arthur Goldberg and Ramsey Clark.
11. Quote in *Myths and Realities*, supra n.8 at 9.
12. Ibid.

Bibliography

Books and Articles

Bagley, William T. *California's Golden Years: When Government Worked and Why*. Berkeley, CA: Berkeley Public Policy Press, 2009.

Ball, Howard. *The Bakke Case: Race, Education, and Affirmative Action*. Lawrence: University Press of Kansas, 2000.

Barnett, Stephen R. "The Emerging Court." *California Law Review* 71, no. 4 (July 1983): 1134–1196.

Bernstein, Shana. "From Civic Defense to Civil Rights: the Growth of Jewish American Interracial Civil Rights Activism in Los Angeles." In *A Cultural History of Jews in California, The Jewish Role in American Life: An Annual Review, Volume 7*, edited by William Deverell, Bruce Zuckerman and Lisa Ansell. West Lafayette, Indiana: Purdue University Press, 2010.

Bollens, John Constantinus, and Geyer, Grant B. *Yorty, Politics of a Constant Candidate*. Pacific Palisades, California: Palisades Publishers, 1973.

Boyarsky, Bill. *Big Daddy: Jesse Unruh and the Art of Power Politics*. Berkeley: University of California Press, 2008.

Brown, Edmund (Pat), with Adler, Dick. *Public Justice, Private Mercy: A Governor's Education on Death Row*. New York: Weidenfeld & Nicolson, 1989.

Buntin, John. *L.A. Noir: The Struggle for the Soul of America's Most Seductive City*. New York: Harmony Books, 2009.

Burke, Robert E. *Olson's New Deal for California*. Berkeley: University of California Press, 1953.

California Deptartment of Justice. *A History of the California Attorney General's Office*. Sacramento: California Department of Justice, 1988.

———. *Opinions of the Attorney General of California Volume 39*. Berkeley, California: California Legal Publication, 1962.

Camarillo, Albert. *Chicanos in California, A History of Mexican Americans in California*. San Francisco: Boyd & Fraser, 1990.

Cannon, Lou. *Governor Reagan: His Rise to Power*. New York: Public Affairs, 2003.

Caughey, John H. "Farewell to California's 'Loyalty' Oath." *Pacific Historical Review* 38, no. 2 (May, 1969): 123–128.

Chang, Helen Y. "Justice Carter's Dissent in People v. Crooker: An Early Step Towards Miranda Warnings and the Expansion of the Fifth Amendment to Pre-Trial Confessions." In *The Great Dissents of the "Lone Dissenter": Justice Jesse W. Carter's Twenty Tumultuous Years on the California Supreme Court*. Edited by David B. Oppenheimer and Allen Brotsky. Durham, N.C: Carolina Academic Press, 2010: 25–36.

Culver, John H., and John T. Wold. "Rose Bird and the Politics of Judicial Accountability in California." *Judicature* 70 (1986): 81.

Dallek, Matthew. *The Right Moment: Ronald Reagan's First Victory and the Decisive Turning Point in American Politics*. New York: Free Press, 2000.

Dollinger, Marc. *Quest for Inclusion: Jews and Liberalism in Modern America*. Princeton, N.J.: Princeton University Press, 2000.

Dreyfuss, Joel, and Charles III Lawrence. *The Bakke Case: The Politics of Inequality*. New York: Harcourt Brace Jovanovich, 1979.

Escobar, Edward J. *Race, Police, and the Making of a Political Identity*. Berkeley: University of California Press, 1999.

Field, Ben. *Activism in Pursuit of the Public Interest: The Jurisprudence of Chief Justice Roger Traynor*. Berkeley, California: Berkeley Public Policy Press for the California Supreme Court Historical Society, 2003.

Gibbs, Jewelle Taylor, and Teiahsha Bankhead. *Preserving Privilege: California Politics, Propositions, and People of Color*. Westport, Conn.: Praeger, 2001.

Halpern, Stephen C. "Symposium: Litigation and Racial Justice." *Law and Courts: Section of the American Political Science Association*, Summer 1996, 4–19.

Hill, Gladwin. *Dancing Bear: An Inside Look at California Politics*. Cleveland: World Pub. Co., 1968.

Holland, Josiah Gilbert. *God Give Us Men*. Inkhorn, Idaho: Cornwall Music Company, 1968.

Hundley, Norris. *Water and the West: The Colorado River Compact and the Politics of Water in the American West*. Berkeley: University of California Press, 1975.

Hurewitz, Daniel. *Bohemian Los Angeles and the Making of Modern Politics*. Berkeley: University of California Press, 2008.

———. "Goody-Goodies, Sissies, and Long-Hairs: The Dangerous Figures in 1930s Los Angeles Political Culture." *Journal of Urban History* 33 (November 2006): 26–50.

Johnson, J. Edward. *History of the Supreme Court Justices of California, Vol. 2.* San Francisco: Bender-Moss, 1966.

Karlen, Delmar. *Appellate Courts in the United States and England.* New York: New York University Press, 1963.

Kengor, Paul, and Patricia Clark Doerner. *The Judge: Williams P. Clark, Ronald Reagan's Top Hand.* San Francisco: Ignatius Press 2007.

Kramer, Sarah Alisa. "William H. Parker and the Thin Blue Line: Politics, Public Relations and Policing in Postwar Los Angeles." Ph.D. diss., American University, 2007.

Liu, Goodwin. "Bakke and the Causation Fallacy." University of Dayton School of Law. http://academic.udayton.edu/race/04needs/affirm18.htm.

Maisel, Louis Sandy, Ira N Forman, and Donald Altschiller, eds. *Jews in American Politics.* Lanham, MD: Rowman & Littlefield, 2001.

Matusow, Allen J. *The Unraveling of America: A History of Liberalism in the 1960's.* New York: Harper Torchbooks, 1986.

McDougal, Dennis. *The Last Mogul: Lew Wasserman, MCA and the Hidden History of Hollywood.* New York: Crown Publishers, 1998.

McWilliams, Carey. *California: The Great Exception.* New York: Current Books, 1949.

_____. *Factories in the Field: The Story of Migratory Farm Labor in California.* Santa Barbara: Peregrine Publishers, 1971.

_____. *A Mask for Privilege: Anti-Semitism in America.* Boston: Little, Brown, 1947.

Medsger, Betty. *Framed: The New Right Attack on Chief Justice Rose Bird and the Courts.* New York: Pilgrim Press, 1983.

Mitchell, Greg. *The Campaign of the Century: Upton Sinclair's E.P.I.C. Race for Governor of California and the Birth of Media Politics.* New York: Random House, 1992.

Mosk, Stanley. *Democracy in America — Day by Day.* New York: Vantage Press, 1995.

Newton, Jim. *Justice for All: Earl Warren and the Nation He Made.* New York: Riverhead Books, 2006.

Rarick, Ethan. *The Life and Times of Pat Brown: California Rising.* Berkeley: University of California Press, 2005.

Reisner, Marc. *Cadillac Desert: The American West and Its Disappearing Water.* New York: Penguin Books, 1986.

Rothmiller, Mike, and Ivan G Goldman. *L.A. Secret Police: Inside the LAPD Elite Spy Network.* New York: Pocket Books, 1992.

Salinger, Pierre. *With Kennedy.* Garden City, New York: Doubleday, 1966.

Sanchez, George J. and Bruce Zuckerman, eds. *Beyond Alliances: The Jewish Role in Reshaping the Racial Landscape of Southern California.* Vol. 9, *The Jewish Role in American Life Series: An Annual Review.* West Lafayette, IN: Purdue University Press, 2012.

Schiesl, Martin. "The Struggle for Racial Equality: Racial Reform and Party Politics in California, 1950–1966." Special Issue, *California Politics & Policy*, 1997.

Shad, Nayan. *Contagious Divides: Epidemics and Race in San Francisco's Chinatown.* Berkeley: University of California Press, 2001.

Sifford, Charlie, and Jim Gullo. *Just Let Me Play: The Story of Charlie Sifford, the First Black PGA Golfer.* Latham, New York: British American Pub., 1992.

Sitton, Thomas. "Urban Politics and Reform in New Deal Los Angeles." Ph.D. diss., University of California at Riverside, 1983.

Sonenshein, Raphael J. "The Dynamics of Biracial Coalitions: Crossover Politics in Los Angeles." *Western Political Quarterly* 42 (June 1989): 333–353.

_____. *Politics in Black and White: Race and Power in Los Angeles.* Princeton, New Jersey: Princeton University Press, 1993.

Starr, Kevin. *Endangered Dreams: The Great Depression in California.* New York: Oxford University Press, 1996.

Stolz, Preble. *Judging Judges: The Investigation of Rose Bird and the California Supreme Court.* New York: Free Press, 1981.

Terrell, John Upton. *War for the Colorado River Vol. I: The California-Arizona Controversy,* and *Vol. II: Above Lee's Ferry–the Upper Basin.* Glendale, California: A.H Clark Co., 1965.

Tuttle, Frederick B. "The California Democrats, 1953–1966." Ph.D. diss., University of California at Los Angeles, 1975.

Vorspan, Max, and Lloyd P. Gartner. *History of the Jews in Los Angeles.* San Marino, California: Huntington Library, 1970.

Weglyn, Michi. *Years of Infamy: The Untold Story of America's Concentration Camps.* New York: William Morrow and Co., 1976.

Yarbrough, Susan. "Bakke Case: The Politics of Inequality." Review of *Bakke Case: The Politics of Inequality,* by Joel Dreyfuss and Charles Lawrence III. *ALSA Forum* 4 (1979–1980): 65–69.

White House Tapes:

Johnson, Lyndon B. Johnson Presidential Recordings. LBJ Telephone Conversation with Edmund G. "Pat" Brown, April 6,1964; 6 min., 16 sec; MP3 Audio. From Miller Center at University of Virginia, http://web2.millercenter.org/lbj/audiovisual/whrecordings/telephone/conversations/1964/lbj_wh6404_03_2860.mp3

Johnson, Lyndon B. *Johnson Presidential Recordings.* LBJ Telephone Conversation with Presidential Aide Lloyd Hand, February 9, 1964; 16 min., 58 sec; MP3 Audio. From Miller Center at University of Virginia, http://web2.millercenter.org/lbj/audiovisual/whrecordings/telephone/conversations/1964/lbj_wh6402_13_1990.mp3

Oral Histories

Bane, Tom. "Oral History Interview with Tom Bane." By Steven L. Isoardi. *California State Archives State Government Oral History Program* (1995).

Belton, Peter J. "A Senior Staff Attorney Reflects on Four Decades With the California Supreme Court (1960–2001) And a Lifetime with Disability." By Germaine LaBerge. *Regional Oral History Office* (2003).

Bradley, Donald. "Managing Democratic Campaigns, 1943–1966: Interview with Donald L. Bradley." By Amelia R. Fry. *Governmental History Documentation Project* (1977–1979).

Broussard, Allen E. "Allen E. Broussard: A California Supreme Court Justice Looks at Law and Society 1964–1996." By Gabrielle Morris. *Regional Oral History Office: University of California Black Alumni Series* (1991, 1992, 1995 and 1996).

Cerrell, Jospeh. "Joseph Cerrell Oral History Interview." By Dennis O'Brien. *John F. Kennedy Library Oral History Program* (June 13, 1969).

Champion, Hale. "Communication and Problem-Solving: A Journalist in State Government." By Amelia Fry. Governmental History Documentation Project (1977, 1978 and 1979).

Clark, John Gee. "John Gee Clark California Legislator, Executive Administrator, and Judge." By Donald J. Schippers. *Oral History Project* (1961 and 1962).

Clifton, Florence McChesney. "*California Democrats, 1934–1950:* California Democrats in the Earl Warren Era." *By Amelia R. Fry. Earl Warren Oral History Project* (1972).

Clifton, Robert. "The Democratic Party, Culbert L. Olson, and the Legislature: California Democrats in the Earl Warren Era." By Amelia R. Fry. Earl Warren Oral History Project (1972).

Cullen, Frank, Sr. "Oral History Interview with Frank Cullen, Sr." By Susan Douglass Yates. State Government Oral History Program (2003).

Fuller, Jean. "Organizing Women: Careers in Volunteer Politics and Government Administration." By Miriam Feingold Stein. Women in Politics Oral History Project (1977).

Gatov, Elizabeth R. "Grassroots Party Organizer to Treasurer of the United States." By Malca Chall. Women in Politics Oral History Project (1978).

Gibson, Phil S. "California Constitutional Officers: Recollections of a Chief Justice of California Supreme Court. By Gabrielle Morris. *Governmental History Documentation Project* (1977).

Goldberg, Abbott B. "California Water Issues 1950–66: Water Policy Issues in the Courts, 1950–1966." By Malca Chall. Governmental History Documentation Project (1979, 1980).

Greenaway, Roy. "Oral History Interview with Roy Greenaway: California Political Activist, 1952–1968." By Amelia R. Fry. State Government Oral History Program (1990 and 1991).

Grodin, Joseph R. "Retrospect Oral History: Justice Joseph R. Grodin. By Committee on History of Law in CA: John Hanft, Mark Pierce, Patricia Seitas, and Kirk McAllister. The California Bar Oral History Series (Sept. 28, 1987).

Hawkins, Augustus F. "Oral History Interview with Augustus F. Hawkins." By Carlos Vasquez. State Government Oral History Program (1988).

Johnson, Gardiner. "Oral History Interview with Hon. Gardiner Johnson." By Gabrielle Morris. State Government Oral History Program (1973 and 1983).

Kenny, Robert W. "My First Forty Years in California Politics, 1922–1962, by Robert W. Kenny." By Doyce B. Nunis. *UCLA Oral History Program* (1960–1962).

Kline, Anthony J. "Oral History Interview with Hon. Anthony J. Kline, Legal Affairs Secretary, 1975–1980." By Germaine LaBerge. State Government Oral History Program (1991).

Kline, Richard. "The Governor's Office Under Edmund G. Brown, Sr.: Governor Brown's Faithful Advisor." By Eleanor Glaser. Governmental History Documentation Project (1977).

McEnery John P. "Oral History Interview with John P. McEnery." By James R. Fuchs. Harry S. Truman Library (March 11, 1970).

Mosk, Stanley. "Constitutional Officers: Stanley Mosk- Attorney General's Office and Political Campaigns, 1958–1966. By Amelia R. Fry. Governmental History Documentation Project (Mar. 1, 1979).

———. "Oral History Interview with Stanley Mosk, Justice of the California Supreme Court, 1964-Present." By Germaine LaBerge. State Government Oral History Program (1998).

Newman, Frank C. "Oral History Interview with Frank C. Newman." By Carole Hicke. State Government Oral History Program (1989 and 1991).

O'Brien, Charles A. "Oral History Interview with Charles A. O'Brien." By Carole Hicke. *State Government Oral History Program* (1987).

Petric, Nicholas C. "Oral History Interview with Nicholas C. Petris." By Gabrielle Morris. State Government Oral History Program (1988 and 1989).

Shirpser, Clara. "One Woman's Role in Democratic Party Politics: National, State, and Local, 1950–1973, Volume 1, Volume 2." By Malca Chall. Women in Politics Oral History Project (1975).

Snyder, Elizabeth. "California's First Woman State Party Chairman." By Malca Chall. Women in Politics Oral History Project (1977).

Zetterberg, Stephen I. "Oral History Interview with Stephen I. Zetterberg, California Democratic Council, Los Angeles County Democratic Central Committee, Democratic Party Politics." By Enid Hart Douglass. State Government Oral History Program (1990 and 1993).

Index of Cases

Allan Bakke v. Regents of the University of California see Bakke v. Regents
American Academy of Pediatrics v. Lungren 242
Arizona v. California 95–96

Bakke v. Regents of the University of California 164, 166, 168–176, 185
Beck v. Bel Air Properties 69
Brosnahan v. Brown 231–232
Brown v. Board of Education 248, 250
Burrows v. Superior Court 155–156

Cabana v. Bullock 218
Callins v. Collins 238
Carlos v. Superior Court 216–218, 226
Cash v. Superior Court 95
City of Berkeley v. Superior Court 188
Curran v. Mt. Diablo Council of Boy Scouts 213

DeFunis v. Odegaard 172
Dillon v. Legg 225

Enmund v. Florida 217

Food Employees v. Logan Plaza 153
Fox v. City of Los Angeles 200
Friends of Mammoth v. Board of Supervisors of Mono County 152
Furman v. Georgia 160

Gratz v. Bollinger 176
Gruter v. Bollinger 176

Hawkins v. Superior Court 196, 231
Henning v. Industrial Welfare Commission. 230
Hi-Voltage Wire Works v. City of San Jose 176, 245
Hill v. NCAA 234, 242

Isbister v. Boys' Club of Santa Cruz 211, 212, 213

Kowis v. Howard 234

Legislature v. Eu 231, 232
Lloyd Corp. v. Tanner 154

Mapp v. Ohio 103–104, 140
Marbury v. Madison 51
Marriage of Carney(In Re) 189–190, 226
Michigan v. Mosely 153
Miranda v. Arizona 69
Molko v. Holy Spirit Assoc. 230
Mooney (In Re) 44
Mooney v. Holohan 44
Moradi-Shalal v. Fireman's Fund Ins. Companies 225
Mosk v. Superior Court 202, 233
Mulkey v. Reitman 139

Olson v. Cory 211

People v. Anderson 159–160, 225
People v. Belous 146
People v. Brisendine 156
People v. Cahan 81–82, 88, 103–104, 140
People v. Caudillo 192–194, n.1, 265
People v. Crooker n.65, 255

People v. Daniels 103
People v. Frierson 160
People v. Krivda 155
People v. Mozetti 155, 156
People v. Shirley 190
People v. Stevie Lamar Fields 217
People v. Tanner 192–197, 199, 202, 205–207
People v. Wein 103
People v. Wheeler 190
People v. Whitfield 235
Pockman v. Leonard 81
Point Lobos Case 48
Price v. Civil Service Commission 173

Raven v. Deukmejian 231–232
Robins v. Pruneyard Shopping Center 154
Roe v. Wade 53
Royal Globe Insurance Company v. Superior Court 215, 225

Shelley v. Kramer 68
Sindell v. Abbott Laboratories 189

Thing v. LaChusa 225
Tison v. Arizona 218
Tony C. (In Re) 156
Tucker (In Re) 151–152
20th Century Insurance Co. et al. v. John Garamendi 235

Warfield v. Peninsula Golf & Country Club 212
Weaver v. Jordan 138, 139
Wirta v. Alameda-Contra Costa Transit District 139
Wright v. Drye 67, 68

General Index

abortion 146, 242
Acuna, Rodolfo 169, 170
Adams, Ida May 56, 61, 62
Addams, Jane 21
Affirmative Action 164–165, 176, 245
Agricultural Labor Relations Act (ALR) 183, 184
Agricultural Labor Relations Board (ALRB) 184, 185
Ahlport, Brodie E. 47
Alexandria, Lorez 123
Allen, David 123
Allen, Steve 124
Allen, Woody 170
Alsop, Joseph 130–131
American Bar Association (ABA) 61, 146, 198, 227
American Civil Liberties Union (ACLU) 24, 29, 31–32, 35, 77, 79, 141, 146, 169
American Federation of Labor (AFL) 29, 31–33, 41, 61, 88, 105
American Federation of Teachers (AFT) 166
American Freedom from Hunger Foundation 39
American Jewish Committee 76, 137
American Jewish Congress 65, 137, 166
American Youth for Democracy 77
Anfenger, Louis 11
Anti-Defamation League (ADL) 74, 76, 166
anti–Semitism 9–10, 20–21; see also Lake Elsinore, CA; A Mask for Privilege; quotas
Antonovich, Mike 180
Arabian, Armand 193, 228, 230, 232–233, 241
Arguelles, John 224–225, 229
Arnaz, Desi 57
Arnold, Dorothy 57
Arvey, Jacob 110
Associated Farmers of California (AFC) 29–30

Bakke, Allan 165–166, 168–170, 176
Balfour Declaration 75
Ball, Joseph A. 53, 84
Ball, Lucille 49, 57
Barrett, Edward L., Jr. 171
Barry, Joan (Berry) 57–58, 62
Bass, Charlotta 67
Baxter, Marvin 228, 230, 233, 241–242, 245
Bay Area Council Against Discrimination 77
Belous, Leon 146
Belton, Peter 138, 167, 187–190, 217, 244
Benson, Mary 140
Ber wanger, Jay 22
Bergen, Polly 118
Bernstein, Leonard 208
Billings, Warren K. 44–45, 101
Bird, (Elizabeth) Rose 6, 161–162, 170, 173, 181, 183–188, 190, 192–196, 198–199, 202–203, 206, 208–211, 214–225, 229, 250
Blackmun, Harry 238
Bloody Thursday 29
B'nai B'rith 11, 17, 74–76, 84, 205, 237
Board of Regents, University of California 46
Boddy, Manchester 36, 74, 80
Bonelli, Frank G. 110
Boot, Max 243
Borough, Reuben W. 29
Bowron, Fletcher 34, 37–39, 74, 76
Boyarsky, Bill 128
Bradley, Don 131, 133
Bradley, Omar 90
Bradley, Tom 69, 127, 209, 215–216, 222
Brand, Edward R. 57
Bregerson, Dianne 84
Brennan, William J. 105, 153, 240, 245, 248
Bridges, Harry 29
Briggs, John 163
Briggs, Ron 163

Briggs Amendment/Initiative 160, 163
Broussard, Allen 156, 197, 206, 208–210, 214, 216–217, 225, 227–228, 230, 233–234, 241
Brown, Edmund "Jerry," Jr. 5, 51, 90, 101, 127, 131, 138, 150, 160, 169, 173, 176–177, 181–187, 207–209, 213, 215, 219, 221, 223, 233
Brown, Edmund G. "Pat" 5–6, 41, 53, 67, 71, 83–84, 87–88, 90–92, 96, 98–103, 107, 109–112, 114–115, 117–123, 125, 127–129, 131–138, 143, 150–151, 181–182, 186, 219, 223, 227
Brown, George, Jr. 150
Brown, Janice Rogers 176, 241–245
Buehl, Steven 187
Bullock, Georgia P. 56
Burger, Warren 151, 155
Burke, J. Frank 35
Burke, Louis H. 137–139, 142–143, 148, 151, 178, 180
Burke, Yvonne Braithwhite 145
Burns, Frank 3, 122, 128, 129, 144
Burton, John L. 91
Burton, Phil 84, 91
Butler, Paul 110
Byrne, William M. 57

Caen, Herb 236–237
Cahan, Charles 81, 83
California Bar Association (CBA) 26–27
California Commission on Judicial Performance 195–197; see also Tanner Commission
California Commission on the Status of Women 90
California Committee for Political Unity (CCPU) 33
California Conference for Democratic Action 77
California Democratic Council (CDC) 83–85, 117, 120–121, 129–131

275

California Department of Consumer Affairs 90
California District Attorneys Association 155
California Dynasty of Communism 107
California Environmental Quality Act 152
California Fair Political Practices Commission 179
California Farmers Association (CFA) 42
California Federation for Political Unity (CFPU) 64
California Judges Association 198
California Real Estate Agents' Association (CREA) 133
California Republican Assembly (CRA) 133
Camp Grant, Illinois 15
Canson, Virna M. 175
capital punishment *see* death penalty
Capone, Al 110
Cardozo, Benjamin 148, 186, 225, 239–240, 248
Carrizosa, Philip 227
Carter, Jesse W. 42, 47, 53, 70, 81–82, 86, 115, 137
Carter, Jimmy 183
Cartwright Act 95
Caruso, Paul 124
Caughey, John 81, 169
Central Arizona Project 97–98
Cermak, Anton 22–23
Cerrell, Joe 133
Chaplin, Charlie 4, 57–58, 62
Chavis, Patrick 176
Chessman, Caryl 46, 70, 100–103
Chin, Ming 241–242, 244–245
Chowchilla kidnapping 191
Christian Anti-Communist Crusade 107
Citizen's Committee for Industrial Justice (CCIJ) 33, 63
Citizen's Committee to Preserve American Freedom 102
Citizens Independent Vice Investigating Committee (CIVIC) 34–36, 49–50
Civil Rights Act of 1964 121, 165, 174
Clark, John C. 57
Clark, Ramsey 144
Clark, Tom 68, 104, 173, 178, 199, 206
Clark, William P., Jr. 5, 174, 177–178, 180, 188–189, 194–195, 198–199, 201–202, 206–207, 211
Clarke, Thurmond 57, 67, 68
Clifton, Florence (Susie) 40
Clifton, Robert 41, 79

Clifton's Cafeteria 33, 38
Clinton, Clifford E. 28, 30, 33–39, 49
Coakley, J.F. 82
Coakley, Tom 117, 118
Coblentz, William 168
Colley, Nathaniel, Jr. 168, 175
Committee of Twenty Five (of FCB) 35, 37–38
Communist Party USA 28
Compassionate Use Act 204; *see also* marijuana
Congress of Industrial Organizations (CIO) 29, 31–33, 38, 41, 48, 62, 76, 88
Constitutional Rights Foundation 141
Coolbrith, Ida 56
Corker, Charles 97
Cox, Archibald 105
Crane, Stephen 58
Cranston, Alan 83–85, 107, 120–122, 127, 129–131, 134, 144–145, 149, 206, 216
Crime Victims for Court Reform 219
Crooker, John 69–71, 100
Crown All Hats store 13
Cusack, James 23

Dairy Workers Union 31
Dalin, David D. 87
Darrow, Clarence 18, 23–24, 208
Davis, Ed 184, 193, 219
Davis, George T. 44, 102
Davis, Gray 5, 246
Davis, James E. 31, 35, 36, 39
Dawson, LeRoy 61–62
death penalty 69–71, 100–103, 159–163
The Deltan 22
Democracy in America — Day by Day 238
Democratic Luncheon Club 56
Democratic National Committeeman 109–111
Democratic National Convention: 1960: 109–112; 1968: 144–145
Denver Hebrew Ladies' Relief Society 11
DES *see* Sindell v. Abbott Laboratories
Desmond, William 105
Detlie, John Stewart 57
Deukmejian, George 5, 156, 160, 208–210, 214–219, 222, 224, 229–230, 232–233
Dewey, Thomas E. 35, 63, 79, 85
dictaphone investigation (illegal wiretapping) 48
Dies, Martin 41
Dies Committee 41, 49–50

DiMaggio, Joe 57
direct democracy 30
Dirkson, Everett 132
Dodd, Martha 21
Dodd, William E. 21
Dolan, Maura 244
Dollinger, Marc 76
Douglas, Helen Gahagan 61–62, 74–75, 80
Douglas, Melvyn 42
Douglas, Paul H. 21
Douglas, William O. 103–104
Downey, Sheridan 26, 28, 42, 80
Doyle, Clyde 62
Drye, Frank Lloyd 67

Eagleson, David 224–225, 228–230
Eckstine, Billy 93
Eisenhower, Dwight D. 51, 102, 107, 114, 134, 177, 248
El Congreso 43
Eliaser, Ann 84–85, 130
Ely, Northcutt 97
End Poverty in California (EPIC) campaign 25–26, 28, 40, 42
Endicott, William 195, 199–200
Engle, Clair 84, 116, 119–121, 131–132
Epstein, Norman L. 92
Equal Rights Amendment (ERA) 56 see also women's rights
Ervin, Sam 132
Escobar, Edward J. 59
Ettelson, Lee 125
Eu, March Fong 145, 219–220
Evans, Hugh A. 208
Exclusionary rule 81–82, 103–104, 127, 135, 156; *see also* People v. Cahan
Executive Order 8802 66
Executive Order 10925 164
Executive Order 11246 165
Exner, Judith 125

Fair Employment Practices Commission (FEPC) 77, 164
Fairbanks, Robert 195, 198–199
False bottoms (cosmetics) 90–91
Fay, Eugene 52
Federal Bureau of Investigation (FBI) 5–6, 63–64, 80, 86, 88, 90, 102–103, 107, 111, 115–116, 123–126, 142, 144, 186; *see also* Hoover, J. Edgar
Federation for Civic Betterment (FCB) 35–37
Feinstein, Dianne 179
Feldman, Eddie 124
Fields, Freddie 124
Fitts, Buron 36

Flournoy, Houston 183
Fontaine, Joan 57
Ford, John Anson 29–30, 34, 37–38, 42
Fortas, Abe 144
Foutz, David 44
Frankfurter, Felix 104, 243
Fulton, Kenneth 43–44

Gabor, Zsa Zsa 57
Gampell, Ralph 187
Gann, Paul 219
Gardner, Ava 57
Garland, Gordon 48–49
Garland, Judy 4, 57–58
Gates, Darryl 127
gender vs. sex 212–213
George, Ronald M. 3, 91, 208, 212–213, 232–235, 241–246
Gibson, Phil, S. 5, 25, 40, 42–43, 47, 50, 52, 64, 82, 95, 101, 104, 134–136, 138, 182, 186, 234
Giesler, Jerry 58, 60, 62
Ginsberg, Ruth Bader 212
Glendale Young Republicans 117, 133
Goldberg, Arthur J. 54, 144, 153, 164, 169, 186, 221
Goldberg, B. Abbott 97
Gomez-Quinonez, Juan 169
Gompers, Samuel 105
Great Depression 22, 24, 26, 238
Greenhouse, Linda 247
Grimes, Leonard M. 181
Grodin, Joseph 3, 6, 136, 138, 202–203, 208, 211–212, 214, 216–219, 221–222, 224
Groman, Harry 205

Hackett, Buddy 118
The Hague 56, 141, 157, 206, 208; *see also* International Court of Justice at The Hague
Hahn, Kenneth 110
Ham and Eggs Movement 28
Hanawalt, Willis 171
Hand, Lloyd 128
Hanna, Byron C. 74
Hansen, John 138
Harper, Arthur C. 30
Harris, Robert Alton 162–163
Hart, Gary 236
Hartzmark (Hartzmark), Elias 9
Hartzmark (Hartzmark), William 10
Hartzmark (Hartzmark), Yetta 10, 12
Hatch, Orrin 174
Hawkins, Augustus 43, 92, 107
Hayworth, Rita 73
Healey, Don 33, 38
Heller, Eleanor 80

Hellman, Isias 76
Henry, Robert H. 240
Heydenfeldt, Solomon 137, 222
Hicks, Frank 19
Hillcrest Country Club 54, 93, 232
Hillings, Patrick 85–87
Hilton, Barron 124
Hofstetter, Patricia 84
Hollifield, Chet 62
Hollywood Cultural Committee 77
Hollywood Independent Citizens Committee of Arts, Sciences and Professions 77
Hollywood League for Democratic Action 77
Hollywood Theatre Alliance 77
Holmes, Oliver Wendell, Jr. 234–235, 248
Hoover, Herbert 23
Hoover, J. Edgar 5–6, 64, 88, 102, 111, 116, 124, 126; *see also* FBI
Hoskin, Carl C. 34–35
House Committe on Un-American Activities (HUAC) 29, 41
Houser, Frederick W. 50
Hufstedler, Seth 197
Hufstedler, Shirley 97, 183, 197
Hughes, Charles Evans 15
Humphrey, Hubert H. 110, 145
Hutchens, Robert Maynard 21, 22
Hutton, Betty 58
Hynes, Captain "Red" 31

Independent Progressive Party (IPP) 79
Industrial Workers of the World (IWW) 29
International Court of Justice at The Hague 56
Israel 73, 74, 78, 130, 136, 156, 158, 162, 183

Jackson, Henry M. "Scoop" 115
Jacobs, Frances Wisebart 11
Jacoby, Norman 81
Jagels, Ed 219
Jarvis, Howard 219
Jeffries, Harold 52
Jenkins, Leon 176
Jessel, George 118
Jewel, Howard 91, 107
Jewish Federation of Greater Los Angeles 78
John Birch Society 107, 109, 133, 193
Johnson, Lyndon B. 91, 122, 128, 130, 131, 134, 141, 144, 164, 165, 174, 247, 250
Johnson, Phillip E. 222
Jordan, Barbara 170
Jordan, Frank 131, 133

Jourdan, Sabrina (Laurelle Jane Stevenson) 122–128, 142, 235
Judging the News 56
Judicial retention elections: (1978) 195; (1982) 208–209; (1986) 214ff.; (1998) 243

Kaiser, Leland M. 132
Karger, Fred 219
Karl, Harry 124
Karlen, Delmar 105
Kaufman, Marcus 224–225, 229–230
Kaus, Otto 156, 205–206, 208–209, 214, 221
Kennard, Joyce 3, 228–230, 234, 241–242, 245
Kennedy, Edward "Ted" 113, 153
Kennedy, Jacqueline 131
Kennedy, Joan 113
Kennedy, John F. 3, 5, 54, 105, 110, 111–120, 125, 127, 130, 134, 142, 144, 150, 164–165
Kennedy, Robert F. 3, 5, 115–116, 130, 142, 144, 150, 159
Kenny, Robert W. 33, 40, 42, 47, 49, 51, 60, 68
Kent, Roger 179
Khan, Sammy 118
Kincaid, Clarence 57
King, Billie Jean 158
King, Coretta Scott 170
King, Martin Luther, Jr. 94, 124, 144, 244
Kleps, Ralph 136, 186, 187
Kline, J. Anthony 3, 183
Knight, Goodwin 5, 82, 83, 87, 137
Knowland, William F. 87, 119
Knowles, Harper 41
Kopp, Quentin L. 131, 202
Korshak, Sidney 110
Koufax, Sandy 114
Ku Klux Klan (KKK) 17, 211
Kuchel, Thomas 116–117, 132, 144
Kynette, Earle E. 31, 34, 36

L.A. Weekly 235
Labor's Non-Partisan League 33, 38, 41, 64
Lake, Veronica 57
Lake Elsinore, CA 98–99; *see also* anti-Semitism
Lamarr, Hedy 57
Landreth, Harold 52, 57
Langdon, William H. 47
Larabee, Lawrence 37
Lascher, Ed 202
Laski, Harold J. 75
Lawford, Pat 113
League for Peace and Democracy 18
Leigh, Janet 113

Leitch, Kenneth 63
Levering Act of 1959 80–81; *see also* Loyalty Oath
Lewis, Anthony 203, 220
Linde, Hans 153, 172
Loeb, Leon 76
Loew, Jacob 76
Lomax, Almena 3, 241
Los Angeles Committee for the Protection of the Foreign Born 103
Los Angeles Committee on Palestine 74
Los Angeles County Federation of Labor 108
Los Angeles County Political Commission 77
Los Angeles County Trade Union Commission 77
Los Angeles Jewish Federation Council 78
Los Angeles Police Department (LAPD) 5–6, 31–32, 34, 36, 39, 63, 81–83, 88, 90, 103, 113, 122–124, 126–127, 193, 219
Low, Harry W. 198
Loyalty Oath 77, 80–81, 83, 85–86; *see also* Levering Act
Lucas, Malcolm M. 162, 210–211, 214, 216, 217–218, 223–225, 229–234, 241
Lumbard, Edward 105
Lynch, Thomas C. 90–92, 111, 178
Lyons, Henry 137

MacArthur, Roderick 42
Mahoney, Harry 32
Mahony, Roger 185
Maio, Dennis Peter 238
Mansfield, Mike 132
Manson, Charles 159
Manuel, Wiley 173, 184, 188, 189, 194, 195, 196, 199, 202, 205, 206
marijuana 122, 204
Marks, Marlene Adler 4, 72, 87
Marshall, Thurgood 68, 91
Martin, Dean 114
A Mask for Privilege 75–76, 167
Mathis, Johnny 123
McAdoo, William Gibbs 28, 42
McCarthy, Bob 84–85
McCarthy, Eugene 144
McCarthy, Joseph 21, 50
McCarthy, Leo T. 202, 223
McCarthyism 4, 80, 117
McCauley, Norma 69, 70
McComb, Marshall 137–139, 142–143, 146, 148, 150, 153, 180, 182, 187, 234
McDaniel, Hattie 67
McDonald, Tom 3, 91, 113, 122–123, 129–130
McEnery, John P. 49

McGovern, George 145
McGucken, Joseph T. 59
McKaskle, Paul L. 171
McKesson, William R. 101
McLain, George 121
McLaine, Shirley 145
McVeigh, Timothy 240
McWilliams, Carey 30, 42, 49, 60, 62, 75–76, 90, 119, 167
Medsger, Betty 199
Medvene, Ed 197
Melvoin, Mike 123
Merriam, Frank 26, 35, 41–42, 80
Metro-Goldwyn-Mayer (MGM) 25–26
Metropolitan Squad 31
Mier, Golda 183
Miller, Loren 67–68
Mr. Kon Ton's nightclub 123, 127
Mitchell, Aaron 147
Mitchell, Katharine 26, 141
Moffitt, James K. 46
Mohr, Gus 27
Monroe, Marilyn 125
Mooney, Thomas J. "Tom" 44–45, 102
Morain, Dan 220
Mosk, Abraham 13
Mosk, Earnest 13
Mosk, Edward 1, 3, 6, 12 13–14, 17–18, 24–25, 51, 54–55, 57–58, 60, 62, 71, 73, 74, 77, 80, 93, 140, 146–147, 205, 223, 227, 241
Mosk, Fern 1, 62, 74, 93, 147, 205
Mosk, Helen Edna (Mitchell) 3, 23, 26–27, 43, 54, 62–63, 66–67, 73, 78, 85–87, 93, 97, 110, 112–113, 115, 119, 126–127, 129, 140–145, 147, 157–158, 178, 182, 205–206, 208–209, 237
Mosk, Julie 147
Mosk, Kaygey (Mosk) 1, 54, 236–237, 244–246
Mosk, Matthew 147
Mosk, Minna (Perl) 10–19, 55, 73, 93, 99, 129, 141, 147, 205
Mosk, Paul 10–11–14, 16–19, 54, 205
Mosk, Phillip 13
Mosk, Richard 1, 18–19, 23, 25, 43, 54, 60, 62, 64–65, 67, 69, 78, 84, 87, 90, 93, 95–96, 109, 112–113, 115, 118, 120, 129, 138, 145, 147, 179, 182, 184, 186, 188, 197–198, 206, 208, 219–221, 228, 235, 244, 246
Mosk, Sam 12–13
Mosk, Sandra Lee "Sandy" (Bunditz) 129, 147, 246
Mosk, Susan Jane (Hines) 143, 208, 209, 227, 229, 236, 246

Mosk, Tom 205, 227
Mosk Doctrine 6, 149, 153–156, 231
Motion Picture Cooperative Buyers Guild 77
Motion Picture Democratic Committee 77
Murphy, George 132–134, 149–150
Murray, Olga 138, 167, 213
Muskie, Edmund 145

narcotics, illegal and Kennedy administration 115
National American Palestine Committee 74
National Association for the Advancement of Colored People (NAACP) 68, 91, 94, 157, 166, 168, 175, 176
National Association of Attorneys General 100
National Civic League (NCL) 30
National Council of Jewish Women 26
National Jewish Hospital 11
National Lawyers Guild 77, 102
National Municipal League (NML) 30, 31, 32, 33, 35, 40, 41, 73
Nelson, Helen 90
New Deal 29
Newman, Frank C. 154, 161, 173, 187, 192, 194–196, 198, 200, 202, 204, 206
Nixon, Richard M. 5, 80, 86–87, 102, 112, 114–115, 117, 144–145, 151, 160, 208, 210
no-fault divorce 57
Noble, Robert 28, 34
Northern California Political Action Foundation 179
Nye, Clement D. 57

O'Brien, Charles 85, 91, 122, 178–179
O'Brien, Larry 113
O'Connor, J.F.T. 42
O'Connor, Sandra Day 183
O'Donnell, Ken 113
O'Donnell, Pierce 198
Office of Federal Contract Compliance Programs (OFCCP) 165
Office of Strategic Services (OSS) 54
Ogren, Oscar 18
Olivier, Laurence 115
Olson, Culbert 4, 26, 33, 35, 39, 40–52, 56–57, 64, 76, 78, 85–86, 100, 109, 120, 182, 223
Olson, Richard 43
Omaha Friendship Club 74
Overholt, Ron 246

Owens, Trudy 145
The Owl 19, 24

Pacht, Isaac 43, 78
Pacific Legal Foundation 231
Palestine Liberation Organization (PLO) 157
Palmer, A. Mitchell 18
Palmer, Harland 36
Palmer Raids 18
Panelli, Edward A. 214–216, 223, 225, 230, 233, 241
Paonessa, Alfred 53
Parker, William H. 82–83, 88, 90, 103–104, 126–127
Parras, George E. 208
Part, Marvin 169
paternity suits 57
Patterson, Ellis 33, 41–42, 46, 62, 64
Pauley, Edward 110
Peace Officer Standards and Training 99
Peace Officers Association of California 82
Pearson, Drew 138
Peek, Paul 137, 139, 143
Peoples' Front (aka Popular Front) 29
Percodan 113
Perl, Bessie 10, 12
Perl, Dave 10, 14–18, 23–25, 54–55, 62, 76, 205
Perl, Morris 7, 9, 10, 12
Perl, Rolla (Hartzmark) 6–7, 9–12, 14–15, 23, 25, 55, 99
Person, Arthur 18
Peters, Raymond E. 137–138, 148, 151–152, 177, 180
Petris, Nicholas, C. 120, 182
Philbrick, Howard R. 48
Philibosian, Robert 219
Phillips, Morton 119
Phillips, Pauline (aka Dear Abby) 119
The Phoenix 22
Pierce, Fred R. 146
Ping Yuen 94–95
Poche, Marc 184, 211
Political Reform Act of 1990 231–232
Porter, Carley V. 120
Porter, John C. 31
Poulson, Norris 74
Powell, Gregory U. 159
Powell, Lewis F., Jr. 172–173
President's Commission on Equal Employment Opportunity (PCEEO) 164
Prettyman, E. Barrett, Jr. 115
Prinzmetal, Isidore 58
Professional Golfers Association (PGA) 93–94, 245
Proposition 1 (anti-picketing) 41

Proposition 8 "The Victims' Bill of Rights" 155–156
Proposition 9 (California Fair Political Practices Commisson) 179
Proposition 14 (Repeal of Rumford Fair Housing Act of 1962) 133, 134, 139, 140, 143
Proposition 15 "Free Television Act" 138–139, 143
Proposition 18 (right to work) 88
Proposition 25 "Ham and Eggs" 28, 42
Proposition 115 (independence of state constitution) 230, 231
Proposition 209 (affirmative action) 176, 245
Prussion, Karl 107; *see also* California Dynasty of Communism
Public Records Act 232

Quevedo, Eduardo 43
quotas 6, 20, 75, 164, 167, 172–174, 206, 212, 216, 223

Racanelli, John 199
Radin, Max 48
Radoff, Esther 14–16, 18, 24–25, 54–55, 205
Rafferty, Max 144–145
Randolph, A. Philip 66
rape 100, 160, 190, 192, 193, 258n43
Rat Pack 114
Rau, Edward 26
Raum, Arnold 68
Raymond, Harry 34, 36
Reagan, Ronald 5, 47, 76, 85, 90, 143, 145, 147, 150, 151, 159, 160, 177, 178, 179, 181, 183, 206, 208, 210, 223, 224, 230, 233
Red Squad (Spy Squad) 31, 36
Reddin, Betty 113, 129
Reddin, Tom 113, 127, 243
Reeves, Beatrice 38
Regan, Edwin J. 114
Rehnquist, William 154, 173
Reilly, George 84
Reinhardt, Stephen 3, 85, 131
restrictive covenents 4, 60 66–68, 72, 76, 79, 92, 95, 170, 173
Reynolds, John W. 135
Reynoso, Cruz 6, 152, 207–210, 214, 216–219, 221–222, 224
Richards, Richard 83, 117
Richardson, Frank K. 173, 178, 189, 194, 196, 202, 206, 209, 210
Richardson, H.L. "Bill" 193, 196, 206
Ridder, Hank 128

Rifkind, Simon H. 96
Riga, Latvia (Livonia) 9
Roberts, Bill 219
Roberts, John 247
Robinson, Edward G. 74
Robinson, Sugar Ray 65
Rochester, George 25
Rockford, Illinois 14–20, 24, 71–73, 246
Rockwell, George Lincoln 116
Rogan, Mary 91
Rogan, Richard 91
Roosevelt, Franklin Delano 17, 21, 23, 26, 28, 42–43, 46, 51, 63, 66, 74 136
Roosevelt, James 51, 77, 79–80, 121, 129
Rosanoff, Aaron J. 43
Rose, David 57, 58
Rosenbaum, Ernest 205–206
Rosenthal, Benjamin 43
Rousselot, John H. 106–107
Rousso, David P. 178
Rumford, William B. 133
Rumford Fair Housing Law of 1962 92, 133
Ruth, Babe 22

Salinger, Pierre 130–134, 142
Sampson, Irene 123
San Antonio, Texas 13–14, 24, 71
San Quentin Prison 36, 45, 48, 102, 159
Scalia, Antonin 212
Schaefer, Walter 105
Schauer, Rey B. 50, 62–63, 135, 137–138, 140
Schecter-Mendoza, Hope 145
Scheinman, Benjamin 57
Schmitz, John 174
Schumann, Frederick L. 21
Schwartz, March 149
Schwarz, Fred 107, 108, 107
Scotch Plaid Tailors 11
Scott, Joseph 58, 62
Screen Office Employees Guild 77
Seawell, Emmett 42, 47
Selznik, David O. 74, 76
Shary, Dore 75, 76
Shaw, Frank L. 4, 31, 32, 34, 35, 36, 37, 38, 39, 40, 49, 73, 81, 125
Shaw, Joe 31, 37
Sheinbaum, Stanley 223
Shelley, John F. 130, 143
Shenk, John 243
Shriver, Sergeant 91
Siempre! 116
Sifford, Charlie 93–94, 245
Silberberg, Mendel B. 78
Silver, Herman 73
Silvers, Phil 118
Silverstein, Gordon 247

Sinatra, Frank 114–115, 231
Sinclair, Upton 21, 25–26, 28, 33, 40–43, 79
Sirhan, Sirhan 144, 159
Sleepy Lagoon 59
Sloss, M.C. 137
Smith, Arlo E. 101
Smith, Gerald L.K. 77
Smith, Stan 158
Smith, Steve 113
Smith, William French 151
Souter, David 248
Southern California Women Lawyers Association (SCWLA) 84
Southwestern Law School 25–26, 40, 171, 185–186
Spinelli, Ethel Leta Juanita (the Duchess) 45
Sproul, Robert Gordon 48
Stagg, Amos Alonzo 22
Starr, Kevin 26, 98
States' rights (new) 6, 104, 154; *see also* Mosk Doctrine
Stauffer, Ted 57
Stephenson, Dwight 52
Stevens, Charles S. 175
Stevenson, Adlai 110, 111, 244
Stolz, Preble 95
Stone, Harlan F. 56
Stone, Richard 208
Story, Harold 35
Strawbridge, Nancy 91
Stricko-Neubauer, Tara Wynn 217
Sullivan, Frank 44
Sullivan, Raymond L. 137, 148, 151, 181

Tanner Commission 195–202
Teamsters (AFL) 32
Temple, Shirley 41
Temple Beth El 17
Tenney, Jack 77
The Hague 56, 141, 157, 206, 208; *see also* International Court of Justice at The Hague
Therapeutic Abortion Act of 1967 146; *see also* abortion
Thorpe, Vince 122, 129
Thurmond, Strom 145
Tobriner, Matthew 42, 136–138, 146, 148, 152, 161, 167–168, 173, 180, 182, 184, 188, 194–196, 199–202, 206–208, 214, 225, 234, 236
Tobriner, Michael C. 236
Townsend Plan 28
Traynor, Roger J. 48, 134–138, 142–143, 145–148, 150–151, 180, 182, 186, 222, 224–225, 234
Truman, Harry S 65, 68, 75, 79–80, 86, 110, 118, 244
Tunney, Gene 150
Tunney, John 150, 208
Turner, Lana 4, 57–58

United Farm Workers (UFW) 170, 183, 184
United States Information Agency (USIA) 103
University of California, Los Angeles (UCLA) 1, 25–27, 54, 67, 81, 169
University of Chicago 21–23, 25, 205, 212, 246
University of Southern California (USC) 54
Unruh, Jesse (Jess) aka "Big Daddy" 3, 5, 110, 112, 120–122, 128, 130–131, 144–145, 150–151, 178–179
Unruh Civil Rights Act 92, 211, 212, 213, 243

Vale, Rena M. 49, 50
Van Camp, Brian 179
Vasconcellos, John 169
Velachi, Joe 116
Victims' Bill of Rights 156, 209
Vinegar, Leroy 123
Vinson, Fred 68
Vista Del Mar 36
Voorhees, Jerry 61
Voshell, Robert E. 48
Voting Rights Act of 1965 134, 165

Walker, Herbert V. 101
Wallace, George 145, 157, 222
Wallace, Henry 51, 79
Wapner, Joseph A. 227
Wapner, Mrs. Joseph (Mickey) 259n31
Warren, Earl 5, 17, 26, 42, 45, 48, 50–52, 59–60, 65, 70, 79–80, 83–84, 90, 105, 107, 116–118, 120, 129, 134, 136, 140, 144, 146–148, 151–153, 177, 222–223, 248, 250
Warschaw, Carmen 97, 121, 145
Warschaw, Louis 259n31
Waste, William H. 42, 47
Water rights 84, 89, 95–98; *see also Arizona v. California*
Watergate scandal 179, 181
Waters, Maxine 174
Watt, James 206
Watts riot 126, 134
Waxman, Henry A. 172
Weaver, Robert C. 134
Webb, U.S. 44
Weinberg, A. 81
Weinberger, Caspar 85
Welch, Robert 107, 108
Werdegar, Kathryn M. 241–242, 245
Weygandt, Don 124
White, Walter 175
Williams, Franklin H. 91, 175
Williams, G. Mennen 142
Williams, Samuel L. 91
Willoughby, Thomas H. 200, 202
Wilshire Boulevard Temple 3, 26
Wilshire Country Club 26
Wilson, Pete 5, 162, 184, 210, 230, 233, 241, 243
Wilson, Woodrow 15, 44
Winchell, Joan 93
Wirin, A. I. (Abraham Lincoln) 29, 32, 77, 81, 102, 103, 146
Witkin, Bernard 26, 148
Women for Legislative Action 103
Women's rights 56; *see also* gender vs. sex
Wood, Parker 177, 184
Works Project Administration (WPA) 43
World War I 16, 29, 59, 61
World War II 39, 67, 72, 76, 78, 95, 130, 208, 229, 247
Wright, Donald R. 150–152, 159, 167, 177–178, 180–182, 186–187, 214, 250
Wyman, Eugene 111, 131
Wyman (Weiner), Rosalind (Roz) 72
Wynn, Keenan 58

Yorty, Samuel 30, 32, 33, 38, 39, 80, 123
Younger, Evelle J. 91, 177, 184, 185
Yugoslavia 73

Zacharias, Jim 24, 208
Zangara, Giuseppe 23
Zanuck, Darryl F. 76
Zarky, Norma G. 146
Ziffren, Mickey 205
Ziffren, Paul 82, 111–112
Zimmerman, Bill 223
Zoot Suit riots 59

www.ingramcontent.com/pod-product-compliance
Ingram Content Group UK Ltd.
Pitfield, Milton Keynes, MK11 3LW, UK
UKHW050540150426
5217IPUK00026B/2009